A Poetic History of the Oceans

A Poetic History of the Oceans

Literature and Maritime Modernity

By

Søren Frank

BRILL

LEIDEN | BOSTON

Originally published in 2022 as Volume 98 in the series Textxet: Studies in comparative literature.

 This is an open access title distributed under the terms of the CC-BY-NC 4.0 license, which permits any non-commercial use, distribution, and reproduction in any medium, provided the original author(s) and source are credited. Further information and the complete license text can be found at https://creativecommons.org/licenses/by-nc/4.0/

The terms of the CC license apply only to the original material. The use of material from other sources (indicated by a reference) such as diagrams, illustrations, photos and text samples may require further permission from the respective copyright holder.

This book was supported by THE CARLSBERG FOUNDATION.

Cover illustration: Holger Drachmann: *Havet i oprør. Skagens Gren*. 1907. Oil on canvas. 62,2 x 115,5 cm. Acquired 1991. © 2019 Skagens Kunstmuseer | Art Museums of Skagen.

The Library of Congress Cataloging-in-Publication Data is available online at https://cata log.loc.gov
LC record of the hardback edition available at https://lccn.loc.gov/2022941719

Typeface for the Latin, Greek, and Cyrillic scripts: "Brill". See and download: brill.com/brill-typeface.

ISBN 978-90-04-54639-4 (paperback, 2023)
ISBN 978-90-04-42669-6 (hardback)
ISBN 978-90-04-42670-2 (e-book)

Copyright 2022 by Søren Frank. Published by Koninklijke Brill NV, Leiden, The Netherlands.
Koninklijke Brill NV incorporates the imprints Brill, Brill Nijhoff, Brill Hotei, Brill Schöningh, Brill Fink, Brill mentis, Vandenhoeck & Ruprecht, Böhlau, V&R unipress and Wageningen Academic.
Koninklijke Brill NV reserves the right to protect this publication against unauthorized use.

This book is printed on acid-free paper and produced in a sustainable manner.

*This book is dedicated to my parents,
Aase Marie Frank (in loving memory) and Jens Peter Frank*

Contents

Acknowledgements XI
List of Illustrations XV
Endorsements XVIII

Introduction 1
1   Embarking with Martin Andersen Nexø   1
      1.1   *The Strait of Gibraltar*   3
      1.2   *Transition and Simultaneity*   6
      1.3   *Maritime World Pictures*   9
2   Amphibian Comparative Literature on a Terraqueous Globe   11
      2.1   *The Forgotten Sea*   13
      2.2   *Revision, Actualization, Crisis*   16
      2.3   *Saltwater Literatures*   23
      2.4   *Geographical Scales*   26
      2.5   *Historical Timelines*   28
      2.6   *Blue Ecologies*   35
      2.7   *Method and Structure*   42

1   History   48
   1   Theocentrism   50
       1.1   *The Biblical Tradition*   50
       1.2   *The Greek-Roman Tradition*   53
       1.3   *"The Seafarer"*   57
   2   Anthropocentrism   58
       2.1   *"The Saga of the Greenlanders"*   60
       2.2   *Luís Vaz de Camões*   66
       2.3   *William Shakespeare*   73
       2.4   *Jens Munk*   78
       2.5   *Daniel Defoe*   90
       2.6   *James Fenimore Cooper*   92
   3   Technocentrism   113
       3.1   *Jules Michelet*   113
       3.2   *Jonas Lie*   127
       3.3   *Joseph Conrad*   140
   4   Geocentrism   142
       4.1   *Nostalgia or Dystopia*   143
   5   The Four World Pictures in *Moby-Dick*   146
       5.1   *Historical Time and Broad Present*   150

	5.2	*Theocentrism* 154
	5.3	*Anthropocentrism* 159
	5.4	*Technocentrism* 163
	5.5	*Geocentrism* 167

2 Rhythm   172

1. The Maritime between Homelessness and Homeliness 173
2. Rhythmanalysis at Sea 178
3. Cosmic and Cultural Rhythms at Sea 187
4. External and Internal Rhythms 192
5. Rituals 195
6. Internal Arrhythmia 196
7. Knowledge, Teaching, Writing 198

3 Technology   202

1. The Shipwreck of the *São João* in 1552 202
2. Technology, Literature, and the Ocean 205
3. Martin Heidegger's Technologies 217
4. Don Ihde and Technological Forms of Experience 225
5. Technology in *Typhoon* 231
   - 5.1 Sail and Steam 232
   - 5.2 Steamship Experiences in *Typhoon* 243
6. Science and Technology in *Vingt mille lieues sous les mers* 265
   - 6.1 The Making of a New Literary Profile and a Novel 266
   - 6.2 Science Adventure Fiction 268
   - 6.3 Progress and Mastering 270
   - 6.4 Vraisemblance 272
   - 6.5 Ambiguities 280
   - 6.6 Apollonian Order, Dionysian Fertility 282

4 Materiality   287

1. Immersion in the Dissolve in *Leviathan* 287
2. Forces of Sea and Abyss in *Les Travailleurs de la mer* 291
   - 2.1 Humans and Things 292
   - 2.2 Vital Materialism 304
   - 2.3 Endings and Narrators 308
   - 2.4 Fooling and Receiving Mercy 313
   - 2.5 Cosmography of Work 320

5 Anthropocene 325

1. Coal in Wales, Whales at the Pole 325
2. The Anthropocene 327
3. Anthropocene Aesthetics 335
    - 3.1 *Time, Discontinuity, Probability* 336
    - 3.2 *Space, Discontinuity, Nation-State* 340
    - 3.3 *Human, Humans, Non-Humans* 342
4. Exceptionalism, Growth, and Stock in *En hvalfangerfærd* 351
5. Psychohydrographies of Cataclysm in *The Drowned World* 362
    - 5.1 *Science Fiction and the Anthropocene* 374
    - 5.2 *Surrealism and the Anthropocene* 379
6. Empire of Thalassa in *Havbrevene* 382
    - 6.1 *Evolution, Devolution* 383
    - 6.2 *Icarus, Bruegel, and the Echo Chamber of Reception* 387
    - 6.3 *Life, but not Human* 407
    - 6.4 *Anthropomorphism* 408

Conclusion 413

Bibliography 423
Index 442

Acknowledgements

My biggest debt of gratitude goes out to the Carlsberg Foundation. In 2007, it supported me with a three-year postdoc grant and thus made it possible for me to embark on the first expeditions of this large book project. Then, in April 2019 I received a Semper Ardens grant, again by the Carlsberg Foundation, which made it possible for me to complete the book. Finally, a publication grant from the Carlsberg Foundation made it possible to publish the book not only as a hardback edition, but also as a paperback edition and a digital Open Access edition.

In 2011, I had the privilege of holding a six-month Senior Fellowship at the Internationales Kolleg für Kulturtechnikforschung und Medienphilosophie (IKKM) at the Bauhaus-Universität, Weimar, in Germany. At the IKKM, I want to thank Bernhard Siegert for inviting me; I am also indebted to Oliver Tege, my personal assistant in Weimar; among my Senior Fellow colleagues, I would like to thank and Linda D. Henderson, Brian Larkin, Reinhold Martin, and Joseph Vogl; among the scientific and administrative staff I particularly want to thank Jörg Braun, Michael Cuntz, Ulrike Engelbert, Lorenz Engell, Laura Frahm, Kristina Hellmann, Harun Maye, Leander Scholz, André Wendler, and the entire Herman Melville Group.

While writing the book, I benefitted from two intense periods at Stanford University in 2008 and 2013. Here, and at an early stage of the project, I held stimulating talks with Joshua Landy, Margaret Cohen, and Robert Pogue Harrison. I also want to reserve a special thank you for Margaret Tompkins, who contributed to making my stays at Stanford so enjoyable. Above all, I owe my deepest gratitude to Sepp Gumbrecht.

Several colleagues from abroad have been important to me while writing this book: Julie K. Allen (Brigham Young), Per Thomas Andersen (Oslo), Sibylle Baumbach (Innsbrück), César Domínguez (Santiago de Compostela), Knut Ove Eliassen (Trondheim), Jesper Gulddal (Newcastle), B. Venkat Mani (Madison), and Thomas G. Pavel (Chicago). I also wish to thank Mary K. Bercaw Edwards (Mystic) for making maritime existence as tangible as possible to me, and Peter Michael Martin (Mattapoisett) whose paper cutting art on *Moby-Dick* was a revelation to me that summer of 2015 in Tokyo—both were also kind enough to invite me to stay with them during my Melville Tour in the autumn of 2016. Thank you as well to Dawn Coleman (Knoxville), Timothy Marr (Chapel Hill) and John Bryant (Hofstra) for stimulating conversations on Melville.

In Denmark, I wish to thank Christian Benne and Frederik Tygstrup at Copenhagen University as well as Frits Andersen, Tore Rye Andersen, Mads

Anders Baggesgaard, Jakob Ladegaard, Svend Erik Larsen, Dan Ringgaard, Karen-Margrethe Simonsen, and not least Mads Rosendahl Thomsen, all at Aarhus University.

I owe a big thank you to the board of the San Cataldo convent on the Amalfi Coast, Italy, who granted me a two-week writing retreat in the summer of 2017. I went back to San Cataldo in 2018, and both stays were crucial for the book's progress. In 2019 and 2020, I also benefitted from two stays at Ørslevkloster thanks to its lovely staff and beautiful setting. Thank you as well to the entire 3ROceans group in Trondheim and abroad.

At the University of Southern Denmark, my home university, I owe a big thank you to Sten Pultz Moslund, Anders Engberg-Pedersen, Erik Granly Jensen, Torsten Bøgh Thomsen, Benjamin Boysen, Rasmus Thorning Hansen, Leif Søndergaard, and the late Jørgen Dines Johansen, all present or previous colleagues in Comparative Literature; to Peter Simonsen, Moritz Schramm, Bo Kampmann Walther, Rune Graulund, Kathrin Maurer, Lars Ole Sauerberg, Lars Handesten, Anne-Marie Mai, Rita Felski, Lars Bøje Mortensen, Christian Høgel, Esben Nedenskov Petersen, Alexandra Holsting, Malene Breunig, Anita Nell Bech Albertsen, Jon Helt Haarder, Hjørdis Brandrup Kortbek, and Kirsten Drotner; to Sophy Kohler and Marlene Marcussen, my two talented and former PhD students; to Michael Karlsson Pedersen, who set me on the Conrad-Heidegger-Ihde track; to Johs Nørregaard Frandsen, Per Krogh Hansen, Anne Jensen, Lars Grassme Binderup, Simon Møberg Torp, Lone Granhøj, Lotte Bloch, Peter Hemmersam, Karen Fog Rasmussen, Ingelise Nielsen, and Signe Østergaard Christensen.

I am especially grateful to my two colleagues Sofie Kluge and Adam Paulsen, both in Comparative Literature. Sofie was so kind to let me stay in her apartment in Athens for two weeks to write. While in Athens, I also benefitted from the hospitality of the Nordic Library. Adam read two of the book's chapters intensely, and I profited greatly from his comments.

I would like to express my gratitude to the students who attended my three seminars on maritime literature and culture in 2010, 2013, and 2015. Our fruitful discussions have seeped into this book. Also a big thank you to the students with whom I created www.melville.dk

At Brill, I wish to thank Clovis Jaillet and Masja Horn, my two editors, and Theo d'Haen who was kind enough to invite me into the "Textxet: Studies in Comparative Literature" series. I also want to express my gratitude to the two anonymous readers of my manuscript for their generous reviews and perceptive suggestions. Pamela Starbird deserves special praise for her meticulous work on the manuscript.

ACKNOWLEDGEMENTS   XIII

Finally, I wish to thank Agnes, Marie, and Sofie for their patience (and occasional impatience), trust, and love.

Some of the chapters in this book have previously been published in different versions in journals and anthologies. Elements of "Histories" were published as "Litteraturhistoriske fragmenter: Billeder af havet" in *Digtning og virkelighed: Studier i fiktion*, an anthology edited by Søren Frank, Leif Søndergaard, and John Thobo-Carlsen (Odense: Syddansk Universitet, Institut for Kulturvidenskaber, 2013). The chapter on Cooper builds on a Danish article, "7. januar 1824: James Fenimore Cooper og den maritime romans fødsel" published in *Kritik* 198 (2010). Elements of the chapter on Jonas Lie first appeared as "The Tensions between Domestic Life and Maritime Life in Sea Novels" in *Navigating Cultural Spaces: Maritime Places* edited by Anna-Margaretha Horatschek, Yvonne Rosenberg, and Daniel Schäbler (Amsterdam: Rodopi, 2014) and later as "Jonas Lie mellem det maritime og det hjemlige: Stedets rolle i *Lodsen og hans Hustru*, *Rutland* og *Gaa Paa!*," co-written with Marlene Marcussen, in *K & K* 118 (2015). My reading of *Moby-Dick* featured in an early version as "Melville's Broad Present: Nostalgia, Presentiment, and Prophecy in *Moby-Dick*" in *Aktuel Forskning* (March 2015). I have also drawn on ideas and passages published in "The Seven Seas: Maritime Modernity in Nordic Literature," which appeared in *Nordic Literature: A Comparative History*, edited by Tom DuBois and Dan Ringgaard (Amsterdam: John Benjamins Publishing Company, 2017). "Rhythms" was published in an early Danish version as "Maritime rytmer: En analyse af livet ombord på skibet" in *Stedsvandringer: Analyser af stedets betydning i kunst, kultur og medier*, an anthology edited by Malene Breunig, Søren Frank, Hjørdis Brandrup Kortbek, and Sten Moslund (Odense: Syddansk Universitetsforlag, 2013). It was also published in a later revised version in English, "Rhythms at Sea: Lefebvre and Maritime Fiction," in *Rhythms Now: Henri Lefebvre's Rhythmanalysis Revisited*, edited by Steen Ledet Christiansen and Mirjam Gebauer (Aalborg: Aalborg Universitetsforlag, 2019). The chapter on Jacobsen's *Havbrevene* draws on "Her regerer havet" published in *NLvT* 2 (2021). Finally, the chapter on Hugo's *Les Travailleurs de la mer* came out in a Danish version as "Havets og dybets kræfter i *Les Travailleurs de la mer*: Forvarsler om det antropocæne og Victor Hugos ambivalente antropocentrisme" in *Passage* 37.3 (2022). I wish to thank all the publishers and editors for permission to recycle and reuse the material.

A note on translations: With only a few exceptions, I cite from the English translations of non-English sources, and if I have modified the translation, I state it in the footnote. Whenever I quote from a non-English text and I reference the original title in the footnote, it is my own translation.

A note on titles: As noted above, I usually cite non-English sources in their English translation. However, when referring to non-English translated titles in my book, I sometimes use the English title (e.g., *Toilers of the Sea* and *Twenty Thousand Leagues Under the Sea*), sometimes the original title (*Les Travailleurs de la mer* and *Vingt mille lieues sous les mers*), the latter because I wish to maintain a multilingual dimension in the book.

Illustrations

Figures

1 Vilhelm Melbye, *A Spanish xebec and other commercial craft in the Mediterranean off Gibraltar at sunset* (1873). Photo: © 2013 Christie's Images Limited. 3
2 Caspar David Friedrich, *Der Mönch am Meer* (1810). Nationalgalerie, Staatliche Museen zu Berlin. Photo: © bpk/Nationalgalerie, SMB/Andres Kilger. 36
3 Carl Rasmussen, *Sommernat under den Grønlandske Kyst circa Aar 1000* (1875). Photo: © Bruun Rasmussen Kunstauktioner. 61
4 Title page and first page of diary from the 1624 first edition of Munk's logbook, *Navigatio, Septentrionalis*. © Det Kgl. Bibliotek/Royal Danish Library. 80
5 Title page from the Hakluyt Society's 1897 English edition of Munk's *Navigatio Septentrionalis*, edited by C. C. A. Gosch. © Widener Library, Harvard University. 84
6 Title page from first edition of Daniel Defoe's *Robinson Crusoe* (1719). © British Library. 85
7 Pages from Jens Munk's original diary from the North-West Passage Expedition in 1619–1620. On the page to the right, Munk has added "31 dead" in the left margin. Additamenta no. 184. © Det Kgl. Bibliotek/Royal Danish Library. 88
8 J. M. W. Turner, *A Paddle-steamer in a Storm* (c. 1841). © Yale Center for British Art, Paul Mellon Collection. 192
9 The foundering of the *São João*. Image from the 1735 edition of Brito's *História trágico-marítima*. © John Carter Brown Library. 205
10 The Codex Mendoza. MS. Arch. Selden. A. 1, excerpt of fol. 063r. © The Bodleian Library, Oxford. 209
11 Gustave Caillebotte, *Les plaisanciers aviron sur l'Yerres* (c. 1877–c. 1879). © Bridgeman Images. 210
12 J. M. W. Turner, *Snow Storm—Steam-Boat off a Harbour's Mouth*, exhibited 1842. © Tate. 262
13 1ère Carte and 2e Carte in *Vingt mille lieues sous les mers*, 1871 edition, drawings probably by Jules Verne. Gallica. © Bibliothèque nationale de France. 276
14 Édouard Riou, "Le cortège suivait toujours la frégate" (1871). Gallica. © Bibliothèque nationale de France. 278
15 Alphonse de Neuville, "Paysage sous-marin de l'île Crespo" (1871). Gallica. © Bibliothèque nationale de France. 279
16 Screenshot from *Leviathan* (2012). 288
17 Screenshot from *Leviathan* (2012). 288

18 Screenshot from *Leviathan* (2012). 289
19 Screenshot from *Leviathan* (2012). 289
20 Gustave Doré, "The Last Breakwater." For *Toilers of the Sea* published in 1867 by Harper and Brothers, New York, and Sampson Low, Son, and Marston, London. 294
21 Gustave Doré, "The Fight with the Devil-Fish." For *Toilers of the Sea* published in 1867 by Harper and Brothers, New York, and Sampson Low, Son, and Marston, London. 295
22 Victor Hugo, "Naufrage" (1864–66). Manuscrits, NAF 247451, fol. 116. © Bibliothèque nationale de France. 296
23 Victor Hugo, "La Pieuvre" (1864–66). Manuscrits, NAF 247452, fol. 382. © Bibliothèque nationale de France. 297
24 "Black rivers"—coal wagons at Barry Docks. Image printed in *En hvalfangerfærd*. 325
25 William Lionel Wyllie, *Barry Docks, South Wales* (c. 1900). Amgueddfa Cymru, Cardiff. © National Museum Wales. 326
26 Population, 1300 to 2021. Sources: Gapminder (v6), Hyde (v3.2), and The UN (2019). 332
27 Global atmospheric CO_2 concentration. Source: National Oceanic and Atmospheric Administration (NOAA). 333
28 Average temperature anomaly, Global. Source: Hadley Centre (HadCRUT4). 334
29 Yoknapatawpha County. The map, hand-drawn by William Faulkner, appeared at the end of the first edition of *Absalom, Absalom!* (New York: Random House, 1936). Albert and Shirley Small Special Collections. © University of Virginia Library, Charlottesville, Virginia. 343
30 Geological time spiral. Joseph Graham, William Newman, and John Stacy, "The geologic time spiral: A path to the past," version 1.1, U. S. Geological Survey General Information Product 58, poster, 1 sheet. 344
31 The Blue Marble. Apollo 17 crew, "The Earth seen from Apollo 17," photograph taken by either Harrison Schmitt or Ron Evans on December 7, 1972, while Apollo 17 was en route to the Moon at a distance of about 29,000 kilometers. 345
32 Whaleboat with a good catch. Image printed in *En hvalfangerfærd*. 356
33 Max Ernst, *Europe After the Rain II* (1940–42). © Wadsworth Atheneum, Hartford, Connecticut. 373
34 Paul Delvaux, *La Vénus endormie* (1944). Presented by Baron Urvater 1957. Tate. © Fondation Paul Delvaux, St. Idesbald, Belgium/DACS, London 2020. 381
35 Paul Delvaux, *Ecce homo* (1949). © Fondation Paul Delvaux, St. Idesbald, Belgium, c/o Pictoright Amsterdam 2022. 382

ILLUSTRATIONS   XVII

36   Dorte Naomi, *Icarus* (2018). © Dorte Naomi.   389
37   Pieter Bruegel the Elder, *Landscape with the Fall of Icarus* (c. 1558/1560). Musées royaux des Beaux-Arts de Belgique, Brussels, Belgium. © Bridgeman Images.   392
38   Circle of Pieter Bruegel the Elder, *The Fall of Icarus* (c. 1590–95). © Le Musée et Jardins Van Buuren, Brussels.   398
39   Simon Novellanus after Pieter Bruegel the Elder, *River Landscape with Daedalus and Icarus* (c. 1595). © The Trustees of the British Museum.   399

Table

1   The coexisting world pictures in *Moby-Dick*.   171

Endorsements

"Combining a capacious vision of the long history of oceanic narratives in Western culture with incisive analysis of recent scholarship in the "blue humanities," *A Poetic History of the Oceans* provides an excellent overview of oceanic literature and culture. At this book's core lies a brilliant reading of *Moby-Dick* as model for four distinct historical iterations of Western imaginations of the sea. In reading Melville's novel as simultaneously theocentric, anthropocentric, technocentric, and geocentric, Frank shows how this American classic opens onto global vistas. Beyond an innovative analysis of the English-language canon, however, this book also brings Scandinavian writers and texts forward into their rightful places as oceanic pioneers. The introduction of figures such as Jens Munk, Jonas Lie, Martin Andersen Nexø, and Siri Ranva Hjelm Jacobsen suggests how much scholars and readers can learn from this book."

Steve Mentz, Professor of English, *St. John's University*, New York, USA

"*A Poetic History of the Oceans* has compelling qualities: a fascinating topic, incredible erudition, an innovative, wide-ranging approach, and a seductive, reader-friendly style. The quality of the scholarship is remarkable, both concerning the works examined and the thinkers and literary critics that are consulted and cited. Given the superb treatment of the topic, the wealth of information, and the theoretical insights, Frank's book could very well become a classic in its field."

Thomas Pavel, Professor of Romance Languages, Comparative Literature, Committee on Social Thought, *University of Chicago*, USA

Introduction

1   Embarking with Martin Andersen Nexø

On a November day in 1902, after having traveled around Italy for some months, the Danish author Martin Andersen Nexø set off from Sicily toward the south coast of Spain by sea. Although it was the penultimate month of the year, the sun continued undeterred to emit rays of heat upon the Mediterranean. With a temperature ranging from 15–17° C, this sea, whose name literally means "between land," was still relatively friendly to swimmers. Its color expressions oscillated alluringly between shining opal, the shade of pale milk, warm indigo, the black of sluggish tar, shimmering crystals, and "a sullen green, opaque and viscous, like molten bottle-glass."[1] The crew and passengers sometimes glimpsed the gleaming back of a shark from the ship's rail, or blooms of transparent jellyfish moving rhythmically and synchronously forward below the surface of the water.

Instead of traveling with a passenger steamer, to save money Andersen Nexø traveled on board a dirty Dutch freighter laden with raisins, prunes, oatmeal, and dried fish. However, shortly after departure he realized he had been cheated by a Sicilian "king," who had arranged the trip for the Dane. The three hundred marks Andersen Nexø paid for the journey by cargo ship turned out to be twice the fare of a passenger steamer. Andersen Nexø had made his first trip to Southern Europe in 1894–96. The primary purpose of that twenty-month journey was for convalescence, but during this journey Andersen Nexø's career as a writer gathered pace, as we can read in the fourth and last volume of his memoirs, *Vejs Ende* (1939; End of Road).[2] This time, the author was on an educational journey through the poorest regions of southern Europe to collect impressions and gather new fuel for his gradually growing authorship. His experiences from the two journeys were transformed into the travelogue *Days in the Sun* (orig., *Soldage*, 1903).

Andersen Nexø's farewell to Italy was dry-eyed, not only because of his unfortunate experience with the deceitful Sicilian. Italy was, despite the nation's unquestionable beauty, "a little too picturesque, a little too idyllic" for the Danish author's taste. "The countless tourists," Andersen Nexø further remarked, "have transformed it into something resembling a bedraggled

---

[1] Martin Andersen Nexø, *Days in the Sun*, trans. Jacob Wittmer Hartmann (1903; New York: Coward-McCann, 1929), 3.
[2] Martin Andersen Nexø, *Vejs Ende, Erindringer II* (København: DSL/Borgen, 1999), 521–31.

poodle performing idiotic tricks." In addition, he found the land "embroidered over, bedeviled, as it were, by all the painters, poets and philosophers in the world. [...] As in China, you dare not spit for fear of hitting an ancestor, nor draw a breath freely for sheer tradition."[3] So, Andersen Nexø looked forward to the more virginal and anarchic character of Andalusia. The relatively undescribed landscape in the southern region of Spain promised literary potential. The more rebellious nature of the population appealed to Andersen Nexø (who was inspired by the radicalism of figures such as Georg Brandes and Friedrich Nietzsche) and was aligned with his socialist temperament and ideals. In Italy, the poor may have been visible and vocal to some extent, but they were also half-buried under and drowned out by high culture. As a result of the comparative cultural "nudity" of the landscape and the population, the lower classes of Andalusia were much more noticeable, clear, and authentic. Before revisiting Spain, Andersen Nexø had to undergo a sea voyage of several days. Despite the high fare and less comfortable conditions where travelers slept "in little canteen rooms right over the screw," and the author's sleep was often disturbed, because his head collided "with some sharp projecting iron,"[4] the voyage was a pleasant and inspiring experience for Andersen Nexø.

On a general level, *Days in the Sun* and his other works are focused on other and more pressing topics than depicting maritime existence and grappling with the poetics of the ocean. The travel account in *Days in the Sun* is a symbolic *Bildungsroman* in which Andersen Nexø discovers an ideal type of human, the heroic, fully molded, and pure Alfonso M., who was based on a true person. In that sense, *Days in the Sun* anticipates the author's subsequent multi-volume novels about Pelle (1906–10) and Ditte (1917–21), both of which were terrestrial, had a didactic tone, and showed a blend of social realism and idealistic utopianism with their empathic portrayal of two heroic landbased workers. Nevertheless, *Days in the Sun* contains ten pages that arguably emulate some of the best in the Nordic tradition of sea literature, from the sagas of Icelanders and Jens Munk to Jonas Lie, Holger Drachmann, Amalie Skram, and Aksel Sandemose and, more recently, to Jens Bjørneboe, Jón Kalman Stefánsson, Morten Strøksnes, Maja Lunde, and Siri Ranva Hjelm Jacobsen. Arguably, these passages from *Days in the Sun* come close to emulating those by hypercanonical maritime writers such as Herman Melville and Joseph Conrad in aesthetic quality and nautical sensibility. In addition, they comprise a high concentration in a very limited space of two significant and complex

---

3   Andersen Nexø, *Days in the Sun*, 1.
4   Andersen Nexø, *Days in the Sun*, 3.

INTRODUCTION

FIGURE 1   Vilhelm Melbye, *A Spanish xebec and other commercial craft in the Mediterranean off Gibraltar at sunset* (1873)
PHOTO: © 2013 CHRISTIE'S IMAGES LIMITED

histories, the *history of ideas* and the *history of technology*, at a time when both these histories were undergoing radical changes.

1.1   *The Strait of Gibraltar*

During the passage to Cadiz, the Dutch steamer called in at Port of Málaga to load figs, raisins, and sweet Málaga wine. The crew and passengers were supposed to pick up their first mail in three weeks, but that turned out to be in vain. The seafarers crossed the narrow Strait of Gibraltar, "the submarine threshold that connects the ranges of Andalusia with those of North Africa, erecting an invisible but effective line between two seas,"[5] the Mediterranean and Atlantic. After having been underway a week or so, the steamer reached the bay of Cádiz. The city of Cádiz is located on the southern coast of Spain between the Mediterranean Sea and the Atlantic Ocean. In the three decades prior to Andersen Nexø's journey, the status of this borderland area had changed significantly due to the rising hegemony of steam power.

It is possible to visualize this change by comparing Vilhelm Melbye's painting *A Spanish xebec* (1873) (Figure 1) and the following passage from *Days in the Sun*:

---

5   Andersen Nexø, *Days in the Sun*, 9.

> Far out ahead of us stand countless columns of smoke rising skyward like great pines; hundreds of factories could be located there. But this is one of the highways of the ocean. Under the smoky pine nearest us rises a hull coming our way, it passes us and disappears in the strait—and another, and another, and so on, forever. Black ten-thousand-ton steel monsters push forward with the aid of twin-screws steamers, gasping, spewing forth ugly yellow water from the side and leaving behind a wake of cinders, kitchen waste and glistening coal dust over which the choking smoke pall hangs suspended, bluish black like a stormy sky. These great coal steamers are heading for Gibraltar, Malta and Port Said. [...]
>
> Steam has given the ocean trodden paths. As far as the eye can reach backwards and forwards—all the way to the faintest traces of smoke from steamers still many miles off in the horizon—a straight, endless line of ships all plow the same narrow strip. It looks as if they were going around the earth in single file.
>
> But further out on the great watery mirror sailing vessels are moving arbitrarily in all directions. Far away, a majestic ship sails past with white sails billowing from all four masts; sky-high it rises and skews toward us like a dazzling iceberg. Little cutters with lateen sails cross the ocean in all directions; they look like white birds skimming the surface of the water with the tip of one wing.[6]

These passages in *Days in the Sun* constitute a literary snapshot condensing the tense relationship between the old era of sailing ships and the new era of steamships. To paint it with a broad brush, it was a time of transformation from a fading anthropocentric world of adventure, contingency, and daring, to an emerging technocentric world of calculation, realism, and routine.

Possibly inspired by Melbye's journey to Spain in the 1850s, *A Spanish xebec* shows the Strait of Gibraltar as a world of sail with numerous vessels cutting through the lively waves, whereas Andersen Nexø's 1902 tableau freezes a state of transition between two worlds, the world of sail and the world of steam. Andersen Nexø's perspective from the Bay of Cádiz extends back to the Mediterranean and its ancient history of myths, coastal seafaring, and *Non Plus Ultra*, and forward toward the Atlantic and the New World, oceanic seafaring, and *Plus Ultra*. We sense the future of global modernity through the implied mapping, routinization, and systematization expressed through "trodden paths," "straight, endless line," "plow the same narrow strip," and "in single file."

---

6 Andersen Nexø, *Days in the Sun*, 11, 13; translation modified.

Yet traces remain of the world of yesterday with its greater contingency and planlessness ("arbitrary directions") and its multitude of sailing ships, tellingly compared with phenomena in nature, an iceberg and white birds. In contrast to the gracious sailing ships, Andersen Nexø emphasizes the monstrous aspect of modern technology, when he mentions "gasping" "Black steel monsters," "ugly yellow water," "cinders, kitchen waste and glistening coal dust," "the choking smoke pall."

But is it not strange that Andersen Nexø, previously so critical towards Italy, because it had developed into a series of tableaus, creates a tableau himself with this snapshot? The Italian tableaus were idyllic, a series of excessively romantic paintings, but his tableau of Cádiz is an explosive, vibrating, and contrasting image that fuses the organicism and romanticism of the near past with the automatism and industrialism of the near future. With this tableau, and with his description of the life and traffic of the Bay of Cádiz, Andersen Nexø invites us to witness the inner contrasts and tensions of his era and of modernity at large. Despite great tensions and conflicts, the two worlds did coexist from the early 1800s to the early 1900s. On the one hand, the birth pangs of the emerging steamship epoch were arduous yet representative of an irreversible process of increased mechanization; on the other hand, the death cramps of the sailing ship epoch were endlessly protracted. Even when the balance between sail and steam had indisputably tipped to the latter's advantage around the mid-nineteenth century, the old world of sailing ships, seafarers, and distinctive nautical practices refused to die in real life and in the imagination.

But why was that? Firstly, the maritime world with its organization, technology, and infrastructure was a heavy organism to transform. One example is the resilience of the commercial sailing ship amidst the steady development and perfection of the steamship, a resilience that was financially motivated and premised on speed that was faster than many steamships. Considerations of higher speed often outweighed those of higher risk. The transition from sail to steam was also hampered when steamship sailors started to establish unions. Sailing ship sailors had never done that and only began forming unions after steamship sailors set the example. Shipping companies generally avoided unionization for as long as possible, since it introduced friction into an unregulated system that favored owners and merchants.

Secondly, those involved in this world of sail—shipowners, officers, ordinary sailors, dockers, office clerks and more—were quite conservative when it came to embracing the new technology. For ordinary sailors, life on a sailing ship was hazardous, whereas steam technology contributed to securitizing working at sea. However, with the new technology new dangers emerged, such as the risk of explosions, and that, together with the monotony of work and the claustrophobia of working in the engine room, made some sailors shy away from steamships. Shipowners were annoyed with the increase of control, regulation, and legislation that accompanied steam technology. On July 7, 1852, the US Senate discussed a bill entitled "An act to provide for the better security of the lives of passengers on board of vessels propelled in whole or in part by steam." As Senator Davis of Mississippi pointed out: "Life in steamers cannot be better secured without measures which [...] excite the distrust, if not the hostility, of the owners of such vessels. They prefer the unrestrained liberty of managing their affairs according to their discretion, though a mercenary spirit may, and often does, triumph over all sympathy for those exposed to destruction from explosions and other causes."[7]

Thirdly, authors writing about life at sea often had personal experiences with the world of sailing ships. By writing about sailing, the writers kept the image of the world of sail alive in the imagination of their readers, even when that world was disappearing. Authors who had experienced both worlds, including Melville and Conrad, as well as Drachmann and Sandemose, had deeply felt and nostalgic sentiments for the old world, and often felt antipathy towards the new world and its transformative practices. It is no coincidence that Melville's last work, the posthumously published *Billy Budd, Sailor (An Inside Narrative)*, begins with the nostalgic phrase "In the time before steamships ..."[8]

1.2   *Transition and Simultaneity*

Andersen Nexø's Cádiz tableau is a snapshot that captures an irreversible transition between two historical epochs, the past of sail and the future of steam. The two world pictures of the tableau were interlocked throughout most of the nineteenth century and constituted an epochal tension. In that sense, the snapshot and the image it evokes of the nineteenth century calls for two different readings of time and temporality. On the one hand, the tableau exemplifies "historical time," the historical consciousness that according to Reinhart Koselleck emerged in the second half of the eighteenth century and

---

[7] *The Congressional Globe: The Debates, Proceedings, and Laws of the First Session of the Thirty-Second Congress*, vol. XXIV, part II (City of Washington: John C. Rives, 1852), 1667.
[8] Herman Melville, *Billy Budd, Sailor (An Inside Narrative)*, *Billy Budd, Sailor and Other Uncompleted Writings*, *The Writings of Herman Melville*, vol. 13, eds. Harrison Hayford, Alma A. MacDougall, Robert A. Sandberg, and G. Thomas Tanselle, historical note by Hershel Parker (Evanston and Chicago: Northwestern University Press and the Newberry Library, 2017), 3.

dominated the era in which Andersen Nexø lived.⁹ Here, the tableau points to a historical process that leaves a useless past behind and promises a future of new possibilities. Progress is inevitable, and sail will eventually make way for steam. On the other hand, the image is an example of "broad present," the temporal consciousness that Hans Ulrich Gumbrecht describes as the way in which we conceptualize time, present, and history today.¹⁰ "Broad present" differs from "historical time" in that we are now flooded with past epochs no longer discarded as useless. Instead of being an open horizon of possibilities, the future has now become closed and menacing. Read through the temporality of "broad present," Andersen Nexø's snapshot of his own present condenses not so much a *transition* between two epochs as the continuous *simultaneity* of the two epochs. The tableau encompasses both temporalities.

Previously in *Days in the Sun*, there is a description supporting the idea that the dominating historical consciousness in Andersen Nexø's maritime world, "historical time," was challenged, or even supplanted, by the temporality of "broad present":

> It is lovely to be sailing, with ocean and nothing but ocean on all sides as far as the eye can see. Mile after mile of watery surface passes under the ship's bow and glides past astern, but far off on the horizon new wastes of water appear as fast as we can put them behind us. It is as if we are going nowhere, and yet the ship is pounding undeterred, and the screw turns—wading through eternity must be something like this.¹¹

Andersen Nexø describes the ship's journey as a struggle without movement. The Dutch cargo steamer crawls monotonously forward, but because the ocean appears to be infinite, the journey does not seem to be making progress despite concepts of transition such as "passes under" and "glides past astern." On the contrary, and anticipating the closed futurities later conceptualized by Sartre as closed doors, by Camus as the ceaseless toil of Sisyphus, and by Beckett as a waiting for Godot, the crew and passengers were seemingly going "nowhere."

---

9   Reinhart Koselleck, "'Space of Experience' and 'Horizon of Expectation': Two Historical Categories," in *Futures Past: On the Semantics of Historical Time*, trans. Keith Tribe (New York: Columbia University Press, 2004).

10 Hans Ulrich Gumbrecht, *Our Broad Present: Time and Contemporary Culture* (New York: Columbia University Press, 2014); Hans Ulrich Gumbrecht, *After 1945: Latency as Origin of the Present* (Palo Alto: Stanford University Press, 2013).

11 Andersen Nexø, *Days in the Sun*, 2; translation modified.

In *A Poetic History of the Oceans*, the temporal configurations of "historical time" (irrelevant past, transitory present, open future) and "broad present" (engulfing pasts, broad present, closed future) are important tools for analyzing humanity's varied entanglements with the technologically mediated and mysterious world of the sea. They are useful when examining nautical sources from the period when steam replaced sail. As Carl Schmitt observes in *Land and Sea* (orig., *Land und Meer*, 1942), the nineteenth century was a time during which the ocean was metaphorically transformed from a large fish into a machine.[12] Arguably, this period represents the heyday of maritime fiction, certainly in novelistic form, including authors such as James Fenimore Cooper, Herman Melville, Victor Hugo, Jonas Lie, Jules Verne, and Joseph Conrad. But "historical time" and "broad present" are also relevant when we discuss writers from earlier epochs (e.g., Homer, Horace, Camões, and Jens Munk) and the two directions taken by writers in the post-Conrad era, the one *nostalgic* and oriented towards the sea of the *past* (e.g., Aksel Sandemose, C. S. Forester, Jens Bjørneboe, Patrick O'Brian, William Golding, Amitav Ghosh, Carsten Jensen, and Franzobel, of whom we shall read a few cursorily), the other *dystopic* and oriented towards the sea of the *future* (e.g., Alfred Döblin, J. G. Ballard, Morten Strøksnes, Maja Lunde, Kim Stanley Robinson, and Siri Ranva Hjelm Jacobsen, of whom we shall focus on Ballard and Jacobsen).

The reader familiar with the field of Blue Humanities will recognize some of the above names, but probably not all of them. Blue Humanities, Oceanic Studies, Maritime History, as well as the other disciplinary labels employed to describe the history of human interactions with the oceans have experienced an upsurge in recent decades. Also characteristic of this fertile development is that it has unfolded predominantly within the scholarly communities of the Anglophone West. More recently, there is increasing interest in the maritime global south, including the Indian and Pacific Oceans and their roles in the societal history of the East. *A Poetic History of the Oceans* has its emphasis on Western sources and material, but one of its primary innovations in the Blue Humanities discourse is to tell the story of Western sea literature and culture through a Nordic lens. One contribution is through the analysis of Scandinavian sources in a Western or global context alongside more well-known and canonical sources, thus introducing these texts to a readership to whom they have been relatively unknown; the other is by insisting through a reading of an early Nordic saga on a softening of the temporal break around

---

12   Carl Schmitt, *Land and Sea*, trans. Simona Draghici (1942/1954; Washington DC: Plutarch Press, 1997), 54.

INTRODUCTION

1500 traditionally associated with the oceanic turn, since Vikings were forerunners of transoceanic voyaging several centuries before Columbus, da Gama, and Magellan set sail for distant shores. Through the perspectives provided by Nordic writers and sailors, it is my hope that *A Poetic History of the Oceans* serves not only an introduction to oceanic literature in the West, but also an intervention in and contribution to the expansion of the scholarly discourse concerned with this literature.

1.3   *Maritime World Pictures*

In my analysis of the selected nautical sources, whether written texts, paintings, a film, novels, logbooks, poems, or history books, my intention is to extract from them their *maritime world picture*. This world picture is made up of the following elements: a temporal configuration (the figure of time and the conception of past, present, and future); an articulation of a distinct relationship between gods, humans, nature, and technology; an image of the ocean; and poetics. What are the implications of a sea ruled by gods in *The Odyssey* as compared to the powerful presence of a writing and acting "I" in Munk's *Navigatio Septentrionalis* (1624) and Defoe's *Robinson Crusoe* (1719)? In the shipwreck of the *São João* in 1552, what role is attributed to technology as compared to the role of modern technology when Captain MacWhirr leads the *Nan-Shan* safely through a hurricane in Conrad's *Typhoon* (1902)? In what ways do nature and the Earth's history return with a vengeance in Ballard's *The Drowned World* (1962) and Jacobsen's *Havbrevene* (2018; The Sea Letters), and where does this leave humanity? Why does Melville resort to lyricism in ecologically sensitive passages and use descriptive realism and encyclopedic forms at other times in *Moby-Dick* (1851)? And why do we find aesthetic strategies similar to Melville's in Michelet's *La Mer* (1861), Hugo's *Les Travailleurs de la mer* (1866), and Verne's *Vingt mille lieues sous les mers* (1869–70/1871)?

Questions such as these indicate some of the topics I address in this book about the poetic history of the oceans. In the following, I discuss why the ocean is important for the writing of cultural history and in the ways in which a Blue Humanities approach is a relevant and crucial method, given that we inhabit what Melville called "this terraqueous globe."[13] The main object of analysis is literature in several languages and from different periods engaging with the maritime and oceanic worlds and portraying maritime and marine actors (i.e., conjunctions of human and nonhuman life). In this analysis, I promote what

---

13   Herman Melville, *Moby-Dick; or, The Whale, The Writings of Herman Melville*, vol. 6, eds. Harrison Hayford, Hershel Parker, and G. Thomas Tanselle (Evanston and Chicago: Northwestern University Press and the Newberry Library, 1988), 64.

I call an *amphibian comparative literature*. This method is characterized by its capacity to accommodate "both kinds of life" (ἀμφί, amphí, "of both kinds," and βιος, bios, "life"): life above water and life under water, the human and the nonhuman, even the organic and the inorganic, and the prehuman and the posthuman. This capacity is crucial in the encounter with literary works that depict an increasingly wet and unstable world in which humans are powerful agents yet also increasingly impotent creatures. Specifically, amphibian comparative literature succeeds at zooming in on components other than human characters and anthropogenic plots. It also focuses on and embraces nonhuman actors, objects and hyperobjects, and terrestrial as well as aquatic life. For amphibian comparative literature, the novel is for example not merely "the modern *bourgeois* epic" (Hegel) and a *bio*graphical form (Lukács), it is also a *geo*graphical form and the epic of the whale (e.g., Moby Dick) and the steamship (e.g., La Durande).

While the chapters on history, rhythm, and technology focus on representations of sailors and their seagoing vessels and what is usually referred to as *maritime history*, the chapters on history, materiality, and the Anthropocene epoch venture into *oceanic history* by turning this "longstanding historiography of humans, vessels, and exploration toward an analysis of complex relations between elements (winds, tides, currents), ocean life (mammals, fish, crustaceans, birds, plants), and human activity in and on the seas." If the former is primarily defined by a lateral perspective focusing on the horizontal movements across the ocean's surface, the latter is characterized by its vertical approach. However, in our case the well-known critique of the vertical perspective as being potentially imperial and disembodied is countered by the fact that the perspective from outer space—the one usually associated with a vertical methodology—is replaced by a perspective from the undersea: *animal, vegetal, and mineral* instead of imperial, and a space of *immersion and entanglement* instead of a space of disembodiment. It is perhaps symptomatic that the editors of *Oceanic Histories* (2018), all historians by training, leave out aesthetic representations when they emphasize that oceanic historiography "overlaps with geographies, cartographies, astronomies, ethnographies, climatic studies and natural histories."[14] *A Poetic History of the Oceans* is an attempt to supplement omissions of the endlessly rich and varied archive of how humans have engaged poetologically and epistemologically with the ocean.

---

14   Sujit Sivasundaram, Alisan Bashford, and David Armitage, "Introduction: Writing World Oceanic Histories," in *Oceanic Histories*, eds. David Armitage, Alisan Bashford, and Sujit Sivasundaram (Cambridge: Cambridge University Press, 2018), 13, 25.

2 Amphibian Comparative Literature on a Terraqueous Globe

It has become common to state quantitative facts when attempting to convince readers of the importance of the ocean and the relevance of Blue Humanities. So as not to disrupt that tradition, here are a few of the most referenced facts: over seventy percent of Planet Earth is covered by oceans, less than thirty percent by landmasses; like Planet Earth, nearly seventy percent of the human body is composed of saltwater; half of the world's human population lives within one hundred miles from an ocean; and roughly ninety percent of our planet's biosphere lives under water. The French historian Jules Michelet summed it up in *La Mer* (1861): "On the surface of the globe, water is the generality, the earth is the exception."[15] As early as 7–23 AD, the Greek geographer Strabo acknowledged in his *Geography* that "we are amphibious, and belong no more to the land than to the sea."[16] Recently, the German philosopher Peter Sloterdijk called the uneven balance between land and sea "the fundamental globographical fact of the Modern Age," observing that the Magellan expedition's logbook by Antonio Pigafetta helped bring "the Ptolemaic belief in the predominance of land masses, to a sensational end." Sloterdijk adds that "it never became clear whether it was an evangelical or a dysangelical one," thus indicating that we are yet to come to terms—historically, culturally, philosophically, existentially—with living on a blue planet.[17]

Historiography, for example, continues to be primarily a terrestrial practice executed *on* and conceived *from* land. But perhaps this is only logical if we stop to think about it. Is it not true that history, cultural history, and literary history are all historiographical practices *by* humans *about* humans? And although we humans may still sense a genetically informed evolutionary intimacy with marine life forms, an intimacy stretching back into deep time, we have gradually and irreversibly morphed into land creatures. From our present rung on

---

15 Jules Michelet, *La Mer* (Paris: Librairie L. Hachette et Cie, 1861), 9–10. To my knowledge, there are three English translations of *La Mer*: an anonymous from 1861 (New York: Rudd & Carleton), which is very liberal in its approach; one by W. D. Davenport Adams from 1875 (London: T. Nelson and Sons), which is better than the anonymous one, but still problematic; and one by Katia Sainson from 2012 (Los Angeles: Green Integer), which I haven't had the chance to consult. But as a consequence of the questionable quality and fidelity of the two early translations, I have chosen to refer to the French text and translate quotations myself.

16 Strabo, *The Geography of Strabo*, trans. H. L. Jones (1917; Cambridge, MA: Harvard University Press, 1949), 29.

17 Peter Sloterdijk, *Spheres II: Globes*, trans. Wieland Hoban (1999; South Pasadena: Semiotext(e), 2014), 805, 807, 805.

the evolutionary ladder, there is no going back. The sea has become an inhospitable and uninhabitable place for humanity, at least for humanity in its current form of *homo sapiens*. However, the imbroglio between humans and oceans, a relationship of both *intimacy* and *separation*, implies that the ocean is both the condition and boundary of our lives.

Although humans live on land and write cultural histories, novels, poems, and stories about their life on land, we must insist on two important corrections to the above. First, despite their terrestrial starting point, human history and culture, including literature, are profoundly entangled with the watery world. For eons, the oceans have connected countries and continents, provided food and other material resources for humans, spawned the cultural imagination of humanity, and offered their coastal regions to humans, who have been strongly inclined to build their residences right at the edge where land and sea meet. Even if we were to keep insisting on an anthropocentric and terrestrial focus when writing cultural histories, these histories would be highly inadequate and incomprehensive if they did not respect the human-ocean entanglements: "Living on land we sometimes forget the sea's dominance of our physical and cultural histories. We should remember," Steve Mentz reminds us.[18]

Second, it is too constricted to postulate that the historiographical practices of historians and scholars in cultural and literary studies focus exclusively on humans and their terrestrial existence. The history of the planet and the history of literatures across epochs and languages include both the nonhuman and the aquatic. However, our understandings of history and of literary and cultural history are too often terrestrial rather than terraqueous or aquatic, and human-centered rather than amphibian or nonhuman, because our historiographical practices have been too anthropocentric and terrestrial. A Blue Humanities approach not only "names an off-shore trajectory that places cultural history in an oceanic rather than terrestrial context," it also turns "to the sea to place human histories in more-than-human contexts."[19]

A Poetic History of the Oceans moves geographically between land and sea and between human and nonhuman perspectives and contexts. I examine the role of the oceans in planetary and human history, and I explore how writers, artists, sailors, philosophers, and historians have attempted to negotiate two of the most pressing challenges of the ocean, one epistemological, the other poetological: *How to know the unknowable? How to give shape to that which is*

---

18 Steve Mentz, *At the Bottom of Shakespeare's Ocean* (London and New York: Continuum, 2009), 97.
19 Steve Mentz, "Blue Humanities," in *Posthuman Glossary*, eds. Rosi Braidotti and Maria Hlavajova (London: Bloomsbury, 2018), 69, 70.

shapeless? Navigators, pilots, and scientists used lead lines to sound the depths of the fathomless ocean. Writers, driven by the alluring yet impossible fantasy of knowing what is unknowable, used their lead pencils (of graphite) and their quills and ink in their ambitious attempts to both *match* and *figure* the vast waters and reach into (physical and psychological) bottomless spaces, where human bodies and minds had never before ventured. From these depths, they brought back strange things and visions—what Hester Blum has labelled a specific "model of knowledge" rooted in the material world and in which imagination always has an "empirical basis"[20]—that demanded a new aesthetic grammar and vocabulary emphasizing obscurity over clarity and process over progress. To Conrad, the central imperative of the writer was thus to make the reader see: "To see, to see!"[21] This aesthetic challenge and the ability *to see* were for Conrad intimately linked with going *to sea*. Life at sea resulted in a productive distortion of landlocked epistemologies of clear vision. It also led Conrad to elevate the sailor's epistemology of embodied vision to a metaphor for a "beclouded" humanity. This theory of an oceanic thinking applicable to humanity as such is captured by Gaston Bachelard's formula, "the true eye of the earth is water."[22] To Holger Drachmann, the Danish writer and marine painter, the sea has an eye that is "wet,"[23] and in an early text, an obituary to his teacher C. F. Sørensen, Drachmann speaks of "'salty' water" and "'wet' water" when characterizing Sørensen's paintings.[24]

2.1 *The Forgotten Sea*

But why this blue-green and amphibious comparative approach? What insights will it yield? These questions are not simply rhetorical. They are legitimized, because the facts evidencing planetary oceanic primacy are counteracted by a development of even greater importance. During the twentieth

---

20 Hester Blum, *The View from the Masthead: Maritime Imagination and Antebellum American Sea Narratives* (Chapel Hill: The University of North Carolina Press, 2008), 2, 3.

21 Joseph Conrad, *The Mirror and the Sea: Memories and Impressions—A Personal Record: Some Reminiscences, Collected Edition of the Works of Joseph Conrad* (1906/1912, 1923; London: J. M. Dent & Sons, 1975), 87.

22 Gaston Bachelard, *Water and Dreams: An Essay on the Imagination of Water*, trans. Edith R. Farrell (Dallas: Pegasus Foundation, 1983), 31; also quoted in Mentz, *Ocean*, 19.

23 Holger Drachmann, "Havets Sang," in *Ungdom i Digt og Sang* (København: Gyldendal, 1879), 204.

24 Holger Drachmann, "Nogle erindringsord," *Ude og Hjemme*, 1879. Quoted from Mette Harbo Lehmann, "Havet som selvportræt: Maleren Holger Drachmann," in *Jeg er hav: Holger Drachmann med pen og pensel*, ed. Mette Harbo Lehmann (Skagen: Skagens Kunstmuseer, 2019), 15.

century, especially after World War II, the advent of diesel engines, airline travel, aerial warfare, space travel, containerization, and the automation of ports gradually led to what artist Allan Sekula has labelled "the 'forgetting' of the sea" in our cultural imagination.[25] After having been perceived as a theater of divine forces to be feared and avoided in ancient times, a glimmering surface promising new lands and riches during the age of sail, and a place of fascinating depths partly familiarized by scientific discoveries and controlled by humans through technological inventions from the mid-nineteenth century, the sea gradually transformed itself from a powerful presence in human history to a place of personal recreation and impersonal containerization. To Mentz, in the post-World War II era, the ocean was left in the care of "maritime museums, the novels of Patrick O'Brian, and sentimental films."[26] There is not necessarily something wrong with, say, a sentimental movie such as *The Blue Lagoon* (1980), a novel such as *Master and Commander* (1969), or a museum such as the twentieth-century version of the Musée national de la Marine in Paris. But Mentz' constellation of maritime museums, O'Brian's novels, and sentimental films arguably signal a somewhat "antiquarian" approach to the sea in history.[27]

In 1947, when the forgetting of the sea was already well under way, it was still possible for the American poet Charles Olson in *Call Me Ishmael*, a short and elegant meditation on *Moby-Dick*, to imagine a world history whose central topics, geographies, and structure would comprise the Mediterranean (Homer), the Atlantic Ocean (Dante), and the Pacific Ocean (Melville).[28] Only half a century after Olson, Michael Taussig regretfully pointed out that such a historiographical vision now seemed almost unthinkable.[29] If we momentarily accept the Eurocentrism in Olson's vision and suspend the knowledge we now possess of how the Polynesian "sea people" four thousand years ago ventured out into the Polynesian Triangle, then the problem with Olson's dream was not so much the chronological imagining of the vision (from the Mediterranean to the Atlantic to the Pacific), nor was the principal problem his list of Euro-American male authors associated with a specific geography. Although the Polynesian explorers-turned-settlers had a complex and varied nautical vocabulary in terms of natural and technical phenomena bearing witness of their

---

25   Alan Sekula, *Fish Story*, 2nd ed. (1995; Düsseldorf: Richter Verlag, 2002), 51.
26   Mentz, *At the Bottom of Shakespeare's Ocean*, ix–x.
27   Friedrich Nietzsche, *On the Uses and Disadvantages of History for Life, Untimely Meditations*, trans. R. J. Hollingdale (1874; Cambridge: Cambridge University Press, 1983).
28   Charles Olson, *Call Me Ishmael* (San Francisco: City Lights Books, 1947), 117–19.
29   Michael Taussig, "The Beach (A Fantasy)," *Critical Inquiry* 26, no. 2 (2000): 250.

highly developed seafaring culture, it seems they had no name for the ocean as a whole, no concept of a high seas zone beyond their immediate environment and possession, and no knowledge of writing. They were a prehistoric people with no literature as we know it from the likes of Homer, Dante, and Melville. Despite their impressive place sensitivity and conception of the ocean as "road map" divided into a web of distinct places and differentiated pathways,[30] they did not possess the global vision, with which the Pacific experiences endowed Melville.[31] As Taussig saw it, the actual problem was the very topic of Olson's dream: *the ocean*.

To some extent, Taussig was right. Even Olson's magnificent vision could be rubricated as "antiquarian" in the decades that followed its publication, a mere attempt to write history for the sake of history. In 2000, when Taussig published his fantasy, and today as well, very few people have firsthand experiences with ships and the sea. Airspace has not only replaced the sea as the medium through which ordinary people travel but has also become the space used by nation-states to protect and expand territorial sovereignty and where empires exercise world dominance. In addition, the sea and its resources provide a livelihood for fewer and fewer people, yet not many of us consider that many of our material possessions were at some point inside containers aboard the colossal ocean freighters that cross the seven seas relatively unnoticed despite their monstrous size. However, is it not characteristic of these times that water plays an increasing role in the self-understanding and branding of many cities, and that we appreciate living close to water? Yes, this may very well be true, but the urban harbors and canals are merely domesticized and tamed versions of the great ocean: "In New York, as in major ports from Liverpool to Los Angeles, the ocean isn't the heart of the city anymore."[32] Mentz mentions specifically how the Port of New York has been relocated from downtown Manhattan (the harbor area where Ishmael meditates on the necessity of going to sea to prevent a potentially suicidal melancholy from getting the better of him) to Newark, New Jersey. The sea is no longer interweaved with our lives in any "elementary" sense. We do not live on the sea, but distant from it or on the edge of it.

---

30 Philip E. Steinberg, *The Social Construction of the Ocean* (Cambridge: Cambridge University Press, 2001), 52–60.
31 Christina Thompson, *Sea People: In Search of the Ancient Navigators of the Pacific* (London: William Collins, 2019), 9, 18–20.
32 Mentz, *At the Bottom of Shakespeare's Ocean*, x.

2.2 Revision, Actualization, Crisis

So why insist on the centrality of the sea? Why ask what insights will emerge from a combined Blue Cultural Studies and Amphibian Comparative Literature approach? A response can be divided into two main strands, one historical, the other contemporary, and each with multiple sub-answers. The first answer emphasizes that the sea has played an immensely undervalued role in history, especially in the history of modernity. If modernity has traditionally been framed through progress, rationality, and the freedom and autonomy of the individual, an oceanic perspective enables us to discover a "shipwreck modernity" defined as "a catastrophe-ridden epic of ocean-fueled expansion and its attendant disasters."[33] The second answer underlines that we are now living at a point in time when the sea, after the "hydrophasia"[34] of much of twentieth-century humanities scholarship, once again assumes a crucial role in the planet's history, although our awareness of this have come about under sinister omens of plastic oceans and rising sea levels. So, paradoxically, what Olson dreamed of in 1947 but Taussig did not believe possible in 2000, an oceanic world history, is in fact in the process of materializing through numerous important publications in different fields such as history, cultural studies, literary studies, science and technology studies, and environmental studies. I call it a paradox, because Blue Humanities is born out of the climate crisis and forecasts of flooding, and this negative premise was never part of Olson's historiographical dream. However, in terms of relevance, a crisis is never a bad starting point for any scholarly method.

Let us begin with addressing the historical argument, which is grounded less in crisis than in revisionary ambitions and a prospective actualization of certain structural, epistemological, and poetological characteristics of maritime history that resonates particularly well with our fluid modernity.[35] From the time of Homer's Ulysses and Vergil's Aeneas to the beginning of the twentieth century, when people looked at the sea from the coast or the harbor, the sight they saw was very different from ours. What we see nowadays is a blank surface or one with a solitary vessel or a couple of insignificant dots spotted in the distance occasionally. Back then, as evidenced by scenes of the waters outside Cádiz depicted in Andersen Nexø's *Days in the Sun* and Vilhelm Melbye's *A Spanish xebec and other commercial craft*, visions bursting with life and movement and crowded with sailors and ships, with schooners and steamers.

---

33   Mentz, "Blue Humanities," 72.
34   Margaret Cohen, "Literary Studies on the Terraqueous Globe," *PMLA* 125, no. 3 (2010): 658.
35   Zygmunt Bauman, *Liquid Modernity* (2000; Cambridge: Polity Press, 2012); John Urry, *Mobilities* (Cambridge: Polity Press, 2007), especially 161–62.

Bearing in mind the radical shift that the maritime world has undergone since the beginning of the twentieth century, it is no wonder that we came to suffer from a very specific type of Martin Heidegger's concept of *Seinsvergessenheit* or "the forgetfulness of Being": *Meeresvergessenheit* or hydrophasia.

When the twentieth-century forgetting of the sea develops into a general blindness towards the sea's historical role, we face a genuine problem: *To us, modernity is terrestrial, not nautical.* This is true whether we consider modernity to begin with the Renaissance, the Age of Reason, the Enlightenment, or the Industrial Revolution. The developments traditionally related to modernity, here summarized by Michel Foucault, are all predominantly terrestrial: a questioning or refutation of tradition; the valorization of individualism, personal freedom, and formal equality; a confidence in social, scientific, and technological progress; rationalization, standardization, and professionalization; a movement from feudalism or agrarianism toward capitalism and the market economy; industrialization, urbanization, and secularization; and the advance of the nation-state, representative democracy, the bourgeoisie, and public education.[36]

However, nautical modernity prioritizes the ocean instead of the urban, and this makes possible a series of revisions of how we traditionally frame modernity. On ships, education was practical, not intellectual, and took place on the masthead and on the deck, not in lecture halls or at a desk: "a whale-ship was my Yale College and my Harvard," Ishmael claims in *Moby-Dick*.[37] Life at sea was everything but democratic, often dictatorial, or at least strictly hierarchical and feudal. The regularity and orderliness of bourgeois life stood in stark contrast to the exceptional and often brutal living conditions on board ships. And if maritime nationalism is an integral part of the seafaring world, this world was fundamentally global, transnational, or stateless. While landlubbers became increasingly secular and rational, sailors remained superstitious and open to the mysteries of the (divine) mechanisms of the sea. Admittedly, with the advent of steamships and the subsequent division of labor between sailors on deck and engineers and stokers in the engine room, the maritime world followed the path of industrialization and, over time, professionalization, but despite safer conditions, ship life remained very different from the monotony of factory life. The maritime world was no doubt a driving force in the development of global capitalism, but in some areas of commercial shipping more collective principles of solidarity reigned. Faced with the immensity of the

---

36   Michel Foucault, *Discipline and Punish: The Birth of the Prison*, 2nd ed., trans. Alan Sheridan (1975/1977; New York: Vintage, 1995).
37   Melville, *Moby-Dick*, 112.

ocean, eternal in its substance when perceived with human eyes, sailors were less inclined than humans on land to subscribe to the idea of progress. And while the ocean with its vast horizons lured with promises of freedom and escape from the strict conformity of social conventions on land, sailors soon discovered that ship life was a collective phenomenon, and that any hopes of individual autonomy and personal freedom were subjected to mightier forces, not least the powers of nature and the captain. Finally, if land people questioned and rejected traditions, life and labor on board ships were largely based on the transfer of experiences, practices, and traditions from one generation to the next.

In some historical sources there are glimpses, also well-known ones, of insights into a modernity that is not exclusively terrestrial, though. In the beginning of the seventeenth century, Francis Bacon listed in a now famous passage in *Novum organon* (1620) gunpowder, the printing press, and the compass as three technological inventions that had "altered the whole face of things right across the globe." According to Bacon, there was "no empire, no sect and no star," which had "exerted a greater effect and influence on human affairs than these mechanical innovations."[38] The compass was actually a Chinese invention dating back to the middle of the third century BC, and it was initially used as a harmonizing tool in line with the principles of *feng shui*. It was probably not until the eleventh century that the compass was employed as a maritime navigational instrument and made possible what Carl Schmitt has called "that elemental turn towards the sea that was completed in the sixteenth and the seventeenth centuries."[39] The first known reference to the compass as a navigational instrument is in Zhu Yu's *Pingzhou ketan*, written between 1111 and 1117, in which we learn that the ship's pilots "are acquainted with the configuration of the coasts; at night they steer by the stars, and in the day-time by the sun. In dark weather they look at the south-pointing needle."[40]

---

38 Francis Bacon, *The instauratio magna part II: Novum organum and associated texts*, ed. Graham Rees and Maria Wakely (1620; Oxford: Oxford University Press, 2004), 195.
39 Schmitt, *Land and Sea*, 19; translation modified.
40 Zhu Yu, *Pingzhou ketan* (1111–1117; Shangwu yinshuguan, 1936), 2.2b, quoted from Joseph Needham, *Science and Civilization in China: Volume 4, Physics and Physical Technology, Part 1, Physics* (Taipei: Caves Books Ltd., 1986), 279. For a discussion of Zhu Yu's comments on the compass, see also Friedrich Hirth, *The Ancient History of China: The End of the Chóu Dynasty* (New York: Columbia University Press, 1908), 133–34; Joseph Needham, *The Shorter Science & Civilisation in China: 3* (Cambridge: Cambridge University Press, 1986), 27–29. Both Hirth and Needham mention that Zhu Yu in connection with his remark about the compass must refer to the period 1086–1099, during which his father lived in Canton. However, they disagree about the nationality of the mentioned pilots or

Bacon, who had adorned the title page of *Novum organum* with two sailing ships, on their way from the Mediterranean Sea to the Atlantic Ocean, passing through the Pillars of Hercules at the Strait of Gibraltar,[41] did not overestimate the importance of the roles played by the compass and the maritime transportation networks in the development of global modernity.[42] Nor did G. W. F. Hegel, when, two hundred years later, in his *Elements of the Philosophy of Right* (1821) he distinguished sharply between "the earth, the firm and *solid* ground" as "a precondition of the principle of family life" and the sea as "the natural element of industry":

> for the ties of the soil and the limited circles of civil life with its pleasures and desires, it substitutes the element of fluidity, danger, and destruction. Through this supreme medium of communication, it also creates trading links between distant countries, a legal [*rechtlichen*] relationship which gives rise to contracts; and at the same time, such trade [*Verkehr*] is the greatest educational asset [*Bildungsmittel*] and the source from which commerce derives its world-historical significance.[43]

It is worth noting that rather than considering the sea as a barrier, Hegel emphasized its *connective potential*. Rivers and oceans "are *not natural boundaries*" but "link humans together."[44] Also, his chosen concepts resonate with the way we today speak about the World Wide Web. In the last part of the important § 247, he attributed the blossoming creativity and growing wealth in nations such as Denmark, Norway, Sweden, and England to their openness toward and active exploitation of the sea, whereas hydrophobic and navigation-frightened countries such as Egypt and India had sunk into superstition.

From the time of Christopher Columbus, Vasco da Gama, and Ferdinand Magellan, a time during which Western man became restless and showed transgressive propensities, and "the notion of a largely terran earth was

---

captains: Hirth believes that they are Arabic and Persian sailors, while Needham thinks they are Chinese.

41 According to myth, the pillars originally bore the inscription "Nec Plus Ultra" or "Non Plus Ultra," which means "no(thing) further beyond." This was a warning to seafarers not to venture into the Atlantic. After the "discovery" of America, the pillars were used in the Spanish Coat of Arms, but the motto was now changed by Charles V into "Plus Ultra" meaning "further beyond."

42 Cohen, "Literary Studies on the Terraqueous Globe," 657.

43 G. W. F. Hegel, *Elements of the Philosophy of Right*, ed. Allen W. Wood, trans. H. B. Nisbet (1821; Cambridge: Cambridge University Press, 2003), 268.

44 Hegel, *Philosophy of Right*, 268.

replaced with that of the oceanic planet," to the beginning of the twentieth century—an era that stretched over more than four centuries—the maritime world played a key role in the development of mercantilism, capitalism, and colonial expansion. Prior to the emergence of the railroad networks in the beginning of the nineteenth century, merchandise, humans, and information had already been travelling across the seven seas for three centuries, thus emphasizing "the considerable predominance of sea voyages over those on land" during the early accelerations of globalization.[45] They had benefitted from what the Dutch jurist Hugo Grotius called *"mare liberum"* (the freedom of the sea or the free ocean) in a book by the same title, published for the first time in 1609.[46] Admittedly, nations such as Spain, Portugal, the Netherlands, Great Britain, France, and later the United States also fought against each other's military and mercantile fleets for the purpose of controlling trade routes and securing access to important coasts and harbors.

Mare liberum provoked immediate counter-reactions in what came to be known as the "Battle of the Books," for example Seraphim de Freitas' *De justo imperio luistanorum asiatico* (The Imperial Right of the Portuguese in Asia) (1625), whose title conveys its main argument, and John Selden's *Mare Clausum* (1635), which argued for the English crown's legal jurisdiction over maritime routes and resources in the waters surrounding England. While de Freitas agrees with Grotius that the ocean is a distinct space that cannot be possessed and endowed with all the rights of exclusion that are usually claimed by a sovereign, he differs from Grotius by asserting that navigation is not a right bestowed upon everyone by natural law, and that sovereigns may rightfully exercise their power in adjacent waters in ways that limit the freedoms of navigation and trade. So, while Grotius acknowledges that stewardship over ocean-space might theoretically be proclaimed by individual states but that it must in such cases be executed on behalf of the community of states, because access to ocean resources is guaranteed to all under natural law, then Freitas proposes that the right to command over the deep sea should be shared among competent sovereigns. These sovereigns gain exclusive *usufruct* rights but not property rights over specific long-distance trade routes.

Selden focuses on demonstrating the legitimacy of states claiming their neighboring waters as fully incorporated territory within the state. To Selden, and seemingly in opposition to Grotius and Freitas, a state may possess

---

45 Sloterdijk, *Spheres II: Globes*, 804, 804.
46 Hugo Grotius, *The Freedom of the Seas: or, The Right Which Belongs to the Dutch to Take Part in the East India Trade*, ed. James Brown Scott, trans. Ralph van Deman Magoffin (1609, 1633; Union, NJ: The Lawbook Exchange, 2001).

ocean-space. In fact, however, he is arguing for a set of rules similar to those advanced by Grotius for situations in which a state or sovereign could, in effect, own a portion of the ocean. Grotius and Selden both propose systems in which rights to private property are superimposed by regulations preventing usurpation of rights to common usage. These systems then contrast with Freitas, who argues that the sea is common property but susceptible to private usufruct. Philip E. Steinberg sums it up: "Freitas envisions a world in which competing powers claim quasi-sovereignty over specific ocean routes and take on responsibility for policing these routes; Grotius implies that this quasi-sovereignty belongs to the community of nations; and Selden—by implication of omission—suggests a *laissez-faire* regime in which states may cooperate or compete freely, so long as they do not hinder navigation."[47] During the mercantilist era of channeled circulation and trade control, the dominant construction of ocean-space was closest to the one promoted by de Freitas, since states, including the Dutch and the English, continued to assert exclusive rights to parcels of the ocean. Eventually, a resolution to the "Battle of the Books" was reached that combined Grotian *mare liberum* in the deep sea with Seldenian *mare clausum* in coastal waters.

The seafaring world was alluring with its promise of stimulating the emerging human curiosity through geographical exploration.[48] It also made promises of wealth and power: "From the start, the oceanic adventure entangled its actors in a race for hidden chances to access opaque distant markets." The adjectives are important here, for with "hidden" and "opaque" Sloterdijk emphasizes a new risk mentality that, together with curiosity, spurred Western man on. Governments and trading companies invested enormous sums of money in exploration, research, and development, thus contributing to making the maritime world into a technological and scientific frontline of modernity: "During that time, anyone who claimed to understand the world had to think hydrographically."[49]

Although ocean-space was uninhabited by humans and functioned for them primarily as a surface across which extensive trade happened *between* nations on land, Steinberg regards it as "a unique and specifically constructed space *within* society." From a spatial-juridical perspective, it could be claimed

---

47   Steinberg, *The Social Construction of the Ocean*, 98.
48   For an examination of curiosity's importance for Modernity as an autonomous period significantly distinct from Antiquity and the Middle Ages (characterized as they were by theological absolutism), see Hans Blumenberg, *The Legitimacy of the Modern Age*, trans. Robert M. Wallace (1966, 1976; Cambridge, MA: The MIT Press, 1999), 227–453.
49   Sloterdijk, *Spheres II: Globes*, 812, 811.

that the oceanic precedes the terrestrial. As a result of *Mare liberum*, Grotius is considered the founder of the law of the sea and of modern international law in general. It is also important to bear in mind that this treatise, motivated by legal questions concerning the high seas, appeared four decades before the Peace of Westphalia (1648), which served as a blueprint for the modern political system of multiple, sovereign, territorially defined states: "If global politics and law simply are rules that emerge from anarchic interactions among predefined state-actors, 'international' law could not have been conceptualized prior to the formalization of the states that allegedly are the essential units of the system," Steinberg points out.[50] During the early modern period, fluid ocean-space played a key role in the subsequent imaginary and judiciary conceptualizations of societal space during the eras of mercantilism and industrial and postmodern capitalism, not least as a spatial alternative to what is termed the "territorial trap."[51] This concept signifies a conception of the world as naturally divided into preexisting, territorially defined nation-states in which the ocean is reduced to a secondary status as an extra-state space.

There is a significant discrepancy between this brief account of genuine maritime importance and the blindness towards the sea expressed by some of the most influential cultural theorists from the mid-nineteenth century to the end of the twentieth century. Philosophers and thinkers such as Karl Marx, Friedrich Engels, Walter Benjamin, Georg Simmel, and Michel Foucault all contributed to delineate what Margaret Cohen has called "a geography of modernity that was primarily land-based" characterized by a focus "on *terra firma*, on territorialized spaces like the nation state, the city, the colony, the home, and the factory."[52] If Simmel paved the way for the Mobilities Studies of today, his groundbreaking analysis of sensuous stimuli, fast movements, and the need for punctuality was based exclusively on the urban environment of the new metropolises. And if Foucault produced an influential paper on sea and ships, he ultimately consigned the ship to a marginal (heterotopic) position in the cultural history of the West, instead emphasizing terrestrial places such as the prison and the asylum. In short, theoretically and rhetorically, the sea was considered an extra-societal, anti-civilizational, and void space. In reality, of course, both deep sea and coastal waters have provided societies with crucial

---

50 Steinberg, *The Social Construction of the Ocean*, 23, 31–32.
51 John Agnew, "The territorial trap: the geographical assumptions of international relations theory," *Review of International Political Economy* 1 (1994): 53–80.
52 Margaret Cohen, "Fluid States: The Maritime in Modernity," *Cabinet* 16 (Winter 2004–2005): 75.

resources—not least connectivity, fish, and minerals—which gradually made active stewardship and governance necessary.

The cultural theorists were not alone in their attempts to marginalize the sea. The majority of literary historians in the twentieth century were their accomplices. The hydrophasia in literary studies, perhaps we could even call it the *thallasophobia* (not merely a forgetting of the sea, but a fear of the sea with its uncertain moorings), meant that scholars often overlooked the important role played by the ocean in literature and literary history as the *concrete place and medium* for 1) narrative action, 2) the unfolding of historical, national, and political conflicts, and 3) global communication and exchange. But is this a problem? Perhaps the marginalization of the ocean in literary historiography is merely a natural consequence of literature being fundamentally earthbound. Come to think of it, was it not Hegel, who in his lectures on aesthetics in the mid-1830s (and despite his highly developed oceanic sensibility in 1821) characterized the novel as "the modern *bourgeois* epic," thereby implicitly excluding the ocean, industry, the fluid, and the ship from the sphere of the novel?[53]

2.3 Saltwater Literatures

In Denmark, Holger Drachmann implicitly echoed Hegel's conception of the novel in his story "Ørnen" (The Eagle), but at the same time he expressed a heartfelt desire that Danish literature would break with the yoke of the bourgeois ethos:

> rather than the persistent spinning of a tale's thread in a web around "the family's" dinner table or supper table, one should once try to relocate one's weaving industry out into the open air where the wind blows and where the web is swung up and down by light, elastic threads that are infinitely extendable and receptive to the enveloping influence of free nature in the guise of fresh and full colors [...] And maybe the time will come when the writer becomes more of a traveler who sees and experiences than a mere writer who writes.[54]

Nordic writers such as Jonas Lie, Alexander Kielland, Amalie Skram, Johannes V. Jensen, and Aksel Sandemose responded to Drachmann's wish for a windy and colorful literature in a series of fine maritime novels and stories.

---

53   G. W. F. Hegel, *Aesthetics: Lectures on Fine Art*, vol. 2, trans. T. M. Knox (1835–38; Oxford: Clarendon, 1998), 1092; translation modified.
54   Holger Drachmann, "Ørnen," *Poetiske skrifter IV: Sømandshistorier* (København: Gyldendalske Boghandel Nordisk Forlag, 1927), 29.

Internationally, the maritime world had stimulated the imagination of writers and readers, and a wide range of saltwater books and stories were in circulation from the sixteenth century and onwards. Sea journeys unfolded in environments that only few had access to but which influenced the lives of so many people and aroused the curiosity of the reading audience of landlubbers. In addition, the global sea journeys converged historically with the invention of the printing press, and many pseudo-sailors combed maritime travel literature, fictional and factual, to find exotic adventures and specific information about new worldly events and developments.

Based on such observations, it is problematic that writers who have included the sea as an elemental component of human existence and planetary history in their works have been met with a critical-analytical gaze more oriented towards the earthly soil than towards the sea and the ship. Let me mention four examples of such optical distortions. First, the canonical studies of Daniel Defoe's *Robinson Crusoe* (1719), subsequently influencing many later interpretations, read the eponymous hero as an iconic figure who heralds or even incarnates a new type of human: *homo economicus* (Karl Marx, Ian Watt) or the colonizer (James Joyce).[55] Second, if James Fenimore Cooper, who wrote the first genuine maritime novel in literary history, *The Pilot: A Tale of the Sea* (1824), is remembered at all in this age of hypercanonization, he is more remembered for his novels featuring Native Americans set in the wilderness and forests, the Leatherstocking Tales, than for his eleven nautical novels, which earned him the most praise in his lifetime. Third, readers of *Moby-Dick*, especially those taking a Marxist approach, translate the maritime constellation *Pequod*-Ahab-crew into a terrestrial constellation of factory-manager-workers. According to Saul Bellow, the reason for this is a tendency among many readers to over-interpret and read symbolically when there is no reason to do so. This manifests as a problematic will to territorialize the oceanic and transform a fish into a dog.[56] Fourth, Jonas Lie is best remembered in Norway

---

55   Karl Marx, *Das Kapital: Kritik der politischen Ökonomie*, Vol. 1 (1867; Berlin: Dietz Verlag, 1962), I, I, 4; Ian Watt, *The Rise of the Novel* (London: Chatto and Windus, 1957), 60–92; James Joyce, "Daniel Defoe," trans. (from Italian manuscript) and ed. Joseph Prescott, *Buffalo Studies* 1 (1964): 24–25.
56   Saul Bellow, "The Search for Symbols, a Writer Warns, Misses All the Fun and Fact of the Story," *New York Times*, February 15, 1959. Melville does in fact describe the *Pequod* as "a floating factory," and American whaling in the 1840s could rightly be called an industry, but the point is that life on board the *Pequod* is much more than a factory-like life. As Carl Schmitt observes in *Land and Sea*: "A ship is no swimming piece of land, just as a fish is no swimming dog," 51; translation modified.

for the bourgeois novel *Familjen paa Gilje* (1883; *The Family at Gilje*), whose subtitle *Et Interieur fra Firtiaarene* (*A Domestic Story of the Forties*) emphasizes its domestic topography. When scholars direct their attention towards Lie's *Lodsen og hans Hustru* (1874; *The Pilot and His Wife*), it is more often referred to as the first novel of marriage in Norwegian literature than as the first maritime novel in Scandinavian literature.[57] In sum, a series of reading strategies has dominated the reception of maritime writers: 1) forgetting the sea, 2) prioritizing land over sea, and 3) translating maritime matters into familiar earthbound matters.

This said, an oceanic turn within literary studies is unfolding, exemplified in books by literary historians such as Ian Baucom, Josiah Blackmore, Hester Blum, Wolf Burkhardt, Cesare Casarino, Margaret Cohen, Bernhard Klein, Gesa Mackenthun, Steve Mentz, and John Peck. Earlier, scholars such as Monique Brosse, Robert Foulke, and Thomas Philbrick have published substantial works on maritime literature, but despite their obvious qualities, these publications remained relatively peripheral in their time because of the general atmosphere of hydrophasia in the Humanities. Within historical and cultural studies, recent decades have also offered a series of important publications documenting the central role of the sea, by scholars including David Abulafia, David Armitage, Thomas Benjamin, Paul Butel, Alain Corbin, John R. Gillis, Paul Gilroy, Peregrine Horden and Nicholas Purcell, Peter Linebaugh and Marcus Rediker, John Mack, Philip E. Steinberg, and Christina Thompson. Prominent philosopher Peter Sloterdijk has returned to the ocean its historical, conceptual, phenomenological, epistemological, and poetological importance in the development of globalization.

---

57   In the first English translation of the novel, *The Pilot and His Wife*, the translator Mrs. Ole Bull for example adds without evidence in the original the subtitle *A Norse Love Story* (Chicago: S. C. Griggs and Company, 1876). In Arne Garborg's biography, *Jonas Lie: En udviklingshistorie* (Kristiania: H. Aschehoug & Co. Forlag, 1893), the ocean is assigned a considerable role in Lie's life and work, but the author nonetheless ends up focusing his reading of *Lodsen og hans Hustru* on the marriage, just as he in his description of the novel as a threshold novel between past and future refers the ocean to the past while the question of woman's role in marriage is considered an element of the future, that is, as the novel's "modern" impulse. In *Essays on Scandinavian Literature* (New York: Charles Scribner's Sons, 1895), Hjalmar Hjorth Boyesen characterizes *Lodsen og hans Hustru* as "an everyday story in the best meaning of the word, a story about marriage between ordinary people [...] and what makes it even more interesting is that it also has a certain significance in regard to the question of women's role," 143. However, Boyesen also acknowledges Lie's treatment of the maritime as an important factor behind the fact that Lie gradually became known in Norway as "the poet of the sea," 144.

2.4   Geographical Scales

It is time to redirect our attention from the problems associated with hydrophasia to the benefits of wearing maritime lenses. In what ways can the view from a ship's deck disclose suppressed histories of modernity and reconnect us to existential dimensions that we thought we had lost? How can observations from a masthead qualify the discussions of highly topical challenges such as ecology and the climate crisis and create the foundation for a genuinely new methodology? In other words, how can the maritime lenses help us reach new understandings on both the level of description (knowledge) and the descriptive level (method)? In terms of our revisionist purpose, such nautically oriented histories offer new spatial and geographical scales as a supplement to the well-known territorial spaces of the nation and the colony, the city and the countryside, the factory and the household, and the public and the private. Through the maritime perspective, these earthbound places are supplemented with spatial components such as oceans and continents, islands and archipelagos, and coasts and ships. Introducing these spaces makes it possible to 1) *connect old and familiar landmasses in new ways*, for example, the Finnmark and southern Europe with the Gulf Stream acting as a medium of connection as in Jonas Lie's *Tremasteren "Fremtiden"* (1872; The Barque "The Future"); 2) *connect new and different spaces*, for example whaling ship, Nantucket, the United States, and the Pacific as in Melville's *Moby-Dick*; and 3) *to discover alternative historical timelines*.

If the nineteenth-century historical and realist novel—examples include Walter Scott's *Waverley* (1814), B. S. Ingemann's *Valdemar Seier* (1826), and Alessandro Manzoni's *I promessi sposi* (1827/1842)—contributed decisively to nation-building through the creation of imagined and symbolic national communities,[58] nautical novels of adventure—Defoe's *Robinson Crusoe*, Verne's *Vingt mille lieues sous les mers*, and Conrad's *Lord Jim* (1900)—mapped and explored some of the planet's more distant regions.[59] Their spatial elephantiasis meant that these novels and others like them replaced the historical novel's centripetalization of the nation with centrifugalizing forces emphasizing each nation's entanglement with other nations, with an outside, and with alterity. As Mentz observes, the appreciation of alterity in the form of the posthuman and nonhuman is made possible by a Blue Humanities approach, which transforms traditional maritime history—characterized by "its passion

---

58   Benedict Anderson, *Imagined Communities: Reflections on the Origin and Spread of Nationalism* (New York: Verso, 1983); Franco Moretti, *Atlas of the European Novel 1800–1900* (1997; London: Verso, 1998).
59   Cohen, "Literary Studies on the Terraqueous Globe," 658.

for technical exactitude and [...] conservative historiographical methods"—into a posthuman oceanic history: "Literary critics, environmental scholars, sea-level activists, poets and artists are turning to the sea to place human histories in more-than-human contexts. Oceanic perspectives replace stories of national expansion or decline with multiple vectors of movement, so that human history becomes a story of multiple estrangements rather than progressive settlements."[60]

A Nordic example of multiple estrangements and national borders being penetrated or flooded by global waves consisting of foreign impulses is found in Lie's *Tremasteren "Fremtiden"*:

> By its thousands of ships, the sea supplies Norway with a jetsam of ideas of our time from all countries [...]. Just as the warm Gulf Stream carries wreckage and jetsam up north, the currents in human affairs in the past centuries have also sat down the most different sorts of wrecked lives from life in the south on the coasts of Nordland and the Finnmark.[61]

In this passage, Lie stresses how the northernmost region of Norway, traditionally considered isolated, is to be conceived as a contact zone in which human, material, and immaterial elements come together. It is a peripheral zone, but it is also an absorbing sponge, which, at the northernmost turning point of the Gulf Stream, is in a position to enjoy the benefits of being part of a planetary oceanic system of circulation.

It is also characteristic of the maritime novel that it rarely represses the brutal traces from European imperialism, as has been claimed about Jane Austen's domestic novels.[62] Instead, it explicitly confronts the inner tensions, conflicts, and paradoxes of modernity. Chinua Achebe accused Conrad of being "a bloody racist" in his 1975 lecture on *Heart of Darkness* (1899),[63] but in this novel Conrad nonetheless allowed Marlow to overtly reflect on the brutality of contemporary Western imperialism, just as he suggested that London, England, and Western civilization have an equally primitive and "dark" origin as the African continent. One further example from Conrad's work is the tale

---

60 Mentz, "Blue Humanities," 70.
61 Jonas Lie, *Tremasteren "Fremtiden" eller Liv nordpaa: En fortælling* (Kjøbenhavn: Forlagt af den Gyldendalske Boghandel, 1872), 1, 2.
62 Edward Said, *Culture and Imperialism* (New York: Alfred A. Knopf, 1993), 95–115; Cohen, "Literary Studies on the Terraqueous Globe," 658.
63 Chinua Achebe, "An Image of Africa: Racism in Conrad's 'Heart of Darkness,'" *Massachusetts Review: A Quarterly of Literature, the Arts and Public Affairs* 18 (1977): 788.

"Falk" (1903) in which Conrad thematized cannibalism. Through his protagonist Christian Falk, Conrad showed that cannibalism is a practice that we can ascribe to both the so-called barbarian and the so-called civilized white man. That it has become custom to brand Conrad reactionary, conservative, and old-fashioned does not change the fact that the dark sides of imperialism and colonialism—for example racism, exploitation, and violence—are addressed directly and with no attempt to shy away from these themes in many of his works.

Finally, the nautically oriented history can also offer us new and more dynamic maps of the literary market, of authors, readers, publishers, book sellers, and critics connected through the circulation of books, poetics, and genres. As Margaret Cohen has shown in "Traveling Genres," it is only possible to grasp the significance of the maritime novel as one of the most important genres in the nineteenth century, if we employ an Atlantic lens.[64] The maritime novel emerged in the United States and then traveled across the Atlantic, first to Great Britain and then to France, before it returned to the United States. These crossings happened from the beginning of the 1820s to the end of the 1840s, from Fenimore Cooper (USA) to Captain Marryat (England) and Eugène Sue (France), and from there to Edgar Allan Poe, Richard Henry Dana, Jr., and Melville (USA). Later, the genre travelled back to France, where Victor Hugo and Jules Verne contributed to the genre with important novels, and to the Nordic countries, Spain, Italy, and South America. What is interesting about such a transoceanic perspective is that it offers a potentially fruitful counter-narrative to what literary historians traditionally label as the nationalist novel of the nineteenth century. It is not only the maritime novel's themes and geographical universe that are inevitably transnational, global because oceanic, the same is true of its form and poetics, which developed in a tense space of appropriations, imitations, and ruptures—with national refractions of course—on its journeys across the seven seas.

2.5 Historical Timelines

The maritime perspective helps to make spatial revisions and create new geographical constellations of a more rhizomatic character. In a cultural-theoretical sense, this results in an emphasis on the interstices and (open or blocked) connections between nations and cultures, which therefore cannot be considered autonomous and sealed-off islands: multi- is replaced by inter- and trans-, the national by the regional and the global, the singular by the plural.

---

64 Margaret Cohen, "Traveling Genres," *New Literary History* 34, no. 3 (2003): 481–99.

By evading the logics of the "territorial trap" and sovereignty as markers of geographical and historical distinctions, oceanic histories can be not only transnational, transareal, or translocal but also transtemporal and transhistorical in scope. The deep histories of oceans and seas provide alternative and arguably better frameworks for historical understanding than such Eurocentric categories as modernity and the Enlightenment. Deep time, understood as both past and future and materialized through the ocean, is a significant engine behind the watery visions we encounter in *The Drowned World* and *Havbrevene*, which I will analyze in chapter five. To Ballard and Jacobsen, adopting an aquatic standpoint, the ocean *is* (in) history, not outside history, it *is* (within) time, not beyond time.

Staying on more familiar ground, the maritime perspective also makes possible a revision of the traditional timelines of modernity that we usually divide into periods such as the Reformation, the Enlightenment, the Industrial Revolution, and the Democratic Revolutions. In the maritime world, this same period, between the early 1500s and the mid-1800s, converges with the period beginning with the first transoceanic sea journeys made by European explorers towards the end of the fifteenth century and ending with the shift from sail to steam in the mid-nineteenth century. In one sense, we can regard this period of almost four hundred years as a continuity. In terms of transport technology, it is united under what we can call the Global Age of Sail.[65] The continuity does not imply that we cannot divide the age of sail into different periods, though. The maritime timeline of Age of Sail has its own important events. It is different from, yet closely interwoven with, the traditional timeline of modernity. The two timelines both stabilize and reconfigure each other.

As Margaret Cohen has taught us, the years 1759, 1795, and 1807 are each associated with an important invention that helped make life at sea safer. In 1759, the English carpenter John Harrison succeeded in optimizing the chronometer he had first begun to develop and build in 1730, so it was now precise enough to keep track of time on longer sea journeys and thus made it possible to calculate longitude during a crossing.[66] In 1795, the Scottish doctor Gilbert Blane, the chairman of the British Navy's "Sick and Hurt Board," persuaded the British Admiralty that lemon juice should be a mandatory part of sailors'

---

65   Margaret Cohen, "Literary Studies on the Terraqueous Globe," 659.
66   The prehistory of the chronometer can be traced back to the Dutch scientist Christian Huygen's first attempts to construct a chronometer in 1673, just as both Jeremy Thacker and Henry Sully, both English watchmakers, in 1714 and 1716 respectively had tried without success to construct a chronometer that was precise enough and could resist the vicissitudes of the sea.

daily food ration to avoid scurvy, then the most frequent cause of death among sailors.[67] And in 1807, the American engineer Robert Fulton's steamship *North River Steamboat* made its first journey on the Hudson River. This journey not only marked the beginning of a commercially successful ferry service between New York City and Albany, NY, a distance of 240 kilometers, it also launched the proliferation of steamship transportation during the nineteenth century. The consequence of the three inventions was an increased routinization of ocean traveling. The chronometer, the intake of vitamin C, and steamship transportation are scientific and technological developments, which we on land categorize under period concepts such as the Enlightenment and the Industrial Revolution. In that sense, these maritime inventions and dates contribute to a stabilization and strengthening of the traditional and general history of modernity.

However, the three events also function as disturbing interventions in other and more specific histories of modernity. In literary history, for example, we can consider the maritime inventions of 1759, 1795, and 1807 as crucial components of that overall routinization of the global waterways, which led to changes in the poetics of the novel. At first glance, it may seem somewhat bizarre that chronometer, lemon juice, and steamship have played an important role in the evolution of the novel's form, but this is the case as Cohen has convincingly argued. In the time before the chronometer, before the routine treatment of scurvy, and before the steamship, the sailing ship was one of the most dangerous places for humans to inhabit. The sailor who possessed the abilities to navigate securely on the sea was a cultural icon, gifted as he was with practical skills of heroic dimensions intended to assist in dangerous and hazardous situations. The heroism of this figure was unequivocally praised in a series of modern adventure novels descending from Defoe's *Robinson Crusoe* and *Captain Singleton* (1720). In the 1820s, 1830s, and 1840s, and much to the pleasure of numerous readers, many heirs to Defoe's protagonists could be found in the works of authors such as Cooper, Sue, Marryat, and Dana, but also in works by lesser-known authors such as William Leggett, Captain Frederick Chamier, Edward Howard, William N. Glascock, Édouard Corbière, Emile Souvestre, Théodore Pavie, Lieutenant Murray Ballou, Ned Buntline, and Charles Kingsley.

---

67 The Polish scientist Johann Bachstrom and the Scottish surgeon James Lind had already proved in 1734 and 1747 respectively that scurvy could be treated by the intake of lemon juice, but it was not until Gilbert Blanes legal intervention in 1795 that the prevention was institutionalized in the navy.

With the routinization of ship life, which really kicked in during the 1840s, the heroic sailor and the literary celebration of him lost their cultural magnetism and fascination for both authors and readers. With the shift from sail to steam, the heroic sailor was transformed into a museum relic, an anachronistic figure in the age of disenchantment. Until then, maritime fictions had contributed to the literary landscape with a captivating and timely poetics founded on action and adventure, but this poetics gradually lost its raison d'être. A crisis emerged in what had until then been a relatively unproblematic convergence between literary form and maritime material. The crisis was a consequence of the modernization of certain maritime practices, and it resulted in a new narrative genre that Cesare Casarino has called "some form of protomodernism."[68] When Melville published *Moby-Dick* in 1851, the genre became full-blown. Not that Melville's whaling novel did not have predecessors, but neither Poe's *The Narrative of Arthur Gordon Pym of Nantucket* (1838), nor Melville's own *Mardi: and A Voyage Thither* (1849), or Cooper's last sea novel, *The Sea-Lions: The Lost Sealers* (1849), possessed the formal complexities and semantic depths that characterize *Moby-Dick*.

Moby-Dick, *Pym*, *Mardi*, and *Sea-Lions* all originated from the nation that in the early 1820s had created the maritime novel in close connection with what Thomas Philbrick has called American "maritime nationalism."[69] Both Poe and Melville, perhaps also Cooper in the last years of his life, understood the tension that emerged between the aesthetic of maritime fiction and its thematic appeal and increasing cultural and historical obsolescence of this genre. Melville in particular twisted the form of the novel out of joint by inaugurating a series of alternative explorations, although he did so without abandoning the sailor and his border-transgressive life and labor. These explorations consisted of diving into the most obscure zones of language, poetics, hermeneutics, and the human mind, but the previous poetic orientation toward the surface of the sea, maritime history, was now also complemented with a curiosity toward the underwater world and *oceanic history*. Modernizers of the poetics of maritime fiction discovered that the human mind's endlessly receding depths and strange life were mirrored in the submarine dimension of the ocean, and they found this to be a vast source of inspiration.

In the maritime narrative tradition, Hugo and Conrad were the next to challenge the Mariana Trench of representation and meaning production. If

---

68   Cesare Casarino, *Modernity at Sea: Melville, Marx, Conrad in Crisis* (Minneapolis: University of Minnesota Press, 2002), 9.
69   Thomas Philbrick, *James Fenimore Cooper and the Development of American Sea Fiction* (Cambridge, MA: Harvard University Press, 1961), 2, 42–56.

Moby-Dick constitutes the American version of the simultaneous culmination and subversion of the maritime novel, the French and English versions of this concurrence of apex and sabotage are works such as *Les Travailleurs de la mer*, *The Nigger of the "Narcissus"* (1897), *Lord Jim*, "The Secret Sharer" (1910), and *Vi pynter oss med horn* (1936; *Horns for Our Adornment*), the latter by Aksel Sandemose. The link between processes of maritime modernization and poetics of the novel not only enables us to explain that Melville, Hugo, Conrad, and Sandemose annexed new territories in the historical evolution of the novel, new territories, which in the cases of Melville, Hugo, and Conrad would later become associated with modernism (and, in the Sandemose example, become an integral part of modernism). It also enables us to explain *why* they did it; or, perhaps even more precisely, why they felt *compelled* to do so, and this even ahead of their time.

Such alternative timelines, made possible through the maritime lens, also enable us to accentuate other and possibly even new dimensions of modernity. As noted by Cohen in "Literary Studies on the Terraqueous Globe," one of the defining chronotopes of modernity is the extremely dangerous, but also potentially productive places that from a temporal perspective exist at the absolute forefront of a present in constant motion, and from which knowledge is always developing and is therefore incomplete. According to Cohen, the fascination of modernity with this chronotope enables us to re-think the importance of Robinson Crusoe. Instead of connotations of primitivity and a regression to a mere natural state, which are what first comes to mind when we look at the original frontispiece with Robinson depicted in clothes of goatskin, the image also allows for a different interpretation of Robinson as a person who experiments and breaks new ground. The ideas of an unspoiled natural state held by Enlightenment thinkers, not least Rousseau, is supplemented with an alternative vision of nature as an admittedly harsh but also genuinely fertile zone that is available for human explorations and practices.

It required incredible skills in the art of action to survive in such places, where knowledge constantly changed and vibrated in its incompleteness. Philosophers has a name for the particular intelligence that characterizes persons who excel in action: *practical reason*. The sailor, especially the sailor who knew how to navigate, was a hero because of his practical reason. Thanks to Descartes, modernity has primarily been defined by and understood through an intelligence famous for its abstract and calculating rationality, with neutral, scientific knowledge being the most celebrated form of this intelligence. But this type of reason is just one of several tools of knowledge that characterize those persons who thrive in the dynamic frontier zones of modernity. Other tools and perhaps more relevant ones are the senses, intuitions, experiences, feelings, and the body.[70] A literary character who embodies the shift away from a Cartesian, disinterested, and bodyless rationality towards a reason based on intuitions, experiences, and embodied local knowledge is Cooper's John Gray, the protagonist in *The Pilot*, whom we shall learn more about later. The Danish navigator Jens Munk, famous for his North-West Passage expedition in 1619–20, is another example that I also examine more closely.

Practical reason, understood as the ability to act in singular *hic et nunc* situations, has been considered differently in different historical periods. The processes of secularization have resulted in a belief in the efficacy and potency of human action (an important characteristic of historical time's open future). This differs from the ancient understanding of practical reason. The modern version of practical reason thrives in vibrating border zones characterized by great unpredictability but also by discoveries, profit, and inventions. In contrast, the ancient version is shaped in a worldview that respects the limitations of humans, which at the same time entails the limits of the divine because of a prevailing logic of reciprocity. In those times, the border was an undesirable place to be for humans, even for those who possessed practical reason.

As Cohen observes, the reappraisal of practical reason as a valuable element in modernity's hierarchy of faculties and abilities enables us to recognize the extraordinary quality and superiority that distinguish literature's heroes of composed action and cunning deeds. Again, Robinson is the obvious example, but so are Jens Munk, John Gray, Ahab, Gilliatt, Nemo, Salve Kristiansen, Rejer Jansen Juhl, Thomas MacWhirr, Henry Whalley, and Wolf Larsen. Cooper's pilot is a hero who acts, and with limited technological resources he uses his embodied reason to navigate extremely dangerous and unpredictable situations at sea. By overcoming challenges and solving problems for his own personal gain—not money and wealth as in *Robinson Crusoe*, but personal fame—he mobilizes his reason (understood here as a future-oriented modality of calculation and action), but also his patience and composure, his ingenuity, his creativity, his body, and his courage. The employment of practical reason to solve problems and to profit from it characterizes the protagonists in the adventurous stories that unfold at sea and on land. It is a device that links a variety of genres across history, genres that also share a tainted reputation among critics and academics, including the chivalric romances and the picaresque novels, perhaps even the Greek idealistic novels, as well as spy novels, detective novels, and science-fiction novels in the nineteenth, twentieth, and

---

70 Cohen, "Literary Studies on the Terraqueous Globe," 660.

twenty-first centuries. The valorization of practical reason invites us to rethink how we estimate the different poetics of the novel.

Among optimistic apologists of Western modernity, freedom of movement is considered one of the decisive premises of progress and perfectibility. From the disenchanted perspective of the Frankfurt School, the project of progress and the freedom of movement are inextricably linked with human dominance over nature, which ends in scenarios of catastrophe. However, Cohen claims that the historical epoch known as the global Age of Sail defined by overseas journeys offers a third (and more morally ambivalent) concept than progress and dominance: *adventure*. Not exclusively a project (as with progress and human dominance), adventure is also a discourse, a narrative, and (with Raymond Williams) a "structure of feeling." Adventure understood as a constellation comprising a particular discourse, a narrative practice, practical reason, and a (transindividual) structure of feeling has played an equally important role in modernity as concepts and phenomena such as calculation and scientific reason.

The adventure constellation is yet another example of how Oceanic Studies and Blue Humanities complicate our previous understanding of modernity. In novel studies, the adventure constellation assists scholars in redefining their understanding of the genre. Historically, novels of suspense and adventure have been among the most popular forms among readers but some of the most denigrated by scholars. A probable explanation for this divergence is that adventure novels lack the conflictual and psychologically profound topic and individual that characterize works such as Richardson's *Pamela* (1740) and, especially, Rousseau's *Confessions* (1782/1789). Coinciding historically with Rousseau's commencement of his confessional project in the 1760s are James Cook's preparations for adventure and ambition to transgress the limits of dynamic knowledge through explorations of the globe's distant regions. In bestselling narratives about Cook's journeys, the exploration of biography, inner feelings, and private life promoted by Richardson, Rousseau, and their descendants are replaced by problem solving, observation of the objects and nature in the outer world, and a struggle for survival in dangerous, unknown territory. The history of maritime modernity compels scholars of the novel to reinstate the adventure novel and the adventure constellation on the maps of modern epistemology.

Scandinavian writers such as Lie, Skram, and Sandemose were not the only ones to answer Drachmann's call for an "open-air" literature as opposed to a "dinner-table" literature. Many internationally established writers had published this type of literature long before Drachmann wrote "Ørnen" in 1874. This implies that the problem of "the 'forgetting' of the sea" is not so much a result of a lack of empirical material as it is a result of a lack of institutional and disciplinary inclination. In *A Poetic History of the Oceans*, I examine some of this empirical material and attempt to counter the forgetting of the sea by adapting the methodology of Blue Humanities and an Amphibian Comparative Literature.

2.6 Blue Ecologies

One of the most important implications of adapting a Blue Humanities approach is the transformation of ecology *from green to blue*. The ocean radicalizes some of the dilemmas in environmentalism and makes them stand out more clearly. Ideas of human control, sustainable growth, and harmony between humankind and nature are seriously questioned, when blue ocean replaces green pastures as a starting point for any discussions on ecology and environment. As Mentz has pointed out, "our newer fables of ecological harmony can't keep us dry."[71] The wet nightmares of environmental destruction and the instability associated with the stingy saltwater of the oceans inundate any cheerful dreams of environmentalism associated with topoi such as the beach and the park. The beach is a model place for withdrawn contemplation and safe transactions between the ocean and the human as exemplified in Caspar David Friedrich's *Der Mönch am Meer* (Figure 2), and the park is a traditional place of carefree loafing as exemplified in Walt Whitman's "Song of Myself" in *Leaves of Grass*.

In his book on Shakespeare's ocean, Mentz references Pierre Hadot's distinction in *The Veil of Isis* (2004) between a Promethean and an Orphic relationship to nature: "The ocean epitomizes Orphic nature. An oceanic perspective speaks to our emerging sense that crisis, not stability, defines the world in which we live now. Supplementing our 'green' cultural turn with a 'blue cultural studies' that looks at our world through the deathly, inhuman, magical lens of the sea can begin rebuilding narrative and interpretive practices to respond to our uncertain future."[72] Mentz's interpretation of Hadot— the ocean as epitomization of an Orphic, instable, and deathly nature—is too simple and does not really convey the nuances of Hadot's definitions of the Orphic and the Promethean attitudes, which both have affiliations with the ocean. Mentz' description seems to suggest that the Friedrich and Whitman scenes, characterized by their safe distance and jubilant untroubledness respectively, belong to the Promethean discourse on nature. However, this

---

71 Mentz, *At the Bottom of Shakespeare's Ocean*, 96.
72 Mentz, *At the Bottom of Shakespeare's Ocean*, xii–xiii.

FIGURE 2   Caspar David Friedrich, *Der Mönch am Meer* (1810). Nationalgalerie, Staatliche Museen zu Berlin
PHOTO: © BPK / NATIONALGALERIE, SMB / ANDRES KILGER

would be a mistake. Although *Der Mönch am Meer* and the green park scenes in "Song of Myself" in no way fit Mentz's description of Orphic nature, they do both fall into Hadot's Orphic category, but belong to a more peaceful class within that category.

But how does Hadot define the two different relationships to nature? If the Promethean approach to nature is "voluntarist," the Orphic is "contemplative."[73] This is why Friedrich's painting belongs to the Orphic orientation. It is a contemplation of the relationship between humans and an opaque and mysterious nature, at once fascinating and terrifying, which is immune to human efforts of omnipotence. A crucial distinction between Friedrich and other Orphic works of art and literature—those alluded to by Mentz—is the difference between a safe distance from and an immersion within the potentially terrifying and deathly natural forces of the sea. Examples include J. M. W. Turner's *Snow Storm* (1842) and specific chapters in Melville's *Moby-Dick*, for example "The Castaway" (chapter 93). Although the experiences of Melville's

---

73   Pierre Hadot, *The Veil of Isis: An Essay on the History of the Idea of Nature*, trans. Michael Chase (2004; Cambridge, MA, and London: Harvard University Press/Belknap, 2008), 317.

Pip and Friedrich's monk can be regarded as being of an Orphic nature, Pip's experiences with the ocean were vastly different from those of the monk.

Of the Promethean relationship to nature, Hadot writes: "If man feels nature to be an enemy, hostile and jealous, which resists him by hiding its secrets, there will then be opposition between nature and human art, based on human reason and will. Man will seek, through technology, to affirm his power, domination, and rights over nature." The Promethean approach to nature is linked to modern technology and is also a metahistorical phenomenon that was characterized by strategies of magic and mechanics that were mobilized to violate, torture, or ruse nature of its secrets or resources. To Hadot, both the Promethean and Orphic approaches to nature have positive attributes. "The moral motive force of the Promethean attitude" is for example "the desire to help humanity," but there is also the danger that the "blind development of technology and industrialization, however, spurred on by the appetite for profit, places our relation to nature, and nature itself, in danger."[74]

Prometheus committed hubris by stealing fire from Zeus, and his nemesis consisted of being chained to a rock where an eagle ate his liver by day. The liver regenerated by night and the cycle repeated endlessly. Promethean figures featured later in this book include Captain Ahab and Captain Nemo. Greek theogonies, centering gods (*theós*) and decentering man (*anthropós*), warned against Promethean transgressions and human overconfidence. In contrast, the biblical "Book of Genesis" instructed mankind to "subdue" the earth and to "have dominion" over all other living creatures.[75] Historically, but especially by German Romantics such as Schiller, Christianity has been regarded as an accomplice in the mechanistic representation and subsequent desacralization of nature, perhaps most obvious personified by Newton. Following the origin stories of the Abrahamic religions, which gave humans a privileged place at the center of divine creation, "Copernicus and Darwin built new narratives from scientific evidence and humans became just another animal on just another planet orbiting just another ordinary star."[76] The shifting power relations between gods, humans, science and technology, nature, and planet will be an important topic in several chapters of this book.

Of the Orphic relationship to nature, Hadot writes: "If, on the contrary, people consider themselves a part of nature because art is already present in it,

---

74 Hadot, *The Veil of Isis*, 92, 98.
75 *The Holy Bible*, "Book of Genesis," KJV King James Bible 1611 (London: Robert Barker, 1611), 1:28.
76 Erle C. Ellis, *Anthropocene: A Very Short Introduction* (Oxford: Oxford University Press, 2018), 1.

there will no longer be opposition between nature and art; instead, human art, especially in its aesthetic aspect, will be in a sense the prolongation of nature, and then there will no longer be any relation of dominance between nature and mankind. The occultation of nature will be perceived not as a resistance that must be conquered but as a mystery into which human beings can be gradually initiated." If the Promethean approach is characterized by an artificial modification of perception—experimental physics is an example—then the perception that orients the Orphic approach is "naïve" according to Hadot. Instead of magic, mechanics, and technology, humans here employ "only reasoning, imagination, and artistic discourse or activity to contemplate nature." Instead of violence, Orpheus penetrates the secrets of nature through "melody, rhythm, and harmony": "Whereas the Promethean attitude is inspired by audacity, boundless curiosity, the will to power, and the search for utility, the Orphic attitude, by contrast, is inspired by respect in the face of mystery and disinterestedness." To Hadot, the positive attribute of the Orphic orientation is its fundamental respect for nature and ability to maintain what he calls "a living perception of nature." If the danger in the Promethean approach had to do with a potential destruction of nature and of our relationship to it, the Orphic approach comprises its own danger of "primitivism."[77] I said before that Captain Ahab and Captain Nemo incarnate the Promethean attitude, but it is also characteristic of both *Moby-Dick* and *Vingt mille lieues sous les mers* that they comprise elements of the Orphic orientation, for example in the form of poetic language miming the wonders and generative force of the undersea world. Other works such as Michelet's *La Mer* and Ballard's *The Drowned World* are also characterized by the coexistence of scientific and aesthetic perceptions, of a technologically driven quest to unveil the secrets of nature and a poetic ambition to match and figure the mysterious splendor and horror of nature.

In strong alliance with the ocean, the concept of the Anthropocene—a concept that refers to a new epoch in planetary history during which humanity has become a geological force—profoundly changes our understanding of the contemporary ecological crisis. Not so long ago we still tended to perceive of the environment as something external to us, an entity that surrounds us, and a place where humans went to extract resources, deposit waste, or enjoy untouched spots of virginal nature. Any environmental degradations were referred to as externalities. Nature in its various forms—natural parks, ecosystems, environment, and sustainable development—was considered important

---

77   Hadot, *The Veil of Isis*, 92, 95, 96, 98.

but essentially separate from us. The hyperobject of the ocean and the concept of the Anthropocene come together in their dual challenge of our idea of separation and our belief in sustainable growth. The environment has now been replaced by the Earth system. If industrial modernity promised to liberate us from the inertia of nature, of its cycles and its limits, and to empower us in a world of unlimited progress, the limited and self-regulating Earth is now making a somber return. Earth history insistently and violently returns into human history, smashing the distinctions between nature and society and reorganizing the principles of the human condition and human freedom.

Blue Humanities in the age of the Anthropocene view humans not as masters and owners of nature but increasingly as beings entangled within the vast feedback loops of the Earth system. The dominant discourse of sustainable growth based on the deep-rooted and stubborn belief in linear and inexorable progress is being challenged by critics of excessive consumerism and profit-driven enterprises. In turn, the progressionists accuse these critics of wanting to return the world to a bygone romantic era of innocence. If there is a growing sense of crisis in our present, this may in fact be a too vague diagnosis. Why? Because crisis implies a transitory state, but according to Christophe Bonneuil and Jean-Baptiste Fressoz, the Anthropocene represents a *point of no return*. They claim that the future of planet Earth, including all its living creatures and species, is at stake, and neither the liberal, nor the social democratic, or the Marxist visions of a bright future bear any similarity with this highly unstable development strewn with so-called tipping points that characterize our contemporaneity.[78] Consequently, we may be forced to think and act outside and beyond those political visions and fiscal systems that we have been used to for almost two hundred years.

The ocean and seafaring are reminders of humanity's profound entanglements with nature and the nonhuman, of the illusion of any deep, essential split between humans and their environment. If the ocean alienizes our globe, it is in the sense of making it *unfamiliar* to us, *not separate* from us. The sea is at the same time the condition (entanglement) and boundary (unfamiliarity) of our human existence. What Melville called the "masterless ocean"[79] constantly reminds us that we control neither ocean nor globe: "It defines the world as it is, not as we'd like it to be. […] The sting of salt reminds us that the world isn't a happy story," says Mentz. Indeed, there are beneficial outcomes of our ecological era. The increasing awareness of a greater mutuality between the planet's

---

78 Christophe Bonneuil and Jean-Baptiste Fressoz, *The Shock of the Anthropocene: The Earth, History and Us*, trans. David Fernbach (2013; London: Verso, 2017), 20–21.
79 Melville, *Moby-Dick*, 457.

different elements and parts, the softening of anthropocentric concerns and the dispersion of agency, and a deepening sense of intimacies instead of separations are potential lifebuoys that we may grab hold of as the inhabitability of the planet increases. However, as Mentz has also pointed out, "hopes for a dry life, an easy, pastoral, sustainable relationship between nature and culture, seem as unlikely as a full season of calm seas. It's not that we don't want it. It's not that we shouldn't work toward it. It's that we won't get it." As scientists discovered in the nineteenth century, the ocean is the conductor of the planet's climate, acting both as thermostat and driving force in ways we still cannot accurately predict. In an Anthropocene era of climate change that has left behind the relative stability of the Holocene, the world is becoming bluer, wetter, and messier. This is also why "our newer fables of ecological harmony can't keep us dry."[80] Nor can the old fables.

If neither the old nor the newer fables of ecological harmony (say, Virgil's *Georgics*, Whitman's *Leaves of Grass*, Ernest Callenbach's *Ecotopia*, and Kim Stanley Robinson's *Pacific Edge*) can keep us dry, then we need what Mentz has labelled wet fables that both match and figure the great oceans and their role in Earth's history. In addition, we need a method with which to read such fables. The good news is that we have these stories already. Instead of fables of ecological harmony, let us call them *fables of blue ecology*. While some of them are newer (e.g., *The Drowned World*, *The Sharks*, *Blå*, and *Havbrevene*), some are also old and perhaps in need of new readings (e.g., *The Odyssey*, *The Aneid*, "The Saga of the Greenlanders," and *Navigatio Septentrionalis*). What I call an *amphibian comparative literature* within the emerging blue cultural studies offers the proper methodological approach to these fables and to the conceptual, intellectual, and ethical challenges posed by a bluer planet. Just as literature and literary criticism cannot cure cancer, they are likewise unable to shield coastal residences from tsunamis and hurricanes and prevent the melting of the ice caps. However, our Western culture is defined by a persistent struggle with living in dynamic, unpredictable, (semi)aquatic environments. This struggle has been waged on the battlefields of language and narrative forms as much as on the battlefields of science and engineering. Amphibian comparative literature embraces the nonhuman dimensions and scales of literature, the terrestrial and the aquatic spaces as well as the organic and the inorganic actors.

In *Ecocriticism* (2004), Greg Garrard surveys the field's most prominent metaphors and tropes. Among them are the pastoral, the wilderness, the

---

80   Mentz, *At the Bottom of Shakespeare's Ocean*, xiii, 96, 97, 96.

apocalypse, and dwelling. It becomes clear from the book's table of content and the specific content of the chapters that the ocean has only played a minor role in ecocriticism. Ecocriticism has been green ecocriticism, but time has come to turn it blue: "Shifting our focus from the supposed stability of land, with its pastoral and georgic master narratives, to a broader vision that embraces the maritime world and what Melville calls 'this terraqueous globe' will mean abandoning certain happy fictions and replacing them with less comforting narratives. Fewer gardens, and more shipwrecks."[81] To Mentz, this means replacing landlocked stories of human struggles to cultivate, calculate, and control nature—that is, agricultural and pastoral visions of sustainability and predictability—with water-logged stories of human improvisations and collaborations with a disorderly world in flux and nautical visions of menacing and capricious environments. Amphibian comparative literature approaches these stories with a belief that they can assist us in *welcoming* and *withstanding* saltwater-propelled turmoil.

Oceanic space is more-than-human. As a hyperobject, and despite its contemporary forms of plastic ocean and mounting ocean, the ocean challenges any aspirations of unconditional anthropocentrism. Plastic ocean and mounting ocean result from anthropogenic behavior, but they now seem to strike back against humanity, leaving us impotent in the face of ocean-driven climate change. In the confrontation and entanglement with the ocean, human actors are translocated from controlling and disembodied heights and plunged into the depths of ambiguity, flux, dissolution. Seafaring and maritime existence are, with Sloterdijk's words, "a resolutely anti-contemplative and deduction-hostile knowledge programme. The *experimentum maris* provided the criterion for the new understanding of world experience."[82] It is because of this experimental and empirical dimension of the maritime that the nonhuman and posthuman environment of the ocean is of great value in this era of anthropogenic climate change. Since the Earth's history has fallen back into human history and destroyed the Enlightenment dream of separating society from nature, humans have found themselves living in an increasingly unstable and destructive environment, whose physically overwhelming manifestations resemble the flux and fluidity of the masterless ocean more than the solidity and stability of cultivated land. The ecological crisis resembles a shipwreck in that they both produce feelings of disorientation and disruption. In many of the texts and sources analyzed in this book, the reader encounters

---

81   Mentz, *At the Bottom of Shakespeare's Ocean*, 98.
82   Sloterdijk, *Spheres II: Globes*, 813.

unembellished visions of humans, most of them male sailors, trapped between divine decree, natural forces, and inadequate assurances of individual agency and technological assistance. Nautical tales depicting the practical labors of sailors in crisis—often denigrated in rational modernity yet celebrated by writers from Homer, Munk, and Cooper to Hugo, Conrad, and Bjørneboe because imperative for survival—represent valuable stories of how humans endure when faced with uncontrollable nonhuman powers. As sea levels rise, and numerous hurricanes wreck seaside residences in the Anthropocene, we have become increasingly aware of the upsetting and bewildering entanglements of humans and oceans. No one has been better at depicting and fabricating these entanglements than writers and artists, sailors and scientists, then and now.

2.7 *Method and Structure*

A Poetic History of the Oceans does not perform a deep dive into specific works or authors, nor into any limited historical epoch, nor any national cultural and literary history. If the book dives deeply, it is into a transnational, planetary, and cross-historical phenomenon: the Ocean. I have chosen this approach because we understand this phenomenon *not only* through Herman Melville's *Moby-Dick*; through biblical sources such as "Genesis" and "Revelation"; through Jules Michelet's *La Mer*; the handwritten diary of Jens Munk; through J. G. Ballard's *The Drowned World*; through J. M. W. Turner's marine paintings; through anonymous accounts of Portuguese shipwrecks; Siri Ranva Hjelm Jacobsen's fictional letter exchange between the Atlantic Ocean and the Mediterranean Sea; and through scientific graphs of CO_2 emissions, deforestation, and global temperatures documenting the entrance into the Anthropocene epoch. No, we understand the Ocean better through the multifaceted *combination* of all these sources and documents and artworks.

In that sense, and because it incorporates all the above and many more, *A Poetic History of the Oceans* is deliberately comparative across periods, languages, nations, genres, and disciplines. The book is not an exercise in comparativism for the sake of comparativism. Rather, it is motivated by the aim of mobilizing what have been separated poetological engagements with water, distanced from each other through time, space, and language despite their obvious interrelations, temporal and spatial entanglements, and human and nonhuman networks. Institutionally, the distancing has occurred because area studies and language-based literature studies are naturally rooted in political realities such as nations and empires. The ocean requires a different take.

Admittedly, comparativism may lead to elisions on some levels, but it is hoped that there are gains on others. Suitable to the book's topic, *A Poetic History of the Oceans* commits itself methodologically to waves and geographical continuity more than to trees and geographical discontinuity.[83] Although the tree mechanism of nations plays a role, such as when Jonas Lie Scandinavizes James Fenimore Cooper's form of the American nautical novel (Cooper's *The Pilot* becomes Lie's *The Pilot and His Wife*), the dominant mechanism in *A Poetic History of the Oceans* is the wave mechanism of the world and the planetary ocean, of World Ocean. Methodologically speaking, the ocean as prism and protagonist catalyzes a new operational vocabulary in which territories give way to *relations*,[84] compartments to *entanglements*,[85] earth to *water*, mountains to *oceans*, distinctions to *distortions*, and clarity to *obscurity*.[86]

There are no doubt Americanists with far greater knowledge of Melville than mine, just as there are entire books devoted to *Moby-Dick* alone; the same can be said about Victor Hugo and *Les Travailleurs de la mer* and about Jules Verne and *Vingt mille lieues sous les mers* within French Studies; surely, biblical scholars and historians can supplement my selection of only a few ancient sources and two texts by Michelet and Munk with much more additional material, and they would also be able to nuance my readings of the selected sources and texts; scientists would definitely be capable of explaining the mathematical mechanisms and deep data behind their graphs better than I can. However, recalling Émile Durkheim's famous dictum that *comparison* may be to the social sciences what *experiment* is to the natural sciences, I want to transplant that idea into the humanities. By bringing these varied sources and approaches together and comparing them (that is, performing what Durkheim labelled an "indirect experimentation"[87]) and by applying a distinct epistemological and poetological framework through which to read them (How to know the unknowable? How to give shape to that which is shapeless?), I hope that Melvilleans, scholars of French literature, biblical scholars, historians, and scientists as well as many other experts and scholars may learn something new from the relations and entanglements forged by this book between their respective fields of expertise and other fields, whether these are literary works, authors, periods,

---

83   Franco Moretti, "Conjectures on World Literature," *New Left Review* 1 (2000): 66–68.
84   Ottmar Ette, *ZwischenWeltenSchreiben: Literaturen ohne festen Wohnsitz* (Berlin: Kadmos, 2005), 9–26.
85   Anette Werberger, "Überlegungen zu einer Literaturgeschichte als Verflechtungsgeschichte," in *Kulturen in Bewegung: Beiträge zur Theorie und Praxis der Transkulturalität*, eds. Dorothee Kimmich and Schamma Schahadat (Bielefeld: transcript, 2012), 111–143.
86   Steve Mentz, *Ocean* (New York: Bloomsbury, 2020), xv–xviii.
87   Émile Durkheim, *The Rules of Sociological Method: And Selected Texts on Sociology and its Method*, 2nd ed., ed. and intro. Steven Lukes, trans. W. D. Halls (1982; Basingstoke: Palgrave Macmillan, 2013), 101.

or disciplines. And, as once reasoned by Fernand Braudel with a reference to Henri Pirenne, as a work of *synthesis* and an attempt at a "new thalassology," my book will hopefully inspire new crops of specialized research.[88]

The comparative approach fosters different questions. How does a reading of Melville's *Moby-Dick* benefit when its final apocalyptic vision of a flood is compared with a biblical deluge, and with the flood scenarios in Hugo's *The Toilers of the Sea*, Ballard's *The Drowned World*, and Jacobsen's *Havbrevene*, and what insights will emerge by performing such a comparison within a framework of the Anthropocene? How can a reading of Michelet's *La Mer* profit from a poetological and aesthetic sensibility and a comparison with the oceanic visions in *The Toilers of the Sea*, Verne's *Twenty Thousand Leagues under the Seas*, and Carson's *The Sea Around Us*? How do different generic modes in Munk's *Navigatio*, Defoe's *Robinson Crusoe*, and Jacobsen's *Havbrevene*—diary, fake diary, anthropomorphized epistle—influence their epistemologies, their oceanic thinking? How can an eyewitness account of a Portuguese shipwreck in the sixteenth century not only inform readings of that same nation's heroic epic, *Os Lusíadas*, but also of later works of technological crisis such as Conrad's *Typhoon* and Verne's *Twenty Thousand Leagues*?

A Poetic History of the Oceans comprises five chapters with three longer chapters on history (chapter one), technology (chapter three), and the Anthropocene (chapter five) punctuated by two shorter chapters on rhythm (chapter two) and materiality (chapter four). There is alternation within and between the chapters of human and nonhuman scales. The chapters on history and technology primarily activate human perspectives, whereas the chapters on rhythm, materiality, and the Anthropocene address the sea and maritime existence from perspectives less human and more nonhuman, prehuman, and posthuman.

"History" examines how Western humanity has perceived the ocean from ancient times to the present. In this chapter and drawing from a wide variety of sources from the Bible, Homer, and Horace to Jens Munk, Herman Melville, Jonas Lie, Jens Bjørneboe, and many more, I outline four so-called maritime world pictures that also represent four historical periods: theocentrism (–1450), anthropocentrism (1450–1850), technocentrism (1850–1945), and geocentrism (1945–). Each maritime world picture comprises a certain perception of the sea, a distinct relationship between gods, humans, technology, and nature, a specific temporal configuration, and to some extent also a particular poetics

---

88   Fernand Braudel, *The Mediterranean and the Mediterranean World in the Age of Philip II*, vol. 1, trans. Siân Reynolds (1949; 1972; Berkeley: University of California Press, 1996), 15.

of the sea. While the above periodizations signal a historical framework that is valid in its overall structure and content, two comments are appropriate: first, the temporal boundaries between the periods are flexible just as the specific characteristics of one period may appear in moderated form in other periods; second, the world-picture constellation comprising ocean perception, figure of time, poetics, and the gods-human-technology-nature relationship is also conceived as a general analytical tool—a methodology—with which maritime sources, especially literary ones, can be approached. At the end of the chapter, I read *Moby-Dick* as both a summation and deconstruction of the preceding (self-consciously simplified) stage-by-stage historical narrative of sea writing.

In "Rhythm," I examine how oceanic and maritime rhythms embrace humans in a bodily and affective sense, making them feel and experience the sea and maritime existence. Analyzing rhythms entails a shift from meaning to presence. Rhythms are not meant to be hermeneutically interpreted. There are no hidden meanings beneath a surface. Instead, they can be analyzed as phenomena that temporally structure our experiences and bodily affect us, and instead of asking what they mean, we should ask whether or not they function and how they work. Ship life is a privileged place from which to analyze rhythms because the sailor is highly exposed to winds, waves, and currents, to sunrise and sunset, and to the seasons; besides such natural rhythms he is also subjected to stringent cultural rhythms and protocols. Rhythmanalysis is reciprocally a relevant method with which to examine the cosmic and cultural rhythms of seafaring. Examples could be a burial at sea in Jack London's *The Sea-Wolf* (1904), the monotony of steamship life in Malcolm Lowry's *Ultramarine* (1933), the militaristic discipline in Jens Bjørneboe's *The Sharks* (1974), a calm sea in Samuel T. Coleridge's "The Rime of the Ancyent Marinere" (1798), the furious weather in Joseph Conrad's *Typhoon*, and the psychological disharmony in his *The Nigger of the "Narcissus."* Rhythmanalysis assists us in getting a better sense of how it feels to be on board an ocean-going vessel by drawing us closer to the physical and empirical dimensions of the mariner's life. The natural and social rhythms of life at sea are supplemented by the aesthetic rhythms of language, form, and style, with which writers attempt to mime and produce oceanic life, which is itself a profoundly rhythmic phenomenon. So, in addition to the cultural and natural rhythms of oceanic existence, I explore the aesthetic rhythms of maritime literature.

Assisted by philosophers and scholars such as Martin Heidegger, Don Ihde, Peter-Paul Verbeek, and Langdon Winner, "Technology" discusses the historically diverse human engagements with the sea, as they have been mediated through different premodern and modern technologies. The central argument of the chapter is that maritime existence is per definition technological. This was the case, when humans ventured out in canoes using muscles and paddles as propellers of motion, and it also applies to the sixteenth century when Portuguese *carraca*, large merchant sailing ships, sailed between Lisbon and India. I analyze an anonymous eyewitness account of the shipwrecking of one such carrack, the *São João*, which foundered because of an unfortunate combination of technological breakdown and critical weather conditions. At the time of Jules Verne and Joseph Conrad, the maritime world had become intensely technological. While the Frenchman is traditionally considered a writer hailing the possibilities of scientific and societal progress as well as geographical advancements made possible by the invention of new technologies, Conrad is regarded the archetypal reactionary critic of modern technology as it leads to alienation, disenchantment, and moral corruption. We see how these perceptions of Verne and Conrad are only partly correct, and I give nuance by showing how Verne exhibits ambivalent and complex attitudes to modern technologies in *Vingt mille lieues sous les mer*, and how Conrad finds positive human experiences on board a steamship in distress in *Typhoon*.

The chapter on "Materiality" focuses on the intense maritime entanglements between humans and nonhumans and between organic and inorganic matter. An initial discussion of the aesthetic strategies of maritime immersion in the experimental documentary *Leviathan* (2012) by Lucien Castaing-Taylor and Véréna Paravel frames the subsequent analysis of Victor Hugo's ode to the sea and the abyss, *Les Travailleurs de la mer*. Drawing on theories on vibrant matter by Jane Bennett, the dissolve by Stacey Alaimo, stone by Jeffrey J. Cohen, things by Bill Brown, and stuff by Maurizio Boscagli, I situate Hugo's protomodernist novel in the context of the new materialism. This context allows for an informed discussion of some of the novel's most important themes such as the relationship between gods, humans, technology, and nature, the status of work and workers in society and nature, and the tension between creation and effacement.

In "Anthropocene," I examine the role of the ocean and how writers have imagined it in different ways in the age of the Anthropocene. The chapter comprises a longer discussion of different theories and poetics of the novel—including those by Franco Moretti, Amitav Ghosh, Thomas Pavel, and Ted Underwood—and of the genre's (in)capacity to embrace and match the challenges posed by the Anthropocene, on the one hand a new world order produced by a powerful humanity, on the other hand a condition in which humans have now been left impotent in the face of potentially catastrophic Earth system processes run amok. I have selected three primary sources for discussion: Aage Krarup Nielsen's travelogue *En hvalfangerfærd: Gennem troperne til Sydishavet* (A Whaling Voyage: Through the Tropics to the Antarctic Ocean), published in 1921; J. G. Ballard's science-fiction novel *The Drowned World* from 1962; and *Havbrevene*, an epistolary novel by Siri Ranva Hjelm Jacobsen published in 2018. The generic variety is intentional as it allows me to show the representational limitations and strengths of different formats when confronting the maritime Anthropocene. Regarding Nielsen's travelogue, a work that celebrates human endeavors and technological development and envisions nature as stock and resource, we can now read it as an early warning of species extinction and fossil fuel-driven climate change thanks to our growing awareness of having entered the Anthropocene. In Ballard's novel, rising sea levels have led to a flooding of the planet, and humans—not the cause behind this new water-world—are now trying to come to terms with their new watery environment. To Ballard, a transformation of the human species in such conditions of inundation is preferable to attempts of species preservation. Finally, in Jacobsen's book, the Mediterranean Sea and the Atlantic Ocean are sisters sending letters back and forth to each other. *Havbrevene* is also a book about the climate crisis and rising sea levels, but as in Ballard's novel, the role of humans is downplayed, allowing instead for a master plan on a higher level to appear. The plan's outcome is a posthuman blue planet on which the saltwater ocean is envisioned as a fertile incubator for new life.

CHAPTER 1

History

In Western history, from Greek-Roman antiquity to the present, the sea has served as a horizontal screen on which humanity's cultural imagination has projected its changing social and metaphysical phantasms. For centuries, humans considered the substance of the sea to be unchanging and regarded its form as constantly changing. The sea's fluctuating appearance has been subject to multiple interpretations throughout human history. Michelet, author of the influential and poetic *La Mer*, points to the ocean's substantial solidity and claims it is humans and their perception of the ocean that change: "The element which we call fluid, mobile, and capricious, does not really change; it is regularity itself. What is constantly changing is man."[1] If claims about the ocean's constancy can be challenged in the light of climate change, microplastic, and the Anthropocene, Michelet does have a point in singling out the radical difference in temporal scale between the ocean and human history. With the briefness of human lives follows a fundamental mutability of humankind's relationship to the ocean. As humanity changes through the centuries, so do conceptions of the sea. The changing interpretations take the form of symbolic representations of the sea in a variety of sources ranging from religious texts, poems, epics, and prose stories to paintings, movies, diaries, logbooks, travelogues, and treatises of history, natural history, and philosophy. In this chapter, I analyze a selection of exemplary representations of the sea drawn from some of these sources, aiming to outline the paradigmatic semantic shifts of the ocean in the cultural history of the West.

This first chapter is divided into two parts. One is a delineation of a history of four maritime world pictures through multiple sources. The other is a reading of Herman Melville's modern epic, *Moby-Dick; or, the Whale* (1851), that aims to show how the four different world pictures coexist in the novel. To anticipate the main argument of the first part, the historical framework comprises four different paradigms in which the components of gods, humans, technology, and nature constitute variable hierarchies among themselves. While the paradigms are serial and chronological, they never exist in their pure form but overlap and interpenetrate throughout history. Abstractions like the one I am about to perform—extracting world pictures of "oceanic thinking"

---

[1] Michelet, *La Mer*, 11.

from historical periods—always entails the loss of historical details, nuances, and ambiguities. But rising above the muddy waters of daily history bring clarity. Questions of clarity versus detail aside, the four maritime world pictures should first and foremost be regarded in their operational capacity and valued by their potential to serve as models of analysis.

The first paradigm, which dominated until the mid-fifteenth century, is *theocentric*. After this period of religious orientation and supremacy, an *anthropocentric* perspective in which humans challenged for and occupied the center prevailed until the middle of the nineteenth century, when a *technocentric* perspective characterized by the dominance of a technological mode of being replaced it. Technocentrism has only intensified since the nineteenth century, but a new planetarianism whose perspective is *geocentric* emerges in the second half of the twentieth century. Joachim Radkau has called the period beginning around 1970 "the age of ecology," others talk about "the great acceleration" around 1945 that catapults the Earth into a new geological era called the Anthropocene.[2] In this geocentric epoch, planet Earth takes center stage. In the first period, mankind is subject to the forces of the sea, which are believed to be expressions of divine will. During the second period, a more equal and collaborative relationship between humans and ocean emerges, and humans begin to consider the sea to be a force of nature rather than a theater of divine dramas. In the third period, humans gain greater control over the sea through developments in transport technology, not least the replacement of sail by steam, just as scientific mappings, analyses, and prognoses assist humans in their efforts to tame the unruly ocean. The emerging fourth period is characterized by an increased awareness of planet Earth being one coherent, vulnerable, and admirable ecosystem that is governed by the ocean as engine and thermostat. Increasingly, our way of thinking and talking about the world and its past, present, and future configurations is filtered through what Timothy Morton has labeled "the ecological thought."[3] In this book, ecological thought implies that the ocean is an elementary component, and the planet is more blue than green.

The dominant theories of modernity from the mid-nineteenth century and onwards by Marx and Engels, Simmel, Benjamin, Foucault, and others defined it as a terrestrial phenomenon and thus marginalized the role of the sea. With

---

2 Joachim Radkau, *The Age of Ecology: A Global History*, trans. Patrick Camiller (2011; Cambridge: Polity Press, 2014); J. R. McNeill and Peter Engelke, *The Great Acceleration: An Environmental History of the Anthropocene since 1945* (Cambridge, MA: Harvard University Press, 2014).
3 Timothy Morton, *The Ecological Thought* (Cambridge, MA: Harvard University Press, 2010).

Martin Heidegger we can say part of our "forgetfulness of Being" is due to our suffering from a "forgetfulness of the sea." However, this hydrophasia is being increasingly challenged by a rediscovery of the crucial role of the ocean. This rediscovery relates to the ocean's role in the world-historical evolution that took off in the mid-fifteenth century and today has culminated in an age of globalization, migration, and mobility. In addition, it is associated with our growing ecological awareness of the planet's existential struggle for survival in the age of the Anthropocene.

In the second part of the chapter, I show how the uniqueness and complexity of *Moby-Dick* is a result of Melville's incorporation of all four world pictures. The coexistence of different historical paradigms of "oceanic thinking" in *Moby-Dick* is not only visible as world pictures entailing different perceptions of the ocean and of time. They are also articulated in distinctive literary styles and tonalities. This points to the significance of literary form and aesthetics in the representational history of the ocean in Western history. Together with the historical framework of the four different paradigms and their characteristics, my reading of *Moby-Dick* and its coexisting world pictures is intended to create a productive starting point from which further discussions and analyses can unfold in the subsequent chapters.

1   Theocentrism

1.1   *The Biblical Tradition*

The notion of a primordial sea is common to most cultures, but it is in the Christian tradition that the idea of the sea as something terrifying, demonic, and chaotic is most evident. The primary sources are biblical texts, originating from an agrarian society, such as "The Book of Genesis," "The Book of Psalms," "The Book of Job," and "The Book of Jonah," but also the classical (Patristic) interpretations of these biblical texts.[4] In "The Book of Psalms," we learn that "the floods of ungodly men made me afraid," and later it says: "Then the channels of waters were seene, and the foundations of the world were discovered: at thy rebuke, O LORD, at the blast of the breath of thy nostrils."[5] "The Book of Genesis" depicts Creation as a series of divinely sanctioned distinctions whose

---

4   Alain Corbin, *The Lure of the Sea: The Discovery of the Seaside 1750–1840*, trans. Jocelyn Phelps (1988; 1994; London: Penguin, 1995), 1. In the following I draw on material and arguments from Corbin's erudite book.
5   *The Holy Bible*, "The Book of Psalms," 18:4, 18:15.

purpose is to transform the formless into form. It portrays the primordial universe before Creation as a dark and desolate hydro-vacuum, a fluid, undifferentiated, and endless deep over which the spirit of God hovered. The formless soup symbolized the unknown and was therefore terrifying. God then created light and separated it from the darkness, and thus the distinction between day and night. Subsequently he created a vault that separated the waters, and the sky and earth emerged as separate spheres. Then "God said, Let the waters under the heaven be gathered together unto one place, and let the dry land appear: and it was so. / And God called the drie land Earth, and the gathering together of the waters called hee, Seas: and God saw that it was good."[6]

It is possible to summarize this notion of the sea from the Christian tradition by noting the absence of any ocean in the Garden of Eden. Nor is there any place within the closed landscape of Eden from which one can behold a vast ocean. According to church fathers such as Saint Basil the Great, Saint Ambrose, and Saint Augustine, trying to understand the mysteries of the sea borders on sacrilege, and is comparable to wanting to penetrate God's impenetrable nature.[7] Substantially, the sea is regarded as a residue of the primordial soup of chaos. Symbolically, it is a sign of the incompleteness of Creation. The sea is the extension of an original, formless chaos into a postdiluvian age and represents an ante-civilizational disorder.

It is unsurprising that the fall of man is followed by a flood, the Deluge. This is a punishment executed by water, and it represents a temporary return to chaos. No consensus exists as to where the water came from: some believe it came from the sky where the clouds make up a fluid and penetrable border between air and water; others believe it came from the earth itself where the coasts form a more sedentary, yet still porous border between land and sea. To the pious souls in the theocentric period, the sea with its noise and sudden ferocity remains a reminder of the state of sin of the first humans and their later obliteration in the waves. It is symptomatic that fire, not water, functions as the cleansing element in the apocalypse in "The Book of Revelations." With the return of Christ, the sea has disappeared: "It is part of the Johannine

---

6 *The Holy Bible*, "The Book of Genesis," 1:9–10.

7 See for example the first conversation about the sea between Ariste and Eugène in Père Dominique Bouhour, *Les Entretiens d'Ariste et d'Eugène* (Paris: Mabre-Cramoisy, 1671), 1–51, especially 37–38. Père Bouhour's neoclassical text disseminates the theocentric tradition's perception of the sea, but it also positions itself in the anthropocentric tradition in which the sea begins to be valued both as an aesthetic object and as a medium of communication in terms of commerce and discoveries.

apocalypse's promise that, in the messianic fulfillment, there will no longer be a sea," says Hans Blumenberg.⁸

The terrifying image of the return of the punishing, chaotic, and endless waves represents a leading motif in Western art until the seventeenth century, in works such as Michelangelo's fresco in the Sistine Chapel, *Diluvio universal* (1508–10), in Antonio Carraci's painting *Il Diluvio* (1616–18), and in Nicolas Poussin's *L'Hiver/Le Déluge* (1660–64). Even for artists such as J. W. M. Turner (*The Deluge*, 1804–05), Théodore Géricault (*Le Déluge*, 1818), Francis Danby (*The Deluge*, 1837–39), and Gustave Doré (*Le Déluge*, 1866), who belong in the anthropocentric and less hydrophobic age, the biblical flood and the terrifying headwaters were often-used motifs. The motif has reemerged as a central topos in our era of climate crisis and rising sea water levels, for example in the fascinating works by visual artists such as Monica d'Alessandro (*Blue Planet*) and Josh Keyes (*Phantom*, 2016).

Maritime disasters in the form of inundation also played a significant role in natural histories and in geology until the first half of the nineteenth century. In 1768, the Reverend Alexander Catcott, an English geologist and theologian, thus attempted a line-by-line commentary to the Old Testament's story of the deluge in his *Treatise on the Deluge*. Catcott found the story fully satisfactory because he considered the Bible to be a scientific source. To him, "the *foundation* for *all true Philosophy*" is "the Knowledge of the *natural State of the Earth*." However, Catcott's ontology compromises the apparent geological basis of this statement and his book in general by his incorporation of theological parameters. His purpose was to offer evidence that a "Flood of Waters" once drowned the Earth, and to convince the reader that the Deluge was the most important event in history: "Now of all events that have happened to the Earth, there is none that has made greater noise in the world, or has left such evident marks of its Reality, as that of a *Flood of Waters*, in which the whole Globe was drowned." He explicitly collected his evidence from three sources: "The *Evidence*, deducible for this great Event, may be said to be *Threefold*: First, *The Scripture*. Secondly, *Heathen History*. Thirdly, the *Natural State of the Earth*."⁹ It makes sense to read this list as a hierarchy in terms of importance, the Scripture being more significant than history and geology.

---

8   Hans Blumenberg, *Shipwreck with Spectator: Paradigm of a Metaphor for Existence*, trans. Steven Rendall (1979; London and Cambridge, MA: The MIT Press, 1997), 8; see also W. H. Auden, *The Enchafèd Flood: or, The Romantic Iconography of the Sea* (New York: Vintage, 1950), 6–7.
9   Alexander Catcott, *A Treatise on the Deluge* (London: E. Allen, 1768), 1–2.

1.2 The Greek-Roman Tradition

In ancient Greece, Homer considered Oceanus to be the origin of everything. Oceanus circumscribed the world and thus marked its limits, but he was himself limitless. Poseidon, who was associated with the Mediterranean, was the nephew of Oceanus. He was not a very powerful god and had a dual function as god of horses and sea god. His power was relativized by this functional split and by the fact that he had several competitors as sea god, for example Triton, Pontus, Nereus, and Thalassa, a female primeval spirit of the sea. As sea god, Poseidon was considered both a destroyer and benefactor. One of the extant Homeric hymns is a hymn to Poseidon:

> I begin to sing about Poseidon, the great god,
> mover of the earth and fruitless sea, god of the deep
> who is also lord of Helicon and wide Aegae. A two-
> fold office the gods allotted you, O Shaker of the
> Earth, to be a tamer of horses and a saviour of ships!
>
> Hail, Poseidon, Holder of the Earth, dark-haired
> lord! O blessed one, be kindly in heart and help
> those who voyage in ships![10]

In terms of the distinctive (anti-)oceanic thinking of theocentrism, the hymn depicts the sea as barren and therefore not of particular interest to or benevolence toward humans. Humans depend on Poseidon to save their ships and help the crews, indicating belief in a god-governed universe.

Admittedly, there are occasional examples of a more positive, even anthropocentric world picture in the Greek sources, including some that comprises the ocean. One of the most famous chorus songs in ancient Greek tragedy serves as an example of this. I am referring to Sophocles' *Antigone* (441 BC). "Wonders are many, and none is more wonderful than man," the chorus begins before continuing with specifics: "the power that crosses the white sea, driven by the stormy south-wind, making a path under surges that threaten to engulf him." But also, the sea's counterpart, the earth, "doth he wear, turning the soil with the offspring of horses, as the ploughs go to and fro from year to year." Furthermore, "he snares" "the light-hearted race of birds, and the tribes of savage beasts, and the sea-brood of the deep, [...] in the meshes of his woven

---

10 Anonymous, "XXII to Poseidon," in *Hesiod, The Homeric Hymns and Homerica*, ed. and trans. Hugh G. Evelyn-White (London: William Heinemann Ltd./New York: The Macmillan Co., 1914), 449.

toils, he leads captive, man excellent in wit." Man is an autodidact who controls cities and states through "speech, and wind-swift thought." In short, "he hath resource for all; without resource he meets nothing that must come: only against Death shall he call for aid in vain; but from baffling maladies he hath devised escapes."[11] The chorus song displays great faith in man and his capacities. It reminds us of the passage in "The Book of Genesis," in which God said to Adam and Eve on the fifth day: "Be fruitfull, and multiply, and replenish the earth, and subdue it, and have dominion over the fish of the sea, and over the fowle of the aire, and over every living thing that mouveth upon the earth."[12] However, in both cases an even stronger theocentrism outweighs anthropocentrism. After all, God was the creator of the world and created Adam in his image. In Sophocles, humans are still required to "honour the laws of the land" and to uphold "that justice which he hath sworn by the gods"[13] The polis and the Olympian gods supersede humans in the hierarchy of the Greek world picture. There is also a possible irony underlying the chorus song's praise of humanity. The song is as an implicit commentary to Antigone's and Creon's virtues, both the laudable ones (commitment to the family, commitment to polis) and the problematic ones (hubris).

Ancient Greek literature generally depicts the ocean as a place of mystery and a place to avoid. In Homer's *The Odyssey*, Eurycleia advises Telemachus against embarking on a sea journey to look for Odysseus: "Nay, abide here in charge of what is thine; thou hast no need to suffer ills and go a wanderer over the unresting sea." To this, Telemachus answers: "Take heart, nurse, for not without a god's warrant is this my plan." The exchange confirms the hydrophobia of the Greek world picture. Telemachus rejects Eurycleia's prudent advice and opens an anthropocentric possibility, but he still refers to the goodwill of the gods as a prerequisite for his venture. Together with Jason, Odysseus was one of the first seafaring adventurers in the history of Western literature, but nostalgia and homesickness made him prefer a life on land to a roaming life on the Mediterranean. Understood as a theater for divine powers, the sea in *The Odyssey* also functions as a source of obstacles for Odysseus, continuously hindering his efforts to return to his island home of Ithaca. Poseidon personifies these powers: he "continued to rage unceasingly against godlike Odysseus." The other Olympian gods also will the sea to perform different functions. On Athena's request and after many years of passivity, they decide to intervene

---

11   Sophocles, *Antigone*, in *The Tragedies of Sophocles*, trans. Richard C. Jebb (1904; Cambridge: Cambridge University Press, 1912), 332–64.
12   *The Holy Bible*, "The Book of Genesis," 1:28.
13   Sophocles, *Antigone*, 367–69.

in Poseidon's persecution of Odysseus and help the latter "return home to Ithaca."[14]

Odysseus had to suffer "many [...] woes [...] in his heart upon the sea," before he could rejoin Penelope, his wife. The ocean is more often an adversary than a helper. This is because Odysseus is guilty of blinding Polyphemus, the son of Poseidon. The personal relationship between Odysseus and Poseidon's family determines Poseidon's role, and by extension, the role of the ocean in *The Odyssey*, yet perceptions of the sea and Poseidon's role in *The Odyssey* do not necessarily serve as an example of how all of Antiquity viewed the sea. However, in general the ocean is associated with a purposiveness. Despite the ocean's contingent and unpredictable nature stemming from Poseidon's idiosyncratic propensities, it still possesses the teleology of an underlying power: "but he took from them the day of their returning," it says about Poseidon's divine power over Odysseus and his men.[15] Everything is significant, everything is endowed with a meaning, and everything happens with a purpose, even if this purpose is down to one god's egoistical desire. In Hesiod's agricultural almanac *Works and Days* (c. 700 BC), there is a similar mistrust of Poseidon when Hesiod rebukes his brother Perses for seeking new opportunities by sea voyaging. If Hesiod discourages embarking on sea journeys, he accepts their existence and perhaps even their necessity. *Works and Days* is full of sound advice on how to go about maritime enterprise and praxis.[16]

The theocentric world picture comprised an oceanic model of fragmentation. If we move forward in time to the stoic tradition, humans were encouraged to stay within the boundaries of the known. This meant that they should abstain from the hazardous and contingent sea journey. Horace, for example, considered navigation to be an outright crime against the gods. In *Tadel und Lob der Seefahrt* (1970; Criticism and Praise of Seafaring), Titus Heidenreich describes this as a belief in a "nautical original sin."[17] In his *Odes* (23 BC), Horace complained that humanity defied the laws of heaven by venturing on reckless and sinful sea journeys:

> Heaven's high providence in vain
> Has sever'd countries with the estranging main,

---

14   Homer, *The Odyssey*, trans. A. T. Murray (1919; Cambridge, MA: Harvard University Press/London, William Heinemann Ltd., 1945), II, 369–70; II, 372; I, 20–21; I, 17–18.
15   Homer, *The Odyssey*, I, 4; I, 9.
16   Hesiod, *Works and Days*, in *Hesiod, The Homeric Hymns and Homerica*, l. 618–94.
17   Titus Heydenreich, *Tadel und Lob der Seefahrt: Das Nachleben eines antiken Themas in den romanischen Literaturen* (Heidelberg: Carl Winter, 1970), 30.

If our vessels ne'ertheless
With reckless plunge that sacred bar transgress.
Daring all, their goal to win,
Men tread forbidden ground, and rush on sin.[18]

In another ode, Horace implores a ship to return to port:

O luckless bark! new waves will force you back
To sea. O, haste to make the haven yours!
[...]
O, shun the sea, where shine
The thick-sown Cyclades![19]

The Horatian image of the sea is of something terrifying and chaotic. Like Ovid and Seneca, Horace despised *oceanus dissociabilis*, the dividing ocean, which separated humans from other humans and from the gods. It was not the division Horace despised; it was the ocean. In both cases, humans/humans and humans/gods, a divinely sanctioned and "natural" law ordained the division. It was not a coincidence that people were separated from each other, nor that the divine and human worlds were divided.

Evidently, there was more than one perception of the sea in the theocentric epoch of the cultural history of the West. Both the Greek and Roman civilizations were maritime and industrious cultures. In recent decades, new research has expanded our knowledge about Western and non-Western premodern maritime cultures.[20] However, besides stressing the general prevalence of theocentrism in these cultures, their maritime praxis was primarily coastal, not oceanic, and the sea was looked upon with distrust, at least in Western culture. The sea was a divine reminder of the mortality and limitations of humans and that their natural habitat was *terra firma*.

---

18   Horace, *The Odes and Carmen Saeculare of Horace*, trans. John Conington (23 BC; London: George Bell and Sons, 1882), I, iii. In the Latin original, the expression "the estranging main" refers to "oceano dissociabili."
19   Horace, *The Odes*, I, xiv.
20   See e.g. David Abulafia, *The Boundless Sea: A Human History of the Oceans* (London: Allen Lane, 2019); David Abulafia, *The Great Sea: A Human History of the Mediterranean* (2011; London: Penguin, 2012); Peregrine Horden and Nicholas Purcell, *The Corrupting Sea: A Study of Mediterranean History* (Oxford: Blackwell, 2000); Albin Lesky, *Thalatta: Der Weg der Griechen zum Meer* (New York: Arno Press, 1973); Sebastian I. Sobecki, *The Sea and Medieval English Literature* (Cambridge: D. S. Brewer, 2008); Christina Thompson, *Sea People: The Puzzle of Polynesia* (London: William Collins, 2019).

1.3 "The Seafarer"

A later example that belongs to the theocentric paradigm is the Old English poem "The Seafarer" (c. 975) in which the sailor is a figure calling for compassion because of the hardships experienced:

> how I often endured / days of struggle, / troublesome times, / [...] the terrible tossing of the waves, / where the anxious night watch / often took me / at the ship's prow, / when it tossed near the cliffs. / [...] a hunger tears from within / the sea-weary soul. / This the man does not know / for whom on land / it turns out most favourably, / how I, wretched and sorrowful, / on the ice-cold sea / dwelt for a winter / in the paths of exile, / bereft of friendly kinsmen, / hung about with icicles; / hail flew in showers. / There I heard nothing / but the roaring sea, / the ice-cold wave. / [...] Indeed he credits it little, / the one who has the joys of life, / dwells in the city, / far from terrible journey, / proud and wanton with wine, / how I, weary, often / have had to endure / in the sea-paths.[21]

A basic elegiac tone characterizes these lines—*troublesome, anxious, hunger, wretched, exile, terrible, weary*. But to the anonymous composer of the poem, the associations with the sea can never be completely negative, because the sea is, always has been, and always will be a place of adventure and a source of new ideas and rebirths.

We must admire the seafarer because of what could anachronistically be labeled his Faustian nature. Note the terms such as *urges, go forth, longing, strives, widely, eager, unsated*, and *unresisting*:

> the wish of my heart urges / all the time / my spirit to go forth, / that I, far from here, / should seek the homeland / of a foreign people—/ [...] he always has a longing, / he who strives on the waves. / [...] And now my spirit twists / out of my breast, / my spirit / out in the waterways, / over the whale's path / it soars widely / through all the corners of the world—/ it comes back to me / eager and unsated; / the lone-flier screams, / urges onto the whale-road / the unresisting heart / across the waves of the sea. / [...] God set that spirit within him, / because he believed in His might. / Man must control his passions / and keep everything in balance, / keep

---

21   Anonymous, "The Seafarer," Anglo-Saxons Net, accessed September 7, 2021, http://www.anglo-saxons.net/hwaet/?do=get&type=text&id=Sfr.

faith with men, / and be pure in wisdom. / [...] Let us ponder / where we have our homes / and then think / how we should get thither.[22]

"The Seafarer" acknowledges that God is the source of man's *Wanderlust* and expansive desire. But the poem that ties in with the elegiac tradition and belongs to the tradition of wisdom literature (e.g., "The Book of Job" and "The Book of Proverbs") also calls for prudence by encouraging man to carefully consider where he belongs and how he can arrive in his place of belonging. The poem's answer to the first question is in heaven. The answer to the second is by stoically controlling his passions and desires, not least his transgressive urge. Compared to the stoic Horace and the hydrophobic biblical texts, we can trace a more positive perception of the sea and a more prominent role of the human in "The Seafarer." The oceanic thinking that develops in the next period entails a further reconfiguration of the hierarchy between gods, humans, technology, and nature.

∴

To summarize, in the theocentric epoch the dominant element in the gods-humans-technology-nature constellation is the gods. The epochal motto is Non Plus Ultra, *and the ocean is considered a barrier and believed to host monsters. Sea journeys are generally associated with high risks not worth taking. This is the era of oar and sail in which humans are reminded to know their limits.*

2   Anthropocentrism

Carl Schmitt once characterized the time around 1500 by its "elemental turn towards the sea" and as "the first, complete, space revolution on a planetary scale."[23] Schmitt's oceanic turn converges with what Ottmar Ette has referred to as the first of "four main phases of accelerated globalization" between 1450 and 1550:

---

22   "The Seafarer."
23   Schmitt, *Land and Sea*, 19, 33; translation modified. We should distinguish between two different "oceanic turns." The one referred to by Schmitt is the practice of sailing the seven seas that became a prime mover in global history from 1450 and onwards. The other oceanic turn refers to the increased attention on the ocean in academia in recent decades.

It is the phase of European colonial expansion, which was mainly sustained by the powers of the Iberian Peninsula and which opened up the "New World" for the Europeans with the so-called discovery of America in 1492. Up until the midsixteenth [sic] century, far from remaining confined to America, this led to an enormous expansion of European political power, as well as creating trade routes on a truly global scale. The asymmetrical nature of European/extra-European relations expressing itself in this first phase was to become the starting point for subsequent phases of accelerated globalization. It led to structural asymmetries in military, economical, political, bio-political and cultural relations, a fact which can still be clearly felt today.[24]

The period between 1450 and 1550 launched an era dominated by anthropocentrism that lasted until approximately 1850. During these four centuries of sail, heroism, and discoveries, the surface of the sea glittered enchantingly and lured humans with tantalizing adventures, and then, during the nineteenth century of steam, mathematization, and routinization, glitter morphed into grid.

The new mentality had at least three different yet interrelated consequences. First, a network model replaced the former model of fragmentation. Second, the winds previously regarded as threatening were now hailed as being full of promise and possibilities. In Camões' *The Lusíads* (1572), the Portuguese sailors are thus "Emboldened by opposing winds."[25] Third, the concept of contingency underwent a semantic transformation from being associated exclusively with risk to being linked also with chance and opportunity for territorial, intellectual, scientific, religious, and economic expansion.[26] "What could have motivated the move from land to sea but a refusal of nature's meager offerings, the monotony of agricultural labor, plus the addictive vision of quickly won rewards, of more than reason finds necessary [...]—the vision, that is, of opulence and luxury?"[27] Blumenberg composes these sentences on

---

24 Ottmar Ette, "European Literature(s) in the Global Context: Literatures for Europe," in *Literature for Europe?*, ed. Theo D'haen and Iannis Goerlandt (Amsterdam and New York: Rodopi, 2009), 126–27.
25 Luís Vaz de Camões, *The Lusíads*, trans. with introduction and notes Landeg White (1997; New York: Oxford University Press, 2001), I, 27.
26 Ulrich Kinzel, "Orientation as Paradigm of Maritime Modernity," in *Fictions of the Sea: Critical Perspectives on the Ocean in British Literature and Culture*, ed. Bernhard Klein (Aldershot and Burlington: Ashgate, 2002), 39–40.
27 Blumenberg, *Shipwreck with Spectator*, 9.

a negative background of Hesiod. In *Works and Days*, he delineated an image of landbased human life that contrasted with Blumenberg's vision of maritime adventure: "The earth bears them victual in plenty, and on the mountains the oak bears acorns upon the top and bees in the midst. Their woolly sheep are laden with fleeces; their women bear children like their parents. They flourish continually with good things, and do not travel on ships, for the grain-giving earth bears them fruit."[28]

To mention but a few significant journeys and writings that document Blumenberg's "move from land to sea," 1450–1850 was the era of Christopher Columbus' four voyages (1492–1504) and the logbooks that accompanied them; of the Magellan Expedition's circumnavigation of the globe (1519–22); of Richard Hakluyt's *The Principal Navigations, Voiages, Traffiques and Discoueries of the English Nation* (1598–1600); of Vitus Bering's two Kamchatka Expeditions (1725–43); of Louis Antoine de Bougainville's circumnavigation of the globe (1766–69) followed by the publication of his logbook *Le voyage autour du monde, par la frégate* La Boudeuse, *et la flûte* L'Étoile (1771), saturated with the latest knowledge in the fields of anthropology, geography, and biology; of La Pérouse's scientific expedition around the world (1785), which tragically ended in shipwreck but still produced *Voyage de La Pérouse autour du monde* (1797); of Captain Frederick Marryat's *Frank Mildway* (1829), the first English maritime novel that was followed by more than a dozen new ones; of Eugène Sue's *Kernok le pirate* (1830), the first French maritime novella, to which Sue added a few more, some of novel length; of Dumont d'Urville's three scientific voyages (1822–25, 1826–29, and 1837–40); of Thomas Beale's *The Natural History of the Sperm Whale* (1839); and of John Franklin's fatal Northwest Passage Expedition (1845).

2.1 "The Saga of the Greenlanders"

Just as extra-European alternatives to my framework of European timelines and world pictures exist (the Chinese and the Polynesians had practiced oceanic navigation in the centuries before the so-called "oceanic turn"), so intra-European exceptions can also be found. The increasing global importance of the oceanic waterways from 1450 and onward marked "a shift from the Mediterranean culture of self-restraint to the Atlantic civilization of transgressive individualism."[29] This shift had been anticipated in the Nordic region during the Viking Age that spanned from the late eighth century to the second

---

28 Hesiod, *Works and Days*, l. 232–37.
29 Kinzel, "Orientation as Paradigm of Maritime Modernity," 44.

FIGURE 3   Carl Rasmussen, *Sommernat under den Grønlandske Kyst circa Aar 1000* (1875)
PHOTO: © BRUUN RASMUSSEN KUNSTAUKTIONER

half of the eleventh century.[30] During this period, Odinist Vikings embarked on adventures in technologically advanced ships, plundering and colonizing areas of the Faroe Islands, Iceland, Greenland, England, Scotland, France, Russia, and Wineland (Figure 3). They were the "last rebels" of Europe before Christianity turned hegemonic.[31] For historical reasons, the Vikings were never impeded by the Christian concept of original sin and the story of the deluge nor the Stoic philosophy of moderation. First, ancient biblical, Greek, and Roman texts had not yet exerted any notable influence in the Nordic regions. Second, the Christianizing of the Nordic countries officially happened in the second half of the tenth century without this resulting in any rapid diminishing of the old habits of thought. In addition, we now know that the Vikings were favored with a climate much milder than the one characterizing the Nordic countries and waters today.

Stories about these border-transgressive maritime journeys of territorial ambition and knowledge expansion exist in different types of contemporary textual sources, for example accounts written by monks, poems, and runic

---

30   For a discussion of the temporal boundaries of the Viking Age, see Else Roesdahl, *The Vikings*, 3rd ed., trans. Susan M. Margeson and Kirsten Williams (1987; London: Penguin, 2016), 9–11.

31   Jeanette Varberg, *Viking: Ran, ild og sværd* (København: Gyldendal, 2019), 14.

inscriptions, just as place names and archeological findings can help us map the expanding world of the Vikings. Among the most famous sources are the sagas of the Icelanders, also known as the family sagas. Written between 1200 and 1400 and relating events that took place between 930 and 1030, the so-called saga era, the sagas are the historical novels of their time. It is often difficult to decide where facts about the Viking Age with its maritime raids end and fiction begins, not least because the family sagas and other canonical texts such as Saxo's *Gesta Danorum* (c. 1200) were entangled in propagandistic machinations with the purpose of promoting a certain person or family regarding claims to power or land.

The sagas of the Icelanders and the world picture they conjure up have endowed the Nordic peoples and the subsequent Nordic maritime literature with a quality characterized by a reluctance to surrender to the more doctrinal influences of antiquity and Christianity from the south. In a preface to the family sagas, the Danish Nobel Prize recipient Johannes V. Jensen sees a direct connection between the family saga mentality and his own epoch: "we have once again come out under the open sky. Movement was a fundamental feature in the old Nordic character as opposed to the Christian chastening that made peasants into wooden men; movement has come back. The world is open."[32] To Jensen, there exists a primordial Nordic mobility and worldliness to be contrasted with a Christian slave mentality originating from Jerusalem and Rome. The slave mentality is unnatural to the Nordic peoples, asserts Jensen, claiming that it infected them temporarily and not permanently. Then, as Lewis Mumford has pointed out, a technological invention occurred that made it possible for less courageous people to take up the mantle from the Vikings. In the fifteenth century, the three-masted ship was invented, and its ability to beat against the wind was a precondition for the oceanic turn in the post-Viking Age: "long ocean voyages were at last possible, without a Viking's daring and a Job's patience."[33]

One of the sagas most maritime is "The Saga of the Greenlanders" (*Grænlendinga saga*). It presumably dates from c. 1200–1230 (or as late as c. 1300) and recounts events occurring between 970 and 1030 during the transitional phase when Christianity was being introduced in the North as the official religion. Together with "Saga of Eirik the Red," it is one of the two principal literary sources of information regarding the Norse exploration of North

---

32 Johannes V. Jensen, "Forord," in *De islandske sagaer*, vol. 1, ed. Johannes Larsen (1930; København: Gyldendals Bogklub, 2001), 11.
33 Lewis Mumford, *Technics and Civilization* (1934; Chicago and London: University of Chicago Press, 2010), 121.

America. Relating the first documented voyages across the Atlantic in which the peoples of Europe and America met for the first time, the two sagas:

> differ from each other in a number of details, *Eirik the Red's Saga* agreeing more frequently with other written sources, such as *Heimskringla*. Neither work is among the best sagas, and yet in their blending of myth and historical tradition are typical of the genre. Modern archaeology, especially the work of Helge and Anne Stine Ingstad in the 1960s at L'Anse aux Meadows in northern Newfoundland, has confirmed that explorers from Greenland and Iceland spent time in North America and constructed buildings of the sort found in Iceland. *The Saga of the Greenlanders* attributes the first sighting of America to a merchant named Bjarni Herjolfsson, who in about 985 went off course on his way to Greenland, whereas *Eirik the Red's Saga* gives the credit to Eirik the Red's son Leif, who made the discovery through a similar accident about 1000. Altogether, *The Saga of the Greenlanders* describes six trips to America, including Bjarni's sighting and an extensive expedition by Leif. *Eirik the Red's Saga* mentions only three.[34]

"The Saga of the Greenlanders" relates the colonization of Greenland by Eirik the Red and his followers and describes six expeditions further west. The first, accidental, is led by Bjarni, the following four by Eirik's children—Leif, Thorvald, Thorstein, and Freydis—and the last by Thorfinn Karlsefni Thordarson.

In "The Saga of the Greenlanders," Leif Eiriksson and his fellow seafarers are converted into Christians by Norway's King Olaf Tryggvason. The king sends Leif and his crew to Greenland to convert the "heathen" to Christianity. However, adventurousness was a long-established trait not to be immediately eradicated by the Christian fear of the sea. There are clear traces of the complex co-existence of Odinism and Christianism in the text, one obvious example being the difference between Leif and his father Eirik. Where Eirik was a hard-edged old Viking, who left Norway because of killings, was banished from Iceland because of classic family skirmishes, including more killings, and resented Christianity, Leif was the one charged with the difficult duty of converting Greenland to Christianity.

---

34   Robert Kellogg, "Introduction," in *The Sagas of Icelanders: A Selection*, ed. Önólfur Thorsson (New York: Penguin, 2001), xxxii.

In 985, when Bjarni Herjolfsson sets out from Norway with the intention to reach Greenland, we get the first glimpse of a genuine Viking perspective of the sea: "Our journey will be thought an ill-considered one, since none of us has sailed the Greenland Sea." For Bjarni and his crew, remaining within the limits of the well-known is not an option, and after three days land is no longer in sight. Over several days and nights, extensive fog banks and constant hard winds from the north make them lose their bearings and veer off course. Instead of reaching Greenland, they accidentally end up on the eastern coasts of North America. After approaching three different landmasses, which Bjarni refuses to explore, they finally reach a fourth landmass that turns out to be Greenland. Tellingly, Bjarni is later mocked for his *lack of curiosity*, the main objection being that he has no interesting *stories* to tell: "Bjarni told of his voyage, during which he had sighted various lands, and many people thought him short on curiosity, since he had nothing to tell of these lands, and he was criticized somewhat for this."[35]

Bjarni's lack of an exploratory mentality feeds the imagination and curiosity of his fellow Greenlanders. Leif Eiriksson purchases Bjarne's ship and embarks on a new voyage, the first proper expedition, with 35 (oars)men. They first make landfall at Helluland (Stone-slab land, probably southern Baffin Island or northern Labrador), then Markland (Forest Land, southern Labrador), and finally Vinland (Wineland, possibly the St Lawrence Valley, but more likely the coast of New England):

> Their curiosity to see the land was so great that they could not be bothered to wait for the tide to come in and float their stranded ship, and they ran aground where a river flowed into the sea from a lake. When the incoming tide floated the ship again, they took the boat and rowed to the ship and moved it up into the river and from there into the lake, where they cast anchor. They carried their sleeping-sacks ashore and built booths. Later they decided to spend the winter there and built large houses.[36]

Landnám, settlement, was of course part of Viking thought, but later during Thorfinn's expedition it becomes clear how easily the Nordic settlers evacuate their little colony. After some violent encounters with American Indians (*Skraeling jar*), they realize they would never be able to live peacefully on

---

35   "The Saga of the Greenlanders," trans. Keneva Kunz, in *The Sagas of Icelanders*, 637, 638.
36   "Saga of the Greenlanders," 639.

the land they "discovered." Instead, it is a fundamental curiosity—"I wish to explore the land,"[37] says Leif—along with mercantile ambitions (cf. "booths," and later "grapevines," "grapes," and "milk and milk products") that drives the Vikings to embark on dangerous transoceanic voyages in uncharted waters and unexplored territories. The anonymous author lauds Leif for his navigational skills, acute perceptiveness, and practical seamanship. This is demonstrated when Leif spots fifteen shipwrecked people and heroically rescues them from starvation and drowning.

Following Leif's expedition to Vinland, which was the source of many stories that incited his fellow Greenlanders to venture forth, his brother Thorvald felt that the land should be further explored. On Leif's ship, which had formerly been Bjarne's ship, Thorvald now embarks on a third journey with thirty men and women, but Thorvald is killed in an encounter with native people. This prompts Thorsten (Leif and Thorvald's brother) to set out on yet a journey to bring back Thorvald's body. However, after drifting aimlessly on the sea for an entire summer, Thorsten makes landfall at Lysufjord, Greenland, where he is struck with a disease and dies. The fifth expedition, carrying sixty men and five women, is led by Thorfinn, who marries Gudrid, Thorsten's widow. In Vinland, Gudrid gives birth to their son, Snorri, the first child born in North America by a European couple. The sixth and final expedition is one spearheaded by Freydis together with two other skippers, the brothers Helgi and Finnbogi: "Discussion soon began again of a Vinland voyage, since the trip seemed to bring men both wealth and renown."[38]

What makes "The Saga of the Greenlanders" one of the most maritime of sagas? First, it recounts six maritime expeditions on relatively few pages. Second, and more substantially, what makes the presence of a new maritime world picture evident in this family saga is the devotion of the anonymous author to navigational and geographical accuracy and the extolling of practical seamanship as a heroic skill along with the willingness of the Greenlanders to navigate the landless ocean, venture into uncharted waters, and explore seascapes, and to overcome the constant fear of shipwreck. In Leif Eiriksson, we thus see *discovery*, *naming*, and *exploration* coming together centuries before the official beginning of the Age of Discovery. Anette Lassen has observed that in the family sagas, sea voyages are not undertaken for the sake of pleasure, but she also concludes that "sailing is a necessary condition"[39] in the lives of Icelanders in the saga era.

---

37 "Saga of the Greenlanders," 639–40.
38 "Saga of the Greenlanders," 648.
39 Anette Lassen, *Islændingesagaernes verden* (København: Gyldendal, 2017), 95.

This unique composite of features endows "The Saga of the Greenlanders" with originality and a genuine oceanic thinking, which would further evolve by subsequent writers across several nations. One of them was Portuguese.

2.2 Luís Vaz de Camões

One of the first truly canonical literary works of the maritime anthropocentric era is Camões' *Os Lusíadas*, the national epic of Portugal. Published in 1572, it centers on Vasco da Gama's crucial discovery of the sea route to India in 1497–1498, which catapulted the Portuguese nation into the global pole position of naval empires: "Within just seventeen years of Vasco da Gama's epic voyage, the Portuguese held and dominated all the most important sea routes and trading networks of the Indian Ocean, the Persian Gulf, and the South China Sea. It was a ruthless demonstration of naval might, and the first instance of a new concept of empire built on control of the oceans."[40] It has been widely established by historians that the entire Indian Ocean region had widespread sea connections for thousands of years prior to the arrival of Vasco da Gama in 1498. So, when da Gama and his crew entered the Indian Ocean, it already had the attributes of an integrated commercial arena. In *The Lusíads*, this is acknowledged by Camões when he shows in the first canto how the expectation of entering an uncharted territory is annulled by the crew's experience of populated waters and busy harbors. However, as Steinberg observes, the deep sea was relatively insignificant for the societies of the region with long-distance trade remaining marginal to the economies and empires round the Indian Ocean at the beginning of the early modern period: "While the sea was a presence in Indian Ocean social life, it was constructed as a special place of trade, external to society and social processes. [...] The sea was a source of diversionary consumer goods, but not a source of social power."[41]

The conception of the sea as a featureless extra-social space of distance and immune from state power changed with the arrival of the Portuguese. They launched a *political* model that combined trade, monopolies, and sea domination. This model projected power across the sea in order to claim rights to trade routes and distant lands, challenging the softer religious and cultural models of connection and affiliation that characterized the Indian Ocean region prior to the arrival of the Portuguese.[42] Eventually, the Portuguese model, together with the similar Spanish model and, to a lesser extent, the Italian city-state models,

---

40 Landeg White, "Introduction," in Camões, *The Lusíads*, ix.
41 Steinberg, *The Social Construction of the Ocean*, 45, 46.
42 Ram P. Anand, *Origin and Development of the Law of the Sea* (The Hague: Martinus Nijhoff, 1983), 17; referenced by Steinberg.

would come to be associated with something uniquely European.[43] However, there is also a difference between the Portuguese and the Spanish enterprises. Since the Indian Ocean was already striated with a flourishing trading network dominated by Muslims at the time of Vasco da Gama's arrival, this "geopolitical situation in Portugal's sphere of influence demanded a more outwardly aggressive stance" than in the Spanish case of Atlantic trade control.[44]

Camões did not travel with da Gama, but in 1553, at the age of twenty-eight, he became the first major European writer to cross the equator and experience Africa and India firsthand. Camões' personal experience of voyaging and not least seeing, feeling, smelling, tasting, and hearing other continents is significant. It contributes to anchoring his work in the real world. When reading *The Lusíads*, our eyes should be lowered "*Earthwards*" because Camões' objective is to convey to the reader how the Portuguese "would dwarf / Legends."[45] If Camões' geographical proximity to the world in which the events of his epic unfold is important, so is the temporal distance between the voyages of da Gama and Camões. By the time of the latter, the Portuguese empire was already in decline. In *The Lusíads*, this results in an undercurrent of elegy and nostalgia running beneath the customary heroic tone of the traditional national epic, born out of Camões' awareness of having come past the peak of national power.

Camões was heavily indebted to Vergil's *The Aeneid* (29–19 BC) and Homer's *The Odyssey*, but when reading *The Lusíads* one cannot but acknowledge the dramatic change that has occurred from the Greek-Roman versions of the ocean to Camões' 1572 version. The change primarily concerns the relationship between gods and humans. Camões replicates the classical epics by portraying the gods and goddesses of Greece and Rome watching over the voyage of Vasco da Gama. The gods and goddesses of Homer and Vergil showed split allegiances during the journeys of Odysseus and Aeneas, and the same holds true of *The Lusíads*. Here, Venus supports the Portuguese while Bacchus, representative of the East, resents the intrusion upon his territory by the hubristic Portuguese. However, Jupiter foretells great fortunes for the sons of Lusus in the East, so Bacchus, seeing that the Portuguese are on the verge of making landfall in India, asks for Neptune's help. The sea god then summons a council of sea gods who decide to assist Bacchus by unleashing formidable winds to sink the Portuguese armada. Vasco da Gama, fearing the destruction of his

---

43 Satish Chandra, "Introduction," in *The Indian Ocean: Explorations in History, Commerce, and Politics*, ed. Satish Chandra (New Delhi: Sage, 1987), 26; referenced by Steinberg.
44 Steinberg, *The Social Construction of the Ocean*, 87.
45 Camões, *The Lusíads*, I, 9, 30.

caravels, prays to his Christian God, but it is Venus who intervenes and helps the Portuguese by sending the Nymphs to seduce the winds into tranquility. After the storm, the Portuguese armada sights Calicut, and Vasco da Gama gives thanks to God. The crew of Lusíads have succeeded and reached India.

If this resumé gives the impression of Camões copying the classical template of a divine theater, there are significant deviations from this template. Camões practically reverses the previous hierarchy between gods and humans. Before elaborating on that, I would like to draw attention to three additional distinctions between the Portuguese and the Greek-Roman epics since Camões implicitly and explicitly draws so heavily on Homer and Vergil. The three distinctions all spring from Vasco da Gama insisting to the Sultan of Malindi that his voyage is superior to those of Ulysses and Aeneas. For one, he asks the sultan,

> Do you imagine that Aeneas and subtle
> Ulysses ever ventured so far?
> Did either of them dare to embark on
> Actual oceans? For all the poetry
> Written about them, did they see a fraction
> Of what I know through strategy and action?[46]

These lines draw a sharp distinction between the coastal practices of Ulysses and Aeneas and the oceanic practices of Vasco da Gama. The significance of this distinction cannot be overestimated. It is symbolically underlined by the fact that Camões begins his epic *in medias res* with the Portuguese already in the Mozambique Channel where no one had ever preceded them. The topopoetics of the opening of *The Lusíads* positively emphasizes Portugal's geographical and oceanic leadership as compared to their predecessors.

The mention of "strategy and action" in the last line of the stanza leads us to the second distinction made by da Gama: his seafaring skills were superior to those of Ulysses and Aeneas. In the following stanza, the Portuguese navigator mocks Homer for "Inventing Circe and Polyphemus / Sirens who make men sleep with song," a critique of Ulysses' credentials as a sea captain. Vergil and Aeneas are derided for letting the crew "sail under canvas and oar / To the Cicones, leaving their / Shipmates in that lotus-befuddled realm, / Losing even their pilot at the helm."[47] These lines express the growing sensibility

---

46   Camões, *The Lusíads*, V, 86.
47   Camões, *The Lusíads*, V, 88.

towards the ocean and maritime life during this period as *empirical* domains ruled by *contingency* that require practical, hands-on skills. To Bernhard Klein, "Camões' sea is not only a global stage for 'heroic' deeds of empire but also a genuinely modern space, keyed to the improvisational skills of the mariner, in whose nautical 'traffic' that very modernity is simultaneously shaped and exhibited."[48] Through da Gama and his crew, we get a glimpse of the sailor-navigator's new professional pride, a paradigmatic shift that was announced by the narrator as early as in the first cantos: *"Abandon all the ancient muse revered, / A loftier code of honour has appeared."* This code of honor makes Venus admire the Portuguese sailors for being "Such strong people! Such bold expedients! / To terrorize the very elements!"[49] Throughout the epic, the paradigm shift gains more and more concreteness, as the poem displays a new oceanic thinking by evoking what Klein summarizes as "the partial vision of the voyager, the incomplete knowledge, the absence of a secure and certain telos."[50]

To genuine oceanic practice and honorable seamanship, da Gama adds a third distinction between himself and his predecessors:

> Let them fantasize, of winds leaping
> From wine-skins, and of amorous Calypsos;
> Harpies who foul their own banquets;
> Pilgrimages to the underworld;
> However they polish and decorate
> With metaphor such empty fables,
> My own tale in its naked purity
> Outdoes all boasting and hyperbole.[51]

With Camões, we are transplanted from the world of myth, fable, and hyperbole into a modern world of history, tale, and "Plain Truth."[52] Does this qualify Camões' work as a "modern epic" in Moretti's sense? That is, as a work haunted by two contrasting impulses, the ancient ambition of coherence and totality and the modern consciousness of fragmentation and incompleteness. Not exactly. *The Lusíads* is too serious in its laudatory nation-building aspirations

---

48 Bernhard Klein, "Camões and the Sea: Maritime Modernity in *The Lusiads*," *Modern Philology* 111, no. 2 (November 2013): 159.
49 Camões, *The Lusíads*, I, 3; II, 47.
50 Klein, "Camões and the Sea," 172.
51 Camões, *The Lusíads*, V, 89.
52 Camões, *The Lusíads*, V, 23.

to qualify as a "modern epic." But in its abandonment of the mythological foundations of the epic genre for a new epic of reality, in its departure from the coastal to the oceanic space, and in its replacement of the god-interfered seamanship for the professional skill-based seamanship, *The Lusíads* launches a transformation of the previous maritime world picture of theocentrism into one of anthropocentrism.

This only becomes clearer as one progresses through the ten cantos. The crucial question concerns Camões' use of the classical gods and goddesses. Two parallel scenes exist in *The Lusíads*, one set on Mount Olympus and one in Neptune's underwater palace. In both cases, the gods debate whether or not to let the Portuguese proceed with their transgressive voyage. First, Jupiter, supported by Venus and Mars, grants them a safe harbor on the eastern coast of Africa to overhaul their ships. Then, in Neptune's palace, Bacchus persuades the sea gods to intervene by releasing furious winds against the sailors to prevent them from reaching India. In this competition, Venus is victorious and rewards the sailors with the pleasures of the Isle of Love. Vasco da Gama keeps referring his struggles to a more cosmic (that is, nonpersonal, nonidiosyncratic, non-Greek/Roman) struggle between good and evil and never fails to thank Providence for guiding and protecting him. But, as Landeg White asks, "What are we to make of this fusing of Christian and pagan myth?"[53]

One tradition of commentary has read the pagan examples as allegories to reconcile the classics and Christianity. What is important is how to understand allegory. The reconciliatory tradition understood allegory as a one-to-one translation between classical myth and Christianity (e.g., Jupiter was God, Venus was the Virgin Mary, Bacchus was Satan). However, this does not make much sense, especially when it comes to Venus' seductive-erotic behavior. Perhaps it would be more fruitful to operate with a more flexible, nonreductive understanding of allegory and to read what Camões actually says about the gods. At one point, the narrator thinks back on "Those immortals whom men of antiquity. / In their love of great deeds, imagined / Living there on starry Olympus," and he concludes that they

> Were enjoying only those rewards
> The world bestows for the superb,
> Deathless achievements of heroes
> Who, though human, became divine;
> Jupiter, Mercury, Phoebus, and Mars,

---

53 White, "Introduction," xv.

HISTORY

> Aeneas, Romulus, and the two Thebans,
> Ceres, Pallas, Diana, Juno, they
> Were all composed of feeble human clay;
>
> But fame, trumpeting their exploits
> Everywhere added strange titles
> Such as gods, demigods, immortals,
> Deities, heroes, and the like.[54]

Dismissing the pagan gods as nothing more than poetic creations, these lines could be interpreted as a confirmation of the reconciliatory tradition and its reductive allegorical reading, perhaps even indicating that they were incorporated at the behest of the Inquisition.

However, their message is authoritatively repeated a little later by Tethys, when she shows da Gama the entire universe in the shape of the Ptolemaic system of concentric spheres:

> Here dwell in glory only the genuine
> Gods, because I, Saturn and Janus,
> Jupiter and Juno, are mere fables
> Dreamed by mankind in his blindness.
> We serve only to fashion delightful
> Verses, and if human usage offers
> Us more, it is your imagination
> Awards us each in heaven a constellation.[55]

Apart from the relegation of the classical gods and goddesses to "mere fables," Tethys' guided world tour in canto ten of Europe, Africa, the Middle East, India, China, Japan, some islands in the Pacific and Indian Oceans, and finally the two Americas and Antarctica is assigned an enormous world pictorial significance by White: "Tethys explains to the Portuguese the momentous consequences of their voyage to India in demonstrating to mankind the dimensions and wealth of the planet mankind inhabits. Nothing quite like this happened again until December 1968, when the Apollo 8 spacecraft showed us the first pictures of Earth taken from space."[56] Indeed, Vasco da Gama's voyage launched a spatial

---

54 Camões, *The Lusíads*, IX, 90–92.
55 Camões, *The Lusíads*, X, 82.
56 White, "Introduction," xi.

revolution on a planetary scale in which the ocean and seafaring were indispensable factors.

It is important to remember that the classical gods and goddesses in *The Lusíads* never gets anything done: "There is no need for the reader to believe that it was Venus who prevented the fleet entering harbour at Mombasa, or Bacchus who called up the hurricane. Da Gama has no difficulty in explaining all that befalls him in terms of a quite different set of beliefs (nor has the modern reader in attributing Portuguese setbacks to a mix of commercial jealousy and natural disasters)." Camões deliberately uses his poetic license—the license to create gods and goddesses as enjoyable fabrications—in order to achieve different effects of world pictorial consequence that would not have been possible in a more prosaic narrative of the journey: "The debates on Mount Olympus and in Neptune's underwater palace allow him to emphasize the significance of da Gama's achievement as a turning-point in human history, comparable to mankind's legendary first voyage in pursuit of the Golden Fleece, or to the attempts by Daedalus and Icarus to fly."[57] Again, the difference is that da Gama's achievement is *real* whereas the projects of the Argonauts and Daedalus-Icarus are myths.

Halfway through the epic, Bacchus warns his colleagues that

> You have seen with what presumption
> Daedalus assaulted the very heavens;
> You observed the Argonauts' mad ambition
> To tame the sea with sail and oar;
> Then, daily, you swallow such
> Insults, that very soon, I promise you,
> Of the vast oceans and the heavenly span
> They'll be the gods, and you and I but Man.[58]

Bacchus' warning merely anticipates what Camões' *The Lusíads* ultimately confirms: the reversal of the hierarchy between gods and humans. To some extent, the reversal is arguably conditioned by the fact that Camões was the first major Western artist to transgress the Christian boundaries and visit the orient and the tropics. This gave him a strong belief in human potentiality and encouraged him to throw off the shackles of the classical pantheon of selfish and dominating gods and goddesses. His confrontation with the radical

---

57 White, "Introduction," xv–xvi, xvi.
58 Camões, *The Lusíads*, VI, 29.

otherness of the non-Christian worlds of Africa and India probably only reinforced the Christian framework of his thinking. But as with other Renaissance writers, Dante notably, it was a new Christian *humanism* that emerged in his writings alongside a perspective from below, that of "the world of oceanic travel and the seafaring realities experienced by the common mariner."[59]

2.3 William Shakespeare

An example of the semantic shift of the word contingency can be found in Shakespeare's comedy *The Merchant of Venice* (1596–98/1600). The drama probes the tensions between (and ironic inversions of) punishment and mercy, revenge and forgiveness, and literality and pliability. The intrigue evolves on a backcloth of maritime mercantilism and speculation. Shylock loans Bassanio 3,000 ducats to enable him to court Portia, money that Antonio vouches for but is then unable to pay back in due time, which makes Shylock demand his bond, a pound of flesh from Antonio's bosom. Antonio, the royal merchant of Venice, owns several ships that have all embarked on mercantile adventures and are situated at different locations around the globe at the beginning of the play.

In the very first dialogues, Shakespeare creates a veritable *mood of contingency*—closely linked to the maritime backcloth and his sophisticated use of a nautical vocabulary—that determines the underlying atmosphere of the rest of the play. Salarino ascribes Antonio's sadness to the fact that his "mind is tossing on the ocean," worrying about his argosies (large merchant vessels). Salanio follows suit and shows understanding for Antonio's distracted humor, admitting that if it were him who had

> such venture forth,
> The better part of my affections would
> Be with my hopes abroad. I should be still
> Plucking the grass to know where sits the wind,
> Peering in maps for ports, and piers, and roads.
> And every object that might make me fear
> Misfortune to my ventures, out of doubt
> Would make me sad.[60]

---

59 Klein, "Camões and the Sea," 179.
60 William Shakespeare, *The Merchant of Venice*, fully annotated and with an introduction by Burton Raffel (New Haven and London: Yale University Press, 2006), I, i.

Shakespeare implicitly shows that Antonio's mindset has changed its spatiotemporal structure from a here-and-now to a then-and-there and even to a more undefined when-and-where. Antonio's mind wanders outwards in space to his ships, which are not *here* in Venice but out *there* on the seven seas, although he is not sure exactly *where*. His mind also drifts forward in time from the present *now* to a future *then* that will announce the return of his ships to Venice and bring him great wealth, although he is uncertain exactly *when* this will happen.

The overall uncertainty is emphasized by Salanio and Salarino's combined list of nearby objects that beg to be read as signs of danger: to Salanio, leaves of grass morph into weathercocks and remind him of the harm that winds may cause the ships; an hour-glass containing sand makes Salarino think of shallows and flats and the threat of immobilization; and a church's stones conjure up images of rocks splintering a vessel's fragile sides causing its precious spices and silks to be scattered on the water, "now worth this, / And now worth nothing," entirely subject to the whims of fortune. The general atmosphere of nervousness, anxiety, and chance is even articulated stylistically by Antonio in the play's opening lines, when he muses on his sadness: "But how I caught it, found it, or came by it, / What stuff 'tis made of, whereof it is born, / I am to learn."[61] The contingency and uncertainty on the content level is echoed in the frantic rhythm and paratactic structure of the lines that reproduce the activity of his mind "tossing on the ocean," skipping from one short-lived crest to the next unable to locate a solid place to rest and find reassurance.

In Shakespeare's drama, the action does not take place on the ocean, its setting is not a ship, and its main characters are not sailors. But thanks to its archipelagic structure and waterfront location, Venice was for centuries a dominant maritime city-state in Europe. Its decline was set in motion around 1500, in part because of Vasco da Gama's discovery of the India sea route. Shakespeare's drama is set in the sixteenth century when the dominance of Venice was waning, yet it is simultaneously a period during which maritime merchants became full-blown transoceanic traders with merchant fleets around the globe. Although *The Merchant of Venice* neither teems with sailors nor ships, nor has scenes at sea, an oceanic sense of unpredictability and hazard nevertheless seeps into every scene of the play.

The Merchant of Venice portrays mercantile seafaring as risky business, but Shakespeare's ocean has also become a new medium for financial gain. Its contingent nature represents both *risk* and *chance*. What is more, whether it

---

61   Shakespeare, *The Merchant of Venice*, I, i.

turns out to be one or the other can now be prognosticated. The transformed conception of the ocean (the condition of possibility for there and where supplanting here) and the emerging calculating spirit (the condition of possibility for then and when supplanting now) are both expressed by Shylock when he characterizes Antonio's financial adventures at sea as being dangerous, but nevertheless worth the risk (if a risk is a risk, a risk worth taking becomes a chance):

> My meaning in saying he is a good man, is to have you understand me that he is sufficient, yet his means are in supposition. He hath an argosy bound to Tripolis, another to the Indies, I understand moreover (upon the Rialto) he hath a third at Mexico, a fourth for England, and other ventures he hath squandered abroad. But ships are but boards, sailors but men, there be land rats, and water rats, water thieves, and land thieves—I mean pirates. And then there is the peril of waters, winds, and rocks. The man is notwithstanding sufficient.[62]

The passage conjures up a global geography where merchant ships navigate the seven seas and forge new or reinforce already existing trade routes with distant nations. Shylock's cadenced reasoning emphasizes the intrinsic ambivalence of sea journeys as being both hazardous and potentially profitable. The Jew refers to "the peril of waters, winds, and rocks" as well as to water thieves and land thieves, both pirates in Shylock's mind. According to Joan Ozark Holmer, there is an irony here, which the audience of Shakespeare's time may have been better equipped to understand. In his treatise *A Discourse upon Usury* (1572), Thomas Wilson thus describes interest gotten from moneylending as "a gaynefull piracie, contrarye to nature." To Wilson, usury is a sin, and the person who lends for gain is "an heretique" just as a person who acknowledges usury to be a sin yet practices it "is straighte wayes a land pyrate."[63]

---

62   Shakespeare, *The Merchant of Venice*, I, iii.
63   Thomas Wilson, *A Discourse upon Usury*, ed. and historical introduction R. H. Tawney (1572; London: Frank Cass & Co., 1962), 326, 327; Joan Ozark Holmer, *The Merchant of Venice: Choice, Hazard and Consequence* (New York: Macmillan Education, 1995), 148–49. Holmer mentions that Wilson's book may have influenced Shakespeare more generally, "especially its sustained development of the importance of charity and mercy as antidotes to usury, and perhaps even more significantly, the historical and moral interrelation of Jews and usury," and also that it acted as a source for some particulars, which "include Wilson's euphemistic use of 'usance', his 'land pirate' cited from Baldus [Baldus de Ubaldis, an Italian expert in Medieval Roman Law, S. F.], his repeated use of 'cut throat', the recurrent imagistic use of 'dog/cur' and 'devil' imagery for usurers as well as the 'biting/feeding'

Shylock's conclusion, "The man is notwithstanding sufficient," implies that when everything is taken into account Antonio is good for the money. The new spirit of calculated risk, so important for the emergent insurance industry, is not restricted to Shylock, though. Antonio dismisses Salarino's belief that his sadness is caused by his thinking about his "merchandise":

> Believe me no, I thank my fortune for it,
> My ventures are not in one bottom trusted,
> Nor to one place, nor is my whole estate
> Upon the fortune of this present year.
> Therefore my merchandise makes me not sad.[64]

The discourse is a blend of investment banking and gambling. Antonio has spread his bets or investments on several ships at several locations, and he has not invested all his assets in this year's expeditions. He contradicts himself later, when he says to Bassanio: "Thou knowst that all my fortunes are at sea, / Neither have I money, nor commodity / To raise a present sum."[65] Whether Shylock is aware of Antonio's risky gamble is not so important. His explicit logic (expressed in the above quote) suggests that he does not know that Antonio has risked everything on his current expeditions. But taking Shylock's obsession with revenge into account—rather a pound of flesh from Antonio than getting his ducats back—he could be updated on Antonio's fragile "supposition" and therefore agree to grant Bassanio the loan.

One could argue that Antonio has taken sufficient precautions by spreading his money and investments on several ships, but news of the highly unlikely outcome reach Venice:

> *Bassanio* [...] But is it true, Salerio,
> Hath all his ventures failed? What, not one hit,
> From Tripolis, from Mexico and England,
> From Lisbon, Barbary, and India,
> And not one vessel scape the dreadful touch
> Of merchant-marring rocks?
> *Salerio* Not one my lord.[66]

---

motif and what appears to be his unique emphasis on the 'heart' and the usurer's taking of hearts from his victims' bodies." Holmer, *Merchant of Venice*, 316, note 8.

64   Shakespeare, *The Merchant of Venice*, I, i.
65   Shakespeare, *The Merchant of Venice*, I, i.
66   Shakespeare, *The Merchant of Venice*, III, ii.

The divine framework, which included fortunes and coincidences but were basically static and an expression of God's or the gods' overriding will, is here replaced by a world in which humans, by using their rationality and skill, can calculate probabilities for gain and loss, which are no longer unequivocally regarded as outcomes of divine will. And, as it happens, the news turned out to be fake. Portia to Antonio:

> And I have better news in store for you
> Than you expect. Unseal this letter soon,
> There you shall find three of your argosies
> Are richly come to harbor suddenly.
> You shall not know by what strange accident
> I chancèd on this letter.[67]

After all, *The Merchant of Venice* is a comedy, and the mood of contingency flows from the determining background of hazardous maritime enterprises into the intrigue and its small-scale machinations of receptions of news and letters.

During the anthropocentric age, humans still considered the ocean threatening and destructive. However, the prime mover behind this gradually changed from God or the gods to nature itself. This implies a more positive view of the ocean that invites humans to prove their courage and demonstrate their skills. As John Peck has shown, Richard Hakluyt's *The Principal Navigations*, published at the same time as *The Merchant of Venice*, illustrates very clearly the mental and discursive shift towards the ocean that happened in this period. In Hakluyt's text, the emphasis shifts from a mysterious and unknown world on and beyond the oceans to a world that is increasingly known, explored, and mapped. In Hakluyt, we can thus identify a movement "from re-narrating legends to recording history" similar to the one we saw in Camões. Also, the experiential suppresses the allegorical and symbolic representations of sea journeys. James Cook's *Journals* and his three Pacific voyages in the second half of the eighteenth century are yet another step, a threshold moment, in the development towards the later technocentric world picture. If the English with Hakluyt felt they knew the world more and better, they began with Cook and his scientifically motivated journeys to feel they also controlled it.[68]

---

67 Shakespeare, *The Merchant of Venice*, V, i.
68 John Peck, *Maritime Fiction: Sailors and the Sea in British and American Novels, 1719–1917* (Gordonsville, VA: Palgrave Macmillan, 2001), 16.

2.4 Jens Munk

Only two decades after Hakluyt's famous collection was published and Shakespeare's drama set in Italy was performed, Danish arctic explorer and sea captain Jens Munk set sail from Tøjhushavnen in Copenhagen with two ships, *Enhiørningen* and *Lamprenen*. The purpose of Munk's royally sanctioned expedition, funded by Christian IV, the King of Denmark, was to discover the Northwest Passage. On their departure on May 9, 1619, the two vessels carried sixty-four men between them. *Enhiørningen* was abandoned and later crushed by the ice. Only Jens Munk and two other men survived the journey; the rest of the crew died of scurvy in Hudson Bay. The three survivors reached Bergen, Norway, on September 25, 1620, after sixty-seven days on *Lamprenen*, sailing from Hudson Bay in search of a route home. Upon their arrival, their suffering from severe scurvy, starvation, and cold showed. After a period of imprisonment in Bergen until the middle of December, Munk returned to Copenhagen on Christmas Eve. Munk was not satisfied with the outcome of the expedition, but he had no reason to question his own efforts. However, the expedition was regarded a disaster by the king and the elite, and the public soon followed suit, and Munk received a chill welcome from Christian IV. He never again enjoyed the full trust of the king, nor his respect.

Four years after his homecoming, and despite his disrepute, Munk managed to get his diary from the strenuous voyage published under the title *Navigatio, Septentrionalis. Det er: Relation eller Bescriffuelse, om Seiglads oc Reyse, paa denne Nordvestiske Passagie, som nu kaldis Nova Dania, igiennem Fretum Christian at opsøge*.[69] The diary-logbook has been translated into English by the Hakluyt Society as *Navigatio Septentrionalis: That is, A Relation or Description of a Voyage in Search of the North-West Passage, now called Nova Dania, through Fretum Christian*.[70] The title continues with considerably more information as titles of that time used to do. Empirical information had become a significant part of the new world picture, which meant that exact dates, participants, purpose, plot summary, place names, place nam*ing*, etc. had to be displayed on the title page (Figure 4).

---

69 Jens Munk, *Navigatio, Septentrionalis. Det er: Relation eller Bescriffuelse, om Seiglads oc Reyse, paa denne Nordvestiske Passagie, som nu kaldis Nova Dania, igiennem Fretum Christian at opsøge* (København: Heinrich Waldkirch, 1624).

70 Jens Munk, *Navigatio Septentrionalis: That is, A Relation or Description of a Voyage in Search of the North-West Passage, now called Nova Dania, through Fretum Christian*, in *Danish Arctic Expeditions, 1605 to 1620, In Two Books, Book II: The Expedition of Captain Jens Munk to Hudson's Bay in Search of a North-West Passage in 1619–20*, ed. with notes and introduction C. C. A. Gosch (London: The Hakluyt Society, 1897).

One of the most striking elements when reading Munk's logbook, especially if one has the tradition of earlier maritime sources present in one's mind, is the insisting presence of an "I." Admittedly, as the images above show, there are markers on the title page of *Navigatio Septentrionalis* ("sailing north") and the first page of the diary that point to more conventionally important powers than *ánthropos*. First, the title page makes the obligatory and celebratory reference to "Voris Allernaadigste Herre / Konning Christian den Fierde" (Our Most Gracious Majesty King Christian the Fourth), the benefactor of the expedition, and further down the king's name is mentioned again, now as the one who has sanctioned the publication. Second, on the first page of the actual "Relation," the title is repeated in a slightly different version, and Munk then adds the following words: "Udi den Hellig Trefoldigheds Naffn: AMEN" (In the Name of the Holy Trinity, AMEN). Third, between the title page and the diary, a three-page long dedication to Christian IV is inserted. This was a typical gesture of the period and can also be seen in Columbus' 1492 logbook, which features a dedication to the Spanish king.

In the case of *Navigatio*, doubt is raised as to whether Jens Munk wrote the dedication himself. The Danish historian Thorkild Hansen ascribes the dedication to the book's publisher, Henrich Waldkirch, in *Jens Munk* (1965):

> When he that same autumn publishes his diary from Hudson Bay provided with a comprehensive dedication to the king, it is unreasonable to regard these tirades as a proof of a good relationship between the two. Stylistically, there exists a gulf between Munk's scarce, concrete prose in the diary and the Germanic pompousness in the convoluted sentences of the dedication. He has not written one word of it all. The dedication is authored by the book's publisher, the German Heinrich [sic] Waldkirch, it is the printer's routine homage to the king. On the other hand, "Navigatio Septentrionalis" does not comprise any of the forewords that were also a standard ingredient in the publications at that time, and in which erudite people in Latin or Danish, in prose or verse, accounted for the author's life and praised his merits. Such a thing was not possible in this case. In 1624, no one finds it favorable to account for Munk's merits, and the story of his life comprises such embarrassing moments that another century passes before it can be printed in Denmark.[71]

---

71   Thorkild Hansen, *Jens Munk* (1965; København: Gyldendal, 1989), 464.

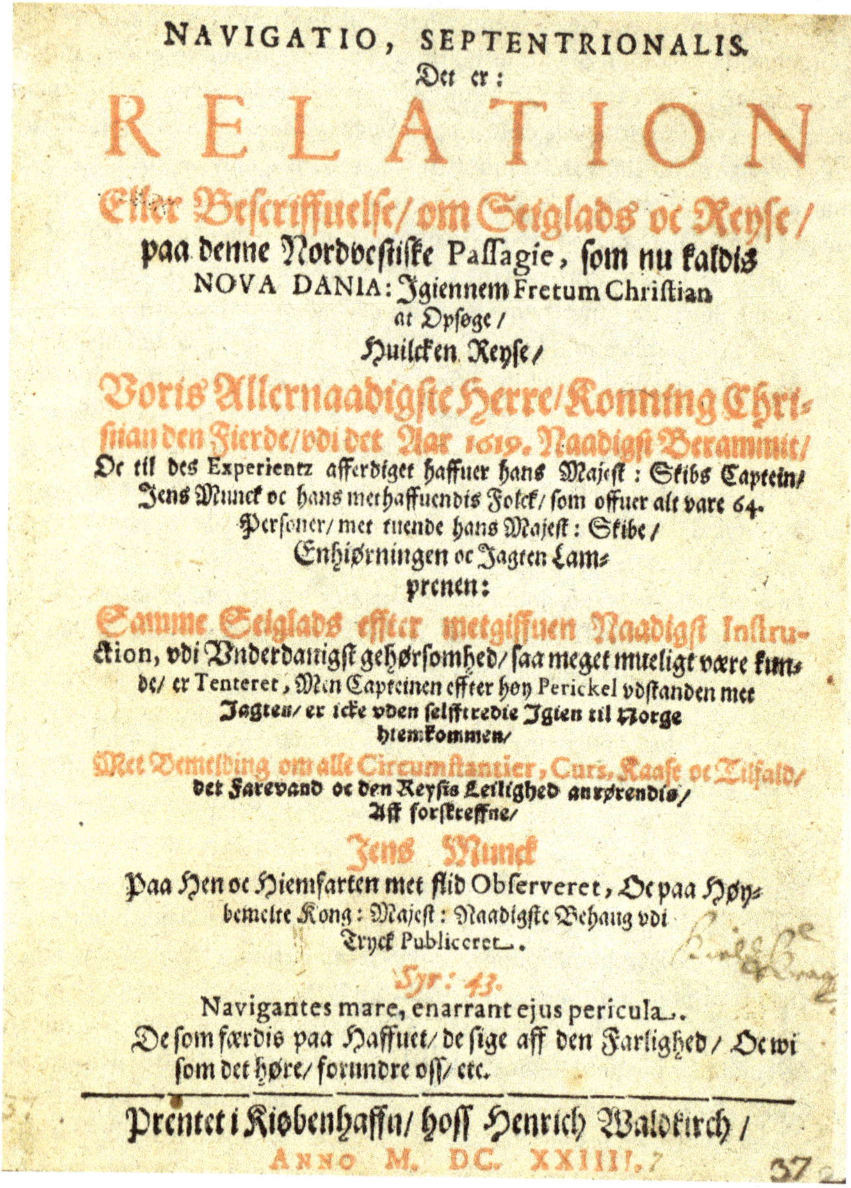
NAVIGATIO, SEPTENTRIONALIS.
Det er:
RELATION
Eller Beſcriffuelſe/ om Seiglads oc Reyſe/
paa denne Nordveſtiſke Paſſagie, ſom nu kaldis
NOVA DANIA: Igiennem Fretum Chriſtian
at Opſøge/
Huilcken Reyſe/
Voris Allernaadigſte Herre/ Konning Chri-
ſtian den Fierde/ vdi det Aar 1619. Naadigſt Berammit/
Oc til des Experientz afferdiget haffuer hans Majeſt: Skibs Captein/
Jens Munck oc hans methaffuendis Folck/ ſom offuer alt vare 64.
Perſoner/ met tuende hans Majeſt: Skibe/
Enhiørningen oc Jagten Lam-
prenen:
Samme Seiglads effter metgiffuen Naadigſt Inſtru-
ction, vdi Vnderdanigſt gehørſomhed/ ſaa meget mueligt være kun-
de/ er Tenteret, Men Capteinen effter hoy Perickel vdſtanden met
Jagten/ er icke vden ſelfftredie Igien til Norge
hiemkommen/
Met Bemelding om alle Circumſtantier, Curs, Kaaſe oc Tilfald/
det Farevand oc den Reyſis Leilighed anrørendis/
Aff forſkreffne/
Jens Munck
Paa Hen oc Hiemfarten met flid Obſerveret, Oc paa Høy-
bemelte Kong: Majeſt: Naadigſte Behang vdi
Tryck Publiceret.
Syr: 43.
Navigantes mare, enarrant ejus pericula.
De ſom færdis paa Haffuet/ de ſige aff den Farlighed/ Oc wi
ſom det høre/ forundre oſſ/ etc.
Prentet i Kiøbenhaffn/ hoſſ Henrich Waldkirch/
ANNO M. DC. XXIIII.

FIGURE 4 Title page and first page of diary from the 1624 first edition of Munk's logbook, *Navigatio, Septentrionalis*
© DET KGL. BIBLIOTEK/ROYAL DANISH LIBRARY

It is obvious from the three examples (title page, dedication, and first page of diary) that *Navigatio Septentrionalis* frames Munk's expedition and his account thereof with references to God and King, but two important factors already relativize their role and status here in the preliminary pages of the

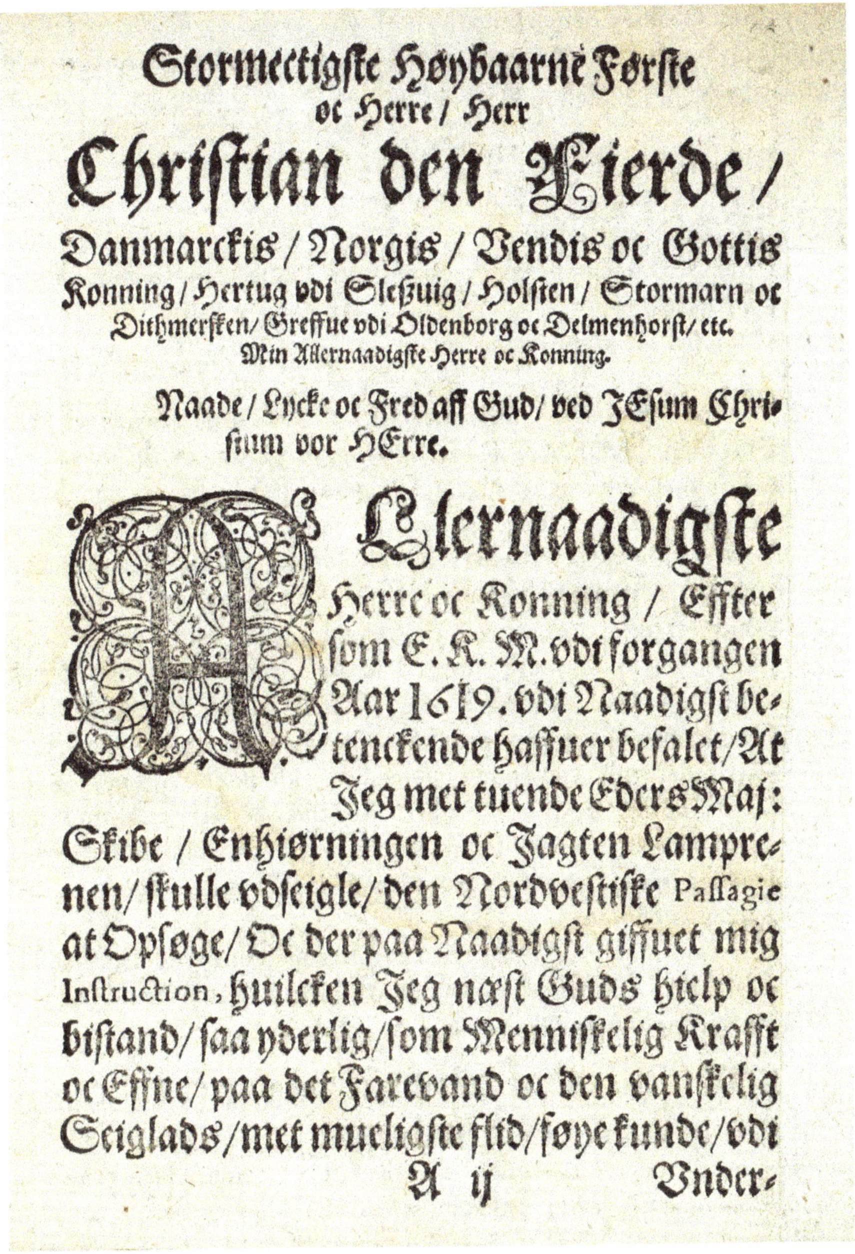

> Stormectigste Høybaarne Første
> oc Herre / Herr
> # Christian den Fierde /
> Danmarckis / Norgis / Vendis oc Gottis
> Konning / Hertug vdi Sleßuig / Holsten / Stormarn oc
> Dithmersken / Greffue vdi Oldenborg oc Delmenhorst / etc.
> Min Allernaadigste Herre oc Konning.
>
> Naade / Lycke oc Fred aff Gud / ved JEsum Christum vor HErre.
>
> **A**llernaadigste Herre oc Konning / Effter som E. K. M. vdi forgangen Aar 1619. vdi Naadigst betenckende haffuer befalet / At Jeg met tuende Eders Maj: Skibe / Enhiørningen oc Jagten Lamprenen / skulle vdseigle / den Nordvestiske Passagie at Opsøge / Oc der paa Naadigst giffuet mig Instruction, huilcken Jeg næst Guds hielp oc bistand / saa yderlig / som Menniskelig Krafft oc Effne / paa det Farevand oc den vanskelig Seiglads / met muelig ste flid / føye kunde / vdi
>
> A ij   Vnder-

FIGURE 4   (*cont.*)

diary, one is conventionality, the other the authorship of the comprehensive dedication.

Reading Munk's diary, it becomes evident that King and Lord play marginal roles in the sailors' drama of life and death. I have selected five consecutive entries from the diary, dating from the beginning of the journey (May 9, 16, 18, 25, and 30, 1619), that can help us identify Munk's style and the maritime world picture that dominated in Munk's lifetime and in the anthropocentric age in general:

> [...] I, Iens Munck, in the name of God, sailed with the said two ships, from Copenhagen into the Sound, on the 9th of May; and there were then on the ship *Enhiörningen* forty-eight, and, on the sloop *Lamprenen*, sixteen persons.
>
> I waited for wind in the Sound until the 16th of May, which was Whitsunday. I then sailed out of the Sound.
>
> On the 18th of May, it happened, early in the morning, while we were sailing along, that one of my men, as he was walking on the deck, suddenly jumped overboard a distance of quite two fathoms and plunged his head under water, without, however, as it appeared, sinking so quickly as he desired. But, as it blew hard, no one could save him, which I should much have wished. He, therefore, went down and was lost.
>
> On the 25th of May, when off Lister, the sloop sprang a leak, so that I was obliged to run into Karmsund, in order there to discover the leak in that vessel; and, on examination, I found that three bolt-holes had been left open by the carpenters, and afterwards filled with pitch; which defect I thereupon caused to be remedied without delay, in order to be able to continue the voyage. While I stayed there at Karmsund, one of my two coopers died; wherefore I caused three young men to be engaged at Skudenes, in the place of those who had died, so as to maintain my full complement of men.
>
> On the 30th of May, I sailed from Karmsund, further to continue my voyage, and shaped our course West-North-West for Heth Land, which we accordingly passed on the 2nd of June.[72]

As is clear from the five entries, Jens Munk is central for the logbook, both in his role as an ordinary human being and in his capacity of navigator and captain of the expedition. Munk is the driving force behind the actions that need to occur and the decisions that must be made, whether these actions and decisions are active or reactive. It is also Munk who authors the logbook by hand with pen and paper.

---

72 Munk, *Navigatio Septentrionalis*, 5–6.

We know that Christopher Columbus was the author of a logbook on his first voyage on board the *Santa María*. Upon his return to Spain in 1493, Columbus presented the original manuscript to Isabella I of Castile who kept it and had a copy made for Columbus. The manuscript has not been seen since 1504. The texts that exist in various editions and under different titles are based on copies, some summaries, others direct transcripts, made by Bartolomé de las Casas, perhaps from Columbus' personal copy. Two problems arise from this: first, there are parts of the diary, perhaps large parts, missing; second, how much of what remains is Columbus's own words, how much de las Casas'? In the case of Vasco da Gama, we do not know if he authored a logbook. The manuscript that goes by the name of *Journal of the First Voyage of Vasco da Gama to India, 1497–1499*—anonymous and undated, although paleographic analysis dates it to the first half of the sixteenth century—is the only known copy of a journal believed to have been written on board the ship during da Gama's first voyage to India. The lost original of the journal most often has been attributed to Álvaro Velho, who accompanied da Gama on the *São Gabriel*. Again, uncertainties about completeness and voice arise and, in this case, we also know for certain that the original source was authored by a soldier, not the captain (which is not a devaluation, rather a matter of perspectival difference).

In the case of *Navigatio Septentrionalis*, we know that Jens Munk was the author, and we even have access to the original handwritten manuscript composed while on board *Enhiørningen* and *Lamprenen* and camped in Hudson Bay. As the entries demonstrate, every time Munk uses "I" it is associated with a specific everyday situation that calls for the "I" to act in a practical and coolheaded manner. On May 16, he demonstrates the patience required when faced with the whims of nature, and as soon as the winds are favorable follows human action. Two days later, when one of his men "suddenly jumped overboard," Munk first discloses his surprise at human caprice. However, this is immediately followed by a combined desire to act (save the man) and a recognition that nature makes action impossible. So, for Munk the natural conclusion is that it is time to move on with the expedition. Note also Munk's insertion of "therefore" (in the Danish original the word is "saa"), which linguistically performs a world ruled by causality. The next entrance in the logbook is a week later, when "the sloop sprang a leak." Here, Munk discovers technical problems that turn out to be caused by human error, but they are soon fixed through human ingenuity, resolve, and skill. We also get a sense of Munk's keen efforts to comply with time schedule, and when the first deaths

NAVIGATIO SEPTENTRIONALIS:

THAT IS, A

RELATION

OR DESCRIPTION OF A VOYAGE

In Search of the North-West *Passage*, now called
NOVA DANIA, through *Fretum Christian*;

WHICH VOYAGE

OUR MOST GRACIOUS MAJESTY KING
CHRISTIAN THE FOURTH WAS GRACIOUSLY PLEASED
TO COMMAND IN THE YEAR 1619;

And, in order to accomplish it, sent out his Majesty's Sea
Captain, Iens Munk, together with a Crew numbering in all
64 Persons, in two of His Majesty's ships, *Enhiörningen*
and the Sloop *Lamprenen*;

WHICH SAME

EXPEDITION WAS, SO FAR AS WAS POSSIBLE,
Carried out with most implicit obedience to the *Instructions*
Graciously given; but the Commander, after incurring great Peril,
returned back to Norway with the Sloop and only two others;

COMPRISING AN ACCOUNT OF ALL THE CIRCUM-
stances, Courses, Directions, and Occurrences, concerning that
Sea and the Particulars of that Voyage;

BY THE SAID

IENS MUNCK

Diligently observed on the Journey there and back, and
published by His said Royal Majesty's Most
Gracious Command.

ECCLUS. 43.

Navigantes mare, enarrant ejus pericula.

They that sail on the sea tell of the Dangers thereof; and, when we hear it
with our ears, we marvel thereat, etc.

Printed in Copenhagen by Henrich Waldkirch.
ANNO M. DC. XXIIII.

1

FIGURE 5   Title page from the Hakluyt Society's 1897 English edition of Munk's *Navigatio Septentrionalis*, edited by C. C. A. Gosch
© WIDENER LIBRARY, HARVARD UNIVERSITY

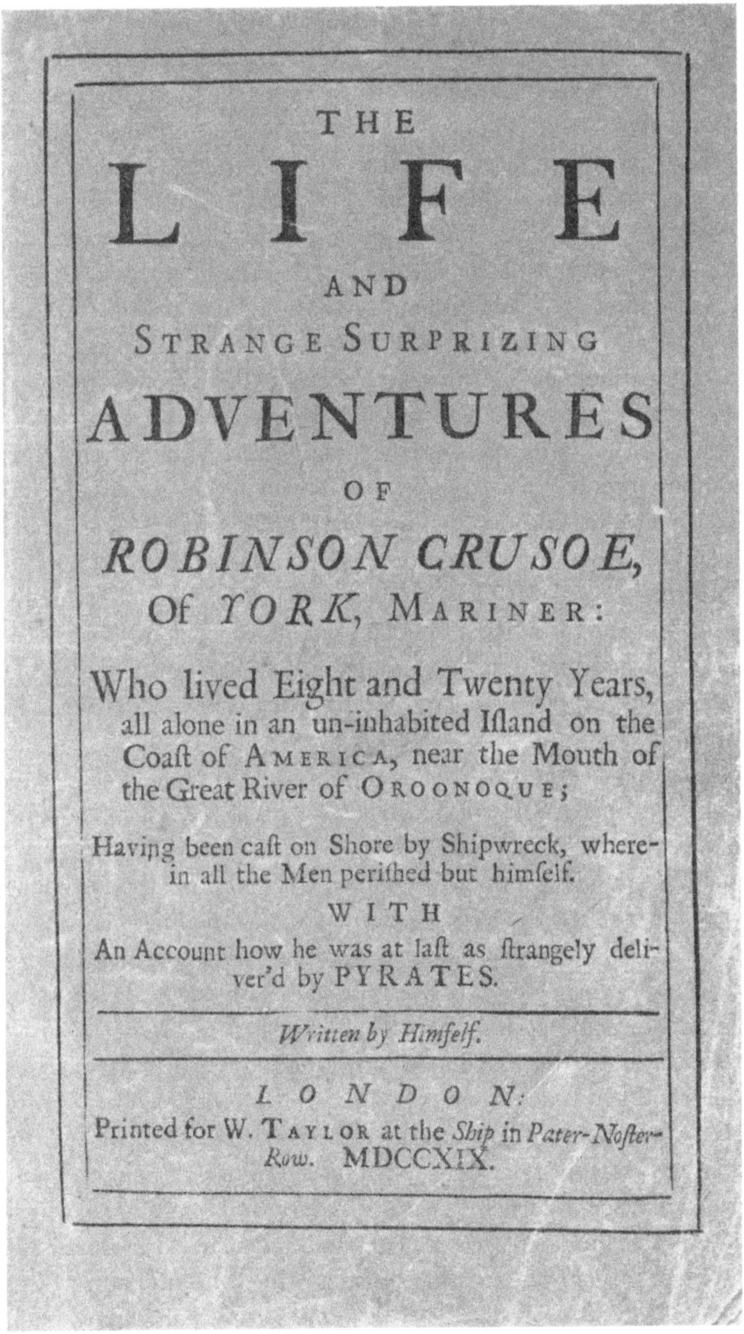

THE

LIFE

AND

STRANGE SURPRIZING

ADVENTURES

OF

ROBINSON CRUSOE,

Of YORK, MARINER:

Who lived Eight and Twenty Years,
all alone in an un-inhabited Island on the
Coast of AMERICA, near the Mouth of
the Great River of OROONOQUE;

Having been cast on Shore by Shipwreck, wherein all the Men perished but himself.

WITH

An Account how he was at last as strangely deliver'd by PYRATES.

Written by Himself.

LONDON:
Printed for W. TAYLOR at the *Ship* in *Pater-Noster-
Row.* MDCCXIX.

FIGURE 6   Title page from first edition of Daniel Defoe's *Robinson Crusoe* (1719)
© BRITISH LIBRARY

among the crew occur, Munk solves the problem straightaway by hiring new crew members.

The style of Munk's logbook is characterized by rigor, the listing of facts, and the logic of causality ("then," "so that," "in order there to," "I thereupon caused to," "in order to," "wherefore I caused," "so as to," "accordingly"). This poetics not only testifies to a certain world view, but it also performs it. The matter-of-fact style converges well with the informational poetics of the title page. Fast forward a hundred years to 1719, and it is evident that the title page of Defoe's *Robinson Crusoe* follows the same principles as Munk's title page (except for the royal references on the latter). For both, it is about the individual, empirical facts, the journey to unknown territories, and authenticity. God is not completely absent in Munk, but almost. Throughout *Navigatio*, Munk refers to God twenty-two times and to Christian IV twelve times. "I," on the contrary, features far more than two hundred times. In situations in which God is invoked, he is not portrayed as a power that punishes humans for their transgressive behavior (the discourse of punishment for example dominates in the "relation" of the shipwreck of the Portuguese galleon *São João* in 1552, as we shall see in the technology chapter) but as a being to whom one prays for mercy and assistance in relation to one's hardships. The problems that occur during the voyage are put down to human error or whims of nature, not as the result of human nemesis or original sin.

The three aesthetic strategies—"I," matter-of-factness, soft God—signal an anthropocentric universe in which humans, in this case a sea captain and proven arctic explorer with several expeditions already behind him, come close to equaling God and productively coping with nature. Munk's actions and style of writing are signs of a *new human* who self-consciously and aided by a practical rationality trusts its abilities to navigate geographically, temporally, practically, and epistemologically as one goes along. It is legitimate to ask whether egocentrism and the orientation towards facts are not dictated by the literary form itself, the diary-logbook. What is more, are they not conditioned by the fact that it is the captain of the expedition with all his authority who produces the logbook and documents the expedition? The form and the author certainly play significant roles. With form follows specific conventions. But if we consider the period in general, other literary forms are in use in which images of the sea and humans converge with Munk's. One of the most famous examples is Defoe's *Robinson Crusoe*. The alert reader will probably object that Robinson, like Munk, writes a diary-logbook, so how can Defoe's book add anything to the anthropocentric argument? There is a crucial difference between the two cases, though. If Munk, an experienced sea captain, wrote in the format he was familiar with and which was expected of him, Defoe *chooses* the format he finds the most appropriate (for Crusoe) to mediate the world picture he wishes to convey. In Munk, to a certain extent at least, the format and the author admittedly dictate a particular empirical style and anthropocentric world picture. In Defoe, it is the other way around: here, the world picture dictates the format.

Considering the bad standing Munk found himself in upon his return from Hudson Bay, it is a proof of his strong willfulness that he succeeded in getting his diary from the 1619–20 expedition published. Miraculously, the original manuscript has survived. Not only did Munk guard it closely during the many difficulties of the expedition and kept it intact until his death, but the manuscript has outlived its author by centuries. Munk's original diary that traveled with him on *Enhiørningen* and *Lamprenen* may be viewed today at the Royal Danish Library in Copenhagen (Figure 7).

The publication of the diary, the survival of the original diary, and the content of the diary show Munk to be an exceptionally determined individual. Hansen demonstrates how Munk was driven by his desire for royal and societal recognition, more specifically for regaining his family's lost status as nobility. In *Jens Munk*, Hansen claims to have submitted excerpts from the manuscript to an expert in handwriting without disclosing the identity of the diary's author. Hansen's motif is the biographer's desire to get closer to his subject's personality. Initially, Hansen describes Munk's handwriting as "solid and regular, with feebly mounting lines and especially characterized by the thick slant lines initiating that part of the words beginning with s. There are practically no corrections." But Hansen is not satisfied with relying on what he can extract from the diary and Munk's handwriting. The image, he laments, "is incomplete, and it shows him only in glimpses, a taciturn and reserved man, mild by nature but blunt, clearsighted, determined, and yet with an enigmatic rupture in his mind, a defect somewhere in the strong will. Is this correct?"

The expert's analysis is then quoted: "The handwriting has a high level of form. On the one hand, it is dominated by an imaginative gift, a visionary power, and an aggressive vivacity, on the other hand by a sensitive softness, warmth, and empathy." The expert (who could be a fictional person and thus a narrative strategy employed by Hansen to proliferate authorship and thereby enhance authenticity and narratorial authority) goes on to emphasize the complexity of Munk's character. This complexity is determined by the strong antagonisms within him, which makes him a genuinely modern human: on the one hand, "passionate and unruly temperament," "divided and anxious," "a constructive and flying imagination," "nourished all kinds of dreams of greatness," on the

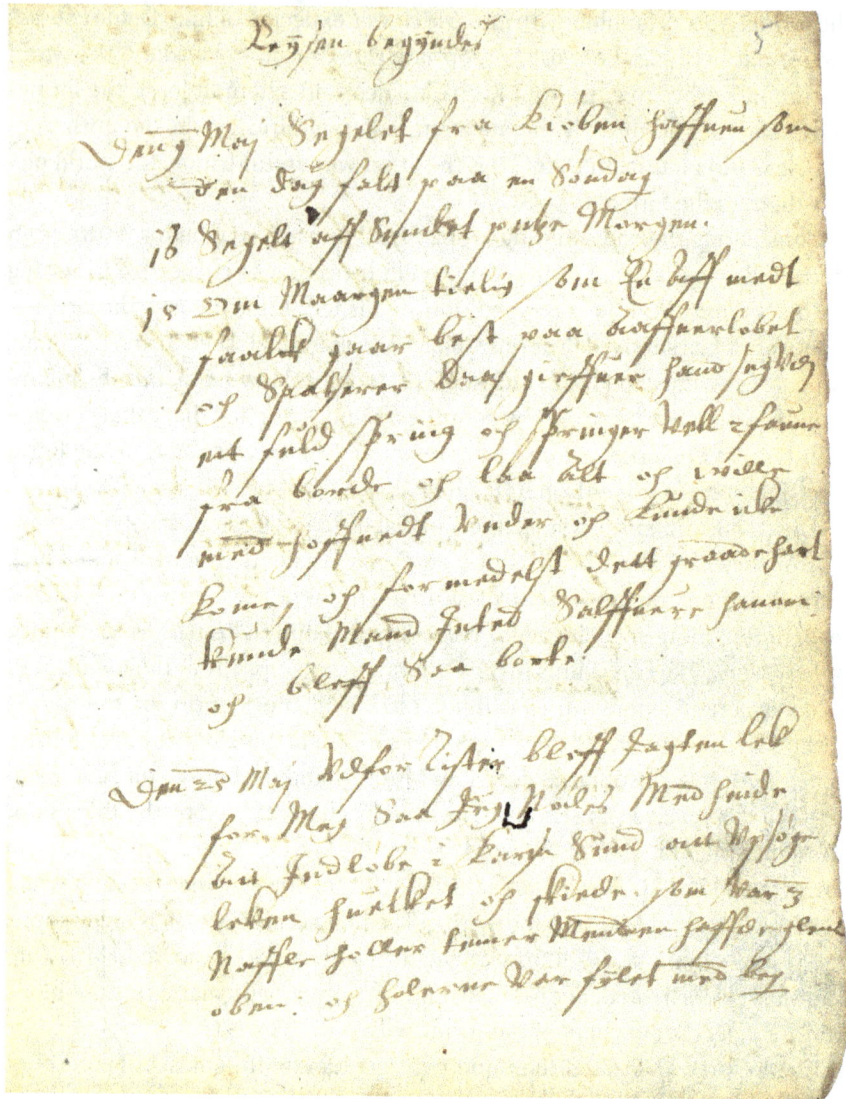

FIGURE 7   Pages from Jens Munk's original diary from the North-West Passage Expedition in 1619–1620. On the page to the right, Munk has added "31 dead" in the left margin. Additamenta no. 184
© DET KGL. BIBLIOTEK/ROYAL DANISH LIBRARY

other hand "a sharp and sober mindset," "ability to combine and talent for calculation," "a stamina beyond normal," "class and aura," "self-reliant and secure," "it is the case itself, that interests him," "possesses a true will to sacrifice himself and is capable of suffer great deprivation," and despite "a solid religious

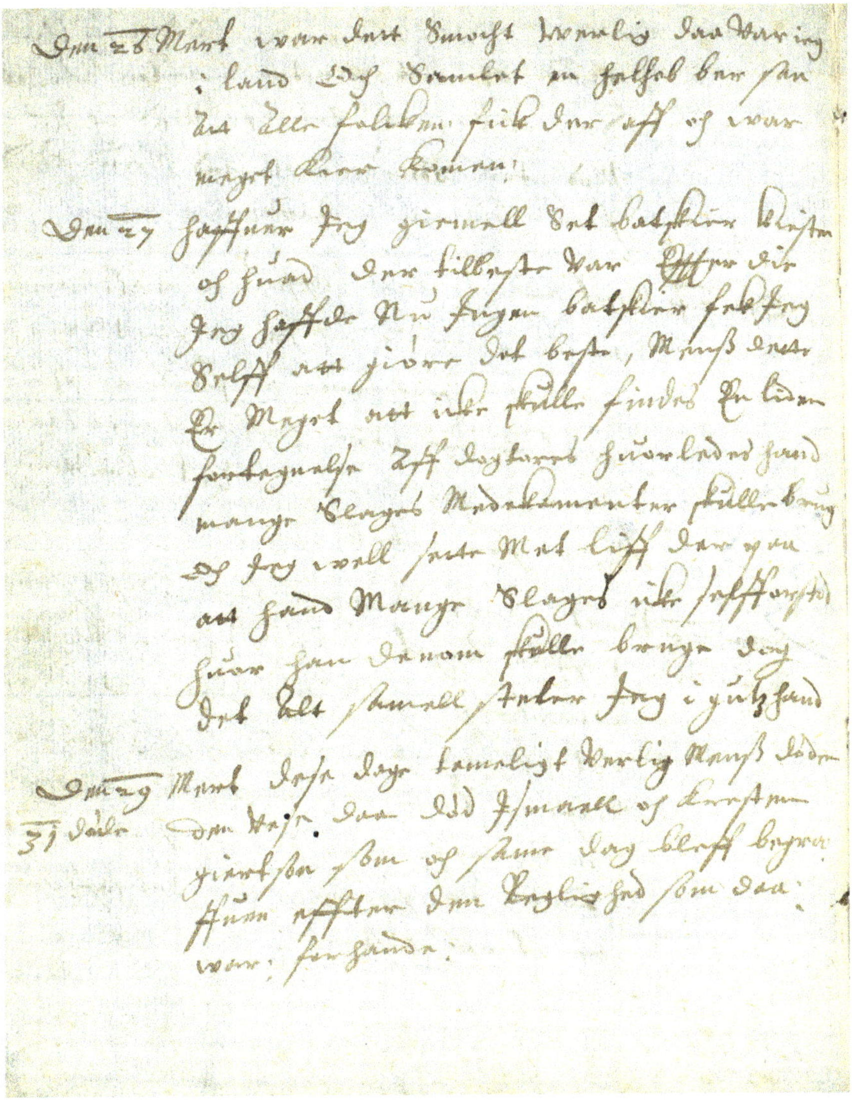

FIGURE 7 (cont.)

conviction" he also "doubted himself."[73] What this amounts to is that Thorkild Hansen portrays Jens Munk as a fusion between Nemo and Hamlet. As such, Munk serves as a Scandinavian icon of anthropocentric modernity.

---

73   Hansen, *Jens Munk*, 18, 18, 19, 19.

2.5 Daniel Defoe

Hakluyt's emphasis on observation and registration, which Cook took up and further developed in the late-eighteenth century, also influenced the first English novel, Daniel Defoe's *Robinson Crusoe* (1719). Defoe borrows a template from older maritime literature such as Philip Sidney's *Arcadia* (ca. 1580), Barnaby Riche's *Apolonius and Silla* (1581), and Robert Greene's *Alcida* (1588), published only two decades before Hakluyt's work. As Frank Watson remarks in *The Sailor in English Fiction and Drama, 1550–1800* (1931), these texts include "kidnapping by pirates, a formula storm, a shipwreck and spar rescue, capture of the ship, a change of identity, a remarkable reunion, and railing at love followed by love."[74] Watson observes that these texts are structured by a narrative template inherited from the Greek idealistic novel (e.g., Heliodorus' *Aethiopica*) rather than by the real world of ships and sea. Sidney, Riche, and Greene all sense the new significance of the maritime world, but according to Watson they are having trouble establishing a connection between inherited forms and the new reality. We would say that Hakluyt and Munk are more aligned with this reality of flux and contingency, but the question is where to place Defoe?

Crusoe experiences storm, shipwreck, and capture. In the beginning of the novel, having embarked on a ship from Hull bound for London, Crusoe attempts to interpret and situate his first storm at sea in a religious framework: "as I had never been at Sea before, I was most inexpressibly sick in Body, and terrify'd in my Mind: I began now seriously to reflect upon what I had done, and how justly I was overtaken by the Judgment of Heaven for [...] the Breach of my Duty to God and my Father." The young rascal promises that "if it would please God here to spare my Life," he will return as the prodigal son to his Father's house and abide by his advice to follow "the middle Station of Life" free of tempests and unnecessary hazards. But Crusoe's mind is, like Antonio's, restlessly "tossing on the ocean," and after having survived the storm a little calm and sun is enough to make him forget his recent hardships and vows. He embarks on a second journey and runs into a second storm. At first, upon seeing "Terror and Amazement in the Faces even of the Seamen themselves" and overhearing the Master of the ship praying, Defoe still maneuvers within a religious system of interpretation, the storm being a sign from God meant to punish the sinful. Crusoe's fainting during the stressful hours is his way of concretizing his own human irrelevance and feebleness in the confrontation

---

74 Frank Watson, *The Sailor in English Fiction and Drama, 1550–1800* (New York: Columbia University Press, 1931), 51.

with a nature that is governed by divine judgments. After their unthinkable rescue, the sacred morale is driven home by the Master when he urges Crusoe to return to his family and "not tempt providence" anymore.[75]

If the opening pages of *Robinson Crusoe* preserve a Christian tradition of reading the ocean as a scene of terror and punishment, this is the point in the story where a significant displacement of world pictures occurs. Within ten lines, Defoe transplants the reader from a theocentric universe of divine signs and warnings as exemplified by the Master of the ship telling Crusoe that he "might see a visible Hand of Heaven" against him, to an anthropocentric universe of prosaic objects and open futures exemplified by Crusoe's words following the Master's warning: "We parted soon after; for I made him little Answer, and I saw him no more; which way he went, I know not. As for me, having some Money in my Pocket, I travelled to *London* by Land."[76] As John Peck has rightly observed, Crusoe's words not just imply a resolution to ignore the warning: "There is an assertion of fact, of what is tangible—Money, Pocket, London—against a conception of experience that presumes to see a symbolic or allegorical meaning in everything."[77] The assertion of empirical facts continues on the island. Admittedly, Crusoe is shocked and frightened upon his arrival on the island and activates his old habit of interpreting incidents as signs of a divine will and predetermined plan. But through the writing of his diary, a counterpart to a ship's logbook, he transforms what he initially interpreted as the outer world's intangible allegorical meaning into tangible and verifiable facts. His *handwriting* consisting of dates, catalogues of his stock, descriptions of events, locations, objects, and natural phenomena, as well as thoughts and feelings, makes him capable of performing this anthropocentric and ordering transformation of his world picture.

With *Robinson Crusoe*, Defoe introduced another significant innovation to the history of the novel: the restlessness of his protagonist. This was a new personal trait that emerged with the mercantile, geographic, and intellectual expansions during the eighteenth century, and it trumps almost any fear of the chaotic manifestations and life-threatening powers of the ocean. Defoe sees and understands this new personality trait, just as he sees and understands the ocean's fundamental importance for the emerging mercantile order of society. However, three things relativize the novel's status as a full-blown maritime novel: first, Defoe stays mainly on land to depict Crusoe's conquest and mastery

---

75   Daniel Defoe, *Robinson Crusoe*, edited with an introduction by Thomas Keymer, notes by Thomas Keymer and James Kelly (1719; Oxford: Oxford University Press, 2008), 9, 11, 15.
76   Defoe, *Robinson Crusoe*, 15.
77   Peck, *Maritime Fiction*, 18.

of the island; second, he sees Crusoe more as a gentleman and businessman than a proper sailor; third, the ocean in *Robinson Crusoe* is relegated to being an abstract medium of connection rather than being the primary scene of the plot. But this is in line with the construction of ocean space during mercantilism: an extra-societal and void space whose only positive attribute was its surface that ensured the facilitation of transport, trade, and circulation. The life of seamen aboard ships and the life of the underwater world were of little interest to Defoe or to most of his contemporaries during the early modern period.

In *Fire Down Below* (1989), a nautical novel set in the early nineteenth century, William Golding has two of his characters, English aristocrats with a neoclassical mindset, reason about the ocean:

> Most of it you know, sir, is quite unnecessary.
>
> Quite, quite unnecessary! Away with it! There shall be no more sea! Let us have a modest strip between one country and another—a kind of canal –[78]

As a space resistant to socioeconomic progress, modernization, and development, the sea had to be conquered or annihilated. As the Golding characters did, Defoe chose annihilation, but only after his protagonist temporarily conquers the sea through rationalization.

2.6 *James Fenimore Cooper*

With the advent of the Romantic Age, writers become increasingly aware of the positive aesthetic and spatial potentials of the ocean. To the romantics, the ocean was a scene for the manifestation of the sublime and on which humankind could liberate itself from the constraining bonds of terrestrial life, not least of industrialized city life. If a new understanding of the sailing ship and its technology had been underway since the mid-fifteenth century, this awareness culminates during the Enlightenment and Romanticism with their valorizations of progress and nature, respectively. The ocean now becomes associated with industriousness, and navigation is elevated to a laudable skill.

In the time between the publication of *Robinson Crusoe* and the beginning of the Romantic Age, Tobias Smollett opened the eyes of the public to life aboard a ship and the existence of the sailor by accommodating both within the form of the novel. In that sense, Smollett can be regarded a predecessor of James Fenimore Cooper, although his treatment of the maritime is very different from Cooper's. The relatively short period that separates Smollett's

---

[78] William Golding, *Fire Down Below* (1989; London: Faber and Faber, 2013), 312.

Roderick Random (1748) from Cooper's *The Pilot* (1824) allows for two highly contrasting worlds to emerge.

Smollett subscribed to the neoclassical aversion to nature's wild, primitive aspects. Although he unlocked the social world of the ship, he devoted little attention to the sea as an object of wonder and fascination. It was only during storms that Smollett's narrator bothered to peep out the porthole, and then mostly because of the storm's potential for narrative suspense and Christian allegory. As Thomas Philbrick observes, a stormy and windblown sea held no promise of sublimity to Smollett; instead, it represented the return of chaos and incarnated a cruel violence that caused fear and confusion. Nor was the ship an embodiment of grace or a symbol of freedom and national pride as it was for Cooper. Instead, it was a miniature world of a corrupt society, a mental institution in decay and smelling of rot and an overturned "stink-pod," or a claustrophobic prison whose inmates were tormented by madness, "bad provision," fever, fleas, and flogging and controlled by evil and incompetence.[79]

In descriptions of genuine indignation, Roderick recounts numerous examples of sailors being mistreated or sent to their deaths because of inhuman command and insufficient or amateurish medical treatment. One sailor, whose excessive overweight is caused by ascites but interpreted as simple fatness by the captain, is forced to climb the mast. Unable to hold his grip, he plunges into the deep (from which he is uncharacteristically saved). To a sailor who complained about lung pains and spitted blood, the surgeon prescribed "exercise at the pump to promote expectoration; but whether this was improper for one in his situation, or that it was used to excess, I know not, but in less than half an hour, he was suffocated with a deluge of blood that issued from his lungs."[80]

Such passages are unthinkable in James Fenimore Cooper, who wrote many of his works when the Romantic Movement was at its peak in the United States. Philbrick observes that the important role of the sublime in the aesthetics of romanticism induced Cooper to invent a poetics of the sea that did not immediately turn away from destruction and danger horrified, but which could understand incredible power and endless distances as positive values and enjoy them for the feelings of wonder and transcendence that they evoked. The social theories of the Romantics emphasized the importance of the natural environment and stressed the achievement of freedom and individuality as the highest of human values. What was needed was thus a perception of the

---

79   Tobias Smollett, *The Adventures of Roderick Random* (1748; Oxford: Oxford University Press, 1999), 151, 189.
80   Smollett, *Roderick Random*, 158; Philbrick, *Cooper and the Development of American Sea Fiction*, 5–6.

ship that appreciated its gracefulness of movement, considered it possible to escape the corrupting distortions and suppressive restrictions of civilized society, and understood the ship's intrinsic potential for epic heroism in its rivalry with the elements. As for the sailor, the romantic imagination placed him in a titanic setting, which meant he had to be a figure elevated by his lifelong connection with and battle against nature in its most sublime manifestations. He had to possess courage and intelligence worthy of the solidly built and finely balanced ship that he steered.[81]

Cooper achieved all this in the second quarter of the nineteenth century. Next, I turn to Cooper's *The Pilot; A Tale of the Sea* (1824) to examine the circumstances that led to its publication as well as the novel's cultural and historical contexts, its originality, and its position in literary history. Paul Celan once observed that every poem is "datable" and therefore radically historical.[82] The literary work is an event that crystallizes a complex network of historical causes and effects. Its singularity endows it with a genuine fascination that stems from its unpredictable balancing act between necessity and contingency. On January 7, 1824, such a crystalline event occurs in literary history—partly inevitable, partly coincidental, and definitely singular—with the publication of Cooper's *The Pilot*. Marcel Clavel considers the novel to be "the first genuine sea novel" in literary history and associates it with "the creation of the maritime novel."[83]

The Pilot is set at the coast of Northumberland towards the end of 1779, three years after the American Revolution. A mysterious pilot by the name of John Gray (modelled on John Paul Jones, "father of the American Navy") joins an American frigate, over which he subsequently gains command. Gray's mission is to capture prominent English citizens. Two young officers, Edward Griffith and Richard Barnstable, are to assist him. However, early in the novel Griffith and Barnstable learn that their loved ones, Cecilia Howard and her cousin Katherine Plowden, are being kept at a former convent close to the coast, where they live with Colonel Howard, Cecilia's uncle and guardian. Howard, a loyalist from South Carolina, has emigrated to the England of his ancestors, out of disappointment with his native country's secession from its motherland.

---

81 Philbrick, *Fenimore Cooper*, 8–9.
82 Paul Celan, *Der Meridian: Endfassung, Vorstufen, Materialen* (Frankfurt am Main: Suhrkamp, 1999), 8.
83 Marcel Clavel, *Fenimore Cooper and His Critics* (Aix-en-Provence: Imprimerie Universitaire de Provence, 1938), 263, 183–263. See also Marcel Clavel, *Fenimore Cooper: Sa vie et son œuvre: La jeunesse (1789–1826)* (Aix-en-Provence: Imprimerie Universitaire de Provence, 1938), 423, 423–506.

Since Howard knows that two American ships matching the descriptions of Barnstable's schooner and Griffith's frigate have been spotted along the English coast, and because Cecilia and Katherine have previously attempted to flee with Griffith and Barnstable back to Carolina, the colonel has deemed it necessary to keep the ladies incarcerated in the convent. Barnstable and Griffith decide to liberate Cecilia and Katherine, and the plot then evolves as a thematic oscillation between private feelings and patriotic duties as well as a topographic oscillation between scenes on sea and on land. At the end of the novel, the American frigate succeeds in vanquishing three English men-of-war and escapes with Katherine and Cecilia aboard.

In what follows, I establish what is meant by a maritime novel and examine why the publication of *The Pilot* is a singular event crystallized as a combination of accidental and pressing impulses. I also discuss how the novel influences the later tradition. I show what makes *The Pilot* an extraordinary and enjoyable novel and use it as a starting point for a characterization of a literary genre—the maritime novel—that is often consigned to a peripheral role in cultural and literary history. Definitions of a maritime novel (also called sea novel and nautical novel) range from inclusive to exclusive. A representative of the former is John Peck to whom it is sufficient that "the sea and sailors function in the text in a subsidiary role, the novelist using the maritime dimension to bring into focus some fundamental questions about the nature of [...] society."[84] An example of the latter is found in Clavel, who uses *The Pilot* to characterize the maritime novel as a work "that would have as principal scene the ocean, as principal characters seafarers, and whose style would appeal to sailors with its technical precision without putting off the ordinary reader."[85] Clavel's definition actually takes its clue from a passage in Susan Fenimore Cooper's introduction to *The Pilot* in *Pages and Pictures*. Here she refers to her father's idea of a novel "with the scene laid on the ocean, whose machinery should be ships and the waves, whose principal characters should be seamen, acting and talking as such."[86]

To appreciate the newness of *The Pilot* and grasp Cooper's disruption of the tradition and the novel's impact on future works, it makes most sense to hold the novel up against Clavel's exclusive definition. This makes us realize that *The Pilot* is the first novel in literary history with the ocean as primary scene, sailors as main characters, and a style characterized by a frequent use of nautical

---

84 Peck, *Maritime Fiction*, 3–4.
85 Marcel Clavel, *Fenimore Cooper: Sa vie et son œuvre*, 428.
86 *Pages and Pictures: From the Writings of James Fenimore Cooper*, ed. and with notes by Susan Fenimore Cooper (New York: W. A. Townsend and Company, 1861), 73.

terminology. Two fifths of the novel unfold on the sea, which is quantitively less than half. Remaining within a quantitative dimension, two fifths was a substantial increase compared to earlier examples, such as Defoe's *Robinson Crusoe* and *Captain Singleton* (1720), Tobias Smollett's *Roderick Random*, and Walter Scott's *The Pirate* (1822). What matters even more is the qualitative fact that the most significant events in *The Pilot* happen at sea. The novel's primary narrative energy is invested in the ocean.

My focus is on what these three characteristics—ocean, sailors, vocabulary—signify, and what thematical and formal implications they have for *The Pilot* and the maritime novel in general. Most readers familiar with the name Fenimore Cooper no doubt associate him with his wilderness novels, especially the five Leatherstocking Tales of which *The Last of the Mohicans* (1826) is arguably the most famous. It comes as a surprise to many that more than a third of Cooper's thirty-two novels are maritime novels. Not only did he invent the genre, but he also wrote eleven sea novels between 1824 and 1849.

Cooper claimed that the human and commercial traffic towards the western frontier was just a temporary redirection of the traffic towards the Atlantic frontier in the east, and that the destiny of the young nation was closely related to the maritime. In his travel book *Notions of the Americans: Picked up by a Travelling Bachelor* (1828), Cooper's European bachelor observes that "the principal theatre for military achievements open to the people of this country is on the Ocean." By further claiming that "the propensity of the nation is so decidedly maritime" and Americans are "a people more maritime [...] than any that exist, or who have ever gone before them," he predicts that "America is to be the first maritime nation of the earth," and "the tide of emigration which has so long been flowing westward, must have its reflux."[87]

Cooper's maritime novels were considered by many contemporaries to be his greatest achievement. In December 1824, an anonymous critic wrote in *New-York Mirror* about Cooper, *The Pilot*, and the United States that

> he has characterized that skill and resolution from which her future glories are to be derived at sea. [...] Cooper is, body and spirit, a sailor. The ocean is his true element—the deck his home. He confers reality on all his descriptions. We hear the roar of the waves—the splash of the oars—the hoarse language of the seamen. [...] Every movement [...] is visible to our eyes, and we actually take part in the proceedings and conversations

---

[87] James Fenimore Cooper, *Notions of the Americans: Picked up by a Travelling Bachelor*, text established with historical introduction and textual notes by Gary Williams (1828; Albany, NY: SUNY Press, 1991), 331, 316, 22, 24–25.

of the crew. They are all, heart and soul, devoted to their profession and their country. Every thing is done nautically.[88]

The review presents a striking contrast to the present when Cooper's maritime novels are completely forgotten. There are three plausible reasons for this, two related to Cooper and one to the genre. First, Cooper's sea novels suffer from the greater popularity of his wilderness novels. If one knows Cooper's work today, it is most likely due to titles such as *The Last of the Mohicans*, *The Pioneers* (1823), *The Pathfinder* (1840), or *The Deerslayer* (1841). Second, Cooper is an author who has been sacrificed on the altar of hypercanonization. During the second half of the twentieth century, globalization and decolonization led to an expansion and transformation of the western canon. Previously consisting of "major" and "minor" writers, this canon increasingly morphed into a genuine world canon now comprising "hypercanonical," "countercanonical," and "shadow canonical" writers.[89] In that process, Cooper's work has been demoted from major novels to shadow canonical (boys') novels. Third, the maritime novel seems generally to be underexposed when the importance of the genre is taken into consideration. In the words of Margaret Cohen, it is "one of the most important and underdiscussed novelistic forms that appealed to a transatlantic public of the nineteenth century."[90] Cohen's claim begs two separate questions: Why is the maritime novel an underdiscussed genre? Why is it one of the most important forms of the novel in the nineteenth century?

The genre's lack of critical attention is primarily a result of a general blindness to the sea in the dominant landbased theories of modernity. I addressed this problem in the introduction. To answer the second question, there are both generic-formal and historic-thematical reasons for the importance of the maritime novel. Constitutively speaking, Margaret Cohen is right to observe that the genre of the novel is international. Peopled by vagrant heroes whose adventures unfolded in an international space, it is characterized by a cosmopolitan thematics. In addition, the novel is characterized by a nomadic poetics constituted by cross-cultural and supranational transfers and appropriations.

---

88 Unsigned review, *New-York Mirror*, December 1924, quoted from *Fenimore Cooper: The Critical Heritage*, eds. George Dekker and John P. McWilliams (London and Boston: Routledge and Kegan Paul, 1973), 74–75.
89 David Damrosch, "World Literature in a Postcanonical, Hypercanonical Age," in *Comparative Literature in an Age of Globalization*, ed. Haun Saussy (Baltimore, MD: Johns Hopkins University Press, 2006).
90 Cohen, "Traveling Genres," 482–83.

This makes it difficult to contain the genre in nationally organized literary histories. Even in the nineteenth century when the novel's thematic universe was predominantly oriented toward questions of national identity, it is symptomatic that the form was still international (historical realism), with national, regional, and local variations of course.[91]

Cosmopolitan thematics and transnational poetics make it clearer why the maritime novel is one of the most significant novelistic forms in the nineteenth century: Like the modernist novel in the first half of the twentieth century and the contemporary migration novel, the sea novel is international in relation to both geography and poetics. The ocean constitutes a supranational topos on which the plot evolves, and at the same time the topographical *terra infirma* results in a form that not only flows across national borders but is itself inherently fluctuating and restless.

On a general level, the historical relevance of the nautical novel is a result of the genre's close connection to three key concepts in the nineteenth century: colonialism, industrialism, and capitalism. On one level, the genre's importance in the nineteenth century is specifically linked with its depiction of labor aboard the ship. Cooper had a keen eye for the heroic and honorable dimensions of labor, seamanship, and the collective. An example, also treated by Cohen, is in the beginning of *The Pilot* when the American frigate finds itself in terrifying waters called the Devil's Grip. These waters abound with sandbars and rocks and are dominated by a powerful surf and the stormy northeast winds of the North Sea, which prevent intruders from escaping the Devil's Grip. Gray has just come aboard the frigate and is immediately assigned the task of navigating the man-of-war out of the bay.

The scene culminates when the frigate approaches the outermost sandbars. The maneuvering is made even more difficult by the approaching tide and the climax of the storm. Gray decides on the unconventional strategy of increasing the sail area rather than following the standard procedure during a storm, which would be pulling down the sails. The reasoning behind his daring idea is that the frigate needs a high velocity to overcome the combined resistance of the tide and the surf and reach the safety of open sea:

> "Gentlemen, we must be prompt [...]. That topsail is not enough to keep her up to the wind; we want both jib and mainsail."
>
> "'Tis a perilous thing to loosen canvas in such a tempest!" observed the doubtful captain.

---

91 Cohen, "Traveling Genres," 481.

HISTORY

> "It must be done," returned the collected stranger; "we perish without it—[...]."
> [...] There was an instant when the result was doubtful; [...] but art and strength prevailed, and gradually the canvas was distended, and bellying as it filled, was drawn down to its usual place by the power of a hundred men. [...]
> "She feels it! she springs her luff! observe," he said, "[...] if she will only bear her canvass we shall go clear." [...]
> [...] the hardy mariners, knowing that they had already done all in the power of man to insure their safety, stood in breathless anxiety, awaiting the result. [...] The pilot silently proceeded to the wheel, and, with his own hands, he undertook the steerage of the ship. [...] she entered the channel among the breakers, with the silence of a desperate calmness. [...] At length the ship reached a point where she appeared to be rushing directly into the jaws of destruction, when suddenly her course was changed, and her head receded rapidly from the wind [...], and directly the gallant vessel issued from her perils, and rose and fell on the heavy waves of the sea.[92]

Gray's character and the maritime novel in general are founded on action and adventurousness. In that sense, the genre belongs to a tradition that precedes the modern novel, indeed contrasts with many of its dominant forms such as the domestic, introspective, and descriptive novels. This tradition includes Homer's *The Odyssey*, the early Greek novels, and the chivalric novels of the Middle Ages. It is a tradition that valorizes daring, composure, the unpredictable, risk, danger, and adventure.[93] In maritime novels, these attributes are depicted in the life-and-death struggles of the sailors when they, usually assisted by technology, confront enemy armies, brutal pirates, foreign people, and not least nature's destructive forces.[94] In Cooper's writing, it results in a structure that has chase and escape as key narrative components.

As the celebrated passage above indicates, a dramatic energy closely related to the labor executed by the captain and his crew supplements the narrative energy invested in the ocean, and "the nature of work, along with the status of the worker, are among the most urgent social questions of the nineteenth

---

92 James Fenimore Cooper, *The Pilot; A Tale of the Sea*, edited, with historical introduction and explanatory notes by Kay Seymour House (1824; Albany, NY: SUNY Press, 1986), 57–59.

93 Michael Nerlich, *Ideology of Adventure*, vol. 1, tr. Ruth Crowley (Minneapolis: University of Minnesota Press, 1987), 5.

94 Cohen, "Traveling Genres," 485.

century."⁹⁵ In particular, it was the degradation of work that occupied the period's philosophers and economists, Karl Marx and Friedrich Engels in particular. This topic is represented in numerous maritime novels in which the ship is associated with the factory. Examples include Conrad's *Typhoon*, Nordahl Grieg's *Skibet gaar videre* (1924; *The Ship Sails On*), and Malcolm Lowry's *Ultramarine* (1933). This is a particularly strong tradition, after the steamship replaces the sailing ship during the nineteenth century. The labor on a steamship is often organized in a highly hierarchical structure like that of the factory of the industrial age, and the common sailor is engaged in the same kind of hard manual work as the factory worker.

However, the maritime novel offers alternatives to the degradation of work that was taking place in the factories of the industrialized metropolises. In that sense, a counter-modernity seems to be at stake in some of the maritime authors, where the disenchanted world is being re-enchanted. When Melville opens *Billy Budd* with the words "In the time before steamships," he strikes a nostalgic tone and implicitly expresses a desire to re-enchant the world, of recollecting values from a bygone era by *looking back*.⁹⁶ Similarly, in the memoir *The Mirror and the Sea* (1906) Conrad employs a vocabulary of re-enchantment of the virtues of maritime work in alignment with Cooper's vision in the Devil's Grip scene. Conrad speaks of "the *honour* of labour" in relation to the art of seafaring, which he believes "is made up of accumulated *tradition*, kept alive by individual *pride*, rendered exact by *professional* opinion, and, like the *higher arts*, it is spurred on and sustained by discriminating *praise*."⁹⁷

As observed by Cohen, work on a ship is defined by the importance of know-how. Know-how means possessing practical skills and technological acumen, the ability to *use* technology rather than *explain* it. Know-how is "applied knowledge, concrete practice, and results, in contrast to concepts, classification, and abstract truth."⁹⁸ It is vital in situations in which the chain of interdependence between human, technology, and nature is weakened, because technology breaks down or reaches its limit. In *The Pilot*, this happens when the frigate is set to commence the arduous maneuver of exiting the Devil's Grip. A sudden reversal in the weather, where "a distinct but distant roaring announced the sure approach of the tempest" results not only in a somber mood and general confusion among the crew but causes the frigate to become "unmanageable." However, Captain Munson's call for immediate action is rejected by Gray: " 'Tis

---

95   Cohen, "Traveling Genres," 491.
96   Melville, *Billy Budd*, 3.
97   Conrad, *The Mirror and the Sea*, 23, my italics.
98   Cohen, "Traveling Genres," 486.

unnecessary,' he at length said; "twould be certain destruction to be taken aback; and it is difficult to say, within several points, how the wind may strike us.' "⁹⁹ Gray knows that it is imperative to find the proper dialectical rhythm between the forces of nature, human action, and technology. The questions posed by nature can be unpredictable, and an impulsive human response can be fatal. If technology is suddenly taken out of the equation, it is crucial to determine the character of nature before responding to it.

Gray's hesitation and timing—his "composure"—turn out to be the right tactic: "the vessel bowed down heavily to one side, and then, as she began to move through the water, rose again majestically to her upright position, as if saluting, like a courteous champion, the powerful antagonist with which she was about to contend."¹⁰⁰ Gray's know-how functions as a relay that synchronizes humans and nature and leads technology back into its proper place in the equation. The situation demands that Gray is future-oriented and foresighted, but this cannot prevent his ability to hesitate and act carefully and be flexible in response to the demands of the here and now. His boldness is just as much a daring throw into the future (the increase of sail during the storm) as it is the courage to pause and face whatever comes (we shall later see how Conrad's Captain MacWhirr exhibits similar qualities). Cohen again:

> The place of know-how is on the deck, not the desk [...]. The measure of know-how is the outcome of a maneuver, not its justice or nobility. Know-how is an amoral and apolitical knowledge [...]. At the same time, know-how has democratizing political implications, for it is potentially a universal human faculty, available across rank, culture, nationality, race, class, and gender.¹⁰¹

This makes her conclude that "sea fiction might be understood as restoring the integrity of work and envisioning a new classless society founded on the ethos of work, the capacity of know-how."¹⁰²

The important role of know-how helps emphasize the difference between the relative "democracy" on the ship and the fixed hierarchical organization of the factory and society in general. Gray's command of the frigate is a good example. In contrast to Captain Munson and Lieutenant Griffith, Gray does not descend from a distinguished family. Since his true identity is a mystery to

---

99   Cooper, *The Pilot*, 48, 48, 49.
100 Cooper, *The Pilot*, 48, 49.
101 Cohen, "Traveling Genres," 486–487.
102 Cohen, "Traveling Genres," 493.

everyone except for Munson and Griffith, he exemplifies Cohen's point about democratization in relation to class, and beyond that to rank and nationality.

If nineteenth-century factory work was defined by a separation between work and worker and by increasing specialization and manualization, then know-how is *embodied knowledge* that cannot be separated from the sailor. It requires training as well as the ability to coordinate between a series of skills and mental faculties. Embodied knowledge is the union of physical and mental competencies. Instead of intellect and reason, the controlling principle is instinct, paired with know-how and experience. Cooper reflects upon the significance of instinct in *The Two Admirals: A Tale* (1842), one of his later sea novels:

> M. de Vervillin, himself, was a man of respectable birth, of a scientific education, and of great familiarity with ships, so far as a knowledge of their general powers and principles was concerned; but here his professional excellence ceased, all that infinity of detail which composes the distinctive merit of the practical seaman being, in a great degree, unknown to him, rendering it necessary for him to *think* in moments of emergency; periods when the really prime mariner seems more to act by a sort of *instinct* than by any very intelligible process of ratiocination. [...] No—no—your real sea-dog, has no occasion for *thinking*, when he has his work before him.[103]

Instinctual work based on know-how seems to be an imperative skill, because once aboard a ship everything is oriented towards survival instead of profit. The immediate consequence of the labor whose basic ethos is know-how is that survival prevails over profit, which means in turn that labor becomes endowed with a heroic and honorable quality that compensates in part for the general degradation of labor that took place during the nineteenth century.

I now proceed to discuss the impulses that led to Cooper writing *The Pilot*. In his 1849 preface, Cooper underlines the originality of his novel as compared to the literary tradition. At the same time, he admits that the circumstances behind "the conception and execution of this book [...] are the result of sudden impulses and accidents." In 1822, Walter Scott had published *The Pirate*, a novel that in Cooper's own words "has a direct connection with the sea."[104] Only four percent of Scott's novel is set on the sea, but Cooper's primary incentive

---

103 James Fenimore Cooper, *The Two Admirals: A Tale*, historical introduction by Donald A. Ringe, text established by James A. Sappenfield and E. N. Feltskog (1842; Albany, NY: SUNY Press, 1990), 313, 318.
104 Cooper, "Preface. [1849]," *The Pilot*, 5, 5.

for writing *The Pilot* is not so much a desire to augment the number of pages devoted to ship scenes and the ocean as it is the wish for greater nautical precision. Shortly after the publication of *The Pirate*, Cooper attended a dinner party hosted by his friend Charles Wilkes, and during the gathering the guests discussed the identity of the Waverley novels' author.[105] The majority of those present, among them Cooper, claimed that Walter Scott was the author of the novels, but some of the guests echoed the usual arguments of the contemporary skeptics that the Scottish lawyer would have been too busy to publish so many novels containing so much historically accurate and universal knowledge. Their argument was strengthened by *The Pirate*. Its nautical passages excited most of the guests, but their apparent precision excluded Scott from its possible authorship. As Cooper observes in the 1849 preface: "The claims of Sir Walter were a little distrusted, on account of the peculiar and minute information that the romances were then very generally thought to display. The Pirate was cited as a very marked instance of this universal knowledge, and it was wondered where a man of Scott's habits and associations could have become so familiar with the sea."[106]

As the only person present who believed that Scott was the author of the Waverley novels, including *The Pirate*, Cooper had a ready answer. He thus found that there was "much looseness in this universal knowledge, and that the secret of its success was to be traced to the power of creating that *vraisemblance*, which is so remarkably exhibited in those world-renowned fictions, rather than to any very accurate information on the part of their author."[107] As Susan Fenimore Cooper later remarked, no one admired Scott more than Cooper, "but on this occasion he maintained the opinion that 'The Pirate' was not thoroughly satisfactory to a nautical reader; he added that a man accustomed to ships, and the sea, could have accomplished far more with the same materials as those employed in 'The Pirate.'"[108]

Far from solving the problem of the identity of the author of the Waverley cycle, Cooper's answer rather complicated the matter, for now both fractions made common front against Cooper:

> they considered the proportion of nautical matter as a proof of the author's skill; they held that similar scenes introduced very freely into a

---

105 Susan Fenimore Cooper, *Pages and Pictures*, 72; see also Clavel, *Fenimore Cooper: Sa vie et son œuvre*, 423–29.
106 Cooper, "Preface. [1849]," 5.
107 Cooper, "Preface. [1849]," 5.
108 Susan Fenimore Cooper, *Pages and Pictures*, 72.

work of fiction must necessarily become tedious from their monotony, that they could not long be made really interesting to the general reader; professional men might take pleasure in them, but for a landsman, occasional passages by way of brief episodes, admitted for the sake of novelty and variety, must always be sufficient. More than this must necessarily become an error of judgment in any work of fiction.[109]

Cooper was now on his own, but he stubbornly stuck to his belief that a novel whose primary scene is the ocean and whose main characters are sailors who talk and act as such "might be written with perfect professional accuracy, and yet possess equal interest with a similar book connected with the land."[110] According to Cooper, the result of the vivid and entertaining discussion, and of his subsequent conversation with Wilkes, was "a sudden determination to produce a work which, if it had no other merit, might present truer pictures of the ocean and ships than any that are to be found in the Pirate. To this unpremeditated decision, purely an impulse, is not only the Pilot due, but a tolerably numerous school of nautical romances that have succeeded it."[111] So, Cooper uses Scott's novel as a contrast in his attempt to articulate the singularity of his own novel, but *The Pirate* is also the indirect and contingent ("sudden," "unpremeditated," "impulse") cause that prompts the writing of *The Pilot*.

In the first preface to *The Pilot* written in 1823, Cooper comments on Smollett's treatment of the sea. The intention with *The Pilot*, Cooper writes at the time of the novel's publication, is not so much "to describe the customs of a particular age, as to paint those scenes which belong only to the ocean, and to exhibit [...] a few traits of a people who [...] can never be much known." He then adds: "It will be seen, however, that though he has navigated the same sea as Smollett, he has steered a different course [...], that he has considered what Smollett has painted as a picture which is finished, and which is not to be daubed over by every one who may choose to handle a pencil on marine subjects."[112] Compared to the more extensively articulated reservations about Scott's novel, the Cooper of 1823 seems unable to explain the differences between his treatment of the ocean and Smollett's.

In hindsight, we can point to a series of obvious differences between Cooper and Smollett, some of them introduced earlier in this chapter. In *Roderick*

---

109 Susan Fenimore Cooper, *Pages and Pictures*, 72.
110 Susan Fenimore Cooper, *Pages and Pictures*, 72.
111 Cooper, "Preface. [1849]," 5–6.
112 Cooper, "Preface. [1823]," *The Pilot*, 3, 3–4.

Random and also in *Peregrine Pickle* (1751), Smollett limits himself to the British Royal Navy, which is depicted as a massive machine that often destroys the individual. Sailing ship life is characterized by filthiness, brutality, and corruption. In Cooper, by contrast, the maritime sphere is not restricted to the American Navy but includes the entire maritime spectrum from military to mercantile enterprises. Unlike Smollett's sailors, Cooper's sailors are dynamic and heroic, a disparity that seems logical. The American nation's maritime history consisted of such individuals and deeds rather than of an institution's long and glorious history and collective traditions.[113] Another important difference is the quantitative and qualitative role of the sea. Whereas almost half of *The Pilot* occurs at sea, in the case of *Roderick Random* it is only one sixth. In Cooper's works, the ocean is an *elementary* topos where "the sea inter-penetrates with life"[114] as Conrad claims in a homage to his American predecessor. In Smollett, the ocean has more the role of accidental backdrop. In Warren S. Walker's opinion, the ocean was "only the pathway *to* adventure with Smollett, not the pathway *of* adventure. [...] In *The Pilot* and its successors one is made aware for the first time in prose fiction of a relationship between man and sea that transcends mere physical proximity."[115]

However, the most significant difference between Smollett and Cooper lies in their respective tones. To the neoclassical Smollett, heroism is ultimately incompatible with a realistic description of everyday topics. If Smollett's depictions of life at sea comprise realism (brutality, corruption, and filthiness were indeed components in a sailor's life), this realism is relativized by a hyperbolic and satirical tone. One consequence is the stereotype "the naïve and gay sailor with rough saltwater voice, strange manners, and prone to drinking." But this stereotype had outlived itself in the American context. When Cooper set about portraying the American sailors' relationship with the sublimities of wild nature or their disposition for heroic deeds, Smollett's sailor was no longer adequate, and the same was true of Smollett's ship and sea.

Cooper's two reflections on the generic and historical status of *The Pilot* are carried out simultaneously with its publication and again twenty-five years later. There are further reflections on *The Pilot* in some of his other works, for example in the travelogue *Gleanings in Europe: England* (1837), where Cooper describes the novel as "an essay in nautical description, a species of writing

---

113   Philbrick, *Fenimore Cooper*, 3–5.
114   Joseph Conrad, "Tales of the Sea," in *Notes on Life and Letters* (1898, 1921, 1926; London: J. M. Dent & Sons, 1970), 55.
115   Warren S. Walker, *James Fenimore Cooper: An Introduction and Interpretation* (New York: Barnes and Noble, 1962), 25, 74.

that was then absolutely new."[116] The temporal distances between the novel's publication on January 7, 1824, the book on England in 1837, and the self-conscious 1849 preface indicate that the awareness of the originality of his own novel came late for Cooper. His self-awareness was only amplified by the influence exercised by the novel upon its many offspring. As the nineteenth century unfolded, *The Pilot* became the forefather whom numerous English, French, and American descendants attempted to imitate: "Cooper's *Pilot*, though full of national prejudices, has unquestionably led the way in this species of literature," a certain W. N. G. observes.[117] Carl van Doren weighs in: "Not only did he outdo Scott in sheer accuracy, but he created a new literary type, the tale of adventure on the sea, in which, though he was to have many followers in almost every modern language, he has not been seriously surpassed for vigor and swift rush of narrative."[118]

A letter from Charles Wilkes to Cooper dated December 27, 1827, makes clear that years before actually composing *The Pilot* Cooper was occupied with writing a novel that would break with generic conventions and represent an entirely new genre, even before he read Scott's *The Pirate*: "I remember very well many years ago long before you published the Pilot or had even composed it, as it now is, but when [you] had conceived it, you told me that you would write on a nautical subject & [make] the principal scenes on the ocean."[119] Wilkes' words relativizes the role of Scott's novel, also the role Cooper himself ascribed to it in 1849. *The Pilot* is not merely a result of a "sudden impulse" caused by *The Pirate* and its nautical imprecision. It is also a "necessary" result of historical circumstances, personal experiences, and literary influences.

As to literary influence, it is possible to supplement Smollett's *Roderick Random* and Scott's *The Pirate* with Daniel Defoe's *Robinson Crusoe* and *Captain Singleton*, William Falconer's "The Shipwreck" (1762), Philip Freneau's poems—for example "The British Prison Ship" (1780) and "On the Memorable Victory of Paul Jones" (1781)—and Lord Byron's *The Corsair* (1814) and *Childe Harold* (1812–18). On the personal level, the background for *The Pilot* and the precondition for creating a detailed, precise, and truthful maritime novel were

---

116 James Fenimore Cooper, *Gleanings in Europe: England*, historical introduction and explanatory notes by Donald A. Ringe and Kenneth W. Staggs, text established by James P. Elliott, Kenneth W. Staggs, and Robert D. Madison (1837; Albany: SUNY Press, 1981), 10.
117 W. N. G., "Naval novels," in *Marryatt's Metropolitan Magazine*, August 1831, quoted from Kay Seymour House, "Historical Introduction," in Cooper, *The Pilot*, xxxiv.
118 Carl van Doren, *The American Novel: 1789–1939* (New York: MacMillan, 1940), 27.
119 Letter from Wilkes to Cooper, quoted from House, "Historical Introduction," in Cooper, *The Pilot*, xvii.

Cooper's experiences from two periods at sea: the first on board the merchant ship *Stirling* where, at the age of seventeen, he spent eleven months in 1806–07 as an ordinary seaman (experiencing the English Channel and the eastern coast of England first hand); the second as a cadet in the American Navy from January 1, 1808, to May 12, 1810. Furthermore, throughout his life Cooper kept close contact with the American Navy, and for a period of time he had part-ownership of a whaling ship.

On the political level, the ambitions of the United States to become a free and powerful nation played a central role in the conception of *The Pilot*, because American nationalism was closely linked with the ocean and American maritime activities. The maritime nationalism sweeping the country was a result of military and especially mercantile merits. After the peace treaty signed in 1815, the American shipbuilding industry and seafaring exploits entered a golden age that was to last thirty-five years. British hegemony was superseded by American seamen in some of the most important maritime mercantile activities. In 1840, three quarters of the world's whaling fleet sailed under American flags. In maritime science, the United States was also ahead of the older European nations throughout the nineteenth century. In *La Mer*, Michelet acknowledges the American position: "Why has America accomplished, in this respect, so much more than we? America is Desire. She is young, and burns to put herself in connection with the globe." It is one American scientist in particular, M. F. Maury, who Michelet singles out for praise. Maury, "the learned poet of the Sea" and "apostle of the sea,"[120] is also mentioned on several occasions by Verne in *Vingt mille lieues sous les mers*. Maury's *The Physical Geography of the Sea* (1855) was an indispensable source for his depictions of Aronnax and Nemo's explorations of the seabed and the submarine world in general.

It was inevitable that the extensive and varied maritime activity of the Americans would find an expression in a literature whose writers sought to create a national identity. Philbrick claims that it was "the duty of American literature to keep the flame of maritime nationalism burning brightly."[121] Traditionally, *The Pilot* has been read as an example of such a maritime nationalism in the emergence of an American literature. The quoted review from *New-York Mirror* has contributed to this tradition: "he has characterized that skill and resolution from which her future glories are to be derived at sea." Cooper's remarks in *Notions of the Americans* also support a link between *The Pilot* and American maritime nationalism. More recently, Philbrick has argued for such

---

120 Michelet, *La Mer*, 51–52.
121 Philbrick, *Fenimore Cooper*, 2.

a connection: "the sea novel as we know it owes its inception to the meeting of maritime nationalism and romanticism in the imagination of James Fenimore Cooper."[122]

According to Philbrick, the Atlantic Ocean provided the opportunity for American writers to create triumphant national stories and a heroic national identity.[123] There are obvious examples of maritime nationalism in American literature. One is Samuel Woodworth's *The Champions of Freedom; or, The Mysterious Chief* (1816), a novel based on the 1812 War that reflects and feeds "the blaze of glory which now streamed from the ocean."[124] Another is Philip Freneau, who already in 1781 with "On The Memorable Victory, Obtained by the gallant Captain Paul Jones, of *Le Bon Homme Richard*, (or father Richard) over the *Seraphis*, of 44 guns, under the Command of Captain Pearson" had created a strong maritime nationalism and heroism in regard to John Paul Jones. However, Cooper's maritime nationalism in *The Pilot* is much more ambivalent than in the cases of Freneau and Woodsworth. This problematizes Philbrick's argument. As Kay Seymour House correctly observes, "Cooper was interested in character rather than chauvinism."[125]

Cooper creates the perfect conditions for a maritime nationalism in *The Pilot*: an American frigate and schooner close to the English coast; the time is just after the revolution; the introduction of John Gray (recognizable to most contemporary readers as John Paul Jones); and the rescue mission. But as events unfold, the novel does not keep its initial promises. First, in contrast to Freneau, Cooper chooses a fictional starting point for the portrait of John Paul Jones (Jones never commanded raids along the eastern coast of England), and his novel therefore loses the anchorage in real events that is usually a prerequisite for the construction of a national-heroic mythology. It is also significant that Freneau depicts Jones' successful battle against the *Serapis*, while Cooper's novel is the story about an unsuccessful campaign, mostly because Griffith and Barnstable decide to succumb "their public duty […] the purpose of their private feelings." When they choose to liberate Cecilia and Katherine, the patriotic kidnapping mission is transformed into a private rescue operation. Griffith contemplates that the mission "may be the means of rescuing the ladies," but

---

122   Philbrick, *Fenimore Cooper*, 42.
123   Thomas Philbrick, "Cooper and the Literary Discovery of the Sea," *Canadian Review of American Studies* 20, no. 3 (1989): 37.
124   Samuel Woodworth, *The Champions of Freedom; or, The Mysterious Chief* (New York: Charles N. Baldwin, 1816), 79.
125   Kay Seymour House, "The Unstable Element," in *James Fenimore Cooper: A Collection of Critical Essays*, ed. Wayne Fields (Englewood Cliffs, N.J.: Prentice-Hall, 1979), 139, note 8.

that it will simultaneously "fail in making the prisoners we anticipate," and in spite of this, "private feeling, rather than public spirit" ultimately reigns.[126] Subsequently, the plot evolves as an endless series of captures and liberations, which makes Sarah Florence Wood conclude that "the Revolutionary narrative of national becoming simply fails to materialise in *The Pilot*, as the private and romantic plot diverts the mission from its purpose."[127] Wood's point is supported by the novel, when John Gray refers to "the main object of our expedition" as "lost," "sacrificed to more private feelings; 'tis like a hundred others, ended in disappointment."[128]

If the kidnapping plot fails, and the many vicissitudes between captured and liberated slowly transforms the novel from a potential epic narrative to a burlesque melodrama, then the general revolutionary plot, whose central theme is the birth of the nation, remains unfinished. As Wood observes, it was normal for novels about the War of Independence "to connect the Revolution with the War of 1812, constructing a Revolutionary or republican continuum, and embedding a sense of ideological continuity in the narrative structure and nationalistic rhetoric of the text."[129] However, in *The Pilot* there is no link to 1812, because the end of the novel is situated in 1791. Admittedly, prior to his death on board the frigate, Colonel Howard acknowledges the inevitability of American victory and the legitimacy of the new nation. But Howard is not endowed with much enunciatory authority; his words do not possess enough gravitational power to transform the novel into an organic national narrative. On the last pages, we encounter centrifugal counterweights to Howard's potentially centripetal effect, when Cecilia expresses her concern about whether "the new order of things" will succeed and Griffith characterizes the new republic as a temporary "experiment, until time shall mature the new system."[130] As Wood remarks, the novel is more focused on "a moment of historical uncertainty [...] than victory, emphasising provisionality over security as it closes on a note of anxiety."[131] The struggles regarding continuity are further emphasized by the absence of any children. The novel's three romantic stories end differently—Alice Dunscombe and John Gray part for ever, Katherine Plowden and Richard Barnstable choose a shared life at sea, and

---

126 Cooper, *The Pilot*, 87, 85, 157.
127 Sarah Florence Wood, " 'Narrow Passages': Captive Sailors and National Narrative in James Fenimore Cooper's *The Pilot*," *Atlantic Studies* 3, no. 2 (2006): 247.
128 Cooper, *The Pilot*, 345.
129 Wood, "Narrow Passages," 248.
130 Cooper, *The Pilot*, 424, 424.
131 Wood, "Narrow Passages," 248.

Cecilia Howard and Edward Griffith decide upon a life together in Carolina—yet all three couples are childless.

John Gray is no doubt Cooper's most purely conceived Byronic hero with all that entails of freedom and betrayal. On numerous occasions, Cooper emphasizes Gray's rootlessness and landlessness, thus underlining his maritime isolation and position outside the conventional social frameworks. Gray's person is associated with moral ambiguity in that he balances between pirate and champion of liberty, faithless cosmopolitan and loyal patriot, and social duties and selfish ambitions. In Griffith's words: "He was a man who had formed romantic notions of glory, and wished everything concealed in which he acted a part that he thought would not contribute to his renown." As already mentioned, Gray's loyalty towards the United States seems to be driven primarily by the desire to stand out and by selfish motifs, "and perhaps a little also from resentment at some injustice which he claimed to have suffered from his own countrymen," says Griffith at the end of the novel about the English-born Gray. Griffith adds that whereas Gray's deeds deserve the highest praise, "His love of liberty may be more questionable; for if he commenced his deeds in the cause of these free States, they terminated in the service of a despot."[132] Here, Griffith refers to Gray's (and Jones') subsequent travels after the partly failed mission in 1779, which led him in the service of Catherine II against the Turks.

Besides the failed rescue mission, the openness of the ending regarding the national project, and Gray's moral indeterminability, maritime nationalism is relativized by Cooper's decision to set the plot on the eastern coast of England. As a result of this decision, certain aspects of the old world inevitably remain important in his novel; during that phase of the country's existence, the United States still defines itself in relation to England. According to Peck, a general difference can be observed between English and American maritime writers:

> British maritime fiction is generally written from the perspective of the shore; indeed, more often than not it is landbased. American maritime fiction places more emphasis on the voyage, which is often a quest or journey of self-discovery. [...] The British novel has a long history to call upon, and is always aware of a complex social inheritance; the nineteenth-century American novel, by contrast, is the product of, and reflection of, a country still in the process of formation. Consequently, whereas the British maritime novel dwells on family connections and social structures, the American maritime novel focuses more on isolated

---

132   Cooper, *The Pilot*, 425, 426, 426.

individuals, heroes on the edge of a new frontier. This is underlined by a different sense of space. [...] The American sea novel [...] can feel boundless: the distances covered are enormous, and the time spent away from land is lengthy. British sea novels never seem to offer a similar sense of remoteness.[133]

Peck's analysis is generally valid but calls for nuance. If one accepts his broad definition of "maritime fiction" and includes Jane Austen's *Mansfield Park* (1814) and *Persuasion* (1818), Charles Dickens' *Dombey and Son* (1848) and *David Copperfield* (1850), and George Eliot's *Daniel Deronda* (1876) in the category, his characterization of the British version of the genre is correct. However, his definition seems somewhat less valid when writers such as Marryat and Conrad are considered.

Melville fits in better with Peck's characterization of the American variant of maritime fiction than Cooper. The point about the romantic individual converges well with Cooper's first three sea novels in which the reader encounters romantic heroes such as John Gray, Captain Heidegger (the eponymous hero of *The Red Rover*) and Tom Tiller (the Skimmer of the Seas in *The Water Witch*) who were all inspired by Byron's Conrad (*The Corsair*) and Harold (*Childe Harold*). But although the narrative energy of these novels relates primarily to the scenes on the ocean, the reader seldomly senses the infinity of space to the same degree as in Melville. Cooper approaches topographical boundlessness in later works such as *Homeward Bound* (1838) and *The Sea Lions* (1849), but in his first sea novels space is not infinite.

The first sentence of the *The Pilot* implies that the plot plays out in a relatively narrow space:

> A single glance at the map will make the reader acquainted with the position of the eastern coast of the island of Great Britain, as connected with the shores of the opposite continent. Together they form the boundaries of the small sea that has for ages been known to the world as the scene of maritime exploits, and as the great avenue through which commerce and war have conducted the fleets of the northern nations of Europe.[134]

When Margaret Cohen writes that the novel's geography is framed by "the edges of the Atlantic," it seems to be a misreading of what Cooper means by

---

133 Peck, *Maritime Fiction*, 89.
134 Cooper, *The Pilot*, 11.

"the opposite continent": It is more likely the European and not the American continent that Cooper alludes to, and therefore the novel's space is the "narrow passage" of the North Sea and not the boundless Atlantic Ocean. If my interpretation is correct, then it is only partly true when Cohen observes that "Cooper took the codes of historical fiction, pioneered by Walter Scott, to map the boundaries and identity of the nation, and translated them to the supranational space of the open sea."[135] Supranationalism is indeed a theme in *The Pilot*. Gray incarnates it, although ambiguously, and maritime nationalism is constantly disrupted. But the insisting presence of the old nation's social order and conventions sedimented over centuries and the history of the new nation's birth problematizes Cohen's idea of the novel's supranational geography. The same is true for the geographical setting, which is purely coastal.

Scott's landbased framework of national history is noticeable in Cooper's *The Pilot*. What remains the most important is that with *The Pilot* Cooper initiated the first serious novelistic movement onto the ocean. This also marks a movement away from the understanding of a nation as exclusively *terra firma*. This movement was subsequently continued by Poe, Melville, and Conrad, as well as Victor Hugo, Jonas Lie, Alexander Kielland, Amalie Skram, Jules Verne, Jack London, William McFee, Hans Kirk, Aksel Sandemose, C. S. Forester, Nordahl Grieg, Malcolm Lowry, Jens Bjørneboe, William Golding, Patrick O'Brian and, more recently, by Amitav Ghosh and Carsten Jensen. Although the heyday of the maritime novel was between 1824 and the 1920s, the fascination with the sea as a political, historical, and supranational space and with the ship as heterotopia and microcosmos lives on among writers in the twentieth and twenty-first centuries.

⋯

To summarize, in the anthropocentric epoch the dominant component in the gods-humans-technology-nature constellation are humans. Non Plus Ultra *is replaced by* Plus Ultra, *and the ocean is no longer seen as a barrier only, but also as an enchanting passage luring glitteringly with promises of wonder. This is the centuries-long Age of Sail and Discovery during which superstition is replaced with exploration and sea monsters transform into fish. The contingency of ocean voyages is no longer associated exclusively with risk but also with chance.*

---

135   Cohen, "Traveling Genres," 483, 483.

3 Technocentrism

During the nineteenth century, the surface of the sea was transformed from glitter to grid because of modernity's disenchanting propensity to expand, monopolize, and systematize. What had been a relatively unsystematic and thus adventurous enterprise in the Age of Discovery was now converted into a conscious and deliberate maritime program of exploration for exploration's own sake. Discovery became an end in itself.[136] According to Carl Schmitt, the sea changed metaphorically in the course of the century of industrialism: "A fish until then, the leviathan was turning into a machine."[137] Expressing a similar thought, Gilles Deleuze and Félix Guattari observe that the sea was not only the archetype of all smooth spaces, but the first of these spaces to undergo a striation, which increasingly conquered it and transformed it into a grid.[138] Such conceptual and philosophical diagnoses testify to a shift from anthropocentrism to technocentrism. Arguably, the latter is still a dominant mode of "oceanic thinking" today, where ocean travel is associated with transport of merchandise (the most important, yet also partly invisible vein in the postindustrial, globalized world's circulation of goods) or with leisure activities (recreational boating, water sports, and cruises that offer a rationalized attempt to re-enchant an otherwise disenchanted sea and human life).

The technocentric world picture manifests itself in various guises. The obvious one is in works that deal explicitly with the *technological dimensions* of maritime life, but it can also reveal itself through *scientification* and treatments of the *progressive spirit*. In what follows, I read Jules Michelet's *La Mer* (1861) as an example of a work that expresses a scientific view of the sea, drawing on multiple scientific discoveries and discourses from Michelet's own time and the previous centuries. Then I discuss Jonas Lie's novel *Gaa Paa! Sjøfortælling* (1882; Go On! A Tale of the Sea) as an example of the period's obsession with progress. In this historical chapter, I only briefly introduce Conrad as an example of a writer occupied with technology. In the chapter on technology, I will return more thoroughly to Conrad's treatment of technology, a chapter that also comprises a reading of Jules Verne.

3.1   *Jules Michelet*

La Mer is part of a tetralogy on natural history, a subject that increasingly occupied Michelet, after the events of 1848 had left him personally and politically

---

136   J. H. Parry, *The Discovery of the Sea* (1974; London: Weidenfeld and Nicolson, 1975), viii.
137   Schmitt, *Land and Sea*, 54.
138   Deleuze and Guattari, *A Thousand Plateaus*, 387.

disillusioned. In 1856, Michelet published *L'Oiseau*, in 1857 *L'Insecte*, and following *La Mer* in 1861, the last volume, *La Montagne*, came out in 1868. Michelet's book on the sea is part science, part literature: an assemblage of the latest scientific knowledge, in fact a genuine system of knowledge, and articulated in a poetic language, a veritable *hydrography* (from Ancient Greek: ὕδωρ (*hydor*), "water," and γράφω (*graphō*), "to write"), whose tentativeness is dictated by the very subject of his book. In that sense, Rachel Carson also becomes the true heir to Michelet. His main objective in *The Sea* is to invert the negative connotations associated with the sea inaugurated by the classical (and neoclassical) tradition without disrespecting that tradition. His two allies are the sciences and language. Each answer their own question: What is the sea? How to write the sea?

The Homeric and biblical traditions had emphasized the barrenness and darkness of the sea, its sterile and nonhospitable nature, and this line of thinking had continued to dominate Western ideas of the sea. Michelet set out to introduce a more positive and scientifically truer image of the sea, but he did so without eliminating the sea's gloomy aspects. The initial pages of *La Mer* recount the classical tradition's maritime world picture and accept its longevity and endurance. Thirty years before the publication of *La Mer*, Michelet had made references to Homer's "sterile sea" in his journal entries during a visit to the French Atlantic coast.[139] To Michelet, it is a metahistorical fact that the ocean strikes "fear" (*crainte*) into anyone, whether that person is a Homeric sailor, a Horatian stoic, or a contemporary "gallant Dutch seaman":

> Water, for every terrestrial being, is the nonrespirable element, the element of suffocation. Fatal and eternal barrier, which irrevocably separates the two worlds. Let us not be surprised if the enormous mass of waters that we call the sea, unknown and dark in its deep thickness, has always seemed frightening to the human imagination.
>
> The Orientals see in it only the bleak chasm, the *night of the abyss*. In all the ancient languages, from India to Ireland, the name of the sea is synonymous or analogous to the *desert* and the *night*.[140]

It has been pointed out how Michelet's prose with its repetitions, tautologies, accumulations, and hyperboles intensifies the reader's feeling—shared with

---

139   Jules Michelet, *Journal*, ed. by Paul Viallaneix, vol. 1, entries for August 7, 1831 (Paris: Gallimard, 1959), 83.
140   Michelet, *La Mer*, 3.

ancient humankind—that nothing can challenge or change this radical separateness of the sea: "Repetition sometimes represents slight variation (*fatale / eternelle; inconnue / tenebreuse*), sometimes precision and thus gradation in intensity (*l'élément non respirable, l'élément de l'asphyxie*), but often it is the simple accumulation of synonyms: *gouffre* (depths) / *abîme* (abyss). Several modifiers add nothing but emphasis and exaggeration to the sense of their nouns: *enorme masse* (huge mass), *profonde epaisseur* (deep thickness)."[141] Michelet seems to confirm, even reinforce, the classical conception of the ocean as barren and dark (to the ancients, it was the sea that swallowed up the sun at sunset). But this is also a strategic maneuver that helps him emphasize the newness of the maritime world picture that he subsequently develops in *La Mer*.

Following the first page, Michelet continues for a while to throw connotations of fear and darkness after us: "a twilight where only one color persists, a sinister red"; "complete night"; "absolute obscurity"; "a world of darkness." In fact, "it was this which so impressed, so overawed the pioneers of our race. They supposed that life ceased whenever light failed, and that, with the exception of its upper strata, the whole unfathomable profundity, and the bottom—if the abyss has a bottom—was one black solitude."[142] But then, slowly, the tonality and vocabulary start to change, and Michelet introduces the word "life" for the first time. What triggers the shift is the sound of the ocean, a sound that one hears long before being in physical proximity to the water, at first perceived as a mass of monotony, but after a short while recognized as discrete sounds with distinct rhythms:

> Long before we see the sea, we hear and guess the dreaded person. First, it is a distant, dull, uniform noise. And little by little all the noises yield to it and are absorbed by it. We soon notice the solemn alternation, the invariable return of the same note, a strong bass, which increasingly rolls, rumbles. Less regular is the oscillation of the pendulum which measures the time. But here the pendulum does not have the monotony of mechanical things. We feel there, we think we feel there the vibrant intonation of life.[143]

---

141 Linda Orr, *Jules Michelet: Nature, History, and Language* (Ithaca and London: Cornell University Press, 1976), 155.
142 Michelet, *La Mer*, 4.
143 Michelet, *La Mer*, 8.

Sensing its vitality even from a considerable physical distance and from the level of its mere surface, Michelet then leads us into the fluid mass of saltwater and—like a bookish version of Jacques Cousteau, assisted by the works of natural scientists such as Buffon and Maury—shows us light, life, and diversity: "That a prodigious world of life, war, and love, of production of all kinds, stirs within it, we can very well guess and already we know a little of it."[144] The similarities between desert and sea—freedom, solitude, barrenness, stasis—begin to yield to their contrasts: the one a dehydrated territory, static, all surface and exposure; the other, it turns out if one plunges, is a fountain of life and vivacity in its hidden depths, "the symbol of potentiality"; in the one, time ends; in the other, it begins; if one is Omega, the other is Alpha.[145]

But Michelet is a monist, not a dualist. To him, the sea is both beginning and end, life and death. It is "the great Killer and the great Creator," as Pierre Loti observes in his foreword to a 1900 French edition of *La Mer*.[146] The question is how to represent such a world? With the emergence of that question, Michelet's task suddenly doubles. The "what" is supplemented with the "how": "to engineer not simply a shift in value, but the linguistic containment of opposites into one, and of the many into one: to find a single image or, better yet, a word that would embrace the Alpha and Omega and everything in between."[147] Beneath Michelet's new semantic contribution of dynamism, life, and light, a Homeric regime of stasis, death, and darkness remains active. But emphasis is now clearly on saltwater vitality, or at least on endowing vitality with its legitimate place in the marine world. At the same time, it is imperative to Michelet that the ocean retains its unified complexity, and his vision conveys a dynamic balance of opposite forces. His tentative solutions, which are at the same time his refusal to solve the oceanic complication by accepting the dominance of one force over the other, are "verbal proliferation" and "verbal compromise."[148] Linda Orr exemplifies the rhetorical strategy of *proliferation* with a quote from *La Mer* in which Michelet lists a series of phenomena whose distinct appearances counteract oceanic darkness: "Bronzed crabs, radiant sea anemones, snowy porcelain-shells, golden eels, undulating whorls, everything

---

144 Michelet, *La Mer*, 10.
145 Auden, *Enchafèd Flood*, 18–19. The Auden comparison between desert and sea has become quite popular. Orr, for example, quotes it in her reading of Michelet, and Harold Bloom cites it in his reading of Camus' use of the sea.
146 Pierre Loti, "Avant-propos," in Jules Michelet, *La Mer* (Paris: Calmann-Lévy, 1900), xi.
147 Orr, *Jules Michelet*, 156.
148 Orr, *Jules Michelet*, 156.

lives and moves."[149] The rhetorical strategy of *compromise* consists of replacing one of the two components in double-word constellations with a new component (and, sometimes, also transforming that component from adjective to noun) so as to soften the classical tradition's exclusively negative conception of the ocean: "dark sea" (*mer ténébreuse*), Homeric in tone, is transformed into "fertile shadows" (*fécondes ténèbres*); "night of the abyss" (*nuit de l'abîme*) later becomes "abyss of life" (*abîme de vie*), thus avoiding the negative associations with bottomless darkness.[150] Lastly, Orr observes how "the earlier *profonde épaisseur* (deep thickness), hesitates between antithesis and a kind of miraculous logic—*épaisseur transparente* (transparent thickness)—for such depth as the ocean's cannot but fade into opacity eventually."[151]

Despite the antithetical or even oxymoronic tensions of the constellations (e.g., "solidified flow"[152]), Michelet is still searching for one word capable of expressing his new vision of the sea as both Alpha and Omega, light and darkness, and life and death. That is, a word able to merge contrasts without annulling them. As we approach the more scientifically informed chapters, the vocabulary of the classical tradition and Michelet's strategies of proliferation and compromise are supplemented with words from eighteenth- and nineteenth-century science. This is also a shift in focus from the first book, "A Look at the Seas," with its anthropogenic accent on *cultural* history and connotations of subjective tone and approach, to the second book, "The Genesis of the Sea," whose chapter titles such as "Fecundity," "The sea of milk," "The atom," "Shells, mother of pearl, pearl," and "The whale" signal *natural* history. One example of Michelet's conceptual reorientation is the word *mucus*, whose meaning is explained to Michelet by a physiologist: "The best way to understand the mucus of seawater is that it is at the same time an end and a beginning."[153] Another linguistic example of the oscillation between life and death is the variety of expressions that include the root *gelée*, for example *eau gélatinisée, gélatineuse, la gélatine* (cognates of jelly, gelatin). In French, *gelée* conveys positive as well as negative nuances of its etymology (from *gelare*): to freeze and to congeal.[154]

Leibniz's theory of monads serves as a sort of backstory to Michelet's genesis narrative. Leibniz conceived of monads as the smallest building blocks of

---

149 Michelet, *La Mer*, 107.
150 Michelet, *La Mer*, 89, 107, 3, 107.
151 Orr, *Jules Michelet*, 157.
152 Michelet, *La Mer*, 113.
153 Michelet, *La Mer*, 114.
154 Orr, *Jules Michelet*, 157.

the universe, similar to atoms, each of them being a microcosmos, while simultaneously being in complete convergence with the macrocosmic universe. In *La Mer*, a drop of seawater is such a monad:

> Let us witness the divine work. Let us take a drop of seawater. In it, we shall see the primitive creation recommence. God does not operate in such a way today, and in another way tomorrow. My drop of water, I do not doubt it, will through its transformations tell me about the universe. Let us wait and watch.
>
> Who can foresee, guess, the history of this drop of water? Plant-animal, animal-plant, which shall first emerge from it?
>
> This drop, will it be the infusoria, the primitive monad which, agitating and vibrating, soon becomes vibrion? which, rising from rank to rank, polyp, coral or pearl, will perhaps reach the dignity of an insect in ten thousand years?
>
> This drop, will there issue from it that vegetable thread, the light silky down that we would not take for a being, and which already is no less than the first-born hair of a young goddess, sensitive hair, amorous, rightly called: *hair of Venus?*
>
> This is not fable, it is natural history. This hair of two natures (vegetable and animal) where the drop of water thickens, it is indeed the eldest of life.[155]

"This is not fable, it is natural history." Again, Michelet touches on the cultural conceptions of the ocean, the myths and narratives—also narratives of creation—in Western and non-Western cultures. He did so in the first book of *La Mer*. Now, we no longer *look* and *conceive*; instead, we *explore* and *investigate* scientifically. The hair of Venus does not refer to that of the mythological Roman goddess, but to a natural phenomenon discovered scientifically. The same is true of monads. They may refer to Leibniz' monadology, but they are also the scientific name of specific infusoria (tiny aquatic creatures).

These concepts, Venus's hair and monad, are perfect examples of the productive interchange between myth and science, between poetic language and scientific language. There remains one problem, though. Venus's hair does not belong to the domain of algae and animalcules, which are the topic of Michelet's chapter. Instead, it refers to geological or horticultural phenomena. Michelet may be right in asserting that he is not in the business of writing

---

155 Michelet, *La Mer*, 116–17.

fables, but his expertise in the field of natural history can be questioned, at least on the level of detail. Linda Orr speculates that "the sound of signifiers" may have "held priority over semantics," and that Michelet's need to reassure the reader of the scientific veracity of the argument is a sign of his "nervousness; he does think he has gone too far in pure linguistic gymnastics."[156]

This is a recurring challenge. How to represent the ocean? Jens Munk, partly as an outcome of the circumstances of exploration and navigation, invented a modern "I" of action and problem-solving, and chose an empirical vocabulary, opting for a structure of causality and chronology. Cooper, writing in the aftermath of the American War of Independence, when the currency of nationalist thinking dominated the agenda, converted many of the negative connotations associated with the ocean, ship, and sailor of neoclassicism into positive features. The concepts of the sublime and practical rationality served his purpose, as did the forms of romance and historical realism.

To Michelet, a historian by training, the representation of the ocean comes down to questions of language, rhetoric, and form. If there was one domain during the nineteenth century that provided the perfect conditions for fruitful transactions between fable and natural history, it was the ocean. The nineteenth century marks the dual discovery—horizontal and vertical—of the ocean, as explorers and scientists (especially zoologists and marine biologists) voyaged around the globe transforming blank spaces on maps into charted and striated territories and ventured back and forth between submarine spaces and the laboratory. As Helen Rozwadowski observes,

> the years from 1840 to 1880 witnessed a dramatic increase in awareness of the open ocean as a workplace, a leisure area, a stage for adventure, and a natural environment. The Anglo-American world enjoyed a deepening acquaintance with the seashore, with the maritime culture of the high seas, and also with the ocean's depths. Because the deep sea could only be known indirectly, through fishing, whaling, or attempts to dip sampling devices beneath the waves, it is hardly surprising that the same decades also saw the emergence of scientific interest in the depths.[157]

The scientific investigation of the ocean and its depths necessitated investments in technological development because access to submarine spaces

---

156 Orr, *Jules Michelet*, 160.
157 Helen Rozwadowski, *Fathoming the Ocean: The Discovery and Exploration of the Deep Sea* (2005; Cambridge, MA: Harvard University Press, 2008), 4.

required complex technologies. Michelet pays little attention to technology, although chapters on beacons, the harpoon, the law of storms and of the oceans, and man's war upon the races of the sea testify to his acknowledgement of the importance of different technologies in human efforts to know and dominate the sea. A few years later, with Verne's *Vingt mille lieues sous les mers*, modern technology was elevated to the role of heroic protagonist.

Michelet's fascination with and knowledge of maritime scientific discoveries were accompanied by an equally important unfamiliarity with science and scientific language. This hesitation between discursive codes, between fable and science, is precisely what makes *La Mer* such an interesting document of the mid-nineteenth century. In many ways, ocean scientists were cast in the same role as the first humans on the verge of inventing language. They, too, looked at strange and unimaginable creatures and phenomena for the first time, and the scientific tradition of choosing a Latinate term for the discoveries often made way for an even older tradition of poetic evocation:

> the scientist, reverting back to the instincts of his primitive forefathers, simply said what the strange creatures looked like. The scientists, like the first poets, could speak only in metaphors: *mer de lait, étoile de mer, éléphant de mer, orient de la perle, écumeur de mer, fleuves de la mer, voies lactées, ceinture de Venus, piqueur de pierres*. Coming upon the new vocabulary of the sea was like discovering a rare language of ready-made poetry. And the excitement of names generates, in turn, an entirely different text.[158]

Orr's last comment implies an important observation on form. Michelet's new maritime world picture encourages him to employ verbal proliferations and compromises, to create antithetical and even oxymoronic constellations, and to revel in metaphors, poetic evocations, and Vico's legendary language. The boundless living energy inherent in Michelet's new ocean and in the rhetorical strategies employed to present this ocean causes the overall form of the book to splinter into fragments of great intensity. The ruptured linearity is underlined by blank spaces inserted by Michelet that separate the fragments; this compositional tactic mirrors a profound and internal splintering energy. The result: "Michelet's aesthetic becomes more violent. Either he will collapse two opposing words together or he will let the verbal possibilities explode. A passage is composed of zigzags, leaps, and reversals whose only coherence is the

---

158   Orr, *Jules Michelet*, 161.

flexible code of language. Such an endeavor (or discovery) brings Michelet closer to Rimbaud, where he belongs."[159]

Rimbaud regarded the poet as an artist who should find the right language for both form and the formless and as someone capable of accepting the formless as an integral part of the world. In *La Mer*, Michelet regards his topic as a cradle of primitive, fluid-solidified, and semi-(dis)organized life; that is, the sea is the epitome of formlessness. The poetological result is a language with its internal handbrake loosened and a form whose splintering and discontinuity are a consequence of both the energetic language and of the author's attempt to halt by external force—the insertion of white spaces—the uncontrolled proliferations of that language.

La Mer proves to be somewhat unbridled, experimental, and tentative on the level of language and rhetoric, a feature that anchors the book in both Romanticism and Modernism as is also the case with *Moby-Dick* and *Les Travailleurs de la mer*. There is also a genuine systematism governing Michelet's overall scientific vision. In a reading of some of the scientific chapters in the first three books, Michel Serres convincingly shows us Michelet's remarkable ability to synthesize an entire encyclopedia of the sciences, each represented by its leading scientists and concretized in the latest scientific discoveries, into a coherent maritime world picture.[160]

There are five scientific regimes interacting in *La Mer*: geometry, mechanics, physics, chemistry, and biology; physics is divided into three sub-disciplines: barology, electrology, and thermodynamics. These different dimensions all share and contribute to the fundamental structure of reservoir and circulation. To Michelet, the sea is a reservoir of different components (a mixture) that circulates these components in a variety of ways (a movement). The philosophical model emerging from Michelet's book and its systematic use of the five scientific regimes is a theory of *hylozoism*, the belief in the vitality of matter. Michelet's hylozoism combines Abraham Gottlob Werner's *neptunism* (a theory of the sea as primordial soup in both its geological and prebiotic sense) with Félix Archimède Pouchet's *heterogenesis* (a theory of life as a spontaneous generation from nonliving materials). An important outcome of this combination and of the hylozoist model is that, to Michelet, *la mer* is also *la mère*. The

---

159 Orr, *Jules Michelet*, 161.
160 Michel Serres, "Michelet, la soupe," *Revue d'Histoire littéraire de la France* 74, no. 5 (1974): 787–802. Interestingly, Serres suggests that in the first book of *La Mer*, "A look at the seas," a complete theory of observation hides beneath the superficial layers of pathos and anecdote, which stylistically dominate this more subjective and cultural-historical book. However, Serres does not pursue his claim.

sea is the source giving birth and care, the liquid element that generates an immense variety of beings. This birth-death chain is cyclical, not linear, incessantly regenerating the feminine, *la mère*: "the earth is at work, a work of metamorphosis, of transformation, of production, of generation."[161]

To get a sense of Michelet's scientific systematism, it will suffice to summarize Serres' most important insights. Geometry provides Michelet with the tools to outline the sea's basic circles (e.g., the equatorial line) and points on these circles (e.g., near the Antilles and Java, which are both characterized by heat and thus condensation and evaporation). Then, in order for the soup to blend, movement is necessary. Here, the newest developments in the law of mechanics assist Michelet: "Beneath the anecdote and beneath the pathos the text mobilizes with great precision the results of rational mechanics well known at the time."[162] Structurally, there is a horizontal movement guaranteed by currents and tides, which are themselves produced by astronomical forces, and a vertical movement assured by the swells or roll, the tempests, labelled "spasms" by Michelet, especially by the cyclones, the major hurricanes with a circular shape. Laplace's celestial mechanics is combined with Chazallon's law on tides, which draws on Euler's law of vibrant strings defining sinusoidal movements. The geometrical circles are thus supplemented with mechanical circles that form circles of circles at the surface level, whereas the vertical movements ensure the churning and mixing of the seawater and its components. The descriptions of these movements, "the law of tempests," are informed by Maury's work, and they also comprise circular movements, cyclones forming circles of circles, dextrorotatory directions in the southern hemisphere and levorotatory directions in the northern hemisphere.

Moving on from these naturalist sciences that describe the circulation and movements, Serres now discusses the sciences dealing with the production of these movements: barology, electrology, and thermodynamics, which all belong to physics. Barology deals with pressure, and here the interest is on low and high pressures along the equatorial line creating circular winds, perhaps first spotted by Edmund Halley as trade winds. Barology helps Michelet to understand the world as a static and dynamic machine. Electrology deals with electric phenomena that also produce movements, and the image of the world as a static and dynamic machine is now supplemented with an image of the world as an electric machine. The previously mentioned geometrical points, the Antilles and Java, are also the two poles of circulation caused by pressure and electricity. This was, however, not new knowledge. In terms of circulation,

---

161 Serres, "Michelet, la soupe," 788.
162 Serres, "Michelet, la soupe," 790.

thermodynamics provided Michelet with the latest scientific development, and he remains faithful to its vocabulary and insights of for example Carnot and his theorem: "The world that was just before a static machine and an electric machine now becomes a steam machine. The sea functions as a steam machine, it is she that assures the churning of the soup."[163]

As for chemistry, it studies the concentration of the soup, especially of mineral salts. Again, it locates specific points of concentration with Java and the Antilles being the centers of the world. Acting as both attractors and repellers, they create circulation that ensures the dissemination of minerals in the seawater. They are both points of condensation and cycles of displacement. Now, the world is also a chemical machine. Having reached the biological dimension of Michelet's system, Serres emphasizes the recurring structure of circles and points and draws the logical conclusion that in the biological regime, the points of condensation and circulation assume the function of hearts securing the pulsating movement. But Carnot's theorem already had a pulsating mechanism, so why the need for one more? Because the soup is no longer merely a mixture of mineral salts, but also something like the blood of the organism that is the entire earth. The centers are thus hearts that guarantee the vascular circulation of blood, analogically speaking. By further analogy, the centers also function as breasts circulating nourishing milk. The soup is both blood and milk, and the sea in fact comprises a complex system of milky ways. The sea and its movements are not pure chaos; they are made up of channels of circulation determined by laws.

As we saw earlier, Michelet used the word "regularity" about the sea. The final regularity governing the rhythms of movement is the lunar rhythm, which secures the menstrual circulation:

> The world is a static machine, it is a machine of pressure, an electric, chemical, and steam machine; the world is an organism—this without contradiction. The basic philosophy is hylozoism. What is hylozoism if not a mechanism coupled with a vitalism in a synthesized manner and without gap? There are mechanical models of the world, which can pass for elementary models of time, *and* the organicist models. To Michelet, the succession of regions of the encyclopedia leads to the synthesis between mechanism and vitalism. Why should the sciences contradict each other?[164]

---

163 Serres, "Michelet, la soupe," 792.
164 Serres, "Michelet, la soupe," 793.

Serres' reading of Michelet's monism amounts to this: There are centers that function as poles for the circulation of movements in general. More specifically, the poles are for the circulation of liquids through high and low pressures. They are also the positive and negative poles for the circulation of electrical flux. Furthermore, they are either cold or warm sources for the Carnot cycle, which in turn works on any liquids. They are concentrations for the circulation of saline mixtures too. Finally, the poles are hearts for the circulation of blood and breasts for the circulation of milk or the menstrual circulation.

The basic *modus operandi* that applies to all five sciences is that there are reservoirs for the circulation of the soup. The soup is the sum total of the elements analyzed by the scientific sections of the encyclopedia: milk, blood, minerals, electric flux, pressure, etc.: "The basic liquid, given by the primordial soup of neptunism or by Pouchet's heterogenesis, is quite simply the synthesis, the mixture ensured by the horizontal and vertical movements, the synthesis and the mixture of liquids already examined by the science of different temporalities, according to the regions of the encyclopedia."[165] Again, the structure that remains stable across the five sciences mobilized by Michelet consists of reservoir and circulation (point and movement), a set of elements present at a given location and operations distributing these elements within a given space.

Serres' contribution to Michelet studies is the demonstration of scientific systematism, even precision, in *La Mer*. Why is this important? In a Michelet context as well as the broader context of this book, Serres' argument serves as a reliable testimony that allows us to reconsider Michelet's reputation and position (Serres had a prior career as a naval officer as well as a *doctorat* in mathematics; his thesis was on Leibniz and mathematic models). First, the accuracy of Michelet's scientific vision elevates him beyond the rambling idealism and solipsism of Romanticism and places him in the center of the serious and rigorous debates on the ground-breaking science of his lifetime; it even forwards him into present-day discussions on potential fruitful interfaces between the natural sciences and the human sciences. Second, the combination of scientific accuracy with a loose and searching language, a language of fable and poetry, of pathos and anecdote, endows Michelet with a poetological and rhetorical profile that is almost protomodernistic. In *La Mer*, form emerges from the topic; matter dictates the language. To Michelet, no inherited forms would do, just as no dictionary and rule book on language were of much use to him. If Serres succeeds in demonstrating a rigorous application of scientific theories and a systematically worked-through philosophical vision in *La Mer*—the

---

165   Serres, "Michelet, la soupe," 794.

ocean as a *model of regularity*—Michelet's book is still a work marked by ambivalences and tensions because of the representational challenges posed by the ocean—here, the ocean as a *model of formlessness*—in relation to language, rhetoric, and form. Consequently, we can re-establish Michelet as a serious, uncompromising, and innovative poet of the sea who deserves to be mentioned along with Melville, Hugo, Verne, and Conrad.

"Who will be able to interpret them? and what word could translate them?" The representational challenge has to do not only with words and language, but also with perspective and focalization, when Michelet struggles to convey the submarine world of the Anthozoa (e.g., sea anemones and corals) in "Flower of blood" (*Fleur de sang*). It is a universe in which a certain structure of distinctions exists, for example between the animal, the vegetal, and the mineral, between subdivisions within each of the three domains, between colors, between the solid and the soft, and between the eternal and the ephemeral: "Some have the solidity, the quasi-eternity of the tree. The others are flourishing, then wither, like the flower." But it is also a world of constant change, of shifting colors, and of seeming boundary transgressions. In fact, etymologically *anthozoa* exemplifies the latter in that the word comprises flower (*anthos*) and animals (*zōia*): "The soft and gelatinous plants, with rounded organs that seem neither stems nor leaves, affecting the fat, the softness of the animal curves, seem to want us to be mistaken, and to believe them to be animals. Real animals seem to contrive to be plants and look like plants. They imitate everything of the other reign."[166]

While the paragraphs in "Flower of blood" carry underlying structures, these are often drowned out by a language whose words oscillates between the weird-alien and the exotic-beautiful (*nacres, émaux, arbustes, gorgones, isis*) because of their referential obligation and by a syntax whose progression is governed more by prosody than semantics: "It charms, it confuses; it is a vertigo and like a dream. The fairy with the slippery mirages, water, adds to these colors a prism of fleeting tinctures, a marvelous mobility, a capricious inconstancy, a hesitation, a doubt" (*Cela charme, cela trouble; c'est un vertige et comme un songe. La fée aux mirages glissants, l'eau, ajoute à ces couleurs un prisme de teintes fuyantes, une mobilité merveilleuse, une inconstance capricieuse, une hésitation, un doute*).[167] It is as if Michelet's words fragment the flow of the syntax because of their individual alien beauty.

---

166   Michelet, *La Mer*, 143, 140, 139–40.
167   Michelet, *La Mer*, 141.

Each word thus carries a mimetic ambition to describe the marvelousness of the submarine phenomena. But if each of Michelet's words make us pause and enjoy its singular protean variability—the alcyonarian polyp (*alcyon*) is a perfect example, since it comprises mutually exclusive associations such as a protean protozoan, a class of polyps, and a mythological bird that rules over calm[168]—then his sentences reactivate a different kind of flow, in which the reader gets absorbed in the playfulness of language. The syntactical flow is not dictated by a narrative-structural mimesis but a prosodic mimesis. Phonetics is for example more important than proper class distinctions for the syntactical flow. The prosodic mimesis aims to bring the submarine world alive to the reader through rhythms and alliterations that simulate its smooth fluctuations, peaceful attachments, and slow transformations:

> The polyp colony was not actually progressing, but going through every kind of contortion while remaining in place—swelling, disappearing; rocking back and forth or trembling; twisting or stiffening. Even static, the polyps metamorphose as passing lights and colors play on parts of their bodies. Michelet's polyps, in contrast with his spiders, do not reflect a relatively ordered linear evolution, but as incarnations of a proteus present a problem for language: how to represent infinite, spontaneous change in a temporal medium.[169]

Despite being a world of constant metamorphosis, a soup of circulations, nothing much actually happens in Michelet's ocean. The absence of narrative mimesis (perhaps due to a general disinterest in a plot dictated by what-happens-next) mirrors itself in a low frequency of verbs. Instead, *La Mer* is characterized by a nominal and adjectival prose style, where adjectives, nouns, and noun phrases dominate. Michelet the historian ended up doing what literary authors also increasingly felt compelled to do: showing, not telling. The descriptive method employed in these scientific chapters of marine close reading also resulted in a change of pace, slowing down the time span narrated per page—a general development in the history of the novel since the eighteenth century[170]—as Michelet, our undersea tour guide, pans his camera-eyes horizontally and vertically and zooms in on details and zooms out to present the bigger world picture.

---

168 Orr, *Jules Michelet*, 164.
169 Orr, *Jules Michelet*, 171.
170 Ted Underwood, *Distant Horizons: Digital Evidence and Literary Change* (Chicago and London: The University of Chicago Press, 2019), 28.

3.2 Jonas Lie

In 1874, fifty years after Cooper published *The Pilot*, Jonas Lie published *The Pilot and His Wife*, the first maritime novel in the literatures of Scandinavia. In 1880, Lie followed up on his breakthrough publication with *Rutland*, and two years later a third maritime novel entitled *Gaa Paa!* came out. Together with Henrik Ibsen (1828–1906), Bjørnstjerne Bjørnson (1832–1910), and Alexander Kielland (1849–1906), Jonas Lie (1833–1908) is considered one of the "Four Greats," the most influential Norwegian writers of the late nineteenth century. Lie's writings on sea matters were part of a larger contemporary trend in the North comprising authors such as Kielland, Amalie Skram, and Holger Drachmann, all of whom took a keen interest in maritime life. They inspired later Scandinavian writers such as Aksel Sandemose, Jens Bjørneboe, and Carsten Jensen.

In several of Lie's novels, especially the earlier ones, life on board the ship and life at home are interdependent. In that sense, Lie taps into two genres usually considered mutually exclusive: the domestic novel in the tradition of Richardson, Burney, and Austen, and the maritime novel in the tradition of Cooper, Dana, and Melville. This observation allows us to reconsider Lie's position in the Norwegian literary canon and the relationship between the Nordic maritime novel and the international tradition of the genre. Lie's originality lies in his special mixture of the maritime and the domestic—an *oceanization of the domestic* and a *domestication of the maritime*—and in the specific structure of compromise that he creates between the two spheres. This indicates that Lie's maritime novels (and perhaps even Nordic maritime literature in general) have a unique position among internationally renowned predecessors and descendants such as Herman Melville and Joseph Conrad.

Where Melville and Conrad operate with sharp divisions between land and sea, home and ship, and man and woman, the domestic and the female are often granted central roles in Lie's maritime worlds. Therefore, sailor life becomes less errant and less brutal. Furthermore, the structure of compromise means that the traditional reading of Lie as the writer of the home can be nuanced. The domestic reading strategy has led to an inevitable comparison between Jonas Lie and Henrik Ibsen and a resulting repudiation of Lie, who is not considered as modern as Ibsen in matters domestic. Lie's opening of the traditionally male world of the maritime to female characters and qualities and his infusion of maritime breezes into the potentially claustrophobic sphere of the household makes him genuinely modern. In Lie, progress to the Norwegian nation is secured by combining the maritime with a nationalist inclination. Importantly, the traditional maritime sphere is tamed by the female and the domestic and manifested in three forms: pilot (Salve Kristiansen in *The Pilot and His Wife*), routinized coastal merchant ship (Rutland in *Rutland*), and herring king (Rejer Jansen Juhl in *Gaa Paa!*). Lie's talent and his unique artistic profile as the writer of the Norwegian waters was recognized by Ibsen. In a letter dated June 22, 1882, which Ibsen sent to Lie from Rome, he commends his colleague for his accomplishments in *Gaa Paa!*:

> It is a new testament to the fact that in the genre of the sea tale, not a single poet exists in our time who might consider challenging you. The descriptions of the herring fishing are complete masterpieces in every respect; they occupy all senses; I smelled herring when I read them, I saw herring scale glitter in front of my eyes wherever I turned, I thought I stepped into slippery herring guts wherever I walked and stood. This is how it should be done![171]

Ibsen's characterization can serve as a starting point for discussing Lie's position and reception.

Despite Ibsen's praise, it is problematic that Lie's position as a maritime writer is understated in relation to his more domestic profile. *The Pilot and His Wife* is usually referred to as the first marriage novel in Norwegian literature, yet not so often as the first maritime novel in Nordic literature (see note 57). Rather than an expression of reactionary conservatism, Lie's more positive view of the domestic sphere and marriage is a result of him opening the doors and windows of the family household for fresh breezes from the sea and vital impulses from the wider world to enter the home space. Through his introduction of the openness of the maritime in the domestic sphere, he is not a less modern writer than Ibsen. Ibsen's work is set in several claustrophobic houses, where domestic problems are depicted in psychologically subtle ways. Lie may not have depicted these problems with as much sophistication as Ibsen, but he invented a solution—the grafting of the domestic with the mobility and dynamism of the maritime world—that not only salvages the domestic sphere, but which can be considered a modern salvaging.

In his lectures on aesthetics, G. W. F. Hegel characterized the novel as "the modern *bourgeois* epic," as we have already seen. Hegel's choice of concepts reminds us of the novel's roots in the ancient epic tradition of Homer and reveals that Hegel found the novel's historical development to be more closely associated with the nostalgic Ulysses, who longs for home and returns to Ithaka and Penelope, than with the adventurous Ulysses, who continues to

---

171 Henrik Ibsen, *Brev fra perioden 1880–89, Henrik Ibsens skrifter*, Universitetet i Oslo, accessed April 19, 2022, http://www.edd.uio.no/cocoon/ibsenarkiv01_01/BREV_1880-188 9ht%7CB18820622JLi.xhtml.

roam the Mediterranean Sea alone or with the crew. With "bourgeois," Hegel's theory of the novel is defined by the solidity and safety of the home, family life, and the earth; consequently, it excludes the ship, the vagrant sailor, and the ocean, and by extension, the hazards and the fluidity implied by maritime life. Canonized authors such as Melville and Conrad, whose maritime novels and tales are concentrated around the strictly male life on board the ship, have no place in Hegel's history of the novel.

The male universes in Melville's and Conrad's sea novels are traditionally associated with maritime literature. Cooper was also aware of the maritime novel's male profile. In his 1849 preface to *The Pilot*, he admitted with no sign of regret that his novel might not please the preferences of women readers, because his purpose was not to depict emotions but life at sea: "The Pilot could scarcely be a favorite with females. The story has little interest for them, nor was it much heeded by the author of the book, in the progress of his labors. His aim was to illustrate vessels and the ocean, rather than to draw any pictures of sentiment and love."[172] It is possible that Cooper downplayed the female and love as important components of *The Pilot*, but in fact women and love do play a significant role in *The Pilot* and in most of Cooper's subsequent sea novels. In that sense, Cooper still had one leg in the romance tradition from Richardson, Burney, and Austen in which the feminine, family life, and emotions were mandatory elements. With Melville and Conrad, the nautical novel becomes full-blown and one-dimensionally male. In a remarkable and quite symptomatic letter to his friend and mentor, Edward Garnett dated November 5, 1912, Conrad compares the hetero romance "Freya of the Seven Isles" (1912) with the same-sex romance "The Secret Sharer" (1910): "I daresay Freya is pretty rotten. On the other hand The Secret Sharer, between you and me, is *it*. Eh? No damned tricks with girls there. Eh?"[173] As Cesare Casarino correctly points out: "the direct personification of the object of his *ressentiment* in a woman's name reveals that such an object is not constituted merely by an unsuccessful piece of writing but rather by the purported cause of such a failure of writing, namely, the presence and question of woman itself."[174]

If "The Secret Sharer" is clinically cleansed of "damned tricks with girls," women feature in another of Conrad's maritime stories, the short novel *Typhoon*. However, their presence only emphasizes the unbridgeable gap

---

172 Cooper, "Preface. [1849]," *The Pilot*, 7.
173 Joseph Conrad, *The Collected Letters of Joseph Conrad*, vol. 5, eds. Frederick Karl and Laurence Davies (Cambridge: Cambridge University Press, 1996), 128.
174 Casarino, *Modernity at Sea*, 218–19.

between the male world on board the ship and the female world at home. Despite Captain MacWhirr's praiseworthy attempts to bridge the two worlds with his detailed and regular letters (twelve a year), he never succeeds in initiating Mrs. MacWhirr in life on board the *Nan-Shan* or in the varied transactions in harbors around the world. One reason could be the extreme lack of imagination in the letters, characterized by a monotonous enumeration of events without any interpretation or perspective, not even in the letter that describes MacWhirr's dramatic encounter with the typhoon: "Lifting her hands, she glanced wearily here and there into the many pages. It was not her fault they were so prosy, so completely uninteresting—from 'My darling wife' at the beginning, to 'Your loving husband' at the end. She couldn't be really expected to understand all these ship affairs." Immediately after having skimmed the letter, which in content (but not in style) mirrors the novel's most dramatic chapter—the miraculous survival after the ship's encounter with a ferocious typhoon—Mrs. MacWhirr takes her daughter shopping since, as she observes, "There is a sale at Linom's." Even if MacWhirr had possessed greater skills in suggestive writing, it would probably not have led to greater insight or interest from his wife. This is not only because "[t]he only secret of her life was her abject terror of the time when her husband would come home to stay for good," but also and especially because there exists, according to Conrad, a fundamental and unbridgeable experiential gap between the domestic (female) and the maritime (male) spheres. As Mrs. Rout, the chief engineer's wife, exclaims while she reads her husband's letter about the encounter with the typhoon: "How provoking! He doesn't say what it is. Says I couldn't understand how much there was in it."[175]

However, in "Falk: A Reminiscence" (1901/1903), one of Conrad's lesser-known tales, the epitome of a domesticated ship is featured, the German *Diana*. It has "suggestions of a rustic and homely nature," and its cabin ports "might have been the windows of a cottage in the country." But the *Diana* is then sharply contrasted with the cannibal sailor Christian Falk. Falk's marriage to the nameless niece of *Diana*'s owner could, on the face of it, be read as a harmonious union between the domestic and the maritime, between the bourgeois housewife and the transgressive traveler, but it only accentuates the dichotomy between the two spheres because of the niece's anti-bourgeois nature: on the one side are Hermann, the owner of *Diana* who is not only "[n]o hero at all," but also likened to "a small shopkeeper" and "a well-to-do farmer," his wife, their four children, and *Diana*; on the other are Falk, Hermann's

---

175 Joseph Conrad, *Typhoon*, 1902, in *Typhoon and Other Stories*, 1903, in *Collected Edition of the Works of Joseph Conrad* (1923; London: J. M. Dent & Sons Ltd., 1950), 93, 95, 14, 96.

niece, and their mutual love of the five senses: "It seemed to me they had come together as if attracted, drawn and guided to each other by a mysterious influence. They were a complete couple. In her gray frock, palpitating with life, generous of form, Olympian and simple, she was indeed the siren to fascinate that dark navigator, this ruthless lover of the five senses."[176] With his experience of cannibalism, Falk mirrors Marlow's feeling of having stepped over an invisible threshold—an experience and knowledge beyond the bourgeois way of life—upon his return to "the sepulchral city" from the Congo River in *Heart of Darkness* (1899).[177] The niece in "Falk," then, is the opposite of Kurtz's "Intended," whom Marlow feels must be left ignorant of the Congo cruelties perpetrated by Kurtz. The niece represents a female character of great significance in Conrad's work, but the point is nevertheless that Conrad upholds an impermeable border between the bourgeois way of life and a more authentic, nonverbal, and sensuous way of life connected with the maritime enterprise, exemplified among others by Falk and Hermann's niece.

In Melville's *White-Jacket* (1850), the narrator underscores the claustrophobic and purely masculine "world in a Man-of-War" (the novel's subtitle) by never abandoning the ship. Only once during the four hundred pages does the narratorial gaze glide across land to view the magnetic city of Rio de Janeiro, but ultimately opts to retreat to the ship anchored in the bay of Rio after a shrewd double movement of evocation and disregard: "But though Rio is one of the most magnificent bays in the world; [...] and though much might be said of the Sugar Loaf and Signal Hill heights; and the little islet of Lucia; [...] ay, though much might be said of all this, yet must I forbear, if I may, and adhere to my one proper object, *the world in a man-of-war*."[178] Recently, there have been critical attempts to read gender topics and the negotiation of feminine attributes into Melville and Conrad. However, these readings usually concern either homoeroticism[179]—that is, sex with no females involved—or

---

176 Joseph Conrad, "Falk: A Reminiscence," 1901/1903, *The Nigger of the "Narcissus" and Typhoon and Other Stories, Collected Edition of the Works of Joseph Conrad* (1923; London: J. M. Dent & Sons Ltd, 1950), 148, 147–48, 239.

177 Joseph Conrad, *Heart of Darkness*, 1899/1902, *Youth, Heart of Darkness and The End of the Tether, Collected Edition of the Works of Joseph Conrad* (1923; London: J. M. Dent & Sons Ltd, 1960), 152.

178 Herman Melville, *White-Jacket: or, The World in a Man-of-War*, 1850, *The Writings of Herman Melville*, vol. 5, eds. Harrison Hayford, Hershel Parker & G. Thomas Tanselle (1970; Evanston and Chicago: Northwestern University Press and The Newberry Library, 1988), 159–60.

179 Eve Kosofsky Sedgwick, *Epistemology of the Closet* (Los Angeles: University of California Press, 1990).

the symbolical femininity associated with the ship[180] or the sailor (Melville's Billy Budd is exemplary)—that is, so-called feminine qualities but still no females involved. As to Billy, he is explicitly characterized by feminine traits and qualities: "He was young; and despite his all but fully developed frame, in aspect looked even younger than he really was, owing to a lingering adolescent expression in the as yet smooth face all but feminine in purity of natural complexion but where, thanks to his seagoing, the lily was quite suppressed and the rose had some ado visibly to flush through the tan."[181] The point is, though, that even if Billy can be said to introduce femininity on board Melville's ship, it is precisely this femininity that leads to his hanging. The collision between Claggart, the Satan figure of irony and raw masculinity, and Billy, the prelapsarian androgenous angelic figure of youthful innocence and pristine virtue seem tragically unavoidable. To the older and more conservative Melville, no longer as utopian and idealistic as in *Typee: A Peep at Polynesian Life* (1846) and *Omoo: A Narrative of the South Seas* (1847), Billy must be eradicated from the maritime sphere to ward off mutiny, upheaval, and chaos.[182]

In Melville's works there is no room for the female and the feminine on board the ships: "Well, the heart here, sometimes the feminine in man, is as that piteous woman, and hard though it be, she must here be ruled out," observes Captain Vere.[183] As in *White-Jacket*, the insularity of the ship in *Billy Budd* is emphasized through the self-imposed limitations of the narratorial gaze, here symbolically by Vere. The discussion of possible outcomes of Billy's trial among members of the jury takes place in Vere's cabin. Vere takes position in front of the window, preventing the jury members (and the readers) from viewing the ocean, the element that, in the works by Melville and other maritime authors, tends to dissolve all cultural categories and frameworks.[184]

---

180   Lilian Nayder, "Sailing Ships and Steamers, Angels and Whores: History and Gender in Conrad's Maritime Fiction" in *Iron Men, Wooden Women: Gender and Seafaring in the Atlantic World, 1700–1920*, eds. Creighton, Margaret S. and Lisa Norling (Baltimore, MD: The Johns Hopkins University Press, 1996): 189–203.
181   Melville, *Billy Budd*, 8.
182   Andrew Delbanco, *Melville: His World and Work* (New York: Alfred A. Knopf, 2005), 302–03, 312.
183   Melville, *Billy Budd*, 55.
184   Delbanco, *Melville*, 310. For further reading on the sea's dissolving effect on cultural categories, see the letter from Carl Schmitt to Ernst Jünger on September 24, 1941, in which Schmitt writes: "From the sea, our classes and classifications cease." Ernst Jünger and Carl Schmitt, *Ernst Jünger—Carl Schmitt. Briefe 1930–1983* (Stuttgart: Klett-Cotta, 1999), 131. See also Schmitt, *Land and Sea*; and Thomas O. Beebee, "Carl Schmitt's Myth of Benito Cereno," *seminar* 42, no. 2 (2006): 114–34.

In addition to physically blocking the view to the ocean, Captain Vere verbally stages the ship as a closed-off space:

> But do these buttons that we wear attest that our allegiance is to Nature? No, to the King. Though the ocean, which is inviolate Nature primeval, though this be the element where we move and have our being as sailors, yet as the King's officers lies our duty in a sphere correspondingly natural? So little is that true, that in receiving our commissions we in the most important regards ceased to be natural free agents. When war is declared, are we the commissioned fighters previously consulted? We fight at command. If our judgments approve the war, that is but coincidence. So in other particulars. So now. For suppose condemnation to follow these present proceedings. Would it be so much we ourselves that would condemn as it would be martial law operating through us? For that law, and the rigor of it, we are not responsible. Our vowed responsibility is in this: That however pitilessly that law may operate, we nevertheless adhere to it and administer it.[185]

Billy Budd is indeed an "inside narrative," a novella that underlines the heterotopic character of the ship by setting it apart from not only the land and the bourgeois home (earthly culture), but also from the sea (nature).

Traditionally, maritime fiction operates with sharp distinctions between the male, associated with the risky and adventurous life of the sea and the ship, and the female, associated with the safe and bourgeois life of the land and the home. These distinctions are challenged in Nordic maritime fiction, exemplified through a reading of Jonas Lie's *Gaa Paa!* (1882). That challenge, manifested in a domestication of the maritime and an oceanization of the domestic, constitutes Lie's foundation for progress and a progressive nationalism.

Narratologically, *The Pilot and His Wife*, *Rutland*, and *Gaa Paa!* open with rumors that travel from the maritime to the domestic: the town talk about the mysterious pilot who lives secluded on the coast with his wife; about the ship *Rutland*'s transformation from galley to cargo vessel; or, as in *Gaa Paa!*, about a big fish followed by shoals of herring that enter the fjords from the open spaces of the ocean, moving towards land: "The rumor went through the fjords."[186] This movement is characteristic of *Gaa Paa!* The novel evolves as a *Bildungsroman* structured around a compromise between land and sea. The

---

185 Melville, *Billy Budd*, 54–55.
186 Jonas Lie, *Gaa Paa! Sjøfortælling* (Kjøbenhavn: Gyldendalske Boghandels Forlag, 1882), 7.

sea is endowed with qualities similar to those ascribed to it by thinkers such as Hegel and Schmitt. It provides life and dynamism and is associated with a forward movement, qualities that are necessary for the barren and frozen land, which is portrayed as an inhospitable place of confinement that rules out human *bauen, wohnen,* and even *denken*. At the same time, a vagrant life on the seven seas is brutal, rootless, and hazardous, so Lie creates compromise maritime models for his male protagonists in *Gaa Paa!, The Pilot and His Wife,* and *Rutland*. These models are domestications of the purely oceanic: Salve becomes a pilot after many years of reckless roaming; Kristensen, the captain of the *Rutland*, reluctantly accepts a routinized merchant life along the coasts; after formative years on ocean-going vessels Rejer is reduced to "Sildekonge" (herring king) in the Aafjord.

Rejer Jansen Juhl and his home, Hammernæsset, at the bottom of Aafjorden need the ocean's vital impulses to emerge from their stagnated existence. The novel's title, in English "Go On!," refers to the ocean's galvanizing and forward-moving effects and, implicitly, we get a sense of the novel's two formal opposites: the crooked, yet inflexible and stiff forms of the land versus the dynamic and pliable forms of the sea. With this recurrent theme, *Gaa Paa!* is the Lie novel that most clearly thematizes the material difference between land and sea and inscribes this difference and these components in a conflict between the domestic and the maritime in its structure of *Bildung*. *The Pilot and His Wife* is set on Merdø near the coast of Arendal. As a geographic location where land and sea elements meet, it is an elemental part of the ocean that makes it possible for Salve and Elisabeth to unite the maritime and the domestic. In *Gaa Paa!*, the geographic location is characterized by something very different, almost the opposite. Like Merdø, Hammernæsset and Aafjorden are areas of land open to the ocean, but unlike Merdø, they are more connected with the solidity of the land than with the dynamism of the ocean. Aafjorden is not a coast facing the open sea; it is described as "a small narrow fjord arm," a piece of land that has withdrawn from the ocean and only has a narrow access to it because of the fjord.

From the beginning, Aafjorden is described as turned towards the land. Its people are not "children of the sea" but "children of the earth" (Schmitt), or at most children of the narrow fjords and fjord arms. The geographic location is withdrawn from the world of maritime experience, a point emphasized by how as the rumor of the great fish spreads to Hammernæsset, belief in it gradually expires. This expiration is characteristic for Aafjorden in its exclusion of anything foreign, a place that in opposition to the sea is crookedly closed around itself. Rejer's father, Jan Rejersen Juhl, who dies in the beginning of the novel, had for decades been the lock and plug at the bottom of the fjord acting as bulwark against the threatening oceanic impulses of change, risk, and foreignness. But this crookedness has become an unhealthy and inept condition leaving its mark on everything in the place. The landscape is described as "narrow cracks and crevices of shielings all suffering of too much shadow and too little sun"; the cows are "wretched and small with sharp hip bones"; the population is like "a completely pent up, old-fashioned people with oversized large features;" and even the fish are "outdated and big headed." This degenerated and degenerating place is characterized by darkness and shadows. Things do not grow normally; instead, they become crooked and bony. This is underlined by the entire landscape being crooked: "crooked vegetation, crooked alder and birch." The landscape's crookedness is even reflected in the Juhl household, which mirrors its inhabitant, here old Mrs. Juhl: "The heavy, crooked figure who sat there on the flour coffin."[187] The crooked forms and movements characterize the entire place: geography, nature, domestic space, and humans. Countering this confinement is the novel's title, *Gaa Paa!* Its opposite movement—onward and upward—is emphasized by the exclamation mark in the title, indicating progress and dynamism. Instead of succumbing, of bowing down, to live in these low-ceilinged homes, the title urges industriousness and openness.

The movement and progression away from this enclosed society is initiated in the opening pages with the death of old Juhl, who made sure that his family and the people in the community were turned away from the maritime and merely "lived to reproduce and share and spin themselves into a stuck position in the crooks." However, it is worth noting that the rise of the settlement and the family was based on sea journeys to Holland in the eighteenth century by a Juhl forefather. The warped land was founded on the maritime but has since stagnated. Aafjorden withdraws from the ocean, turns its back on oceanic voyages, and degenerates due to inbreeding. The task of the next generation, "Juhlegutten" (the Juhl boy), is to reverse the potentially fatal degeneration. In contrast to his family, Rejer Jansen Juhl is not dark and bent but bears the characteristics of his ancestor, the maritime adventurer. He is upright and fair-featured as opposed to "the settlement's otherwise dark and stocky inhabitants." His physical appearance sets him apart from the crookedness of Hammernæsset, and Rejer does not want to bow down but "to go on, until it cracked." In this trait, his formation is to be found. He distinguishes himself from the rest of his hometown's inhabitants by his uprightness and by daring to look outward to the world. Yet, to be able to return to his native place and renew and confront the crookedness of the coast, he must learn to bend

---

187   Lie, *Gaa Paa!*, 8–9, 12, 30.

and compromise without cracking. This happens through his meeting with the ocean and its dynamism. This formal metaphor (grounded in substantiality, in the elemental saltwater) accompanies Rejer throughout the novel. In the beginning, he is described as the "young slim reed," and following a dream about fish and the sea, his face turns towards the sea and assumes the shape of a ship's stern: "But when he woke up, his face had a singular expression. [...] The sharp-lined face had the appearance of a sharp stern."[188]

Rejer's posture as a "slim reed" reaches a physical completion in the novel's female protagonist, Sara Rørdam, whose last name suggests a union between the maritime and the domestic in that it fuses Rejer's straightness (*rør* means reed) and the mobility of the maritime (*dam* means pond); her given name associates her with the mysticism, energy, and vitality that Rejer admires in Spanish women. The second half of Sara's surname connotes a domesticated ocean since a pond is a piece of enclosed and tamed water. As opposed to the warped and woody women of Aafjorden and Hammernæsset, Sara Rørdam unites the solid and the flexible and therefore the domestic with the maritime. In her physical appearance, she incarnates the union that Rejer seeks. She unites Aafjorden's darkness with Rejer's fair hair: Her hair "was brighter on the inside and darker on the outside." Hence, she adds to Aafjorden an element of foreignness that it needed to progress. She is responsible for transferring Rejer's wish for forward movement to Aafjorden and for relocating the meaning of the title, go on, from the sea to the land: "Well, Sara, just go ahead with it! Put people to work!"[189]

While Sara fuses the maritime and the domestic in Aafjorden, Rejer must complete an educational journey before he can return home and attempt to unite the two dimensions. His journey follows a general separation between sea and land: it is on land that he is tested by being constantly seduced, whether by women, money, or comrades; it is at sea that the forward-moving development happens. In contrast to other maritime novels, for example Edgar Allan Poe's *The Narrative of Arthur Gordon Pym* (1838), where Pym's formation occurs through his encounters with the ocean, specifically a storm and a mutiny on board the ship, Rejer's trials happens on land, and the ship becomes a pause or a respite from these trials. It is telling that the actual sea journey takes up little space in the novel. Instead, Lie elaborates on the visits to harbors, where Rejer tends to spend everything just earned aboard the ship. Rejer's maritime experience is closely linked with the novel's motto "Go on!" Despite the terrestrial setbacks, the dynamism of the maritime enables Rejer to move forward.

---

188   Lie, *Gaa Paa!*, 11, 11, 30, 30, 26.
189   Lie, *Gaa Paa!*, 220, 333.

Rejer's *Bildung* implies that his slim as a reed terrestrial character must learn flexibility. This happens when he becomes a sailor. With a nautical education and experience, Rejer returns to the narrow fjords of Norway and opens them up, setting them in motion. From the beginning, he admires Lind's "free sailor-like nature [...], his sea-fresh, easy way of comporting himself," which contrasts sharply with the crookedness of domestic isolation. By the end of the sea voyages, Rejer with his "innate Juhlian obstinance" is transformed into "a competent sailor and cook as good as an accomplished one!" But opposed to Lind and the Gothenburger who are homeless seamen, Rejer's maritime journeys are merely an intermezzo between leaving and returning to Aafjorden, a means of completing his formation, which consists of a union between the domestic and the maritime enabling him—with the aid of his wife—to generate progress and healthy growth to the warped and barren land. This happens through the maritime. Contrary to his father, Rejer is capable of transforming Aafjorden into a maritime place through herring fishing and "the sluggish pace and the eight meals a day" into "Solid food, few meals, and 'hurry up!'"[190]

With Sara, Rejer succeeds in transferring the maritime mobility to the land. But whereas Sara's flexibility unites the two, Rejer's education ultimately fails. Toward the end of the novel, he breaks, not during a trial on land, but in a struggle at sea. As a result of his ambition, pride, and belief in his own invulnerability, he decides to go fishing with a small crew in bad weather. The men never return. If the ocean was the place of Rejer's progress, the place of soft, round, and moving waves and a pause from the trials of the land, it shows its destructive and sharp face towards the end of the story. The ocean becomes the place where Rejer's boat meets the rocks in the fjord, breaks apart, and founders. The upright hero's last encounter with the ocean shows the waters as "edgy, dark [...] dented!"[191] However, the maritime motto "Go on!" is passed on to Sara and their eldest son, Jan. Regardless of the circumstances of Rejer's death, Lie has oceanized the warped, stagnated land and created the conditions necessary for national progress and growth.

Land and sea are opposed to each other as spaces with contrasting dynamics. To humans, land is the familiar and homely, whereas the sea is the unfamiliar and hazardous. The sea is an element beyond the control of humans, but as both Hegel and Schmitt have pointed out, it is also a dynamic element necessary for the development of human societies and civilizations. In most maritime novels, men leave behind land, home, and female companionship for

---

190   Lie, *Gaa Paa!*, 99, 132, 327.
191   Lie, *Gaa Paa!*, 341.

work or to experience adventure. The family household is typically not present in works by canonized maritime authors such as Melville and Conrad. To their vagrant seamen, the ship functions as a piece of *floating* land. Materially, the sea is anti-domestic, since waves, winds, and currents will always set the ship in motion or wreck it. The forward movement converges with the structure of *Bildung*, in which the hero wishes to leave behind the solidity and security of the domestic sphere to venture forth, voyaging into the unfamiliar, epitomized by the fluctuating and restless form of the ocean. This is the perfect environment for the hero to discover his true identity.

The structure of *Bildung* implies too that the hero returns home and is able to reach a compromise between society and his individuality. In Lie's three maritime novels, the compromise of the traditional *Bildungsroman* between middle class and upper class or between artistic and bourgeois ambitions[192] has been transformed into a compromise between the maritime and the domestic, between the sea and the land. In his introduction to the different stages in Lie's work, Harald Bache-Wiig observes that the coming to terms with the domestic sphere is a result of Lie's female characters: "The women are the key to a harmonious relationship and family life and to the unification of all the constructive and unifying forces in a young nation." My reading enables us to specify that what makes the women in Lie's maritime novels unifying forces is their ability to fuse the maritime and the domestic. As opposed to Ibsen's Nora, Lie's women have no desire to escape their potentially claustrophobic and restricting households. As maritime characters, or as characters able to connect with and incorporate the maritime dimension, they build their homes as an "antidote," a corrective to any form of maritime recklessness.[193] Prior to *The Family at Gilje* (1883), characterized by a restricted home because of a lack of oceanic openness, the domestic spheres in Lie's three maritime novels fuse the dynamic substance of the ocean with the solid ground of the home. The fusion results in a more equal gender balance. Elisabeth, Madam Kristensen, and Sara Rørdam are strong female characters capable of embracing and incorporating their husbands' maritime sphere into the domestic sphere: an oceanized home in *The Pilot and His Wife*; a domesticated ship in *Rutland*; a new fertile land in *Gaa Paa!*

The maritime sphere is dependent upon the domestic sphere. Salve's ship life is determined by the domestic mood; Kristensen's maritime life becomes

---

192 Franco Moretti, *The Way of the World: The Bildungsroman in European Culture* (1987; London: Verso, 2000).
193 Harald Bache-Wiig, *Med lik i lasten: Subjekt og modernitet i Jonas Lies romanunivers* (Oslo: Novus Forlag, 2009), 30, 30.

domesticated by Madam Kristensen's presence; and Rejer's maritime journey is a break from his trials which happen on land. The male journeys with their formative structure result in a return to homes that they graft on to their maritime lives. The coexisting maritime and domestic lives are passed down and their sons take over from their fathers in different yet similar ways: Gjert ends up as a naval officer; Bernt becomes a shipbuilder; Jan Conrad repeats Rejer's credo "Go on!" All three sons unite the land and the sea through their choice of occupation. But in contrast to their fathers, who combined the two spheres through an emphasis on the maritime and a subsequent domestication of their seafaring nature, the starting point for the sons is the land. Their exploitation of the sea is founded on terrestrial terms: by becoming a naval officer and thus contributing to society's valorization of social ascent, by building ships, and by improving the land through herring fishing. In a comparison of the three novels, it is possible to trace a development toward a more pessimistic attitude toward the domestic sphere (an attitude evident in *The Family at Gilje*, in which the maritime sphere is eliminated). About the ending in *Gaa Paa!*, Bache-Wiig observes: "There is something ominous about this weird inner connection between the confined stubbornness and the unlimited and dynamic movement that points forward in the work."[194]

Gaa Paa! is the last of the three maritime novels and the only one not comprising of a union between sailor and home. The household may very well be united with the maritime, and Rejer does succeed in his efforts to create growth and progress for the life on the land, but his credo "Go on!" cannot be bent. It signals a straight arrow that is unstoppable in its linear progression, and in his desire for more growth and progress Rejer ends up losing his life at sea. This development is emphasized in the subsequent novels. *The Family at Gilje* in particular, Lie's most famous novel, depicts a home that "produces homelessness."[195] Inger-Johanna inherits Rejer's drive but also experiences homelessness throughout the novel. In this second phase of Lie's career, there is nothing reconciliatory or restorative about the terrestrial home. Why is that? Because there is no longer any ocean in those works. As soon as the maritime is eliminated, the domestic sphere can no longer unite the sexes and becomes dysfunctional. By extension, the ideology of (national) progress suffers. The domestic and the maritime are interdependent in *The Pilot and His Wife*, *Rutland*, and *Gaa Paa!* Lie creates a compromise in which the home is not an enclosed space and neither sailor nor wife become restless.

---

194   Bache-Wiig, *Med lik i lasten*, 34.
195   Bache-Wiig, *Med lik i lasten*, 35.

3.3   Joseph Conrad

In this chapter, I will only briefly introduce Conrad's stance on technological development since I examine the treatment of technology in Conrad and Verne more thoroughly in a later chapter. There, we shall see how the works of Jules Verne are closely affiliated with the fascination of scientific discoveries in Michelet's *La Mer* and of societal and financial progress in Lie's *Gaa Paa!* In Verne's case, science and progress combined with his editor's vision of a pedagogical-educational encyclopedia come together in his technological inventions. Perhaps the most famous of these are the *Nautilus*, the legendary submarine in Verne's most ambitious maritime novel, *Twenty Thousand Leagues under the Seas*, which features the equally renowned Captain Nemo. In contrast to Verne, who is usually considered a writer with a positive attitude toward technology, Conrad was deeply skeptical of modern technology because of its transformative effects on the maritime world.

Reflections on and depictions of the technocentric sailor life abound in nautical tales from the late nineteenth century and onward. Arguably, Conrad is the writer who has reflected most deeply on the transformation of the ocean from glitter to grid. We encounter these reflections in tales and novels, in his diaries and letters, and in essays. "Ocean Travel" (1923) is an example of the latter, and an important one regarding technocentrism. Here, Conrad catalogues a series of elementary differences between life on board a sailing ship and life on board a steamship:

> The one statement that can safely be advanced about travelling at sea is that it is not what it used to be. It is different now elementally. It is not so much a matter of changed propelling power; it is something more. In the old days, under the machinery of sails, the distinguished and the undistinguished travellers (of whom there were not so very many) were wafted to distant parts of the world by the movement of variable air currents. Now the travelling multitudes are taken to their destination because of the invariable resistance of water to the screwing motion of the propeller, with which fire (that other element) has a lot to do.[196]

There are several interesting points here. First, Conrad uses the word "machinery" in relation to sails. This suggests that Conrad acknowledged the technological dimension of the sail ship, something that I will return to in

---

196   Joseph Conrad, "Ocean Travel," in *Tales of Hearsay and Last Essays* (1928; London: J. M. Dent and Sons Ltd, 1955), 35.

the chapter on technology. Second, he operates with two dichotomies, one between the few and the many travelers, another between variability and invariability. The former distinction tells us something about the accessibility of the sea and maritime life. It used to be only for the dedicated or chosen few, but now it has become available to "the travelling multitudes" and is therefore no longer as special. The latter difference, between variability and invariability, is depicted in two distinct world pictures: one in which organicism, contingency, and a collaborative relationship between ship and sea prevail (wind and sails); versus one in which predictability and monotony gain mastery because the ship dominates nature and the sea (water and propeller).

Third, by referring to fire as "that other element," Conrad suggests that a foreign element has interfered in the hitherto harmonious or at least natural relationship between air and water. In Conrad's elemental philosophy, air and water belong together at sea, whereas fire belongs to the earth on land. Interestingly, Conrad admits to a wonder of progress and a miracle of complexity in the effort that led to the construction of a mechanical machine such as the steamship, but he laments that "it may render life more tame than it should be." He does not fear that applied science will ever succeed in domesticating the inherent wild spark in man, but science makes "the condition of our pilgrimage less exciting," as he says.[197]

Whereas the passenger on board a sailing ship used to break with the conditions of his or her terrestrial life, the steamship passenger transfers these conditions on board the ship and conceives of the ship as a hotel with its typical pseudo comforts and disadvantages of a social life. The only consolation is that there is a set date for release to look forward to. "The modern traveller has never the time to get into an acquiescent mood," Conrad complains:

> It was otherwise with the old-time traveller under sail: he had to become acclimatized to that moral atmosphere of ship life which he was fated to breathe for so many days. He was no dweller in an unpleasantly unsteady imitation of a Ritz Hotel. He would before long begin to feel himself a citizen of a small community in special conditions and with special interests which gradually ceased to be secret to him, and in the end secured his sympathies [...] it had a charm and an intimacy of a settled existence no modern steamship with its long barren alleyways swept by the wind and decorated with the name of promenade decks can give [...] almost all, men and women, became reconciled to the vast solitude of the sea

---

197   Conrad, "Ocean Travel," 35, 35.

untroubled by the sound of the world's mechanical contrivances and the noise of endless controversies. The silence of the universe would lie very close to the sailing ship, with her freight of lives from which the daily stresses and anxieties had been removed, as if the circle of the horizon had been a magic ring laid on the sea. No doubt the days thus enchanted were empty, but they were not so tedious as people may imagine. They passed quickly, and, if they brought no profit or excitement, I cannot help thinking that they were not wasted. No! They were not wasted.[198]

The exclamation mark and the final repetition emphasize a determination in Conrad and his heirs of nostalgic writers of the sea towards salvaging and preserving the existential dimensions and modes of being that modernity has suppressed: place, composure, silence, slowness, boredom, variation, intimacy, solitude, magic, and enchantment.

In the chapter on technology, I will return to Conrad and Verne and read them more thoroughly. My readings will both affirm and nuance the established views of Conrad as a conservative critic of technological development and of Verne as a progressive advocate of science and technology.

∴

To summarize, in the technocentric epoch the dominant component in the gods-humans-technology-nature constellation is technology. This means a perpetuation of the motto Plus Ultra *and the conception of the ocean as a place of passage. This is the era of steam in which the sea is transformed metaphorically from fish into a disenchanted machine, the glitter of the previous age morphing into a grid. The dimensions of risk and chance on sea journeys in the age of sail are supplemented in the age of steam with strong elements of control and calculation. Belief in progress and scientific explorations prevail.*

4   Geocentrism

The evolution of ocean perceptions does not stop at technocentrism. A new planetary consciousness emerges in several writers and thinkers from around 1950. Theocentrism, anthropocentrism, and technocentrism are "world pictures" related not only to the period prior to 1450, to 1450–1850, and to the period after 1850, but also transhistorical perspectives that are found in

---

198   Conrad, "Ocean Travel," 36, 37–38.

different periods. The same is true of geocentrism. It is a perspective we can characterize as epochal for our contemporaneity and is also found in earlier periods. As with all efforts to synthesize in a *longue durée* perspective, our history from theocentrism and anthropocentrism to technocentrism and geocentrism necessarily leaves out nuances and details that potentially challenge the otherwise symmetrical and systematical architecture of this historical chapter. However, I do not consider these potentially threatening nuances and details sufficiently potent to undermine our building, which also serves as a model for various analytical approaches.

4.1   *Nostalgia or Dystopia*

The post-Conrad era of maritime fiction can be roughly split into two diverging paths, a nostalgic path on which writers look to the past to re-enchant an otherwise disenchanted present, and a dystopian path on which writers predict disturbing futures of plastic oceans, rising sea levels, and mass extinction. We shall examine the dystopian path in detail in the chapter on the Anthropocene, especially through readings of *The Drowned World* and *Havbrevene*. To this path also belongs Maja Lunde's novel *Blå* (*Blue*). In what follows, I briefly discuss examples of what we might call the heirs of Conrad. In the wake of the technocentric age, even during that age, we can detect efforts to re-enchant a world gone wrong through industrialization and mechanization. In the ages of technocentrism and geocentrism, nautical literature evokes the sea's eternal splendor and promises of enchantment.

In *Haiene* (*The Sharks*, 1974), a brilliant historical novel by the Norwegian writer Jens Bjørneboe, whose plot unfolds from December 1899 to January 1900, a steamship is repeatedly described patronizingly, for example as "flat iron," "the filthy thing," and "iron box," but it gets even worse:

> Off our bow one morning we saw a column of smoke on the horizon as from a burning ship. In a couple of hours we could descry that it came, not from a sailing vessel, but from a steam'ship'—one of those slow, ridiculous craft whose sole task should be that of tugging real ships in and out of harbours, but which today are allowed to pollute the seas: heavy, lumpy, and smelling just as terrible as they look. [...] It groaned on through the long, clear swells as if it was suffering from a combination of heart disease and asthma.[199]

---

199   Jens Bjørneboe, *The Sharks: The History of a Crew and a Shipwreck*, trans. Esther Greenleaf Mürer (1974; Norwich: Norvik Press, 1992), 127.

The images used by Bjørneboe to convey the sense of steam are entirely negative. The steamship is compared to a double disease, accused of contaminating the ocean, and Bjørneboe is not even willing to use the term ship in connection with steam because of the steamship's slowness and lack of grace and beauty. The novel shows Bjørneboe to be a worthy heir to Conrad's conservative voice in the battle between sail and steam, and in the chapter on rhythm we will see Bjørneboe's attempts to re-enchant the world through scenes of rhythmic harmony and moments of bliss.

In *Mytteriet på Barken "Zuidersee"* (*Mutiny on the Barque Zuidersee*, 1963), the Danish-Norwegian writer Aksel Sandemose expresses yet another criticism of technology in the era of steam. Sandemose published several works on sea life between the 1920s and the 1960s, and if the Bjørneboe example focused on the ship itself, Sandemose reflects upon the relationship between the sailor and the ship in *Mutiny* and points to a difference between sail and steam:

> A sailor today has no particular feelings for his ship; he may have had in the days of sail, when his personal effort meant so much more; but in a machine-driven ship everything is so very impersonal, and this manifests itself all the way down from the command, divided between the skipper and the chief engineer, to the deckhands and the engineroom crew, whose work is so utterly different that, as a rule, the one has little idea of what the other does.[200]

Both Sandemose and Bjørneboe were born when the presence of sailing ships had waned and had little personal experience with sail ships and the age of sail. Still, they position themselves within a powerful tradition of nostalgia, one that still survives in the literature of the sea today. In this tradition, authors remember and portray the sailing era as organic, graceful, and heroic, whereas they associate steamships with disenchantment, artificiality, and fragmentation. Sandemose thus stresses the personal relationship between sailor and sailing ship and complains about the inorganic division of labor on a steamer that is split into two separate worlds: sailors on deck and engineers below deck.

We encounter an example of re-enchantment in Pär Lagerkvist's novel *Pilgrim på havet* (*Pilgrim at Sea*, 1962):

> The sea, which was almost calm, shimmered in many colours; hazy, fleeting colours of indescribable beauty, as if flowers of every kind had been

---

[200] Aksel Sandemose, *Mutiny on the Barque Zuidersee*, trans. Maurice Michael (1963; London: Neville Spearman, 1970), 9.

scattered over its boundless surface, to rock upon it until they slowly faded, paling away in a death of ineffable bliss, melancholy and loveliness. [...] the great and endless sea which is indifferent to all things, which erases all things; which in its indifference forgives all things. Primeval, irresponsible, inhuman. Freeing man through its inhumanity [...]. No fixed goal, no goal at all.[201]

Lagerkvist's maritime vision turns the sea into an epochal and existential metaphor. It becomes a guiding principle for humanity in a godless world of fluid modernity where (Christian and scientific) certainty, doctrinism, and teleology have been replaced by uncertainty, unconcern, and freedom. Neither uncertainty nor unconcern should be understood negatively; rather, they represent the potential for constructing a new mode of being and approach to life in which humans to a greater degree let the world come to them. The sea makes us aware of our nonhuman potential as we recognize the connection between freedom and acquiescence, intensity and composure. As mentioned, common to writers in the technocentric age—Melville, Hugo, Lie, Conrad, Sandemose—and writers in the more geocentric age—Bjørneboe, Ghosh, Carsten Jensen, Lagerkvist, Strøksnes, Lunde, Jacobsen—is their interest in extrapolating the enchanting or re-enchanting potentials of the sea and of maritime existence. Transhistorically, the sea cannot be robbed of this potential for enchantment. Writers react to the disenchanting processes of technocentrism with a compensatory strategy: what is being lost must be regained.

•••

To summarize (and to anticipate the insights in the chapter on the Anthropocene), in the geocentric epoch the dominant component in the gods-humans-technology-nature constellation is Nature and the Blue Planet. This results in a return of the motto Non Plus Ultra *and the conception of the ocean as a coherent ecosystem that is crucially important for the entire planet. This is the era of diesel and inorganic chemicals in which the sea is literally transformed into a plastic ocean or, in some works, is re-enchanted. The former belief in human control over nature is now replaced by a realization of our impotence, and as miscalculation sets in, a suspicion toward calculation develops.*

---

201   Pär Lagerkvist, *Pilgrim at Sea*, trans. Naomi Walford (1962; New York: Random House, 1964), 47, 55, 33.

5   The Four World Pictures in *Moby-Dick*

Having delineated and described a historical framework of four different world pictures, we can now continue with a reading of Herman Melville's *Moby-Dick*. The four world pictures function as a framework that will guide our reading of the novel, but our reading will place concreteness (in the form of different perceptions of time and the ocean and of distinct literary styles and discursive strategies) back into the framework thus making it more complete and solid. I argue that the originality and complexity of *Moby-Dick* stems to a large extent from Melville's incorporation of the four world pictures into his most ambitious novel. It is also in this sense that "*Moby-Dick* dramatizes questions present if underarticulated in maritime writing: What do sailors know? And how is that knowledge registered or measured?"[202] The answer to both these questions posed by Hester Blum is linked to my idea of the coexistence of the four different maritime world pictures.

However, a few elaborations are in order here. It is important to emphasize that my reading of *Moby-Dick* serves as both summation and deconstruction of the above stage-by-stage historical narrative of sea writing. It is my hope that the reader accepts that what I have offered in the preceding pages of this historical chapter is a self-consciously simplified reading of the progress of Western sea writing through four stages: theocentric, anthropocentric, technocentric, and geocentric. Yet, I also believe that my historical narrative captures important epochal differences on top of the undoubtedly strong continuities that characterize historical evolution and, not least, builds a conceptual platform that is analytically operational and fruitful as well as pedagogically necessary. So, by claiming that *Moby-Dick* is a novel that comprises all four modes and historical trends, my intention is to reinforce the value of these historical frames and show by example how a literary writer such as Melville spans and combines them. My global and transhistorical reading method reveals how *Moby-Dick* is especially successful in practicing what Mentz calls an aesthetic of "composture,"[203] which he defines as a recycling of multiple historical trends and layers simultaneously present to form a polychronic system (see also Table 1 at the end of this historical chapter). Literature in general seldom belongs to and exemplifies one narrow historical trend only. In *A Poetic History of the Oceans*, epochal claims such as the four maritime world pictures are not artificially imposed. They serve both a pedagogical, conceptual, and historical

---

202 Blum, *View from the Masthead*, 130.
203 Steve Mentz, *Shipwreck Modernity: Ecologies of Globalization, 1550–1719* (Minnesota: University of Minnesota Press, 2015), ix–xxii.

purpose, but my intention is to prioritize "an accumulated layering of exchange and entanglement," thus turning to "turbulent plurality, a disorienting mixture of weak, attenuated, competing epochs."[204]

Published in 1851, Herman Melville's *Moby-Dick; or, the Whale* straddles the anthropocentric age of adventure, heroism, and enchantment and the technocentric age of industrialization, mathematization, and disenchantment. Belonging equally to two different eras, the age of sail and the age of steam, Melville's novel simultaneously marks the culmination and prefigures the decline of the tradition of sea literature and maritime novels. Arguably, Melville was aware of *Moby-Dick*'s "double consciousness" of being a climax and an anticipation of future demise. Initially, Melville planned no more than a mere whaling version of his former more traditional novels such as *Typee: A Peep at Polynesian Life* (1846) and *Omoo: A Narrative of Adventures in the South Seas* (1847), both of which he referred to as a "plain, straightforward, and amusing narrative of personal experience."[205] However, during the summer of 1850, Melville decided to write what he later would refer to as "a wicked book."[206] The willfulness behind this decision is proof of Melville's re-awakened megalomaniac ambitions. His meeting with Nathaniel Hawthorne at a picnic on Monument Mountain on August 5, 1850, stimulated these ambitions, as did his readings of Shakespeare's dramas, of Milton, Virgil, and Mary Shelley as well as of Goethe, Thomas Carlyle, and William Beckford.[207]

Melville had already once failed to become a genuine writer-artist and not just some documentarist or romance writer yielding to the desires of the audience. His *Mardi: And a Voyage Thither* (1849) flopped, commercially at least. Following that unpleasant experience, he succumbed to the pressures of publishers and readers and returned to a more marketable format. In four months, Melville churned out two novels, *Redburn: His First Voyage* (1849) and *White-Jacket; or, The World in a Man-of-War* (1850). Going by what the author wrote in his journal, he did this so that he could "buy some tobacco."[208] The author

---

204 Mentz, *Shipwreck Modernity*, xi, xiii.
205 Herman Melville, "Letter to Richard Bentley," in *Correspondence*, The Writings of Herman Melville, vol. 14, ed. Lynn Horth (Evanston and Chicago: Northwestern University Press and the Newberry Library, 1993), 132. All subsequent quotes from Melville's letters refer to this edition.
206 Melville, "Letter to Nathaniel Hawthorne, 17 [?] November 1851," 212.
207 Delbanco, *Melville*, 125–31.
208 Herman Melville, "Journal Entry," in *Journals*, The Writings of Herman Melville, vol. 15, ed. Howard C. Horsford and Lynn Horth (Evanston and Chicago: Northwestern University Press and the Newberry Library, 1989), 13. All subsequent quotes from Melville's journals refer to this edition.

self-distanced from these novels by referring to them as "trash"[209] and "two *jobs*, which I have done for money—being forced to it, as other men are to sawing wood."[210] Melville's artistic ambitions were postponed out of necessity. However, the frustration of having to write for the market in combination with inspiration from Hawthorne and Shakespeare led to Melville's ambitious gear shift during the summer of 1850.

Melville's reading of Hawthorne's work and the intimate conversations between the elder Hawthorne and the younger Melville, conversations Melville referred to as "ontological heroics,"[211] made him realize three things: first, that the United States—despite a persistent and asphyxiating dependency on the Old World in cultural and literary matters after decades of political independence—could produce an author as accomplished as the greatest European authors; second, that Hawthorne was close to being the American Shakespeare; third, that he, Melville, could potentially equal or perhaps even supersede "divine William."[212] In short, Hawthorne and Shakespeare activated Melville's artistic ambitions.

If Melville believed that his novel had the potential of being one of the greatest sea novels ever, the pinnacle of a noble literary tradition and written at the high-point of the maritime world's enterprises, many passages in *Moby-Dick* are suffused with a nostalgic tone and an awareness of a world about to disappear—a world of sailing ships, whalers, and sperm lump squeezing. *Moby-Dick* shows us that Melville was endowed with a gift of presentiment regarding the near future and a gift of prophecy regarding the distant future. This maritime world was already undergoing a radical transformation. The heroic sailor battling with the elements or with the aquatic creatures of the sea would become an anachronism and the maritime novel a problematic or even outmoded genre. However, it is not only the nostalgic tone used to depict the old and soon to be extinct world of sail that bears witness of the novel's self-consciousness around the imminent collapse of an entire world and a genre. The conversion from sail to steam and the resulting routinization of ocean travel that was well underway in the mid-nineteenth century were visible on the formal level of Melville's novel just as they re-oriented his thematic concerns.

Instead of being driven forward by a linear plot and written in a traditional romance style like the works of Defoe, Smollett, and Cooper, *Moby-Dick* mixes

---

209   Melville, "Journal Entry," 13.
210   Melville, "Letter to Lemuel Shaw," 138.
211   Melville, "Letter to Nathaniel Hawthorne, 29 June 1851," 196.
212   Melville, "Letter to Evert Duyckinck, 24 February 1849," 119.

a one-dimensional and monomaniacal quest narrative with a multitude of digressions comprising all sorts of stories. This "multiplicity of other things requiring narration"²¹³ ranges from Queequeq's Polynesian family history and the laborious process of extracting whale oil to the Atlantic history of the Nantucketers and a cetological encyclopedia. In a metafictional comment, Ishmael reflects:

> Unconsciously my chirography expands into placard capitals. Give me a condor's quill! Give me Vesuvius' crater for an inkstand! Friends, hold my arms! For in the mere act of penning my thoughts of this Leviathan, they weary me, and make me faint with their outreaching comprehensiveness of sweep, as if to include the whole circle of the sciences, and all the generations of whales, and men, and mastodons, past, present, and to come, with all the revolving panoramas of empire on earth, and throughout the whole universe, not excluding its suburbs. Such, and so magnifying, is the virtue of a large and liberal theme! We expand to its bulk. To produce a mighty book, you must choose a mighty theme.²¹⁴

The stylistic features of this passage, including the use of exclamation marks, the paratactical syntax, and the accumulative sentence length supplement Ishmael's explicitly stated encyclopedic ambition. Melville's novel performs the intermingling of different discourses from sermon, song, dream, meditation, and Shakespearean dialogue to cetology, poetry, travel account, myth, and apocalypse. The formal crisis, or, put in more positive terms, the *invention* of *Moby-Dick* was a consequence of the growing anachronism of the sailing ship mariner and of the narrative potentials of this mariner in relation to action and adventure.

The anachronism also affected the novel's thematic design. *Moby-Dick* was preoccupied with depicting the sailor's battles against nature, against fellow mariners, and against the oceanic kingdom of animals. Alongside these traditional topics of maritime fiction, Melville's oceanic epic explored psychological depths, natural history, racism, epistemology, and cultural diversity in a manner and degree never before seen in sea novels or in any other novel. Melville was fascinated with men who deep-dived ontologically and epistemologically: "Any fish can swim near the surface, but it takes a great whale to go down stairs five miles or more […]. I'm not talking of Mr Emerson now—but

---

213   Melville, *Moby-Dick*, 430.
214   Melville, *Moby-Dick*, 456.

of the whole corps of thought-divers, that have been diving & coming up again with bloodshot eyes since the world began."²¹⁵ With *Moby-Dick*, Melville joined the corps of deep divers of the human mind and the phenomenal world. In the words of Gilles Deleuze, the overwhelming experience meant that he, too, returned to the surface "from what he has seen and heard with bloodshot eyes and pierced eardrums."²¹⁶

The tension between the worlds of sail and steam and Melville's awareness of living in a period of epochal change were infused into *Moby-Dick*. In my view, the result was a novel that pays tribute to four heterogeneous and somewhat incompatible world pictures: theocentrism, anthropocentrism, technocentrism, and geocentrism. In what follows, I elaborate on the distinctions delineated earlier in this chapter between these four world pictures. I attempt to systematize the novel's thematic and formal heterogeneity around these four topics: gods-humans-technology-nature; temporality; worldview; style. This enterprise may seem irreconcilable with Melville's aspirations while writing *Moby-Dick* and even with the book itself. My effort to systematize the overall complexity of the novel is intended to provide a helpful framework through which to read *Moby-Dick* and gain a deeper understanding of the novel and its continued relevance to a world that seems to get wetter.

5.1   *Historical Time and Broad Present*

Before discussing the novel and its coexisting theocentric, anthropocentric, technocentric, and geocentric world pictures, I introduce the concepts of "historical time" (Koselleck) and "broad present" (Gumbrecht), two different conceptions of temporality and past, present, and future that can assist us analytically. The chronotope of "historical time" emerged in the second half of the eighteenth century and became consolidated throughout the nineteenth century, whereas the chronotope of "broad present" emerged during the decade following the end of World War II.²¹⁷ Reinhart Koselleck was the first to historicize the very notions of historical time, historical thought, and historical consciousness and make us aware that the now obsolete chronotope of the nineteenth century was institutionalized so widely and comprehensively that many mistook (and many still confound) it with time itself. Koselleck does so by extracting two anthropological and metahistorical concepts—two formal categories structuring and acting as conditions of possibility for every human

---

215   Melville, "Letter to Evert Augustus Duyckinck, 3 March 1849," 121.
216   Gilles Deleuze, *Essays Critical and Clinical*, trans. Daniel W. Smith and Michael A. Greco (1993; London and New York: Verso, 1998), 3.
217   Gumbrecht, *Our Broad Present*; Gumbrecht, *After 1945*.

relationship with time—from the vocabulary of history and philosophy: experience (*Erfahrung*) and expectation (*Erwartung*). His main point, which has implications for mankind's changing relationship with past, present, and future, is that "the classification of experience and expectation has been displaced and changed during the course of history."[218]

In the introductory chapter of *Our Broad Present: Time and Contemporary Culture* (2014), Gumbrecht summarizes in six points the characteristics of the historical mindset that Koselleck describes.[219] First, the newly historically conscious humankind imagines itself on a linear path moving through time (i.e., time itself does not move). Second, historical thought assumes that all phenomena are affected by change in time (i.e., time is an agent of transformation). Third, moving through time, humankind is convinced to have left the past behind and is skeptical of the value of past experiences as points of orientation (i.e., the past is severed from and considered irrelevant to the present). Fourth, the future presents itself as an open horizon of possibilities toward which humankind is making its way (i.e., the future is the natural and unproblematic next step following the present). Fifth, the present—situated in-between the past (useless experiences) and future (great expectations)—is transformed into a fleeting, almost imperceptible moment of transition (i.e., the present is not essential in itself, but essential only as a difference from the past and as a steppingstone to the future). And sixth, the confined present of "historical time" offered the Cartesian subject its epistemological habitat. Here, Gumbrecht's point is that the transitory present was the site where the subject for the first time in human history felt that it could adapt experiences from the past to the present and the future and then make open choices among the possibilities offered by this future. The ability to select from among these options is both the framework and the condition of possibility for human agency.

Koselleck refers to the transition into the *Neuzeit* ("new time") of European history as a "saddle time" (*Sattelzeit*) taking place between 1780 and 1830 (he sometimes broadens the period to 1750–1850).[220] Koselleck's main thesis on modernity is that it is characterized by an ever-widening gap between humankind's horizon of (future) expectations (*Erwartungshorizont*) and its space of (past) experiences (*Erfahrungsraum*). Premodern man was convinced that his life, played out in an agrarian world dominated by the cycle of nature, would proceed in the same way as the lives of his immediate ancestors. Expectations

---

218   Koselleck, " 'Space of Experience' and 'Horizon of Expectation,' " 259.
219   Gumbrecht, *Our Broad Present*, vii–viii.
220   *Sattelzeit* is a (cognitive) third revolution running parallel with the (political) French Revolution and the (technological) Industrial Revolution.

were nurtured by the experiences of one's fathers, and those experiences then became the experiences of the descendants. Admittedly, events such as the Copernican Revolution and the overseas conquests could have challenged the premodern convergence of experience and expectation. However, according to Koselleck, the Christian eschatology ensured that the horizon of expectations remained confined within clearly defined boundaries. Therefore, at least up until the middle of the seventeenth century, the future continued to be inextricably tied to the present.[221]

Modern man, on the contrary, lives in the conviction that the future can be made; that is, history can be created, and one can creatively intervene into the future. Francis Bacon perceived this in the early seventeenth century, but he was too restricted by the political, technological, and religious frameworks of his time to formulate what later thinkers did in that respect. In the late seventeenth century and throughout the eighteenth century, thinkers such as Leibniz, Rousseau, Kant, and Lessing gave credibility to mankind's potential for secular *perfectibilité*. This paved the way for conceiving of earthly history as a process of continual and increasing perfection. They opened a new horizon of expectation called "progress." Consequently, eschatology was replaced by an open future: "Pragmatic prognosis of a possible future became a long-term expectation of a new future."[222]

The concept of "space of experience" also underwent a transformation in this period. Events such as the Copernican Revolution, technological developments (chronometer, steam engine, and gas lightning to mention but a few), and the discovery of the planet made people realize they lived on a planet defined by the synchronicity of the nonsynchronous and the nonsynchronicity of the synchronous. Diverging temporalities or "ages" coexisted on the planet: history became a question of evolution; geography and society a question of stage.[223] Koselleck concludes:

> It was new that the expectations that reached out for the future became detached from everything that previous experience had to offer. Even the new experience gained from the annexation of lands overseas and from the development of science and technology was still insufficient for the derivation of future expectations. From this moment, the space of experience was no longer limited by the horizon of expectations; rather,

---

221 Koselleck, "'Space of Experience' and 'Horizon of Expectation,'" 263–64.
222 Koselleck, "'Space of Experience' and 'Horizon of Expectation,'" 267.
223 Koselleck, "'Space of Experience' and 'Horizon of Expectation,'" 266–68.

the limits of the space of experience and of the horizon of expectations diverged.[224]

Gumbrecht argues that "historical time" still dominates our way of thinking about time and history today. My point is that when Melville wrote *Moby-Dick* he anticipated the post-World War II chronotope of the "broad present."

What does Gumbrecht mean by broad present? How does it differ from historical time? If we think about it, the ways in which we gain experiences and the ways we act have changed, although we may still be unaware of this change. As to our potential for agency, it is becoming more and more obvious that "the future no longer presents itself as an open horizon of possibilities; instead, it is a dimension increasingly closed to all prognoses—and which, at the same time, seems to draw near as a menace."[225] Several contemporary phenomena contribute to the transformation of the future from an open horizon of expectations and possibilities to a closed and menacing horizon of limited options. The climate crisis, social inequality on a global scale, and international terrorism are but three examples of looming catastrophes.

Our relationship with the past has also changed. If historical time was defined by an ability (or deeply felt desire) to sever the (irrelevant) past from a transitory present, then we are no longer capable of leaving anything behind in our broad present. If in "historical time" the past provided no points of orientation for the present, then our present is swamped with pasts because of digitalization, the internet, and electronic systems of memory. Finally, the broad present entails a new structure of the present, too: "Between the pasts that engulf us and the menacing future, the present has turned into a dimension of expanding simultaneities."[226] Instead of a transitory moment cut off from a relatively useless past and open toward a promising future that one could prognosticate, we now live in an ever-widening present in which we can no longer free ourselves from the past(s), and in which we only meet closed doors to an ominous future.[227]

In this chronotopic configuration, contemporary phenomena such as retro waves (of fashion, design, and music), the Google Books Project with its

---

224   Koselleck, " 'Space of Experience' and 'Horizon of Expectation,' " 266–67.
225   Gumbrecht, *Our Broad Present*, xiii.
226   Gumbrecht, *Our Broad Present*, xiii.
227   Arguably, some of the first literary texts in which the author's thematization of the topics of closed futurity and stalled present could be sensed were Jean-Paul Sartre's *Huis clos* (1944), Albert Camus' *La Peste* (1947), and Samuel Beckett's *En attendant Godot* (1952). See also Gumbrecht, *After 1945*, 25–26, 49. Again, *Moby-Dick* contains elements of this chronotope, as I will demonstrate in a while.

promise of full access to everything that was ever written, and the institutional and private archives of photographs and video recordings make sure that the spreading present is in constant motion. The present is kept dynamic by pasts repeatedly evoked anew. However, the often mutually exclusive, yet coexisting (past) worlds within this present also cause it to lack clear contours. It is not merely a case of the common metahistorical difficulties of not being able to grasp one's present while living in the midst of it. The lack of a clear identity is amplified because of the multiple and diverging pasts expanding the dimensions of this present. Because the contraction of futurity makes it increasingly difficult to act authentically—that is, to act with the conviction that one's actions are an investment in potentially positive future outcomes (no action is possible where no place exists for its realization to be projected)—the mobilization of the present by the different pasts is contrasted by an immobilization of the present by the closure of futurity. The broadening present may offer room (or so we think) to move back into the past and forward into the future, yet such efforts return to their point of departure. What we get is a present that is stagnant, an "unmoving motion" in Gumbrecht's words.[228] If the Cartesian subject reveled in "historical time," because this chronotope allowed its consciousness to project itself meaningfully into the future, Gumbrecht sees a new figure of (self-) reference emerging in the "broad present." This is a subject that is no longer merely or primarily defined by the mind, consciousness, and transcendence, but also by the body, the senses, and *physis*.

5.2 *Theocentrism*

Moby-Dick comprises the four mutually exclusive, yet coexisting world pictures that we have labelled theocentrism, anthropocentrism, technocentrism, and geocentrism. This encyclopedic complexity is one of the reasons for the novel's continued relevance. The *theocentric* world picture permeates the novel but does monopolize it according to Zachary Hutchins: "most studies of *Moby-Dick*, distracted by Melville's apparent Ahabian disregard for behavioral standards derived from mainstream Christian interpretations of scripture, underestimate Melville's interest in preserving and sustaining biblical structure and content within the novel. [...] his writing is so saturated with scriptural references that his entire corpus seems a type of third testament encompassing and extending the Bible."[229] A classical and still influential study by Nathalie Wright, *Melville's Use of the Bible* (1949), highlights the influence of the Wisdom books

---

[228] Gumbrecht, *Our Broad Present*, xiii.
[229] Zachary Hutchins, "*Moby-Dick* as Third Testament: A Novel 'Not Come to Destroy but to Fulfill' the Bible," *Leviathan* 13, no. 2 (2011): 20, 29.

of the Old Testament, particularly the Books of Job, Proverbs, and Ecclesiastes, the latter for example cited explicitly in "The Try-Works" chapter: "No other group of scriptural books is so extensively represented in his pages, or so profusely marked in his Bible."[230] Nevertheless, my focus is mainly on "The Book of Jonah" and Melville's chapter "The Sermon."

Prophetic voices in *Moby-Dick* express a *Non Plus Ultra* approach to the sea, consider the ocean a barrier, and associate seafaring with risk. In addition, the novel carries powerful religious symbolism. Moby Dick is a natural phenomenon, a giant fish to be fought and caught, and more, a sacred creature to be admired from a respectful distance and a marvelous monster to be feared up close. In the novel's *anthropocentric* world picture, Melville lauds the Faustian expansionist drive of mankind, its "immaculate manliness" and "august dignity,"[231] as well as its collaborative, yet agonistic, relationship with nature. Examples of anthropocentrism can be found in the novel's descriptions of the Nantucketers and of the crew's whale hunting. In the *technocentric* universe, we meet Melville's tribute to the efficiency of industrialism and its services to humankind. The descriptions of the whale hunt as a rationalist and capitalist enterprise, "hopes of cash—aye, cash,"[232] fall into this category, and so do those of the ship as a factory and the cetological chapters with their systematization of nature. The *geocentric* universe enters the foreground whenever Melville pays homage to the ocean and to its animal kingdom, and when he evokes the prehuman or posthuman worlds. The shared practice of squeezing sperm lumps becomes a harmonious cosmic experience, whereas the novel's ending depicts human apocalypse and planetary rebirth simultaneously. In the following, I compare the four universes in greater detail. More specifically, I will analyze their image of humanity's relationship to nature, technology, and religion, their temporality, their worldview, and their style. This will allow me to discuss the chronotopic design of the novel and its potential uses of "historical time" and "broad present."

Moby-Dick is undoubtedly one of the novels in the Western canon in which the Holy Scriptures, ancient religions in general, and the classical tradition and its texts have the strongest presence and afterlife. I shall present only one example, but it should provide enough input for us to get an idea of the theocentrism in the novel. In its polyphonic structure and heteroglossic style, we encounter a series of prophetic voices of biblical nature: "For many Christian

---

230   Nathalie Wright, *Melville's Use of the Bible* (Durham, NC: Duke University Press, 1949), 94.
231   Melville, *Moby-Dick*, 117.
232   Melville, *Moby-Dick*, 178.

readers, the Bible's claim to divine authorship identifies every page as the product of a prophetic pen, and *Moby-Dick* likewise invests its multiplicity of narratives with a clearly prophetic voice."[233] Father Mapple draws ominous parallels to Jonah, Ishmael evokes a second Deluge at the end of the novel, and through his insistent warnings to Ishmael and Queequeg against signing up for the *Pequod*, "a stranger" in the chapter entitled "The Prophet" insinuates Ahab's hubristic transgressions of divine boundaries. Common to the three examples is a vision of a millennial future, an anticipation of its completion or failed completion, unfolded in linear, eschatological time.

The example I will discuss is Father Mapple's sermon.[234] Melville exhibits Mapple's unifying ability, his power to centralize, in a double way. Before Father Mapple's entrance into the chapel, the "small congregation of sailors, and sailors' wives and widows" is scattered randomly around the room, each person apparently isolated in his or her individuality: "Each silent worshipper seemed purposely sitting apart from the other, as if each grief were insular and incommunicable." Just before beginning his sermon, now situated in the pulpit, adroitly boarded in a sailorly fashion by the assistance of a rope ladder, Mapple, in "a mild voice of unassuming authority," commands the people to draw together "midships."[235] A former sailor, Father Mapple speaks the *lingua nautica* and reminds us of a captain who has a gathering effect on his crew.

Melville also underlines Mapple's centralizing function through his rhetorical style. Mapple tells the story of Jonah by starting with the ending and then going back to the story's beginning. Endowed with hindsight, the entire story and all its details are present in his mind. He is outside or above time.[236] His sermon becomes a recollective and systematizing narrative in which everything is told at the proper time and place: "the sin, hard-heartedness, suddenly awakened fears, the swift punishments, repentance, prayers, and finally the deliverance and joy of Jonah."[237] This structure corresponds to what Sacvan Bercovitch has called "the American Jeremiad," a Puritan narrative with roots in the Calvinist providential view of history in which recounted beginnings were simultaneously announcements that promised an epiphanic end in the fullness of time. Its purpose was "to direct an imperiled people of God towards

---

233 Hutchins, "*Moby-Dick* as Third Testament," 22.
234 For a more elaborated reading of "The Sermon," see Søren Frank, "Melvilles Ambivalenz gegenüber Vater Mapples Rhetorik und Weitsicht," *Neue Rundschau* 1 (2013): 183–94.
235 Melville, *Moby-Dick*, 34, 34, 41.
236 William Spanos, *The Errant Art of* Moby-Dick: *The Canon, the Cold War, and the Struggle for American Studies* (Durham: Duke University Press, 1995), 87–114.
237 Melville, *Moby-Dick*, 42.

the fulfillment of their destiny, to guide them individually towards salvation, and collectively towards the American city of God."[238] There are no deviations in Mapple's sermon, because he—like the punishing (Puritan) God he believes in and believes that he serves—hovers above the material of his story as well as above the congregation, epitomized in his isolated and elevated position in the pulpit.

As William Spanos points out, the pulpit recalls Bentham's Panopticon from which all details can be monitored and evaluated. In Mapple's sermon, differing considerably from the biblical source in its density of detail, such particulars as Joppa (Jaffa in modern day Tel Aviv), Tarshish (Cadiz), customs papers, passport, passage money, cargo, parricide reward notice, locked cabin, and lamp never escape the gaze of the alert exegete. The numerous details endow Mapple with a godlike narratorial authority and serve to bend his narrative towards preaching "the Truth to the face of Falsehood."[239] All parts act together in supporting the whole. The countless details are semantically confined. If they are unambiguous, they are mentioned to demonstrate the narrator's superior control, all-encompassing knowledge, and omnipresent gaze.

If we compare Mapple's panoramic style to Ishmael's narrative technique, they seem to be opposites. Mapple stays aloof; he never plunges. Ishmael plunges. He explores the watery and fluid depths, what D. H. Lawrence has called "the strange slidings and colliding of Matter," whereas Mapple reaches out for the metaphysical heaven, for eternity. Ishmael also explores horizontally, allowing for digressions and doubts when commenting on details. Mapple is will, idea, and discourse. In contrast, but only occasionally (for Ishmael is also spirit, talk, and idea), Ishmael's "bodily knowledge moves naked, a living quick among the stark elements. For with sheer physical vibrational sensitiveness, like a marvellous wireless-station, he registers the effects of the outer world."[240] Melville's experience of writing on a formal *terra infirma* from August 1850 and onwards splits into two diverging narrative modalities, one stylistically sympathetic to or converging with his own insecurity (Ishmael's ramblings, digressions, and pure bodily apprehensions of the physical world), the other a compensatory counterreaction to the insecurity, necessary in order to fend off chaos and the howling infinite, temporarily at least (Mapple's teleology, linearity, and purely spiritual interpretations of the metaphysical world).

---

238   Sacvan Bercovitch, *The American Jeremiad* (Madison: The University of Wisconsin Press, 1978), 9.
239   Melville, *Moby-Dick*, 48.
240   D. H. Lawrence, *Studies in Classic American Literature* (1923; London: Penguin, 1971), 154, 155.

Instead of Father Mapple's magnetic ability to bend details into prophetic signs of later fulfillment, Ishmael's encounter with details and signs seems to emphasize chance, randomness, and coincidence, such as when he wanders about New Bedford and misses several lodging opportunities before choosing The Spouter-Inn where Queequeg just happens to be staying. It could be argued that this modality of contingency continues throughout the novel until the survival by chance at the end. To Ishmael, the signs are merely presentiments, and as such they are unreliable and highly ambiguous.[241] They are not, as in Mapple's case, clear-cut signatures of truth, but rather vague, fluid pre-structures that invite examination and doubt.

The contrast between Ishmael and Mapple signals a critique of Mapple's interpretation (misreading) of the biblical Jonah story. Mapple disregards the fourth chapter of "The Book of Jonah," the chapter in which God shows his mercy on Nineveh and the pagan inhabitants. And whereas Mapple's Jonah is portrayed as someone terrified of being discovered and who is treated as a criminal, the Bible's Jonah tells his shipmates right away who he is and what he has done. Mapple's Jonah fears that God will punish him, in the Bible he goes below to sleep, seemingly untroubled by his consciousness. Mapple says of Jonah that his repentance is genuine and that he is grateful for his punishment, but in the Bible, Jonah calls for God's help. No model of repentance, he stays angry until death, incensed by God's decision not to punish Nineveh. In that sense, the Jonah of the Bible and Mapple share a belief in the necessity of sacred violence, of identifying scapegoats to cleanse the world. However, this necessity seems undermined by God in "The Book of Jonah," since his logic, and the logic of Ishmael, is anti-sacrificial. In contrast to Mapple's punishing God, this implies a merciful and tolerant God, and, consequently, indicates a disruption between violence and the sacred.

Mapple's sermon takes an unmistakable stand on the need for sacrifices, scapegoats, and violence, whereas "The Book of Jonah" shows a God more compassionate and forgiving. In relation to a sacrificial world vision, Ishmael seems to end up on Mapple's side, although his narrative techniques differ from Mapple's, and though the fulfillment is apparently only temporary. As for *Moby-Dick*, it seems divided between a critique of the practice of victimization and its cleansing effects, on the one side, and the need nevertheless to come up with a victim on the other.[242]

---

241 Spanos, *The Errant Art of Moby-Dick*, 91–92.
242 Giorgio Mariani, " 'Chiefly Known by His Rod': The Book of Jonah, Mapple's Sermon, and Scapegoating," in *Ungraspable Phantom: Essays on Moby-Dick*, eds. John Bryant, Mary K. Bercaw Edwards, and Timothy Marr (Kent: Kent State University Press, 2006), 52–54.

The theocentric world picture in *Moby-Dick* rests on several other sources and chapters than "The Book of Jonah" and "The Sermon" but this will not be examined in depth here. However, I would like to offer a condensed summary of Melville's theocentrism in *Moby-Dick*. The temporality governing most of the theocentric parts of the novel is a linear, eschatological conception of time in which the past is incomplete, the present transitory, and the future (fails to be) complete. It is a universe in which God's will trumps that of humans, who are not yet assisted by modern technology in their confrontations with a divinely administered nature. Melville's tone oscillates between reverence and prophecy depending on nature's manifestations as being either enchanted or apocalyptic. Not yet a fish or a machine, the ocean is perceived as either a marvel or a monster, and Melville conveys this universe in a style that is predominantly either lyrical or allegorical.

5.3   Anthropocentrism

In "Nantucket," Melville heaps praise on the islanders from Nantucket in a manner not so different from the famous anthropocentric chorus song in Sophocles' *Antigone*. Initially evoking the island's geographical and natural characteristics and reaching back to legendary times when Nantucket was settled by American Indians, halfway into the chapter Melville describes the history and evolution of the Nantucketers in recorded time:

> What wonder, then, that these Nantucketers, born on a beach, should take to the sea for a livelihood! They first caught crabs and quahogs in the sand; grown bolder, they waded out with nets for mackerel; more experienced, they pushed off in boats and captured cod; and at last, launching a navy of great ships on the sea, explored this watery world; put an incessant belt of circumnavigations round it; peeped in at Behring's Straits; and in all seasons and all oceans declared everlasting war with the mightiest animated mass that has survived the flood; most monstrous and most mountainous! That Himmalehan, salt-sea, Mastodon, clothed with such portentousness of unconscious power, that his very panics are more to be dreaded than his most fearless and malicious assaults!
>
> And thus have these naked Nantucketers, these sea hermits, issuing from their ant-hill in the sea, overrun and conquered the watery world like so many Alexanders; parcelling out among them the Atlantic, Pacific, and Indian oceans [...]; two thirds of this terraqueous globe are the Nantucketer's. For the sea is his; he owns it, as Emperors own empires; other seamen having but a right of way through it. [...] The Nantucketer, he alone resides and riots on the sea; he alone, in Bible language, goes

down to it in ships; to and fro ploughing it as his own special plantation. *There* is his home; *there* lies his business, which a Noah's flood would not interrupt, though it overwhelmed all the millions in China. He lives on the sea, as prairie cocks in the prairie; he hides among the waves, he climbs them as chamois hunters climb the Alps. For years he knows not the land; [...] at nightfall, the Nantucketer, out of sight of land, furls his sails, and lays him to his rest, while under his very pillow rush herds of walruses and whales.[243]

The perspective is clearly anthropocentric. The undisputed protagonists of the passage are the people of Nantucket, admired and celebrated for their actions and deeds. Their evolution as islanders and people is one of linear progression ("grown bolder"), hegemonic colonization ("overrun and conquered"), steady expansion (from a local interaction with the sea to a global oceanic authority), utilitarian cultivation ("ploughing it as his own special plantation"), and cartographic distribution ("parcelling out").

The relationship between the Nantucketers and nature is partly one of collaboration, partly one of rivalry, more specifically of the Nantucketers' dominance over nature. However, this domination is not unequivocal; the "assaults" and "panics" of both the sea and its most dreaded creature, Leviathan, are still to be feared by humans. Melville portrays an era in which the link between man and nature is still uncontaminated by modern technology. The American Indian settlers embarked upon the Atlantic Ocean in small canoes searching for their lost kin with only the aid of manpower and wind. Later, with their sea-conquering whaling fleet, the Nantucketers colonized the seven seas relying on their extraordinary navigational and seafaring skills, and on the currents, the winds, and the sails.

Before discussing the temporality, worldview, and style of the novel's anthropocentric component, I introduce one more scene to support my analysis. In the whale hunting scenes—the one quoted from below is part of "Stubb Kills a Whale"—the celebratory tone from "Nantucket" is maintained. But instead of the narrator's more physically and temporally distant perspective from outside, Melville transports us into the very action of the whale hunt through an inside perspective attached to the action (i.e., not to the psychology of the whalers) as it unfolds; that is, the narrator is both physically and temporally proximate:

"There go flukes!" was the cry, an announcement immediately followed by Stubb's producing his match and igniting his pipe, for now a respite

---

243 Melville, *Moby-Dick*, 64.

was granted. After the full interval of his sounding had elapsed, the whale rose again, and being now in advance of the smoker's boat, and much nearer to it than to any of the others, Stubb counted upon the honor of the capture. It was obvious, now, that the whale had at length become aware of his pursuers. All silence of cautiousness was therefore no longer of use. Paddles were dropped, and oars came loudly into play. And still puffing at his pipe, Stubb cheered on his crew to the assault.

Yes, a mighty change had come over the fish. All alive to his jeopardy, he was going "head out"; that part obliquely projecting from the mad yeast which he brewed.

[...] "Start her, now; give 'em the long and strong stroke, Tashtego. Start her, Tash, my boy—start her, all; but keep cool, keep cool—cucumbers is the word—easy, easy—only start her like grim death and grinning devils, and raise the buried dead perpendicular out of their graves, boys—that's all. Start her!"

"Woo-hoo! Wa-hee!" screamed the Gay-Header in reply, raising some old war-whoop to the skies [...].

But his wild screams were answered by others quite as wild. "Kee-hee! Kee-hee!" yelled Daggoo, straining forwards and backwards on his seat, like a pacing tiger in his cage.

"Ka-la! Koo-loo!" howled Queequeg, as if smacking his lips over a mouthful of Grenadier's steak. And thus with oars and yells the keels cut the sea. [...] Like desperadoes they tugged and they strained, till the welcome cry was heard—"Stand up, Tashtego!—give it to him!" The harpoon was hurled.[244]

As in "Nantucket," we are dealing with a pre-technocentric bond between man, nature, and animal. This is an enchanted world in the way Max Weber understood it. To Weber, the process of modernity was a constant development towards a more and more disenchanted world. *Entzauberung*, or disenchantment, results from an increasingly rational (as opposed to magical) legitimation of human behavior, which consequently becomes purpose-guided and future-oriented. Rational behavior is always an investment in potential, and sometimes even pre-calculable, future outcomes and thus entails an idea of mankind's greater control of surroundings, an ability to master (or at least reduce or productively cope with) contingency.[245] The transition from an enchanted

---

244 Melville, *Moby-Dick*, 283–84.
245 Max Weber, "Wissenschaft als Beruf," in *Wissenschaft als Beruf. Politik als Beruf, Max Weber-Gesamtausgabe*, vol. I/17, ed. Wolfgang J. Mommsen and Wolfgang Schluchter

world into a disenchanted one produces several side effects, which manifest in relation to temporality, spatiality, and existentiality. Future-orientedness, abstraction, and meaning replace immediacy, concretization, and presence.

Melville's whale hunt belongs predominantly to the enchanted world as does the discourse of "Nantucket." In the hunting scenes, the modus of time is the *hic et nunc* of immediacy. The whalers are absorbed in the present moment of the hunt that involves the bodies, senses, and instincts of all participants. The hunt does not allow time for reflection nor for abstraction or future planning. However, if time in the actual hunting scenes is a temporality of the immediate, the context supplies these scenes with a touch of nostalgia. The reason is the reader's awareness—transported to us by the different world pictures and discourses of *Moby-Dick*—of the enchanted world's termination in the near future. When Ishmael visits the Spouter-Inn, he feels inclined to describe the many exhibited maritime objects—paintings, clubs, spears, and lances—in a language of legend evoking the heroism of whale hunters of the near past: "With this once long lance, now wildly elbowed, fifty years ago did Nathan Swain kill fifteen whales between a sunrise and a sunset."[246] The praxis of the past is here inextricably linked with the description of concrete objects. Remembering presupposes this description, because in Melville description of objects always has an evocative potential. Implicitly, Ishmael nostalgically draws a line between the enchanted near past and present, "the knightly days of our profession,"[247] on the one side, and the disenchanted present and near future on the other.

As for literary style in the anthropocentric universe, Melville employs the style of romance and adventure characterized by an emphasis on human deeds and a relatively linear progression of plot. In these passages, Melville draws on a tradition running as far back as the Hellenistic and Chivalric romances, and closer to his own time on a tradition that includes Defoe and Fielding. It is a tradition that contrasts with the sentimental and psychological tradition of Richardson and Rousseau. Whereas *Pamela* and *Confessions* explore biography, inner feelings, and the intimacy of indoor private life, *Robinson Crusoe* focuses on practical problem solving, on recording the objects of the empirical outdoor world, and on surviving in dangerous and unknown territory.[248]

(Tübingen: Mohr Siebeck, 1922), 49–111; Walter M. Sprondel, "Entzauberung," in *Historisches Wörterbuch der Philosophie*, vol. 2, ed. Joachim Ritter and Karlfried Gründer (Darmstadt: Wissenschaftliche Buchgesellschaft, 1972), 564–65.

246   Melville, *Moby-Dick*, 13.
247   Melville, *Moby-Dick*, 361.
248   Cohen, "Literary Studies on the Terraqueous Globe," 661.

If we think of the defining features of "historical time"—irrelevant past, transitory present, open future—the anthropocentric universe in *Moby-Dick* represents a different temporality. If past experiences had become useless points of orientation in the present during "historical time" (because the future was now expected to be something new), the exploits of the whalers depend on the transmission and internalization of experience and skills from the older generations of whale hunters. The present is a temporality of immediacy and nostalgia, so the future becomes irrelevant and undesirable to a certain degree. If anything, the chronotope of the anthropocentric universe is closer to Koselleck's image of the agrarian world in which space of experience and horizon of expectation were still closely linked and almost converging.

5.4   *Technocentrism*

Moby-Dick also comprises a technocentric universe, which partly overlaps and partly contrasts with the anthropocentric world. Here, Melville writes enthusiastically about the effectiveness and productivity of industrialism and about the comforts it provides for humans. The passages quoted above belonging to the novel's anthropocentric universe contained seeds to "historical time": "Nantucket" in the form of historical progress and human agency, "Stubb Kills a Whale" in the form of human agency, although the horizon of expectation was here less important than the immersion in the here and now action of whale hunting. However, they were examples of a pre-technocentric and enchanted world of (sometimes agonistic) collaboration between mankind and nature. In the technocentric universe, on the contrary, the world is disenchanted, bereft of magic, and governed by rationality. The relationship between humans and nature becomes increasingly mediated through technology, so humans to a larger extent dominate nature and master its contingencies. The modus of time changes from a temporality of immediacy and nostalgia to one of presentiment and future-orientedness. Because of nature's diminished role, *Moby-Dick* is less concerned with man's battles against nature, and this influences the style of the novel. Instead of romance and adventure, the novel reveals traits of realism and protomodernism, when the narrator resorts to the encyclopedia, and the characters gradually turn their attention inward to confrontations with their own psychological depths.

In the nineteenth-century chronotope of "historical time," people realize that time is an agent of transformation and that all phenomena are affected by the change in time. It is no coincidence that it is during this period that literary realism, with its propensity for meticulously describing the appearance and emotions of the characters as well as the design, function, and colors of the objects of the outer world, emerges. Balzac is one of the first authors to depict a world in which history is experienced as inevitable change. To cope with this transitive quality of the present, he develops the art of description. The minute recording of appearances is a way of saving them from their imminent disappearance, or, in Milan Kundera's words: "Man began to understand that he was not going to die in the same world he had been born into." Consequently, everything had to be described before it disappeared. To Kundera, description can therefore be defined as "compassion for the ephemeral; salvaging the perishable." The concreteness of everyday objects, personal trifles, and natural phenomena suddenly become a major topic in novels. This is why Balzac's Paris is nothing like Fielding's London. In Balzac, the squares have their names, the houses their colors, the streets their smells and sounds. Balzac's Paris is the Paris of a specific moment, Paris as it had not been before and as it would never be again. Every scene of Balzac's novels "is stamped (be it only by the shape of a chair or the cut of a suit) by History which, now that it has emerged from the shadows, sculpts and re-sculpts the look of the world."[249]

Melville is part of that same world. He was acutely aware of the radical transformation of the maritime world due to technological developments. A strong discourse in *Moby-Dick* is thus a Balzacian urge to salvage the perishable through description. Melville's choice of naming many chapters after concrete objects (carpet bag, wheelbarrow, cabin table, cassock, lamp, musket, etc.) and devoting large parts of these chapters to meticulously describing these objects can be interpreted in this light. Around each object Melville draws a specific (maritime) culture and praxis, and he feels the urgency of doing so because things are changing and will eventually disappear.

The awareness of inexorable change has as one of its side effects the belief in progress and continual expansion of human knowledge, articulated by Kant as *Fortschritt* and by Koselleck as "long-term expectation of a new future." In the cetological chapters in *Moby-Dick*, Melville is a child of this belief. In "Cetology," Melville's ambition is nothing short of penetrating the "[i]mpenetrable veil covering our knowledge of the cetacea," and he wants to do this by putting before the reader "some systematized exhibition of the whale in his broad genera": "The classification of the constituents of a chaos, nothing less is here essayed."[250] A little later in the same chapter, the narrator stresses that he is merely "the architect, not the builder," and then elaborates on his project, this "draught of a systematization of cetology":

---

249 Milan Kundera, *The Curtain: An Essay in Seven Parts*, trans. Linda Archer (London: Faber and Faber, 2007), 14.
250 Melville, *Moby-Dick*, 134.

HISTORY

> But it is a ponderous task; no ordinary letter-sorter in the Post-Office is equal to it. To grope down into the bottom of the sea after them; to have one's hands among the unspeakable foundations, ribs, and very pelvis of the world; this is a fearful thing. What am I that I should essay to hook the nose of this leviathan! [...] But I have swam through libraries and sailed through oceans; I have had to do with whales with these visible hands; I am in earnest; and I will try.[251]

Melville presents a two-fold legitimization of his ambition of "cetological letter sorting," one *cerebral* ("I have swam through libraries"), the other *practical* ("and sailed through oceans; I have had to do with whales with these visible hands"). In a scientific tradition, he has read everything there is to read about whales, but at the same time his scientific enterprise of defining, describing, and classifying the whale is backed up by empiricism through his own hands-on experiences. The entire style of "Cetology" is maintained in the style of a natural science book and with clear categorizations between the folio whale, the octavo whale, and the duodecimo whale as well as between their respective subgenera. If there is a conviction in the novel's anthropocentric enchanted universe that the whale "eludes both hunters and philosophers,"[252] the ambition in the technocentric universe is *to replace possibility and probability with certainty though comprehensive description.*

A word of caution, though. "Cetology" is, as are other chapters such as "Extracts" and "Etymology" whose objective is encyclopedic, marked by irony and a self-conscious awareness of the encyclopedic ambition's futility. This realization of incompleteness has further implications: "It is significant that the narrative's classification systems are not simply incomplete; they are in draft form, which invites the reader's participation in the work of progress."[253] To Melville, maritime labor, scientific efforts, and works of literature are all collective democratic endeavors.

Another example of technocentrism is found in "The Chart," in which the narrator describes how Captain Ahab with the help of "a large wrinkled roll of yellowish sea charts" "of all four oceans" and "piles of old log-books" is trying to "seek out one solitary creature in the unhooped oceans of this planet." If this seems "an absurdly hopeless task" to most of us, Ahab, on the contrary, "knew the sets of all tides and currents; and thereby calculating the driftings of the sperm whale's food; and, also calling to mind the regular, ascertained seasons

---

251   Melville, *Moby-Dick*, 136.
252   Melville, *Moby-Dick*, 140.
253   Blum, *View from the Masthead*, 130.

for hunting him in particular latitudes; could arrive at reasonable surmises, almost approaching to certainties, concerning the timeliest day to be upon this or that ground in search of his prey." As with the cetology, there is a conviction that "all possibilities would become probabilities" and "every probability the next thing to a certainty."[254] Weber's disenchanted world of pre-calculable futures and rational presents is given poetic voice.

If cetology and cartography contribute to the transformation of the Atlantic into a "settled and civilized ocean," other discourses reinforce the novel's technocentrism. Melville treats the question of money and capitalism with ambivalence. He describes cash as a natural inclination of man ("man is a money-making animal") and celebrates it as a motor that drives progress and expansion. In "The Advocate," Melville resorts to statistics and numbers to draw the reader's attention to the financial and material benefits of whale hunting: "we whalemen of America now outnumber all the rest of the banded whalemen in the world; sail a navy of upwards of seven hundred vessels; manned by eighteen thousand men; yearly consuming 4,000,000 of dollars; the ships worth, at the time of sailing, $20,000,000! and every year importing into our harbors a well reaped harvest of $7,000,000." What could be labeled existential dominance in the anthropocentric sections of the novel is here transformed into utilitarian and financial dominance. Money also dehumanizes the universe as when Stubb yells to Pip, "a whale would sell for thirty times what you would, Pip, in Alabama," just as it implies an elimination of animal species such as the whale, of which it is said that "he must die the death and be murdered."[255]

The influence of technocentrism on the style of *Moby-Dick* does not limit itself to realism in the concrete forms of description and encyclopedia. As the increased role of technology involves the taming of nature, the adventurous style of the anthropocentric universe in which the sailor was in constant heroic battles with nature is replaced by a protomodernist style in which the sailors are physically battling each other or psychologically battling with themselves. However, if Melville occasionally turns away from the traditional discourse of maritime fiction—action and adventure—and instead employs a style of introspection and psychology, he is, like Dostoyevsky, closer to twentieth-century authors such as Rilke, Döblin, and Joyce than to, say, Richardson. In Melville's writing, the ocean provides a context for introspection similar to that of the metropolis in Rilke, Döblin, and Joyce. Paris, Berlin, and Dublin are

---

254 Melville, *Moby-Dick*, 198–99, 199, 200.
255 Melville, *Moby-Dick*, 245, 413, 109, 413, 357.

urban oceans of chaotic impressions and cacophonic multitudes, just as the Atlantic and the Pacific are oceanic metropolises of multiethnic encounters and capitalist ventures. The domestic intimacy of Richardson is replaced with a propensity for madness, schizophrenia, and paralysis. Captain Ahab's soliloquies in this respect are famous: "They think me mad—Starbuck does; but I'm demoniac, I am madness maddened! That wild madness that's only calm to comprehend itself!" Captain Ahab is a precursor for twentieth-century atrocities and genuine technocentrism. Hence, when he exclaims: "all my means are sane, my motive and my object mad,"[256] he appears as an early version of Adolf Hitler and Joseph Stalin, whose inhumanity was accentuated by the very rational processes facilitating it.

In the technocentric universe of *Moby-Dick*, the chronotope of historical time has come to the fore. Now, the past has become increasingly irrelevant in the sense that it is no longer able to provide points of orientation, and the present is transitory, a steppingstone towards an open future of possibilities. This is most manifest in the descriptive, capitalist, and scientific discourses of *Moby-Dick*, although it is sometimes difficult to distinguish these from the anthropocentric universe of immediacy and nostalgia and the geocentric universe of prophecy and menace. The relationship between humans and nature is now so saturated with technology that technology becomes the dominant actor in the triangle, something that entails a general disenchantment of the world. Finally, the styles of adventure and romance give way to both realism (description) and protomodernism (introspection, fragmentation).

5.5   *Geocentrism*

Geocentrism entails an insertion of the terraqueous planet as the most vital component of the novel's cosmos. This reconfiguration of the cosmos in which humans and technology recede in order to make way for nature holds three possible outcomes. First, Melville outlines a genuine *re-enchantment* of the world supported by a poetical and lyrical discourse. One example is the description of sperm lump squeezing in "Squeeze of a Hand":

> It had cooled and crystallized to such a degree, that when, with several others, I sat down before a large Constantine's bath of it, I found it strangely concreted into lumps, here and there rolling about in the liquid part. It was our business to squeeze these lumps back into fluid. A sweet and unctuous duty! No wonder that in old times sperm was such a

---

256   Melville, *Moby-Dick*, 168, 186.

favorite cosmetic. Such a clearer! such a sweetener! such a softener; such a delicious mollifier! After having my hands in it for only a few minutes, my fingers felt like eels, and began, as it were, to serpentine and spiralize.

As I sat there at my ease, cross-legged on the deck; after the bitter exertion at the windlass; under a blue tranquil sky; the ship under indolent sail, and gliding so serenely along; as I bathed my hands among those soft, gentle globules of infiltrated tissues, wove almost within the hour; as they richly broke to my fingers, and discharged all their opulence, like fully ripe grapes their wine; as I snuffed up that uncontaminated aroma,- literally and truly, like the smell of spring violets; I declare to you, that for the time I lived as in a musky meadow; I forgot all about our horrible oath; in that inexpressible sperm, I washed my hands and my heart of it; I almost began to credit the old Paracelsan superstition that sperm is of rare virtue in allaying the heat of anger; while bathing in that bath, I felt divinely free from all ill-will, or petulance, or malice, of any sort whatsoever.

Squeeze! squeeze! squeeze! all the morning long; I squeezed that sperm till I myself almost melted into it; I squeezed that sperm till a strange sort of insanity came over me; and I found myself unwittingly squeezing my co-laborers' hands in it, mistaking their hands for the gentle globules. Such an abounding, affectionate, friendly, loving feeling did this avocation beget; that at last I was continually squeezing their hands, and looking up into their eyes sentimentally; as much as to say,- Oh! my dear fellow beings, why should we longer cherish any social acerbities, or know the slightest ill-humor or envy! Come; let us squeeze hands all round; nay, let us all squeeze ourselves into each other; let us squeeze ourselves universally into the very milk and sperm of kindness.[257]

Melville's language turns lyrical in these geocentric passages, and the scene evokes images of pastoral landscapes, universal brotherhood (including homoerotic pleasure), and cosmic harmony between nature and humankind. The lyricism is continued in "The Pacific" and "The Symphony" in which the synchronicity between ocean, ship, and man and between ocean, whales, and man are depicted in poetically dense prose.

Second, in the style of allegory Melville prophesies an ecological apocalypse in which mankind's Faustianism, its transgressive expansionism and haughtiness (e.g., Ahab's "fatal pride"), triggers an irreversible planetary evolution ultimately resulting in a *posthuman world*. However, if humans are

---

257 Melville, *Moby-Dick*, 415–16.

eradicated, nature is reborn. The novel's famous ending could be interpreted in this way: "then all collapsed, and the great shroud of the sea rolled on as it rolled five thousand years ago." This is a universe of "foolish mortals" in which "science and skill" will never prevent the sea from "insult[ing] and murder[ing]" humans. In this world, "the masterless ocean overruns the globe" and "this antemosaic, unsourced existence," the whale, "must needs exist after all humane ages are over."[258]

Third, the novel operates with a version of history in which not only humankind, but also *nature and the planet are wiped out*. As previously mentioned, Carl Schmitt once remarked that industrialization transformed the ocean from a big fish into a machine. Today, we can see that global consumerism has converted the ocean from machine into plastic. Melville was gifted with "divine intuitions" in that respect; this is why Ishmael often feels "foreboding shivers" running over him. Common to the three outcomes is a basic and, for Melville's time, early ecological awareness and mindset. In the first version, the transgressions and mistakes of mankind can still be remedied; in the second, this is only half true, as it entails an annihilation of humans, whereas "the sea will have its way";[259] and in the third version, the outcome is total destruction.

Our contemporaneity is defined by a growing concern with the negative impacts that human activity has on the environment. From first-hand experiences as well as in his writings, Melville dealt with several geopolitical themes that are now part of early twenty-first century concerns: "Pacific Rim commerce, colonialism, deliberate or careless destruction of indigenous cultures and environments, exploitation of nature, racism, enslavement, immigration."[260] Whales are no longer merely the victims of commercial and industrialized whaling but also of massive and increasing oceanic pollution.

The menacing aspect of the future of "broad present" is obvious here; the future is no longer an open horizon of positive expectations as in "historical time" and the technocentric universe. The temporal modus of the novel's geocentric parts is one of premonition, prophecy, and fatality, "fatal to the last degree of fatality";[261] the point of orientation is the distant future (of destruction). If chance and free will ruled the universes of anthropocentrism and technocentrism, necessity rules the universe of geocentrism. Agency has become problematic or even illusory because no action is possible where no place

---

258 Melville, *Moby-Dick*, 519, 572, 273–74, 457.
259 Melville, *Moby-Dick*, 374, 123, 504.
260 Hershel Parker and Harrison Hayford, "Preface," in Herman Melville, *Moby-Dick; or, the Whale* (New York and London: W. W. Norton, 2002), x.
261 Melville, *Moby-Dick*, 180.

exists for its realization to be projected. The fatalism and skepticism toward human agency in Melville endow his work with a tragic view of history.

Necessity alone does not rule the Melvillean world. One reason that *Moby-Dick* continues to fascinate is its complexity, its holding together of a present that in Gumbrecht's words "has turned into a dimension of expanding simultaneities": "aye, chance, free will, and necessity—no wise incompatible—all interweavingly working together."[262] Chance, free will, and necessity are not the only divergent phenomena coexisting in *Moby-Dick*. It is a novel flooded with pasts belonging to theocentric, anthropocentric, and technocentric universes. Like Gumbrecht's "broad present," *Moby-Dick* lacks clear contours and thus falls into Henry James' pejorative category of "large, loose baggy monsters."[263] But herein lies its longevity, timelessness, and prophetic potential.

Below is a table summarizing this chapter's findings regarding *Moby-Dick* (Table 1). There are overlaps between the categories, concepts, and attributes. This said, the table shows that it is possible to systematize the complexity of the novel. This is conceived as a pedagogical exercise that may help the reader to better grasp the novel. It is also meant as a strategy for understanding why complexity is not simply another word for chaos and what one early reviewer of the English version called an "ill-compounded mixture."[264] In Melville's case, complexity refers to a highly ambitious and serious encyclopedic project comprising an inherent potential for longevity.

---

262   Melville, *Moby-Dick*, 215.
263   Henry James, "Preface to The Tragic Muse," in *The Tragic Muse* (New York: Charles Scribner's Sons, 1922), x.
264   Anonymous (Henry F. Chorley), "*The Whale*. By Herman Melville, Author of 'Typee,' &c. &c.," *London Athenæum* 1252 (October 25, 1851): 1112–13.

TABLE 1 The coexisting world pictures in *Moby-Dick*.

World picture	Theocentric –1450	Anthropocentric 1450–1850	Technocentric 1850–1950	Geocentric 1950–
Chronotope	Eschatological time	Agrarian time (Koselleck)	Historical time (Koselleck)	Broad present (Gumbrecht)
Past	Incomplete	Relevant	Irrelevant	Flooding
Present	Transitory	Immediacy	Transitory	Broad
Future	Complete (failed)	Irrelevant (repeat)	Open (possibility)	Closed (menace)
Figure of time	Linear	Cyclical	Linear	Impasse
Tonality	Reverential/ Prophetical	Nostalgic	Premonitory	Reverential/ Prophetical
Human	Humans	**Humans**	Humans	Humans
Technology	(Technology)	Technology	**Technology**	Technology
Nature	< ≠	> ≈ ≠	> ≠	< ≈ ≠
	God/Nature	Nature	(Nature)	**Nature**
Ontology	Enchanted/ Apocalyptic	Enchanted	Disenchanted	Re-enchanted/ Apocalyptic
Ocean	Marvel/ Monster	Fish	Machine	Fish/ Plastic
Style	Lyrical/ Allegorical	Romance, Adventure	Realism, Protomodernism	Lyrical/ Allegorical

CHAPTER 2

Rhythm

In popular imagination, especially during the period spanning from the oceanic turn around 1450 until the first half of the twentieth century, ship life was enveloped in romantic ideas of unlimited freedom, unbounded movement, and unconditional escape, but also in more realist notions such as hard work, brutal violence, and claustrophobic spaces. In the same period, the sea was simultaneously admired and feared for its formless sublimity, chaotic rage, and mysterious depths. Ship and sea are empty containers into which we can pour whatever content we want. They are endowed with hyper-metaphorical potential. To mention a few examples, some of which we have already touched upon: In "The Book of Genesis," the ocean is initially associated with primeval chaos and later, when materialized as the flood, with punishment for sin.[1] To Horace, the sea represents an earthly reminder of the "sacred bar" between gods and humans and between different peoples, hence his idea of *oceanus dissociabilis*.[2] In Shakespeare's *Hamlet* (1599–1602), the salty waters of the Øresund off the cliffs at Kronborg in Elsinore are associated with and thought to trigger madness.[3] In Hegel's *Philosophy of Right* (1820), the ocean is the condition of possibility for international trade, societal development, and personal *Bildung*.[4] And in James Joyce's *Ulysses* (1922), it is described as the "great sweet mother" and likened to the Ur-womb.[5]

As for the ship, two authors close to each other historically, Tobias Smollett and James Fenimore Cooper, had very different notions of what it represented. In *Roderick Random* (1748), Smollett likened the ship to a miniature version of a corrupt society, and also to a decaying health institution smelling of rot, as well as a prison whose inmates were plagued by fleas, tormented by the whip, and controlled by evil and incompetence.[6] Cooper replaced Smollett's neoclassical mindset with a romantic one and mirrored Hegel's more positive notions of sea and ship, when he considered the ship in *The Red Rover* (1827) as the

---

1   *The Holy Bible*, "The Book of Genesis," 1.2, 6.5–17, 7.17–24.
2   Horace, *The Odes and Carmen Saeculare of Horace*, I, iii.
3   William Shakespeare, *Hamlet*, ed. Ann Thompson and Neil Taylor, Arden Shakespeare (1599–1602; London: Methuen Drama, 2006), 1.4.
4   Hegel, *Philosophy of Right*, 268.
5   James Joyce, *Ulysses* (1922; London: Penguin, 1995), Book 1.
6   Smollett, *Roderick Random*, 150–51, 157–60, 189–90.

incarnation of graceful movement and endowed it with a potential for heroism in its rivalry with the elements.[7] If we return to Horace and the stoic sensibility, he saw the ship as the material symbol of human nemesis and haughtiness—"a luckless bark" he calls it—since it was the vehicle facilitating the transgression of a divinely sanctioned border.[8] Historically more recent is Jens Bjørneboe, who likens the steamship to a patient "suffering from a combination of heart disease and asthma," whereas the sailing ship is endowed with erotic qualities and supreme beauty.[9] As this small-scale historical survey shows, there is no end to the semantic and metaphorical potential and varieties of the sea and the ship.

Apart from the metaphorization of sea and ship, certain attributes are historically associated with the sailor, the ship, and the sea. The sailor was considered a vagrant, rootless creature who was at home anywhere and therefore nowhere. The ship was associated with mobility, not least because it travels the ocean, an ever-changing element on which no human can ever hope to rest or create a permanent abode. These associations are not wrong, but they are incomplete. Marine life has other valuable dimensions, a life determined by ever expanding movements and formless conditions but also by centripetal forces and domesticating rhythms. One objective in what follows is to examine the moments of homeliness and stability that also characterize maritime existence along with its potential risks, conflicts, and breakdowns. Whether the focus is on homelessness or homeliness, the basic premise of this chapter is that rhythms constitute a privileged starting point for analyzing and describing ship life in a nuanced, concrete, and bodily way.

1 The Maritime between Homelessness and Homeliness

In Carsten Jensen's novel *We, The Drowned* (2006), pastor Abildgaard and Albert Madsen discuss the difference between the peasant and the sailor. Albert is convinced that the pastor regards sailors as "the rootless, restless, stateless freebooters," because "Given his shackled life, the farmer fitted the basic Christian vision better than the sailor did. All those messages about bowing your head

---

7 James Fenimore Cooper, *The Red Rover: A Tale*, in *The Writings of James Fenimore Cooper*, ed. Thomas and Marianne Philbrick (1827; Albany: State University of New York Press, 1991), 150, 168, 255–56, 397, 398–99, 414. For a comparison between Smollett and Cooper, see also Philbrick, *Fenimore Cooper and the Development of American Sea Fiction*, 5–6, 72–78.
8 Horace, *The Odes*, I, xiv; I, iii.
9 Bjørneboe, *The Sharks*, 125, 26.

and throwing yourself on the mercy of fate were made for him. Of course a sailor was also subject to the whims of nature, but he challenged the weather and the sea; he was something of a rebel." In opposition to the pastor, Albert highly values this defiance and greatly appreciates the potentially edifying confrontation with all things foreign and different in maritime life. During World War I, while the Marstal fleet was forced to temporarily anchor up in port, Albert fears that the sailors shall "grow as stupid as the farmers" since a farmer "spends his life ploughing the same old furrow."[10]

Albert's conversation with pastor Abildgaard and his thoughts on sailor life mirror a widespread conception of life on board ocean-going ships as one dominated by movement. However, a mobile life is valued differently by the pastor and Albert. Whereas Abildgaard associates it negatively with homelessness, for Albert it conjures up inspiring encounters with new languages, customs, and ways of thinking. Peasant life, which is also grounded in a shared starting point, stasis, contains an axiological duality, too: the pastor's positive "fellowship"[11] emerges from a common language and a shared history versus Albert's negative associations of peasantry with stupidity and place-boundness.

In Yi-Fu Tuan's *Space and Place: The Perspective of Experience* (1977), we come across a similar structural dichotomy signaled in the "space" and "place" of the title. Interestingly, the book's prototypical space is the ocean, whereas place is associated with home on earth. Tuan's ocean has a positive connotation with "freedom," which is partly due to its "limitless horizon and unrestricted space," and partly a result of his determination of space "as that which allows movement." However, "openness, infinity, unrestricted space" can also be threatening, not least because the ocean is undifferentiated and abstract, that is, ungraspable, formless, and placeless. Tuan's home has a positive connotation with "security," partly due to its "stability," partly a consequence of his determination of landbased place as a "pause" and as "centers of felt value where biological needs, such as those for food, water, rest, and procreation, are satisfied." The negative connotation of Tuan's home is that stability and security can also feel too "narrow and restrictive."[12]

My intention in the following is not so much to decide for or against the specific values—freedom and placelessness versus security and narrow-mindedness—that are associated with maritime and domestic (agrarian)

---

10   Carsten Jensen, *We, The Drowned*, trans. Charlotte Barslund with Emma Ryder (2006; London: Vintage, 2011), 262, 260, 260, 261.
11   Jensen, *We, The Drowned*, 261.
12   Yi-Fu Tuan, *Space and Place: The Perspective of Experience* (1977; Minneapolis and London: University of Minnesota Press, 2001), 3–6.

life, respectively. Instead, I would like to nuance the one-dimensional focus on movement, placelessness, infinity, and freedom that dominate conceptions of ship life. An example of this line of thinking is found in Michel Foucault's "Of Other Spaces" ("Des espaces autres") in which he describes the ship as "a floating piece of space" (*un morceau flottant d'espace*).[13] A genuine insider perspective that supports the idea of maritime homelessness is expressed by the American naval captain Frederick Chamier. In his autobiographical *The Life of a Sailor* (1831–32), he describes himself as "a wandering sailor" and claims that he "never felt the luxury of repose excepting in bed."[14]

Somewhat surprisingly, it is possible to find a corrective to this traditional stereotype of the sailor as vagrant, homeless, and restless in Conrad's *Heart of Darkness*. Here, the anonymous narrator describes Marlow as an atypical sailor:

> He was the only man of us who still "followed the sea." The worst that could be said of him was that he did not represent his class. He was a seaman, but he was a wanderer, too, while most seamen lead, if one may so express it, a sedentary life. Their minds are of the stay-at-home order, and their home is always with them—the ship; and so is their country—the sea. One ship is very much another, and the sea is always the same.[15]

The sailor, the ship, and the sea are typically linked with mobility, fluidity, and *terra infirma* as the examples from Jensen, Tuan, Foucault, and Chamier show. My intention is to take seriously Conrad's inversion of the relationship between home and homelessness in the maritime sphere. I do so by examining moments of homeliness and stability amid the fundamental homelessness and instability of maritime life. It is not my aim to disregard the dynamism and insecurity of maritime life, but are there not pauses and stability—the values we usually associate with peasant life, home, and earth—associated with maritime life? If there are, how do these phenomena manifest? In short: *What contributes to the homeliness of the ship and the sea?*

The purpose of this examination is not to blur the ontological differences between land and sea and between home and ship. I do not wish to transform the ship into something terrestrial. By opening our senses to (literature's staging

---

13 Michel Foucault, "Of Other Spaces," *Diacritics* 16, no. 1 (Spring 1986): 27; Michel Foucault, "Des espaces autres," 1967/1984, in *Dits et écrits*, vol. 4 (Paris: Gallimard, 1994), 762.
14 Frederick Chamier, *The Life of a Sailor*, vol. 3 (1831–32; London: Richard Bentley, 1832), 202–03.
15 Conrad, *Heart of Darkness*, 48.

of) the physical, bodily, and material nature of ship life—to the fundamental rhythms that emerge in the assemblage of ocean, ship, sky, crew, aquatic creatures, colors, sounds, and winds—the aim is to reach a more nuanced understanding of what being on board a ship on the open sea really means. This understanding partly supports and partly challenges the traditional image of maritime life as one dominated by directionlessness, drifting, homelessness, and placelessness.

Instead of being considered a superfluous and uninteresting intermezzo between two homes and two pieces of land, the sea journey is granted a value in and of itself. It is not only about bestowing the "away" in the "home-away-home" structure a privileged place; it is more like a genuine inversion of the conceptual values of these places, so "home-away-home" morphs into "away-home-away." The *ship* is home. The sailor is at home on the ship. Melville's *White-Jacket; or, The World in a Man-of-War* (1850) was a radical example. As indicated by the title, the entire world of the narrator-protagonist and the reader is a man-of-war.

Foucault characterized the ship as "a floating piece of space," and in the same lecture says that the ship is "a place without a place" ("un lieu sans lieu").[16] In his definition of the ship, Foucault mobilizes both place ("a place") and space ("without a place"). With Tuan we can say that "a place without a place" indicates that we can associate the ship with form, security, and homeliness, while the ocean is the ultimately placeless. At first glance, it seems logical that the ship is "without a place," first because it is always on the move, second because it moves on a permanently fluid element. But how can we talk about the ship as a "place"? To be mobile, and to be mobile on a fluid surface, does not mean that the ship itself is exclusively "a floating piece of space." Admittedly, the ship floats *on* a "space," on a *terra infirma*, but it is possible that the ship is a "place" with an inner organization and structure.

In order for the ship to move on the ocean, the "smooth space par excellence" as put by Deleuze and Guattari,[17] it is determined by an urgent need for stability, for order and organization, and for being a place with its own placial qualities. These qualities are necessary because the ship is constantly surrounded by the ocean which is the incarnation of flux, "a soup of space" according to Edward S. Casey where place can be lost,[18] and thus a potentially

---

16 Foucault, "Of Other Spaces," 27; Foucault, "Des espaces autres," 762.
17 Gilles Deleuze and Félix Guattari, *A Thousand Plateaus: Capitalism and Schizophrenia*, trans. by Brian Massumi (1980; Minneapolis: University of Minnesota Press, 1987), 479.
18 Edward S. Casey, *Getting Back into Place: Toward a Renewed Understanding of the Place-World*, 2nd ed. (1993; Bloomington and Indianapolis: Indiana University Press, 2009), 3.

annihilating force that threatens the ship with destruction. This becomes clear in Bjørneboe's *The Sharks* when Peder Jensen exclaims: "There I stood on her planks, with the sky above me and the sea below. Great God, what a situation! Upward, the endless space of heaven; downward, the dark, bottomless sea."[19] It is in this sky-plank-sea sense that the ship transforms into a Deleuzian "fold" of the ocean: "inside space conforms to outside space: tent, igloo, boat."[20] The ocean "dictates" the ship, determining its form, organization, and functions. Blum connects the doings of the ocean and mariners in a similar line of thinking that stresses homeliness: "Leisure at sea, like labor, was dictated (and often abbreviated) by the environment. Mariners at rest spent time mending clothing, overhauling gear damaged by use or weather, writing letters home, reading, and telling stories or yarns. Their attention to and concern for order, neatness, and utility speaks to the paradoxical domesticity of life at sea."[21]

Another consequence of wanting to trace moments of homeliness and stability in maritime life is that instead of regarding the ocean as a medium of connection only, the ocean is conceived as a concrete political, historical, material, and symbolic place. If Foucault admits the ship a placial quality, he also says that the ocean is a nonplace—the ship is *sans lieu*. But in contrast to Foucault, I argue that we can ascribe placial qualities to the ocean. As Deleuze and Guattari observe, "smooth space is constantly being translated, transversed into a striated space."[22] This process takes place because the ocean

> was the first to encounter the demands of increasingly strict striation. The problem did not arise in proximity to land. On the contrary, the striation of the sea was a result of navigation on the open water. Maritime space was striated as a function of two astronomical and geographical gains: *bearings*, obtained by a set of calculations based on exact observation of the stars and the sun; and *the map*, which intertwines meridians and parallels, longitudes and latitudes, plotting regions known and unknown onto a grid.[23]

Deleuze and Guattari furthermore claim that "before longitude lines had been plotted, a very late development, there existed a complex and empirical nomadic system of navigation based on the wind and noise, the colors and

---

19 Bjørneboe, *The Sharks*, 16.
20 Deleuze and Guattari, *A Thousand Plateaus*, 478.
21 Blum, *View from the Masthead*, 111.
22 Deleuze and Guattari, *A Thousand Plateaus*, 474.
23 Deleuze and Guattari, *A Thousand Plateaus*, 479.

sounds of the seas."[24] So, prior to mathematization and the emerging scientific gaze there were already practices grounded in know-how and local expertise that contributed to the domestication of the ocean.

2   Rhythmanalysis at Sea

In what follows, my ambition is to show how the ship and the ocean are also territorialized spaces, that is, places. As for the ship, we can ask: What is it that holds the ship together and makes it a place? What contributes to the permanence of a mobile ship? What makes a ship a Latourian "immutable mobile," a transportable object that nevertheless maintains its form while in motion? More generally, how can we get closer to the concreteness of maritime existence, better understand the workings of the sea, and have more than an inkling how the ship functions? How to embrace the conflicting forces of monotony and disruption, confinement versus expansiveness, and culture contra nature in maritime life?

These questions lead to the choice of method. The basic idea of this chapter is that Henri Lefebvre's concept of rhythm and his method of rhythmanalysis developed in *Rhythmanalysis: Space, Time and Everyday Life* (the French original, *Éléments de rythmanalyse: Introduction à la connaissance des rythmes*, was published posthumously in 1992) are privileged points of departure when seeking a firmer grasp of what it means, or, rather, how it *feels* to be on board an ocean-going ship. I examine works by authors such as Samuel Taylor Coleridge, Joseph Conrad, and Jens Bjørneboe. These authors may have fueled the popular imagination with both romantic and realist images of life at sea; that is, with a semantics of the ocean and the ship. They have also provided us with some of the most aesthetically convincing, thematically complex, and existentially specific depictions of maritime existence. The purpose of this chapter is not to discuss the ship's role during the different accelerations of globalization, not to interpret how many symbolic meanings literary and cultural history have ascribed to the ocean, and not to analyze the ocean's vital role for the future of our anthropocene planet. The purpose is, with the help of literary works by Coleridge, Conrad, and Bjørneboe and others, to gain a greater understanding of what maritime existence actually is—concretely, physically, emotionally, and phenomenally—through the concept and phenomenon of rhythm. David Seamon, a proponent of "phenomenological geography," once

---

24   Deleuze and Guattari, *A Thousand Plateaus*, 479.

wrote: "A phenomenological geography asks the significance of people's inescapable immersion in a geographical world."[25] In line with this, I ask the significance of the sailor's temporarily inescapable immersion in the world of the ocean-going ship by performing an analysis of maritime rhythms.

Inherent in this approach is an implicit quarrel with hermeneutics and the primacy of meaning in the humanities. It offers a supplement to our constant interpretation of each and every detail, object, or phenomenon in more and more dubious ways. Lefebvre's method, his attention to the rhythmic (and arrhythmic) character of life, stands in opposition to the majority of the Western philosophical tradition, in which concepts such as representation, meaning, and interpretation have been dominant. Plato comes to mind, and in the early modern world Descartes's sharp distinction between body and mind and his prioritization of the cogito are also examples of this tradition. Contrary to this, the rhythmical has to do with the body and the senses, a striving "for the actualization of contact,"[26] and it does not possess a primary dimension of representation. A rhythm does not refer to anything but itself, which is also why it should not be interpreted. It does not stand for, or *re*-present, a hidden and deeper level of meaning. If anything, it must be sensed and felt, which does not exclude that a rhythm can affect us mentally; subsequently, it must be analyzed in its relationship to other rhythms and in its sensuous and bodily effects on us.

If we instead of looking back on philosophers such as Plato and Descartes confine our attention to the narrower time frame of the last four or five decades, then we also realize that the rhythmanalytical method may offer us a third way, an alternative to what have been two of the most dominant paradigms in literary studies and in the humanities, namely deconstruction and cultural studies.[27] Both paradigms agree that literature is a medium that attempts to represent reality. But to deconstruction this project is basically a *cul-de-sac* because of its radicalization of the Saussurean philosophy of language in which the link between signifier (sound pattern) and signified (concept) is arbitrary. Cultural studies operates with a relatively unproblematic relationship between language and reality, which results in a toning down of the problem of representation in favor of questions that are more concerned

---

25   David Seamon, "Body-Subject, Time-Space Routines, and Place-Ballets," in *The Human Experience of Space and Place*, eds. Anne Buttimer and David Seamon (London: Croom Helm, 1980), 148.
26   Seamon, "Body-Subject, Time-Space Routines, and Place-Ballets," 148.
27   Hans Ulrich Gumbrecht, *Stimmungen lesen: Über eine verdeckte Wirklichkeit der Literatur* (München: Carl Hanser Verlag, 2011), 8–10.

with (identity) politics. Since both paradigms operate with a literature ontology in which representation is central (either as a problem or as something unproblematic), literature must be interpreted. Literature *stands for something*, and this very *re*-presentational structure calls for a semantic determination of literature's statements about reality. Lefebvre's rhythmanalysis, with its predominantly descriptive (rather than interpretative) approach, offers a sobering alternative to the immanent tendency of relativism and subjectivism in hermeneutics. This does not imply that we can or should abandon hermeneutics completely. Focusing on rhythms means that we connect with other dimensions of reality and, in this case, with dimensions of literature and its portrayal of maritime existence beyond the purely semantic.

Arguably, rhythmanalysis is a method that does not offer new knowledge in the way we traditionally conceive of knowledge; that is, as meaning understood as something immaterial, yet essential, that lies hidden below the surface of phenomena, and which it is the task of humans to dig out through an effort of consciousness. Knowledge production on these terms is the task of hermeneutics. Rhythmanalysis instead points to the fact that the conditions for the production of knowledge can differ from how we usually conceive them. This is because rhythmanalysis situates the body and the mind of the analyzer *in* the world instead of mentally and consciously ex-centric to the world. It is also because it does not consider the world a surface that hides a series of semantic deep levels, but a phenomenal world of biological, cosmic, social, and cultural practices, phenomena, and energies that interact. The common denominator for all of those is that each is defined by its unique rhythm. Interactions between these rhythms either result in compromises or conflicts. Rhythmanalysis entails a shift in attention from the immaterial, the semantic, and the mental to the sensuous, the affective, and the bodily. It connects us more directly with the reality, which from the Renaissance and onwards we thought we had lost. Rhythms are not subsumed the paradigm of world representation; rather, they belong to the reality of the world.[28]

---

28   For a similar line of thought, although rhythm is replaced with *Stimmung*, see Gumbrecht, *Stimmungen lesen*, 34. It would be too big a task in this chapter to go deeper into a discussion of the differences and similarities between rhythm and *Stimmung*, but it is perhaps worth noting that a conceptual evolution can be traced in Gumbrecht's work from rhythm in "Rhythm and Meaning" (1988) to presence in *Production of Presence* (2003) culminating with *Stimmung* in *Stimmungen lesen* (2011). What is important here is that they are all part of Gumbrecht's ongoing attempt to propose alternatives to representational thinking and hermeneutical approaches. In terms of analytical operationality, I would say that rhythm is a better and handier concept than *Stimmung*, at least in the way Lefebvre

Besides addressing the questions of rhythm, meaning, and knowledge, I will also discuss, tentatively rather than extensively, the pedagogical challenges of Lefebvre's rhythmanalysis and the challenges it poses for the analyzer to communicate his or her findings. How are we supposed to teach if we are discouraged from interpreting? Hungry for knowledge, how will students react if we suddenly choose not to always serve up the meaning of a text for them? If meaning and interpretation are no longer our main concern, how are we supposed to write our analyses? I address the questions of knowledge, teaching, and writing at the end of this chapter, whereas the first and major part of the chapter will deal with rhythms at sea exemplified through literary examples from maritime fiction. Here the aim is to demonstrate 1) the analytical relevance of rhythmanalysis to the domain of maritime literature and culture and 2) that ship and sea are privileged and obvious places to examine the rhythmic character of human existence and the nonhuman world.

Rhythm and rhythmanalysis share a unique ability to embrace three common but somewhat incompatible approaches to the world: the phenomenological (the world as sensed through the body); the discursive (the world as imagined and mediated through language and culture); and the aesthetic (the world as mediated in an artistic form). In line with this tripartition, Lefebvre claims that rhythms can be 1) biological, cosmic, and natural, and 2) constructed, cultural, and social, and 3) aesthetic, formal, and stylistic. Cosmic rhythms (e.g., seasons and tides) are independent of man. Although Latour and others have convincingly shown how interwoven the natural and the manmade are,[29] it can benefit us analytically to operate with the two spheres as distinct. In addition, humans create socio-cultural rhythms (e.g., meals and working hours), just as they employ aesthetic rhythms in art (e.g., meter in literature, keeping time in music, and patterns in visual arts).

Although rhythms are sometimes humanmade and socially or culturally created, Lefebvre reminds us that rhythms are *sensed* by humans: "The *sensible*, this scandal of philosophers from Plato to Hegel, (re)takes its primacy,

---

unfolds and uses it. The vagueness of *Stimmung* in terms of analytical operationality is evident if one reads the concrete analyses in Gumbrecht's *Stimmungen lesen*.

29 See for example Bruno Latour, *We Have Never Been Modern*, trans. Catherine Porter (1991; Cambridge, MA: Harvard University Press, 1993). Claude Lévi-Strauss already stressed the fragile distinction between nature and culture in *Les Structures élémentaires de la parenté* (Paris: Presses universitaires de France, 1949) and in several of his other works. See also Jacques Derrida's discussion of Lévi-Strauss in "La Structure, le signe et le jeu dans le discours des sciences humaines," in *L'Écriture et la différance* (Paris: Seuil, 1967). The rising significance of "the anthropocene" in the humanities is part of the same argument.

transformed without magic (without metaphysics)."³⁰ Human perception of rhythms is body dependent, and the rhythmical is linked with something both preconceptual and worldly immanent. Lefebvre again: "To grasp rhythm and polyrhythmias in a sensible, preconceptual but vivid way" ("Pour saisir de façon sensible, préconceptuelle mais vive, le rythme et les polyrythmies").³¹ Note here that Lefebvre does not use interpret (*interpreter*), but grasp (*saisir*). It is also worth noting that the English translation (grasp) underlines the physical dimension in Lefebvre's choice of words, but with the French *saisir* it arguably becomes even more clear that Lefebvre links the physical "to grasp" (or seize) directly to a dimension of knowledge, since *saisir* not only means "to grasp," but also "to understand." Knowledge is linked with something we can physically grasp with our fingers, it is actualized through contact, not with something we achieve through a mental process of consciousness (interpretation). Lefebvre continues, providing us with methodological legitimacy to apply rhythmanalysis to maritime fiction and sea life: "To grasp rhythm and polyrhythmias in a sensible, preconceptual but vivid way, it is enough to look carefully at the surface of the sea."

Rhythms may be coded with a cosmic or cultural form, but they are not coded with meaning. They do not come to us from a world whose visual, tactile, aural, olfactory, or gustatory appearance hides a meaning beyond the appearance, which one must decipher or interpret (therefore "without metaphysics"). A rhythm signifies nothing; it simply is, which is one reason that rhythmanalysis promises a descriptive alternative to the interpretational practice of hermeneutics and its immanent intellectual relativism. A rhythm has no (immediate) semantic effect on us; instead, it has what Gumbrecht calls a "presence effect" affecting us through its physical-sensuous constitution and acting (immediately) on and through our body.³²

The rhythmanalytical method rests on basic assumptions, which from the Renaissance onwards have been marginalized in the Western philosophical tradition. First, humans are not ex-centric to the world; second, humans are not purely intellectual, bodiless creatures. The separation between humankind and the world and the creation of the ex-centric man as an observer of

---

30 Henri Lefebvre, *Rhythmanalysis: Space, Time and Everyday Life*, trans. Stuart Elden and Gerald Moore (London and New York: Continuum, 2004), 17.
31 Lefebvre, *Rhythmanalysis*, 79; Henri Lefebvre and Catherine Régulier, "Le projet rythmanalytique," *Communications* 41 (1985): 196. The original French article quoted here does not feature in *Éléments de rythmanalyse: Introduction à la connaissance des rythmes*, the original French book, but a translation of this article is incorporated into the English book.
32 Gumbrecht, *Production of Presence*, xiv–xv, 2, 18, 49, 106–117.

a world of which he is no longer an integrated part laid the foundations for Western man's inclination to see the world as a surface that demands to be interpreted and for the idea that it is only humans who can produce knowledge. Regarding the later emergence of the new self-conscious observer, Gumbrecht remarks:

> If the observer role that arose in early modernity as a key element of the hermeneutic field was merely concerned with finding the appropriate distance in relation to its objects, the second-order observer, the new observer role that would shape the epistemology of the nineteenth century, was an observer condemned—rather than privileged—to observe himself in the act of observation. The emergence of this self-reflexive loop in the form of the second-order observer had two major consequences. Firstly, the second-order observer realized that each element of knowledge and each representation that he could ever produce would necessarily depend on the specific angle of his observation. He thus began to realize that there was an infinity of renditions for each potential object of reference—which proliferation ultimately shattered the belief in stable objects of reference. At the same time, the second-order observer rediscovered the human body and, more specifically, the human senses as an integral part of any world-observation. This other consequence coming from the new observer role would not only end up problematizing the pretended gender-neutrality of the disembodied first-order observer (this question can indeed be regarded as one of the origins of feminist philosophy); above all, it brought up the question of a possible compatibility between a world-appropriation by concepts (which I shall call "experience") and a world-observation through the senses (which I shall call "perception").[33]

The answer from Western philosophy and literature to this problem concerning the relationship between concept-experience and sense-perception was most often that humankind had now lost the world, or at least it had lost its immediate access to the world. The inherent attempt in Lefebvre's rhythmanalysis to overcome metaphysics and circumvent the age of the (linguistic) sign should in this line of thinking be considered an attempt to recuperate the world and the world of things. How? Rhythm combines world-appropriation and experience (we grasp the world through rhythms) with world-observation

---

33   Gumbrecht, *Production of Presence*, 38–39.

and perception (the grasping is not hermeneutical or reflective, but perceptual and immediate).

Regarding maritime life, it is interesting that the principal manner humans, according to Gumbrecht, relate to each other in a presence culture is through the body. They also consider themselves part of the world, not ex-centric to it. Life on board a ship is a bodily rather than a reflexive existence (if reflexive, it is a reflection rooted in empiricism), and the sailor is radically *in* the world and subject to the rhythms of nature. As one character in Cooper's *The Red Rover* exclaims: "What is to happen will happen bodily."[34] Meaning does exist in a presence culture, but according to Gumbrecht it is not produced by humans through an act of world interpretation. Instead, meaning is something that is revealed; something that just happens. The maritime equivalence to this is the epiphanic moments of bodily (and therefore also mentally) bliss, which ship life sometimes offers. Apart from this, it is also characteristic for a presence culture that space is its primary dimension, not time. Finally, Gumbrecht argues that physical violence (understood as bodily obstructions in space, but also understood in a more traditional way) is not a tabooed but a normal phenomenon among people in presence cultures.[35] It is well known that life on board a ship can be extremely brutal and violent, and combined with the ship's threatening surroundings and its architecture, which facilitates a life form in which bodies obstruct other bodies in space, emphasizing the claustrophobic spatial constitution of maritime existence.

Edward Casey has rightly observed that places endow us with stability, memory, and identity.[36] I would like to add that rhythms produce and stabilize places by giving them a memory and a continuous identity. Rhythms act as a resistance to formlessness and pure fluidity because of their dependency on repetitions. Contrary to the so-called "dead" or "naked" repetitions,[37] the return of the self-identical, rhythms are defined by their subtle dose of movements and differences within the very rhythm of repetition. Rhythm is form that becomes form over time, a changing structure that realizes itself in time as pointed out by Émile Benvéniste in the first volume of *Problems in General Linguistics* (1966).

To Benvéniste, the concept of rhythm manages the "vast unification of man and nature under time" and, like Lefebvre, he mentions "the regular

---

34 Cooper, *The Red Rover*, 207–08.
35 For a discussion of the differences between a presence culture and a meaning culture, see Gumbrecht, *Production of Presence*, 78–86.
36 Casey, *Getting Back into Place*, xv.
37 Gilles Deleuze, *Différence et répétition* (Paris: P.U.F., 1968), 37.

movements of the waves of the sea" as a possible etymological impulse in "rhythm," which originally meant "to flow." However, looking closer into this connection, Benvéniste reaches the conclusion that the link is morphologically possible but semantically impossible, because the sea does not actually flow. In fact, rhythm was used in ancient times as a synonym for "form," seemingly the opposite of "to flow." However, Benvéniste returns to etymology claiming that we merely used the wrong sense of "rhythm," that is, "to flow" instead of "form." His next step is now to connect those two. "Form" is not to be understood as "fixed form," but rather as "form in the instant that it is assumed by what is moving, mobile and fluid, the form of that which does not have organic consistency; [...] It is the form as improvised, momentary, changeable." Literally, rhythm means, "the particular manner of flowing" writes Benvéniste. Behind this notion lies the Heraclitean worldview of fluidity, which infuses the very conceptual framework of its contemporaneity: "There is a deep-lying connection between the proper meaning of the term ῥυθμός and the doctrine of which it discloses one of its most original notions."[38] Benvéniste's final step consists of bringing in Plato to make the ends between "form" and "flow" meet:

> We are far indeed from the simplistic picture that a superficial etymology used to suggest, and it was not in contemplating the play of waves on the shore that the primitive Hellene discovered "rhythm"; it is, on the contrary, we who are making metaphors today when we speak of the rhythm of the waves. It required a long consideration of the structure of things, then a theory of measure applied to the figures of dance and to the modulations of song, in order for the principle of cadenced movement to be recognized and given a name.[39]

"Order in movement," "a configuration of movements organized in time," and "cadenced movement" are then Benvéniste's final definitions of rhythm.[40]

Since our objects of investigation are the sea and the ship, and recalling Casey's thoughts on place, could we not ask, with Benvéniste in mind, if rhythm is not primarily a temporal rather than a placial phenomenon? Lefebvre says both yes and no:

---

38 Emile Benvéniste, *Problems in General Linguistics*, vol. 1, trans. Mary Elizabeth Meek (Miami: Miami University Press, 1971), 281, 286.
39 Benvéniste, *Problems in General Linguistics*, 287.
40 Benvéniste, *Problems in General Linguistics*, 287.

concrete times have rhythms, or rather are rhythms—and all rhythms imply the relation of a time to a space, a localised time, or, if one prefers, a temporalised space. Rhythm is always linked to such and such a place, to its place, be that the heart, the fluttering of the eyelids, the movement of a street or the tempo of a waltz. This does not prevent it from being in a time, which is to say an aspect of a movement or of a becoming.[41]

Rhythms can also destabilize and insert amnesia and rupture in a place. Lefebvre labels this phenomenon arrhythmia, which happens when rhythms break down and circumvent synchronization. Lefebvre compares arrhythmia to a pathological condition, to an illness; in addition, he claims that we are usually not aware of rhythms until they become irregular. Rhythms thus comprise both continuity and contrast, identity and difference, and change and repetition, just as each of them is characterized by its own tempo, its own phase, and its own durability.

Whether we speak of rhythm or of arrhythmia, rhythmanalysis contributes to describing life on board a ship in a concrete and material way. In the beginning of *Typhoon*, Conrad characterizes the seaman's life as being "uninteresting" but not without a "mysterious side" and "so entirely given the actuality of the bare existence."[42] Rhythmanalysis can contribute to a description of maritime existence, because rhythms make up the "uninteresting" (monotonous) and the "mysterious" (epiphanic) sides as well as "the actuality of the bare existence." The latter consists of the sensuous conditions, the smells and odors, colors and lights, moods and atmospheres. What occupies or fills "smooth space" is, as Gilles Deleuze and Félix Guattari remark, "intensities, wind and noise, forces and sonorous and tactile qualities."[43] Life on board the ship is an extremely physical existence. The human body is dressed in the material texture of life and the everyday, a texture that is constituted by biological, psychological, natural, and social rhythms.

In this universe, the sailor's body becomes a metronome, a contact zone where linear-social and cyclical-biological rhythms interact, converge, or diverge:

> Cyclical repetition and the linear repetitive separate out under analysis, but in *reality* interfere with one another constantly. The cyclical originates in the cosmic, in nature: days, nights, seasons, the waves and the

---

41   Lefebvre, *Rhythmanalysis*, 89.
42   Conrad, *Typhoon*, 4.
43   Deleuze and Guattari, *A Thousand Plateaus*, 528.

tides of the sea, monthly cycles, etc. The linear would come rather from social practice, therefore from human activity: the monotony of actions and of movements, imposed structures. Great cyclical rhythms last for a period and restart: dawn, always new, often superb, inaugurates the return of the everyday. The antagonistic unity of relations between the cyclical and the linear sometimes gives rise to compromises, sometimes to disturbances.[44]

The point is that not only is rhythmanalysis a productive method for examining ship life, but the ocean-going ship is also a privileged place from which to analyze rhythms. Rhythms in relation to nature, the elements, and the "natural" body as well as in relation to the sociocultural and the "cultural" body become very visible and tangible from the perspective of the ship, because the ferocity of nature and the fragility of humans on the planet are so obvious and deeply felt on the ocean. The calm rhythms of nature, the rhythm of the sailor and the ship in relation to nature, and the sociocultural rhythm on board the ship—that is, the necessity of a mutual rhythm to navigate in relation to the rhythms of the planet—are therefore evidently of vital significance for ship life. In what follows, I examine different types of rhythms and their significations and implications for maritime life.

3   Cosmic and Cultural Rhythms at Sea

In *The Ship Sails On*, Nordahl Grieg compares the novel's steamship with "a warehouse that moves about from port to port,"[45] and in Conrad's *The Nigger of the "Narcissus,"* the *Narcissus* is described as "a high and lonely pyramid," whereas a tugboat is characterized as an "enormous aquatic black beetle."[46] Earlier, Cooper had likened the ship to "one of the bubbles of the element,"[47] a mere water bubble. These are just a fraction of the many striking metaphors authors used to emphasize the ship's intense *exposure* to the cyclical and cosmic rhythms of nature. The cosmic rhythms—days and nights, sunrises and sunsets, months and seasons, waves and tides—occasionally contribute to

---

44   Lefebvre, *Rhythmanalysis*, 8.
45   Nordahl Grieg, *The Ship Sails On*, trans. Arthur G. Chater (1924; New York: A. A. Knopf, 1927), 2.
46   Joseph Conrad, *The Nigger of the "Narcissus": A Tale of the Sea*, 1897, in *Collected Edition of the Works of Joseph Conrad* (1923; London: J. M. Dent & Sons Ltd., 1950), 27.
47   Cooper, *The Red Rover*, 248.

making life on board the ship an appeasing, satisfying, and rewarding experience. This happens for example in *The Nigger of the "Narcissus,"* when "the serene purity of the night enveloped the seamen with its soothing breath, with its tepid breath flowing under the stars that hung countless above the mastheads in a thin cloud of luminous dust."[48] Implied here is a symbiosis between firmament and ship ("enveloped"), and with "soothing breath" and "tepid breath," Conrad stresses the fundamental rhythmic and synchronic nature of the situation. In *Typhoon*, we learn that "every ship Captain MacWhirr commanded was the floating abode of harmony and peace," and in relation to the captain it says that he "could feel against his ear the pulsation of the engines, like the beat of the ship's heart."[49]

In *The Sharks: The History of a Crew and a Shipwreck*, the protagonist Peder Jensen tells us how he and the other crew members "heard the clear, almost transparent lapping of water and waves around the ship's bow and along her sides."[50] This experience of security and harmony, which is mostly aural, is supplemented a few pages further on with a genuine epiphanic moment of synchronicity and joy:

> It's no exaggeration to say that I trembled as I first gribbed the mahogany wheel. [...] Carefully I eased her a quarter of a point off to windward, just to feel the contact, to feel how she minded her rudder. And I felt it, the faint quivering—she too trembled at my touch! A tall flame of happiness went through me, from my feet to my fingertips I felt the trembling of her, of this oneness of hull and rigging—of body and soul, of ropes and wind. It was a great, rushing music: the sea, the ship, and the wind.[51]

Irritation and a feeling of losing one's sense of direction if rhythms are experienced as being too monotonous can replace a rhythmic wellbeing such as Peder Jensen's. In *Typhoon*, the narrator refers to the captain as being "exasperated by the continuous, monotonous rolling of the ship."[52] In Malcolm Lowry's *Ultramarine*, Dana Hilliot loses his sense of time because of the repetitious character of ship life: "Today, or was it yesterday? Two days ago. All the days were the same. The engine hammered out the same stroke, same beat, as yesterday. The forecastle was no lighter, no darker, than yesterday. Today, or is it

---

48 Conrad, *The Nigger of the "Narcissus,"* 14–15.
49 Conrad, *Typhoon*, 4, 66.
50 Bjørneboe, *The Sharks*, 18.
51 Bjørneboe, *The Sharks*, 26.
52 Conrad, *Typhoon*, 26.

yesterday? Yes, two days it must be. Two days—two months—two years."[53] Notice the displacement from "was" to "is" in the repetition of "Today, or was/is it yesterday?" The displacement, or perhaps oscillation between past tense and present tense, subtly emphasizes Hilliot's temporal disorientation on the level of form.

Nature and the cosmos possess destructive forces that expose the fragility of the ship's construction and constitution. Out of necessity, the ship answers to these threats by creating more mechanical, rigid, and linear rhythms in the form of cultural organizations that stabilize the ship. Think of the monotony of certain scripted actions and movements, such as the conventional behavior of the crew toward the officers, the mustering of the crew, or the stoker's feeding the furnace with coal. These actions or movements have to do with what Lefebvre calls "dressage," a schooling or a breeding of the human body that is internalized and "puts into place an automatism of repetitions" in order to fill "the place of the unforeseen."[54] Dressage is a phenomenon whose necessity on board ships is legitimized by the exposure of the ship and its crew. As to being schooled in the ability to step in as buffer or even bulwark against all kinds of unexpected incidents, dressage is a phenomenon implicating that culture (education) comes close to biology (instinct).

To David Seamon, a place emerges *as* place when choreographed by different body movements of which many have become automated and unpremeditated. Seamon calls such movements "body-ballets" performed by "body-subjects." The body has morphed into a subject with its own intentionality, built up through countless repetitions of certain movements. Habits allow for the body to automatically perform tasks without the need for our consciousness and reflection to trigger movement. To many, driving a car has for example become automated to an extent where the body performs small tasks without the person consciously realizing it:

> Without the structure of body-subject, people would be constantly required to plan out every movement anew to pay continuous attention to each gesture of the hand, each step of the foot, each start. Because of body-subject, people can manage routine demands automatically and so gain freedom from their everyday spaces and environments. In this way, they rise above such mundane events as getting places, finding things, performing basic gestures, and direct their creative attention to wider,

---

53 Malcolm Lowry, *Ultramarine*, rev. ed. (1933; London: Jonathan Cape, 1969), 16.
54 Lefebvre, *Rhythmanalysis*, 40.

more significant life-dimensions. [...] Body-subject assures that gestures and movements learned in the past will readily continue into the future. It handles the basic behaviors of everyday living. Body-subject is a stabilizing force, and through it people gain the freedom to extend their world horizons.[55]

The same with sailors. Drilling and dressage is a way of creating what Seamon calls "time-space routines." They are of great significance at sea, because they structure time, organize space, grant sailors a relative freedom from potentially oppressive environments, and free up their cognitive capacities for unforeseen disruptions to rhythmic routines:

> The time-space routine has a certain holistic pattern which, like movement itself, is well described by the word "unfolding." When a person has established a series of time-space routines in his typical daily or weekly schedule, large portions of his day can proceed with a minimum of planning and decision. The person may become attached to these routines; interference, as the above observation indicates, can generate a certain amount of stress. Time-space routines are an essential component of daily living because they appropriate activities automatically through time. They maintain a continuity in people's lives, allowing them to do automatically in the present moment what they have learned in the past. In managing the routine, repetitive aspects of daily living, time-space routines free people's cognitive attention for more significant events and needs. On the other hand, time-space routines may be difficult to break or change. In this sense they are a conservative force which may be a considerable obstacle in the face of useful progress or change.[56]

At sea, the body-subject performing body-ballets and time-space routines are most often required to do so in coordination with other body-subjects. Seamon also has a word for this phenomenon: "The *place-ballet is a fusion of many time-space routines and body-ballets in terms of place.*" Ships are exemplary places for such place-ballets to unfold, or perhaps it would be more correct to say that place-ballets are exemplary choreographies for ships.

---

[55] Seamon, "Body-Subject, Time-Space Routines, and Place-Ballets," 156–57.
[56] Seamon, "Body-Subject, Time-Space Routines, and Place-Ballets," 159.

Ships become ships because place-ballets are performed on them, and place-ballets spring to life on board ships. With their dependency on interpersonal collaboration and rhythmic coordination, place-ballets generate trust or mistrust among the crew members depending on their execution: "Place-ballet, in other words, is an environmental synergy in which human and material parts unintentionally foster a larger whole with its own special rhythm and character."[57]

Dressage or the disciplining of the human body is often more intense aboard military ships than mercantile ships, although according to Bjørneboe the militaristic discipline is a general condition:

> Life at sea is indeed a military world, built on total obedience and submission on the crew's part. The captain is the government's deputy, he has the law on his side, and he is absolute dictator in his little society. He can be brought to trial for brutality or abuse of power, but only when he is back on land. Until then he is sovereign and must be obeyed.
>
> The class difference between officers and crew is an unbridgeable gulf. [...]
>
> Each has his precisely allotted rank and role. Their dictates are harsh, both for crew and command.[58]

Enforced temporal, spatial, and social structures such as shifts, compartmentalizations, and hierarchies also contribute to the territorialization of the ship. It is not just that "Each has his precisely allotted rank and role," each action also has its specific time on board the ship, just as each object and person has a carefully allotted place.

When the two types of rhythms, the cosmic and the cultural, converge in a condition of compromise, what Lefebvre calls "eurhythmia," "the bundle of natural rhythms wraps itself in rhythms of social or mental function" in a metastable equilibrium.[59] But we cannot always count on compromise, sometimes conflicts occur, whether because of accelerations or decelerations, unpredictable as well as predictable natural events, or due to disturbances in the social (atmo)sphere. On board the ship, such arrhythmia, or desynchronization, can have a potentially fatal and morbid outcome.

---

57 Seamon, "Body-Subject, Time-Space Routines, and Place-Ballets," 159, 163.
58 Bjørneboe, *The Sharks*, 205.
59 Lefebvre, *Rhythmanalysis*, 8–9.

4 External and Internal Rhythms

Rhythms both external and internal structure everyday life on board the ship. External rhythms are more cosmic and have to do with the relationship between the vessel and such rhythmic components as sky, ocean, winds, waves, stars, sun, moon, horizon, rain, sea creatures, and often even Heaven and Hell (superstition is an inevitable part of ship life and maritime fiction). Internal rhythms are more social and have to do with the relationships between officers, crew, work, and ship. External rhythms play a greater role on board sailing ships than steamships because of the sailing ship's closer and more collaborative connection with nature, especially the winds. On a steamship such as Turner's paddle-steamer (Figure 8), being more independent of nature, the internal rhythms, especially those between man and man, are of greater significance. Whether we speak of internal or external rhythms, there is usually a hierarchy, a determining rhythm or an original and coordinating aspect, which, like a conductor, regulates the whole ensemble of rhythms.

FIGURE 8   J. M. W. Turner, *A Paddle-steamer in a Storm* (c. 1841)
© YALE CENTER FOR BRITISH ART, PAUL MELLON COLLECTION

When Conrad began writing *Typhoon* in 1899, his creativity was challenged not so much by the depiction of the storm as by the need to come up with "a leading motive that would harmonize all these violent noises, and a point of view that would put all that elemental fury into its proper place." Conrad's solution was the invention of Captain MacWhirr. Throughout the novel, MacWhirr acts as a center of gravity amid chaos. During the climax of the storm, MacWhirr's voice has a reassuring effect on the mate: "And again he heard that voice, forced and ringing feebly, but with a penetrating effect of quietness [...] bearing that strange effect of quietness like the serene glow of a halo [...] in the enormous discord of noises."[60] The calming effect of the voice has nothing to do with meaning. It is not *what* MacWhirr says, but *how* he says it—that is, it has to do with rhythm, sound, intonation, and the bodily effects of the voice rather than its intellectual meaning. The voice as a physical as opposed to a semantic phenomenon plays a significant role in much sea fiction, where it functions as a rhythmical epicenter and either coordinates a potentially polyrhythmic confusion of rhythms, or, as in this case, is opposed to the arrhythmia caused by the typhoon. The crew's songs sung while doing demanding tasks is another example of the voice as a coordinating, collectivizing, and even enhancing force. During rhythmic communal singing, the crew becomes one body.

Language can work in a heterogenizing and cacophonizing way, such as when several national languages coexist on board the ship. Cacophony does not automatically exclude a tolerant form of polyrhythmia. According to Lefebvre, "polyrhythmia always results from a contradiction, but also from resistance to this contradiction—resistance to a relation of force and an eventual conflict."[61] However, it often happens that maritime heteroglossia leads to strife, violence, and murder since the cacophonic surface covers deeper-lying conflicts. In *The Sharks*, Peder Jensen is amazed "that there was so little cohesion, so little solidarity in the forecastle. There was incessant hostility and bickering, eternal factional battles—between group and group, man and man, between races and colours."[62] Ships in maritime fiction are loaded with race conflicts, nationalistic chauvinisms, disciplinary mechanisms, gender role patterns, sexual desire, homophobic anxieties, brutal enforcements of law and order, hierarchical segmentations of space, and endless risks of mutiny.

Without MacWhirr's timely deeds and cold-blooded *in*action, and without his magnetic voice that introduce a determining and stabilizing rhythm

---

60   Conrad, *Typhoon*, vi, 44, 46, 44.
61   Lefebvre, *Rhythmanalysis*, 99.
62   Bjørneboe, *The Sharks*, 102.

during the violent storm, *Nan-Shan*, its crew, and its cargo would have been victims of what Robert Pogue Harrison has called "the sea's irresponsibility, its hostility to memory, its impatience with ruins, and its passion for erasure."[63] Rhythm is a precondition for life; as rhythmless conditions, chaos and formlessness threaten life itself. If chaos and death are found on one end of a scale with rhythm, "cadenced form" (Benvéniste), and life in the middle, then at the opposite end of this scale is another life-threatening phenomenon: stasis. On the ocean, this life-threatening phenomenon manifests itself as calm sea. We can illustrate it like this:

Death ⇐ Storm (Chaos) ↔ **Rhythm** ⇒ LIFE ⇐ **Rhythm** ↔ Calm sea (Stasis) ⇒ Death

Calm sea can immobilize the sailing ship for several days and create an even more oppressive atmosphere on an otherwise already claustrophobic ship.

Movement is a precondition for rhythm. When the sea is calm, movement is absent, and even the mechanized, linear, and monotone hammering of a steamship engine would sound like a heartbeat and indicate a resumption of life itself. In Coleridge's "The Rime of the Ancyent Marinere" (1798), we come upon a description of such a dead calm scene:

> Down dropped the breeze, the sails dropped down,
> 'Twas sad as sad could be;
> And we did speak only to break
> The silence of the sea!
>
> Day after day, day after day,
> We stuck, nor breath nor motion;
> As idle as a painted ship
> Upon a painted ocean.[64]

In his use of repetitions, Coleridge formally mimes the stasis of the situation. Pay especially attention to "down dropped [...] dropped down," "sad as sad," "Day after day, day after day," "nor [...] nor," and "a painted [...] a painted," all syntactical constructions emphasizing enclosure and dead repetition. The

---

63   Robert Pogue Harrison, *The Dominion of the Dead* (Chicago: University of Chicago Press, 2003), 14.
64   Samuel Taylor Coleridge, "The Rime of the Ancyent Marinere," in *Lyrical Ballads*, William Wordsworth and Samuel Taylor Coleridge (1798; London: Henry Frowde, 1911), II, 6; II, 8.

potentially rhythmless scenario is disturbed by sounds that interrupt the monotony, though. The rhythms and rimes of the stanzas also contribute to disturb the dead calmness.

5   Rituals

Rites and rituals sometimes constitute the determining rhythm of ship life. According to Lefebvre, they "have a double relation with rhythms, each ritualization creates its own time and particular rhythm, that of gestures, solemn words, acts prescribed in a certain sequence; but also, rites and ritualizations intervening in everyday time, punctuating it. This occurs most frequently in the course of cyclical time, at fixed hours, dates or occasions."[65] Rituals are temporal incisions into a possibly monotonous everyday life. On board the ship, they imprint an *extra*-everyday rhythm on the everyday, a rhythm that stands outside of the everyday. Rituals only interrupt the everyday momentarily, though. Whether we speak of religious, political, or social rites, they function as a centripetalizing force that strengthen the alliances and compromises between the different rhythms on board the ship. "Burial at sea" is an example of a ritual that takes up a privileged period on the ship, but also, as Blum has shown, that represents a crisis of epistemology and poetics to sailors and sailor-writers, because it is an event that is fundamentally nonmaterialist.[66] We encounter it in many sea stories. Since the ritual of burial is usually an event that trumps all other occupations and doings, and because it is surrounded by much reverence, it acts a coordinating and determining conductor.

In Jack London's *The Sea-Wolf* (1904), there is a burial at sea, but in this scene a dominating rhythm upstages the crew as they carry out the ritual. It is that of Wolf Larsen, the dictator-captain of the *Ghost*. During the established ceremony around disposing of the dead body of a fellow crew member, Larsen fails to respect the associated rituals. On a general level, these are "gestures, solemn words, acts prescribed in a certain sequence." Specifically, they comprise reciting appropriate passages from the Bible and devoting an appropriate time frame for the ceremony to be completed properly as well as for the deceased sailor to be honored decently. A ferocious mix of Spencerian biologism and economism governs Wolf Larsen's primary rhythm. It is a rhythm that is linear and one-dimensionally focused, especially in relation to what concerns personal survival and wealth. Larsen takes leave of his deceased crew member

---

65   Lefebvre, *Rhythmanalysis*, 94.
66   Blum, *View from the Masthead*, 158–92.

with the following words: "'I only remember one part of the service,' he said, 'and that is, "And the body shall be cast into the sea." So cast it in.'"[67]

At first, the crew is confused because of the short duration of the ceremony and Larsen's irreverence. A risk of arrhythmia and conflict exists. Wolf Larsen immediately dominates the crew verbally by ordering them to rid the ship of the body. As in the case of Captain MacWhirr, Wolf Larsen's voice is a physical phenomenon that projects an instruction, which instantaneously makes any hermeneutic activity superfluous. "They elevated the end of the hatch-cover with pitiful haste, and, like a dog flung overside, the dead man slid feet first into the sea. The coal at his feet dragged him down. He was gone."[68] The quickness of the ceremony echoes on the literary-formal level in the brevity of the last sentence: "He was gone."

What strikes the narrator most is the "heartlessness" of the event, and that the dead sailor instantly became "an episode that was past, and incident that was dropped." The sealers, apparently unaffected by the situation, laugh at a story while "the dead man, dying obscenely, buried sordidly," was "sinking down, down—." Later in the novel, the body of Wolf Larsen is transferred to the sea with the same words: "And the body shall be cast into the sea." After which, the novel laconically and prosaically repeats: "It was gone."[69] There is a difference compared to the earlier burial, though. The humanizing and individualizing "He" is replaced by the reified and anonymizing "It."

6   Internal Arrhythmia

Conrad's *The Nigger of the "Narcissus"* is suffused with arrhythmia between man and man. The governing atmosphere on board the ship suggests a pathological, dysfunctional condition. The novel is characterized by Conrad's distinction between the era of steam and the disappearing era of sail. The conflicting structure of the dichotomy—including the tensions between money calculation and mystery, iron and wood, mass and individual, ugliness and beauty, clumsiness and grace—reverberates throughout the novel and dictates its fundamental rhythm. This rhythm can be described as an arrhythmia threatening to paralyze the crew and the ship. As Singleton, the incarnation of the old-fashioned, conservative sailor, remarks: "Ships are all right. It is the

---

67 Jack London, *The Sea-Wolf* (1904; New York: Random House, 2000), 28.
68 London, *The Sea-Wolf*, 28–29.
69 London, *The Sea-Wolf*, 29, 29 279, 280.

men in them!"[70] Singleton's remark is a reminder of the nature of the conflict on the *Narcissus*. A conflict between men, it has psychological dimensions.

Of the many tensions, the decisive one is the tension between egoism and community, especially in relation to work. This tension results in longer periods with arrhythmia and thus threatens the ship's functionality and seaworthiness. Two individual actors are behind this tension: James Wait, the so-called "nigger," and Donkin. Wait suffers from lethal tuberculosis, and with Donkin as his prime accomplice, he involves the entire crew emotionally in his disease. Conrad insinuates that the crew's sympathy with and altruistic behavior toward Wait is motivated primarily by an egoistic drive whose purpose is to conceal an underlying inability to become reconciled with the reality of suffering and death. This inability is very dangerous at sea. The apparent humanitarian sympathies of the crew are founded in their need to feel redeemed and to consider themselves to be good human beings. This philanthropic misunderstanding is also the psychological rhythm that threatens the health of the ship since it negatively influences the work ethic and therefore also the crew's genuine sense of community. Early on, Donkin is designated as the primary villain:

> He was the man that cannot steer, that cannot splice, that dodges the work on dark nights; that, aloft, holds on frantically with both arms and legs, and swears at the wind, the sleet, the darkness; the man who curses the sea while others work. The man who is the last out and the first in when all hands are called. The man who can't do most things and won't do the rest. The pet of philanthropists and self-seeking landlubbers. The sympathetic and deserving creature that knows all about his rights, but knows nothing of courage, of endurance, and of the unexpressed faith, of the unspoken loyalty that knits together a ship's company.[71]

The peaceful environment and mutual trust on board the *Narcissus* gradually lessen because of the crew's ambivalent reactions to Wait and his disease. Torn between suspicion and pity, they ultimately succumb to pity, which corrupts. At the end of the novel, the *Narcissus* regains an eurhythmia of sorts. For this to happen, Conrad tests the crew in a storm, an event that provides an opportunity for collaborative work, a process through which the crew become reconciled with death. *The Nigger of the "Narcissus"* is not exceptional in terms of showing the significance of the internal, psycho-pathological rhythms when

---

70 Conrad, *The Nigger of the "Narcissus,"* 24.
71 Conrad, *The Nigger of the "Narcissus,"* 10–11.

it comes to danger and potential shipwreck. In Lie's *The Pilot and His Wife*, the pilot and captain, Salve Kristiansen, is challenged one night at sea by the forces of nature, yet the principal reason for Salve's shipwreck is not so much due to these natural forces. Rather, it is his jealousy and rage rooted in his personal marital affairs that lead him into navigational hubris and blindness.[72]

The ship is perhaps comparable to "a piece of floating space," and the ocean occasionally assumes the attribute of being "a soup of space." But both spaces are also places with unique placial qualities. If the ship and the ocean oscillate between being space and place—between being movement and pause, freedom and security, threat and claustrophobia—then the maritime rhythms are what determine the direction and tempo of the pendulum. The cosmic-cyclical and the social-linear rhythms jointly endow ship life with form and homeliness. These same rhythms, if broken down, institute disruption, chaos, and potential destruction on board the ship.

7   Knowledge, Teaching, Writing

I have tried to show life at sea as a privileged place from which to examine cosmic and social rhythms and the benefits of reading sea fiction through a rhythmanalytical lens. These benefits have to do with getting closer to the concreteness of maritime existence. Methodologically, this is made possible through a shift in focus from interpreting the multiple (symbolic) meanings of the sea and the ship to an understanding, a *grasping*, of how it feels to be on board an ocean-going ship. I will now discuss 1) what type of knowledge is produced by rhythmanalysis, 2) the problems related to the implementation of rhythmanalysis in the classroom, and 3) the challenges associated with writing a rhythmanalysis.

Besides contributing to a more nuanced understanding of what it means and how it feels to be on board a ship on the ocean, the analysis of maritime rhythms suggests a possible way forward in terms of reading literature and cultural artifacts in new and more rhythmic approach. These are ways that show greater sensibility toward materialities, moods, bodily effects and affects, as well as the immanent rhythm of physical things. What has motivated the rhythmic approach has not been semantics and hermeneutic demands but the experience—understood as immediate, sensuous perception (*Erlebnis*)[73]—of

---

72   Lie, *The Pilot and His Wife*, 236–57.
73   In English, the word "experience" covers both the reflective afterthought, the mental processing and ordering, of something one has experienced, as well as the actual experience,

the world's thingness and of the preoccupation with this experience in literature and culture.

The primary objective of rhythmanalysis is not to produce new, positive knowledge or to revise traditional knowledge. This is the chief aim of hermeneutics. The epistemological project of rhythmanalysis is a rethinking and reconfiguration of the very conditions of knowledge production within the humanities. Lefebvre's aim is "nothing less than to found a science, a new field of knowledge."[74] Again, not to generate new knowledge, but establish a new *field* of knowledge. It is a *saisir*, a *savoir*, and a *connaissance* mediated by the sensuous intrinsic to the world, not by any conscious hermeneutic activity extrinsic to the world. The analysis of "the bundle" of natural and social rhythms "consists in opening and unwrapping the bundle" ("consiste à ouvrir et à défaire le paquet"),[75] not in interpreting it. If we insist on knowledge and new knowledge, then we should differentiate between knowledge as interpretation and semantic meaning and knowledge as grasping and understanding. If we shift our attention from the epistemological to the existential, it is an additional benefit of rhythmanalysis that the experiential-perceptual approach to the things of the world in their preconceptual "thingness" will reactivate an increased sensibility towards the bodily and sensory dimensions of our existence.

The knowledge produced by rhythmanalysis is not a conscious-mental knowledge, an intellectual or semantic knowledge of the essential meaning of an object, whether a city, a text, or a building. Rhythmanalytical knowledge arises through the senses and the human body. It has less to do with what something means than with how something works and what effects something has on us and the other participants in the rhythmic constellation. Rhythmanalysis has to do with force fields, energies, conflicts, compromises, and synchronicities, a sort of Nietzschean world of active and reactive forces, rather than with semantics, meaning, significance, and interpretation. The analyzer observes, listens, feels, tastes, and smells. He or she has an eye for the phenomenal world's lengthy processes and becomings, even for the rhythmic movements of inorganic objects (I examine this in greater detail in the chapter on materialities). Rhythmanalysis counters the inherent relativism and subjectivism in hermeneutical interpretation and represents a more sober

---

which is more immediate and sensuous. In German there is a specific word for each one of them: *Erfahrung* and *Erlebnis* (so too, in Danish: *erfaring* and *oplevelse*).

74 Lefebvre, *Rhythmanalysis*, 3.
75 Lefebvre, *Rhythmanalysis*, 9; Henri Lefebvre, *Éléments de rythmanalyse: Introduction à la connaissance des rythmes* (Paris: Éditions Syllepse, 1992), 18.

and perhaps even more objective alternative to hermeneutics. However, rhythmanalysis is also inherently perspectival, as its starting point is the subjective, rhythmic, and bodily constitution of the person doing the analyzing. It is necessary to uphold a difference between hermeneutics and rhythmanalysis. The inherent subjectivism and perspectivism in rhythmanalysis, expressed here as "Man (the species): his physical and physiological being is indeed the measure of the world,"[76] is more directly and immediately connected to the world than the inherent subjectivism and perspectivism in hermeneutics. Our ears, eyes, and hands are not passive receivers of impressions but are co-creators of the world. According to Lefebvre, they are less arbitrary in their grasping than is mental-conscious interpretation.

The rhythmanalytical approach challenges the traditional way of acting in the classroom. The problem is related to my next and last issue concerning our style of writing. There is a danger that one's rhythmanalysis—whether we develop it in the classroom or in a text—ends up becoming a bit boring. The epiphanic moments of our students and ourselves most often relate to the eye-opening experiences we have when digging out new knowledge and meaning through interpretations. This dimension is ideological and political and often has to do with the message or worldview of the author and the text. I am not saying that this dimension is not important, but rhythmanalysis operates differently and seeks something else, namely the sensuous dimensions of the text and the organization and mediation of these dimensions and rhythms. Our challenge is to encourage our students' receptivity to the aesthetic and rhythmic qualities of art and attach less importance to ideology, ethics, and semantics.

Rhythmanalysis sometimes seems inadequate when we write scholarly articles and books. One reason is that rhythmanalysis is descriptive rather than interpretative. As we know, description is a discursive practice whose value is debated. Description is a stranger in academic texts; it belongs more naturally to textual practices associated with fiction, but even in this context it divides people. Many readers of novels simply skip the descriptions. Instead, they are driven forward solely by the plot, by what Salman Rushdie once called "what-happened-nextism."[77] So why even consider returning to a discursive practice that Balzac, Tolstoy, and Eliot elevated and perfected in the nineteenth century?

---

76   Lefebvre, *Rhythmanalysis*, 83.
77   Salman Rushdie, *Midnight's Children* (1981; London: Vintage, 1995), 39.

What does Lefebvre say on the subject? He rarely touches upon the style of rhythmanalysis in his book. The topic features more prominently in the article on the Mediterranean cities written with Catherine Régulier, which is included in both the French and English editions of the book, but it is still relatively sporadic and undeveloped. In the article, the rhythmanalytical method is described as inevitably transdisciplinary. It is the ambition of Lefebvre and Régulier to unite the scientific and the poetic, or at least to separate as little as possible the two genres and forms of knowledge.[78] Toward the end of the article, they address a potential objection that could be raised against the article's conceptually very high level of abstraction. However, according to Lefebvre and Régulier, this conceptual abstraction was a necessity, because the rhythmanalytical method found itself in an initial phase of conceptual development at the time of writing. Lefebvre and Régulier claim they could easily have avoided these possible objections if they had chosen to. Their solution for avoiding abstraction is important: "either by painstakingly describing a known and privileged place—or by throwing ourselves into the lyricism that arouses the splendor of the cities evoked" ("soit en décrivant minutieusement un lieu privilégié et connu—soit en nous lançant dans le lyrisme que suscite la splendeur des villes évoquées").[79]

Lefebvre and Régulier indicate a rhythmanalytical discourse that will either poetically and lyrically arouse splendor or, through a descriptive approach and style, will capture the rhythmic and sensuous dimensions of a city, a place, or a text and make them comprehensible and graspable. *Saisir* (to grasp) and *susciter* (to arouse) instead of *interpreter* (to interpret). Now, I cannot blame anyone for thinking if this advice is every researcher's worst nightmare. Are we supposed to become authors in the artistic sense of the word? No, this is not what Lefebvre and Régulier are aiming at. What they suggest, perhaps implicitly, is an expansion of our catalogue of academic discourses, just as they urge us to work seriously with our own style and to challenge the traditional academic discourse as a discourse that interprets and analyzes only and nothing more. Academics are also allowed to bring back the world into our writings.

---

78 Lefebvre, *Rhythmanalysis*, 87; Lefebvre, *Éléments de rythmanalyse*, 98.
79 Lefebvre, *Rhythmanalysis*, 100; Lefebvre, *Éléments de rythmanalyse*, 109.

CHAPTER 3

Technology

1   The Shipwreck of the *São João* in 1552

On February 3, 1552, the galleon *São João* left Cochin on the western coast of South India to return to Lisbon. Being a cargo ship, a so-called *carraca* (carrack), the *São João* was employed in the Portuguese merchant fleet. Leaving Cochin, it carried mostly pepper, and also porcelain, beads, tapestries, and other goods. The load could have weighed as much as twelve thousand quintals, but due to ongoing war in the Malabar area, which restricted the Portuguese delegation in its merchant scouring of the southwestern territory of India, the load is supposed to have weighed only seven and a half thousand quintals (three hundred and sixty-seven tons). Nevertheless, the *São João* was still "overladen," the goods reportedly "were worth a *conto* in gold." It was alleged that since Vasco da Gama's discovery of a sea route to India in 1497–98, a ship had never left the Indian coast loaded with so much richness in merchandise.[1]

On board the ship was Capitão Manoel de Sousa Sepúlveda together with his wife *dona* Leonor and two children. Close to six hundred crew members, enslaved people, and passengers accompanied them. After four and a half troublesome months attempting to reach Cape Agulhas, the southernmost tip of Africa, the *São João* shipwrecked off the coast of Natal, at 31°S, near what is now Port Edward on the eastern coast of South Africa. This happened on June 24, 1552. The breakdown of the sailing ship's technological system, which had been in process for quite some time, had fatal consequences. Nature proved to be more powerful than human ingenuity, and over one hundred people lost their lives during the actual wrecking (Figure 9).[2]

---

1   Anonymous, "Naufrage du grand Galion *São João* sur la Côte du Natal en l'année 1552," in *Histoires tragico-maritimes 1552–1563: Chefs-d'œuvre des naufrages portugais*, ed. Anne Lima and Michel Chandeigne, trans. Georges Le Gentil, preface José Saramago (Paris: Chandeigne, 2016), 28, 36, my translation. One *conto* of gold corresponds to one million *cruzados*, that is, gold money worth 400 *réis* at that time.
2   The shipwreck of the *São João* also features in Margaret Cohen's *The Novel and the Sea* (Princeton and Oxford: Princeton University Press, 2010), although it is only treated briefly. The most complete treatment in English of the Portuguese pamphlets relating the India Route shipwrecks can be found in Josiah Blackmore's *Manifest Perdition* (Minnesota: University of Minnesota Press, 2002). Steve Mentz devotes eight pages to the account of the shipwreck of the *São João* in his *Shipwreck Modernity* (2015). My reading has some similarity with Mentz' analysis, which focuses on the pamphlet's undecided position regarding the shipwreck's

We know what happened before, during, and after the wreck, because an eyewitness account has survived for almost five hundred years. In the eighteenth century, the Portuguese historian Bernardo Gomes de Brito collected a series of narrative accounts of the toils and wrecks of numerous Portuguese ships on the India route between 1552 and 1602. The disturbing yet fascinating accounts relate the agonizing sufferings of the survivors and those who perished. They constitute what José Saramago in his preface to a recently published French edition including three of the accounts calls "the tarnished side of the golden medal of the Discoveries and the Conquest." To Saramago, the narratives represent the counterimage of "the triumphalism of the *Lusiads* (1572)" with its "idealized figure of the navigator."[3] Some of the accounts had been published previously as singular pamphlets, but in 1735 and 1736 Brito collected them in two volumes under the title *História trágico-marítima, em que se escrevem chronologicamente os naufragios que tiveram as naus de Portugal, depois que se poz em exercício a Navegação da Índia*, published in Lisbon by Oficina da Congregação do Oratório. Brito's original 1735–36 works contain twelve accounts, six in each volume, and they are printed in chronological order from 1552 to 1602.[4]

The account of the misfortune of the *São João*, "Relação da muy notavel perda do Galeão Grande S. João" (Account of the very great loss of Galeão Grande S. João), was recorded by an unknown author, perhaps based on information from Àlvaro Fernandes, a survivor and guardian of the galleon. It was probably printed for the first time as early as 1554. Most of the account relates the events after the wrecking, when Manoel de Sousa leads the survivors up the coast of Africa. This turns out to be a most difficult march during which they suffer horrendously from thirst and hunger, some are attacked by wild animals such as leopards and snakes, and even eaten. As the journey up the coast continues more and more people die en route.

We are also invited on board the ship during the crucial days and hours of distress, when the crew works hard to rescue the precious cargo and the ship. In the first pages, it becomes clear how dependent the sailors are on the ship's

---

cause between errors of seamanship and technology and a Providential punishment. As the following will show, I emphasize Providential punishment more than Mentz in my analysis of the pamphlet's maritime vision, although the importance of acknowledging a technological dimension of seafaring in the Age of Sail is a significant objective behind my reading.

3 José Saramago, "La mort familière," preface in *Histoires tragico-maritimes 1552–1563*, 10, 16.
4 For further bibliographical details concerning the twelve accounts, see Bernard Martocq, "Note bibliographique sur l'História Trágico-Marítima," *Cahiers d'études romanes*, no. 1 (1998): 19–29, published online January 15, 2013, accessed March 31, 2017, http://etudesromanes.revues.org/3428.

technological system, and how fragile their lives become when this system starts to break down. The narrator and the characters refer to other factors behind their predicament. There are several expressions such as "may God forgive him" and "for our sins"[5] (sin of greed, sin of transgressing the boundaries of their human condition). The religious references endow the account with theocentric characteristics, but the very fact that the Portuguese delegation finds itself in Cochin and in the Indian Ocean also emphasizes the new anthropocentric qualities of audacity and risk willingness that would define the next centuries of European-dominated global history. In that sense, the account expresses the transition from theocentrism to anthropocentrism. On the one hand, it points forward to a new mentality that can be found in, say, *The Merchant of Venice*, but on the other hand it is more rooted in religiously motivated temperance than is Shakespeare's drama.

Twenty-first-century readers are able to see through the sixteenth-century religious veil and discover technology and its failings as the most probable cause of wreckage. Already in 1552, in the time before steamships, the sea journey was a highly technological affair as the first pages of "Naufrage du grand Galion *São João*" show. The sails were a major component of this technology. They not only facilitated motion and speed but also played a vital role in maneuvering the ship: "they spent much time mending them in order to be able to navigate." In the case of the *São João*, the sails having been in a bad condition for quite some time "was one of the causes, the most important one, for their perdition."[6]

During the weeks, days, and hours before the foundering, we register an intense maritime coupling of 1) natural elements such as winds, waves, depth, currents, lightning, rain, and darkness, 2) human factors such as skill, force, cunning, and panic, and 3) technological components such as sails, lead line, pintles, helm, rigging, yards, rope, hawsers, masts, and axe. Due to the high degree of unpredictability—"And the winds blew in such a way that one day they came from the Levant, the next they came from the Ponant"—it is crucial that the humans work together smoothly and appropriately with the technological components and that the components function properly. If not, the risk of wreckage and death increases dramatically: "But the sea remained so high, and the ship fatigued when losing three pintles of the helm, the entire perdition or salvation of the ships depending on this."[7]

Minor destructions multiply and are soon followed by major ones. A wave smashes into the helm, which turns out to be rotten; it breaks in two, making it

---

5 "Naufrage du grand Galion *São João*," 27, 38.
6 "Naufrage du grand Galion *São João*," 28, 27.
7 "Naufrage du grand Galion *São João*," 27–28, 29.

FIGURE 9 The foundering of the *São João*. Image from the 1735 edition of Brito's *História trágico-marítima*
© JOHN CARTER BROWN LIBRARY

practically useless. In an attempt to gain greater control of the ship's steering, the officers decide to cut down the main mast with axes, but the wind beats them to it and blows the mast and its sails violently into the sea. Despite the attempts to repair and reconstruct, the *São João* ends up without masts, sails, and helm. Consequently, the ship is left to the mercy of the winds and the currents, drifting relentlessly towards the coast and its dangerous surf. More than seventy enslaved people and about forty Portuguese lost their lives, when the *São João* broke in two, then in four, and finally sank. Almost everyone else died while marching along the African coast in the months that followed, including the captain, his wife, and their two children. Only a few survived the journey and made it back to Lisbon.

2 Technology, Literature, and the Ocean

The domains of culture and technology have a long history of being looked upon as two separate and distinct worlds, according to Bruno Latour.[8] On

---

8 Bruno Latour, *Aramis, or the Love of Technology* (Cambridge, MA: Harvard University Press, 1996), vii–viii.

the one hand, humanities scholars are reluctant to deal with the cold, steely, artificial, and dead world of technology, as they believe it compromises the warm, emotional, genuine, and living world of human culture, *Geist*, and the *cogito*. This tradition dates back to Plato, in whose works can be found many traces of discomfort with technology and the material arts. On the other hand, engineers tend to regard technology as if its evolution was the very purpose of being, and they care very little about how technological developments affect and transform the human lifeworld.[9]

If there is one world in which this dichotomy between culture and technology makes little sense, it is the maritime world. Technology is embedded in every aspect of maritime culture. This is true of the age of sail and the post-sailing era as well. More accurately, we can speak of different intensities of technological embeddedness during the ages of paddle, oar, sail, steam, and engine power. If the prevailing idea of a fundamental technological, existential, and experiential disruption caused by the replacement of sail by steam during the nineteenth century is somewhat reasonable,[10] it is worth remembering that the sailing ship was arguably the world's most complex technological machine during the four centuries spanning from the mid-fifteenth century to the mid-nineteenth century.[11]

In this chapter, one ambition is to challenge the idea of maritime history as either a dichotomous before-and-after (an enchanted, technology-free past versus a disenchanted, technologically determined present) or a smooth linear progression of ever higher technological complexity. This is not to say that

---

9   Langdon Winner, *The Whale and the Reactor: A Search for Limits in an Age of High Technology* (1986; Chicago and London: Chicago University Press, 1989), 4–5; Peter-Paul Verbeek, *What Things Do: Philosophical Reflections on Technology, Agency, and Design*, trans. Robert P. Crease (2000; Pennsylvania: The Pennsylvania State University Press, 2005), vii, 1.

10 This idea characterizes essays and tales by Joseph Conrad such as "Ocean Travel" (1923) and "The End of the Tether" (1902), critical writings such as Robert Foulke's *The Sea Voyage Narrative* (New York and London: Routledge, 2002) and Tobias Döring's "The Sea is History: Historicizing the Homeric Sea in Victorian Passages" (2002), and J. M. W. Turner's iconic painting *The Fighting Temeraire tugged to her last Berth to be broken up, 1838* (1839).

11 Theodore Ropp, *War in the Modern World* (1959; Baltimore and London: The Johns Hopkins University Press, 2000), 71; Richard Wilk, *Home Cooking in the Global Village: Caribbean Food from Buccaneers to Ecotourists* (Oxford and New York: Berg, 2006), 27; Eve M. Duffy and Alida C. Metcalf, *The Return of* Hans Staden: *A Go-between in the Atlantic World* (Baltimore: The Johns Hopkins University Press, 2012), 33; Pablo E. Pérez-Mallaína, *Spain's Men of the Sea: Daily Life on the Indies Fleets in the Sixteenth Century* (1992; Baltimore and London: The Johns Hopkins University Press, 1998), 63.

before and after are identical; neither is it my intention to say that technological development did not happen and is not happening. On the one hand, it is possible to operate on a metahistorical level at which maritime history and human history are technological per se: "*human activity from immemorial time and across the diversity of cultures has always been technologically embedded.*" On the other hand, it is possible to operate on a historical level at which we distinguish between specific technologies, focusing on "the histories of *technology transfers*"[12] and their existential, experiential, and epistemological consequences (pertaining to action, perception, and thinking, respectively) for the relationship between humans, technology, and nature. There is both *invariance* and *variance*.

Another objective is to avoid the binary extremes of utopianism and dystopianism that often adhere to technology. This is not to say that technology is neutral. Technological artifacts are withdrawn for most of the time, acting as a sort of second nature for humans, but they are never neutral. They transform our perception, our being-in-the-world, says Don Ihde: "*new instrumentation gives new perceptions.*"[13] But if technology and technological evolution have always been part of human and maritime history, then it would be more productive to analyze the distinctive experiences of different technological environments at sea instead of ignoring them or splitting them into two forms, namely an enchanted pretechnological era and a disenchanted technological era. Such an analysis makes it possible to acknowledge that the favored scapegoats in maritime fiction, the steamship and the more exclusive submarine, are just as capable as the sailing ship of producing *positive* experiences of a technologically mediated life at sea.

If maritime history is technological history, then each technological transfer potentially brings with it a double movement of revelation and concealment, amplification and reduction, invitation and inhibition: "We learn something new of the physical world through such differences, and there is 'truth' in each variation."[14] This line of thinking will guide us in a reading of Joseph Conrad's *Typhoon* in which Captain MacWhirr and his steamship the *Nan-Shan* encounter a tropical cyclone in the western part of the Pacific Ocean. We will also analyze *Twenty Thousand Leagues Under the Seas* by Jules Verne, arguably the first novel to embrace and celebrate the potentials of maritime science and modern technology, and compare Verne's take on technological

---

12 Don Ihde, *Technology and the Lifeworld: From Garden to Earth* (Bloomington and Indianapolis, Indiana University Press, 1990), 20, 70.
13 Ihde, *Technology and the Lifeworld*, 56.
14 Ihde, *Technology and the Lifeworld*, 48; Verbeek, *What Things Do*, 195.

development with Conrad's. If Verne is usually considered a utopian writer in the breed of Saint-Simon and his industrial socialism, Conrad is known for his gloomy take on the existential and social consequences of the steamship era. In both works it is possible to nuance any rigid utopian and dystopian tendencies. Before presenting these readings, further elaborations on technology are necessary. I mobilize thinkers such as Francis Bacon, Martin Heidegger, Don Ihde, Langdon Winner, Bruno Latour, and Peter-Paul Verbeek to construct an analytically productive conceptual architecture and closely examine the most interesting challenges pertaining to maritime technologies.

In Latour's *Aramis, or the Love of Technology* (1996), which deals with the rise and fall of an ambitious train system project in Paris, a source called M. Cohen remarks: "A train may well be more complicated than a satellite, technologically speaking."[15] Although the book is about a different transport system, Cohen's statement reminds us that the history of technology is not a linear one-way street that leads toward an ever-higher degree of complexity, at least not if we look at shorter time spans. Objects from the past may well be more technologically complicated than the inventions of now and tomorrow. Their newness and transformational power may certainly have been existentially more remarkable to their contemporaries than some recent inventions are to us at present. Cohen's remark also implies that not only are the present and future technological (satellites), the same is true of the past (trains). If we take Cohen's (and Latour's) argument a bit further, the idea of a technology-free past seems to be a romantic illusion. *Human history is technological history.*

The replacement of sailing ships by steamships during the nineteenth century was made possible by Thomas Newcomen's invention of the steam engine in 1712 and James Watt's improvement of the engine from 1763 and onwards. It triggered a series of fundamental changes within the entire maritime culture, for example a strict division of work between on-deck sailors and below-deck engineers and stokers, a greater degree of predictability in terms of arrival times, and less danger and hazard for the crew. Within the domain of water-borne propulsion, the switch from paddles in the first dugout canoes (Figure 10) to oars in the first rowing boats (Figure 11) represents a parallel evolutionary step. Whereas paddles are held by the paddler and not connected with the vessel, oars are traditionally connected to the vessel by means of rowlocks, which transmit the applied force to the boat. In this system, water is the fulcrum. Paddlers face the front of the canoe. Rowers face the stern of the boat, and as they pull the oar, their entire body contributes to the transmittance of power from oar and water via the rowlock to propel the boat. The two

---

15   Latour, *Aramis*, 15.

TECHNOLOGY

FIGURE 10   The Codex Mendoza. MS. Arch. Selden. A. 1, excerpt of fol. 063r
© THE BODLEIAN LIBRARY, OXFORD

examples—steam replacing sail and oars replacing paddles—are obviously very different, but they share features that help remind us that human waterborne transportation has been a technological affair from the very beginning. By extension, sailors are cyborgs per definition because of their "man-machine hybrid identities" and "private language that entwines human bodies with nonhuman tools."[16]

The social bond between objects and humans is "mysterious,"[17] Latour claims. However, in the maritime world this bond is often characterized by intimacy, familiarity, and confidence, at least for experienced sailors accustomed to seafaring. If not, the ship would wreck, and the crew would drown. The primary reason for this fusion of culture and technology is that the sea is fundamentally a hostile environment for human habitation. Evolutionary speaking, the human species may derive from early life forms that emerged from the sea millions of years ago, but in recorded human history humankind's natural habitat has always been the *terra firma*. The assemblage of the human world (culture) and the marine world (nature) requires a third component: the

---

16   Mentz, *Ocean*, 56.
17   Latour, *Aramis*, viii.

FIGURE 11 Gustave Caillebotte, *Les plaisanciers aviron sur l'Yerres* (c. 1877–c. 1879)
© BRIDGEMAN IMAGES

world of objects (technology). Without these objects of technology—oars, rowlocks, compass, sextant, sail, wheel, masts, echo sounder, life vest, and the ship—humans would be helpless on the ocean and consigned to a landbased existence. Whereas technology-driven transportation could be considered a bonus on land (people could navigate without a GPS and even without a car), it is essential at sea (Ahab could not have travelled far without his maps, sails, and the *Pequod*).

In that sense, the maritime world is a privileged place from which to examine the relationship between humans and technologies. This interface is more intense on the ocean-going ship, and it can produce insights applicable to landbased existence and existence in general. In *The Whale and the Reactor* (1986), Langdon Winner remarks: "The map of the world shows no country called Technopolis, yet in many ways we are already its citizens." Informing Winner's view of human history is a narrative of a progression from low technology to "high technology," also comprising ideas of "a new order" and "a distinctively modern form of power." Winner's diagnosis is true of landbased existence. There, "artificial things now shape our sense of being human."[18] But

---

18 Winner, *The Whale and the Reactor*, ix.

when it comes to seabased existence, sailors have *always already* been citizens not of Technopolis, but of Technoploío (technoships). From the moment humans first embarked on sea journeys, artificial things have been an integral part of, provided a structure for, and reshaped what it meant to be a seafaring human. It is worth remembering, as Thor Heyerdahl does, that: "Man hoisted sail before he saddled a horse. He poled and paddled along rivers and navigated the open seas before he travelled on wheels along a road. Water-craft were the first of all vehicles. With them, the Stone Age world began to shrink. [...] Water-craft were man's first major tool for his conquest of the world."[19] The origins of sailing fades in the depths of prehistory, but there are Scandinavian petroglyphs—stone carvings and paintings depicting ships—that date back to around 5,000 BC (perhaps even 8,000–9,000 BC at Efjorden).

Maritime history challenges Winner's idea of a break between then and now in terms of technological complexity and its impact. Technological developments at sea have never only been about the transformation of what sailors do, but also what people think about the sea, human existence, and seafaring.[20] If Winner advocates a *difference in kind* (old order/new order), I argue for a *difference in degree*. In my view, the metahistorical level stands for invariance, while variance can be found on the historical level. "Individual habits, perceptions, concepts of self, ideas of space and time, social relationships, and moral and political boundaries have all been powerfully restructured in the course of modern technological development," claims Winner.[21] Yes, they have, but this is equally true of the course of "premodern" technological development, especially at sea. Every tweak to an already-existing instrument and technology and every invention of new instruments and technologies made new geographical worlds accessible and opened new *experiential-perceptual* and *existential-practical* worlds to the sailor (and the reader of his exploits). Using new instruments becomes second nature and thus shapes the sailor's life. At the same time, sailors are always aware of the extreme fragility of these second-nature instruments and that everyone's survival depends on their functioning. These instruments had to be as fully integrated as extensions of bodily movement and behavior as possible, with the underlying realization that the instruments could fail or break.

To see how technological innovations were already decisive in so-called premodern times and were also *considered* decisive in early modernity, we

---

19   Thor Heyerdahl, *Early Man and the Ocean: The Beginning of Navigation and Seaborn Civilizations* (London: George Allen and Unwin Ltd., 1978), 19.
20   Winner, *The Whale and the Reactor*, 6.
21   Winner, *The Whale and the Reactor*, 9.

need only recall one of the most quoted passages about the significance of technology:

> Again it helps to observe the force, virtue and consequences of what has been discovered, and that is nowhere more apparent than in those three things which were unknown to the ancients and whose origins, though recent, are dark and inglorious: namely the *Art of Printing*, *Gunpowder*, and the *Mariner's Compass*. For these three have altered the whole face of things right across the globe: the first in things literary, the second in things military, and the third in navigations. From these countless other alterations have followed so that no empire, no sect and no star seems to have exerted a greater effect and influence on human affairs than these mechanical innovations.[22]

Bacon may have intended to characterize the techno-progressive blessings of his time and its immediate past ("recent origins") by referring to these three inventions, but while Gutenberg's printing press was invented around 1440 in Europe, only 180 years prior to when Bacon wrote about it, the Chinese invention of gunpowder dates back to the ninth century,[23] and the compass, another Chinese invention, was invented as early as the middle of the third century BC, although it was probably not used as a navigational instrument before the eleventh century.[24] Two of the three examples referred to by Bacon belong to much earlier epochs than the age of scientific revolution. So, if we buy into Bacon's technological eulogy, his examples and their genealogy emphasize the metahistorical importance of technological inventions and the difficulty of excluding technology from the premodern phase of human history.

If humanists in general have been hesitant to venture into the domain of technology, the situation does not improve if we consider the literary scholarship concerned with maritime fiction. Blindness may be too strong a word, but it seems as if the dimension of a technologically embedded existence on board the ship gets less attention than it deserves considering its importance.[25] The majority of literary scholars occupied with the sea and ships interpret the

---

22 Bacon, *Novum organum*, 195.
23 Brenda J. Buchanan, "Editor's Introduction: Setting the Context," in *Gunpowder, Explosives and the State: A Technological History*, ed. Brenda J. Buchanan (Aldershot: Ashgate, 2006), 2.
24 Hirth, *The Ancient History of China: The End of the Chóu Dynasty*, 133–34; Needham, *The Shorter Science & Civilisation in China: 3*, 27–29.
25 Digital library search engines such as MLA show close to no results if one enters "technology" and, say, "Melville" or "Conrad."

symbolism or semantics of the ocean, the psychology of the interpersonal relationships on board the ship, or the sociopolitical dimension of the seafaring journey.[26] These approaches are productive, but they overlook the existential, experiential, and epistemological significance of technology as a vital and inescapable mediator between man and nature.

Technology fundamentally influences the everyday lives of humans in at least three domains—action, perception, and knowledge—but it does not "stand for something else." Technology does not possess a meaning or symbolic truth hidden beneath its surface that must be retrieved to explain its existential significance for humans. Although genealogies of technologies may reveal crucial decisions comprising ethical and political implications—democratic or totalitarian, centralization or decentralization—such findings have little to do with a symbolism of technology. Instead, they pertain to what Latour labels "network." Technology either works or does not work. Either way, it impacts the human lifeworld in practical and perceptual ways. Technology is never neutral.

The significant role of technologies at sea has generic implications for nautical literature. Maritime fiction is neither Goethe's *Die Leiden des jungen Werthers* (1774) nor is it Oscar Wilde's *The Picture of Dorian Gray* (1890). Goethe's novel focuses on the individual's matters of heart and personal feelings, not least ideal love; it is written in the form of intimacy, subjectivity, and subjective feelings *par excellence*, the personal letter, but it is also completely ignorant of, uninterested in, and cleansed of the technical sphere of life (e.g., how guns work). Wilde's novel implodes into its own mirror of creation and is articulated in a philosophical discourse, and like *Werther* it is unconcerned with the outer world of messy, unruly stuff and its practical-technical constitution. Maritime fiction is neither *Sturm und Drang* nor *l'art pour l'art*. It may contain elements of both: *Sturm und Drang* and *l'art pour l'art* are broader

---

26   See e.g., Ian Baucom, *Specters of the Atlantic: Finance Capital, Slavery, and the Philosophy of History* (Durham and London: Duke University Press, 2005); Blumenberg, *Shipwreck with Spectator*; Casarino, *Modernity at Sea*; Corbin, *The Lure of the Sea*; Alain Corbin, *Le ciel et la mer* (Paris: Bayard Culture, 2005); Alain Corbin and Hélène Richard, *La mer, terreur et fascination* (Paris: BNF, 2004); Paul Gilroy, *The Black Atlantic: Modernity and Double Consciousness* (London: Verso, 1993); Peter Linebaugh and Marcus Rediker, *The Many-Headed Hydra: Sailors, Slaves, Commoners, and the Hidden History of the Revolutionary Atlantic* (Boston: Beacon Press, 2000); Marcus Rediker, *Between the Devil and the Deep Blue Sea: Merchant Seaman, Pirates, and the Anglo-American Maritime World, 1700–1750* (Cambridge: Cambridge University Press, 1987); Marcus Rediker, *Villains of All Nations: Atlantic Pirates in the Golden Age* (London: Verso, 2004); Eric W. Sager, *Seafaring Labour: The Merchant Marine of Atlantic Canada, 1820–1914* (Montreal: McGill-Queen's University Press, 1989); Schmitt, *Land and Sea*.

epochal characteristics of certain thematic and formal propensities, and maritime fiction written in the late 1700s or the late 1800s may be affiliated with such propensities.

Perhaps it is Fenimore Cooper's early sea novels with their young romantic sailor heroes that come closest to Goethe's *Werther* and its idealistic protagonist, while Conrad may be the maritime author whose aesthetic experiments are most comparable to Wilde's aestheticism. It must be stressed, though, that both Cooper and Conrad are intent on depicting the dirty and brutal life on board the ship and the cold and mechanic world of technology, to which neither Goethe nor Wilde came close. Maritime fiction is first and foremost an examination of *man's technologically mediated encounter with nature* and (perhaps less recognized) *his "naturally" mediated encounter with technology*—it may even be a depiction of *nature's challenge of technology and vice versa* in which man's role is minimal. Consequently, maritime fiction is saturated with nature, technology, and the practical human activities that arise in the coupling between the two. As such, the technological dimension constitutes a metahistorical component of maritime fiction (a historical component is then the intensity and concrete design of the technological dimension), independent of historically specific aesthetic and thematic orientations. How technology and technological development are perceived varies from period to period and from author to author, but in nautical literature technology is ever-present.

As with many vital rhythms of life, such as the beating of the heart, technology is such an integrated part of human life that we only notice its existence when it breaks down or is unavailable. This is the case on board the ship. Daily life is often governed by monotony and strictly defined routines involving (or dictated by) technology—the reading of the compass, the measuring of latitude and longitude, the feeding of the stove with coal, the looking out for allies or enemies, etc. In what follows, I use the insights of Martin Heidegger, Don Ihde, and Peter-Paul Verbeek on technology to create a platform from which to elaborate on topics of interest and concepts useful for an analysis of maritime fiction, here Verne's *Twenty Thousand Leagues Under the Seas* and Conrad's *Typhoon*.

In the passage from *Novum Organon*, Bacon considered technology to be more than simply newly invented objects. To Bacon, technology transforms the world. It does so by changing man's perception *of* and behavior *in* the world in that it determines different ways of experiencing the world and of opening it to new practices. In that sense, Bacon is a key figure in the transition from theocentrism to anthropocentrism and technocentrism where the relationship between man and technology becomes crucial for humankind's evolution, progress, and way of uncovering the world. Bacon belongs to the utopian wing among the philosophers of technology. This is not only apparent in his book of utopia, *The New Atlantis* (1627), but also in *Novum Organon*. Just prior to his relatively neutral descriptive enumeration in the printing-gunpowder-compass quote, Bacon shows a more value-laden side when he claims that "discoveries enrich and spread their blessings without causing hurt or grief to anybody."[27] To Bacon and many of his contemporaries during the scientific revolution, technological inventions had positive implications for both humankind and society. The utopian hope of progression through the evolution of technology also characterizes many Enlightenment thinkers and their heirs, for example Marquis de Condorcet and Émile Zola. The discussions between utopians and dystopians have been a constant ever since Bacon. Jules Verne belongs to Bacon's camp, whereas Conrad does not.

I will try to steer clear of the binary utopia/dystopia thinking and instead use Bacon's printing-gunpowder-compass quote as an invitation to examine the different kinds of technological experience that are crucial ways of being in the world. Technological experience is not limited to the post-sailing epoch, and technological experience in the post-sailing epoch—for example the experience of being and working on board a steamship—can have its own positive elements. Which changes in "human affairs" and "the whole face of things right across the globe"—they may be good or bad, positive or negative, but they are certainly *different*—are triggered by technological changes?

Heidegger and Ihde are relevant, because their phenomenological approaches facilitate an understanding of technology as a certain way to uncover the world and as a special form that transforms man's experience of the world. In addition, it comprises both an epistemological and a practical dimension of human existence by prioritizing "a certain interpretation of human *experience* and that, in particular, concerns *perception* and *bodily activity*."[28] In a maritime context, the practical dimension is very important, because ship life historically has been physically demanding and required hands-on skills and a practical rationality. But the perceptive dimension is equally important as a way to comprehend the specific maritime epistemology of "oceanic thinking."

The invention of the compass was evidently of the greatest importance to the maritime-driven transformation of the cartographic appearance and state of the world. Although the compass was a Chinese invention, and although the Chinese had explored the Pacific long before the European transoceanic

---

27   Bacon, *Novum organum*, 194.
28   Ihde, *Technology and the Lifeworld*, 21.

adventures arrived in the late fifteenth century, it is still reasonable to follow Bacon's line of thinking, not only because the subject of this book is maritime history in the Western world, but, more importantly, because it was the European transoceanic voyages that came to define the development of modernity through the planet-transformative actions of nations such as Portugal, Spain, France, the United Kingdom, and the United States. The global center of power shifted sometime during the fifteenth century, perhaps earlier, to the West. The compass assisted the opening of oceanic water transport (in the East and the West), and also made completely new worlds of experience and existence possible for the hitherto earthbound or coastal-bound human being. According to Margaret Cohen, "Bacon was not overstating the importance of saltwater transport networks in the forging of global modernity."[29] During this period, part of humanity morphed into what Schmitt terms "children of the sea," although the majority remained "children of the earth."[30] Although Atlantic journeys had taken place earlier, they were of a more accidental character and certainly not as pervasive. It was the technology of the compass that made the European "discoveries" of and interactions with the non-Western world possible. From then on, ocean voyaging became a global activity.

As previously mentioned, Margaret Cohen takes up the mantle from Bacon and mentions three further discoveries or inventions with decisive importance for life at sea: John Harrison's invention of the chronometer in 1759; the British Admiralty's decision in 1795 to introduce fixed rations of lemon juice to all crew members to prevent scurvy; and Robert Fulton's steamboat journey in 1807 up the Hudson River from New York City to Albany, New York.[31] In *La Mer*, Michelet devotes an entire chapter to the lighthouse, which from around 1830 began to populate the coasts on the world's continents, "saving, and guiding" seamen lost in utter darkness and therefore in danger of shipwrecking due to sandbanks and rocks.[32] Like the compass, these technological inventions and scientific discoveries transformed maritime existence and the sailor's experience of the world, primarily in terms of making life at sea safer, more calculable, and regularized. It is only reasonable to assume that both later and earlier discoveries have also had existentially, experientially, and epistemologically transformative effects.

---

29 Cohen, "Literary Studies on the Terraqueous Globe," 657.
30 Schmitt, *Land and Sea*, 2, 3.
31 Cohen, "Literary Studies on the Terraqueous Globe," 659.
32 Michelet, *La Mer*, 87–97.

3 Martin Heidegger's Technologies

Heidegger elevated technology to a philosophical question. By turning technology into a vital component of man's interpretation of and being in the world, he emphasized its hermeneutical and existential importance to human life. In Heidegger's work there are several books, texts, and passages—from *Sein und Zeit* (1927) and *Der Ursprung des Kunstwerkes* (1935) to "Die Frage Nach der Technik" (1954) and *Gelassenheit* (1959)—dealing with the question of technology and its perceptual and practical human consequences. In Heidegger's work, there is a move from an *ontic and ahistorical* analysis of the capacity of concrete technologies and tools to open up the world in a particular manner to an *ontological and historical* analysis of technology as "world-disclosure" in which any specific technology is simply a manifestation of the world picture that already governs our way of thinking in a specific moment in history.[33] Simply put, Heidegger moves from "beings →Being" (*Sein und Zeit*) to "Being →beings" ("Die Frage").

The most obvious example of a philosophy of technology in Heidegger's work is the famous lecture "The Question Concerning Technology" given in Munich in 1953. The lecture is widely considered to be the first serious contemplation on technology in Western philosophy. Heidegger transcendentally defines technology as a dominating and controlling manner of thinking and engaging with the world. Technology becomes a particular way of world-disclosure (Being) in which reality appears to humans as no more than calculable raw material to be manipulated by humans. However, as early as in *Being and Time*, more specifically in § 15–18, Heidegger discusses through his analysis of tools or equipment (*Zeug*) as "ready-to-hand" (*zuhanden*) man's "being-in-the-world" as an already practically (and nonthematically) oriented existence shaped by the operativity of tools and in which it is possible to see a particular world-disclosure. However, this type of world-disclosure is *a posteriori* (determined by concrete tools, by technologies) whereas the world-disclosure in the lecture is *a priori* (determining the way in which technology appears).

Both texts attempt transcendental determinations of man's technological/technical relationship with the world. In other words, Heidegger uncovers basic pre-structures that are valid at all times (*Being and Time*) or at certain moments in history ("The Question"). Transcendentally means here two different things, though, depending on which temporality governs the analysis. In the lecture, where technology is seen in a specific historical context (that

---

33   Verbeek, *What Things Do*, 62, 65–66, 75, 76, 80.

of Heidegger's contemporaneity, the machine age), transcendental means a pointing backwards to technology's conditions of possibility, in this case specified as the dominating technical world picture. This world picture, described in very negative terms by Heidegger, then determines our understanding of modern technology's relationship to nature as raw material (*Bestand*) to be manipulated and controlled. Another way to put it is that it is not the power station built on the Rhine that causes us to see the Rhine as a source of energy instead of as a beautiful river; it is the fact that we already see the Rhine as a source of energy that causes us to build the power station. The world conceived of as *Bestand* determines our technologies.

In *Being and Time*, it is not technology as such that is submitted to a transcendental analysis in which the ambition is to trace technology back to its conditions of possibility. Instead, Heidegger's focus is the way in which technologies or tools (e.g., a hammer) appear to humans either as ready-to-hand (*zuhanden*) or present-at-hand (*vorhanden*). Ready-to-hand, or handiness, and present-at-hand, or simply present, are the two pre-structured ways in which tools enter into a relationship with humans. They either work unnoticed, or they noticeably don't work. In contrast to the idea of technology in the lecture, tools are not analyzed transcendentally and backwards in terms of their conditions of possibility, but forward in terms of their concrete functions and their manner of opening up new worlds to humans. The hammer implicitly makes us see the world in new and potentially multiple ways; there is not one single and dominating world picture determining the functions and potentials of the hammer.

If both texts draw up transcendental approaches (technology as an inescapable mode of human perception), although in a different manner (tools as positive world openers, or technologies as expressions of a negatively valorized technical Being), there is a difference of temporality between the ahistoricism of *Being and Time* and the historicism of "The Question." This difference is important for the understanding of Heidegger's position *vis à vis* traditional and modern technology and his conception of the evolution of the history of technology. The tool analysis in *Being and Time* is to be considered within Heidegger's agenda of creating a fundamental ontology concretized in the analysis of *Dasein*. The tool analysis is linked to the analysis of "the worldhood of the world" ("die Weltlichkeit der Welt") and thus points forward to one of the constitutive elements in *Dasein*'s "being-in-the-world" ("in-der-Welt-sein"). In *Being and Time*, man is in his thrownness (*Geworfenheit*) already given a world, and this world is either ready-to-hand or present-at-hand. The world is either given in a practical-useful interaction (*Zeug*) or in a distanced, contemplative, and theoretical approach (*Ding*).

In "The Question Concerning Technology," it is a question of the status of modern, industrial technology, a question emerging from more concrete circumstances. In the one, the hammer is central; in the other, it is rather "modern machine-powered technology" that is at issue: "And it is precisely the latter and it alone that is the disturbing thing, that moves us to ask the question concerning technology per se."[34] Heidegger's early tool analysis, the hammer being the most prominent example, is linked to a predominantly craftsman-like and positive understanding of technology, whereas the later analysis of technology, the power station being the most prominent example, is linked to a predominantly industrial and negative understanding of technology. In that sense, Heidegger constructed a metahistorical perspective on man's relationship with technology early in his career (the ahistorical approach in *Being and Time*), whereas the later Heidegger spoke of a rupture between old and new technology (the historical approach in "The Question").

As Verbeek has convincingly shown, the difference in approach is the main reason why Heidegger end up formulating two axiologically very different evaluations of the hammer (positive) and the power station (negative): "Heidegger measures tradition and modernity with different scales. [...] When he compares specific technologies of the past and present with each other, he applies two different standards, reserving a historical perspective for an analysis of modern technologies and an ahistorical perspective for traditional technologies."[35] This internal inconsistency makes it possible to nuance the traditional understanding of Heidegger as someone who nostalgically looks back upon a bygone era of innocent craftsmanship (hammers and mills) and critically and contemptuously observes his own contemporaneity of industrial technology (power stations).

For what would happen if we were to use Heidegger's own ahistorical approach, in which technologies are world openers and things that make Being as an event visible, to an analysis of modern technology? What is the equipmentality of modern technology, its characteristics of such immanent features as its ready-to-hand, present-at-hand, "in-order-to," and "*in terms of* [*aus*] its belonging to other equipment"?[36] What would happen if modern technology was less an expression of *how* coming into being is understood in different

---

34 Martin Heidegger, "The Question Concerning Technology," in *The Question Concerning Technology and Other Essays*, trans. William Lovitt (New York and London: Garland Publishing, 1977), 13–14.
35 Verbeek, *What Things Do*, 75.
36 Martin Heidegger, *Being and Time*, trans. John Macquarrie and Edward Robinson (1962; Oxford and Cambridge, MA: Blackwell, 2001), § 15, 97.

epochs, that is, was less an exponent of a specific sending of being (the Rhine power station could only be built because the Rhine shows itself as *Bestand*, as standing-reserve), and more an expression of the fact *that* reality comes into being, that is, more an exponent of being itself and a thing that makes visible that being is an event that happens?[37]

One of the most fruitful insights of Heidegger's analysis of *Zeug* is that the special human intercourse (*Umgang*) with the world, which Heidegger calls handling (*handtierende*) and using (*gebrauchende*), that is, the ready-to-hand intercourse that is characterized by a "thrusting aside our interpretative tendencies," comprises its own epistemology, "its own kind of 'knowledge'" (*seine eigene "Erkenntnis"*). Humans do not access or gain new knowledge only through theoretical or interpretative elaborations of consciousness, but also through the preconscious workings with their hands and the artifacts in those hands. Furthermore, this *zuhanden* interaction with the world makes the world closer, more habitable, and more familiar to humans. Heidegger thus pinpoints and legitimizes a practical knowledge about the world that is caused by the use—the "something in-order-to ..."[38]—of technological artifacts. Through the technical-handling dealings with the world, humans recognize and perceive the world. Technology is a mode of uncovering the world. Using technology, a specific practical opening of the world takes place, a knowledge that is technologically mediated.

It is important that Heidegger identifies and legitimizes a practical knowledge about the world constituted through the use of equipment, which here applies to a broad conception of technology and technique. Heidegger mentions for example "equipment for writing, sewing, working, transportation, measurement."[39] Although Heidegger famously exemplifies with a hammer (a technique that belongs to the domain of craftsmanship), it is not wrong to conclude that his analysis—the transcendental dimension associated with the pre-structure of ready-to-hand or present-at-hand—applies to technology as such. Inherent in the technical making-use-of the world or in the practical dealings with the world is an epistemological dimension of worldly knowledge through the event of disclosure. Technology is a manner in which the world is revealed to humans. Through the use of technology, a certain practical opening of the world takes place. This opening is at the same time knowledge mediated through technology.

---

37   Verbeek, *What Things Do*, 74.
38   Heidegger, *Being and Time*, § 15, 96, 95, 97.
39   Heidegger, *Being and Time*, § 15, 97.

Technology as tool or equipment (*Zeug*) plays an important role in the epistemological form of knowledge. When a tool is used, something significant happens: "The peculiarity of what is proximally ready-to-hand is that, in its readiness-to-hand, it must, as it were, withdraw [zurückzuziehen] in order to be ready-to-hand quite authentically." The reason for this withdrawal and becoming-transparent of the tool is that it is constantly referring to other and wider contexts or environments than itself. Heidegger says that a tool has a structure of "in-order-to ['etwas um-zu ...']" in which lies "an *assignment* or *reference* of something to something" (*Verweisung*), for example "ink-stand, pen, ink, paper, blotting pad, table, lamp, furniture, windows, doors, room." In addition, equipment always comprises "a manifold of such assignments" (*Verweisungsmannigfaltigkeit*). It is important that the discovery of the relational totality of tools always precedes the discovery of the individual tool. Prior to every tool, a context of use that determines the specific tool is already given. In contrast to the theoretical behavior's "just looking, without circumspection,"[40] the practical behavior operates through a vision of circumspection (*Umsicht*).

The primary orientation or dwelling of our everyday dealings is not (in) the tools themselves: "On the contrary, that with which we concern ourselves primarily is the work—that which is to be produced at the time; and this is accordingly ready-to-hand too. The work bears with it that referential totality within which the equipment is encountered." For this work to be produced, Heidegger also determines the equipment as having a structure of towards-which, and the product itself has the same "in-order-to" structure of the tools endowing it with an essential usability: "The shoe which is to be produced is for wearing (footgear) [Schuhzeug]; the clock is manufactured for telling the time." Apart from the work to be produced, the production itself is a using of something for something. In other words, there is also a reference to materials in that the work is dependent on leather, thread, needles, and the like. Finally, *Dasein*, here the producer or the bearer of the equipment, should also be accounted for in this relational totality: "The work produced refers not only to the 'towards-which' of its usability and the 'whereof' of which it consists: under simple craft conditions it also has an assignment to the person who is to use it or wear it. The work is cut to his figure; he 'is' there along with it as the work emerges."[41] The produced work, its context, its material, and man are four dimensions already inscribed into the tool in terms of its character of

---

40 Heidegger, *Being and Time*, § 15, 99, 97.
41 Heidegger, *Being and Time*, § 15, 99, 99, 100.

reference or assignment, and therefore the tool also constitutes a relational totality. To Heidegger, equipment becomes a distinctive center of gravity that connects and reveals man, world, and nature in a totality of relations endowed with a specific direction: man becomes bearer of the tool, nature becomes material that the tool uses, and the world becomes the product created by the use of the tool, a work-world or Nature (*Werkwelt* or *Umwelt*).

The hidden connection between world and technology—hidden because the world is opened through the transparency of the tool—can only become manifest through a negative experience: "When we concern ourselves with something, the entities which are most closely ready-to-hand may be met as something unusable, not properly adapted for the use we have decided upon. The tool turns out to be damaged, or the material unsuitable." The nonthematized *zuhandene* intercourse with the world can break down if the tool suddenly turns out to be useless as is the case with the compass on Conrad's the *Sofala*, the bolt holes insufficiently filled with pitch on Munk's *Enhiørningen*, and the helm on Captain Manoel de Sousa's the *São João*. Transparency morphs into opacity as when a clean windshield in a car suddenly is hit by a stone and cracks. The tool now points to itself as something present and material that demands attention, as if it was a prompter emerging from her box and entering onto the scene. It becomes conspicuous, obtrusive, or obstinate, says Heidegger. Consequently, the tool's totality of different contexts of assignments—of "in-order-to," "whereof," and "towards-which"—is made explicit through a rupture in the circumspective sounding through the thematization of the circumspection itself, and the environment reveals itself all over again: "With this totality, however, the world announces itself."[42]

With Heidegger's analysis of equipment in *Being and Time*, it becomes clear that technology is a fundamental human activity that functions as a center of gravity around which the world, nature, and man circles in a pre-theoretical and nonthematized totality of understanding that constitutes man's immediate world. This practical approach is more primordial than the theoretical "present-at-hand" approach. It is crucial that this technologically mediated interaction is given not merely a legitimized but a privileged epistemological role in relation to world-disclosure and knowledge of the world.

In "The Question Concerning Technology," the "unconcealment" that governs modern technology "is a challenging [*Herausfordern*], which puts to nature the unreasonable demand that it supply energy that can be extracted and stored as such." Modern technology's challenge happens in a way so as to

---

42   Heidegger, *Being and Time*, § 16, 102, 102–03, 105.

open up for nature's hidden energy, which is then transformed, stored, and distributed. Technology's world-disclosure understood as a challenge is the general designation that also covers ways of disclosing, even "the chief characteristics of the challenging revealing," such as "regulating" (*Steuerung*) and "securing" (*Sicherung*)—that is, different ways to count on and manipulate nature and its energy reserves. The challenging interaction with the world means that nature can always be made available to humans. Nature becomes something that humans can count upon, and such management and control of nature's resources Heidegger calls "standing-reserve" (*Bestand*): "It designates nothing less than the way in which everything presences that is wrought upon by the challenging revealing. Whatever stands by in the sense of standing-reserve no longer stands over against us as object." In modern technology's way of revealing, nature becomes standing reserve. Nature is challenged due to its stock, and this way of revealing is gathered under the concept *Ge-stell*: "It is nothing technological, nothing on the order of a machine. It is the way in which the real reveals itself as standing-reserve."[43]

Bestand points back to Heidegger's earlier analysis of *Zeug*. On the one hand, nature is revealed as a material "in-order-to," on the other hand the world no longer appears as an object. In *Being and Time*, the equipment also entailed a discovery of nature as "natural products" and ready-to-hand through its use and structure of "in-order-to": "The wood is a forest of timber, the mountain a quarry of rock; the river is water-power, the wind is wind 'in the sails.' "[44] This is not a distanced intercourse that transforms reality into a present-at-hand object; instead, it has already included reality and nature into a context of use and assignments. The world, which humans encounter through modern technology, is saturated with the quality of standing-reserve, with nature already implicated in different situations of energy demands. In the famous example of the Rhine and the power station, the river no longer runs freely according to Heidegger: "even the Rhine itself appears as something at our command. [...] the river is dammed up into the power plant." For the modern tourist who wishes to enjoy the Rhine as an aesthetic object, a river in a landscape, the experience is compromised by the fact that it has become "an object on call for inspection by a tour group ordered there by the vacation industry."[45] Even though similarities exist between the analysis of equipment and that of standing-reserve, it becomes evident that Heidegger has moved the emphasis

---

43   Heidegger, "The Question Concerning Technology," 14, 16, 17, 23.
44   Heidegger, *Being and Time*, § 15, 100.
45   Heidegger, "The Question Concerning Technology," 16, 16.

from technology as a primordial and practical way of opening and obtaining knowledge about the world to technology as a way of unconcealment that requires that reality, and especially nature, can be calculated and controlled. Modern technology expresses a mastering of nature.

Throughout "The Question," Heidegger's descriptions of and vocabulary related to modern technology (e.g., "the monstrousness that reigns here") could tempt the reader into believing that the more neutral, even positive Heidegger who wrote *Being and Time* has morphed into a dystopian technophobe or neoluddite. That is a simplification of the complexity of his thoughts. Heidegger's ambition is to distill the essence of modern technology in order to discover its limits and, ultimately, its dangers. Not the danger of specific technologies, but the danger of technology's essence. Since the essence of technology "is by no means anything technological," it is not possible for humans to choose if they want to be part of it or not. Specific technologies are not neutral, but neither is the essence of technology a neutral dimension of Being. It is to be treated as what Heidegger terms "*destining* [*Geschick*]," that is, "a way of revealing" (*ein Weg des Entbergens*),[46] which man has been sent upon and that determines all history. In this idea of being sent on a path, we hear echoes from the earlier fundamental and existential idea of man's thrownness into the world. Here, it implies that humans are given a concrete historical existence, and within the modern world (which Heidegger seems to think begins in the seventeenth century) they have been sent upon a technological path of unconcealment.

Heidegger's emphasis of the historicity of modern technology—and remember that he describes it as monstrous—enables humans to regard it as something historically given. The historicity means that the technological *Gestell* may eventually be replaced by another paradigm; that it is given, means that humans may relate to it more freely. Destining is not an expression of fatalism; instead, it includes two options: either a potential for the freedom to choose alternative paths or a danger of only going down one path.

It is the last option that makes modern technology a topic of some urgency. The danger of modern technology is that humans act and think exclusively within the technological world-disclosure. Captain Nemo of Verne's the *Nautilus* is arguably an example of this. The same with Hauke Haien in Theodor Storm's *Der Schimmelreiter* (1888). Heidegger lists four consequences. Firstly, the reductionist challenging inherent in *Ge-stell* is directed at man, who consequently "comes to the point where he himself will have to be taken as standing-reserve." Secondly, because threatened man begins to see himself as "lord of the earth" meaning "that everything man encounters exists only insofar as it

---

46   Heidegger, "The Question Concerning Technology," 16, 4, 24, 12.

is his construct" (*Gemächte*).[47] Thirdly, this illusion leads to the delusion that man always and everywhere encounters only himself, but Heidegger is quick to correct this delusion:

> *In truth, however, precisely nowhere does man today any longer encounter himself, i.e., his essence.* Man stands so decisively in attendance on the challenging-forth of Enframing that he does not apprehend Enframing as a claim, that he fails to see himself as the one spoken to, and hence also fails in every way to hear in what respect he ek-sists, from out of his essence, in the realm of an exhortation or address, and thus *can never encounter only himself.*[48]

Fourthly, and this is perhaps the most dangerous consequence, modern technology and its destining in the form of Enframing and ordering "drives out every other possibility of revealing": "Thus the challenging Enframing not only conceals a former way of revealing, bringing-forth, but it conceals revealing itself and with it That wherein unconcealment, i.e., truth, comes to pass." The essence of modern technology not only blocks off alternative ways of revealing, but also, by doing so, the possibility for a more primordial revealing. Heidegger writes off a superficial critique of technology that remains on the ontic level: "What is dangerous is not technology. There is no demonry of technology, but rather there is the mystery of its essence. The essence of technology, as a destining of revealing, is the danger."[49] The true danger is not the fact that humans can get hurt, even fatally, because of some machine. Rather, the hegemony of *Ge-stell* threatens to determine human existence in the image of technology's essence and to block any alternative roads thereby denying humans the opportunity to access a more primordial unconcealment and truth.

4   Don Ihde and Technological Forms of Experience

Heidegger exerts a deep influence on the works of Don Ihde, whose overall ambition is to further advance the thinking on the role of technology in human life beyond Heidegger's work. Ihde's starting point is Heidegger's transcendental approach to technology in that he shows how human relations with technology fundamentally color the human experience of and existence in the

---

47 Heidegger, "The Question Concerning Technology," 27, 27.
48 Heidegger, "The Question Concerning Technology," 27.
49 Heidegger, "The Question Concerning Technology," 27, 28.

world. Ihde also believes, as did Heidegger, that technologies are inescapable and have been an integrated part of human life from time immemorial.[50] Since humans have always interacted with technology, it has influenced people's perceptions of and actions in the world continuously throughout human history. This is important, because it immediately eliminates any potential romantic fantasies of a return to a nontechnological state of nature from Ihde's philosophy of technology.

But if Ihde's starting point is Heidegger's transcendental understanding of technology, his correction of and ambition to think further than Heidegger consist of leading his own philosophy of technology in a more empirical direction. This move was partly inspired by what Hans Achterhuis labeled "the empirical turn" and has subsequently inspired Verbeek to further elaborate on both Heidegger's and Ihde's thinking.[51] The empirical challenge to the philosophy of technology implies that thinkers replace their focus on Technology (as essence) with a focus on technologies (in use). In that sense, the transcendental agenda in Heidegger's later writings on technology, especially the search for the essence of technology in "The Question," needs to be supplemented by investigations of concrete technologies and tools. In Ihde's words, a move takes place from "generalizations about *technology uberhaupt*" to an "examination of *technologies in their particularities*."[52] It is still necessary to distinguish between the transcendental approach in *Being and Time* and in Heidegger's later writings. In the latter, transcendentalism means searching for technology's conditions of possibility, which Heidegger found in the historical manifestation of Being as a negatively valorized technological world-disclosure. In the former, the transcendental approach had to do with uncovering the pre-structures of our concrete technologically mediated perceptions and actions—pre-structures such as "ready-to-hand," "present-at-hand," and "in-order-to."

Ihde attempts to position himself between the transcendentalism of the late Heidegger, the transcendentalism of the early Heidegger, and the empirical position by concentrating on what he calls "human-technology-relations." These are meant to capture "the ways we are bodily engaged with technologies."[53] Ihde asks how the human relationship with technology transforms and has always transformed human experience and existence. But technology's transformation of human perception and action is seen within concrete

---

50   Ihde, *Technology and the Lifeworld*, 20.
51   Hans Achterhuis, *American Philosophy of Technology: The Empirical Turn*, trans. Robert P. Crease (1997; Bloomington: Indiana University Press, 2001); Verbeek: *What Things Do*.
52   Ihde, *Technology and the Lifeworld*, 22.
53   Ihde, *Technology and the Lifeworld*, 72.

circumstances, more specifically within concrete technologies (from telescope to telephone). Ihde finds more inspiration in the *Zeug* analysis and its concrete phenomenological analyzes than in the *Ge-stell* analysis. Inherent in that approach is the attempt to steer clear of or navigate between the Scylla and Charybdis of philosophy. Scylla is the classical philosophy of technology entailing "a too-conservative philosophy of alienation" that laments the loss of materiality and authenticity (e.g., the late Heidegger, Karl Jaspers, and Jacques Ellul), whereas Charybdis is the more general philosophical movement consisting of "a too-radical strict linguistic philosophy" claiming that the language in which humans speak about reality determines what counts as that reality (e.g., Michel Foucault, Jacques Derrida, and Judith Butler).[54]

Neither Ihde nor Verbeek rejects the insights of the linguistic turn but consider them to be necessary corrections to a too naïve positivistic and naturalistic thinking. But since the linguistic turn has led to a death of the thing, the time is ripe to reverse the Platonist propensity for immaterialism and counter the linguistic turn by acknowledging the crucial roles of materiality, technology, and things in our everyday lives. According to Ihde, the way to do so is by adopting an empirical method. As Verbeek remarks about the empirical studies: "By researching specific technologies in concrete applications, they have brought to light the fact that technologies have different impacts in different contexts. The supposed determinism of technology appears to be weaker than is presented in the classical picture; while technologies do indeed strongly shape the form and the context in which they function, this happens in a more differentiated and local manner than in the traditional view."[55] A relevant point is that this was in fact what Heidegger initiated (but never completed) in *Being and Time*.

In *Technologies and the Lifeworld*, Ihde lists four different forms of human-technology-relations corresponding to four types of technological experience. The first two are characterized by being technologically mediated perceptions in which humans are related to the world through technology. Ihde labels the first of these perceptions embodiment relations and the second hermeneutical relations. The third form is labeled alterity relations and the fourth is called background relations. The first three forms are to be seen within a human-technology continuum in which the first (embodiment relations) is characterized by a pure ready-to-hand relationship between man and technology (man and technology merge and technology becomes a quasi-I), whereas the third (alterity relations) is characterized by a pure present-at-hand relationship

---

54 Verbeek, *What Things Do*, 2.
55 Verbeek, *What Things Do*, 5.

between man and technology (man and technology stand apart and confront each other, and technology becomes a quasi-other); the second form (hermeneutical relations) is somewhere in-between *Zuhandenheit* and *Vorhandenheit* (technology mediates between man and world, and while technology is not present as itself, it still draws attention to itself by not being embodied but in need of being read or interpreted). Embodiment relations and hermeneutical relations both take place within the human sphere of practical dealings with the world, and the equipment or technologies are neither foreign elements to humans nor in this world but are bound up in familiar and ordinary human practices. In alterity relations, technologies become strange in the sense of being an "other," while in background relations they fade from our consciousness.

Embodiment relations are Ihde's elaboration of Heidegger's *Zeug* analysis, and they have the same structural characteristics: withdrawal and transparency. Humans are granted a mediated access to the world through technologies in such a way that man and technology fuse into a symbiosis. Humans incorporate technologies in their perception of the world so that they no longer are experienced as separate and different. Ihde mentions glasses and binoculars as examples of such embodied ready-to-hand technologies. The diving suits, including the helmets of copper and glass, in *Vingt mille lieues sous les mers* are another example. An important correction of or supplement to Ihde's theory is Verbeek's emphasis of technology's role in co-shaping or constituting both humans and the world. It is wrong to believe that subject and object are just two preexisting poles whose relationship is mediated by technology; more accurately, both humans and the world are products of technological mediation.[56]

The transformative character of embodiment relations has a general dual structure that Ihde terms "an essential magnification/reduction structure."[57] Each embodied technology simultaneously enhances and diminishes human perception and experience. This structure, transcendental in fact, shows very clearly why technology is not neutral. There are always costs to be paid, but at the same time one gains certain advantages. Human experience is both magnified and reduced because the concrete technology or tool organizes perception in a specific manner. Technology manipulates, but it would be wrong to equate manipulation with loss; instead, this basic structure must be acknowledged and included. Nevertheless, Ihde expresses concern by pointing to the fact that

---

56   Verbeek, *What Things Do*, 129–30.
57   Ihde, *Technology and the Lifeworld*, 76.

the reduction is typically ignored, because the magnifying aspect is new and thus intriguing: "What is *revealed* is what excites; what is concealed may be forgotten."[58] Ihde's way of schematically expressing embodiment relations looks like this:

(I-technology) → world

Hermeneutic relations imply "a special interpretive action within the technological context." Here, technologies that represent the world require reading and interpretation. Technology mediates a specific access to the world, but in this case the link is representational and demands a hermeneutical effort. Technology is no longer completely transparent but must be somehow experienced. Humans move towards a more thematized and present-at-hand relationship with the tool, which is now functional through its visibility, although this visibility can be said to represent a different kind of referential transparency. The analysis of hermeneutical relations is Ihde's attempt to adjust Heidegger: "What is emerging here is the first suggestion of an emergence of the technology as 'object' but without its negative Heideggerian connotation."[59] To Ihde, the hermeneutical relation to technology is a no less primordial derivation than the embodied technological relation. Admittedly, a thematized and thus (self-) conscious interpretation of technology is required, but this is merely a new type of transparency in which humans are not overly fixated on the specific interpretation but on the world to which the technology refers.

This type of technological experience is thus perceptually linked to the formalized expression of the concrete technology. Ihde mentions maps and chronometer, and compass, barometer, and manometer can also be mentioned. At the same time, the experience is oriented toward what this expression refers to, namely concrete aspects of the world that one wishes to have hermeneutically and epistemologically enhanced. Technology no longer obtains a perceptual but a hermeneutical or readable transparency: "while, referentially, one 'reads through' the artifact, bodily-perceptually, it is *what* is read."[60] Technology performs a special formalized translation or interpretation of the world that requires reading and therefore also presupposes knowledge about the language or code used by the technology. An interesting diversion from any straightforward readings and interpretations is the risk of the emergence of a

---

58   Ihde, *Technology and the Lifeworld*, 78.
59   Ihde, *Technology and the Lifeworld*, 80, 88.
60   Ihde, *Technology and the Lifeworld*, 43.

more mysterious relationship between technology and reality. This happens when humans are unable to immediately perceive if the formalized referentiality of the equipment works correctly. This happens to Captain Whalley, when the compass is disturbed by the metal and misguides him in *The End of the Tether* (1902). Ihde schematizes hermeneutical relations in the following way:

    I → (technology-world)

Alterity relations are "relations *to* or *with* a technology." Here, the technological artifact becomes a quasi-other that is "stranger than mere objectness but weaker than the otherness found with the animal kingdom or the human one."[61] Such technologies make it possible for humans to relate to them as if they were an "other," although this presupposes that the specific technology possesses some kind of quasi-animation and thus quasi-autonomy, a life of its own. Ihde mentions robots as obvious examples. The *Nautilus* oscillates between quasi-autonomy, representation, and embodiment, the former mostly in cases when observed by outsiders or newly arrived members of the community, while to Captain Nemo and his crew the submarine is either a prosthesis or something to be interpreted. Within this specific sphere of human-technology relations, it is possible to address anthropomorphism and personification. Since humans relate to technology exclusively as otherness, the world withdraws to the background. When Professor Aronnax first sets foot inside the *Nautilus*, its otherness so overwhelms him with wonder that he becomes fully absorbed with the submarine's technological complexities. Only as he becomes more familiar with its workings—as it gradually morphs into an embodiment and hermeneutical relation to him—is he able to focus on the marvels of the underwater world. Alterity relations are expressed in this formula:

    I → technology (-world)

These three technologically mediated relations all stand in the foreground, because each of them includes humans in their way of functioning. Background relations work differently. These are relations that are not central to experience, although they can still be important. Although in the background, they still shape and change human experience. Ihde mentions electrical light or radiator heat as examples of technologically mediated background relations. Another could also be sound, such as the constant background noise of the

---

61   Ihde, *Technology and the Lifeworld*, 97, 100.

winds working the sails or the monotonous rhythm of the steam engine. These relations emphasize and help to clarify that the entire human environment, its *Umwelt*, is saturated by technological relations making the human world into "a kind of near-technological environment." This fourth type of technological experience is just as important as the three foreground types, says Ihde: "Background technologies [...] transform the gestalts of human experience and, precisely because they are absent presences, may exert more subtle indirect effects upon the way a world is experienced."[62] In background relations, man is neither related explicitly to technology nor to the world through technology; instead, technology shapes the context for our experience in a way that is not consciously perceived. They are absent presences, as Ihde writes, but their presence is often felt if they stop functioning for whatever reason. Their formula is:

I (-technology/world)

This typology of Ihde's and the insights of Heidegger's philosophies of technology will now act as a conceptual platform from which to read Conrad's *Typhoon* and Verne's *Vingt mille lieues sous les mers*.

5 Technology in *Typhoon*

In the Conrad analysis, I examine different types of technological-maritime experiences on board a steamship. Conrad is widely regarded as a conservative, disenchanted, and dystopian writer of modernity, a lost romantic who has little good to say about steamships and the moral, mental, and structural changes they bring with them. Nevertheless, in *Typhoon* certain positive qualities of steamship life emerge (possibly contrary to Conrad's intention). Conrad is a key figure in the complex discussion of maritime technology and its evolution, especially concerning the replacement of sail technology with steam technology. In the essay "The Character of the Foe," Conrad confirms Ihde's later idea of human-technology relations, in this case the relationship between humans and ships, and their importance for the human experience of the surrounding world: "And so much depends upon the craft which, made by man, is one with man, that the sea shall wear for him another aspect."[63]

---

62 Ihde, *Technology and the Lifeworld*, 108, 112.
63 Joseph Conrad, "The Character of the Foe," in *The Mirror and the Sea*, 73.

Conrad's observation converges with Ihde's "embodiment relations," in which man and technology almost fuse into symbiosis in the human perception of the world. Conrad's statement signals a hermeneutical phenomenology comprising the idea that in their fusion, man and sailing ship devise a different world than the one that emerges from the merger of man and steamship. In *Typhoon*, I focus on the *Nan-Shan* and the different forms of human experience staged on the ship, both technologically and nontechnologically mediated, the latter becoming especially evident and necessary in the encounter with the typhoon and the crisis in which it situates the crew. This opens for a more general discussion of the limits and limitations of technology.

5.1   Sail and Steam

A recurrent axiological and ideological structure in Conrad's work develops out of the fierce antagonism that he creates between two technological machines, the sailing ship and the steamship, the former often eulogized, the latter repeatedly denigrated. We have already examined the two descriptions in *The Nigger of the "Narcissus"* of the eponymous sailing ship and the steamer tugging the *Narcissus*. An initial contrast between "The short black tug" that "gave a pluck to windward," "then hovered for a moment on the quarter with her engines stopped," and "the slim, long hull of the ship" that "moved ahead slowly under lower topsails,"[64] sets the tone for many of Conrad's dichotomous images of the innocent world of yesteryear and the degraded worlds of now and tomorrow.

One thing is the description of each ship's design, one short, the other long and slim, but Conrad also points to nuances between the movements of the two ships. To give a pluck and to hover give an impression of unsteadiness, whereas the slow movement of the *Narcissus* is harmonious and even graceful. This is emphasized as the sailing ship "became a high and lonely pyramid, gliding, all shining and white, through the sunlit mist," whereas the tugboat

> resembled an enormous and aquatic black beetle, surprised by the light, overwhelmed by the sunshine, trying to escape with ineffectual effort into the distant gloom of the land. She left a lingering smudge of smoke on the sky, and two vanishing trails of foam on the water. On the place where she had stopped a round black patch of soot remained, undulating on the swell—an unclean mark of the creature's rest.[65]

---

64   Conrad, *The Nigger of the "Narcissus,"*.
65   Conrad, *The Nigger of the "Narcissus,"*.

Twice Conrad employs "black" in his portrait of the tugboat, and the "beetle" is evidently uncomfortable in the sunlight, belonging more to the gloomy land than to the sparkling jewelry of the sunlit sea, although its escape towards land is "ineffectual." In addition, the tugboat, negatively called a "creature," pollutes nature, and the foam it momentarily leaves on the water's surface is an unnatural result of "the two paddle-wheels that turned fast, beating the water with fierce hurry."[66] Sailing is associated with aesthetic beauty and majestic harmony, whereas the steam-powered vessel is a grotesque monstrosity that deforms and ruins nature.

A few years later, Conrad repeats the clear distinction between sail and steam in *The End of the Tether*. The steamer *Sofala* is described as experienced and dependable, even wise: "She could always be depended upon to make her courses. Her compasses were never out. She was no trouble at all to take about, as if her great age had given her knowledge, wisdom, and steadiness. She made her landfalls to a degree of the bearing, and almost to a minute of her allowed time."[67] But there are several downsides to her being knowledgeable and functional. Her commander, Captain Whalley, takes little notice of his surroundings and is hardly involved in the steamer's attempt to reach the estuary of a river. The narrator observes the landscape and acts as our camera:

> He could not hope to see anything new upon this lane of the sea. He had been on these coasts for the last three years. From Low Cape to Malantan the distance was fifty miles, six hours' steaming for the old ship with the tide, or seven against. Then you steered straight for the land, and by-and-by three palms would appear on the sky, tall and slim [...]. The *Sofala* would be headed towards the somber strip of the coast [...]. Then on through a brown liquid, three parts water and one part black earth, on and on between the low shores, three parts black earth and one part brackish water, the *Sofala* would plow her way up-stream, as she had done once every month for these seven years or more, [...] long before he had ever thought of having anything to do with her and her invariable voyages.[68]

---

66   Conrad, *The Nigger of the "Narcissus,"* 27.
67   Joseph Conrad, *The End of the Tether*, in *Youth, Heart of Darkness* and *The End of the Tether: Three Stories by Joseph Conrad*, Collected Edition of the Works of Joseph Conrad (1902; London: J. M. Dent and Sons, 1960), 166.
68   Conrad, *The End of the Tether*, 165–66.

The passage offers several answers to why Captain Whalley chooses to remain seated and let his "faithful Serang," "an elderly, alert, little Malay," communicate the orders to the helmsman (Whalley's increasing blindness is not yet revealed to the reader). One reason is that the relative ugliness of the surrounding nature, "the low swampy coast had retained its appearance of a mere smudge of darkness beyond a belt of glitter," makes Whalley indifferent. Another is the monotony and routinization resulting from doing the same thing over and over again for three years: "At any moment, as he sat on the bridge without looking up, or lay sleepless in his bed, simply by reckoning the days and the hours he could tell where he was—the precise spot of the beat. He knew it well too, this monotonous huckster's round, up and down the Straits; he knew its order and its sights and its people." In addition, Captain Whalley's route is coastal, not oceanic, "the low land on the other side in sight at daylight," and after going up the river, "in and out, picking up coastwise cargo here and there, and finishing with a hundred miles' steady steaming."[69] Conrad portrays the *Sofala* as a means of transportation more closely associated with the land than the sea, almost as if she was bound to the shore.

Contrasting the *Sofala* is the *Condor*, "a famous clipper" whose name represents the opposite of earthiness and a passive (sofa) existence: air, adventure, and agility. The clipper used to be under the command of Captain Whalley when he was known as "Dare-devil Harry—Whalley of the *Condor*."[70] Life on the *Sofala* is contrasted sharply with the captain's past exploits:

> Not a very enterprising life for a man [...] who had sailed famous ships [...]; who had made famous passages, had been the pioneer of new routes and new trades; who had steered across the unsurveyed tracts of the South Seas, and had seen the sun rise on uncharted islands. [...] Was there not somewhere between Australia and China a Whalley Island and a Condor Reef? On that dangerous coral formation the celebrated clipper had hung stranded for three days, her captain and crew throwing her cargo overboard with one hand and with the other, as it were, keeping off her a flotilla of savage war-canoes. At that time neither the island nor the reef had any official existence. Later the officers of her Majesty's steam vessel *Fusilier*, dispatched to make a survey of the route, recognized in the adoption of these two names the enterprise of the man and the solidity of the ship.[71]

---

69   Conrad, *The End of the Tether*, 165, 166, 167, 167.
70   Conrad, *The End of the Tether*, 167.
71   Conrad, *The End of the Tether*, 167–68.

With this description of Captain Whalley's adventures on the *Condor*, Conrad reinforces the significance of the name of the vessel. In contrast to the regularity, boredom, and localizability of the *Sofala*, the *Condor* implies a frontier existence for its crew and captain, forging new routes and commercial opportunities in hitherto unmapped territories fluid ("tracts of the South Seas") as well as solid ("uncharted islands"), and navigating between the threat of cannibalism and saving their own lives versus sacrificing the cargo and their profit. Captain Whalley and the *Condor* existed in places whose existence became official only when the government followed up on Whalley's initial transgressive enterprise by sending the steamer *Fusilier* to record the undertaking by mapping their route and thereby transforming it into a potentially future highway for ships and firms. Whalley broke barriers and ventured into uncharted land and seas, others followed to record and regularize them.

In both *The End of the Tether* and *The Nigger of the "Narcissus,"* the difference between sail and steam is a conflict of modernity between the old world of craftsmanship and the modern world of industrialization—that is, between a world of simple experiences in which bodily toil and stable communities are the central components, on one hand, and a complex and obscure world of money controlled by distant companies on the other. Robert Foulke has described the transformation from the former to the latter: "When the Merchant Shipping Act of 1854 formally established the British Merchant Service, many shipowners complained that 'the confidence between the sailor, his officers, his captain, and his owner' had been destroyed. The force of custom was gradually replaced by the rule of law." Already in the 1840s, an increasing bureaucratization of the maritime world intended for making profit and creating competition took place. This happened in the same decade during which the steamship began to pose a threat to the sailing ship, although this development did not really take off until the opening of the Suez Canal in 1869. The positive image painted by Conrad of the unity of shipowner, ship, and crew became challenged when "owners without consciences sent crews to sea in ill-found steam-coffin ships."[72]

The antagonism between the era of sail and the era of steam and Conrad's anxiety towards the future death of the sailing ship involve a diagnosis of broader social and political tendencies, and also point to Conrad's deep-seated existential concerns. The shift from sail to steam has to do with different experiential and perceptual worlds and the existence and practices they make

---

72   Robert Foulke, "Life in the Dying World of Sail, 1870–1910," in *Literature and Lore of the Sea*, ed. Patricia Ann Carlson (Amsterdam: Rodopi, 1986), 74, 75.

possible for humans. In *The Mirror and the Sea*, his collection of autobiographical essays published between 1904 and 1906, Conrad explicitly reflects upon the steamship's transformation of human experience in "The Character of the Foe": "The machinery, the steel, the fire, the steam, have stepped in between the man and the sea."[73] To Conrad, man's existence on the steamship implies the loss of a more direct and unmediated relationship with nature that was still possible on the sailing ship. However, as I have argued, there is always technological mediation going on, also on the sailing ship "machinery." A variation of Conrad's sentence concerning the steamship can be altered to describe the conditions on the sailing ship: "The machinery, the wood, the sails, the wind, have stepped in between the man and the sea."

Central to Conrad's "hermeneutical phenomenology" and existentialist thinking is the man-ship-sea constellation he uses as an elementary model for critical reflection on the transformations of human life at sea. The model clearly resonates with Ihde's idea of "human-technology relations" and of his model "I-technology-world." Conrad's ship becomes the medium through which his characters experience their environment (*Umwelt*), in this case the sea, and experience themselves as perceiving and practically oriented individuals. To Conrad, the steamship results in an isolation of man, because he loses contact with the sea and the ship; instead, he becomes absorbed by the machine and its omnipresent rhythm, noise, and smoke. Implied in Conrad's descriptions and reflections of steamship-mediated existence is an idea of the sailing ship as a completely different mediator. We are to understand life on board a sailing ship as one in which the ship disappears and makes way for an unmediated I-world, which Ihde calls "naked perception." However, as the example of the *São João* showed, Conrad's idea of the sailing ship as a withdrawn and transparent mediator may be questioned.

To Conrad, the steam engine and the by-products of its machinery are the new elements that determine steamship experience. We have already discussed his essay "Ocean Travel" (1923), in which he talks about "the invariable resistance of water to the screwing motion of the propeller."[74] Conrad regards the machine-driven propeller as unnatural, because it does not enter an equal relationship with nature as do the sails in relation to the wind. In contrast, the propeller's conditions of functioning relate to the water's resistance (not its cooperation) and the engine's monotonous and autonomous power (not its variable and contingent power). Based on Conrad's reflections, Foulke draws

---

73 Conrad, "The Character of the Foe," 72.
74 Conrad, "Ocean Travel," 35.

attention to the experiential shift happening with the introduction of the steamship. He outlines a model for "being-on-the steamship" that points to man's isolation and a shift from being active and involved to being passive and uninvolved: "the mechanical nature of the steamship, with its constant vibration produced by the throbbing of the screw, isolates the man from his ship and makes him a spectator rather than a participant in the contest between ship and elements." The consequences for the sailor's work and identity are enormous: "Besides robbing the sailor of his sensory contact with reality, the steamship had taken away his job and turned it over to a mechanic, [...] it made the sailor a specialist—a man tied to a monotonous and not very important round of routine duties."[75]

Foulke continues his argument by referring to some lines from Conrad's "Certain Aspects of the Admirable Inquiry into the Loss of the *Titanic*" (1912), featuring in *Notes on Life and Letters* (1921). According to Foulke, Conrad not only predicts that these new "seamen-mechanics of the future" will be "the legitimate successors of these seamen-sailors of the past," but also, and despite being legitimate successors, that "they are a different breed of men."[76] However, this last sentence does not figure in Conrad's text. How it has entered Foulke's article can only be speculated. This misquotation is worthy of note. Foulke quotes Conrad to support his claim about Conrad's dichotomous thinking on sail/steam, but a detail Foulke misses is that Conrad does not speak about the toilers of marine steam boilers. Instead, he refers to the "comparatively small crews of disciplined, intelligent workers," "resourceful and skilled," of the new internal combustion engine. In other words, Conrad introduces a reflection on the *motor-driven ship* to supplement his usual categories of sailing ships and steamships. "Certain Aspects of the Admirable Inquiry into the Loss of the *Titanic*" confirms the traditional Conradian valorization of sail and steam as positive and negative respectively, but he then adds a positive image of "being-on-the-motor ship."

Foulke's argument that Conrad re-affirms a critical stance on steam in "Inquiry into the Loss of the *Titanic*" is not wrong, he just misses the significant point that Conrad with "seamen-mechanics" refers to combustion-engine engineers and does so positively. Conrad sees them as the "legitimate successors" to the true and idealized seamen-sailors of the past era of sail. He contrasts them

---

75   Foulke, "Life in the Dying World of Sail, 1870–1910," 84, 85.
76   Joseph Conrad, "Certain Aspects of the Admirable Inquiry into the Loss of the *Titanic*," in *Notes on Life and Letters, Collected Edittion of the Works of Joseph Conrad* (1921; London: J. M. Dent and Sons, 1971), 238. Foulke, "Life in the Dying World of Sail, 1870–1910," 85.

with "the unthrifty, unruly, nondescript crowd [...] of men *in* the ship but not *of* her," the marine boiler engineers and stokers.[77] To Conrad, these are

> men whose heavy labour has not a single redeeming feature; which is unhealthy, uninspiring, arduous, without the reward of personal pride in it; sheer, hard, brutalising toil, belonging to neither earth nor sea, I greet with joy the advent for marine purposes of the internal combustion engine. The disappearance of the marine boiler will be a real progress, which anybody in sympathy with his kind must welcome.[78]

It is not the men of steamships who are criticized (at least not here). Conrad is sympathetic to them and their predicament. Rather, it is the technological system that is responsible for their specifically degraded being-in-the-world. Conrad proves to be a sophisticated thinker of the experiential and existential impact of concrete technologies, although his view on sailing ships may be too innocent and neutral in terms of their mediating role.

Returning to the more prominent antagonism between sail and steam, we can identify more clearly what transforms maritime life. Instead of being ruled by the *laws of nature*, maritime life is now ruled by the *laws of mechanics*; instead of being determined by nature's unpredictability and its calls for readiness, it is now determined by the machine's monotony and the precalculated arrival times systematized in trustworthy timetables. Steamship life is infused with what Heidegger calls "calculative thinking," a future-oriented thinking that constantly, on "conditions that are given" and "serving specific purposes," plans ahead (even without numbers, adding machines, or computers) and "races from one prospect to the next" with the anticipation of being able to "count on definite results."[79]

The sailing ship is characterized by what Gumbrecht would call a presence-oriented relationship between man-ship-nature, especially by nature's basic unpredictability. If nature is the pole with the greatest magnetic force in the constellation man-sailship-nature, on the steamship this external orientation shifts towards an internal orientation. The steamship and especially the engine room is now the pole with the greatest magnetic force. The antagonism parallels Heidegger's opposition between the era of technical craftsmanship and the era of industrial technology, between an exclusively practically oriented

---

77 Conrad, "Inquiry into the Loss of the *Titanic*," 238.
78 Conrad, "Inquiry into the Loss of the *Titanic*," 238.
79 Martin Heidegger, "Memorial address," in *Discourse on Thinking*, trans. John M. Anderson and E. Hans Freund (1959; New York: Harper Perennial, 1966), 46.

dealing with the world of the ship at sea and an unconcealment (still practical-intimate) of the world of the ship (at sea), which is now part of an overall and dominant system, the *Ge-stell*. The steamship can be ordered and counted upon, whereas the sailing ship is never fully dependable because determined in a higher degree by nature and its uncontrollable zone bordering up to the *Bestand*. It is important not to automatically indulge in Conrad's nostalgia for the past and pessimism toward the future, but to instead insist upon this: *In the intercourse with modern technology, concrete and legitimate technologically mediated experiences take place, experiences that are simply different from those of the sailing ship.*

To Conrad, the shift from sail to steam was a decisive technologically mediated experiential disruption, here expressed in the essay "Ocean Travel": "The one statement that can be safely advanced about traveling at sea is that it is not what it used to be. It is different now elementally." This feeling made it possible for him to describe with great precision the existential consequences the new steamship had, not least for man's worldly experience: "It is not so much a matter of changed propelling power; it is something more." In both "Ocean Travel" and "The Character of the Foe," Conrad investigates the different experiential forms that can be linked with the steamship. In his own words, he examines the "psychology of sea travel." We have already discussed "Ocean Travel" as an example of a disenchanted thinking about the technocentric epoch, so let me recapitulate: The experiential transformation triggered by steam can be summarized by such words as "tame," "less exciting," "conditions of shore life," "hotel," "sham comforts," "fixed," "definite date," "hold of the land," and "disharmony."[80]

In "The Character of the Foe," Conrad opens up immense temporal vistas of the prehuman past and a distant human future. He initially zooms in on the ocean and its gales, which give to the sea "an appearance of hoary age, lustreless, dull, without gleams, as though it had been created before light itself." The human attachment to the sea is ambivalent, involves both affection and fear, condensed in the hostile gales, which seem to have personalities of their own: "adversaries whose wiles you must defeat, whose violence you must resist, and yet with whom you must live in the intimacies of days and nights." This perspective, Conrad admits, is that of "the man of masts and sail, to whom the sea is not a navigable element, but an intimate companion." Conrad positions himself in (and in sympathy with) the recent past and heyday of sail. Other words associated with the lifeworld of sail are "solitude," "close dependence

---

80   Conrad, "Ocean Travel," 27, 27, 35, 27–28.

upon the very forces," "friendly," "dangerous," and "fellowship."[81] In opposition to this (slightly romanticized) description of sailing ship life, Conrad draws a bleak picture of the steamship life of the present:

> your modern ship, which is a steamship, makes her passages on other principles than yielding to the weather and humouring the sea. She receives smashing blows, but she advances; it is a slogging fight, and not a scientific campaign. The machinery, the steel, the fire, the steam have stepped in between the man and the sea. A modern fleet of ships does not so much make use of the sea as exploit a highway. The modern ship is not the sport of the waves. Let us say that each of her voyages is a triumphant progress; and yet it is a question whether it is not a more subtle and more human triumph to be the sport of the waves and yet survive, achieving your end.[82]

The close and collaborative/colliding relationship with nature is gone and has been replaced by an autonomous ("she advances"), indifferent, and disenchanting ("slogging fight") machine. It is as if steam technology suddenly and disturbingly steps in between man and nature and occupies a spot that was previously empty. Conrad considers the sailing ship a large ready-to-hand and well-functioning tool, a pure embodiment relation like wearing eyeglasses to improve vision. The sea is no longer pure nature with its undulating, rhythmic, and capricious waves; instead, the steamship transforms the sea into a flat, smooth, and frictionless highway. To Conrad, such "triumphant progress" is not a victory to be celebrated, because it is mechanistic and dehumanizing.

The vista is now opened towards the future in that Conrad wonders how future humans will look back on the era of sail. Their ability to feel sympathy is questioned by Conrad in that an "incorrigible mankind hardens its heart in the progress of its own perfectability" and thus becomes less receptive to nature's wonders and to the "soft" machinery of sail that allowed nature to be nature by respecting it. This is different from "the seaman of the last generation" who was "brought into sympathy with the caravels of ancient time by his sailing-ship, their lineal descendant," and who "cannot look upon those lumbering forms navigating the naïve seas of ancient woodcuts without a feeling of surprise, of affectionate derision, envy, and admiration. For those things, whose unmanageableness, even when represented on paper, makes one gasp with a sort of

---

81   Conrad, "The Character of the Foe," 71, 71, 71, 71–72.
82   Conrad, "The Character of the Foe," 72.

amused horror, were manned by men who are his direct professional ancestors." In another look into the distant future, Conrad confirms that the coming seamen "will probably be neither touched nor moved to derision, affection, or admiration," because our "ships of yesterday will stand to their ships as no lineal ancestors, but as mere predecessors whose course will have been run and the race extinct. Whatever craft he handles with skill, the seaman of the future shall be, not our descendant, but only our successor."[83]

If Conrad confirms an antagonistic thinking between sail and steam (the lineage is broken), his vocabulary takes us back to the vocabulary of "Inquiry into the Loss of the *Titanic*" in which he introduced the "seamen-mechanics" of motor-driven ships as *legitimate* successors to the men of sail. If Conrad defines steamship sailors as being "only our successor" and not "our descendant," then the adding of "legitimate" to "successor" in "Inquiry into the Loss of the *Titanic*" indicates that Conrad considers the new "disciplined, intelligent," "resourceful and skilled" seamen-mechanics of the future as the true descendants of the seafarers of mast and sail. If so, the image of a lineage broken transforms into a lineage that, although disrupted, will continue in a different form in parallel with the advent of new technologies and new humans. The era of steam becomes a mere parenthesis in-between the era of sail and the era of combustion engines, a parenthesis characterized by man's physical, arduous, brutal, alienating, monotonous, and unredeeming toil, whereas the work of the man of masts and sail and the seaman-mechanic of the future is characterized by uniting a physical and cerebral dimension and comprising a redeeming potential.

Conrad considers human experience in the age of sail as richer and purer, more harmonious and naked, more primitive and intimate than the experiences humans achieve in the age of steam. Ihde's idea that every mediating technology always implies a double movement of magnification and reduction is given a twist by Conrad: the duality is maintained, but the magnification is linked to sail only, whereas the reduction belongs to steam exclusively. Time and again, the conclusion of Conrad's analysis is that with the advent of steam humanity is denied the richer experience of the world of sail. The steamship is not an "engine" capable of generating possibilities for new *maritime* experiences. The early Heidegger as well as Ihde and Verbeek would perhaps disagree. Instead, steam-power is regarded as a technology that facilitates the transfer of the comforts of land to the space of the ship. With the emergence of the steamship, humanity becomes poorer, because it loses

---

83 Conrad, "The Character of the Foe," 72, 72, 73.

something without gaining anything in return: "Formerly a man setting out on a sea voyage broke away from shore conditions and found in the ship a new kind of home." Seafarers lose the opportunity to escape from the mechanical logic of terrestrial civilization, from "the sound of the world's mechanical contrivances." Romantically, Conrad emphasizes that the steamship deprives man of the possibility of a more primordial accordance with nature; instead, technology increases the distance between humans and nature, and humans become alienated. Conrad's analysis concludes that, through technology, man becomes experientially poorer and more separate from nature. The sailing ship was previously the medium through which man was carried into a harmonious being-in-the-world, but now the steamship has reduced life at sea to a "luxurious prison."[84]

The reduction of experience can be viewed in the context of Heidegger's metering out the *Gefahr* in which modern technology places mankind, especially the danger of reducing human experience exclusively to technological experience (in the form of *Ge-stell*). The question is whether or not this is the right path to take? Should we uncritically accept Conrad's romanticized conclusions? Or is a more constructive approach to be found in Ihde and the early Heidegger? Conrad never frees himself from an interpretation of modern technology, which feeds off the illusion that humanity has had a more natural and nontechnological relationship to the world, the I-world. In his strong bias towards the age of sail, Conrad forgets that the sailing ship facilitates a technologically mediated experience with its own transformative powers.

Foulke draws attention to nostalgia and romance as being "almost ubiquitous in the literature of sail," but it is also one of his key points that "life on board nineteenth-century sailing ships was not the romantic existence which readers of sea literature sometimes imagine." It is Foulke's intention to reconstruct and flesh out "the image of experience in the lost world of sailing ships," which he sees as an embodied world of experience.[85] In that sense, Foulke's ambition, like mine, is to examine the different forms of ship-life experience more closely and without prejudice. To Foulke, we should not blindly trust the literature that deals with sailing ship life, because it is romanticizing and nostalgic. And if the literature about steamship life is often critical and disenchanted, as is Conrad's, the philosophies of technology put forward by Heidegger, Ihde, and Verbeek assist us in bypassing the authorial bias and creating an alternative version of maritime existence. We may suppose that

---

84 Conrad, "Ocean Travel," 35, 38, 36.
85 Foulke, "Life in the Dying World of Sail, 1870–1910," 89, 105, 90.

steamship experiences are just as rich and primordial to humans and present as much legitimacy and necessity as sailing-ship experiences did. We are not obliged to follow Conrad in his romantic conclusions; instead, it becomes possible to examine his descriptions of steamship experiences in a more nuanced and positive light. Why is it that comfort, stability, precision, and safety are negatively valued experiences? The steamship sailor becomes a person who believes in the established order and the functionality of this order. He has no reason to doubt it, because it is given as a result of calculation, planning, and an expectation of compliance with the calculations and plans. This is the contract that the steamship sailor has signed, and as a result his life is less dangerous and exposed. This creates an even greater contrast to the surrounding ocean, which has not lost its potential for violence and destruction.

5.2 Steamship Experiences in Typhoon

Foulke is correct in saying that Conrad only personalizes a steamship in *Typhoon*, but when he says, "only in one other story, 'The End of the Tether,' does he seriously explore steamship life for its own sake,"[86] that is not entirely accurate. *The End of the Tether* is a portrait of "the Dying World of Sail" seen from the perspective of the era of steam and "historical time." *Typhoon* is the only fictional text in which Conrad deals exclusively with steamship existence, which means that he steers clear of the antagonism between sail and steam. *Typhoon* is therefore an obvious choice for examining steamship experiences on their own terms, also because Conrad treats steamship life as being nearly free of all the usual negative valorizations.

In my analysis of *Typhoon*, I employ a dual focus. One line of argument will concentrate on the *Nan-Shan* as a collective and relational environment. The ambition is to describe the different experiences of and mediated through the steamship, not least when the typhoon hits the ship. Another line of argument centers on Captain MacWhirr's experiences of technology, his relationship to the barometer, an instrument that plays a central role in the novel, and his distinct attitude of "composure" that ultimately leads to the rescue of the crew and the ship. My approach falls within the Heideggerian model of everydayness/disruption (*Alltäglichkeit/Störung*). The typhoon is a negative experience and disruption of the average everydayness with its ready-to-hand relationship to tools and their assignment structure. As such, it helps to make visible man's technologically mediated relationship with the world, not least because the disruption destroys the structure of assignments of the in-order-to.

---

86 Foulke, "Life in the Dying World of Sail, 1870–1910," 87.

Before proceeding with the analysis and close reading of the novel, a few comments on its reception will help clarify the contribution of my reading. Conrad scholarship discusses whether *Typhoon* is a good or bad work of literature just as it disagrees on whether the main protagonist is MacWhirr or Jukes, and, importantly, whether MacWhirr is as stupid as Jukes says he is. For different reasons, scholars such as Jacques Berthoud, C. B. Cox, M. C. Bradbrook, Douglas Hewitt, and Albert J. Guerard dismiss *Typhoon* as a minor work,[87] while F. R. Leavis, John H. Wills, Paul S. Bruss, H. M. Daleski, and Jakob Lothe value the novel positively.[88] The following analysis will demonstrate that I belong to the second group, and my main reason for doing so relates to the status of Captain MacWhirr and how Conrad presents him. In his discussion of *Typhoon*, Ian Watt emphasizes how his reading distinguishes itself from the one performed by Leavis. While the latter associated MacWhirr, the chief mate Jukes, and the chief engineer Rout with "heroic sublimity," not least because of the contrast between their ordinariness and the "demented fury" of the typhoon,[89] the former stresses that the novel's "primary aim is to achieve not the sublime but the comic and the humorous."[90]

While acknowledging that Leavis and Watt have valid points concerning the general tone and the specific characterizations in *Typhoon*, my reading moves in a different direction. Instead of Leavis' emphasis on sublimity with its Kantian connotations of the primacy of human rationality and calculation, and instead of Watt's Bachtinian accentuation of the comic and the humorous, I argue that MacWhirr's composure represents a different type of heroism that is best described as a unique combination of Heideggerian *Gelassenheit* (releasement, letting-be) and calculative thinking; that is, of meditation and calculation. My reading will also dispute those readings, for example Bruss', that place Jukes at the center of the novel. It will demonstrate that *Typhoon* is a novel about the relationship between man, technology, and nature; more

---

87   Jacques A. Berthoud, *Joseph Conrad: The Major Phase* (Cambridge: Cambridge University Press, 1978); C. B. Cox, *Joseph Conrad: The Modern Imagination* (London: Dent, 1974); M. C. Bradbrook, *Joseph Conrad: Poland's English Genius* (Cambridge: Cambridge University Press, 1941); Douglas Hewitt, *Conrad: A Reassessment* (Cambridge: Bowes and Bowes, 1952); Albert J. Guerard, *Conrad the Novelist* (Cambridge, MA: Harvard University Press, 1958).
88   F. R. Leavis, *The Great Tradition* (London: Chatto and Windus, 1948); John H. Wills, "Conrad's *Typhoon*: A Triumph of Organic Art," *The North Dakota Quarterly* 30 (1962); Paul S. Bruss, *Conrad's Early Sea Fiction* (London: Associated University Presses, 1979); H. M. Daleski, *Joseph Conrad: The Way of Dispossession* (New York: Holmes & Meier, 1976); Jakob Lothe, *Conrad's Narrative Method* (Oxford: Clarendon Press, 1989).
89   Leavis, *Great Tradition*, 183–85.
90   Ian Watt, *Essays on Conrad* (Cambridge: Cambridge University Press, 2000), 97.

specifically, that it is about how the encounter between a simple-minded captain, modern technology in the form of a steamship, and a furious typhoon initiates a formative development in the captain, but also how his composed temperament is invaluable during the storm and how it remains fundamentally unchanged at the end of the story. It is easy to consider MacWhirr an antihero in Conrad's work, an example of those sailors who do not understand the sea, but this reading is only possible if one reads Jukes' comments and letters as aligned with the attitude of the omniscient narrator. However, Lothe has persuasively demonstrated the complex "modulations of the text's authorial narrative"[91] and how the authorial narrator varies his attitudinal distance to Jukes and MacWhirr throughout the novel. Lothe's detailed analysis of the variations in distance shows that MacWhirr, through his actions (and nonactions), grows in stature both during and after the typhoon, not only because of his battle with the typhoon but also because of his handling of the Chinamen. In that sense, MacWhirr displays heroic and moral sides of his character.

...

Technology is the precondition for man's maritime being. In *Typhoon*, the *Nan-Shan* is a complex totality of different technological tools and instruments, and the ship must be understood as the entire world of experience for the crew and passengers. On the *Nan-Shan*, man dwells completely in a technological environment. The technological experience of the steamship totality can be categorized as an embodiment relation in which the sailor in his entire being is absorbed into the movement and domain of technology. Whatever other technological experiences may emerge, the following embodiment relation is under normal circumstances always valid:

(man-steamship) → nature

The *Nan-Shan* has become the environment (*Umwelt*) of sailors and mechanics in which they usually move around unproblematically and transparently. Ultimately, this means that the above schematization can morph into a background relation in which technology retreats completely from human consciousness and manipulates the environment and man's experience implicitly and constantly. The steamship always colors man's experience of the world,

---

91 Lothe, *Conrad's Narrative Method*, 116.

and during the journey this can never be avoided. Maritime experience is always technological experience.

man (-steamship/nature)

However, this needs to be differentiated. While it is true that everybody on board the *Nan-Shan* is implicated in the abovementioned embodiment and background relations, they experience them in different ways. This has to do primarily with the architecture of the ship (the deck above and the engine-room below) and its division of labor (sailors above and engineers below). The deck and the engine-room determine to a large extent each crew member's concrete experience of the ship's environment and functioning. Each space signals a world completely different from the other space. Conrad draws contrasting images of the two. One is open, clear, and airy, the other closed, dark, and claustrophobic. One belongs to the sailors, the other to the stokers and the engineers, one of whom had "arms like a blacksmith." Each world is determined by a particular intentionality, its in-order-to, and its specific task. One is oriented towards navigation and reading the weather (e.g., through the barometer), the other is one-dimensionally focused on the steam. Rather than complement each other, they seem to be incommensurable: "Who cared for his crimson barometer? It was the steam—the steam—that was going down."[92]

The topology of the steamship consists of two separate worlds of experience. Below it is closed off from nature and the sea, and the engineers experience them indirectly only, for example through increased temperature. Technological experience can thus be schematized like this:

(man-machine) (-nature)

The arrow of technology's mediating capacity is dissolved because focus is no longer directed at anything but the machine. At the same time, it is not a case of an alterity relation, because the machine does not present itself as an "other" to the stokers and engineers. Instead, their bodies are completely absorbed by the ship's steam engines because of the closed-off room with its noises, heat, and emissions that attack the human senses. The embodiment relation of "below" emphasizes the fusion between man and machine and simultaneously tones down any experience of mediation between ship and sea.

---

[92]   Conrad, *Typhoon*, 22, 24.

To Jukes, the second mate, life on board the steamship's deck is "continuous, monotonous." Everything about Captain MacWhirr's ship, also his past ones, exudes calm, peace, and harmony. The captain's everyday life on the *Nan-Shan* is characterized by comfort, convenience, and a certain distance to the sea. Jukes calls it "the easy life."[93] The sailors on deck, like the engineers and stokers in the engine-room, are absorbed by the steamship's mechanical rhythm, but in contrast to the crew below, the sailors do not experience this rhythm as deafening; instead, they are almost hypnotized into a drowsy condition by the sound. The technological experience encloses man and magnifies the sense of calmness and sameness between ship and sea, while simultaneously reducing the experience of the surrounding nature. In that sense, the technological experience of the steamship totality still constitutes the first schematized relation, but nature is somewhat of a background phenomenon, although it remains sensible and visible:

(man-steamship) → nature

The two worlds are separated, but as Conrad mentioned, on the steamship it is the machine that is decisive, and it is obvious how it both encircles and influences sea life above and below deck. Experience through technology, here the steamship, becomes either more atomized and specialized (the *Nan-Shan* reduced to pure machine, the steam engine) or more self-sufficient and disengaged (the *Nan-Shan* reduced to being on vacation). The technologically mediating event or movement, symbolized by the arrow in the schematization of human-technology relations, loses much of its power, becomes softer, so that man and technology constitute an increasingly closed circle. The sea seems to be an unobtrusive reality more distant.

The closed circle points to a possible experience of the steamship as an "other." A movement may be triggered from an almost symbiotic, yet nonthematized, relationship between the crew members and a transparent technology to a technology becoming thematized as an "other" in front of the crew members. When "Mr. Jukes, in moments of expansion on shore, would proclaim loudly that the 'old girl was as good as she was pretty,'" it is a sign of the *Nan-Shan* having accomplished a kind of independent existence and autonomy. It has become part of an alterity relation.

man → steamship (-nature)

---

93 Conrad, *Typhoon*, 26, 17.

The two different worlds of experience, above and below, have consequences for the crew members' existence. Instead of being an integrated and active part of the man-technology-nature constellation on the deck, some have morphed into passive passengers. The activities of others are directed exclusively towards the machine and are therefore reduced to the experiential forms governed by the *Ge-stell*: regulating and securing the ship's advancement (the engine-room).

The basic human-technology relation on the *Nan-Shan* is still the embodied relation: (man-steamship) →nature. Sometimes, this morphs into a background relation: man (-steamship/nature), but this has to be supplemented with an alterity relation: man →steamship (-nature). This shows that the technological experience in the engine-room in condensed form constitutes the essence of steamship experience. Its scheme is precisely the fusion of embodiment relations and alterity relations: (man-steamship) (-nature). The engineers and the stokers in the engine-room, the "black-squad,"[94] realize this experience in its full extent through their work, while the sailors on deck are reduced to idlers and spectators.

All the above-mentioned human-technology relations and experiences are thrown into confusion and broken down during the hurricane. The advent of the typhoon, a tropical cyclone, results in a negative confrontation between the technological relations and human experiences. They are torn out of their transparent context of use and suffer a *Störung*, a disruption. This is where the man-technology-nature theme is revealed as being problematic. Jukes senses this new experience of the steamship. In addition to feeling "unsafe," he feels that the ship's motion is "unfamiliar, unforeseen, and difficult to counteract." What used to be familiar is now strange; tranquility has been replaced with anxiety. Nature, here in the form of the sublime, has begun to challenge man and not the other way around. To the sailors on deck, the challenge with its extreme noise drowns out both man and machine: "It was tumultuous and very loud—made up of the rush of the wind, the crashes of the sea, with the prolonged deep vibration of the air, like the roll of an immense and remote drum beating the charge of the gale." The sailors are no longer isolated from or in a disengaged relationship with nature but separated from each other: "This is the disintegrating power of a great wind: it isolates one from one's kind."[95] Their eyes, ears, and mouths are somehow rendered useless, and what is left of their sensitivity is their ability to smell and, more importantly, feel with their entire bodies the ship and nature.

---

94   Conrad, *Typhoon*, 7, 17.
95   Conrad, *Typhoon*, 56, 36–37, 40.

The typhoon makes the man-steamship-nature relation explicit by capturing the sailors in between the increasing destruction of the steamship and the destructive beatings of the sea. The steamship experience has been torn out of its *Zuhandenheit*, its transparent condition, and now confronts the sailors in the form of a strange and insecure world. The three components in the relation are blown apart, each exhibited in its autonomous existence: the sailors are fragile, on the verge of death; the *Nan-Shan* is battling steadily, but also slowly disintegrating; nature is forceful and destructive: "The men on board did not count, and the ship could not last. This weather was too impossible." On deck, the sailors become more and more isolated, so much so that they may diminish in number and ultimately disappear from the relation between steamship and ocean:

(man) steamship-nature

The battle instigated by the hurricane is now a battle between steamship and nature in which man has become an unnecessary and superfluous component. The disruption emphasizes that the sailors on deck are passive spectators to what is anthropomorphically described as a fight: "The seas in the dark seemed to rush from all sides to keep her back where she might perish. There was hate in the way she was handled, and a ferocity in the blows that fell. She was like a living creature thrown to the rage of a mob: hustled terribly, struck at, borne up, flung down, leaped upon."[96]

Below deck everything is different. The engine-room is now an ambiguous space whose features are summarized in the following way: "A loud and wild resonance, made up of all the noises of the hurricane, dwelt in the still warmth of the air." The space is shaken by the noises produced by the typhoon, but the room is somehow able to absorb these noises in its mechanical tranquility and rhythms. This is also why Jukes—the crew member who crosses the border between upstairs and downstairs—is "bewildered" by "the comparative vastness, peace, and brilliance of the engine-room." The engine-room upholds its isolated existence and becomes a shelter from the storm; there, nature's violence has not taken over man. The previously outlined closed relation below deck is upheld, although nature is no longer present parenthetically, but is completely open and perceptible:

(man-technology) -nature

---

96   Conrad, *Typhoon*, 45, 47.

This is also why the crew members of the engine-room can continue working unimpeded in their attempt to keep the fire burning, as that maintains the steam pressure and, ultimately, their chances of survival: "the fires out, the ship helpless." The task is still "the steam—the steam." Here, the negative disruption underlines a steamship experience that intensifies the relationship between man and machine because of nature's pressure from the outside. In defiance of the typhoon, "the engines worked their steel limbs headlong or slow with a silent, determined smoothness." In contrast to the sailors on deck who are drowned out and dissolved by nature, the machine and its human servants continue their work almost as if nothing extraordinary had happened. A certain monotony and continuity are upheld amid the tropical cyclone's disintegrative forces. During the hurricane, MacWhirr even likens "the pulsation of the engines" to "the beat of the ship's heart."[97] The anthropomorphism—inorganic machine transformed into organic human—is an example of a more positive image of steamships in Conrad's work.

It is primarily the sailors on deck who are called upon to relate to nature, and we will now turn our attention to their world of experience, which is characterized by a coming to the forefront of the man-technology-nature relation. More specifically, this is represented by the case of Captain MacWhirr, and especially his technological experience linked to a reading of nature through a barometer. Here, technology's mediating factor becomes important again, now in the form of a small instrument, because nature's previous background status is replaced by its violent and inevitable presence, which jolts the captain out of his lethargy and comfort. What is of interest is that MacWhirr relates to nature primarily through a technological medium, the barometer. He does not root his experience of the surrounding world on what Ihde called a "naked face-to-face experience," that is, "the direct, nontechnologically-mediated dimension of experience,"[98] but on Ihde's hermeneutical relation:

man → (technology-world)

It is of course questionable if such exposed nontechnological experiences are possible on the steamship since every experience here is embedded in technology. Nevertheless, the typhoon suddenly makes it possible to enter a direct relationship with nature.

---

97   Conrad, *Typhoon*, 68, 71, 61, 70, 66.
98   Ihde, *Technology and the Lifeworld*, 15, 16.

This happens when Jukes falls overboard: "All the time he was being tossed, flung, and rolled in great volumes of water." As a result of the tropical cyclone, the sea has suddenly become just as present as the steamship. But MacWhirr relates to nature with downcast eyes. He "seldom looked up," the narrator informs us. There are several reasons for MacWhirr's behavior, the two most important being his unwavering trust in his ship's seaworthiness and strength as well as the fact that the sea itself "had never put itself out to startle the silent man, who seldom looked up, and wandered innocently over the waters with the only visible purpose of getting food, raiment, and house-room for three people ashore."[99] This lack of a more direct and unmediated approach to nature culminates when the typhoon blinds MacWhirr and prevents him from seeing nature, even in moments when he attempts to see:

> He was trying to see, with that watchful manner of a seaman who stares into the wind's eye as if into the eye of an adversary, to penetrate the hidden intention and guess the aim and force of the thrust. The strong wind swept at him out of a vast obscurity; he felt under his feet the uneasiness of his ship, and he could not even discern the shadow of her shape. He wished it were not so; and very still he waited, feeling stricken by a blind man's helplessness.[100]

The typhoon does not change much for MacWhirr since he is used to having an indirect or distanced relationship to nature. At first, this is a genuine problem for him: an actual blindness and inadequacy whose concrete expression is the condition of false comfort and lethargy. Later, the blindness transforms into a qualified way of seeing which turns out to be the salvation of him and the crew.

The problem arises because his instrument, the barometer, cannot help him decode nature. When MacWhirr cannot interpret the signs of nature as a forewarning about a coming typhoon, he seems inexperienced. The problem of readability is directed toward the barometer. The situation requires hermeneutical competences because the barometer mediates nature in the following manner:

> MacWhirr → (barometer-nature)

---

99   Conrad, *Typhoon*, 42, 18.
100 Conrad, *Typhoon*, 40.

The barometer needle's position is a sign of the present and future weather. It is both a diagnosis and a prognosis. MacWhirr

> stood confronted by the fall of a barometer he had no reason to distrust. The fall—taking into account the excellence of the instrument, the time of the year, and the ship's position on the terrestrial globe—was of a nature ominously prophetic; but the red face of the man betrayed no sort of inward disturbance. Omens were as nothing to him, and he was unable to discover the message of a prophecy till the fulfilment had brought it home to his very door.[101]

Inherent in this type of technological experience is a formalization of specific aspects of nature. Something is reduced, something is magnified, but what is magnified requires deciphering. It serves as an example of Heidegger's calculative thinking: Nature is quantified, and man can count on nature by being able to predict it. Nature can be counted and counted upon. As a result, the typhoon announces its arrival at this early point in the novel. Because MacWhirr has never seen such a dramatic barometer fall before, he rejects it or simply cannot read it correctly. The barometer loses its hermeneutical transparency, and the instrument points toward itself as something useless. The typhoon's disruption is revealed by the barometer, yet in MacWhirr's case, its indication cannot be read accurately.

After the typhoon hits the *Nan-Shan*, MacWhirr returns to the barometer to read it once again. Something has changed, not on the barometer, which still stands very low, but in MacWhirr who now seems better equipped to understand and accept the signs of first one reading and then another:

> It stood very low—incredibly low, so low that Captain MacWhirr grunted. [...]
>
> His eyes looked at it, narrowed with attention, as if expecting an imperceptible sign. [...] There was no mistake. It was the lowest reading he had ever seen in his life.
>
> Captain MacWhirr emitted a low whistle. [...] Perhaps something had gone wrong with the thing!
>
> There was an aneroid glass screwed above the couch. He turned that way, struck another match, and discovered the white face of the other instrument looking at him from the bulkhead, meaningly, not to be

---

[101] Conrad, *Typhoon*, 6.

TECHNOLOGY 253

> gainsaid, as though the wisdom of men were made unerring by the indifference of matter. There was no room for doubt now. [...]
>
> The worst was to come, then—and if the books were right this worst would be very bad. The experience of the last six hours had enlarged his conception of what heavy weather could be like. "It'll be terrific," he pronounced, mentally. He had not consciously looked at anything by the light of the matches except at the barometer; and yet somehow he had seen that his waterbottle and the two tumblers had been flung out of their stand. It seemed to give him a more intimate knowledge of the tossing the ship had gone through. "I wouldn't have believed it," he thought. And his table had been cleared, too; [...] all the things that had their safe appointed places—they were gone [...]. The hurricane had broken in upon the orderly arrangements of his privacy. This had never happened before, and the feeling of dismay reached the very seat of his composure. And the worst was to come yet![102]

Between the first and second look on the barometer, MacWhirr has undergone a learning process. He is now better able to equate the barometer's position with the empirical conditions of nature, the typhoon. As a result of his immediate experience of a tropical cyclone, MacWhirr has expanded his hermeneutical competences and technological vocabulary. The typhoon has clarified the hermeneutical skills that are presupposed for the barometer to make sense, not through a theoretical process, but a practical and concrete process.

Ultimately, the barometer has not served its purpose; instead, it has been a kind of measuring device able to chronicle the development of MacWhirr, from inexperienced to experienced, from blind to seeing, from an inaccurate interpreter to an accurate one. However, the technological experience only reaches its completion when Captain MacWhirr returns to the barometer to re-read it. Only then is its hermeneutical transparency restored, and only then does he understand the meaning of its expression. But Captain MacWhirr's enhanced hermeneutical proficiency is not enough to lead the *Nan-Shan* safely through the hurricane. It only helps MacWhirr to get a better understanding of the enemy's magnitude. The still missing ingredient for the ship to get through the storm without wrecking is to be found in MacWhirr himself as a personal trait.

During the typhoon, nature arouses the sense of the sublime in the main characters. This is emphasized by the narrator's use of words that all point to liminal experiences in which perceptions of the outer world and mental

---

102 Conrad, *Typhoon*, 84–85.

processes cannot find solid ground to stand upon. Before the actual hurricane, Jukes writes in the logbook: "Ship rolling heavily in a high cross swell," but immediately adds to this matter-of-fact statement: "Heavily is no word for it." The addition marks the beginning of language's inability to represent human experience. Shortly after this, the narrator notices the sea to be "as black as the sky,"[103] indicating that our perceptual distinctions are about to disappear. During the hurricane, sublimity is time and again suggested through numerous words and phrases of which I shall only cite a selection: "deep vibrating noise," "confused clamour," "avalanche," "burst of lightning," "formidable and swift," "vial of wrath," "explode," "beyond the powers of his fancy," "the immense flurry of the elements," "tremendous uproar," "appalling helplessness," "senseless, destructive fury," "enormous discord of noises," "impenetrable obscurity," "unchained fury," "ferocity," "a profound trouble to their souls," "wild and appalling shrieks," "excessive tumult," "the gathered weight of crashes menaced monstrously," "tumult of strangled, throaty shrieks," "desperate confusion," "Rancorous, guttural cries," "stunning shock," "sudden booming gusts," "tearing crash and a swirling, raving tumult," "as if going over the edge of the world," "like the inside of a tower nodding in an earthquake," "blind panic."[104]

When Jukes reappears on deck after his mission to create order amongst "the Chinamen," he "discovered he could detect obscure shapes as if his sight had become preternaturally acute. He saw faint outlines." Calm and order are reemerging. The shapes may be obscure, but still, they are shapes. The wind having disappeared, Jukes' senses reactivate one by one. He breathed the smoke from the funnel, he felt "the deliberate throb of the engines" throughout his body, he heard distinct sounds, and he saw "dimly the squat shape of his captain." However, what has been endured was only the first round of the fight. After having re-gained a little strength in the hurricane's core, the second round announces itself through "a colossal depth of blackness hanging over the ship," and "Jukes could no longer see his captain distinctly." Between parts V and VI, Conrad introduces an ellipsis in the story's chronological progress by choosing not to depict the second half of the fight. Instead, he laconically states at the end of part V that Captain MacWhirr was spared the "annoyance" of losing his ship, and in the beginning of part VI we hear about the *Nan-Shan*'s arrival in Fu-chau on "a bright sunshiny day."[105]

---

103 Conrad, *Typhoon*, 26.
104 Conrad, *Typhoon*, 36, 39, 40, 41, 42, 44, 45, 46, 47, 52, 53, 57, 62, 63, 74, 78.
105 Conrad, *Typhoon*, 80–81, 81, 88, 90, 91.

In *Kritik der Urteilskraft* (1790), Kant sketches two types of the sublime, one mathematical, one dynamical. In both cases, the experience of the sublime consists of a feeling of the superiority of human reason over nature. To Kant, reason is a supersensible faculty with the power to triumph over nature, the latter being doomed to belong to the sensible-phenomenal sphere: *"That is sublime which even to be able to think of demonstrates a faculty of the mind that surpasses every measure of the senses."* Kant adds: "Nature considered in aesthetic judgment as a power that has no dominion over us is *dynamically sublime*."[106] It is the dynamical sublime that is most relevant in *Typhoon*. Kant's examples include cliffs, volcanoes, hurricanes, and the boundless ocean. The sense of the dynamically sublime emerges when humans experience nature as threatening, yet simultaneously find themselves in a position of safety, which causes them to not feel threatened. Associated with the sublime is not only a sense of pleasure (resulting from not being in real danger and from the superiority of reason over nature), but it also involves displeasure as we become aware of our physical powerlessness in the encounter with nature's might.

To Kant, objects may be called beautiful, but they cannot be called sublime, because sublimity "is not contained in anything in nature, but only in our mind." The source of the beautiful is in nature, whereas the source of the sublime is exclusively in us: "the object serves for the presentation of a sublimity that can be found in the mind; for what is properly sublime cannot be contained in any sensible form." Natural phenomena such as earthquakes or typhoons pass through our sensory perception. As a result of their might and violence, they surpass our imaginative faculty and lead to a cognitive collapse. They "make our capacity to resist into an insignificant trifle in comparison with their power," and as a result "we found our own limitation in the immeasurability of nature and the insufficiency of our capacity to adopt a standard proportionate to the aesthetic estimation of the magnitude of its domain." However, the collapse also leads to a new and purely reason-determined cognition. The experiences of the limits of our senses and our inadequacy make us realize that we possess a supersensible capacity and strength (the mind, ideas): "we gladly call these objects sublime because they elevate the strength of our soul above its usual level, and allow us to discover within ourselves a capacity for resistance of quite another kind, which gives us the courage to measure ourselves against the apparent all-powerfulness of nature."[107]

---

106   Immanuel Kant, *Critique of the Power of Judgement*, The Cambridge Edition of the Works of Immanuel Kant, ed. Paul Guyer, trans. Paul Guyer and Eric Matthews (Cambridge: Cambridge University Press, 2000), 134, 143.
107   Kant, *Critique of the Power of Judgement*, 147, 129, 144, 145, 144–45.

Kant was inspired by Edmund Burke's ideas of the sublime. While Burke focused on the origin of the feeling of the sublime (the sensuous world), Kant was interested in "the *destination* of our faculty," where the feeling of the sublime takes us (the world of ideas and the superiority of our reason): "Thus nature is here called sublime merely because it raises the imagination to the point of presenting those cases in which the mind can make palpable to itself the sublimity of its own vocation even over nature."[108] With Kant, we discover a capacity for resistance that encourages us to measure ourselves against nature's supposedly omnipotence:

> in our own faculty of reason [we found] another, nonsensible standard, which has that very infinity under itself as a unit against which everything in nature is small, and thus found in our own mind a superiority over nature itself even in its immeasurability: likewise the irresistibility of its power certainly makes us, considered as natural beings, recognize our physical powerlessness, but at the same time it reveals a capacity for judging ourselves as independent of it and a superiority over nature on which is grounded a self-preservation of quite another kind than that which can be threatened and endangered by nature outside us, whereby the humanity in our person remains undemeaned even though the human being must submit to that dominion.[109]

Humans (defined as natural beings) may be overwhelmed and die, but humanity (exceptional because of reason) survives and triumphs over nature. Kant concludes:

> we can become conscious of being superior to nature within us and thus also to nature outside us (insofar as it influences us). Everything that arouses this feeling in us, which includes the *power* of nature that calls forth our own powers, is thus (although improperly) called sublime; and only under the presupposition of this idea in us and in relation to it are we capable of arriving at the idea of the sublimity of that being who produces inner respect in us not merely through his power, which he displays in nature, but even more by the capacity that is placed within us for judging nature without fear and thinking of our vocation as sublime in comparison with it.[110]

---

108 Kant, *Critique of the Power of Judgement*, 145.
109 Kant, *Critique of the Power of Judgement*, 145.
110 Kant, *Critique of the Power of Judgement*, 147–48.

In sea literature and marine paintings, nature often appears in forms capable of arousing feelings of the sublime, not least when the sea is experienced as terrifyingly chaotic and threatening. In "The Chronotopes of the Sea," Margaret Cohen labels this specific chronotope of sea literature "white water" and offers a correction to the Kantian model of the sublime:

> White water, of course, figures prominently in the Romantic conception of the sublime, and the related notion of the oceanic, where pleasure is derived from the prospect of terror, boundlessness, and obscurity. But within the narrative chronotope of white water, characters do not enjoy the contemplative distance necessary for the sublime. A character's removed and aesthetic stance toward the struggle to survive would be a road to certain death.[111]

Cohen introduces a different kind of sublimity that we could call *the maritime sublime*. To Kant, the epistemological conflict associated with the sublime—the capacity to grasp genuine terror, boundlessness, or obscurity—is ultimately solved by reason and thereby confirms reason's sovereignty and capacity to totalize nature conceptually, for example through concepts such as the infinite. An aesthetic distance to the natural object is upheld in order not to be destroyed. In contrast, Cohen argues that to the sailor facing the hurricane on board the ship everything is a matter of life and death. The sailor encounters the sublime nature physically, head-on, without the comfort of contemplative distance and the sanctuary of reason's abstractions. The maritime sublime overwhelms the sailor's senses with matter. It causes a mental state of conceptual and ideational vacuum without any possibility of escape (epistemological problem) and a physical state of numbness in which speech dissolves, the ears are blocked, and the eyes are blinded (phenomenological problem). The liminal experience is both cerebral and corporal. If the sailor occupies a distanced position as a detached observer with a transcendent perspective, he will lose sense of the lethal potential of the sea and jeopardize his survival.

This is not exactly the case in *Typhoon*, though. Through Captain MacWhirr, Conrad shows that having a certain distance to nature perceived as sublime is a necessary supplement for survival. But the distance is more Heideggerian than Kantian. In *Typhoon*, the experience of the sublime emphasizes the limit of concepts, but Conrad also mobilizes it to expand this limit. MacWhirr

---

111 Margaret Cohen, "The Chronotopes of the Sea," in *The Novel, vol. 2: Forms and Themes*, ed. Franco Moretti (Princeton, NJ: Princeton University Press, 2006), 658.

undergoes a hermeneutical education that was underpinned by empirical and sensuous experiences. This dual education—one corporeal, one intellectual—makes MacWhirr capable of letting his perception of nature's sublimity form a correction and extension of his concepts. The sublime experience is integrated into MacWhirr's larger experiential context: "The experience of the last six hours had enlarged his conception of what heavy weather could be like."[112]

Early on, MacWhirr tries to understand the storm through a theoretical reference work:

> without taking the time to sit down he had waded with a conscious effort into the terminology of the subject. He lost himself amongst advancing semi-circles, left- and right-hand quadrants, the curves of the tracks, the probable bearing of the centre, the shifts of wind and the readings of barometer. He tried to bring all these things into a definite relation to himself, and ended by becoming contemptuously angry with such a lot of words, and with so much advice, all head-work and supposition, without a glimmer of certitude.[113]

MacWhirr cannot understand what he reads. He is unable to integrate the meaning of the words into his horizon of understanding, because they do not relate to himself. It is only when MacWhirr has experienced the typhoon that he manages to fuse this experience with the theory and signs mediated by the reference work and the barometer and thereby achieve a new understanding of what a storm is. MacWhirr is a rather one-dimensional man, who values practicality above all else, and who only understands a phenomenon when it strikes him physically.

The disruption is not the novel's final statement. The transition between the parts V and VI reveals that the *Nan-Shan* managed to survive the tropical cyclone. But perhaps the survival is not the novel's final statement either? Perhaps we could examine the *manner* in which the *Nan-Shan* manages to stay afloat? This is where Captain MacWhirr takes center stage. The disruption is not completely isolated from the rest of the tale's more everyday episodes. The typhoon as *Störung* functions as a correction causing MacWhirr to integrate two separate experiential dimensions. He is only able to do so because the relationship between man, technology, and nature is set in a particular way. The human relationship with nature must be distant, in a way more Heideggerian

---

112   Conrad, *Typhoon*, 84.
113   Conrad, *Typhoon*, 32–33.

than Kantian, and it needs to be mediated in a certain way. If those conditions of the relationship are not met, man would be overpowered and fatally injured, or drown.

At first, MacWhirr's steamship existence is characterized by a mediated and distanced relationship to nature, first through the totality of the *Nan-Shan* itself, then through the barometer, his downcast eyes, and the reference book. This detached relationship becomes impossible to uphold during the typhoon when these media are inaccessible, either because his senses have been blocked or because his hermeneutical competency is inadequate, or they are insufficient because the typhoon makes it impossible to walk around (or sit) with downcast eyes. The typhoon demands a supplement to the technologically mediated revealing of the world; it demands a revealing that is distanced but distanced in a different way. Conrad uses the word "composure" to characterize MacWhirr's specific attitude, and this can be further elaborated through Heidegger as a particularly productive combination of his concept of *Gelassenheit*, which is a nontechnological manner of revealing (usually translated as "releasement" or "composure"), and his idea of "calculative thinking."

The calm collected attitude is associated with MacWhirr from the beginning, but it is valorized in two opposite ways throughout the novel. At first, the narrator and Jukes contribute to the ridiculing of MacWhirr. His calm is here an expression of a "bashfulness" bordering on the ludicrous and associated with the comfortable life. It is implied in his wearing "a brown bowler hat, a complete suit of brownish hue, and clumsy black boots" as if "unable to grasp what is due to the difference of latitudes," and it is condensed in the image of his "elegant umbrella of the very best quality, but unrolled." When Jukes acts as MacWhirr's maid by helping him unfold the umbrella, Rout, the chief engineer, "would turn away his head in order to hide a smile." The negative and positive evaluations of MacWhirr's attitude are contained in one sentence: "Having just enough imagination to carry him through each successive day, and no more, he was tranquilly sure of himself." No imagination and no ability whatsoever to understand figural speech, yet also self-reliant, dutiful, and reliable. This combination of characteristics is the reason that every ship under MacWhirr's command is a "floating abode of harmony and peace."[114]

In the negative evaluation of MacWhirr, his calmness is a consequence of steamship life and, ultimately, of his inexperience in relation to technology and nature. But during the typhoon, MacWhirr's calmness transforms into a footing for stability and decisiveness and, ultimately, for survival. The experience

---

114   Conrad, *Typhoon*, 3, 3, 3, 4, 4, 4, 4.

of the maritime sublime pushes the challenge of the technological revealing of the world (until then inhabited by MacWhirr) to its limit. Consequently, the calculative relationship to the world, the *Ge-stell*, must be supplemented by a new position, *Gelassenheit*, to ensure survival. MacWhirr is suddenly equipped with a dual attitude: on the one hand, a technologically mediated revealing of the world, calculative thinking, on the other hand a withdrawal from things (instruments, tools, technologies) that reveals the world in a different way, *Gelassenheit*.

MacWhirr's "composure" comprises both. It signals an attitude of calculative-calm thinking, a mixture of mental activity and passivity, of future-orientedness and being-in-the-here-and-now. The attitude is a unique maritime coded position in which the future-oriented calculative thinking is supplemented with presence-oriented and calm thinking. In the "Memorial Address," in which Heidegger develops his ideas of *Gelassenheit* and meditative thinking as an alternative to calculative thinking, he describes *Gelassenheit* or releasement in the following way: "We let technical devices enter our daily life, and at the same time leave them outside, that is, let them alone, as things which are nothing absolute but remain dependent upon something higher. I would call this comportment toward technology which expresses 'yes' and at the same time 'no,' by an old word, *releasement toward things*."[115] This attitude does not open nature through challenging but instead cautiously lets nature encounter man. Releasement (also called abandonment or letting-be) becomes the attitude capable of resisting the danger (*Gefahr*) of a humanity that adopts an exclusively technological-revealing approach to the world. Michelet observes something similar in "Conquest of the Sea," the chapter in *La Mer* that discusses (the limits of) the scientification of the ocean, in relation to a typhoon: "Enmeshed, it is no longer possible to go back; it holds you."[116] Ultimately, science (understood as calculative thinking) and daring (understood as future-orientedness) alone or paired would allow the typhoon to dominate; when combined with *Gelassenheit* and know-how, survival is possible.

Through this analysis based on Ihde's human-technology relations, it seemed as if the possibility for a distanced and contemplative gaze had disappeared within the *Ge-stell*, but perhaps this was too hasty a conclusion. Through the composed (*gelassene*) attitude, it is possible to establish a necessary distance to nature's overwhelming forces. This distance is the basis for decision-making and survival. The calculative attitude is always reaching out in(to) the things,

---

115 Heidegger, "Memorial Address," 54.
116 Michelet, *La Mer*, 299.

but supplemented by the calm attitude, this reaching out in the things can be withdrawn temporarily to create an overview and a short timespan for reflection. Composure allows for this withdrawal in order to create an overview and is deeply anchored in things and nature's dangers. Nature thus forces man into abandoning the attitude of maintaining a technologically revealing approach alone; instead, it makes us accept that this attitude needs to be supplemented with a withdrawal to make possible a space for meditative thinking, a space for survival.

During the typhoon, MacWhirr remains calm. To Jukes, he is transformed into a solid rock to which the roaming and panicking first mate can hold on for dear life. The calmness manifests on several levels, for example through the captain's voice, which comprises "that strange effect of quietness like the serene glow of a halo." MacWhirr's calmness and passivity is no longer charged with comfort; instead, it is endowed with a sacred light and offers a potential for survival. MacWhirr has been formed and educated by the hurricane, so that his "composure" is now ready to be expressed in its true oxymoronic constitution: "Face it. [...] Keep a cool head."[117] MacWhirr unites the challenging attitude ("Face it" indicates reaching out for things) and the collected attitude ("Keep a cool head" signifies withdrawal and meditation) into the attitude of composure, which is what prevents the *Nan-Shan* from shipwrecking. In the encounter with the devastating force of the tropical cyclone, man needs to have a mediated relationship with nature, not merely through concrete technologies, but also through himself. Man as seaman must withdraw from nature's violent tumult and look inward to remain in the world. Through the typhoon, Conrad points to a freedom in man in relation to technology and to the *Ge-stell*, which is necessary for his survival. Technology cannot rescue humanity; only humanity can rescue humanity.

J. M. W. Turner's painting *Snow Storm—Steam-Boat off a Harbour's Mouth* from 1842 (Figure 12) foregrounds the relation between technology (steamship) and nature (the ocean) and can therefore serve as a useful framework for understanding Conrad's *Typhoon*. Both works have the same objectives: to emphasize the limits of technology in relation to nature and to show that nature constitutes a particular correction to technology. Turner's painting conveys his lifelong fascination with the forces of nature; at the same time, it is an example of his fervent engagement with the development of nineteenth-century steam technologies. More specifically, *Snow Storm* thematizes the limits of technology through the destructive potential and centrifugal forces of

---

117 Conrad, *Typhoon*, 46, 89.

FIGURE 12   J. M. W. Turner, *Snow Storm—Steam-Boat off a Harbour's Mouth*, exhibited 1842
© TATE

nature. These forces are formally articulated by an almost cyclonic configuration of wind, water, snow, foam, and mist that results in the spiraling entrance into the painting. The vortex pattern was perhaps inspired by contemporary scientific developments on magnetic energy fields and advances in meteorology.[118] The technique forces the viewer into focusing on a steamship in distress, but also results in the ship being engulfed by nature and almost disappearing.

The painting was not well received by Turner's contemporaries. An exception was John Ruskin who praised it for being "one of the very grandest statements of sea-motion, mist, and light, that has ever been put on canvas."[119] It eventually became iconic because of its unique rendering of the chaotic forces of the wind and the waves, as they round upon a manmade machine. Its fame is also a result of Turner's rejection of the physical and rational distance so

---

118   William Rodner, "*Snow Storm—Steam-Boat off a Harbour's Mouth 1842*. Painting by J. M. W. Turner," in *Encyclopedia of the Romantic Era, 1760–1850*, vol. 2, ed. Christopher John Murray (New York and London: Fitzroy Dearborn, 2004), 1063.
119   John Ruskin, *Modern Painters*, vol. 1, in *The Complete Works of John Ruskin*, vol. 3, ed. E. T. Cook and Alexander Wedderburn (1843; London: George Allen, 1903), 571.

important in Kant's theory on the sublime. The 67-year-old painter was (supposedly) not only on board the *Ariel*, but he also asked the crew to strap him to the mast so that he could closely observe and feel what turned out to be a four-hour storm which he feared he would not survive with his life intact.

The typhoon educates MacWhirr, and he realizes the need to complement the technological approach to the world with a contemplative approach. Turner produced his paintings some fifty years before Conrad wrote his sea stories, yet they are both romantics in the sense that they see the conflict between nature and technology from the perspective of nature. Technology will always constitute a fall from a more natural and primordial state. To find what is genuinely human, it becomes important for Turner and Conrad to examine the limits of technology. To Conrad, the genuinely human is always to be found on the sailing ship (MacWhirr is a special case), because this "machinery" functions in concurrence with man and nature.

It is possible to locate Heidegger within this horizon in that he, too, operates with a kind of naturalness—the ready-to-hand attitude—that can be disrupted by the theoretical-thematized approach. This relationship becomes more complicated with modern technology, through which the challenging idea of nature as standing-reserve becomes dominant. Within this historical moment of being, Heidegger is also searching for more primordial forms of relating and revealing. He proposes the attitude of releasement, of letting-be, that results in a more detached and composed relationship with the technological world. In Conrad and Heidegger, there is a constant search for the primordial and for what is uniquely human. Technology in its modern variant seems to be enemy number one. The experience of the typhoon is to Conrad what the experience of anxiety is to Heidegger. Both experiences tear man away from his technologically mediated and everyday approach to the world, isolate him, and let him be confronted with his abandonment to the world (*Geworfenheit*) and his freedom of opportunities (*Entwurf*). This condition is un-homely (*unheimlich*) in the same way as the *Nan-Shan* suddenly becomes a stranger, because the sailors can no longer feel at one with or take refuge in what was their familiar environment. The intrusion of the negative emphasizes man's freedom regarding the technological world-disclosure—in Conrad, this is precisely the addendum that makes possible the rescue of the ship—but it also points to the finitude and inadequacy of humans when faced with the forces of nature and the surroundings. Realizing that the technological and calculative opening of the world is given within a limited and historical context that is man's signals the impossibility of maintaining a hegemonic relationship to nature. Since man is final, he can never calculate everything. Conrad and Heidegger are not only critics of technology, but they are also explorers of the limits of technology because they constantly maintain a perspective of human finality and freedom that can never be leveled.

Like Heidegger, Conrad shows that it is when man is in grave danger that he is able to find the saving (*Rettende*): "But human reflection can ponder the fact that all saving power must be of a higher essence than what is endangered, though at the same time kindred to it."[120] Through a new attitude, man is able to see that the saving (the possibility for another world-disclosure) stands in a special relationship to danger and its possible reduction to only one world-disclosure. By realizing the essence of technology and technology's reduction (in Heidegger man becomes standing-reserve, in Conrad passenger), it becomes possible to relate to it freely. So, when the technologically implicated and nature-challenging man seems to be most absorbed and occupied, a turn is possible that opens man in a new way. Heidegger calls this new and freer opening toward things and nature *Gelassenheit*. During the typhoon, such a turn happens, but in the distinct maritime way in which technology is united with the calm attitude. Maritime life is always already technologically coded and mediated, and there is in this life a constant focus on survival in the struggle between life and death. In that sense, the two "settings"—calculation and meditation—are united in one state of being, MacWhirr's composure.

In the "Author's Note" to *Typhoon and Other Stories*, Conrad discusses how he transformed the hurricane story from "mere anecdote" into genuine art: "I felt that to bring out its deeper significance which was quite apparent to me, something other, something more was required; a leading motive that would harmonize all these violent noises, and a point of view that would put all that elemental fury into its proper place. What was needed of course was Captain MacWhirr."[121] Three things are important here: "deeper significance," "leading motive," and "point of view," all of which converge in the attitude of composure. The *deeper significance* has to do with Conrad's probing into the question of the roles of humans and technology, and the limits of technology in relation to nature. The *leading motive* is MacWhirr, who, like a conductor, manages to centralize the divergent rhythms (as conceived by Lefebvre) and, not least, unite the complementary viewpoints of calculative and meditative thinking into a single *point of view*, the composed attitude. Composure becomes Conrad's salvaging of a unique maritime-technological form of experience that is an acceptable and nonreductive world-disclosure with a capacity for safeguarding (but not guaranteeing) the sailor's survival in his encounters with extreme

---

120 Heidegger, "The Question Concerning Technology," 33–34.
121 Conrad, "Author's Note," in *Typhoon and Other Stories*, vi.

natural phenomena. This makes *Typhoon* into one of the great existentialist novels and most profound explorations of the role of technology as a mediator between humans and the surrounding environment.

6 Science and Technology in *Vingt mille lieues sous les mers*

The works of Jules Verne and Joseph Conrad share the same fundamental interest and structure: the relationship between humans and the natural world as mediated by technology. However, their attentiveness toward humans took separate directions, their visions of the natural world contrasted, and their attitudes toward modern technology differed. Conrad's primary interest is the physical, psychological, and existential predicaments of shipborne men and life at sea. He sees steam technology as muddying, even destroying, the purer and more primordial experiential relationship between humans, sailing ships, and the ocean. In Conrad's oeuvre, *Typhoon* is a rare example of a more positive attitude toward modern technology. Verne's focus is on the capacity of manmade technological machines to assist humans in transgressing the geographical and spatial boundaries of the known worlds. In Verne, the psychological dimensions of his characters are of lesser importance than their actions and observations of the exterior world.

If Conrad uses the outer world of technoships at sea as a setting from which to explore the inner worlds and interpersonal relationships of his characters, Verne uses state-of-the-art and not-yet-accomplished technological developments as vehicles for human explorations of the white spaces of the physical world. The natural sciences then assist Verne in describing and inventorying its riches and resources. In Conrad, focus is on the human predicament. But it is the mysterious laws of a withdrawn, noncommunicating, and hostile universe that governs his worlds, reducing humans to impotent, insignificant, and yet fascinating creatures who grapple to comprehend the obscure mechanisms that determine their individual fates. In Verne, focus is on technology's capacity to open up new outer worlds. Manmade technological inventions make humans into industrial masters of and consubstantial with a pliant world made transparent and communicative through science. In Verne, there are no uninhabitable spaces, only uninhabited ones.[122] Assisted by technology and language, Nemo and other Verne characters become demiurges, something we almost never see in Conrad. As world-makers, they *"make space into a language"* and

---

[122] Jules Verne, *The Adventures of Captain Hatteras*, transl., intro., and notes William Butcher (1864–65; Oxford: Oxford University Press, 2005), 284.

"contribute to the world's genesis through nomination."[123] Verne would later, post-1871, become less optimistic about progress, mastery, and transparency.

6.1   The Making of a New Literary Profile and a Novel

Jules Verne combined the seriousness of scientific documentation and the didactics of educational instruction with the qualities of fiction, which gave him a profile as "popularizing writer." This was encouraged, perhaps even constructed and dictated, by his editor Pierre-Jules Hetzel after he received Verne's manuscript to *Cinq semaines en ballon*, his first novel, which was published in 1863.[124] The duo's idea was to create a symbiosis between the novelistic form and the natural sciences by meticulously incorporating the totality of knowledge accumulated during the previous and ongoing geographical explorations. The concept for the series *Voyages extraordinaires*, in stark contrast to *l'art pour l'art*, was natural history mediated as science adventure fiction, a picturesque encyclopedia. It was an ambitious, optimistic, and somewhat utopian project. Fundamentally, it was also a commercial agreement, a literary production in the economic sense with two to three works to be written per year. The agreement seems to have suited Verne's bourgeois temperament.[125]

Thirty-seven years before the publication of Conrad's *Typhoon*, on July 25, 1865, George Sand (1804–1876) sent Jules Verne (1828–1905) a letter of thanks for sending her his two most recent novels, *Voyage au centre de la terre* (1864/1867) and *De la terre à la lune* (1865). Sand appreciated his writing and urged Verne to pursue his imaginative explorations of the world by turning to the depths of the sea in his next novel, making submarine adventures possible by the creation of diving devices perfected by the young writer's scientific imagination.[126] The elder Sand, whom Verne admired, is often credited with playing a decisive role in the genesis of *Vingt mille lieues sous les mers*, first serialized from March 20, 1869 to June 20, 1870 in *Le Magasin d'éducation et de recreation*, and published as an illustrated novel on November 16, 1871. As Jacques Noiray remarks in his "Préface" to Gallimard's 2005 edition of the novel, it is possible that Verne obeyed "a deeper logic of his own imagination."[127] After the aerial

---

123   Michel de Certeau, "Writing the Sea: Jules Verne," in *Heterologies: Discourse on the Other*, trans. Brian Massumi (Manchester: Manchester University Press, 1986), 143.
124   Jacques Noiray, "Préface," in Jules Verne, *Vingt mille lieues sous les mers* (1871; Paris: Gallimard, 2005), 10–11.
125   Jean Chesneaux, *Une lecture politique de Jules Verne* (Paris: Maspéro, 1971), 12.
126   George Sand, *Correspondance*, letter no. 11807, July 25, 1865, ed. Georges Lubin (Paris: Classiques Garnier, 1985), 322–23.
127   Noiray, "Préface," 9.

novels *Cinq semaines en ballon* and *De la terre à la lune*, the surface-nautical novel *Les Aventures du capitaine Hatteras* (1864–65/1866), and the underground novel *Voyage au centre de la terre*, it would have been a logical next step—with or without Sand's advice—to compose an underwater novel, following the same formula as the previous novels: an extraordinary voyage saturated with adventures and trials framing an exploration of unfamiliar or unknown worlds through the medium of a new locomotion apparatus (after balloon, space gun, brig, train, and steamboat).

The inner, personal, and artistic logic was supported by outside, social, and market forces. Among the public there was an enormous interest in scientific landmarks, technological innovations, and barrier-transgressing voyages. Curiosity regarding the underwater world was particularly fervent during the 1860s. An important source for Verne (as it was for Michelet), and an example of a scientific landmark publication that resonated with the public, was Matthew Fontaine Maury's *The Physical Geography of the Sea* (1855). Additionally, several submersible ships had already been on display in Paris. The increased attentiveness towards submarines and the speed of experimentation was due in part to their rising significance in the American Civil War. The submersible vessels employed during that war were all still dependent on human power to move. The world's first submarine to be propelled by mechanical power, the French *Plongeur* by Admiral Siméon Bourgois and naval engineer Charles Brun, was launched on April 16, 1863, and inspired Verne's design of the *Nautilus* in terms of form, size, and functions. There was also a real *Nautilus* created by the American Samuel Hallett, displayed in 1858 and later during the 1867 World Exhibition. Hallett named his submarine in homage to Robert Fulton who invented the world's first submarine in 1800 and named it *Nautilus*.[128]

Sand may have urged Verne to explore the oceanic depths, but she alone did not catalyze *Vingt mille lieues*. As Noiray put it, "the surprising thing would have been if this novel had not been written."[129] The fact that Verne had published a short story in 1861, "San Carlos," which features a bizarre submersible vessel, relativizes Sand's role even more. If Conrad drew on personal experiences from sea voyages and anecdotes circulating among the sailing community, Verne plunged into scientific textbooks and visited exhibitions to examine the latest hardware on display. Verne also had the maritime world close by. He was born on an island surrounded by two branches of the Loire River in Nantes, an important shipbuilding town in Verne's lifetime. His brother was a naval officer

---

128   Noiray, "Préface," 10.
129   Noiray, "Préface," 10.

and helped him plot the mechanics of the *Nautilus*, and Verne owned a ship and used it extensively during the years he worked on *Vingt mille lieues*.

6.2 Science Adventure Fiction

Almost all of Verne's novels are adventure novels, and several have been labeled as science fiction. *Twenty Thousand Leagues Under the Seas* qualifies as both, although the science-fiction tag has been challenged by Verne scholar and translator William Butcher: "Verne is *not* a science-fiction writer: most of his books contain *no* innovative science."[130] Verne was inspired by several contemporary submarines, perhaps the *Plongeur* most of all. He visited the 1867 World Exhibition that featured section models and complete models of the *Plongeur*, which he is supposed to have observed carefully.[131] Verne's novel cannot qualify as science fiction if one understands science fiction to be a work of fiction that comprises not-yet invented technological machines. But the truth is that the all the submersible ships built prior to the publication of *Vingt mille lieues* were extremely primitive compared to Verne's *Nautilus*.

After two years of further experimentation, especially trying to solve the problem of a lack of stability, Bourgois and Brun abandoned the *Plongeur* project in 1865, largely unhappy with the result, and the French navy disarmed it on June 20, 1867. Jacques Payen remarks, "The true beginnings of the submarine dates to the end of the nineteenth century, first with the *Gymnote* by Gustave Zédé from 1888, then especially the *Gustave Zédé* from 1893, and finally the *Narval* by Laubeuf in 1899."[132] Submersible vessels existed around 1870 when Verne published *Vingt mille lieues*, but his *Nautilus* was much more advanced than the *Plongeur*, Hallett's *Nautilus*, and Fulton's *Nautilus* as well as all other existing submarines. Verne's *Nautilus* was a machine of the future that helped inspire the technological breakthroughs of the 1880s and 1890s. This is precisely what George Sand meant when she urged Verne to create diving devices and perfect them by using his scientific imagination. The science was already underway, but for it to advance it required not only further technological experiments, but also the vivid imagination of a writer with Verne's unique talents.

---

130   William Butcher, "Introduction," in Jules Verne, *Twenty Thousand Leagues under the Seas*, translated and with introduction and notes by William Butcher (1869–70/1871; Oxford: Oxford University Press, 1998), ix.
131   William Butcher, "Appendix" and "Explanatory Notes," in Verne, *Twenty Thousand Leagues under the Seas*, 383, 391–92; G.-L. Pesce, *La Navigation sous-marine* (Paris: Vuibert & Nony, 1906), 290–96; Jacques Payen, "De l'anticipation à l'innovation: Jules Verne et le problème de la locomotion mécanique," *Culture Technique*, no. 19 (1989): 310.
132   Payen, "De l'anticipation à l'innovation," 310.

If we consider Darko Suvin's classical work on science fiction, which we shall examine more extensively in the chapter on the Anthropocene, one of the most surprising claims in *Metamorphoses of Science Fiction* (1977) is that the genre of science fiction is not dependent on the innovation of new technologies but on cognitive estrangement. While Suvin agrees with Butcher on Verne not being a true science-fiction writer, he does so for a different reason than Butcher's *"no innovative science"* argument. To Suvin, there is in authors such as Verne and H. G. Wells a prevalence of anti-cognitive impulses, for example a fetishization of machines and gadgets that degrade the crucial estrangement to formal and superficial sensationalism. In Suvin's Marxist influenced thinking, the *Nautilus* serves merely as a new strain of opium for the people.[133]

Two interventions are possible. First, it is generally acknowledged that Verne's primary interest was never science and technology as such, but rather the prospects made possible by science and technology to make new spaces in the form of geographies, hydrographies, and aerographies accessible to humankind as well as their implications for political society in its entirety.[134] Second, Suvin's argument that cognitive estrangement primarily emerges from "a narrative novum (the dramatis personae and/or their context) significantly different from what is the norm in 'naturalistic' or empiricist fiction," and also bearing in mind his comment on science fiction's "concern with a domestication of the amazing," makes it difficult not to associate *Vingt mille lieues sous les mers* with science fiction. The novum is obviously the context of the submarine world, which represented one of the last frontiers not yet crossed by humans, and the project of Verne and Hetzel was to familiarize the amazing undersea world. In addition, Verne mobilizes estranging perspectives that challenge the norms governing society at large. The *oceanic perspective*, the view from the aquatic depths, represents an alternative to the terrestrial "Ptolemaic-type closed world picture,"[135] by challenging the idea of human exceptionalism. The *submarine perspective*, the view from the *Nautilus* and through the eyes of Captain Nemo, also conjures up an alternative social model comprising echoes of the *quarante-huitarde* tradition, utopian socialism, nationalist liberation movements, and libertarian individualism.

Let us not delve into technological and generical details here. Some sources already quoted can be consulted for more on the evolution of submarines and the accompanying micro-technologies. With regard to genre, a flexible solution

---

133 Darko Suvin, *Metamorphoses of Science Fiction: On the Poetics and History of a Literary Genre* (Yale University Press, 1977), ix.
134 Butcher, "Introduction," xiv; Chesneaux, *Une lecture politique*, 21, ch. 2.
135 Suvin, *Metamorphoses of Science Fiction*, 3, 4, 6.

could be *science adventure fiction*,¹³⁶ as this categorization is outside the fixed definitions of science fiction "proper." At the same time, it acknowledges the major role of science in Verne's novels.

6.3 Progress and Mastering

My main objectives are to discuss the role maritime technologies play in transforming the relationship between humans and the natural world and how a technologically mediated experience of the sea is configured aesthetically. Jules Verne's *Voyages extraordinaires* in general (the series comprises more than sixty novels), and *Vingt mille lieues sous les mers* in particular, inscribe themselves in two interdependent ideological currents that dominated the societies of Europe and the United States during the nineteenth century: the quasi-religion of scientific and technological progress and the aspiration to master the planet, which included mapping the parts of the planet as yet unknown to these societies.

Later in his career, from around 1870–71, the optimism that characterizes Verne's early work is replaced with a more pessimistic view of progress and the potential for science and technology to support progress, growth, and exploitation. The novel that marks the turn is *Le Chancellor*, which Verne began to write in 1870 and published in 1874–75.¹³⁷ In *Vingt mille lieues*, arguably the last work of Verne's first period, he glorifies both currents, progress and mastering, although not without the occasional reservation. As Jean Chesneaux has shown, Verne's thinking is inspired by the optimistic ideology of Saint-Simonianism characterized by its commitment to the exploitation of the world's natural resources and of capitalist and colonial conquest.¹³⁸

Nemo's praise of Ferdinand de Lesseps, the developer of the Suez Canal, which opened in 1869, the same year that Hetzel initiated the serialized publication of *Vingt mille lieues* in *Magasin d'éducation et de récréation*, is a testimony of the novel's Saint-Simonianism: "He does more honour to his nation than the greatest of sea-captains! Like so many others, he began with obstacles and disappointments, but has triumphed because he has the necessary will-power."¹³⁹ Navigators such as James Cook, Comte de La Pérouse, Louis Antoine de Bougainville, and Dumont d'Urville are often referred to by Nemo or Aronnax, all of them considered heroes in their efforts to explore the globe and expand our knowledge about it. Verne's admiration for past discoveries

---

136 Cohen, *The Novel and the Sea*, 214.
137 Butcher, "Introduction," ix–x.
138 Chesneaux, *Une lecture politique*, ch. 4; Noiray, "Préface," 13.
139 Verne, *Twenty Thousand Leagues Under the Seas*, 215.

and the accumulation of knowledge, shows respect for the past and a pedagogical strategy, as well as a subscription to the belief in the positivity of further progress and future discoveries. His inclination towards the past is simultaneously a sign of the potential of the future.

Nemo's voyage is an attempt to resume and transgress the explorations of the English Cook and the French d'Urville in Oceania and the Antarctic. It is precisely by virtue of the *Nautilus*, Nemo's awe-inspiring submarine and technological wonder, that, in the words of Aronnax "a still greater marvel" than "the most fabulous and mythological of creatures" because "a man-made phenomenon,"[140] Verne is able to push further than his predecessors. Cook and d'Urville were restricted spatially as well as temporally, which left their explorations fragmentary, limited, and unfulfilled. Their expeditions had a natural expiry date, manned as they were by land-committed scientists, sailors, and family men, and subject to the demands that only *terra firma* can supply in the long run (fresh water, fruits, and vegetables, materials for clothing, tools, etc.). The expeditions also had natural geographical and hydrographical limits as the ships were reliant on the surface of the sea for movement and unable to cross masses of ice.

As machine and literary device, the *Nautilus*, a genuine *prosthesis* of Nemo and his crew, becomes Verne's mediator of hitherto unexplored worlds:

(crew-*Nautilus*) → underwater world

The structure is the same that determined the starting point for the crew's experience of the ocean aboard the *Nan-Shan* in *Typhoon* before different events, especially the typhoon, resulted in variations on the basic structure. In *Twenty Thousand Leagues*, Verne introduces a completely new relationship between the three components:

(crew-*Nautilus*-underwater world)

Not only is the submarine able to access spaces no human has ever accessed, but it is also able to inhabit them. The *Nautilus* is not only a prosthesis of the crew, but it also forms an *organic unity* with the ocean.

As a self-supporting ecosystem that requires oceanic substances and nothing more for its continued existence, there is no time limit on the voyage of the *Nautilus*. This enables Verne to *totalize* what had up to then been fragmentary

---

140 Verne, *Twenty Thousand Leagues Under the Seas*, 45.

and incoherent knowledge (which is even the case in Michelet who had no *Nautilus*, only books and personal surface experiences, and who never ventured into the Antarctic regions, nor did he circumnavigate the globe). Verne's underwater voyage is genuinely global and a recapitulation and completion of a century's disconnected conquests, now organized in a conclusive epistemological system and explication of the (submarine) world. What is new and truly extraordinary about *Vingt mille lieues sous les mers* is the world of the underwater depths and, by implication, the potential planetarity of its vision. With the *Nautilus*, Verne is able to complement the familiar heights with the unfamiliar depths and the visible with the invisible. From this amazing achievement emerges this crucial question: Does it affirm and amplify human mastery and smoothen out alterity, or does it position humans alongside the nonhumans and emphasize genuine alterity? Is Verne's vision global or planetary, or both?[141]

The point of view in *Vingt mille lieues* is radically different from anything seen before in literary history. In the mid-twentieth century, Günter Grass was celebrated for creating a perspective from below through the character of Oskar Matzerath in *Die Blechtrommel* (1949). Grass's point of view was from below in a generational-altitudinal and social sense, primarily the child's perspective from an altitude of approximately one meter, but also the perspective of a member of the German merchant middle-class. Verne's point of view is from below in a veritable elemental(-altitudinal), spatial, and species sense. With the *Nautilus*, and through the narrator Aronnax and Captain Nemo, Verne invents an all-embracing vision that unites worlds above and below. It is a dual point of view that is simultaneously inverted-inverting, decentered-decentering, and displaced-displacing—in short, radically different-differentiating and strange-estranging. It is a perspective that borders on the nonhuman and approaches a superhuman techno-geographical-hydrographical epistemology, at once geographical-hydrographical and detached from the challenges of nature thanks to the invention of a technological marvel.

6.4 *Vraisemblance*

So far, we have dealt mainly with the marvelous and the extraordinary. It is important to stress that *Vingt mille lieues* taps into the register of vraisemblance. The rootedness in a world that is *radically different* yet *not impossible* (Suvin's formula for science fiction)[142] was part of the pedagogical and didactic

---

141 Gayatri Chakravorty Spivak, *Death of a Discipline* (New York: Columbia University Press, 2003), 72.
142 Suvin, *Metamorphoses of Science Fiction*, viii.

ambitions of *Voyages extraordinaires*, and Verne mobilized vraisemblance through different strategies. The world depicted may seem improbable, but the *means* of conveying it needed to be reliable. Like every other first-person narrator, Aronnax is intertwined with his own subjectivity (middle-class, academic), but generally he is a reliable narrator who transmits to the reader what he *sees and feels*. Sometimes, he misinterprets things, but then Nemo, Conseil, or Ned Land usually clarify things for us. This belatedness is comparable to that which structures Marlowe's perceptions in *Heart of Darkness*.[143] But if the delay between perception and understanding in Conrad's novel was the result of an underlying epistemology of fragmentation and transience finding expression in an impressionistic aesthetics, in Verne's novel the delay is an effect of the strangeness of the things observed in combination with Aronnax's temperament. Although a man of science and precision, Aronnax is also someone astounded by flora and fauna (and a machine) not previously known to humans. This makes his misinterpretations even more human and understandable.

Aronnax's scientific background endows him with reliability, and the reader does not have to worry about him telling tall tales or imagining things. Add to this that *Vingt mille lieues* is written in the form of a journal, the marine form par excellence, and that its style is characterized by precision. If the scientific impulse vouches for accuracy and objectivity, the journal format rests on detailed chronology. Admittedly, if one examines the temporal design of the novel closely, mistakes and irregularities in Aronnax's chronology can be found. But the most important aspect of this type of vraisemblance is not the veracity of the dates, but the very practice of dating. In addition, we can point to three types of near-convergence. The first is between Aronnax's experiences and his writing them down. This endows the novel with intensity, presence, and even an emotional dimension that supplement the scientific neutrality. The second is between the voyage and the editing of the novel. This partially collapses the distinction between narrator and author and thus underlines the reliability argument. The third is between the end of the voyage and the publication, which enforces the impression of veracity. With its events taking place in 1866–67, *Vingt mille lieues* is the documentation of immediate history, very near the present of the first readers.

The chronological precision and the story's temporal proximity to the year of publication is supplemented by geographical precision. Throughout the

---

143 Ian Watt, "Impressionism and Symbolism in Heart of Darkness," in *Joseph Conrad: A Commemoration*, ed. Norman Sherry (London: Palgrave Macmillan, 1976), 37–53.

narrative, islands, cities, continents, mountains, bays and so forth are conscientiously named, located, and described by Aronnax: "At three a.m. on 26 November, the Nautilus cut the tropic of Cancer at longitude 172°. On the 27th it passed within sight of the archipelago of Hawaii, where Captain Cook met his death on 14 February 1779. We had then covered 4,860 leagues from our starting point. When I arrived on the platform that morning, I sighted Hawaii two miles to leeward, the biggest of the seven islands forming the archipelago."[144] The novel features two maps showing the route of the *Nautilus*, thus allowing for the geographical nominations and descriptions to be further determined topographically. The voyage is geometrically outlined and geographically and hydrographically mapped. As a scientific endeavor, cartography is added to the list of other practices in the novel. It functions as an exemplary act of the taking possession of the natural world by humankind. A map represents the scientific and technological domination of humans over surrounding nature.

Verne's novels were richly illustrated, and *Vingt mille lieues* is no exception. Besides the two maps (Figure 13), the novel abounds with drawings by Alphonse de Neuville (1835–1885) and Édouard Riou (1833–1900), engraved by Henri Théophile Hildibrand (1824–1897) (Figure 14 and 15). While many of the illustrations depict familiar phenomena and scenes (e.g., "Le cortège suivait toujours la frégate" and "Ned Land avait environ quarante ans"[145]), some of them also serve to *naturalize the unnatural*. The drawings are initially founded on Verne's text and its descriptions. Words determine illustrations. At the same time, as a result of their detailed, realistic style, the illustrations create a feedback loop. Their visuality lends credibility to the descriptions. Illustrations verify the words. The radically different, yet not impossible, wonders of the submarine world—even the giant squids that had not yet been scientifically accepted at the time—are conveyed precisely as *not impossible*.

In Verne, the fantastic is usually a result of existing, yet up to that point inaccessible, realms of reality (the undersea, the moon, the inner core of the Earth, etc.), which have been made accessible though scientific and technological progress. The spaces opened up for human exploration by the Vernian machines are thus both real and realistic, whereas the machines have futuristic components. The *Nautilus* is not a completely new innovation, but it is more advanced than contemporary examples of submarines. Although the *Nautilus* does not yet exist on the material plane, it is assuredly a nineteenth-century machine, and not of the twentieth or twenty-first century. This makes Verne

---

144 Verne, *Twenty Thousand Leagues Under the Seas*, 122.
145 Pages 17 and 24 in the original 1871 edition and pages 73 and 83 in the 2005 Gallimard edition. Unfortunately, no illustrations are printed in the 1998 Oxford edition.

an author of the *futur proche* (near future), not of the *futur lointain* (distant future). Conversely, Conrad is an author of the *passé recent* (recent past).

I have previously suggested that Verne and Conrad had different accentuations in the constellation of humans, technology, and nature. Although both authors employ technology and technological developments to examine the changing relationships between humans and the natural world, Conrad is traditionally considered an author more interested in the human understood as an individual person with a singular fate, whereas Verne's focus is on the general progress of civilization through scientific and technological inventions. The role of the individual character as a singular person is sometimes questioned in Verne scholarship, and the characters are seen as types, carriers of ideas and representatives of a class or a nation.[146] In the last stages of preparing the manuscript for publication, Verne indicated in a letter to Hetzel that he saw revisions of some of Riou's illustrations necessary in order for them to convey the spirit of the vision more accurately: "I have received the sketches of Riou. I have some observations to make. I will write to him while I return them to him. I think that it is necessary to make the characters much smaller and show the salons much more *in large*. These are just corners of a salon that do not convey the idea of the wonders of the *Nautilus*. He will have to draw all the details with extreme finesse."[147] To Verne, the *Nautilus*, together with the undersea world, was clearly conceived as one of the novel's protagonists alongside the more traditional choice of human protagonists (Aronnax and Nemo).

If science in the form of machine (the *Nautilus*) and a series of disciplines (geography, geology, hydrography, ichthyology, etc.) is a crucial element of Verne's vision, he nevertheless had to endow science with a novelistic existence.[148] To do so, Verne anchors science in the human characters, first of all in Aronnax, a doctor and a professor affiliated with the Muséum national d'histoire naturelle in Paris where he studied under Milne-Edwards, and in Captain Nemo, the chief engineer of the *Nautilus* and a *savant*. In the previous novels, the *savants* all had certain comic traits (e.g., Samuel Fergusson in *Cinq semaines* and Otto Lidenbrock in *Voyage au centre de la terre*), but in *Vingt mille lieues* business is more serious with Aronnax and Nemo. Similarly, adventure had primacy and science a secondary role in the previous novels; geography,

---

146 Marie-Hélène Huet, *L'Histoire des* Voyages extraordinaires*: Essai sur l'œuvre de Jules Verne* (Paris: Minard, 1973), 12, 172.

147 *Correspondance inédite de Jules Verne et de Pierre-Jules Hetzel: 1863–1886*, vol. I, 1863–1874, eds. Olivier Dumas, Piero Gondolo della Riva, and Volker Dehs (Genève: Slatkine, 1999), folios 128–129, letter 60, p. 89. Date probably end of December 1868.

148 Noiray, "Préface," 21.

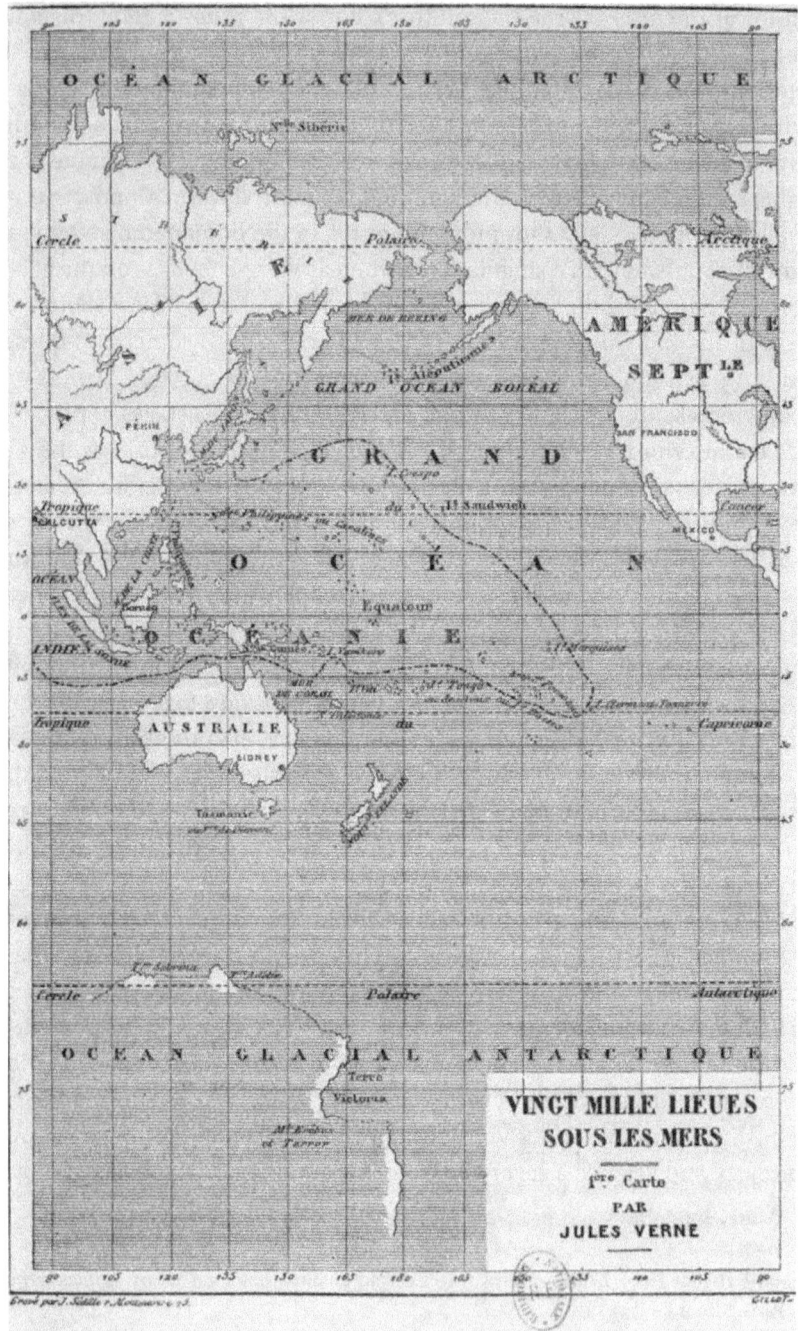

FIGURE 13   1ᵉʳᵉ Carte and 2ᵉ Carte in *Vingt mille lieues sous les mers*, 1871 edition, drawings probably by Jules Verne. Gallica.
© BIBLIOTHÈQUE NATIONALE DE FRANCE

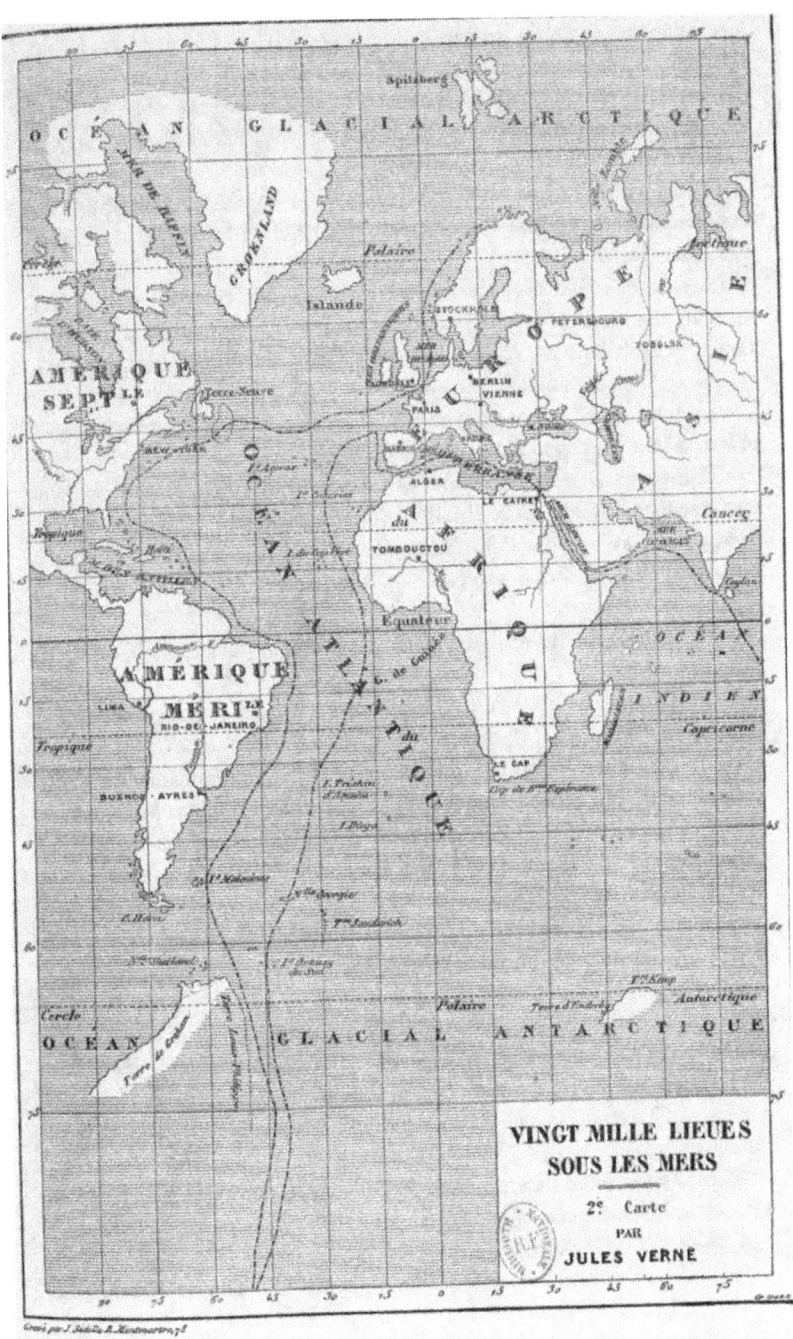

FIGURE 13   *(cont.)*

FIGURE 14   Édouard Riou, "Le cortège suivait toujours la frégate" (1871). Gallica
© BIBLIOTHÈQUE NATIONALE DE FRANCE

FIGURE 15 Alphonse de Neuville, "Paysage sous-marin de l'île Crespo" (1871). Gallica
© BIBLIOTHÈQUE NATIONALE DE FRANCE

geology, algebra, and ballistics undergirded the adventure plots. In *Vingt mille lieues*, science is elevated to primary focus in that it absorbs state-of-the-art knowledge from several domains such as ichthyology, conchyliology, botanic, geology, hydrography, and meteorology. As in Michelet's case, this scientifically infused encyclopedic impulse (here incarnated by Aronnax and Nemo and verified through the *Nautilus*) makes *Vingt mille lieues* into one of the most authentic novels about life under the sea.

6.5   Ambiguities

It has been suggested that Aronnax and Nemo represent two opposite sides of Jules Verne, one side identifying with Aronnax's logical and systematic aspects, perhaps also his humanist ethos, the other aspiring to emulate Nemo's imaginative, energetic, and free spirit. Furthermore, the temperamental divergence between the two protagonists may even be transferred to the relationship between Verne and Hetzel, the latter embodying both the literalness and realism of Aronnax and the political idealism of Nemo.[149] Whereas Aronnax represents the ideal of a measured, balanced, and reasonable science, which is legitimized by its respect for moral values and religious principles on which the bourgeois society are founded, Nemo is a more complex character oscillating between a seductive and charismatic visionary power and a superhuman, almost satanic temptation of omnipotence and complete knowledge.[150] His moral compass is compromised by his anthropocentric yearning to unveil "the last secrets" of "our planet" and to not only "contemplate the works of the Creator in the midst of the liquid element, but also to penetrate the most fearful mysteries of the ocean." This is accompanied by a demonic anger when his personal secrets are in danger of being disclosed: "You came and discovered a secret that no man on earth must penetrate—the secret of my entire existence."[151] There is an obvious parallel between Aronnax and Ishmael and between Nemo and Ahab. Although Melville's duo is fleshed out more extensively, Ishmael is endowed with a greater artistic virtuosity and sensibility than Aronnax and Ahab embodies a deeper and more complex darkness than Nemo.

Verne's creation of Captain Nemo contributes to making *Twenty Thousand Leagues* a novel of unresolved dilemmas and intense paradoxes. He is Verne's Ahab or Kurtz, transgressing the boundaries of our traditional "earthbound science"[152] and earthly ethics, balancing between a self-expressed idealism of oceanic freedom and a latent, unacknowledged despotism of his own:

---

149   Butcher, "Introduction," xxix.
150   Noiray, "Préface," 22–23.
151   Verne, *Twenty Thousand Leagues Under the Seas*, 65, 123, 65.
152   Verne, *Twenty Thousand Leagues Under the Seas*, 65.

> The sea is everything. It covers seven-tenths of the terrestrial globe. Its breath is healthy and pure. It is a spacious wilderness where man is never alone, for he can feel life throbbing all around him. The sea is the environment for a prodigious, supernatural existence; it is nothing but movement and love; it is a living infinity, as one of your poets has said. And indeed, sir, nature is present there in its three kingdoms, animal, vegetable, and mineral. [...] The sea is nature's vast reserve. It was through the sea that the globe as it were began, and who knows if it will not end in the sea! Perfect peace abides there. The sea does not belong to despots. On its surface immoral rights can still be claimed, men can fight each other, devour each other, and carry out all the earth's atrocities. But thirty feet below the surface their power ceases, their influence fades, their authority disappears. Ah, sir, live, live in the heart of the sea! Independence is possible only here! Here I recognize no master! Here I am free![153]

Nemo's overture to the sea, recycling thoughts and passages from Michelet, is expressed on a background of tragic personal experiences of loss of family (a wife and two children) and political persecution. Nemo, Latin for nobody, is a freedom fighter, a Byronic hero, who supports the liberation struggles of small nations against the hegemonic oppression of great nations, concretely assisting the Cretan struggle for independence from his undersea world. But Nemo's behavior and treatment of Aronnax, Conseil, and Ned Land as prisoners reveal an autocratic streak. Together with Nemo's libertarian idealism, the motto of the *Nautilus*, *mobilis in mobile* (moving within a moving element), contrasts sharply with the forced immobilization of his guests. His autocratic streak also surfaces in his notion of ocean territories as his personal estate: "Sometimes I go hunting in the midst of this element thought inaccessible to man, and pursue the game living in my underwater forests. My flocks, like those of Neptune's old shepherd, graze without fear on the immense ocean plains. There I have a vast property which I alone farm and which is always replanted by the hand of the Creator of all things."[154] Here, Crusoe's name joins those of Ahab and Kurtz on the list of Nemo's spiritual brothers.

Nemo's overture has an additional point of interest, which has to do with the novel's use of different temporalities. Verne and his protagonists are usually considered to be high priests of progress, and rightly so. But the linearity inherent in this pseudo-religion of the nineteenth century—the steady advancement of scientific knowledge and territorial discovery—is supplemented by

---

153 Verne, *Twenty Thousand Leagues Under the Seas*, 68–69.
154 Verne, *Twenty Thousand Leagues Under the Seas*, 67.

a circular temporality embodied by the ocean as an organism responsible for both beginning and end. Verne activates two temporal scales, a human scale of progressive discoveries and an oceanic circular scale of births, deaths, and rebirths. The irony is that it is the former which has made it possible to uncover the latter. There is a third temporality in the novel expressed by Nemo in relation to his presentation of his library to Aronnax: "In my eyes, your modern artists are not to be distinguished from the ancients: they could be two or three thousand years old and I mix them all up in my mind. The great masters are ageless." In Nemo's library, time comes to a standstill. He compares it to death, a condition in which "chronological differences are erased."[155] Instead of a linear or a circular temporality, Nemo articulates a stable and static coexistence of different temporal layers in which neither progress nor movement is possible. It is important to bear in mind that Nemo's voyage with the *Nautilus* has seen him work on ameliorating the flaws and holes in Aronnax's two-volume *Les Mystères des grands fonds sous-marins* (*The Mysteries of the Ocean Deep*), and he lures Aronnax with promises of specific sights that will enable the French professor to upgrade his own work. In that sense, the idea of a library in which time stands still is undermined by the fact that Nemo and Aronnax constantly contribute to increasing the knowledge contained in the library. Finally, we should remember that "the straight line forms a circle": the progressive spirit's figure of linearity has the encyclopedia as its ultimate goal, that is, a circular instruction (from Greek, ἐγκύκλιος παιδεια, *enkyklios paideia*) and thus an attempt to encircle all knowledge. However, as we shall see, and as Michel de Certeau also acknowledges, "The circle is not perfect. Fiction cuts across it."[156]

6.6 Apollonian Order, Dionysian Fertility

The Faustian drive in Nemo and Aronnax is linked with the pedagogical commission assigned to Verne when the *Voyages extraordinaires* was conceived with Hetzel. How does one convey the results of this *wanting to see everything* and *wanting to know everything*, including the things beyond the limits of the mere terrestrial? Verne resorts to the catalogue, a classical literary technique also employed in *Moby-Dick* and *La Mer*: He galvanizes the potentially dry listings with an imaginative impulse: "These long zoological or botanical enumerations, these long descriptions of volcanic, geological, or meteorological phenomena are also, paradoxically, the opportunity for Jules Verne to give free rein to his poetic fantasy, to get intoxicated with technical

---

155   Verne, *Twenty Thousand Leagues Under the Seas*, 72.
156   de Certeau, "Writing the Sea," 147, 148.

terms with strange assonances."[157] The countless enumerations and classifications of phenomena—didactic in purpose and a privileged literary form capable of rendering totality—are sometimes overtaken by verbal avalanches in which alliteration, rhyme, and rhythm triumph over referentiality and scientific precision. One reason may be that Verne finds the scientific nomenclature "a little arid," as Aronnax remarks when commenting on the classificatory obsession of Conseil. We hear of "hyaline Cydippes," "comatulids," "triangular donaxes, tridentate Hyalinae," "opercular pectens," "*Cynthiae*," "*Carinariae*," "Cavolines," "periwinkles, Janthinae, cinerairia, petricola, Lamellariidiae, cabochons, Pandoridae, etc." So, quite often, the enumerations display a serious scientific mode as well as a poetic note: "pediculate, foliaceous, globular, and digitate," "snooks; oriflamme mullets with yellow heads; parrot fish, labra, triggerfish, gobies, etc.," "periwinkles, delphiniums, screw shells, ianthines, ovules, volutes, olives, mitre shells, casques, murexes, whelks, harps, winkles, Triton's shells, cerites, spindle-shells, wing shells, scorpion shells, limpets, hyales, and *Cleodora*: all delicate and fragile shells that science has baptized with its most charming names."[158] As Jacques Noiray has observed, the last sentence testifies to Verne's ambiguous relationship with science, or *scientific language*. Verne was fascinated by scientific discoveries and the powerfully persuasive systematization emerging from the classificatory efforts in for example zoology and botany, and he was intent on remaining faithful to scientific traditions. He realized that the scientific tradition was entangled in different discourses and rhetorical traditions. In *Fathoming the Ocean*, Helen Rozwadowski convincingly shows the intense circulatory impacts between travel narratives by explorers, novels by writers, and scientific publications by researchers. It was not only the popular forms that adapted systematic insights and vocabulary from science books such as Maury's and Darwin's, scientific publications likewise borrowed rhetorical strategies, narrative forms, and language from explorers and writers such as Cook, Defoe, and Dana.[159] As we saw in Michelet, the scientist encountering a phenomenon for the first time oscillated between latinate terms and ready-made poetry. Science and fable were constantly crossing each other's domains. Aronnax's reference to the scientific practice of baptizing with "charming names" shows Verne's ironic gesture toward the Apollonian-global ambitions of science. He reacts against the serious classifications by spawning a variety of poetic effects through regroupings and reconfigurations of the scientific terms (most evident in the original

---

157 Chesneaux, *Une lecture politique*, 28; see also Noiray, "Préface," 27–33.
158 Verne, *Twenty Thousand Leagues Under the Seas*, 240–41, 210–11, 74.
159 Rozwadowski, *Fathoming the Ocean*, 1–35.

French text). Verne produces effects of sound and rhyme (*"des littorines, des dauphinules"* / *"des janthines, des ovules"*); word play (*"des ovules, des volutes, des olives"*); association of ideas (*"des mitres, des casques," "des buccins, des harpes"*); and unexpected evocations that return the reader to a heroic imagination (*"des casques, des pourpres, des buccins"*), reminding us that the voyage of the *Nautilus* takes place under the sign of a grand epic inherited from the Roman antiquity.[160] Verne's catalogues, far from being mere explications of already filled-out scientific files, are written passages full of humor and fantasy that bear witness to his creative and literary ambition to match and figure the ocean's fertility of the ocean.

If Hetzel wanted Verne to write didactic novels, Verne complied with his publisher's demands and conveys extensive knowledge through the pedagogical form of the catalogue. The catalogue signals a belief in the accumulation of information and progress. It formally articulates the genuine spirit of the encyclopedia. *Twenty Thousand Leagues* is a utopian book, as the advancement of knowledge is infinite, never complete (Verne's listings often end with "and so on" and "etc."). The enumerative form is an emblem of knowledge and an effect of the richness of the documentation utilized by Verne and his publisher. It guarantees seriousness and methodological rigor and stands as a quantitative proof of the novel's scientific quality. Superabundance is necessary for the encyclopedic ideal of totality.

Verne is also a literary writer with ambitions transgressing the mere didactic. Of Nemo's complete oceanic existence Verne once wrote: "I believe that this 'absolute' situation will give much depth to the work. Oh! my dear Hetzel, if I don't succeed with this book, I'll be inconsolable. I've never held a better subject in my hands."[161] As Verne's enthusiastic and anxious letter indicates, he was aware of the thematic potentials inherent in the novel's unique spatial setting. The massive liquid space and the amazing wonders of the undersea creatures likely played essential roles in shaping the novel's aesthetics by coercing a creative and poetic approach to the discoveries of scientific voyages. In numerous passages, Verne's prose discloses uncertainties and ambiguities in the otherwise sober and sedimented scientific language. This causes it to morph into fantasies or exhibit signs of aesthetically motivated choices of bizarreness and melodiousness. Like Michelet, at times Verne seems caught up in self-referential linguistic games in which strangeness becomes its own qualification and quality.

---

160 Noiray, "Préface," 30.
161 *Correspondance*, folios 71–72, letter 49, p. 80. Date probably end of March 1868.

FIGURE 16   Screenshot from *Leviathan* (2012)

FIGURE 17   Screenshot from *Leviathan* (2012)

and why the directors had to experiment with film language (Figure 16, 17, 18, and 19).

One of the most striking experimental elements of the film is its use of multiple points of view, most of which avoid the traditional human-eye perspective. The soundtrack, almost wordless, also contributes to the film's originality. There is a deliberate shying away from human gaze and sound and a movement toward a more centrifugal or distributive perception: " 'It was more corporeal, more embodied than the most frenetic vérité footage,' he said. 'There's

In *Vingt mille lieues sous les mers*, Verne combines the serious and didactic transmittance of state-of-the-art scientific knowledge of the ocean and its submarine lens with a poetic treatment of the very same liquid undersea world. Whereas the former represents an Apollonian, *global* desire to master nature by ordering and classifying it, the latter represents a Dionysian, *planetary* desire to mime the creative and reproductive forces in nature's endless becoming. The enumerations are unable to classify the enormity of nature. If the catalogue formally equivalates the infinite expansion of nature's fertility and orders this expansion, it is nevertheless an exercise that can never be completed. The accumulation of words is always unable to keep up with the endless accumulation of objects to be studied and the continuous generation of new forms in nature. The disorder of the world will always exceed the order of language. Verne's encyclopedic ambition remains a utopian mission, because any book representing the sea truly would have to be amorphous and endless.

The inability of scientific language to dominate the exuberant profusion of species is also a qualitative problem. In addition to the insufficiency of the catalogue as form, there are no words available to describe the strangeness and wonders: "And what a sight! What pen could ever describe it?" "What indescribable sights," "What a sight! How can I depict it!" "And now, how can I possibly record the impression made on me by this excursion under the waters? Words are inadequate to recount such marvels! When even the artist's brush is incapable of depicting the unique effects of the liquid element, how could a pen begin to portray them?"[162] Verne's problem is two-pronged: not *enough* words and not the *right* words to represent "this prodigious, inexhaustible wet-nurse."[163] In response to this twofold challenge Verne mobilizes passages of astonishing lyricism. It is a lyricism that sometimes has an elegiac tonality because it expresses the impotence of language when confronted with such marvels. At the same time, the elegiac tone transfers the enthusiasm of witnessing the marvels to the reader's mind. It is here *Vingt mille lieues sous les mers* abandons the language of pure denotation (nomenclatures, classifications) for a more expressive figurative language; it is here classification is replaced by *making the reader see and feel* the extraordinary newly discovered splendors under the sea. Verne morphs science and scientific language into fable and poetic language. Michel de Certeau has observed that Verne's writings are "closer to Borges' 'fictions' than to Michelet's 'resurrections,'" and he traces in Verne "the interlinkage of the imaginary and the collection, in other

---

162   Verne, *Twenty Thousand Leagues Under the Seas*, 93, 209, 257, 108.
163   Verne, *Twenty Thousand Leagues Under the Seas*, 68.

words the labor of fiction within the library."[164] Michelet's project and prose may be more poetic in *La Mer* than de Certeau acknowledges; nevertheless, his comment recognizes the twin forces of science and fable and that scientific sources are being haunted by inventions in Verne. As a result, *Vingt mille lieues sous les mers* is a novel that strives for Apollonian order and global-universal systematization and produces Dionysian fertility and planetary variety. The *Nautilus* made it possible for Verne to simultaneously pursue his pedagogical and poetic ambitions.

---

164   de Certeau, "Writing the Sea," 139.

CHAPTER 4

Materiality

1 Immersion in the Dissolve in *Leviathan*

The expression "You had to be there" offers an easy way out for those unable to verbally convey their experience, often of something hilarious, at other times of something that has made an impression. But there is some truth in the expression. Words can only do so much, even if they are skillfully combined with intonation and timing by a master storyteller who is physically present. It is difficult for words to express an experiential totality that would include smell, sound, light, temperature, mood, and touch. Words on paper are what authors have as their primary, if not only, tool. Filmmakers work in a medium that communicates with us through our senses of sight and hearing. Still, movies cannot convey smells and temperature, nor can they touch you physically in the strict sense of the word.

Leviathan (2012), a documentary film directed by Lucien Castaing-Taylor and Véréna Paravel of the Sensory Ethnography Lab at Harvard University, is an experimental work about the North American fishing industry. But experimental in what way? And why? Paravel provides us with a clue in Dennis Lim's review of the film, which also features brief interview clips with the directors: "The film became a physical reaction to the experience of being out at sea." Paravel's statement points to the inevitable link between maritime experience and poetics, between being aboard an industrial fishing trawler at sea and the experimental character of the film language in the documentary. Explicitly, Paravel tells us that she and Castaing-Taylor came to associate being at sea with a very corporeal experience, and that they felt compelled to transfer that feeling into the film. Implicitly, her description tells of an experience that was physical in a strange and unsettling way. This is backed up by her co-director, who tells us why they chose to discard 50 hours of landbased footage with fishing industry workers: " 'Once we started filming on the boat, we lost interest in land,' Mr. Castaing-Taylor said. 'There was something going on out there that was much more cosmic and profound.' "[1] The sense of an ontological and epistemological sea change explains why the film had to be experimental

---

1 Dennis Lim, "The Merger of Academia and Art House: Harvard Filmmakers' Messy World," *The New York Times*, August 31, 2012, accessed September 9, 2021, https://www.nytimes.com/2012/09/02/movies/harvard-filmmakers-messy-world.html?pagewanted=all&_r=0.

© SØREN FRANK, 2022 | DOI:10.1163/9789004426702_006
This is an open access chapter distributed under the terms of the CC BY-NC 4.0 license.

MATERIALITY 289

FIGURE 18   Screenshot from *Leviathan* (2012)

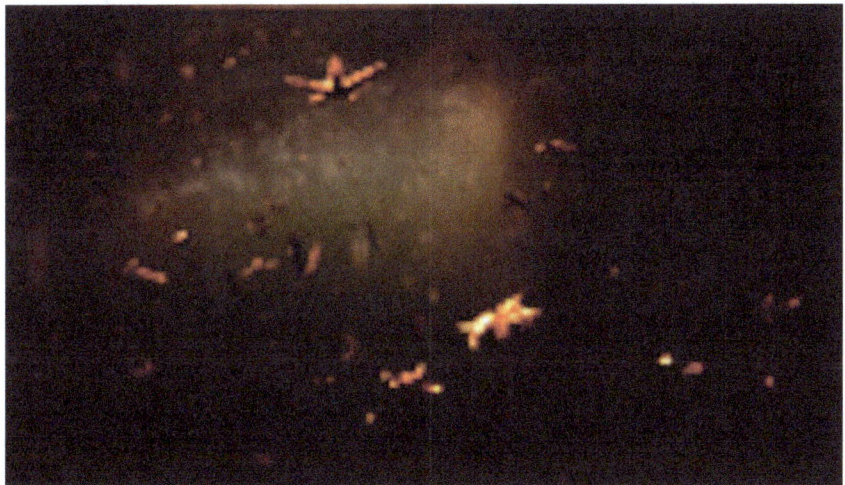

FIGURE 19   Screenshot from *Leviathan* (2012)

this charge of subjectivity. But at the same time it renounces any directorial intent,'" Castaing-Taylor tells Lim.[2] These techniques of sensory experience simulation became possible through the use of small water-resistant action cameras, the so-called GoPro, that were mounted on sailors, fish, trawlers, and other objects to capture the raw images and natural sounds, among them the

---

2 Lim, "The Merger of Academia and Art House."

clanking of metal chains, the splashing of violent waters, and the churning of industrial machines. Sometimes, when the splashing water hits the camera lens, it seems to be splashing us in the eyes.

The directors of *Leviathan* do not tell viewers, "You had to be there," because the documentary takes you there. You are immersed in the brutally tough life of fishermen on industrial ships; the intense dynamics between fishing trawler, ocean, and sky; the salty forces of waves; and the predatory formations of seagulls. The film violently plunges the spectator into its universe of visual and aural stimuli whose concentration overpowers you and whose fragmentary editing estranges you. Are immersion and estrangement not incompatible? Not in this case. The spectator is simultaneously estranged from a *terra firma* existence and immersed in an unfamiliar oceanic universe. Through the operations of color and light, more specifically the blend of intensified and washed-out colors and a persistent darkness or obscurity, combined with other poetological techniques such as multiple and (humanly and especially nonhumanly) embedded points of view, natural sounds, and nonlinear composition, Castaing-Taylor and Paravel succeed in generating a hallucinatory effect. One critic, unconvinced of the film's qualities, suggested an alternative title, *David Lynch, Gone Fishin'*.[3] Despite the derogatory intention, that is not too far off. Castaing-Taylor has admitted that while the film "is utterly a documentary, and in the sense that we gave over the camera for part of it, it's perhaps even more documentary, less mediated by the filmmakers, [...] it also doesn't feel like a documentary to me. It feels more like a horror film or science fiction."[4]

Why are the effects of hallucination and estrangement a measure of success when, as Lim remarks, "most documentaries prize clarity"?[5] For two reasons, one ontological, the other epistemological. Being on board a ship in the middle of the ocean (deep-sea fishing has one of the highest mortality rates of any occupation) can, ontologically speaking, be compared to a strange, almost hallucinatory experience. This can be explained not only because of losing firm ground under one's feet, but also by referring to Stacy Alaimo's ideas of being "exposed" and "dwelling in the dissolve" as theorized in *Exposed: Environmental Politics and Pleasures in Posthuman Times* (2016).[6] To exemplify, Alaimo refers to persons

---

3 Stephanie Zacharek, " 'Leviathan': Of Fish And Men, Without Chats," *National Public Radio*, February 28, 2013, accessed May 21, 2018, https://www.npr.org/2013/02/28/172981501/leviathan-of-fish-and-men-without-chats?ft=1&f=1045.
4 Lim, "The Merger of Academia and Art House."
5 Lim, "The Merger of Academia and Art House."
6 Stacy Alaimo, *Exposed: Environmental Politics and Pleasures in Posthuman Times* (Minneapolis and London: University of Minnesota Press, 2016).

affected by the Chernobyl disaster in 1986 as "totally exposed." In that situation, the human body's protective membranes, especially the skin, became powerless against surrounding forces, here lethal radiation, penetrating their bodies as if boundaries did not exist. Alaimo's example shows on a more general level that human bodies, also in less drastic situations, are in constant interaction with a myriad of nonhuman matter that undermines the seemingly solid boundaries between us and it. This happens when we eat food, inhale air, produce vitamin D through metabolism because absorbing sunlight through our skin, or simply by existing in the world. We inhabit this world of constant exchanges, blends, and crossings, not between two sharply separated flanks, human and nonhuman, but between every single agentic component in a relational force field. We dwell in the dissolve, which is the opposite of a hierarchical binary structure with us on one side and nonhuman life and matter on the other.

Leviathan forms and reveals this flatter universe. The images of sky and ocean may suggest a vertical scale of the most extreme heights and depths, but the film advocates that ultimately, seagulls and fish are made of the same substance. When Castaing-Taylor and Paravel zoom in on the furrowed brow of a fisherman, they hold the close-up image for a while so that the human eye of the fisherman increasingly resembles something that belongs to a sea creature. The visual tactic of close-up and retaining the frame conveys a world picture in which humans are being levelled ontologically, becoming closer with other living species. The film is a radical experiment, thematically in that it re-thinks the relationship between humans, nature, and technology by promoting a vision of dwelling in the dissolve, and formally in that it succeeds in conveying this vision through a variety of aesthetic technics of immersion.

2 Forces of Sea and Abyss in *Les Travailleurs de la mer*

In the following, I will continue the discussion of the relationship between humans, nature, things, and technology and of how this relationship can be aesthetically configured by reading Victor Hugo's *Les Travailleurs de la mer*, first published on March 12, 1866. The three-volume novel was released simultaneously in Brussels and Paris, and while it was received positively and even had bestseller status in the Channel Islands at one point, it gradually fell into obscurity; however, it has recently been acknowledged by a few but important scholars as an important work in the history of the novel.[7]

---

7 Victor Brombert, "*Les Travailleurs de la mer*: Hugo's Poem of Effacement," *New Literary History* 9, no. 3 (Spring, 1978): 581–590; Victor Brombert, *Victor Hugo and the Visionary Novel*

In the "Preface," Hugo frames *Les Travailleurs de la mer* by contrasting it with two of his previous novels, *Notre-Dame de Paris* (1831) and *Les Misérables* (1862). Hugo's starting point for comparison is "the three struggles in which man is engaged," but that "are, at the same time, his three needs." Whereas *Notre-Dame de Paris* and *Les Misérables* depict mankind's struggles with and needs for religion and society, respectively, *Les Travailleurs de la mer* is a portrayal of mankind's struggle with and need for nature. To Hugo, in mankind's struggle with and need for religion, we find a solution in faith that leads to the construction of temples (Notre-Dame); in mankind's struggle with and need for society, we find a solution in creation that leads to the building of cities (Paris); and in mankind's struggle with and need for nature, our solution is subsistence in the form of plow and ship (the steamship Durande in *Travailleurs*).

However, with every solution comes a danger against which mankind ought to fight: if faith is one side of religion's coin, superstition is the other; if creation is one side of society's coin, prejudice is the other; and if subsistence is one side of nature's coin, the elements are the other. Faith, creation, and subsistence are anthropocentric solutions, but superstition, prejudice, and the elements are three exterior forces, *fatalities*, that govern our lives: "A triple *ananke* weighs upon us: the *ananke* of dogmas, the *ananke* of laws, the *ananke* of things." *Les Travailleurs de la mer* is from the outset distanced by its author from religion, faith, temples, superstition, and dogmas (*Notre-Dame de Paris*) and from society, creation, cities, prejudice, and laws (*Les Misérables*); instead, it is linked with nature, subsistence, plow, ship, elements, and things. Cultural anthropological spheres such as religion and society and cultural constructions such as temples and cities are not entirely absent in the novel, but as Hugo indicates in the "Preface," nature, ship, elements, and things (the exterior fatality) are, together with "the supreme *ananke*, the human heart" (the interior fatality), crucial agentic and almost fatal forces governing the novel's universe.[8] The question is who gets the upper hand?

2.1 *Humans and Things*

Les Travailleurs de la mer is closely associated with Victor Hugo's nineteen-year exile (December 11, 1851–September 5, 1870), the majority of which he spent on Guernsey in the Channel Islands after also having lived in Brussels and on Jersey. The novel began to incubate during a two-week holiday on the tiny

---

(Cambridge, MA., and London: Harvard University Press, 1984), 40; Graham Robb, *Victor Hugo* (1997; London: Picador, 1998), 414–16; Cohen, *The Novel and the Sea*, 189–200.

8 Victor Hugo, *The Toilers of the Sea*, trans. James Hogarth (1866; New York: The Modern Library, 2002), xxvii.

island of Sark in the summer of 1859, and it was written between June 1864 and November 1865. *The Toilers of the Sea*, set on Guernsey and in its surrounding archipelago, is a strange, composite, and undecided novel in both a thematic and formal sense. On the one hand, written as a traditional plot-driven story involving human protagonists, it is a story of failed romantic love, human isolation, deceit, and financial ruin. On the other hand, composed in some sections as a treatise on natural history and in others as philosophical essay, it is a poetic portrayal of organic forces and inorganic potencies undermining or supplementing human agency. The novel's critical reception has often ignored these thematic and formal ambiguities and has instead focused on the human protagonists and the themes of the human-centered storyline. In many readings of the novel, "the supreme *ananke*, the human heart," carries more weight than nature, things, and the elements.

In a comparison between Hugo's novel and Conrad's *The End of the Tether*, J. H. Stape notices their mutual concern "with marginality and alienation, with the betrayal of trust, heroic self-sacrifice, and the encounter with a hard fate."[9] Stape focuses on themes rooted in individual man and his relationship to his fellow humans or nature. Switching media, Gustave Doré's two illustrations for the 1867 English editions of the novel, "The Last Breakwater" (Figure 20) and "The Fight with the Devil-Fish" (Figure 21), subscribe to the same line of thinking with their emphasis on Gilliatt, the heroic romantic outsider. By foregrounding Gilliatt, sharpening his profile, and blurring everything around him, Doré accentuated his principal role.

In contrast, the majority of the thirty-six illustrations made by Hugo, which he never specifically intended for *Les Travailleurs* but nevertheless incorporated into the original 1866 manuscript, portray scenes in which humans are either absent or, if present, invisible and backgrounded. Hugo's drawings, exemplified below by "Naufrage" (Figure 22) and "La Pieuvre" (Figure 23), demonstrate his attentiveness to nonhuman elements and their potency.

In "Naufrage," the technique of misting or obscuring applies not only to the surrounding ocean and sky but also to the ship in the center of the image, making a comparison with Turner's style in *Snow Storm* inevitable. Hugo's fascination with unruly matter and stuff was not limited to the represented vision; it also manifested in his choice of materials of representation. Graham Robb informs us that Hugo supplemented the traditional materials of charcoal, graphite, ink, gouache, and gum with substances such as blackberry

---

9 J. H. Stape, "'The End of the Tether' and Victor Hugo's 'Les Travailleurs de la mer,'" *The Conradian* 30, no. 1 (Spring 2005): 71–80.

FIGURE 20   Gustave Doré, "The Last Breakwater." For *Toilers of the Sea* published in 1867 by Harper and Brothers, New York, and Sampson Low, Son, and Marston, London

juice, caramelized onion, burnt paper, soot from the lamp, toothpaste, and—according to Georges Hugo, Victor's grandchild—saliva; there have been hints of even less respectable materials: "Anyone who investigates the origins of a new style should expect to find a mess. Hugo scribbled, smudged, scratched and toyed. He was a lover of substances and textures—inanimate and

MATERIALITY 295

FIGURE 21   Gustave Doré, "The Fight with the Devil-Fish." For *Toilers of the Sea* published in 1867 by Harper and Brothers, New York, and Sampson Low, Son, and Marston, London

human."[10] Hugo's vision of shipwreck, which cannot be characterized as a harmonious relationship between all parts nor as a transcendent spirit merging

10   Robb, *Victor Hugo*, 391, 394.

FIGURE 22 Victor Hugo, "Naufrage" (1864–66). Manuscrits, NAF 247451, fol. 116
© BIBLIOTHÈQUE NATIONALE DE FRANCE

the diversity of elements, brings to mind Deleuze's phrase: "Ontologically one, formally diverse."[11] The misty quality draws all elements closer to each other on

---

11   Gilles Deleuze, *Expressionism in Philosophy: Spinoza*, trans. Martin Joughin (1968; New York: Zone Books, 1992), 67. See also Jane Bennett, *Vibrant Matter: A Political Ecology of Things* (Durham and London: Duke University Press, 2010), xi, who cites this phrase of Deleuze's.

FIGURE 23 Victor Hugo, "La Pieuvre" (1864–66). Manuscrits, NAF 247452, fol. 382
© BIBLIOTHÈQUE NATIONALE DE FRANCE

an ontological level, although the individual shapes are discernable. The contrast between Doré's and Hugo's devil-fish images is as obvious as that between "The Last Breakwater" and "Naufrage." The former centralizes Gilliatt; the latter excludes him.

However, even Hugo was wavering. If a large portion of his thirty-six illustrations suggests a world in which humans are reduced to minor ripples on the oceanic canvas of universal history and, as a result, depict nature and the inorganic matter of human constructions (e.g., ships) as forceful and dynamic actors, then the genealogy of the novel's title seems to point in the opposite direction. With the original tentative title, *L'Abîme* (The Abyss), Hugo signaled a disanthropocentric thinking like that depicted in his illustrations. To Hugo, "the abyss," a concept used several times in the novel, refers to immeasurable oceanic depths and mysteriously vivacious caverns, that is, to concrete physical places. Together with expressions and sister concepts such as "somber force beneath," "darkness," "invisible world," "irreducible obscurity," "immensity," and "shadows,"[12] "abyss" also refers to the innermost workings and enigmatic mechanisms of life, matter, and the universe as such. Hugo's preferred title thus emphasizes a world of relational forces in which human agency is only one force, energy, or effect among many others. But with Hugo's switch of title from *L'Abîme* to *Les Travailleurs de la mer*—a switch insisted upon by the publishers of Lacroix, Verboeckhoven et Cie in Brussels for commercial reasons—it could be argued that a more anthropocentric world picture is heralded, one in which "the human heart" reigns supreme.

It seems a fair assumption that the eponymous toilers, or, perhaps more appropriate, *workers* of the sea are humans, more specifically, the "weather-wise" sailors and semi-amphibian persons mastering "sea gymnastics"[13] such as Mess Lethierry, Rantaine, Sieur Clubin, and Gilliatt. This assumption is not wrong. Besides, the title has an air of First International (1864–1876) and Émile Zola about it. The naturalism of the latter was on the verge of a breakthrough with the publication of *Thérèse Raquin* (1867) and, especially, of the second edition published the following year that included Zola's foreword in which he introduces naturalism for the first time.[14] However, it is important to dismiss the idea of a collective novel relating the everyday tasks of fishermen in the mold of Melville's *Moby-Dick* or Hans Kirk's later *Fiskerne* (1928; *The Fishermen*), although portrayals of these people do appear in glimpses in the novel's introductory part (first added in 1883). It could also be argued that with *travailleurs* Hugo maintains a reference to the broader forces and energies of maritime life forms and organisms including crabs, rocks, steamships,

---

12 Hugo, *The Toilers of the Sea*, 369, 370, 378.
13 Hugo, *The Toilers of the Sea*, 311, 362.
14 Yves Gohin, "Préface," in Victor Hugo, *Les Travailleurs de la mer* (1866; Paris: Gallimard, 1980), 8.

octopuses, and seaweed, all of which are oceanic workers in their own right as they influence and uphold or destroy the ecology of the sea.

That the workers (in plural) of the title perhaps refer more to nonhuman than human actors is supported by Hugo's decision to portray the mariners as loners and isolated individuals. This choice was determined in part by the modernization of maritime life, a theme that runs through Hugo's novel and is most clearly expressed through the Durande's success in outmaneuvering the island's sailing ships. "The telos of *La Durande*," Margaret Cohen states in her labor-oriented reading of the novel, "is the vast, depopulated container ship of the turn of the twenty-first century."[15] The themes of sail versus steam and of technological development unites Hugo with Melville, Verne, and Conrad, but Hugo's mariners are strikingly different from the mariners hailed by his three colleagues.

Melville focused on and emphasized the values of collaboration and community on board sailing vessels; Conrad did so too, or, in the texts dealing with life on board steamships, he bemoaned the decline of those values; Verne followed a similar trend, although in his case the reader was invited on board a submarine. Admittedly, the *Nautilus* is captained by an isolated individual, but Nemo depends on and encourages teamwork on board his underwater vessel. In Melville, Ahab's charisma, thoughts, and deeds set him radically apart from his crew, but in large portions of the novel Ishmael is oriented towards the collective work of the crew. Ahab, if endowed with superhuman characteristics, is never praised for them as Gilliatt is. In Conrad, no such supermen sailors exist. Outsiders such as Marlow and MacWhirr are not celebrated because of their heroism, craft, skills, and cunning; instead, they are ordinary men, some of whom are endowed with a gift of *seeing* a modern world in the process of becoming disenchanted and *telling* about it. MacWhirr is a special case, not really able to see, certainly not to tell, but in a way, he is celebrated because of heroic deeds made possible by his composure, yet also portrayed sufficiently ludicrous to disqualify him as a hero in the mold of Hugo's outsider-hero. Gilliatt has more in common with Robinson Crusoe, also with Hemingway's old man, but Gilliatt is not a reader of the Bible like Crusoe, and instead of comprehending the values of the civilization he has just left, Gilliatt discovers the immanent immensity of the universe that he affronts, and which engulfs him.[16]

---

15   Cohen, *The Novel and the Sea*, 192.
16   Gohin, "Préface," 10.

The indecisiveness or disagreement in relation to the choice of title and the ambiguity of the meaning of *travailleurs*/toilers in the final title sustains a stimulating tension between anthropocentric and geocentric (and hydrocentric) propensities in *Les Travailleurs de la mer*. This is backed up by the novel's formal qualities. On one level it is a traditional and plot-driven story of (disillusioned and failed) romantic love between an orphaned outsider, Gilliatt, and a sweet, pretty, and carefree girl, Déruchette (a diminutive form of Durande, the one the daughter of Lethierry, the other his steamship). On another level, the novel contains long passages that turn away from the anthropo-story, some of which are best characterized as natural history, travel guide, anthropological treatise, philosophical essay, or aesthetic manifest, others as technological handbook, craftsman user manual, or nautical compendium. Plot, human deeds, and interpersonal relations take center stage in most of the novel, but frequently and for quite long stretches this anthropocentric world picture with its period belief in societal progress, human agency, and personal liberty is challenged or even undermined. This happens when Hugo zooms in on a plethora of nonhuman forces and energies attributed to organic and inorganic matter alike, which activate temporalities that are different from traditional human-centered temporalities. Examples of "vibrant matter," as Jane Bennett calls it, are seasons, clouds, fog, wind, flowers, grass, granite, foam, waves, seaweed, reefs, underwater caverns, engines, and a steamship. In that sense, *The Toilers of the Sea* contradicts Jeffrey J. Cohen's claim in *Stone: An Ecology of the Inhuman* (2015) that "a narrative in which it might figure as something more than an ancillary device, a protagonist rather than a prop, has yet to appear." Hugo's novel is precisely such "a multifaceted narrative of cross-taxonomic relation"[17] in which stone, most notably in the shape of a reef, the Douvres, but also the deceptive mirages and formless formations of granite, rocks, and cliffs along the eroding coastline, plays a crucial and actively plot-shaping role.

The most clear-cut example of a longer section in which the traditional anthropocentric plot is supplanted by a nonanthropocentric plot predominantly governed by nonhuman forces is the novel's first chapter, a sort of overture, "The Archipelago of the Channel" (p. 5–55). Other examples are "Book I: The Reef" (p. 239–81), "Sub Re" (p. 289–94) and "Sub Umbra" (p. 294–99) from "Book II: The Labor," and "The Winds From the Ocean" and "The Combat" from "Book III: The Struggle," all of which are part of the novel's second and middle part, "Gilliatt the Cunning." In "The Archipelago of the Channel," examples

---

17   Jeffrey Jerome Cohen, *Stone: An Ecology of the Inhuman* (Minneapolis and London: University of Minnesota Press, 2015), 5.

abound of an object-based historiography and anthropology showing Hugo's preoccupation not merely with thinking of and with things but also with rendering thought thing-like: we are thus presented with *disanthropocentric history* (e.g., "The Atlantic wears away our coasts. The pressure of the current from the Pole deforms our western cliffs"), *geological survey* (e.g., "Granite to the south, sand to the north; here sheer rock faces, there dunes"), and *elemental-biological determinism* (e.g., "The wind carries away miasmas and brings about shipwrecks").[18] Tellingly, this introductory chapter did not feature in the first English translations of the novel and became part of the English edition only with the first complete translation published in 2002, the bicentenary of Hugo's birth. Nor did it feature in the 1866 French original due to editorial decisions, which overruled the author's intention of including it as an overture; it was not included until the "*ne varietur*" edition that Hetzel-Quantin published in 1883 as volumes XI and XII in *Œuvres complètes*, two years before Hugo's death. The exclusion of "The Archipelago of the Channel" during the first seventeen years of the French edition and during the first 136 years of the English edition explains the focus of the critical reception on the novel's human-centered plot elements and themes concerning its Byronic hero. It also accentuates Hugo's uncertainty regarding the relationship between the agentic powers of humans and nonhumans.

Reading Hugo's novel today, one is struck by passages comprising unmistakable anthropocene features and remarkable affinities with flattened ontologies characterized by human-nonhuman equality and a more dispersive agency. In his "Introduction" to the 2002 unabridged English translation of *The Toilers of the Sea*, Graham Robb claims that Hugo's introductory chapter "is still the best general guide to the Channel Islands."[19] By asserting its continued relevance more than a century after its composition in May 1865, Robb opens up a question of the chapter's vision of archipelagic temporality, implying a layer of stasis or an extremely slow rhythm of barely perceptible changes. "The Archipelago of the Channel" evolves on an entirely different time scale than traditional novelistic plots. It is not restricted to the lifespan of an individual or the timeframe of two or three generations but operates within the time of human history or on the vaster scale of lithic or geological time: "The configuration of an island changes over time. An island is a construction by the ocean. Matter is eternal; not its aspect. Everything on earth is being perpetually moulded by death: even extra-human monuments, even granite. Everything changes shape, even the

---

18 Hugo, *The Toilers of the Sea*, 5, 6, 20.
19 Graham Robb, "Introduction," in Victor Hugo, *The Toilers of the Sea* (New York: The Modern Library, 2002), xix.

shapeless. Edifices built by the sea crumble like any other. The sea, which has built them up, also demolishes them."[20] Such temporality affects the chapter's speed of action. In some passages, Hugo describes the immensely slow biological, geological, and hydrological processes of coagulation and change in the nonhuman world as these processes stretch out over millennia. In other sections, Hugo morphs into a cultural anthropologist and registers the slow sedimentations and transformations of human customs, languages, and practices on Sark, Guernsey, and Jersey over centuries. Three examples: "Each man is his sovereign, not by law but by custom"; "Since the seventeenth century these islands have had fraternal feelings for the whole world; they glory in hospitality. They have the impartiality of a place of asylum"; "These peoples have preserved from their earlier activities as smugglers a proud liking for risk and danger."[21]

Importantly, Hugo's cosmology does not propose a bifurcation of the human and inhuman domains despite their respective calculable and incalculable temporalities. As Cohen persistently maintains in *Stone*: "the lithic is not some vast and alien outside. A limit-breaching intimacy persistently unfolds."[22] If the ecological project entails thinking beyond anthropocentricity and thus requires amplified historical and geographical scales, Cohen observes that such

> expanded frames risk emphasizing separations at the expense of material intimacies. In both eco-theory and object studies, much critical writing on the inhuman is animated by an ardor for an unpeopled world. While the project of this book is disanthropocentric, assuming a world irreducible to its human relations and not existing for any particular purpose, its methods stress alliance, continuity, and mutual participation over elemental solitariness and human exceptionalism.[23]

As we shall see, Hugo struggles with this tension between alliance and bifurcation, but even if the tension remains unresolved in *Les Travailleurs de la mer*, the insistent presence of nonhuman actants such as saltwater, rocks, crabs, and wind makes the novel one of the greatest meditations on a universe of vibrant matter.

---

20 Hugo, *The Toilers of the Sea*, 49.
21 Hugo, *The Toilers of the Sea*, 42, 45, 54.
22 Cohen, *Stone*, 2.
23 Cohen, *Stone*, 9.

At certain moments in the novel, Hugo challenges the idea that humans (and humans aided by their technological inventions) occupy the central position in the world, contrary to the worldview that dominated during ages of Enlightenment (think of Kant's confidence in rationality) and Romanticism (think of Fichte's pure idealism): "these Trinacrias are immune to reshaping by man," the narrator reminds us.[24] There exist dimensions of the world that are immune to human interference. The challenge to anthropocentrism is executed partly through Hugo's verbal and visual creation of scenarios devoid of humans, partly through his depictions of scenes comprising human action, but in which human agency is then compromised through its entanglement with nonhuman forces that either resist or assist it. But there are also instances in which Hugo reverts to a more conventional anthropocentric belief in scientific progress, moral perfectibility, rationality, and human freedom characteristic not only of the ages of Enlightenment and Romanticism, but of the traditional understanding of modernity as such: "A geological formation that has at its base the mud of the Deluge and at its summit the eternal snows is, for man, a wall like any other: he cuts through it and continues beyond."[25] It is this tension between a human-centered world picture and sophisticated acknowledgements of the nonhuman world's unruliness and impact on humans and history that will be my focus in what follows. To anticipate, we will examine how Hugo, partly as an outcome of his personal experiences of being existentially and bodily exposed to the archipelago of the Channel Islands, is on track to reveal and produce a flattened ontology and to foresee the Anthropocene, and that he also sometimes backtracks and returns to what he must have felt as the more confident thematic and formal frameworks of anthropocentrism and the novel of what-happened-next.

To create a solid platform from which to read the novel, I will continuously entangle it with concepts from the materialist theories of thinkers such as Jane Bennett ("vibrant matter"), Bill Brown ("a sense of things"), Jeffrey J. Cohen ("stone"), Maurizia Boscagli ("stuff"), and Stacy Alaimo ("exposed"). These scholars share a resistance toward anthropocentrism and a dual belief in the agentic impacts of nonhuman forces operating in nature, bodies, and artifacts and their capacity to act as powerful counterweights to the narcissistic impulses inherent in human language and thought.

---

24 Hugo, *The Toilers of the Sea*, 52.
25 Hugo, *The Toilers of the Sea*, 50. For a discussion of modernity as defined by rationality, progress, and freedom of the individual, its three most determining concepts, see Dag Østerberg, *Det moderne: Et essay om Vestens kultur 1740–2000* (Oslo: Gyldendal, 1999), 11–12.

2.2   Vital Materialism

First things first. The form of materialism employed here is not the one linked to philosophers such as Marx and Adorno, who were proponents of an egocentric materialist thinking in which matter was always a sign of a hidden human agenda, often imperialist, capitalist, and oppressive. Admittedly, such materialism would function well as an underlying assumption in a reading of *Les Travailleurs de la mer*. Legitimate foci could be topics such as 1) the corruptive influence of money between human business partners; 2) the decisive influence of money on marriage plans; 3) the fetishization of material objects such as steam engines and steamships; 4) the significance of steamships in the global circulation of goods; 5) the significance of the division of labor on board the steamships as compared to the sailing ships; and 6) the role of technology in the human illusions of progress, mastering nature, and gaining wealth. However, a different form of materialism emerges from vitalist thinkers such as Lucretius, Spinoza, Nietzsche, Bergson, and Deleuze, none of whom were ever really occupied with the historical materialist ambition of analyzing the workings of human power to disclose social hegemonies. Instead, they articulate a materialism made up of nonhuman, thingly forces and are occupied with the material agency of biological bodies and technological artifacts. To my knowledge, a new materialist approach has not yet been applied to Hugo's novel.

But why is such a theory analytically fruitful? Because vital materialism strongly resonates (without converging seamlessly) with the world picture emerging in Hugo's novel where—as Bill Brown has remarked on a more general note—"our relation to things cannot be explained by the cultural logic of capitalism," and "the human interaction with the nonhuman world of objects, however mediated by the advance of consumer culture, must be recognized as irreducible to that culture."[26] A similar line of reasoning can be found in Maurizia Boscagli's *Stuff Theory* (2014): "The older materialism insists that under the system of capital every object is always already commodified; the new materialism insists on the fungability of matter and on the plasticity possible at the moment of subject-object interaction."[27] Again, *The Toilers of the Sea* legitimates a reading focusing on consumption and commodities, on capitalist money culture (Lethierry's business, Rantaine's theft followed by Clubin's

---

26   Bill Brown, *A Sense of Things: The Object Matter of American Literature* (Chicago and London: The University of Chicago Press, 2003), 5–6, 13.
27   Maurizia Boscagli, *Stuff Theory: Everyday Objects, Radical Materialism* (New York and London: Bloomsbury, 2014), 4.

theft, Gilliatt's poverty versus Ebenezer's inherited fortune). However, Hugo also proposes a genuine material-elemental cosmology of greater ontological importance and epistemological depth in which the human and nonhuman become entangled.

An important objective in vital materialism is to patch together the human-made slit in the world between "dull matter (it, things) and vibrant life (us, beings)" and to encourage us to pay attention to "the vitality *of* matter and the lively powers *of* material formations." Bennett's project of mattering humans and of humanizing or vitalizing matter, also essential in Brown's thing theory, entails philosophical consequences and spurs politico-ethical benefits. Along with a flattening reconfiguration of the relationship between humans and nonhumans and between organic and inorganic matter resulting in "a more *distributive* agency," vital materialism promotes "a cultivated, patient, sensory attentiveness to nonhuman forces operating outside and inside the human body."[28] The latter is important because without

> proficiency in this countercultural kind of perceiving, the world appears as if it consists only of active human subjects who confront passive objects and their law-governed mechanisms. This appearance may be indispensable to the action-oriented perception on which our survival depends [...], but it is also dangerous and counterproductive to live this fiction all the time [...], and neither does it conduce to the formation of a 'greener' sensibility.[29]

The fiction of human exceptionalism is dangerous, says Bennett, because "the image of dead or thoroughly instrumentalized matter feeds human hubris and our earth-destroying fantasies of conquest and consumption."[30]

Bennett's formulations on the philosophical and political projects of vital materialism are pertinent gateways into Hugo's novel. At times, the narrator conveys images of a world in which an active-effective Gilliatt confronts seemingly passive objects—a steamship, its engines, waves, winds, reefs, seagulls—and cunningly exploits their law-governed mechanisms. To survive, or not to survive, that is the question. Gilliatt's conviction of his heroic qualities, his self-reliance as Emerson would say, is mandatory here. It is a seductive idea of the role and ability of humans in the world. But to environmentalists then and

---

28   Bennett, *Vibrant Matter*, vii, ix, xiv.
29   Bennett, *Vibrant Matter*, xiv.
30   Bennett, *Vibrant Matter*, ix.

now, this idea also facilitates and legitimizes potentially destructive behavior against the planet. To a certain extent, Hugo seems aware of this. At other times, the narrator introduces perspectival changes from ego-point of view to geo-point of view, from the perspective of Gilliatt to that of a subterranean current of microbiological energies and forceful matters. Through these multiple points of view, the narrator introduces blue and green sensibilities and reveals the illusory nature of an egocentric universe.

One way to illustrate this duality within the novel is by comparing Stape's summary of the plot (quoted, although in abridged form, from Graham Robb's 1997 biography *Victor Hugo*) with a passage from the novel itself. First Stape/Robb:

> a reclusive Guernsey fisherman called Gilliatt falls in love with the daughter of a local shipowner. The shipowner, Mess (Monsieur) Lethierry, has two passions: his daughter, Déruchette, and his steam-ship, *La Durande*. The latter is deliberately run aground by its trusted captain, Clubin. The captain's plan is to fake his own death and steal the 75,000 francs he was carrying back to Lethierry. The passengers and crew abandon ship, admiring Clubin's selflessness ... Only then does it dawn on the hypocrite that he has struck the wrong reef and is marooned, not on Les Hanois, a mere mile off the coast, but on the lugubrious Douvres, a full 5 leagues from Guernsey. But before the sea can claim him, a mysterious, rag-like thing moving swiftly underwater grabs him by the leg and pulls him to his death.
>
> Back on Guernsey, the shipowner's daughter offers her hand to anyone who can save the ship. Gilliatt sets off and spends the larger part of the novel dislodging the steamer from the two stone pillars of Les Douvres [...]. At the end, Gilliatt returns in triumph to find that Lethierry's daughter is enamoured with an Anglican vicar. He relinquishes his prize, removes the last obstacle to the marriage, and, sitting in his rock armchair, watches the newly-weds sail over the horizon as the tide washes over him.[31]

Then Hugo:

> There are vast movements of heavenly bodies, the family of the stars, the family of the planets, the pollen of the zodiac, the *quid divinum* of

---

31   Stape, "'The End of the Tether' and Victor Hugo's 'Les Travailleurs de la mer,'" 75; quoted from Robb, *Victor Hugo*, 413–15.

currents, emanations, polarizations, and attractions; there are embraces and antagonisms, the magnificent flow and ebb of a universal antithesis, the imponderable at liberty amid the centers; there is sap in the globes, light outside the globes, there are wandering atoms, scattered seeds, fertilization curves, meetings for coupling and for combat, unimagined profusions, distances that are like dreams, dizzying movements, worlds plunging into the incalculable, prodigies pursuing one another in the shadows, a mechanism in permanent operation, the breathing of spheres in flight, wheels that can be felt turning; scholars make conjectures, the ignorant believe and tremble; things are there, and then withdraw; they are unassailable, they are out of reach, they cannot be approached. We are convinced to the point of oppression. We are faced with some mysterious dark reality. We can grasp nothing. We are crushed by the impalpable.[32]

Before commenting on the two passages, this comparative exercise raises a question. Is comparing two different sources, one a critical reading, the other the novel, problematic when trying to figure out what the novel is about? No, because my point is not to show that Stape's summary is wrong, and the novel is wiser than the critic. Stape's condensed selection of Robb's even longer summary and discussion (which, admittedly, shows in passages excluded by Stape a refined sensitivity toward Hugo's nonhuman universe and formal transgressions) is an adequate summary of the anthropocentric plot level in the novel. An objection to Stape's summary could be that the implicitly human-centered approach covers only half the truth about the novel. This other half can be sensed in the passage by Hugo quoted above in which a different plot level is summarized. This is the plot level of the nonhuman, yet vitalist material universe of cosmic scope.

In Stape's trimmed summary, the focus and starting point are the human characters (Gilliatt, Mess Lethierry, Déruchette, Sieur Clubin, Ebenezer) and intersubjective themes (love, passion, fraud, heroic deed, disappointed love, self-sacrifice, marriage, and suicide). Yes, we also learn about the Durande (intentionally not italicized in the novel to signal its humanoid quality), but the summary refers to the steamship as a mere vehicle for human transport under human control. Stape never mentions the archipelago and the steamship as protagonist-actants. The introductory chapter is bypassed in silence, and the 60,000-word, 134-page depiction of Gilliatt's entanglement with nature and technology at the Douvres is reduced to less than two lines.

---

32   Hugo, *The Toilers of the Sea*, 297–98.

A different plot unfolds in the passage quoted from the novel. No humans feature until the last few lines where "we" are crushed. The perspective is initially cosmic yet embedded. As the narratorial gaze gradually zooms in on the human world, the epistemological register morphs from knowledgeable planetary and galactic perspectives to a human point of view unable to grasp the universe or anything in it. The world is a buzzing force field of active and reactive intensities, of antithetical movements and propensities, of flux and stasis. No beginning-middle-end, just middle. It is a world simultaneously made up of the immense and the minuscule—planets and atoms, stars and seeds—and of wheels continuously turning and mechanisms constantly running. At one point Bennett says, "I want to highlight what is typically cast in the shadow: the material agency or effectivity of nonhuman or not-quite-human things."[33] This could also be read as Hugo's intention in writing *Les Travailleurs de la mer*. He often refers to "the shadows," "a mysterious dark reality," and in the passage above he highlights the darkness, sheds light on shadows, so readers can contemplate a world of vibrant matter, material agencies, and nonhuman things. Hugo's visions into the impalpable inner workings of the universe reveal they are oppressive and threaten to crush us. They may not destroy us as living creatures, but they destroy our illusions of human sovereignty and exceptionalism.

2.3 *Endings and Narrators*

To determine the novel's commitment to vital materialism, its position between egocentric and geocentric world pictures, it is helpful to compare it with *Moby-Dick*, more specifically the endings and choices of narrator. We have already discussed Melville's ending with its apocalyptic vision of a posthuman world triggered by a combination of human hubris (Ahab's) and whale-driven revenge (Moby Dick's): "Now small fowls flew screaming over the yet yawning gulf; a sullen white surf beat against its steep sides; then all collapsed, and the great shroud of the sea rolled on as it rolled five thousand years ago."[34] These closing lines follow a scene in which the *Pequod* and its crew members in their respective whaleboats—Ahab, Tashtego, Stubb, etc.—are all swallowed up by the ocean. *Les Travailleurs* ends similarly with the ocean slowly engulfing the human protagonist: "At the same moment the head disappeared under the water. There was now nothing but the sea."[35] As in Melville's novel, there is a vision of nature's survival and continuity combined with man's downfall.

---

33 Bennett, *Vibrant Matter*, ix.
34 Melville, *Moby-Dick*, 572.
35 Hugo, *The Toilers of the Sea*, 430.

There are also important differences. First, the ending of *Moby-Dick* is not the passage just quoted, but an epilogue written by Ishmael explaining what happened after the sinking of *Pequod* and the perishing of its crew. Melville's choice of a dramatized narrator necessitates the survival of this narrator-character. A narrator meeting his death at the end would have a problem of reliability regarding all that has been narrated up until that death. An exception could be if his manuscript was found and published by someone else, but in Ishmael's case that would be near impossible because of the place of the shipwrecking. For the sake of reliability, found manuscripts are usually framed by another story explaining how the manuscript was found and why it has been published. In *Moby-Dick* there is no such frame. Another and more pertinent problem in Ishmael's case is that he has told large parts of his story in retrospection, from a narratorial vantage point set after the story ends with the foundering. Melville's choice of narratorial strategy ultimately compels the survival of his narrator. Throughout the novel Ishmael is a very human narrator-character with person-bound perspectives on, engagements in, and experiences with life and life at sea. Although Melville inconsistently oscillates between *vision avec*, *vision par derrière*, and *vision du dehors*, the narratorial perspective is mostly linked closely with Ishmael as character (*vision avec*). If Melville's novel hints at a posthuman world dominated by nonhuman matter, forces, and energies, this hint is nevertheless articulated by a human survivor. Ishmael gets the last word.

Victor Hugo chose a different enunciatory tactic. Instead of a first-person narrator, he opted for a third-person narrator. It could be argued that this narrator very often does not even act as a human being but rather as a sort of nonhuman observer employing a perspective close to and embedded in the world of vibrant matter. The choice of third-person narrator allows Hugo to let his human protagonist die without violating any internal narrative logic. Ishmael survives, Gilliatt drowns. In that sense, *Les Travailleurs* proposes a more radical quarrel with anthropocentrism than *Moby-Dick*. In Melville's version: "the great shroud of the sea rolled on as it rolled five thousand years ago"—except that we would never know this if we were not told so by the narrator-character, and except that it does so, "rolled on," parallel with the survival and continuous life of this same protagonist-narrator. So, only posthuman to a certain degree. In Hugo's version: "There was now nothing but the sea." End of story.

Or is it? If Melville relativizes his novel's posthuman and nonhuman signals through the necessary survival of Ishmael, Hugo's opposite treatment of Gilliatt does not mean the annihilation of the human world as such. When Gilliatt, resigned to losing Déruchette and even actively contributing to her marriage with Ebenezer and their subsequent escape on the *Cashmere*, chooses to end his own life by allowing the rising tide to engulf him, he not only sees as his last vision in life the *Cashmere* slowly disappearing into the horizon and thus carrying off Déruchette and Ebenezer to a presumably happy life together, but he also meets his destiny by an act of free will. In that sense, the novel's last words, at first glance unequivocally signaling a posthuman and nonhuman world, are, as in Melville's case, relativized by Hugo. Still, it makes sense to distinguish between Melville and Hugo. While Ishmael survives, Gilliatt perishes; and while Melville employs a human first-person narrator, Hugo opts for a more-than-human third-person narrator. Both the destiny of the protagonist and the enunciatory tactic point to the radicalism of Hugo's project.

The theme of (human) effacement staged by Hugo at the end of *Les Travailleurs* is in fact a recycling of the novel's beginning, which introduces the same theme. Gilliatt's transient existence and the ephemerality of the human condition are captured in a beautiful and evocative scene in which Déruchette writes Gilliatt's name in snow, a fragile substance unsuitable for any lasting inscription whatsoever. That the name "Gilliatt" is doomed to dissolve in the melting snow is a harbinger of Gilliatt's drowning in the rising tide at the end of the novel. It is also a metafictional commentary on the precarious durability of texts, although this play on textual and personal annihilation is countered by Hugo's description of the Douvres rocks, which form a giant H for *Homme* or for Hugo. The repetition of human effacement underlines the novel's devotion to the theme of geocentrism, but it also has formal implications. The similarity between beginning and end means that Hugo replaces traditional novelistic narrativity and sequential structure with an order of simultaneity "that cancels the double rule of events and chance."[36]

With the implication that Hugo's enunciatory strategy is better capable of simulating (and thus transporting the reader into closer proximity with) a nonhuman world of material forces, his narrator is nevertheless still bound to and by human language and its latent narcissistic constraints whenever he attempts to convey the energies and dynamics of matter. How does Hugo solve this paradox of suggesting the potency of the nonhuman and expressing it *as* a human and *in* a human language? More specifically, how does Hugo go about "the task of developing a vocabulary and syntax for, and thus a better discernment of, the active powers issuing from nonsubjects"? Bennett suggests that it requires "a certain willingness to appear naïve or foolish," but according to her, this is an entirely legitimate strategy since the awareness of vital materiality she seeks to bring to life "already found expression in childhood experiences of a

---

36   Brombert, "Hugo's Poem of Effacement," 581.

world populated by animate things rather than passive objects." Consequently, she urges us "to cultivate a bit of anthropomorphism—the idea that human agency has some echoes in nonhuman nature—to counter the narcissism of humans in charge of the world."[37]

This rhetorical strategy, if viable, is good news to authors and literary scholars. For centuries writers have been attempting to breathe life into their surroundings through metaphors and analogies, perhaps more often their natural surroundings (e.g., forests, animals) than their environments of inert matter (e.g., rocks). However, Bennett has not solved the paradox. Anthropomorphism can be seen as a means of creating echoes of human agency in nonhuman matter, but it could just as well be considered yet another anthropocentric strategy. It is not certain that Bennett is aware of this, although she comes close to admitting it here: "Though the movements and effectivity of stem cells, electricity, food, trash, and metals are crucial to political life (and human life per se), almost as soon as they appear in public (often at first by disrupting human projects or expectations), these activities and powers are represented as human mood, action, meaning, agenda, or ideology. This quick substitution sustains the fantasy that 'we' really are in charge of all those 'its.' "[38] It is unclear whether Bennett sees the relation between anthropomorphism and, for example, "represented as human mood." But representing matter—whether granite, steamships, or storms—as human moods (something Bennett has a negative opinion of) is one way of anthropomorphizing the nonhuman world (of which Bennett has a positive opinion). The problem is that such a strategy "sustains the fantasy that 'we' really are in charge of all those 'its.' " The conclusion is that anthropomorphism is an extremely delicate balancing act; to successfully perform it, the writer evokes the vitality of matter and reaffirms anthropocentrism.

Les Travailleurs de la mer teems with anthropomorphisms. This is no coincidence. The question is whether they feed egocentrism or whether they simulate the vitalist dynamics of a subterranean world of matter. This is where the choice of narrator and narratorial perspective becomes important. Which experiential technique does Hugo's enunciatory strategy represent? How does he convey the fictional universe?

Early on in "The Archipelago of the Channel," the narrator employs a martial discourse to convey the war-like relationship between nature and people in Guernsey. Human-built "fortifications" are "*invaded* by sand and *attacked* by the waves," although some "little houses" are in fact "capable of *withstanding* a

---

37 Bennett, *Vibrant Matter*, ix, xiii, vii, xvi.
38 Bennett, *Vibrant Matter*, x.

cannonball," just as "windmills" are "*dismasted* by storms." The narrator talks of rabbits "setting man at *defiance*" with the help of their "*friend* the ocean" that "isolates them": "*Fraternal* relations of this kind are found throughout nature," the narrator concludes. In a description of rock formations along "the formless coast," the narrator constantly anthropomorphizes the formations into images of "a tripod," "a lion," and "an angel," first seeing "a smile," then "a distorted grin."[39] The sections on coastal rock formations, compared in their architectural design to Caliban rather than Venus or the Parthenon, that is, to human figures or human-built constructions, comprise an entire aesthetic theory on beauty and the sublime. These anthropomorphisms serve a dual purpose: they *familiarize* alterity, the natural and animal worlds otherwise ungraspable for humans, by investing it with recognizable patterns; and they *invigorate* these nonhuman worlds by assigning them humanoid purposes. Familiarization and invigoration are anthropocentric endeavors that paradoxically intend to disanthropocentricize the world by dispersing agency into the nonhuman world.

The introduction of the Durande reminds us of Hugo's technique of blurring in his etching "Naufrage" (), and it happens through anthropomorphizing the ship:

> Sometimes in the evening, after sunset, when night mingles with the sea and twilight invests the waves with a kind of terror, there could be seen entering the harbor of St. Sampson, menacingly churning up the water, a shapeless mass, a monstrous form that whistled and spluttered, a hideous thing that roared like a wild beast and smoked like a volcano, a kind of hydra slavering in the foam and trailing a wake of fog, hurtling toward the town with a fearful beating of its fins and a maw belching forth flames. This was Durande.[40]

We must acknowledge the anthropocentrism inherent in this passage since someone is communicating the tableau to us. But we can then ask what kind of tableau is communicated? There is a humanoid purposefulness in nature and an ability to produce emotion or affect as when "twilight *invests* the waves with a kind of *terror*." Otherwise, the focus is on the steamship. Apart from not being italicized (traditionally, italics signals that the name refers to a ship and not a person), Durande is attributed with intentions or at least with having certain effects on anyone seeing or hearing it/her enter the harbor: she is shapeless, monstrous, and menacing because noisy. In describing her aural and

---

39   Hugo, *The Toilers of the Sea*, 6, 8, 12, 13, my italics.
40   Hugo, *The Toilers of the Sea*, 96.

visual outlook, the narrator borrows qualities from both organic (animal) and inorganic (geological) nature: she roars like a wild beast and her funnel emits smoke like a volcano. The dual registers are repeated with hydra and fog, fins and flames. The narrator commingles humanmade technology and nature in the form of organic and inorganic matter. Metaphors and analogies conjure up a world picture of correspondences which serve the narrator in his attempts to break down the barriers between three nonhuman spheres—technology, organic nature, inorganic nature—to create a flatter ontology in which they all spring from the same substance.

2.4 Fooling and Receiving Mercy

So far, my approach to the question of egocentrism (aided or hindered by technocentrism) versus geocentrism has seemingly been informed by a logic of either/or. But vital materialism is less concerned with adversaries than with forces and energies affecting each other through support or opposition, each following its own tendency, but hooking up with others in temporary groupings. Humans are not necessarily in opposition to artifacts and nature, though they can be. They coexist on a horizontal rather than on a vertical plane. Intimacy outweighs incongruity, association trumps separation.

Near the end of *Les Travailleurs*, Gilliatt performs miraculous deeds by surviving in hazardous natural surroundings while at the same time dismantling the wreck of the Durande and salvaging its steam engines, funnels, and propellers. A potent anthropocentrism is evident when Gilliatt exclaims to the abyss, "Fooled you!"[41] Hugo's lone romantic outsider hero and superman mariner is a modern Faust or Prometheus conquering nature and emulating the divine. Gilliatt's triumphant outburst follows his solitary ten-week ordeal and his survival of a relentless and ferocious hurricane. When Gilliatt is victorious in a subsequent encounter with a giant octopus trying to suck his body dry of blood, human dominance over nature, animals, and inert matter seems secured.

But just when Gilliatt is ready to return to land, something unexpected happens, which strikes him with terror: his paunch leaks, ultimately leaving him "at the mercy of the abyss."[42] Hugo's anthropocentric project in which he "wanted to glorify the work, the will, the devotion, all of which makes man great,"[43] exemplified through Gilliatt and his superhuman efforts, is shattered. Gilliatt falls back on a more horizontal plane of unruly stuff:

---

41 Hugo, *The Toilers of the Sea*, 343.
42 Hugo, *The Toilers of the Sea*, 368.
43 Victor Hugo, *Correspondance*, vol. II, 1849–1866, ed. Cécile Daubray (Paris: Albin Michel, 1950), 537.

> For the first time Gilliatt felt helpless and at a loss. An obscure fatality was now his mistress. With his boat, with the engines of the Durande, with all his toil, with all his success, with all his courage, he was now at the mercy of the abyss. He had no means of continuing the struggle; he was now purely passive. [...] The makeshift contrivance for stopping the leak was now within the power of the sea. How would this inert obstacle behave? The fight was now to be carried on by this contrivance, not by Gilliatt; by a scrap of material, not by human will. [...] The matter was now to be determined by a struggle between two mechanical quantities. [...] He was now merely a spectator of his fate [...]. He had hitherto been the directing intelligence; now, at this supreme moment, he had given place to a mindless resistance.[44]

His anthropocentric "Fooled you!" is replaced with a more compliant "Have mercy!":

> For two long months the consciousnesses and providences that exist in the invisible world had watched the contest. On one side were ranged the vast expanses of the ocean, the waves, the winds, the lightning, the meteors, on the other one man; on one side the sea, on the other a human soul; on one side the Infinite, on the other an atom. There had been a battle. And now perhaps this prodigious effort was to be wasted. This extraordinary heroism was to be reduced to impotence.[45]

Mercy is an act that can only be bestowed upon us from the outside and something larger than us: "Defeated by the immensity, he was making his submission."[46] But this is not the time and place in the novel where Gilliatt meets his death by allowing the tide to engulf him as he watches the *Cashmere* disappear in the horizon. Not only does Gilliatt manage to survive the hurricane and kill the octopus, but he also succeeds in returning to the harbor of St. Sampson with Mess Lethierry's steam engines and his 75,000 francs, a deed that signals a resurrection of the novel's anthropocentrism (and in a certain sense, Gilliatt's suicide merely contributes to this anthropocentrism).

So, what happens between Gilliatt's discovery of the leak and his arrival in St. Sampson? How does Gilliatt survive after he "felt his whole being dissolving in the cold, in fatigue, in impotence, in prayer, in darkness, and his

---

44 Hugo, *The Toilers of the Sea*, 368.
45 Hugo, *The Toilers of the Sea*, 370.
46 Hugo, *The Toilers of the Sea*, 370.

eyes closed"?[47] His killing the devilfish, the *pieuvre*, and his withstanding the hurricane are made possible through a combination of luck, skill, experience, and cunning. However, his ultimate survival after having faced the leak and the hurricane turns out not to be an act of human will. When Gilliatt begs for mercy, he *receives* it. But how? From what source? The answers can be found in the following quote:

> Some hours passed.
>
> The sun rose in all its brilliance. Its first ray lit up a motionless form on the summit of the Great Douvre. It was Gilliatt.
>
> He was still stretched out on the rock. This naked body, cold and rigid, no longer shivered. The closed eyelids had a pallid hue. It would have been difficult for an observer to decide whether it was a living body or corpse.
>
> The sun seemed to be looking at him.
>
> If this naked man was not dead, he was so close to death that the least cold wind would be enough to carry him off.
>
> The wind began to blow, a mild, life-giving wind: the spring breath of May.
>
> Now the sun was rising higher in the deep blue sky; its rays, falling less horizontally, took on a tinge of red. Its light became heat. It enveloped Gilliatt.
>
> Gilliatt did not move. If he was breathing it was with a faint respiration that would barely tarnish a mirror.
>
> The sun continued its ascent, now shining less obliquely on Gilliatt. The wind, which had originally been merely mild, was now warm.
>
> The rigid naked body was still without movement, but the skin now seemed less pallid.
>
> The sun, approaching the zenith, fell vertically on the summit of the Great Douvre. A prodigality of light streamed down from the sky, and was joined by the vast reverberations from the serene ocean. The rock began to warm up, and conveyed some of its warmth to the man.
>
> A sigh stirred Gilliatt's chest: he was alive.
>
> The sun continued its caresses, which were now almost ardent. The wind, which was already the wind of midday and of spring, drew close to Gilliatt, like a mouth breathing gently on him. He moved.

---

47   Hugo, *The Toilers of the Sea*, 370.

> The sea was ineffably calm. Its murmur was like the lullaby of a nurse cradling a child. The waved seemed to be rocking the reef to sleep.
>
> The seabirds, now familiar with Gilliatt, fluttered anxiously above him—no longer with their former wariness but with an air of tenderness and sympathy. They uttered little cries, as if calling to him. A seagull, which seemed fond of him, was tame enough to perch near him and began to talk to him. He seemed not to hear. It jumped onto his shoulder and gently pecked at his lips.
>
> Gilliatt opened his eyes. The birds, pleased but still shy, flew off.
>
> He stood up, stretched like a lion awakened from sleep, ran to the edge of the summit platform, and looked down at the defile between the two Douvres. The paunch was still there, intact. The plug had held: the sea had probably not troubled it much. All was saved.[48]

While it is possible to read a religious or spiritual force or spirit into the scene, I would argue that the language, largely a language of anthropomorphisms, points in a more material-ecological and cosmic direction.

Before examining the passage in closer detail, we will briefly discuss how three prominent scholars have read the novel and Gilliatt's struggle with the Infinite. Surprisingly, none of them pay any attention to the crucial scene that begins with the leak and ends with "All was saved." Instead, they focus on the preceding scene during which Gilliatt succeeds in dismantling the Durande and transferring engines, funnels, and propellers onto his own paunch after many challenges. To Victor Brombert, Gilliatt's heroic engineering deeds make *Les Travailleurs* into an "allegory of salvation and rebirth" in that the "engine is literally 'delivered.' "[49] Gilliatt's efforts also legitimize Margaret Cohen's attention to individual labor and marine craftmanship,[50] but Cohen does not seem interested in the importance of what Brombert recognizes as Hugo's "cosmic choreography" in which every "atom is the worker of the inconceivable, the incommensurable work."[51]

In his biography of Victor Hugo, Graham Robb remarks that "*Les Travailleurs de la mer* can be read in several ways and tamed to a gentle allegory." Robb lists four such readings, the first being rooted in the author's comments: "Hugo claimed that it showed the final victory of Prayer over 'that most formidable of despots: the Infinite.' " The second allegorical reading considers the novel a

---

48 Hugo, *The Toilers of the Sea*, 371–72.
49 Brombert, *Victor Hugo and the Visionary Novel*, 141.
50 Cohen, *The Novel and the Sea*, 191–93.
51 Brombert, "Hugo's Poem of Effacement," 584, 585.

metaphor for the nineteenth century, suggesting that the novel's English title would benefit from "workers" because of its political connotations instead of the more poetic choice of "toilers," while emphasizing the novel's preoccupation with technical progress, creative genius, and hard work overcoming the ghastly inertia of the material world. In that sense, Gilliatt's engineering project—to conquer gravity—becomes a symbol of the spiritual mission of freeing oneself from the burden of original sin. The third reading sees the novel as "the only great memorial in Hugo's work to his second daughter: a huge, obsessive monolith looming over the tidier, poetic mythology arranged around Léopoldine."[52] While Hugo in several poems had mourned and tried (in vain) to reconcile himself with the loss of Léopoldine who drowned in 1843 at the age of nineteen, *Les Travailleurs* can be read as an ambiguous tribute to Adèle II, who had eloped to Canada to be with her beloved Albert Pinson (who never repaid her affections that eventually morphed into obsession). The final reading suggested by Robb is to consider the novel an allegory for the Second Empire: the wrecked Durande is the ship of State, Clubin is Napoléon III, and Gilliatt is Hugo.

Cohen's focus on human labor produces excellent readings of maritime novels and prose texts, not least because they always establish a persuasive bond between the theme of labor and its implications for the poetics of the novel. But in her reading of *Les Travailleurs*, Cohen neglects the cosmic, atomistic perspective in Hugo's theory of work, in which atoms are not merely a metaphor for humans but also refer to "the consciousnesses and providences that exist in the invisible world." If Brombert's reading explicitly articulates this cosmic perspective as a central element, he nevertheless stops his analysis of Gilliatt's struggles on the reef when Gilliatt delivers the engines. Brombert neglects the fact that not only does Gilliatt *deliver* but he himself is *delivered* by external forces.

Robb's four pathways for understanding the novel are viable readings, but it is necessary to challenge his first suggestion concerning the triumph of religion and prayer over nature and things. One problem with Robb's reference to Hugo is not his translation from Hugo's letter to Pierre Véron (dated late March or April 1866), but his use of the word "Prayer," which is actually nowhere present in Hugo's letter. Instead of referring to Prayer, Hugo writes that he wanted to prove that "will and understanding are sufficient, even for the atom, to triumph over that most formidable of despots: the Infinite." This is doubly important. First, Hugo's letter leaves out religion entirely; second, it emphasizes not

---

52   Robb, *Victor Hugo*, 414, 414, 415.

only human but also atomistic will and understanding as crucial factors in any struggle with what he labels *"things."* Another important point in the letter is also that no matter how heroic a struggle and triumphant an outcome, the human heart—here, Déruchette's love—is always more merciless (*implacable*) than any abyss: "what escapes the ocean does not escape the woman: I wanted to show that when it comes to being loved, *doing everything* is vanquished by *doing nothing*, and Gilliatt by Ebenezer."[53] This important tweak—from Robb's idea of human Prayer to Hugo's actual words about human and atomistic will and understanding, and then the relativization of Gilliatt's triumph because of the mercilessness of Déruchette's love for Ebenezer—has consequences for Robb's second allegorical reading. Is it correct that Gilliatt's hard work ultimately overcomes gravity?

The main reason for the critics' focus on the human individual and his triumph is their inclination to read the scene (if they read it at all) in which Gilliatt begs for mercy as a mere parenthesis between the scenes of fooling the Abyss/the Infinite and returning triumphantly St. Sampson. However, the lengthy quote above from the two-page chapter "There Is an Ear in the Unknown" is of vital importance if we are to understand the true vision of *The Toilers of the Sea*. At first glance, Hugo's vocabulary signals a dichotomic scenario: on one side, activity, movement, warmth, deep colors, and life expressed through the sun, the sky, the sea, the winds, the waves, the rocks, and the seabirds; on the other side, passivity, rigidity, coldness, pale colors, and death, all associated with Gilliatt, who is more corpse than living body. But gradually, the barrier separating the nonhuman elements and the human is penetrated through the force of matter's vitality, especially the solar energy. What starts out as a scene of incongruity slowly turns into a scene of intimacy in which Hugo mobilizes a "cross-ontological fellowship."[54]

The mobilization happens primarily through anthropomorphism. The initial image of a rising, brilliant sun set against the motionless, naked, and cold body of Gilliatt is set in motion by Hugo's first use of anthropomorphism: "The sun seemed to be looking at him" establishes a connection between the two spheres, initiates a breakdown of the barrier between them, and from then on, as the sun continues to rise and increase the temperature on the Douvres, an intense transfer of life-giving impulses upon Gilliatt begins. At first, Gilliatt is no different from the cold and hard rocks on which he surrendered himself to sleep and possible death. But as the sun rises and gives off its heating rays,

---

53   Hugo, *Correspondance*, vol. II, 537.
54   Cohen, *Stone*, 8.

the rocks grow warmer and transfer heat to Gilliatt. The wind, too, becomes "a mild, life-giving wind," then it turns from "merely mild" to "warm."

Gradually, the entire setting collaborates on what seems an intentional effort to breathe life into Gilliatt. The sea begins to reverberate and simulate the rhythm of the heartbeat, its "murmur was like a lullaby of a nurse cradling a child," while the "waves seemed to be rocking the reef to sleep" to prevent it from threatening Gilliatt. The only organic matter apart from Gilliatt, the seabirds, now repay his earlier generosity towards them by sending him "tenderness and sympathy," uttering "little cries, as if calling to him. A seagull, which seemed fond of him, was tame enough to perch near him and began to talk to him [...] and gently pecked at his lips." This physical touch from an animal is the last in a series of collaborations among vital matters that help bring Gilliatt back to life. It is as if the roles are inverted in *Les Travailleurs*: The sun, a material phenomenon, is elevated by Hugo to a godlike creature that in close cooperation with its assistants—the winds, the rocks, the waves—incubates the human, an organic phenomenon. Even if we admit that Hugo's vision includes a God as the ultimate creator and force behind the sun's life-giving powers, the vision diverges from the biblical idea of human superiority in the realm of the Earth. In *Les Travailleurs*, nonhumans and humans are entangled, and even if Hugo creates one of the most powerful scenes in literary history of an isolated human's struggle against and triumph over gravity and the Infinite, he still supplements this scene with one of equal importance, the scene of Gilliatt's merciful deliverance by benevolent cosmic forces. Antagonism is followed by alliance.

It could be argued that Gilliatt's triumph over nature and his deliverance of and reclaiming authority over a broken technology as well as the subsequent deliverance of Gilliatt through benevolent cosmic forces are both visions of little significance, because the ultimate triumph is reserved for the human heart, the supreme *ananke*, and concretized in Déruchette's love for Ebenezer. The novel's ending converges well with Hugo's remarks about the omnipotence of a woman's love in his 1866 letter to Pierre Véron. However, both ending and letter must be read with certain precautions. Robb's suggestion that *Les Travailleurs* can be read as a monument to Hugo's second daughter Adèle is perfectly legitimate. But the elopement scene in the novel, in one sense a tribute to love, is clouded in ambiguity because of the grief felt by her father over her elopement and the development of her feelings for Pinson that evolved into pathological obsession.

Still, it is possible to buy into the reading that Hugo suggests in his letter, in which he emphasizes that human love conquers all. After his heroic and superhuman efforts, what topples Gilliatt is the marriage of Adèle and Ebenezer and their presumed happiness. It is true that his suicide is the result of his conscious choice. Whereas his deliverance on the rocks was a result of nonhuman cosmic forces, his suicide is the result of Gilliatt taking his destiny into his own hands. Marriage and suicide confirm anthropocentrism, perhaps even a bourgeois anthropocentrism. However, we must recall the crucial scene in which Gilliatt discovers the potentially fatal leak, resigns himself to his fate, and falls asleep only to wake up refreshed and discovering that the paunch has not sunk. This scene confirms *Les Travailleurs de la mer* as a novel of deep human and nonhuman entanglements. If the novel is a homage to the supreme *ananke*, the human heart, it is also an acknowledgment of the intimacy that exists between humans, rocks, ships, waves, winds, and birds. The drama of human love does not unfold on a background of inert matter but evolves through constant alliances with vibrant matter.

2.5 Cosmography of Work

The theme of effacement commences and terminates the human storyline of the novel. In Part I, "Sieur Clubin," Gilliatt's name is written in snow, and it is only a matter of time and temperature before the traced name and the human footprints vanish. In Part III, "Déruchette," Gilliatt commits suicide by drowning. The theme of effacement is also found in the overture of the novel and plays a significant role in the very first lines of the later incorporated and immensely important "The Archipelago of the Channel" that precedes the three parts:

> The Atlantic wears away our coasts. The pressure of the current from the Pole deforms our western cliffs. This wall that shields us from the sea is being undermined from Saint-Valery-sur-Somme to Ingouville; huge blocks of rock tumble down, the sea churns clouds of boulders, our harbors are silted up with sand and shingle, the mouths of our rivers are barred. Every day a stretch of Norman soil is torn away and disappears under the waves.[55]

Effacement, deformation, and disappearance are transplanted from the human sphere (Gilliatt) to the sphere of nature in the various shapes of meteorology, geology, and oceanography. The spatial scale is explicitly global (the Atlantic, the Pole, Guernsey), and in the workings of nature we sense a temporal vista that extends over several millennia (the year 709 and "earlier times"

---

55 Hugo, *The Toilers of the Sea*, 5.

are referred to a little later). Hugo depicts a global system, a material cosmography, characterized by a "tremendous activity" that has "terrible consequences," for example "erosion," due to its "power," "violence," and "aggression."[56] It is a tableau emphasizing how the sheer physical power of the ocean dominates the earth.

Still on the first page, Hugo signals his intention to include both spheres, the human and the nonhuman, in his novel's world picture, not as two incongruous and incompatible spheres radically separated, but as two spheres operating in great intimacy with each other and with constant "cross-ontological"[57] spillover or overlap: "The industry of the sea, which created ruin, has been succeeded by the industry of man, which has made a people."[58] However, it soon becomes clear that the structure of destructive nature and constructive mankind also exists in its inverted form of constructive nature and destructive mankind. Apart from the double effacement of Gilliatt, other examples of human destruction and deformation include Clubin's intentional foundering of the Durande, the unsteady loyalty of the local people and their superstitions and distrust of anything queer. What is of interest here is the vibrant material cosmography created by Hugo in which human intentions and natural forces of destruction and creation work constantly with and against each other in complex entanglements of cosmic scope.

The vision of a dynamic world in which processes of destruction and construction are in incessant motion, clearly inspired by Michelet, is articulated in a *longue-durée* perspective: "The configuration of an island changes over time. An island is a construction by the ocean. Matter is eternal; not its aspect. Everything on earth is being perpetually moulded by death: even extra-human monuments, even granite. Everything changes shape, even the shapeless. Edifices built by the sea crumble like any other. The sea, which has built them up, also demolishes them."[59] In this scenario dominated by geological forces, mankind plays its part. In some remarkable pages, Hugo anticipates contemporary anthropocene discussions of humanity as a telluric force with earth-remodeling powers: "The sea builds up and demolishes; and man helps the sea, not in building up but in destroying. Of all the teeth of time the one that works hardest is man's pickax. Man is a rodent. Everything is modified or changed at his hand, either for the better or for the worse. Here he disfigures, there he transfigures. [...] man can carve up nature. The scar of human work can be

---

56   Hugo, *The Toilers of the Sea*, 5.
57   Cohen, *Stone*, 8.
58   Hugo, *The Toilers of the Sea*, 5.
59   Hugo, *The Toilers of the Sea*, 49.

seen on the work of God."⁶⁰ Contrary to a wound that heals invisibly, a scar is a lasting visible physical record of past actions, damage, or events.

If scar is a negatively loaded word, Hugo immediately shifts the mood of the argument by focusing on the praiseworthy qualities and accomplishments of man, now cooperating with nature instead of injuring it:

> It seems that a certain power of achievement is granted to man. He appropriates the creation to humanity. Such is his function. He has the necessary boldness; one might also say the necessary impiety. This collaboration with nature is something offensive. Man, a short-lived being who is perpetually dying, takes on the infinite. Against all the ebb and flow of nature, against elements seeking to communicate with other elements, against the vast navigation of forces in the depths man declares a blockade. [...] He has his idea of fitness, and the universe must accept it. [...] A universe is a mass of raw material. The world, which is God's work, is man's canvas.
>
> Everything limits man, but nothing stops him. He responds to limits by jumping over them. The impossible is a frontier that is perpetually receding.
>
> A geological formation that has at its base the mud of the Deluge and at its summit the eternal snows is, for man, a wall like any other: he cuts through it and continues beyond.⁶¹

This is humanity imagined as sovereign, assigned the role as the supreme project maker to whom the world is but a stage, an inertia to be overcome. The metaphor of "world as canvas" implicates humanity's separation from the world. Incongruity is emphasized over intimacy. Hugo comes close to articulating anthropocentrism in its purest form. He goes even further in his eulogy:

> Once upon a time he did all this work for Xerxes; nowadays, less foolish, he does it for himself. This diminution of foolishness is called progress. Man works on his house, and his house is the earth. He disarranges, displaces, suppresses, knocks down, levels, mines, undermines, digs, excavates, breaks up, pulverizes, effaces this, abolishes that, and rebuilds with what he has destroyed. Nothing makes him hesitate—no mass, no blockage, no obstacle, no consideration for splendid material, no majesty of

---

60 Hugo, *The Toilers of the Sea*, 50.
61 Hugo, *The Toilers of the Sea*, 50.

nature. If the enormities of creation are within his reach he tears them down. This aspect of God that can be ruined tempts him, and he mounts an assault on immensity, hammer in hand. Globe, let this ant of yours have his way.[62]

If positive words and expressions such as "progress" and "less foolish" signal Hugo's admiration for humanity, there seems to be a movement in the passage towards irony and critique of our hubristic treatment of earth and our spoiled behavior. This becomes explicit in the following passage:

Let us not, however, exaggerate our power. Whatever man does, the great lines of creation persist; the supreme mass does not depend on man. He has power over the detail, not over the whole. And it is right that this should be so. The Whole is providential. Its laws pass over our head. What we do goes no farther than the surface. Man clothes or unclothes the earth; clearing a forest is like taking off a garment. But to slow down the rotation of the globe on its axis, to accelerate the course of the globe on its orbit, to add or subtract a fathom on the earth's daily journey of 718,000 leagues around the sun, to modify the precession of the equinoxes, to eliminate one drop of rain—never! What is on high remains on high. Man can change the climate, but not the seasons.[63]

In the next chapter, we will return to the discussion of maritime fiction in the Anthropocene at length. Clearly, Hugo's passages here strike chords that resonate with problems and challenges defining the Anthropocene. What vision does Hugo promote here? How does he envision humanity's planetary role? How far can human agency go?

It is remarkable how close Hugo comes to articulating some of the core dilemmas and by now established truths about mankind's telluric power. At the same time, it is telling that Hugo situates man's impotence chronologically *before* what we now refer to as tipping points. These temporal junctures mark points of no return, characterized by a time *before* (defined by human actions of telluric magnitude that have produced the tipping points) and by a time *after* (during which mankind has now become impotent, unable to prevent, halt, or even control potentially fatal processes in the Earth system). In *Les Travailleurs*, tipping points do not exist, because Hugo sets a limit to the

---

62 Hugo, *The Toilers of the Sea*, 50–51.
63 Hugo, *The Toilers of the Sea*, 51.

powers of human agency: humans may cause climate to change, but we cannot manipulate the seasons; humans may control the detail, but never the Whole; we only decide Earth's garment, but we have no say in the lines of creation; our sphere is the surface, not the supreme mass.

Hugo is right in many ways. In contemporary discussions of the consequences of the Anthropocene, scientists speak of a record of human actions traceable on the geological surface of the planet. There is nothing suggesting that planet Earth will stop its law-bound rotation around the sun or its volcanic activities no matter how much humans wreak havoc on its climactic system. Today, the greatest fears seem to be an uninhabitable planet and human extinction caused by human actions. Is this a scenario envisioned by Hugo? Not really. *Les Travailleurs* may be a novel in which nonhuman matter plays a significant role, but Hugo does not imagine human extinction as a result of harmful anthropogenic actions. Arguably, the main difference between Hugo and contemporary worst-case scenario thinkers of the Anthropocene is the introduction of tipping points as markers of points of no return after which the Earth's evolution may result in an uninhabitable, posthuman planet. Hugo's idea of a fundamental separation between detail and whole, between surface and lines of creation, has been challenged today with the discovery of the Earth system in which details and surfaces are directly linked with the whole—not in a cosmological-astrological sense, but in a planetary sense. Today, we know that climate change affects seasonal rhythms as we know them today and as they define specific locations. We are also aware that the scars on the earth's surface inflicted by humans will not only be visible for thousands of years to come, but that they will disturb and perhaps even destroy the ecology of the Earth system.

So, Hugo did not or could not conceive that human actions could be so extensively ecologically damaging that the result would be a posthuman world. Nevertheless, in the novel's last words there is a commitment to nature, a pledge that signals a posthuman planet. On the new anthropogenic earth in "The Book of Revelations," "there was no more sea."[64] In contrast, Victor Hugo envisions an entirely different new world at the end of his novel: "There was now nothing but the sea." If God eradicated the wet, unruly sea from dry earth in his efforts to create orders and distinctions, Hugo promotes another image of order: "everywhere the profound order of nature's great disorder."[65]

64   "Book of Revelations," *The King James Bible*, 21.1.
65   Hugo, *The Toilers of the Sea*, 430, 9.

CHAPTER 5

Anthropocene

1 Coal in Wales, Whales at the Pole

In October 1920, a strike by coal miners and railway workers was looming in Great Britain and threatened to paralyze national and international trade and traffic. On any given day at Barry Docks in Cardiff, Wales, hundreds of train wagons loaded with coal were lined up in several adjacent rows of seemingly endless length. As these rows of wagons moved forward, it gave the onlooker an impression of black rivers flowing peacefully alongside each other (Figure 24). At the estuary of these rivers of coal, in dock basins on the verge of the Atlantic Ocean, hundreds of fuel-consuming steamships on their way to near and far away places around the globe each day waited impatiently for giant cranes to load thousands of tons of coal from the train wagons into their cargo holds (Figure 25).

On a Friday in early October 1920, the Danish doctor Aage Krarup Nielsen (1891–1972) arrived in Cardiff on the Norwegian whaler *Solstrejf* (Sunbeam). Its destination was the area of the Antarctic Ocean around Deception Island and in the Belgica Strait (now Gerlache Strait) which was a hunting ground for whalers. Nielsen and the ship's Norwegian crew entered Barry Docks just

FIGURE 24   "Black rivers"—coal wagons at Barry Docks. Image printed in *En hvalfangerfærd*

FIGURE 25　William Lionel Wyllie, *Barry Docks, South Wales* (c. 1900). Amgueddfa Cymru, Cardiff
© NATIONAL MUSEUM WALES

as the British newspapers multiplied their daily editions announcing the imminent strike with ever increasing intensity and the shouting of numerous newspaper boys. The strike was soon officially declared by the coal miners' union—their "Triple Alliance" partners, the unions of railway and transport workers, threatened to follow suit—and would result in the imprisonment of all ships for an indefinite period. According to Nielsen, *Solstrejf* managed to escape into the Atlantic as the last ship out of Barry Docks. The drawback was a lack of fuel, since the short time span and emerging coal crisis meant that Wilson, the coal company, could only provide 50 tons of coal, a mere one per cent of the initial agreement of 5.000 tons. However, as Wilson was an international company with offices around the globe, the captain of *Solstrejf* was told by Wilson's Cardiff representative to make a stop at Dakar and later at Montevideo, where the ship would receive the rest of the fuel needed before continuing the long journey to the rich whaling grounds near the South Pole.

Aage Krarup Nielsen's first published writings came out as a series in the newspaper *Politiken* between January 10 and August 14, 1921. They were travel letters from his voyage on the *Solstrejf*, which lasted from October 1920 to May 1921. In the same year, the articles were published in Nielsen's first book, *En hvalfangerfærd: Gennem troperne til Sydishavet* (A Whaling Voyage: Through the Tropics to the Antarctic Ocean).[1] Nielsen had just passed his medical exam in early 1920 and subsequently worked as a doctor between March and September in Ibestad, Norway. He became bored and so signed up as one of the two doctors on the whaling expedition. After his return from the Antarctic Ocean, he continued to travel the globe and write vividly about his experiences. He published several books, some of which are translated into English, German, Dutch, and a few more languages. *En hvalfangerfærd* has been translated into German, but not into English.[2]

Reading *En hvalfangerfærd* at a time of increasing awareness of living in the Anthropocene or the Age of Ecology characterized by climate change and the sixth extinction, three components of Nielsen's travelogue immediately stand out: coal, whales, and the ocean. *En hvalfangerfærd* provides insight into a historical period during which coal circulated the globe as cargo while simultaneously being burned in massive amounts as fuel[3] and whales were being killed in vast numbers in the Antarctic Ocean. The transportation and burning of coal are never questioned by Nielsen. In 1920, the great threat to the machinery of first world societies was a lack of coal to burn, whereas today we have come to realize with Thomas Hylland Eriksen that "the marriage of the steam engine and fossil fuels was the killer app of the nineteenth century."[4] The killing of whales only receives attention, really just a few remarks, as a potential problem in an afterword written for the 1935 edition. Here, but nowhere in the first edition of the book, Nielsen reflects upon how the technological progress in whaling since 1921 has contributed to a numerical acceleration in ship weight, crew members, whales killed, and oil volume.

2 The Anthropocene

In this chapter, I establish a link between the Anthropocene and the maritime world to show 1) the mutual infiltration of these two phenomena and 2) how maritime fictions experiment with representing the Anthropocene

---

1 Aage Krarup Nielsen, *En hvalfangerfærd: Gennem troperne til Sydishavet*, 2nd ed. (1921; København: Gyldendal, 1935).
2 The German translation, *Durch die Tropen zum Südpolarmeer: Eine Fahrt mit Walfischfängern*, came out with Gyldendal in Berlin in 1923 and was translated by Julia Koppel.
3 Sarah Palmer, "Coal and the Sea," in *The Sea in History: The Modern World / La Mer dans l'Histoire: La Période Contemporaine*, ed. N. A. M. Rodger (Woodbridge: The Boydell Press, 2017), 115–25.
4 Thomas Hylland Eriksen, *Overheating: An Anthropology of Accelerated Change* (London: Pluto Press, 2016), 36.

condition aesthetically. The Anthropocene signifies two things: first, a new geological epoch (the Earth has moved out of its former geological epoch called the Holocene); second, human activity is responsible for this exit (humankind has become a global geological force). It has been pointed out that the Anthropocene is, paradoxically, "the sign of our power, but also of our impotence,"[5] "power" signifying that it is humans who have caused the transition, "impotence" acknowledging that some of the processes set in motion by human activity have accelerated beyond our control.

As a concept, the Anthropocene was used by biologist Eugene F. Stoermer in the early 1980s, although it was presumably in use more informally already in the 1970s. Scientists in the Soviet Union used it as early as 1960, perhaps even sooner.[6] In 1948, Fairfield Osborn claimed in his much read *Our Plundered Planet* that mankind had become for the first time "a *large-scale geological force*" and even named the entire third chapter "The New Geological Force: Man."[7] He did not use the concept of the Anthropocene, but his emphasis of humankind as a geological force aligns Osborn's writing with how the Anthropocene is defined today. Another precursor was the concept "noösphere" coined in 1924 by Vladimir Vernadsky, Pierre Teilhard de Chardin, and Edouard Le Roy and further elaborated in the former's *Biosfera* from 1926. In his 1924 book *La Géochimie*, Vernadsky wrote about a "psychozoic era, era of Reason," thus emphasizing the human factor.[8] Actually, the line of thinking behind today's understanding of the Anthropocene is traceable at least as far back as 1873. Back then, geologist, paleontologist, and priest Antonio Stoppani in his *Corso di geologia* proclaimed to be living in "the anthropozoic era," because the emergence of humans had introduced "a new telluric force, which, due to its power and universality, does not faint in the face of the major forces of the globe."[9] Even in George Perkins Marsh's *Man and Nature* from 1864, similar thoughts on humans as a geological force can be found, although Marsh—who lived in Italy and knew Stoppani and his work—admits in a revised 1874 edition of his work that he had not gone as far as Stoppani did in 1873.[10]

---

5   Bonneuil and Fressoz, *The Shock of the Anthropocene*, xi.
6   *Doklady: biological sciences sections*, vol. 132–135 (1960), American Institute of Biological Sciences, 640.
7   Fairfield Osborn, *Our Plundered Planet* (Boston: Little, Brown and Company, 1948), 29, 32–47.
8   Vladimir Vernadsky, *La Géochimie* (Paris: Librairie Félix Alcan, 1924), 342.
9   Antonio Stoppani, *Corso di geologia*, vol. 2 (Milano: G. Bernardoni and E. G. Brigola, 1873), 732.
10 George Perkins Marsh, *The Earth as Modified by Human Action: A Last Revision of "Man and Nature"* (1864; 1874; New York: Charles Scribner's Sons, 1885), 584.

The popularization of the Anthropocene as a concept took off when it was proposed in 2000 as a new epoch in Earth's history by a group of scientists, including Stoermer, led by the Nobel Prize laureate Paul Crutzen.[11] The Anthropocene is characterized by certain effects and side effects brought about by a variety of human activities. For Crutzen, the most significant of these activities is the anthropogenic emission of greenhouse gases, which in 2000 had increased atmospheric levels of carbon dioxide by 30 percent and methane by more than 100 percent, causing substantial changes in global temperature and climate. Crutzen and countless scientists have also pointed to the exponential growth of the planet's human population and its exploitation of 30–50 percent of the planet's land surface, the clearance of tropical rain forests, the transformation of waterways through dam building and river diversions, the growing production and use of (semi-)synthetic and slowly degradable substances such as plastic, as well as the accelerated increase in energy use. "The consequences are, among others, acid precipitation, photochemical 'smog' and climate warming," the latter estimated to reach between 1.4–5.8 °C in the current century.[12]

The Anthropocene is yet to receive the official stamp of approval from the International Commission on Stratigraphy (ICS) and the International Union of Geological Sciences (IUGS). But in recent years, a growing number of scholars in both wet and dry sciences have accepted the term (or proposed alternative terms such as Capitalocene) as one that signifies a new epoch in Earth's history. Debate as to when this epoch began is ongoing. Two symbolic dates lead the race. One is 1784 when James Watt succeeded with an approved version of his steam engine, an achievement many have come to see as contributing significantly to catapult the Industrial Revolution. The other is July 16, 1945, when the Trinity test in New Mexico, related to the Manhattan Project, detonated a nuclear device, which to many marks the beginning of the nuclear age. Others, but they count as a minority in the research community, have proposed the kickoff of agriculture 10,000–15,000 years ago as the beginning of the Anthropocene, or, more precisely, the clearing of forests and conversion of land to cropping about 8,000 years ago and the development of irrigated rice cultivation about 5,000 years ago. Finally, there are those who date the beginning of the Anthropocene back to the end of the Pleistocene era and the wave of extinctions of that era's megafauna, the so-called Quaternary extinction

---

11   Paul J. Crutzen and Eugene F. Stoermer, "The 'Anthropocene,'" *IGBP Newsletter* 41 (2000): 17–18. See also Will Steffen, Jacques Grinevald, Paul Crutzen, and John McNeill, "The Anthropocene: Conceptual and Historical Perspectives," *Philosophical Transactions of the Royal Society A* 369, no. 1938 (2011): 842–67.
12   Paul J. Crutzen, "Geology of Mankind," *Nature* 415, no. 6867 (2002): 23.

event eliminating a range of large mammals, which happened most intensely between 13,000 BC and 8,000 BC, although extinctions also happened before this period.

I agree with Crutzen, Malm, Bonneuil and Fressoz, Eriksen and others that it makes most sense to date the beginning of the Anthropocene to the second half of the eighteenth century when several environmentally damaging human activities (made visible by recent data and statistical graphs documenting those activities) began to accelerate. Among those scholars who prefer situating the beginning of the Anthropocene around 1800, many acknowledge the substantial impact of post-1945 "worldwide industrialization, techno-scientific development, nuclear arms race, population explosion, and rapid economic growth" on the Anthropocene by referring to the postwar era as "the Great Acceleration of the second phase of the Anthropocene."[13] It has been suggested that the first phase, the initial acceleration (1784–1945), and the second phase, the great acceleration (1945–2000), have been followed by a third phase characterized by a growing attentiveness of human impact on the environment at the global scale and first attempts to create global governance systems to manage humanity's relationship with the Earth system.[14] More philosophically formulated, Timothy Morton has characterized the growing awareness of our own destructive role as an "ecognosis": "It is like becoming accustomed to something strange, yet it is also becoming accustomed to strangeness that doesn't become less strange through acclimation. Ecognosis is like a knowing that knows itself," "an awareness of things I can't shake off."[15]

Through human enterprises at sea, the maritime world has played a role in bringing about this new epoch, and some of the effects of the Anthropocene have now begun to destabilize the oceanic environments on the planet. Rising sea levels, escalating amounts of plastic debris, and increasing acidification are but three of numerous consequences triggering a plethora of other damaging processes. The oceans are at one and the same time scenes of causes and arenas of effects, but without ever really having had the power of determination in the matter. In *La Mer*, Michelet claimed a temporal constancy of the ocean and argued that it was only mankind that changed (and changed its view of the

---

13   Steffen et al., "The Anthropocene: Conceptual and Historical Perspectives," 845. See also McNeill and Engelke, *The Great Acceleration*. McNeill and Engelke belong to those who date the beginning of the Anthropocene to 1945.
14   Will Steffen, Paul Crutzen, and J. R. McNeill, "The Anthropocene: are humans now overwhelming the great forces of Nature?" *Ambio* 36 (2007): 614–21.
15   Timothy Morton, *Dark Ecology: For a Logic of Future Coexistence* (New York: Columbia University Press, 2016), 5, 123.

ocean as well, as we have seen in the history chapter): "The element which we call fluid, mobile, and capricious, does not really change; it is regularity itself. What is constantly changing is man."[16] Until recently, most people would have agreed with Michelet, but no more. Michelet turned out to be too optimistic on the ocean's behalf.

It has now become evident that the ocean has undergone physical-chemical changes (temperature, microplastic, acid) since 1800, and even more so since 1945, on a scale that we never thought possible. These changes were caused by human activities. The idea of a boundless dumping ground capable of absorbing the pressures of human activities, the idea of the ocean as the quintessence of permanence, has been irreversibly shattered. Concretely, the world's population has more than tripled since the middle of the twentieth century (from 2.6 billion in 1951 to 7.9 billion in 2022) (Figure 26), whereas populations of sharks, tuna, swordfish, and many other ocean creatures have dropped by 90 percent; cities, farms, factories, and fishing fleets have boomed in both volume and efficiency while coral reefs, mangrove forests, and sea grass meadows have been reduced to half their size.[17]

What role can aesthetic products and the humanities, more specifically literary and cultural studies, possibly play in understanding the Anthropocene and its very tangible challenges and dangers? After all, these challenges, dangers, and the epochal phenomenon itself seem to be of such complexity and scope that only hard data and science can save us from our own misdeeds. But as Bonneuil and Fressoz have shown in *The Shock of the Anthropocene* (2013), history proves that handing over the keys to "Spaceship Earth" to the engineers of the Earth system and opting for a managerial variant of possible solutions to climate change could in fact be seen as repeating what brought us here in the first place. Bonneuil and Fressoz oppose what they call the official (scientist) narrative, which goes like this: We, the human species, unconsciously destroyed nature, but our eyes have now been opened by Earth system scientists so that we finally understand better. However, *measuring* does not equal *understanding*. This story of awakening, say Bonneuil and Fressoz, is a fable of a blind past and a clear-sighted present that is historically false and problematic: false, because it depoliticizes the long history of the Anthropocene; problematic, because it serves to credit our own excellence.[18]

---

16 Michelet, *La Mer*, 11.
17 Sylvia Earle, introduction to Rachel Carson, *The Sea Around Us* (1951; New York: Oxford University Press, 2018), x.
18 Bonneuil and Fressoz, *Shock of the Anthropocene*, xii–xiii.

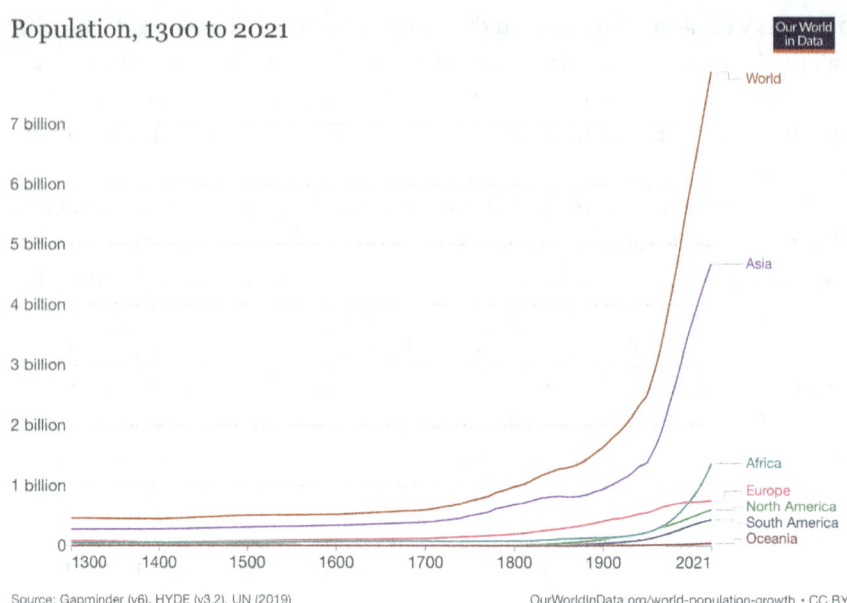

FIGURE 26 Population, 1300 to 2021
Note: Max Roser, Hannah Ritchie, and Esteban Ortiz-Ospina, "World Population Growth," Our World In Data, 2013, most recent substantial revision in May 2019, accessed April 20, 2022, https://ourworldindata.org/world-population-growth
SOURCES: GAPMINDER (V6), HYDE (V3.2) AND THE UN (2019)

Following this skeptical line of thinking towards a scientist-managerial solution, for example in the form of giant geo-engineering projects, aesthetic products can serve as an archive of stories from which not only the political but also the ethical and existential histories of the Anthropocene can be reconstructed and remembered, and in which mankind's exceptionality has been challenged. As to literary and cultural studies, they offer proven methods for analyzing this reconstruction, remembering, and challenging. Writing a novel may not solve the actual challenges of the Anthropocene, nor will an analysis of that novel, but novels and other aesthetic products may serve as translators of graphs and hard data (Figure 26, 27, and 28) thereby offering their readers a mediating *rewiring* of the spheres of abstraction (numbers, statistics, globality) and concretion (experience, existence, locality). Writers and artists may grapple with questions concerning the politics of the carbon economy and the extinction of species, but they may also link such questions to human cultural practices (e.g., flight travel), imagination (e.g., cosmopolitan), and desires (e.g., freedom) and their potential complicity in the Anthropocene.

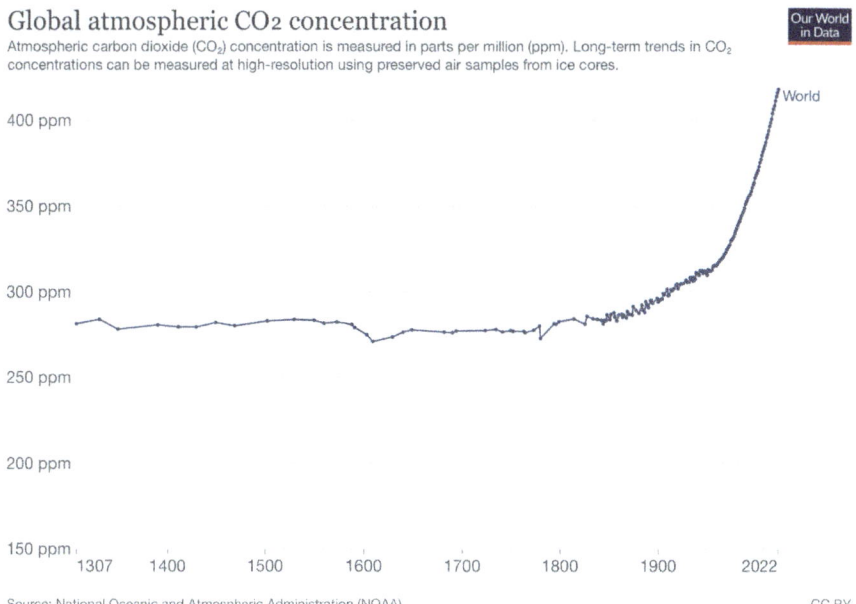

FIGURE 27   Global atmospheric CO_2 concentration
Note: Hannah Ritchie, Max Roser, and Pablo Rosado, "CO_2 and Greenhouse Gas Emissions," Our World in Data, May 2017, last modified August 2020, accessed April 20, 2022, https://ourworldindata.org/co2-and-other-greenhouse-gas-emissions.
SOURCE: NATIONAL OCEANIC AND ATMOSPHERIC ADMINISTRATION (NOAA)

"Scientists have built up data and models that already situate us beyond the point of no return to the Holocene, on the timetable of geological epochs. They have produced figures and curves that depict humanity as a major geological force. *But what narratives can make sense of these dramatic curves?*"[19] The narratives called for by Bonneuil and Fressoz serve not only as translators of data and mediators between science and everyday life. They potentially carry their own epistemological benefits, producing a different type of knowledge through their languages, forms, and points of view—a knowledge more embedded, more experiential, more concrete, and more existential—than the one characteristic of scientific discourse. To "make sense" signifies not only acts of giving *meaning* to something, but also making that something *sensuous*. As Ottmar Ette has argued, literature comprises its own distinct *Lebenswissen* (knowledge for living/knowledge of life) because of its unique capacity to

---

19   Bonneuil and Fressoz, *Shock of the Anthropocene*, xii (my italics).

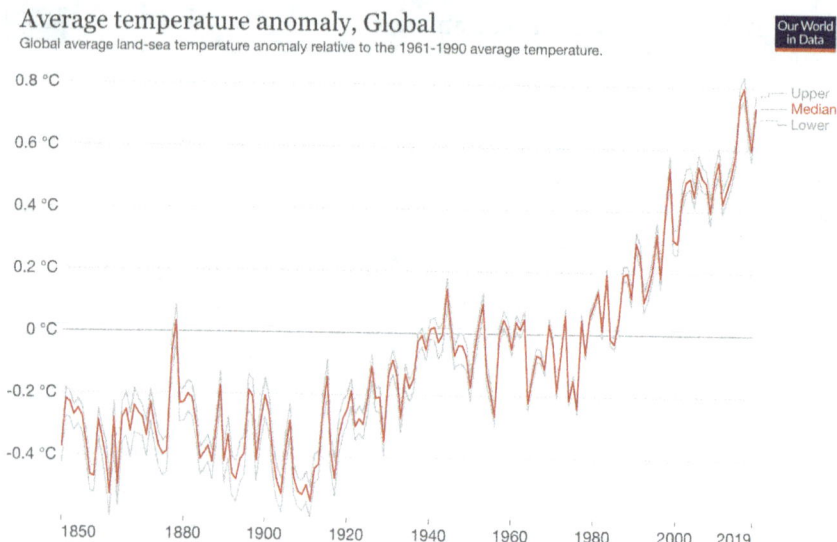

FIGURE 28   Average temperature anomaly, Global
Note: Ritchie, Roser, and Rosado, "CO₂ and Greenhouse Gas Emissions," accessed April 20, 2022.
SOURCE: HADLEY CENTRE (HADCRUT4)

circulate—without the obligation to synthesize or systematize—a plurality of epistemological codes, including scientific ones, and fragments of life knowledge from diverse traditions.[20]

I will read three texts of different genres: Nielsen's travelogue *En hvalfangerfærd* (1921), in which depictions of the burning of fossil fuel and the hunting of whales point forward to contemporary pollution and species extinction respectively; J. G. Ballard's *The Drowned World* (1962), a science fiction novel speculating on human reactions to rising sea water levels; and Siri Ranva Hjelm Jacobsen's *Havbrevene* (2018; The Sea Letters), written in the epistolary form as an exchange between the Atlantic Ocean and the Mediterranean Sea and thematizing the Anthropocene through the focalization of the oceans themselves. While these brief summaries should give an indication of why the works are all thematically relevant for this chapter, it is also important to underline that the generic variety of this selection is intentional, as is the combination of less and

---

20   Ottmar Ette, "Literature as Knowledge for Living, Literary Studies as Science for Living," trans. Vera M. Kutzinski, *PMLA* 125, no. 4 (2010): 986–87.

more canonized works. The generic variety will allow me to show a broader range of discursive strategies that writers mobilize when confronted by maritime life and the Anthropocene. Combining works of which some are more canonized (*The Drowned World*), some less so (*Havbrevene*), and some rather obscure (*En hvalfangerfærd*), enables me to illustrate how wide-ranging the topic of the maritime anthropocene is when the archive is scrutinized. In addition, in writing this book part of my ambition is to draw attention to maritime works by Scandinavian authors.

In my readings a recurring question is how the works anticipate or respond to some of the key challenges posed by the Anthropocene, such as climate change, pollution, species extinction, and responsibility. My analysis combines a focus on these thematical dimensions with an attention to the formal and aesthetic dimensions of the works. What do they have to say about the Anthropocene? How do they express it? Can it even be put into words? This leads to a discussion of the benefits and pitfalls of specific representational strategies *vis à vis* the immense challenges that humankind faces in the era of the Anthropocene. Does anthropomorphism bring humans closer to the nonhuman world and facilitate empathy and care, or does it disrespect the genuine otherness of nonhuman matter, instead demonstrating the dangerous anthropocentrism that brought about our predicament in the first place? Is science fiction merely useless and inaccurate speculation, or does the genre offer valuable insights into future scenarios through specific aesthetic strategies? In general, how can a travelogue, a science-fiction novel, and an epistolary novel help fill out the *missing history* in the graph of rising CO_2 emissions—that is, the missing history of human experiences and behavior; of animal and non-animal perspectives; of how we got here; of who is responsible for doing what and when; of individuals and groups; of nations and corporations; of social and ethnic hierarchies; and, not least, of what to do now?

3   Anthropocene Aesthetics

It has been suggested by several scholars, and by the artists themselves, that writers and filmmakers face various problems of representation when portraying the history of the Anthropocene. In a mixture of lament and puzzlement, Amitav Ghosh has observed that the practices of "poetry, art, architecture, theater, prose fiction, and so on"—creative forms that have otherwise had no problems in responding to "war, ecological calamity, and crises of many sorts"—apparently "prove so peculiarly resistant" to the consequences of climate change. "What is it about climate change," Ghosh continues, "that the mention of it should lead to banishment from the preserves of serious fiction?"[21] To answer this, we need to take a closer look at the characteristics of climate change and the Anthropocene. What are their temporal and spatial structures? When did they begin? How do they evolve? Where do they emerge, and where do they strike? However, the problem of representation does not lie on the side of the represented only. It also has to do with the aesthetic and discursive strategies of the cultural forms that represent. Is there something about "serious fiction" that causes it to banish climate change from its universe? Is there something inherent in the novel that prevents it from facing the challenges posed by the Anthropocene? Is it possible Ghosh is not completely right about serious fiction's exclusion of the climate crisis? Could it be that humans are unable to fully grasp the effects of climate change let alone convey it through language?

3.1 Time, Discontinuity, Probability

One of the main representational challenges facing writers and artists depicting climate change has to do with questions of scale, not least time scale. Our contemporary predicament of a warming world involves a high risk of future violent scenarios if or when the so-called tipping points are reached and transgressed.[22] But the Anthropocene also carries with it what Rob Nixon calls a "slow violence" and this has been happening for a couple of centuries. Normally, we understand violence as sudden disruptions of states of equilibrium (that is the temporal dimension of violence) and as events that evolve visibly and explosively between living and nonliving bodies (that is the spatial dimension of violence). Slow violence, on the other hand, is gradual instead of immediate. It unfurls virtually unnoticeably over long periods of time, not as spectacular body-to-body conflicts but through the medium of entire ecological networks. A time scale of such dimensions and the slow, imperceptible processes evolving along its path are difficult to capture in a novel, a poem, or a movie.[23] It may be more accurate to say that the history of these forms has *de facto* been circumscribed predominantly by the time scale of the human individual or a few human generations, not the continuity of geological time.

---

21 Amitav Ghosh, *The Great Derangement: Climate Change and the Unthinkable* (Chicago and London: The University of Chicago Press, 2016), 10, 11.
22 Bonneuil and Fressoz, *Shock of the Anthropocene*, 25.
23 Rob Nixon, *Slow Violence and the Environmentalism of the Poor* (Cambridge, MA: Harvard University Press, 2011); Andreas Malm, *Fossil Capital: The Rise of Steam Power and the Roots of Global Warming* (London: Verso, 2016), 8–9.

The representational challenges are linked not only with the phenomena to be represented (e.g., the causes and effects of global warming, emissions of greenhouse gases, the dissemination of micro plastics) but also with certain constraints in the aesthetic forms intended to represent these phenomena. In the case of literature, Ghosh asserts that a "grid of literary forms and conventions [...] came to shape the narrative imagination in precisely that period when the accumulation of carbon in the atmosphere was rewriting the destiny of the earth." An important component of this grid was the boosting of *probability*, the modern novel's twin and a sort of anti-narrative device.[24] Ghosh supports this by referring to Franco Moretti's description of this development in the "serious century" as a simultaneous concealment of exceptional moments and foregrounding of everyday details. Observation triumphs over action, telling makes way for showing. *Don Quixote* and *Candide* are followed by *Père Goriot* and *Ulysses*. To Moretti, this double movement, also united in and staged through what he calls "fillers," is to be understood as a rationalized aesthetic strategy to convey *"the kind of narrative pleasure compatible with the new regularity of bourgeois life."* Ghosh's point is that the effects of climate change do not align with a narrative form which, from the nineteenth century and onwards, has solidified into exposing the uniformity of the everyday. In Moretti's words, it is "a world of few surprises, fewer adventures, and no miracles at all."[25] The crown example of the bourgeois novel is Flaubert's *Madame Bovary* (1857), which is masterfully composed as a symmetrical geometry of nonevents.

Interestingly, the valorization of regularity over exceptionality in the modern novel is paralleled in the sciences, as shown by Stephen Jay Gould in *Time's Arrow, Time's Cycle* (1987). Gould analyzes how the catastrophist narrative of history of the earth, exemplified by Thomas Burnet (c. 1635–1715) and his idea of events of "unrepeatable uniqueness," was replaced by a gradualist narrative of the earth, championed by James Hutton (1726–1797) and Charles Lyell (1797–1875), that privileged slow processes evolving over time at regular, predictable rates. Together with Pierre-Simon Laplace's (1749–1827) development of the Bayesian interpretation of probability, the gradualist thought regime is an Enlightenment-influenced attempt to promote a worldview in which humankind was in greater control of its destiny and nature.

It is no coincidence that gradualism triumphed during a period that we now refer to as the end of the Holocene era (9,700 BC–c.1800) with its uncharacteristic

---

24   Ghosh, *Great Derangement*, 7, 16–19.
25   Franco Moretti, "Serious Century: From Vermeer to Austen," in *The Novel*, vol. 1, ed. Franco Moretti (Princeton, NJ: Princeton University Press, 2006): 372, 381, 381.

climactic stability compared to that of the previous Pleistocene era (2,588,000 BC–9,700 BC). The problem with gradualism as total explanation is that earth history contains many examples of evolutionary fractures caused by unpredictable geological and natural catastrophes. Nevertheless, the gradualist theory held sway until quite recently.[26] Ghosh, in line with Latour's "purification" thesis, sees this as a typical example of modernity's insistence on rendering other or older so-called "primitive" forms of knowledge obsolete. However, an acknowledgment of "both and neither" (Gould's formulation) as a more legitimate truth now seems to have reached consensus.[27] But if geological historiography has been forced by scientific evidence to accept improbable and exceptional events as narrative components, this does not apply, claims Ghosh, to the "serious" modern novel, which continues to hide its narrative scaffolding of exceptional moments.[28]

The rise to prominence of probability as aesthetic category in the modern novel and of gradualism in science converges with two other interdependent stories, both suggested by Ted Underwood with the help of collaborators, large text corpora, and digital tools. The first is the novel's gradual move away from biography in the period spanning from 1750 to 1950. Whereas biography is characterized by an emphasis on social generalization and collectivity, in novels we encounter a gradual specialization in "descriptions of bodies, physical actions, and immediate sensory perceptions in a precisely specified place and time." Whether this was formally achieved through Jane Austen's invention of a way to preserve the psychological closeness to the subjective world of the characters as Defoe and Richardson did, without resorting, as they also did, to fake autobiography (Ian Watt), or, a bit later, to making sight paramount as the nineteenth-century realists did (Peter Brooks), or, even later, through the decline in omniscient narration in the early twentieth century, Underwood says that this is not really important. These devices, however distinct and innovative they may be in their own historical moment, contribute to the same general move away from biography and toward narrowly focused descriptions of the appearance, activities, and perceptions of individuals.[29]

---

26 Examples of catastrophist theories that were initially met with skepticism or even rejection but are now widely accepted are Alfred Wegener's theory of continental drifts (1912) and Luis and Walter Alvarez's asteroidal theory of dinosaur extinction (1980).
27 Ghosh, *Great Derangement*, 19–22; Stephen Jay Gould, *Time's Arrow, Time's Cycle: Myth and Metaphor in the Discovery of Geological Time* (1987; London: Penguin, 1988), 191.
28 Ghosh, *Great Derangement*, 23.
29 Underwood, *Distant Horizons*, 26, 30–31.

The slow changes in the descriptive vocabulary of fiction, here characterized by an increased density of concrete diction, is closely connected with changes in pacing—that is, with changes in the relationship between time of narration and narrated time. This is the second story. Interestingly, an average page in an eighteenth-century novel often covered several days of action, whereas an average page in twentieth-century novels typically describes a period of only thirty to sixty minutes.[30] What does that tell us? It fits well with Ghosh's claim (based on the novel's actual historical development, not its inherent generic potential): "The *longue durée* is not the territory of the novel."[31] But there is more. The evolution of the novel shows a dramatic and continuous slowing down and contraction of its time span toward our present. Whereas Ghosh contrasts the limited temporality of the novel with the more unbounded temporal horizons of the epic, Underwood compares the evolution of the novel with that of biography. The latter shows a relatively stable curve between 1700 and 2000 in which an average page covers between a week and a month (more often the latter). Both epic and biography thus help to highlight the specifically singular evolution of the novel. Two things stand out: *concretization of individual perspective* and *contraction of narrated time*.

Before we proceed to discuss the spatial scale and specific works of literature, it is appropriate to consider whether there is a discrepancy, or even an incompatibility, between Andreas Malm's insistence on slow violence and Ghosh's preference for catastrophism? Malm seemingly determines that books and films are unsuited media for embracing and depicting the gradual accumulation and delayed consequences of human actions in the Anthropocene. For Ghosh, the issues are the novel's preoccupation with the regularity and slowness of the everyday and its forgotten potential to narrativize catastrophism and the unexpected. Can the two characteristics meet or are they contradictory? I would say the first. Malm's focus is on human history and the steady accumulation of past actions and their delayed and destructive effects striking us as "so many invisible missiles aimed at the future."[32] A work of fiction must be able to embrace this long history of accumulating missiles. If fiction is to depict a warming world, it should cover the entire Anthropocene era, if not more. If the large chunks of coal in train wagons at Barry Docks in 1920 have become invisible for us today, the task of contemporary fiction is to make us see them again in all their future-oriented destructive power. Although Malm's

---

30   Underwood, *Distant Horizons*, 28.
31   Ghosh, *Great Derangement*, 59.
32   Malm, *Fossil Capital*, 7.

focus is on the past, he does not forget the present and the future. They are the times the missiles strike.

The same holds true of Ghosh, only it is the other way around. Without neglecting the determining role of the past ("cumulative human actions"), Ghosh focuses on the present and future effects of global warming: "the freakish weather events of today, despite their radically nonhuman nature, are nonetheless animated by cumulative human actions." These events are potentially violent in the sudden, explosive sense; they are not everyday events, but unprecedented ("freakish"). The problem, says Ghosh, is that the unprecedented is becoming the norm: "it appears that we are now in an era that will be defined precisely by events that appear, by our current standards of normalcy, highly improbable: flash floods, hundred-year storms, persistent droughts, spells of unprecedented heat, sudden landslides, raging torrents pouring down from breached glacial lakes, and, yes, freakish tornadoes." Nineteenth-century realism depicted reality as regularity; today, reality threatens to become increasingly extraordinary on a daily basis. It follows that employing realist devices (backgrounding exceptional moments and foregrounding everyday details) to conjure up reality would ultimately be a concealment of the real.[33]

The two challenges faced by writers, encompassing a vast accumulative past comprising delayed effects and portraying these effects of potentially catastrophic character in the present and future, are not mutually exclusive; they only have different points of temporal emphasis and poetological requirements. But can these challenges be met? Or are works of literature inherently incapable of *longue durée* and catastrophism? Are there genres and forms better suited for these issues than others? Before answering these questions, we need to consider the role of space in the Anthropocene and fiction.

3.2   *Space, Discontinuity, Nation-State*

According to Ghosh, in contrast to the epic, the novel suffers from contraction, not only in time, but in space too. He draws on a long tradition here, including Benedict Anderson's argument about the close connection between the novel and the nation-state in *Imagined Communities* (1983), and further elaborated upon by Moretti in *Atlas of the European Novel* (1997). With unprecedented and highly improbable Hurricane Sandy fresh in his mind, Ghosh spends a few pages on discussing the problematic geographical locations of megacities such as Mumbai, New York, and Hong Kong and of nuclear power plants such as Fukushima Daiichi. What was the underlying episteme that allowed surveyors, cartographers, engineers, and politicians to disregard knowledge, experiences,

---

33   Ghosh, *Great Derangement*, 32, 24, 23.

and even warnings from the past, and then encouraged them to build cities and nuclear power plants on *naturally* dangerous sites close to the capricious sea or in earthquake-prone areas?

Ghosh's speculations made me recall the famous exchange between Voltaire and Rousseau following the Lisbon earthquake on November 1, 1755. Voltaire exhibited an increasing anger and pessimism in *Poème sur le désastre de Lisbonne* (1756), producing a vicious attack on Leibniz's idea of "le meilleur des mondes possibles" and Pope's dictum "Whatever is, is right." Rousseau maintained in the letter to Voltaire (August 18, 1756), which he wrote as a response to his poem, a more optimistic belief in a divine and universal order. One of Rousseau's main points was the social component of and the degree of human hubris and culpability in the disaster. Rousseau questioned the human habit of constructing twenty thousand houses of six or seven floors so close to one another and so close to the waterfront. He argued that the damage would have been much reduced if the inhabitants of Lisbon had been more equally dispersed and less densely housed. Rousseau also criticized human vanity and greed, which cost them their lives when, instead of seeking refuge immediately, they prioritized gathering their garments, money, and other material belongings.

In addition to a predatory hubris in relation to the planet and its resources associated with European Enlightenment thought, Ghosh points to "a habit of mind that proceeded by creating discontinuities," "a way of thinking that deliberately excludes things and forces ('externalities') that lie beyond the horizon of matter at hand: it is a perspective that renders the interconnectedness of Gaia unthinkable."[34] This same logic of spatial discontinuity is mirrored in the novel when its geographical scope is restricted to the nation-state or local settings that function as microcosmic models of the nation-state or larger regions. Following the principles of the probable and the real, the function of these settings is inevitably to emplace the reader and to evoke a sense of place, which means that connections to the wider world are often backgrounded. The novelistic setting often becomes "a self-contained ecosystem."[35] Ghosh's line of thinking ties in well with that of Ursula Heise to whom such systems are expressions of "ecolocalism" (as opposed to "eco-cosmopolitanism"), "an excessive investment in the local" (as opposed to "a deterritorialized environmental vision").[36] This contrasts with the epic, which is frequently characterized by

---

34 Ghosh, *Great Derangement*, 56.
35 Ghosh, *Great Derangement*, 61.
36 Ursula K. Heise, *Sense of Place and Sense of Planet: The Environmental Imagination of the Global* (Oxford: Oxford University Press, 2008), 9, 10.

the inclusion of multiple universes or settings and a spatial boundlessness. Novelistic universes owe their sense of being real precisely to their circumscription and particularity—think of Brittany in Balzac's *Les Chouans* (1829/1845), Faulkner's Yoknapatawpha County (Figure 32), and Gilead in Atwood's *The Handmaid's Tale* (1985)—although circumscription and particularity do not prevent the novels from synecdochally signaling larger geographies.

Ghosh claims that serious fiction shies away from representing the creation of the continents, just as it rarely refers to the passage of thousands of years. Connections and events on this scale are "absurd within the delimited horizon of a novel."[37] The problem for a novelist is that the Anthropocene is a world characterized by unrelenting and unavoidable spatiotemporal continuities, by effects and events triggered by forces that are quite simply immense because historically accumulated and geographically unbounded (Figure 33 and 34). The novel has historically sided more with Gilead than Gaia, more with June 16, 1904, than deep time.

Does it have to be like that? Are contraction and discontinuity inherent generic features of the novel, or is the genre elastic enough to transgress its hitherto *de facto* spatiotemporal boundaries? Is the novel able to go against the trend of the gradual decrease of narrated time documented by Underwood? As we are entering a post-Westphalian era of waning state sovereignty and increasing transnational traffic,[38] will the "serious" novel be able to follow us into this increasingly decompartmentalized era? Or are there other genres, for example the travelogue, science fiction, or the epistolary form, better suited for the Anthropocene?

3.3   *Human, Humans, Non-Humans*

There is an additional topic to discuss before initiating our analyses of the literary works. As noted, the so-called "serious" novels are most often characterized by a logic of probability as well as spatiotemporal contraction and discontinuity. This implies that the Anthropocene, defined as unthinkable events unfolding in a global, interconnected space and rooted in a protracted, accumulating time, cannot be an integrated part of these novels. In addition, the "serious" novel is also the genre of the *anthropos*. Inspired by Hegel's idea of the novel as the "modern *bourgeois* epic," Georg Lukács held that the modern novel from Cervantes and onwards is a biographical form focusing on the human individual. *Problematic subject* and *contingent (godless) world* make up

---

37   Ghosh, *Great Derangement*, 61.
38   Wendy Brown, *Walled States, Waning Sovereignty* (2010; New York: Zone Books, 2017).

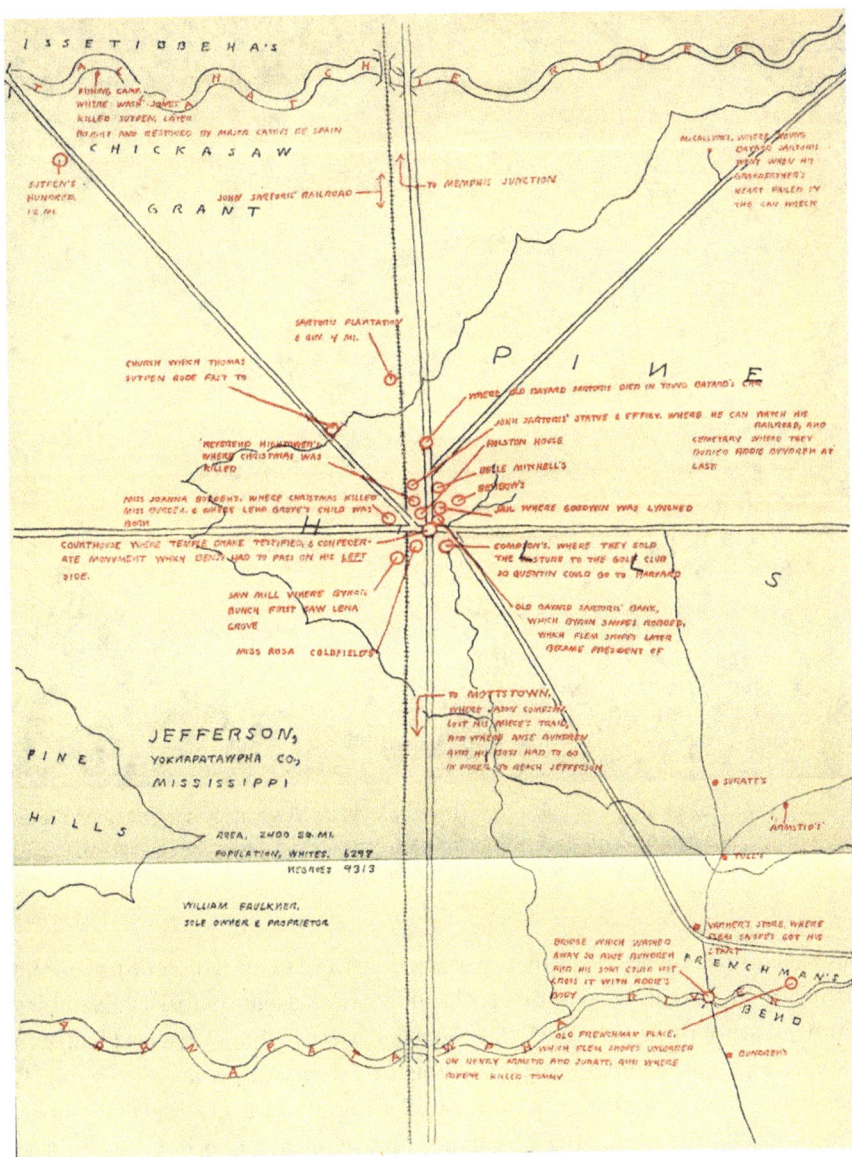

FIGURE 29   Yoknapatawpha County. The map, hand-drawn by William Faulkner, appeared at the end of the first edition of *Absalom, Absalom!* (New York: Random House, 1936)
ALBERT AND SHIRLEY SMALL SPECIAL COLLECTIONS. © UNIVERSITY OF VIRGINIA LIBRARY, CHARLOTTESVILLE, VIRGINIA

FIGURE 30   Geological time spiral. Joseph Graham, William Newman, and John Stacy, "The geologic time spiral: A path to the past," version 1.1, U. S. Geological Survey General Information Product 58, poster, 1 sheet

the skeleton of Lukács' early theory of the novel and in his later writings on the historical and realist novels, this anthropocentric baseline subsists. Examples from Lukács' writings include Walter Scott's *Waverley* (1814), Gustave Flaubert's *L'Éducation sentimentale* (1869), Leo Tolstoy's *Anna Karenina* (1873–77), J. P. Jacobsen's *Niels Lyhne* (1880), and Henrik Pontoppidan's *Lykke-Per* (1898–1904). These novels are characterized by an impressive social scope, but they are also circumscribed by a limited spatiotemporal boundary (a region, a city, a lifetime) and focused on the biography of the individual (Edward, Frédéric, Anna, Niels, Per).

More recently, Thomas Pavel has built on Lukács' early theory and reemphasized the importance of the human individual in the history of the novel: "By imposing a breach between characters and their surroundings, the novel is the first genre to reflect on the genesis of the individual and the establishment

FIGURE 31 The Blue Marble. Apollo 17 crew, "The Earth seen from Apollo 17," photograph taken by either Harrison Schmitt or Ron Evans on December 7, 1972, while Apollo 17 was en route to the Moon at a distance of about 29,000 kilometers

of a common morality."[39] Pavel's *La Pensée du roman* (2006), arguably the most impressive theory of the novel since Lukács and Bakhtin, is also carried by an anthropocentric idea.[40] And Ghosh, who subscribes to the premises of these theories without referring to them explicitly, sees a direct link between the novel's anthropocentrism and the beginning of the Anthropocene: "it was in exactly the period in which human activity was changing the earth's

---

39 Thomas Pavel, "The Novel in Search of Itself: A Historical Morphology," in *The Novel*, vol. 1, ed. Franco Moretti (Princeton, NJ: Princeton University Press, 2006): 3.
40 Thomas Pavel, *La Pensée du roman* (Paris: Gallimard, 2006).

atmosphere that the literary imagination became radically centered on the human."[41]

But if the human *in singular* has been the novel's main constituent in some of the most canonical novels and influential theories of the novel, where does this leave humans *in plural* such as "men in the aggregate,"[42] "the collective,"[43] and the "crowded canvas,"[44] and nonhumans such as whales, typhoons, seals, oceans, rocks, factories, deserts, mountains, forests, and ships? The Anthropocene may be animated by human actions (the epoch is a sign of our power), but whenever "nature" strikes back with a vengeance, it tells us that nature has a radically nonhuman character and is no longer mastered by a deified humankind (the epoch is just as much a sign of our impotence). Again, is the novel as a genre elastic enough to venture into a more disanthropocentric or multianthropocentric territory now that an awareness of the Anthropocene, of our own impotence or limited powers, and of the powers or agencies of nonhuman forces are on the rise?

The manner in which the modern novel has administered its dualistic structure of problematic subject and contingent world—that is, opting for an anthropocentric model emphasizing a fissure and hierarchy between the individual and the world (of institutions, things, and animals)—brings to mind Bruno Latour's definition of modernity in *We Have Never Been Modern* (1991). To Latour, modernity is first and foremost characterized by a practice (unacknowledged by the moderns themselves) of "partitioning" between the spheres of nature/science and society/culture. Supplementing this internal divide within modernity is an external divide between the moderns and the premoderns, between the practice of partitioning and a practice of overlapping. If the former is unacknowledged by the moderns, the latter represents the conception of the premoderns by the moderns. The external divide is defined by the moderns and their practice of partitioning.

A second important enterprise of modernity is "purification" that safeguards the sphere of nature from being entangled with that of society and ensures that only scientists have access to it. This initiates a countermovement in which culture laborers, writers for example, focus solely on human matters. Latour recounts reading a newspaper one morning: "Fortunately, the paper

---

41   Ghosh, *Great Derangement*, 66.
42   John Updike, "Satan's Work and Silted Cisterns," in *Odd Jobs: Essays and Criticism* (New York: Knopf, 1991), 564, quoted in Ghosh, *Great Derangement*, 77. The concept is employed as derogatory by Updike, but reclaimed as laudatory by Ghosh.
43   Ghosh, *Great Derangement*, 78.
44   Nixon, *Slow Violence*, 87.

includes a few restful pages that deal purely with politics [...], and there is also the literary supplement in which novelists delight in the adventures of a few narcissistic egos ('I love you ... you don't'). We would be dizzy without these soothing features. For the others are multiplying, those hybrid articles that sketch out imbroglios of science, politics, economy, law, religion, technology, fiction."[45] Tongue in cheek or not, Latour confirms Ghosh's idea of novels as egocentric contractions.

To Latour, the problematic consequence of these processes of modernity is an inability and unwillingness to properly deal with, genuinely accept, and fully accommodate what he calls hybrids and quasi-objects, phenomena that have increasingly come to define our present and which dominate news media, although they have always existed. Recent examples include holes in the ozone layer, dead whales washed ashore because of plastic blocking food from traveling from stomach to intestine, the production of the documentary *Leviathan*, the response to Covid-19, and global warming. These events are impure, compound entanglements that are constituted as networks in which knowledge, interest, justice, and power interact with the global and the local, the human and the nonhuman: "To shuttle back and forth, we rely on the notion of translation, or network. More supple than the notion of system, more historical than the notion of structure, more empirical than the notion of complexity, the idea of network is the Ariadne's thread of these interwoven stories."[46]

But is it really the case, as argued by Ghosh and to a certain degree by Latour, and as implied in canonized theories of the novel by Lukács and Pavel, that novels are constricted historically to human lifetimes and geographically to nation-states, narcissistically focused solely on the human individual and matters anthropocentric, thus seemingly incapable of spatiotemporal expansion and of handling hybrids, animals, things, and nonhumans? In *Les Travailleurs de la mer*, Victor Hugo navigates in geological time, evoking the slow rhythms of rock formations and the flux of atoms and particles. Nonhuman phenomena such as the steamship Durande, the ocean, and the sun are protagonists given importance equal to that of Gilliatt and Mess Lethierry and endowed with similar agentic potential. Melville's *Moby-Dick* is a composite novel in which human narcissism, megalomania, and perceptiveness are combined with natural history, whaling manual, and material culture, oscillating between the human life span and deep time, between the narrow space of the *Pequod* and the immensity of the seven seas. Limited in space to the village Macondo,

---

45 Latour, *We Have Never Been Modern*, 2.
46 Latour, *We Have Never Been Modern*, 3.

Gabriel Garcia Marquez's *Cien años de soledad* (1967) expands its narrated time to cover seven generations of the Buendía family, and like other novels in the magical realism genre, it excels in hybrids and quasi-objects blurring the boundaries between the natural and the cultural, the scientific and the imagined, the human and the nonhuman, and the profane and the sacred.

True. Novels that challenge the novelistic framework put forward by Ghosh and others can be found, but these are exceptions, not the rule. The initial reception of *Moby-Dick* underlines its status as an exception. The same is true of the publication history and critical reception of *Les Travailleurs*. The question of reception points to a possible divergence between the practices of writing and reading, between what novelists have written about (and how they have written about it) and what critics and scholars have focused on. Could it be that novels are far more extensive, hybrid, and nonanthropocentric than we have come to believe, and that it is interpretative preferences that have restricted their scope? I believe that both cases are legitimate. The novel has tended towards contraction, observation, and anthropocentrism, and *Moby-Dick* and *Les Travailleurs* are exceptions. Yet many novels, which have been read as examples of spatiotemporal discontinuity and egocentrism because of habit or critical trends, could benefit from being revisited with a new attention towards networks, imbroglios, and ecocentrism. Edward Said managed to complicate the image of Jane Austen as an author who wrote domestic novels by pointing to networks (perhaps not exposed by Austen, but nonetheless visible yet undiscovered by critics) of colonial economy unfolding between manor home and plantation, country and city, nation-state and empire in *Mansfield Park* (1815).[47] And Lawrence Buell challenged the view of Henry David Thoreau's *Walden; or, Life in the Woods* (1854) as being no more than an exemplary performance of Emerson's "self-reliance" and notion of "the age of the first person singular" by showing an intricate movement in both the published work and its genesis between egocentrism and ecocentrism, I and nature, poetic discourse and natural history, and Concord in the mid-1800s and universal history.[48]

As a gateway into the subsequent analyses, and as something that nicely wraps up the previous discussions of the novel and the Anthropocene, I will briefly look at differing reactions to a more recent work of so-called petrofiction, Abdel Rahman Munif's *Cities of Salt* (orig. *Mudun al-Milh*, 1984), a novel

---

47 Said, *Culture and Imperialism*, 80–97.
48 Lawrence Buell, *The Environmental Imagination: Thoreau, Nature Writing, and the Formation of American Culture* (Cambridge, MA, and London: Harvard University Press, 1995), 115–79.

(the first in a pentalogy) that portrays the oil industry in Arab countries. In *The Great Derangement* (2016), Ghosh compares his own 1992 assessment of the novel to two other reactions to Munif's novel: John Updike's review, entitled "Satan's Work," in *The New Yorker* on October 18, 1988 (immediately after the fatwa issued against Salman Rushdie for his novel *The Satanic Verses*), and Rob Nixon's analysis in *Slow Violence and the Environmentalism of the Poor* (2011), a text that generally informs Ghosh's further discussion of the novel as a genre.

In a striking passage, Updike expresses strong reservations about Munif's book:

> It is unfortunate, given the epic potential of his topic, that Mr. Munif ... appears to be ... insufficiently Westernized to produce a narrative that feels much like what we would call a novel. His voice is that of a campfire explainer; his characters are rarely fixed in our minds by a face or a manner or a developed motivation; no central figure develops enough reality to attract our sympathetic interest; and, this being the first third of a trilogy, what intelligible conflicts and possibilities do emerge remain serenely unresolved. There is almost none of that sense of individual moral adventure—of the evolving individual in varied and roughly equal battle with a world of circumstance—which since "Don Quixote" and "Robinson Crusoe," has distinguished the novel from the fable and the chronicle; "Cities of Salt" is concerned, instead, with men in the aggregate.[49]

The passage is striking for several reasons. First, the formulation "insufficiently Westernized" inevitably smacks of a colonial us-versus-them mindset that divides the world. "They" are doomed to failure when attempting to write in forms that have been developed and refined over centuries by Western authors. Second, and more relevant for our discussion, Updike presents a series of formal objections, most notably against narratorial voice and characterization, the former presumably having a tone too didactic and unsophisticated, the latter lacking profoundness and individuality. Third, it is remarkable how close Updike comes to repeating Lukács and anticipating Pavel with formulations like "the evolving individual in varied and roughly equal battle with a world of circumstance" and "individual moral adventure."

---

49   Updike, "Satan's Work," 76–77. The passage is also quoted by Ghosh and parts of it by Nixon.

In fact, Updike's verdict and reasonings point to a conception of the novel in line with the one that Ghosh has outlined in *The Great Derangement*, which features regularity, description, the individual human. But Ghosh then begins to change his perspective from *de facto* to *de jure*. First: "It is a fact that the contemporary novel has become ever more radically centered on the individual psyche while the collective—'men in aggregate'—has receded, both in cultural and fictional imagination." But then: "Where I differ from Updike is that I do not think that this turn in contemporary fiction has anything to do with the novel as a form: it is a matter of record that historically many novelists from Tolstoy and Dickens to Steinbeck and Achebe have written very effectively about 'men in the aggregate.'"[50]

Ghosh is a novelist and clearly a fan of the genre, but he has been frustrated by the paths taken by the novel at certain moments in its history, just as he problematizes the way it has been read and theorized by Western critics. Munif's *Cities of Salt*, Tolstoy's *War and Peace* (1869), Melville's *Moby-Dick*, and Émile Zola's *Germinal* (1885)—all classics, three of them "modern epics" as theorized by Moretti—prove that the novel is elastic enough to supplement regularity with *unexpectedness*, showing with *telling*, the human with the *nonhuman*, the individual with the *collective*, partitions with *networks*, and spatiotemporal contraction with *expansion*. As Nixon remarks about space in Munif and Updike:

> Updike's regionalism is internal to the nation and his imagination contoured to a particular strip and social stratum of America's northeast corridor, whereas Munif is a transnational regionalist whose imagination roams from Morocco to Iran. Munif's fascination with epic, tectonic convulsions is at the furthest remove from the assumed solidity—emotionally deep but geographically narrow—that Updike cites as his own creative foundation [his house, S.F.]. [...] Munif knew no such house. Imaginatively, he was housed and fed by homelessness; he never possessed a categorical nationality or a conclusive homeland.[51]

Cities of Salt challenges the conventional spatial contraction of many Western novels and sidesteps the processes of partitioning and purification characteristic of Western modernity. It operates with hybrids as it registers "the collisions (and collusions) between old religious cosmologies and new ones, between

---

50   Ghosh, *Great Derangement*, 78–79.
51   Nixon, *Slow Violence*, 88.

the preachers and the preachers of profit, between damnation or paradise in the afterlife and the satanic or redemptive possibilities created by an unearthly oil-rush."[52]

We are now well-equipped to analyze works of different aesthetic formats that share an interest in the ocean. First, we return to Aage Krarup Nielsen's travelogue, *En hvalfangerfærd* (1921); then I analyze J. G. Ballard's *The Drowned World* (1962), a science fiction novel about a solar cataclysm causing a rise in temperatures and sea levels; finally, I analyze Siri Ranva Hjelm Jacobsen's *Havbrevene* (2018), an epistolary novel consisting of letters between the Mediterranean Sea and the Atlantic Ocean. My primary focus will be on the relationship between the ocean and the Anthropocene and how this relationship is aesthetically mediated.

4   Exceptionalism, Growth, and Stock in *En hvalfangerfærd*

En hvalfangerfærd (A Whaling Voyage) was written at a time when the maritime world of ships, sailors, and their endeavors still captivated readers. Nielsen's combination of marine themes with accounts from harbor cities on different continents satisfied the early twentieth-century reader's curiosity regarding exotic places and people. However, traveling and writing for the first time in the decade of Conrad's death, Nielsen is aware of the transformation undergone by the maritime world during the previous decades: "We have long since gotten used to considering it a sad but undeniable truth that the romance and sense of glittering adventure, which surrounded sailor life in the old days, have practically disappeared nowadays. The steam engine and all the prosaic techniques that later followed have killed them." The passage is Conradian in its nostalgic longing for the old days acknowledged to be "irrevocably past." Nevertheless, Nielsen finds comfort in the fact that there still exists "a small spot on this mechanized and blasé earth where the expedition of ships across the world's oceans still means a voyage into the unknown and still possesses the adventure and excitement of those days— the month-long and vibrating uncertainty that comes with great risk and mighty chance."[53] Here, Nielsen anticipates what Conrad wrote in the March 1924 issue of *National Geographic*, the year of his death, about his childhood

---

52   Nixon, *Slow Violence*, 87.
53   Nielsen, *En hvalfangerfærd*, 7.

fascination with the "exciting spaces of white paper" on maps, "the blank of my old atlas."⁵⁴

En hvalfangerfærd employs the discourses of economy and natural resources and combines them with a laudatory approach to the traditions and contemporary conditions of Norwegian whaling. Nielsen writes from the colonial perspective of a white, European male, and some passages describing his encounters with citizens in Dakar and Rio de Janeiro would be considered racist today. His attitude towards sailors and ship life tends to be romantic. He recycles Fenimore Cooper's characterization of sailing ships as "majestic" to describe the steamship *Solstrejf*.⁵⁵ Like Conrad, Nielsen maintains a strong desire for the continued existence of competent seamanship. Unlike Conrad, he has an unsentimental relationship with whales. Conrad often sharpened his pen and tongue when confronted with the exploitation of natural and human resources. It left him with "the distasteful knowledge of the vilest scramble for loot that ever disfigured the history of human conscience and geographical exploration. What an end to the idealized realities of a boy's daydreams!"⁵⁶ Nielsen is rarely concerned about the effects of our vile scrambling for loot: "When the number of whales in the Arctic Ocean decreased severely as a result of intense hunting, new hunting grounds had to be searched for."⁵⁷ The matter-of-factness emphasizes the understanding that humans rank higher than animals, and when a spot on earth is emptied of its natural resources, humans can just move on to the next not yet exploited blank spot.

En hvalfangerfærd is not about climate change. Nevertheless, with our knowledge of the Anthropocene and its history, Nielsen's travelogue can be read as a text that registers the human activities and the mindset that have since been revealed as the root causes of the climate crisis and the mass extinction of species, both of which have already radically transformed our contemporary world and threaten worse. *En hvalfangerfærd* was composed prior to our awareness of the Anthropocene epoch, but it offers valuable insights into our current predicament by presenting us with a sliver of political and environmental history from around 1920.

With Andreas Malm we can say that the "many invisible missiles aimed at the future" are being produced and at work in *En hvalfangerfærd*. They may

---

54   Joseph Conrad, "Geography and Some Explorers" (1924), in *Tales of Hearsay and Last Essays, Collected Edition of the Works of Joseph Conrad* (1928; London: J. M. Dent and Sons, 1955), 13, 15.
55   Nielsen, *En hvalfangerfærd*, 11.
56   Conrad, "Geography and Some Explorers," 17.
57   Nielsen, *En hvalfangerfærd*, 7.

have been invisible to Nielsen and his contemporaries, but they have become visible to us today. The most significant missiles are the belief in *human exceptionalism*, the confidence in *capitalistic growth*, and the reliance on *nature as stock*. These attitudes come together in more concrete missiles: the burning of coal and the killing of whales. Another way of identifying the mechanisms governing the world view expressed in *En hvalfangerfærd* is to engage the three different geographical modes of thinking described by Conrad in "Geography and Some Explorers": 1) the speculative, fabulous geography, which dates back to "the mediæval mind playing in its ponderous, childish way with the problems of our earth's shape, its size, its character, its products, its inhabitants," 2) the militant, acquisitive geography beginning with the discoveries of the New World in 1492 and the Pacific Ocean in 1513, "an ugly tale" dominated by "reckless cruelty and greed" and peopled by "pertinacious searchers for El Dorado," and 3) the scientific, triumphant geography, which starts with James Cook's first voyage in 1768 and is governed by a quest for truth through experiment and hands-on experience.[58]

Nielsen constantly mobilizes the discourse of adventure by referring to hazards, risks, and the excitement of the hunt. This vocabulary is closely affiliated with Conrad's third geographical spirit. The explorers progress through trial and error, and the period is dominated by "a ruling passion expressed by outward action marching perhaps blindly to success or failure, which themselves are often undistinguishable from each other at first."[59] However, with its future-bearing missiles of human exceptionalism, capitalistic growth, and nature as stock, and despite Nielsen's attempts to link up with the world of the third geography, the scientific, *En hvalfangerfærd* belongs primarily to Conrad's second geographical spirit.

Conrad labels his second geography "militant." Kingdoms, states, and armies are concepts used by Conrad to characterize the second geographical spirit, yet monetary concepts play a more significant role in its vocabulary: "The voyages of the early explorers were prompted by an acquisitive spirit, the idea of lucre in some form, the desire of trade or the desire of loot, disguised in more or less fine words."[60] When comparing the Spanish and Portuguese motifs and principles with those of the earlier endeavors of the Basque whalers and the Vikings, Conrad's words echo Michelet's in *La Mer*: "They were more preoccupied with conquests to make and treasures to take than about proper discoveries." Michelet refers to the fact that the Portuguese replaced the "really bold

---

58   Conrad, "Geography and Some Explorers," 2, 4, 3, 10.
59   Conrad, "Geography and Some Explorers," 1.
60   Conrad, "Geography and Some Explorers," 10.

and genius" seaman Bartholomew Diaz with Vasco da Gama, "a great lord of the king's house, and, above all, a soldier." Plunder surpasses adventure, even in the case of Magellan: "A discount on pepper was the primitive inspiration behind the most heroic voyage ever made on this planet."[61] In Nielsen's travelogue, financial gain also take priority over military acquisitions and the spirit of adventure. *En hvalfangerfærd* subscribes to a *monetary* geography.

However, we can be more precise. In the beginning of "Geography and Some Explorers," before distinguishing between the three geographies, Conrad discusses the differences between geometry and geography. Although geography has had its extravagantly speculative phase, its primary formal expression is the map, grounded in the forms of experiential, phenomenal reality since the end of medieval times. In contrast, geometry's primary formal expression is the shape, founded in an ideal world of "accurate operations" able to spawn "a long array of precise, no doubt interesting, and even profitable figures" that are based on "exact configuration."[62] To Conrad, both geometry and geography are sciences, but one is a science of the desk, the other a science of the deck. In addition to being less a militant than a monetary geography, *En hvalfangerfærd* has a scientific impulse that is not so much geographical as it is *geometrical*. Admittedly, *Solstrejf* carries two scientific explorers, Mr. Cope and Mr. Wilkins, who are heading for the Pole on an expedition whose purposes are mapping territories and the migration routes of whales and observing their reproductive conditions, but they are also hopeful of establishing goldmines and coalmines in the future. Apart from being infiltrated with "the idea of lucre," the scientific work of Cope and Wilkins takes up little space in the travelogue, which upholds a steady attentiveness to money matters.

Nielsen describes Larvik, Tønsberg, and Sandefjord as "home for nearly the entire industry that has brought back huge values to Norway, and which owns such proud old traditions and memories of bold and competent seamanship." On its route, *Solstrejf* stops in Cardiff, Dakar, Rio de Janeiro, and Montevideo, and after four and a half months in the Antarctic and nine months away, the whaler returns to Larvik a few days before the Norwegian national day on May 17, 1921. The space covered in the travelogue is a maritime space that transcends national territory. However, it could also be argued that Nielsen expands the Norwegian territory all the way into the Antarctic Circle: "there is not an ocean where Norwegian whalers have not at some point hunted."[63] The narrative structure of home-away-home constitutes a movement from the familiar to

---

61   Michelet, *La Mer*, 283, 285.
62   Conrad, "Geography and Some Explorers," 1.
63   Nielsen, *En hvalfangerfærd*, 7, 8.

the unknown and back again. This circularity, which implies a domestication of the unknown, supports the idea of human mastery of nature and space and signals success. In *En hvalfangerfærd*, there is no Moby Dick to overpower crew and ship, no typhoon to initiate de-anthropocentrism, no astral cataclysm to off-set biological devolution. Like Conrad's third geography, it is a story of triumph. But the triumphalism is not genuinely scientific; instead, it is monetary, buoyed by a geometrical mentality of numbers, figures, and precision. Such a mentality distances humans from the alive-and-kicking, phenomenal world of nature and animals, and it strengthens the idea of human exceptionalism.

The world depicted by Nielsen is agonistic and competitive. Those who catch the most whales and collect the most sperm oil in the shortest time get the greatest rewards. They come in kroner, up to 15 million for a full cargo of oil when prices were at their highest: "Day and night, the oil—a glistening bold and still running stream—is pumped down into the large tanks of the ships. All 1,100 men divide and calculate and fantasize about gold and the moon." The market is sensitive and sometimes unpredictable, but companies and crews can generally rely on larger quantities to equal larger income. Speed matters, too, since every day and hour count: "The day is not counted in hours, it is counted in 'whales,' and the week is not counted in days, but in 'oil barrels.'" Every delay is a source of distress: "For the large whaleships it would mean disaster to be stuck here for a longer period of time. In a short while the hunting begins down there on the ground, it only lasts a few months, and during these months whales worth many millions must be caught. Each day wasted means a heavy loss."[64]

Financial gains and losses are constantly weighed up to calculate anticipated profits. During an unplanned stop in Rio due to technical problems, it is decided to load the coal there instead of in Montevideo: "We'll take the missing 2,500 tons of coal in Rio while the repair work is done, in order to save four days in Montevideo, despite the fact that the coal in Rio costs about 140,000 kroner more, so one can understand how much four days earlier arrival to the hunting ground is estimated." The cost of the entire whaling expedition, prices for the ships excluded, is estimated at around 20–30 million kroner, but the prospective value of a full cargo is between 60 and 70 million kroner. One blue whale is worth an average of 15,000 kroner, but whales have been caught whose oil value amounted to 50,000 kroner. During a typical season in the period of Nielsen's voyage with *Solstrejf*, 4,000 whales are caught, resulting in around 200,000 barrels of sperm oil (Figure 35). As Nielsen dryly notes, the

---

64   Nielsen, *En hvalfangerfærd*, 77, 73, 17.

FIGURE 32 Whaleboat with a good catch. Image printed in *En hvalfangerfærd*

value of a human life down here "is worth a lot less between brothers than a blue whale."[65] For a doctor, this results in primitive working conditions.

---

65 Nielsen, *En hvalfangerfærd*, 55, 74.

After almost nine months, Nielsen can settle the accounts: "We return home with the largest oil cargo that *Solstrejf* has ever managed during its twelve years as a whaler. We know nothing about how things have been 'on earth' during the months we have been down there, but we are full of beautiful hopes in regard to the value of our cargo. A year ago, it would have amounted to 10–11 million kroner, and why should the price not be as good this year?" One more record has been set. A shooter has killed ninety-nine blue whales. With a combination of fixed minimum wages and performance pay, a reward system is in place that promotes a geometric-numeric exploitation of nature: "It is a healthy and sensible principle that makes the ground rather barren in relation to Bolshevik semen. Here people work hard and energetically, but they are also paid fairly and generously. Everyone comes to feel as a shareholder in the enterprise."[66] This passage from the travelogue underlines the vision of capitalist growth, and with its focus on collectivism (here, driven by money, not by bolshevism), it also signals a formal difference from the individualism of the "serious" novel.

En route to the Antarctic whaling grounds, *Solstrejf* visits Dakar on the west coast of Africa. Here, as in Rio, Nielsen leaves the ship and enters the city where he resumes his anthropological tasks of meeting and talking with locals and visitors, registering the distinctive customs and traditions of the place, tasting the local food, traveling on the public buses, visiting institutions, and, not least, writing about it all: "Strange characters appear here in Dakar and disappear again to another spot on the globe just as suddenly as they arrived, or for some inexplicable reason, they get stuck on this random spot of Africa. Vagrant destinies whose adventure and experiences could provide enough material for many a novel where the author would not have to add anything but the chapter titles."[67] In this passage, Nielsen shows a metafictional awareness of the formal difference between the novel and the travelogue, the former committed to conveying the adventures and experiences of individual destinies, while the latter—as a result of its anthropological and documentary purpose—can focus on collectives (say, a crew) and the mechanisms of an industry (say, whaling). Nielsen does employ novelistic strategies such as the narrative structure of home-away-home, but his travelogue distances itself from the use of individual protagonists and shies away from the otherwise ubiquitous theme of love in novels.

If the adventure discourse requires certain typical plot devices—suspense, action, encounters with exotic otherness—these devices are transplanted

---

66   Nielsen, *En hvalfangerfærd*, 106–07, 73.
67   Nielsen, *En hvalfangerfærd*, 30.

from an individual level of self-discovery to an anthropological level of communal interest. In that sense, and bearing in mind the characteristics of the Anthropocene and Ghosh's concern with the individualistic narcissism of the "serious" novel, there are elements immanent to the travelogue format, for example a legitimate commitment to portraying an industry without being obliged to install a centripetalizing human protagonist, that allow Nielsen to register what we are able to see today as some of the collective, hybrid mechanisms—the burning of coal and killing of whales in the whaling industry around 1920—that eventually led to our current predicament of threatening climate changes and the sixth mass extinction.

However, if the adventure discourse in the travelogue format allows Nielsen to move away from individualism, it is still a discourse that supports an anthropocentric vision of human exceptionalism. There are plenty of passages in *En hvalfangerfærd* lauding human enterprises. As mentioned, there is no Moby Dick in the travelogue, but there is a blue whale acting almost as clever and cocky as the legendary sperm whale. The difference is that the Norwegian whalers succeed where Ahab never did. They eventually kill the whale. Also, when the engine is close to breakdown, Nielsen informs us that "It is a very difficult and seldomly competent piece of work that has been achieved here, and 'Master' and his men, who have now for several days worked hard at it, have the right to be proud of the result." At the end of the voyage, accounts settled, Nielsen supplements the monetary discourse with a chivalric one concluding that the men have "accomplished their duties in a dignified manner." Finally, he claims in the afterword that he has been proven right in his previous prophecy about the Norwegian whalers "not letting themselves be cowed by dark days and times of adversity."[68] *En hvalfangerfærd* is a eulogy to Norwegian whalers, to their audacity, skills, and solidarity, and to the whaling industry's acquisitive and monetary spirit.

During the stopovers in Dakar and Rio, Nielsen reflects on the level of financial development, infrastructural adeptness, and productive efficiency regarding natural resources. Back home, the fruit dealer "carefully weighs a small, bumped banana and notes that it weighs for exactly 0,28 kroner," while a few miles outside Rio there exists "millions of wonderful fruits rotting because nobody bothers to pick them." And while the infrastructure in Rio with its impressive freeways extending for hundreds of kilometers enable people to visit beautiful locations, "there exists in the interior of the country values worth millions, which cannot be exploited because there still are no roads

---

68   Nielsen, *En hvalfangerfærd*, 39, 107, 113.

and railroads."[69] This acquisitive gaze, here in the form of "the desire of loot" and natural resources, is a constant in Nielsen's travelogue, most pertinent of course in the chapters on hunting on the whaling grounds of Antarctica.

There are moments when Nielsen pauses to wonder if or when the natural resources will come to an end. If Melville dismissed the idea of whale extinction because he could neither imagine the degree of human population growth nor the speed or degree of technological development, Nielsen shows a genuine concern, especially with the consequences of technology for the stock of whales. There is an indecisiveness as to whether nature is too fecund to let human exploitation disturb its processes or is vulnerable to a degree that such exploitation could ultimately lead to species extinction. The temporal distance between the 1921 text and the 1935 afterword is significant. In 1921, Nielsen seems generally undisturbed by the efficiency of their enterprise in regard to number of whales killed. Instead, he sees it as a cause for celebration: "Everywhere the ocean abounds with these wonderful Giants, and throughout the whole day the entire whaling fleet tows one rich prey after the other back to the motherships [...]. One sees boats crawl slowly into the harbor towing as many as eight large whales, and at bow and stern, even at buoys in the harbor, entire flotillas of slain whales are moored."[70]

Nielsen describes the hunt in detail and is concerned with the suffering of the whales in situations where the exploding grenade does not kill the whale immediately. His solution is telling: "Inevitably, the idea emerges—for both humane reasons and practical considerations—that it must be possible to construct a grenade that besides its explosive contained a sufficient quantity of a fast-acting toxin so as to kill or at least paralyze the animal in a matter of moments, and without making the oil useless."[71] There are two important distinctions here; considerations both humane and practical at stake. Clearly, the latter trumps the former. The second distinction supports this. The whale can be killed in two ways by the new grenade, either ruining the oil or saving the oil. The latter again trumps the first. The principle of killing whales is not questioned; what worries Nielsen is only the way in which it is done. The worry is ultimately a monetary-geometrical concern about efficiency, and "for humane reasons" is only a positive side effect. Not killing whales at all is not considered an option.

The degree of concern with species extinction increases in the 1935 afterword in which Nielsen has an opportunity to look back on the development

---

69   Nielsen, *En hvalfangerfærd*, 49.
70   Nielsen, *En hvalfangerfærd*, 77.
71   Nielsen, *En hvalfangerfærd*, 93.

in the whaling industry over the last fourteen years. It is "staggering" in terms of "the dividends from the hunt" and "the utilization of the whales."[72] Again, the development is primarily numerical, an increase in number (barrels, tonnage, whales, territory etc.). Their catch of 4,000 whales in 1920–21 had increased ten years later to 25,000 killed whales. Seven boiling stations grew to twenty-eight, and they also doubled or tripled in size. Twenty-five whale boats became 150. The 1,000–1,100 Norwegian whalers increased to 10,000 whalers in 1930–31, and the 200,000 barrels ten years earlier had increased to 2,250,000 barrels.

The downside was that supply outgrew demand. The whaling industry had overproduced massively. The world market could not buy such large quantities: "To continue with this unlimited slaughtering of whales and overwhelming production of oil would sooner or later and inevitably lead to the ruin of companies and the extinction of whales." This is quite an acknowledgment. It comes on the book's next-to-last page, in an afterword published fourteen years after the first edition. Something had happened. Expansive growth on all fronts. It is worth noticing that it is monetary consequences of overproduction that leads Nielsen to speculate about species extinction. Would this question have been raised at all if the market could have absorbed the increased amount of oil? The solution was a one-year pause after which the Norwegian companies agreed upon a quota system ultimately resulting in annual productions about half the size of the 1930–31 season, which is still more than a million barrels of oil and more than 10,000 killed whales per year. This means, as Nielsen puts it, "that Norwegian whaling once again rests upon a more healthy and solid foundation even though profits are only modest compared to those of the golden days."[73]

The technological development led to a decrease in experiential quality and the disenchantment of sailor life. Nevertheless, Nielsen concludes on a triumphant and anthropocentric note:

> But there is one thing that even the most complete technology has not been able to change: To this day, the activities of the gigantic boiling stations in the Antarctic involve the admirable efforts of the hardy and dauntless seafarers—the dizzying risk and great chance. To this day, the hunt for whales—the whale boats' race with the ocean's snorting and diving giants, to the moment when the canon blazes—comprises

---

72 Nielsen, *En hvalfangerfærd*, 113.
73 Nielsen, *En hvalfangerfærd*, 116, 116.

the same quivering excitement. To this day, a whaling voyage is the big adventure.[74]

Nielsen's last word refers to the book's initial passages and underlines the travelogue's continuous commitment to an anthropocentric triumphalism mediated through the discourse of adventure.

En hvalfangerfærd is dominated by a *monetary geography and geometrical scientific impulse*. From the perspective of the Anthropocene, this worldview plays a significant role in the creation of three future-bearing missiles in the concrete forms of human exceptionalism, capitalistic growth, and nature as stock. The possible effects of these missiles, as seen from within the contemporary framework of the Anthropocene, come in the forms of climate change (the burning of coal) and mass extinction (the killing of whales).

...

During the twentieth century, maritime fiction as we have come to understand it through the models of Melville and Conrad withdrew even more from the literary scene. With the advent of the steamship and the motorship, life at sea became increasingly routinized and safe, and authors gradually lost interest in maritime life. Air traffic was the new mode of transportation. Although the flight cabin never replaced the ship as a microcosmic setting of interest in literature, aviation contracted the globe and reoriented the attention of authors towards the new and closer connections between faraway landbased localizations such as the world's great metropolises. A direct heir to the oceanic ship, understood as a circumscribed space floating upon limitless space, emerged with the spaceship, a favorite topos in science fiction.

It would be wrong to claim the total disappearance of the maritime and the ocean from post-Conradian literary history. If we survey that history, we see an interesting development in which authorial interest in the ocean splits into *two directions*. One is the continuation of the Melvillean and Conradian models of portraying sailor life on board ocean-going ships. But since this model has lost its attraction in relation to contemporary sailors and ships, these novels are all historical and often nostalgic. Authors who followed this direction include Aksel Sandemose, Patrick O'Brien, Pär Lagerkvist, Jens Bjørneboe, William Golding, Carsten Jensen, and Amitav Ghosh. The other direction is literature whose primary subject matter is not sailor life and whose primary setting is not

---

74   Nielsen, *En hvalfangerfærd*, 117.

the ocean-going ship. The author is not interested in the ocean as a medium for human endeavors, exploits, and industry. Instead, the author's attention is on the ocean as a planetary, often punishing, apocalyptic force of nature beyond human control. This type of literature is often dystopic, often set in the future, and writers include J. G. Ballard, Stephen Baxter, Kassandra Montag, Maja Lunde, and Siri Ranva Hjelm Jacobsen. Kevin Reynolds' *Waterworld* (1995) and Roland Emmerich's *The Day After Tomorrow* (2004) are filmic examples. If maritime fiction in its prime from Fenimore Cooper to Conrad was set mainly in the present, in the post-Conrad era it is set either *nostalgically in the past* or *dystopically in the future*. In the former, the ocean is a scene of human industry; in the latter, seawater is transformed into a climatic effect. In both cases, maritime fiction comments on the challenges of contemporary society.

5   Psychohydrographies of Cataclysm in *The Drowned World*

J. G. Ballard is one of the usual suspects when literary critics, scholars, and fellow writers, among them Ghosh, list novelists who have successfully engaged with climate change and the Anthropocene. In Ballard's case, this happened decades before the popularization of the concept of the Anthropocene, which means he is often ascribed a prophetic gift. Ballard, though, prefers to see himself as "an investigator and a sort of early warning system" instead of a prophet.[75] This makes sense because of the strong resonances between *The Drowned World* (1962) and contemporary scholarly predictions of rising sea levels and "worst-case scenario" floodings. Ballard's drowned world—a world characterized by extremely high temperatures and a sea level rise that has inundated the first six storeys (50–60 feet) of the Ritz Hotel in London—corresponds to a world that many present-day readers imagine to be a likely near-future postapocalyptic global-warming scenario.

However, there is an important difference between Ballard's world and our world. In the novel, human activities in the form of extensive burning of fossil fuel are not the cause of the temperature rises that have melted the polar ice caps and caused sea levels to climb. Instead, climate change in *The Drowned World* was initially catalyzed by "a sudden instability in the Sun" some 60 or 70 years ago leading to a "series of violent and prolonged solar storms lasting several years." These storms then "enlarged the Van Allen belts and diminished

---

75   J. G. Ballard, "Reality is a Stage Set," interview by Travis Elborough, *The Drowned World* (1962; London: Fourth Estate, 2014), 177.

the Earth's gravitational hold upon the outer layers of the ionosphere. As these vanished into space, depleting the Earth's barrier against the full impact of solar radiation, temperatures began to climb steadily, the heated atmosphere expanding outwards into the ionosphere where the cycle was completed." Later, a second cataclysm happened when the "entrained ice-seas of the Antarctic plateau broke and dissolved, tens of thousands of glaciers around the Arctic Circle, from Greenland and Northern Europe, Russia and North America, poured themselves into the sea, millions of acres of permafrost liquefied into gigantic rivers."[76] From the first page, the reader is introduced to a world, which is postapocalyptic, but not posthuman—yet. *The Drowned World* unfolds in a setting that reflects some of the likely *effects* of the Anthropocene (rising temperatures and sea levels), whereas its *causes* (human activities such as gas emissions and deforestation) play no role. Ballard *imagines the possible psychobiological effects of the geophysical and hydrophysical effects.*

As opposed to many contemporary cli-fi novels, *The Drowned World* neither engages in climate blame games nor in discussions of how to reverse the processes, how to mitigate the situation, and who should manage such tasks. Ballard devotes only two pages to the past which is understood as the progression of accumulative causes behind the two "gigantic geophysical upheavals."[77] These upheavals, resulting in extreme heat and flood waters, just happened—abruptly, accidentally, and without human intervention. They happened first on an astrophysical scale (solar storms), then on a geo- and hydrophysical scale (melting of polar ice), and the processes they set in motion are irreversible and unpreventable. Consequently, the planet is exiting one ecological model and entering a new one. Ballard leaves it at that and directs his interest towards this question: What are the evolutionary and psychological consequences in the present and in the future for humans and for planetary life as such and their ability to adapt to the new ecological paradigm? But if the past understood as an accumulation of anthropogenic climate-destructive missiles aimed at the future—that is, the role of the past in the Anthropocene—is of no interest to Ballard, the past nevertheless occupies a crucial role in his novel. On the one hand, the past is an *evolutionary past* from which all life forms descend; on the other hand, the past is also an *evolutionary outcome* to which future developments shall ultimately return us (more on this enigmatic claim to come).

The Drowned World is set sometime around 2045 in what used to be London, a city now flooded, abandoned, and morphed into tropical lagoons and jungles.

---

76   J. G. Ballard, *The Drowned World* (1962; London: Fourth Estate, 2014), 21, 22.
77   Ballard, *Drowned World*, 21. I supplement Ballard's "geophysical" with "hydrophysical" because of water's important role in the novel.

It is a world often haunted by fierce storms and heavy rainfall, teeming with vegetation, insects, mammals, reptiles, amphibians, and submarine creatures. The lagoon has been overtaken by fungus, moss, gymnosperms, fern-trees, Mato Grossos, massive olive-green fronds, Sargasso weed, and orange-sized berries. Huge flies, giant Anopheles mosquitos, and colonies of wolf spiders coexist with large hammer-nosed bats and marmosets as well as with iguanas, snakes, lizards, crocodiles, alligators, basilisks, and caimans. Occasionally, the lagoon smells of dead vegetation and rotting animal carcasses, and the entire setting resembles "a confounded zoo." Birdlife seems to be less plenteous, probably because of the sun's relentless force, although we do hear about some "sentinel birds, Nile plover and stone curlew."[78] Throughout the novel Ballard makes references to a series of geological periods, epochs, and eras (and does not always attribute these concepts correctly): the Paleozoic era, the Carboniferous period, the Pennsylvanian period, the Triassic period, the Mesozoic era, and the Paleocene epoch.

A scientific survey unit consisting of researchers and military personnel has been sent to the area around London. The majority of them are installed at a base station, and the scientists—two biologists, Dr. Kerans, the protagonist, and Dr. Bodkin—perform their work at a testing station. The military, commanded by Colonel Riggs, is there to patrol the region and chart locations such as harbors and keys that might once again become geopolitically important in the future. The scientists' task is to carry out environmental research in the form of mapping the alterations in flora and fauna and analyzing "the emergent lines" of their recent evolution. The underlying purpose is to be better able to adapt to the new world. After having worked their way northward across the European lagoons for three years, six months of which have been spent in inundated London, the group have been told to return to their more permanent base, Camp Byrd, in the Arctic. Apart from the Antarctic, this is the only region still sufficiently hospitable for human habitation: "Apparently the water-level is still rising; all the work we've done has been a total waste—as I've always maintained, incidentally," Colonel Riggs tells Dr Kerans.[79] All other regions of the planet are flooded and too hot.

The cast of *The Drowned World* is all male except for Beatrice Dahl, the friend and lover of the novel's protagonist. Dr. Robert Kerans resides in a luxury penthouse suite at the former Ritz Hotel, whereas Miss Dahl resides in the apartment in which she grew up. The novel is told by a third-person narrator

---

78 Ballard, *Drowned World*, 17, 86.
79 Ballard, *Drowned World*, 8, 15.

and combines descriptions of the evolutionary processes in the postdiluvian nonhuman environment with a plot comprised of weird human actions and explorations of the psychological transformations of the main characters. *The Drowned World* is a complex meditation on time. Each of the three discursive components carry different temporalities: of preservation or transformation, of progression or regression, of linearity or cyclicality, and of fragmentation or continuation.

Ballard's interest in human psychology has led many scholars to claim the primacy of inner space over outer space in his fiction.[80] In interviews and essays, Ballard often seems to support such a view: "The dream worlds invented by the writer of fantasy are external equivalents of the inner world of the psyche," he claims in "Time, Memory and Inner Space" (1963).[81] However, we should be careful of such a ranking, because as Thomas S. Davis rightly remarks, "it is impossible to reduce *The Drowned World*'s version of species transformation to the merely personal as it loops psychology, biology, and geology over and into one another."[82] I will add hydrology to Davis' three concepts. Ballard's fiction, including *The Drowned World*, is preoccupied with the dynamics of the inner worlds of its characters, but it constantly demonstrates a strong reciprocity between the physical environment and the human psyche. While the quote from "Time, Memory and Inner Space" may be read as if the physical landscapes and seascapes of his books are mere projections of psychological landscapes, Ballard's fiction shows the relationship between them to be, if not actually inversed, more complicated (in the etymological sense of them being *folded together*, entangled, intertwined). In the same essay, Ballard evokes memories of his childhood in a flooded Shanghai thus implying that experiences of such extraordinary (hydro)physical environments have had a deep impact on his mental and imaginative life.

It must be emphasized that Ballard in *The Drowned World*, and also in other early works such as *The Drought* (1965) and *The Crystal World* (1966), is preoccupied with the relationship between an extraordinary environment, often characterized by cataclysmic events, and how humans respond psychologically to the new situation. Exterior geo- and hydrophysical processes infect interior psychological processes. His concept of "inner space" refers not to pure interiority or psychological depth but to what is often referred to in *The*

---

80   See for example Jim Clarke, "Reading Climate Change in J. G. Ballard," *Critical Survey* 25, no. 2 (2013): 16.
81   J. G. Ballard, "Time, Memory and Inner Space," in *The Drowned World*, 184.
82   Thomas S. Davis, "Fossils of Tomorrow: Len Lye, J. G. Ballard, and Planetary Futures," *Modern Fiction Studies* 64, no. 4 (Winter 2018): 673.

Drowned World as a "zone of transit," a relay mediating between the inner world of the mind and the outer world of reality. If preservation of the human species presupposes and necessitates a dichotomous and unrelenting antagonism between humans and nature, the "zone of transit" introduces a transformative and hybrid model to humans comprising the dimensions of geology, hydrology, biology, and psychology, a model characterized by metabolism, entanglement, and exposure. It is no coincidence that "most of the people still living on in the sinking cities were either psychopaths or suffering from malnutrition and radiation sickness."[83] Here, Ballard lists effects of psychological, biological, hydrological, and geological origin.

Ballard's rising seawater is a material element in an outer world which, combined with increasing temperatures, generates a biological evolution that really is a devolution. Ballard's drowned world is on track to return to a second Triassic period, a posthuman world in which an evolutionary reboot will happen sooner or later: "The steady decline in mammalian fertility, and the growing ascendancy of amphibian and reptile forms best adapted to an aquatic life in the lagoons and swamps, inverted the ecological balances," and as "Kerans sometimes reminded himself, the genealogical tree of mankind was systematically pruning itself, apparently moving backwards in time."[84] On the path to this new beginning, minor signs of temporal reversal supporting the devolutionary design show up. While Kerans shaves in front of a mirror, the narrator informs us that although he was forty, because of chemical processes his appearance was that of someone ten years younger. Also, the timing device on Beatrice's generator runs backwards. As we shall see, a similar (d)evolutionary reboot scenario is presented in *Havbrevene*, although without the Ballardian interest in the psychodynamics of the human species.

---

83   Ballard, *Drowned World*, 12.
84   Ballard, *Drowned World*, 23. Ballard refers to the transition between the Permian and the Triassic geological periods as well as between the Paleozoic and Mesozoic eras. The transition marked the Permian-Triassic extinction event, also called the End-Permian Extinction and colloquially known as the Great Dying, which happened approximately 252 million years ago (see also the Graham-Newman-Stacy time spiral above). It is planet Earth's most severe known extinction event, with up to 96% of all marine species and 70% of terrestrial vertebrate species becoming extinct. It was also the largest known mass extinction of insects. Some 57% of all biological families and 83% of all genera became extinct. The exact causes are difficult to establish, but it is likely that both catastrophic and gradual processes contributed: the first include one or several major bolide (meteor) impact events, increased volcanism, and sudden release of methane from the sea floor, while the second comprise sea level change, increasing ocean anoxia (oxygen depletion), and increasing aridity (drought). See "Permian-Triassic extinction event," accessed January 28, 2020, https://en.wikipedia.org/wiki/Permian–Triassic_extinction_event.

The watery world also has an inner equivalent that fluidizes the inner selves of the characters and sets them in regressive motion to their individual childhoods—"Perhaps these sunken lagoons simply remind me of the drowned world of my uterine childhood"—and earlier, to the beginnings of organic life, by reconnecting them with the Rolland/Freudian "oceanic feeling": "Kerans felt, beating within him like his own pulse, the powerful mesmeric pull of the baying reptiles, and stepped out into the lake, whose waters now seemed an extension of his own blood-stream. As the dull pounding rose, he felt the barriers which divided his own cells from the surrounding medium dissolving, and he swam forwards, spreading outwards across the black thudding water ..."[85] The barriers upholding the distinctions between the preconscious, the conscious, and the unconscious in Kerans' inner world dissolve, as do the barriers that separate him from the outer world.

The quote also illustrates my assertion that in Ballard the past is ultimately an evolutionary outcome of future developments. Christopher Daley and Nicholas Ruddick consider *The Drowned World* to be more indebted to the theories of psychoanalysis and surrealism than to the theory of evolution with its implications of deep time. To them, the novel is a reaction to the closing down of the past as an avenue of human interest following the invention of nuclear weaponry.[86] The post-1945 threat of nuclear extinction undoubtedly played a vital role in transforming the future from an open field of potentialities into a *cul de sac*. Time as such, also Darwin's geological time, became irrelevant in the face of total destruction. Ballard's novel has a nuclear age mood. We hear of solar radiation storms and biological mutations. However, planetary wipe-out due to the detonation of atomic bombs is not compatible with Ballard's drowned world, a world that continues in the form of what we now call Anthropocene scenarios of (futile) human struggles in extreme environmental conditions.

In contrast to Daley and Ruddick, I argue that Ballard collapses the future into familiar vistas of the deep past (of geological time). The future, understood as clocks moving forward, is directed towards the past, understood as evolution moving backward: "we are re-assimilating our own biological pasts."

---

85 Ballard, *Drowned World*, 28, 71.
86 Christopher Daley, "The Not So Cozy Catastrophe: Reimagining the British Disaster Novel in J. G. Ballard's *The Drowned World* (1962) and Brian Aldiss's *Barefoot in the Head* (1969)," in *Apocalyptic Discourse in Contemporary Culture: Post-Millennial Perspectives on the End of the World*, eds. Monica Germanà and Aris Mousoutzanis (New York and London: Routledge: 2014): 138; Nicholas Ruddick, *Ultimate Island: On the Nature of British Science Fiction* (Westport, CT: Greenwood Press, 1993), 155.

Evolution is, ultimately, *devolution*. When Kerans exclaims, "Is there any point? We know all the news for the next three million years,"[87] it is a realization of a closed future and an anticipatory insight into a geological-biological reset. It is precisely under circumstances such as a watery and warming world that different temporal avenues, including geological time, become worthy of Ballard's reexamination. Sigmund Freud and Max Ernst are important for understanding Ballard's vision of a twofold crisis of the human and the nonhuman world, but so is Charles Darwin.

A fundamental dilemma for the characters who are able to reflect on their predicament more deeply, is whether to fight for species *preservation* (a familiar plot for readers of apocalyptic fiction) or to embrace species *transformation* (arguably, one of Ballard's most recurring trademarks).[88] As a means of preserving the human species, a return to Camp Byrd in the Arctic Circle, more specifically in Northern Greenland (Colonel Riggs's choice), is one option. Remaining at the Ritz Hotel, as Kerans, Beatrice, and Bodkin choose to do at first, is another. The freebooter Strangman, who enters the lagoon with his motley crew of multi-colored castaways and semi-domesticized alligators, represents a third model of preservation. Staying at the Ritz to survive would probably have a shorter time frame for success than the options chosen by Riggs and Strangman, but Camp Byrd and constant roaming are ultimately short-term fixes as well, unable to withstand the pressures of the astral upheaval and the environmental extremities. Kerans knows this. In *The Drowned World*, the Holocene human is unfit for the post-Holocene (Anthropocene) planet. We know it too, because the first sentence of the novel informs us immediately: "Soon it would be too hot."[89]

If none of these three options—remaining in the lagoon, returning to Camp Byrd, or freebooting in the flooded European cities—are viable solutions to species preservation, what is? The short answer is nothing. Species preservation is ultimately impossible in *The Drowned World*. When, in the final lines of the novel, Kerans is likened to "a second Adam searching for the forgotten paradises of the reborn sun," we are not to interpret this as a new beginning, or a second chance for humanity. Rather, it signals a fundamental metamorphosis of the human species and the eventual extinction of humans in their current form. Kerans has gradually come to accept this. In contrast to Colonel Riggs and Strangman, who cling to the preservation of species, the reoccupation of lost cities, and the maintenance of old systems, displaying what Beatrice labels

---

87 Ballard, *Drowned World*, 91, 15.
88 Davis, "Fossils of Tomorrow," 671.
89 Ballard, *Drowned World*, 7.

"a total lack of adaptability,"[90] Kerans realizes the inevitable and chooses to face the reality of species transformation and eventual annihilation.

If Kerans' acceptance of species transformation is not a real choice because of the inherent evolutionary determinism, he has nevertheless *embraced* it and come to terms with it as a given:

> His time there had outlived itself, and the air-sealed suite with its constant temperatures and humidity, its supplies of fuel and food, were nothing more than an encapsulated form of his previous environment, to which he had clung like a reluctant embryo to its yoke sac. The shattering of this shell, like the piercing doubts about his true unconscious motives set off by his near drowning in the planetarium, was the necessary spur to action, to his emergence into the brighter day of the interior, archaeopsychic sun. Now he would have to go forward. Both the past, represented by Riggs, and the present contained within the demolished penthouse, no longer offered a viable existence. His commitment to the future, so far one of choice and plagued by so many doubts and hesitations, was now absolute.[91]

When the narrator refers to past, present, and future, they are to be understood from Kerans' perspective. To Kerans, the past (Riggs and Camp Byrd) and the present (the lagoon and a demolished Ritz penthouse suite) are no longer viable models for living; only moving forward into the future (traveling south) is. As mentioned, this personal route into the future is simultaneously a transspecies pathway into deep time.

Lieutenant Hardman's case serves as an illustration of what is in store for Kerans as he moves further south and further into Triassic deep time. Hardman shows signs of physical-biological metamorphosis due to an adjustment of his metabolism. Early on, we learn that his "tough self-sufficiency [...] was as strong as ever, if anything stronger," that he has a "large-jawed face," and that "there was little sweat on his face and bare chest" despite the heat. Later, when Hardman disappears and Riggs and his crew chase him, he "swung himself like an acrobat down the drain-pipe to the parapet below," and then they "saw Hardman swinging around the banisters four floors below, hurling himself from one landing to the next in a single stride." The connotations with apes are obvious. He is also likened to "a wounded water-buffalo." Towards the end

---

90   Ballard, *Drowned World*, 175, 80.
91   Ballard, *Drowned World*, 147.

of the novel when Kerans stumbles upon a barely human Hardman, his hand resembles "a skeletal green claw" and "a crab." Hardman eats "voraciously," is reduced to a memory-less organism sensitive to the sun's rays and pestered by flies. His language has regressed to the military simplicity of giving disconnected orders. Hardman's physical-biological devolution, like that of Beatrice Dahl, who at one point looks "like a sleeping python,"[92] is paralleled by a psychological-biological transformation mirroring the external landscape of the early Triassic period.

Kerans' realization that staying at the Ritz is futile and that he needs to head south has been underway for quite some time, initiated by his introduction to Bodkin's theory of Neuronics, the central nerve system (CNS), and archaeopsychic time, as well as his first experience with the dream that Beatrice, Bodkin, Hardman, and half of the crew have all experienced before him. Even before these events, Kerans compares the growing isolation and self-containment of the others with "all animal forms about to undergo a major metamorphosis" and likens his own state of being to "a careful preparation for a radically new environment, with its own internal landscape and logic, where old categories of thought would merely be an encumbrance."[93]

The pretext for Bodkin's explanation of his theory (arguably the most science fictional passages in the novel as the they are passages of scientific theory and discourse, but they are fictional, not factual) to Kerans is the latter's correct summing up of their work during the last three years, a work involving the examination of five thousand species in the animal kingdom and tens of thousands of new plant varieties: "Well, one could simply say that in response to the rises in temperature, humidity and radiation levels the flora and fauna of this planet are beginning to assume once again the forms they displayed the last time such conditions were present—roughly speaking, the Triassic period."[94] Bodkin agrees:

> Everywhere the same pattern has unfolded, countless mutations completely transforming the organisms to adapt them for survival in the new environment. Everywhere there's been the same avalanche backwards into the past—so much so that the few complex organisms which have managed to retain a foothold unchanged on the slope look distinctly anomalous—a handful of amphibians, the birds, and *Man*. It's a curious thing that although we've carefully catalogued the backward journeys of

---

92 Ballard, *Drowned World*, 38, 36, 64, 65, 65, 170, 171, 173, 25.
93 Ballard, *Drowned World*, 14.
94 Ballard, *Drowned World*, 42.

so many plants and animals, we've ignored the most important creature on this planet.[95]

Bodkin does not suggest the possibility of a complete reversal of the biological process nor that humans are regressing into Cro-Magnons.

His intuition is that it is not only the external landscape that is changing. The déjà vu sensations felt by crew members, of recognizing and of remembering the swamps and lagoons, are examples that support Bodkin in his belief that humans carry within them "innate releasing mechanisms literally millions of years old, which have lain dormant through thousands of generations but retained their power undiminished." Our instinctive loathing of spiders and fears of snakes and reptiles are because "we all carry within us a submerged memory of the time when the giant spiders were lethal, and when the reptiles were the planet's dominant life form." Bodkin's point is that the innate releasing mechanisms (the IRMS) are not just mental processes, but timecodes "carried in every chromosome and gene. Every step we've taken in our evolution is a milestone inscribed with organic memories."[96]

There is an analogy here between Freudian psychology (the individual) and Bodkinian/Darwinian evolutionary theory (the species); in Ballard's novel the latter trumps the former:

> Just as psychoanalysis reconstructs the original traumatic situation in order to release the repressed material, so we are now being plunged back into the archaeopsychic past, uncovering the ancient taboos and drives that have been dormant for epochs. The brief span of an individual life is misleading. Each one of us is as old as the entire biological kingdom, and our bloodstreams are tributaries of the great sea of its total memory. The uterine odyssey of the growing foetus recapitulates the entire evolutionary past, and its central nervous system is a coded time scale, each nexus of neurones and each spinal level marking a symbolic station, a unit of neuronic time.[97]

Bodkin claims that moving progressively down the central nervous system corresponds to descending into the neuronic past.

Each physical segment, such as a junction between two vertebrae, represents concrete evolutionary transitions. These transitions are hybrid structures in

---

95   Ballard, *Drowned World*, 42.
96   Ballard, *Drowned World*, 43, 43, 43.
97   Ballard, *Drowned World*, 43–44.

which geological, hydrological, biological, physical, and psychological processes are entangled:

> I am convinced that as we move back through geophysical time so we re-enter the amnionic corridor and move back through spinal and archaeopsychic time, recollecting in our unconscious minds the landscapes of each epoch, each with a distinct geological terrain, its own unique flora and fauna, as recognisable to anyone else as they would be to a traveller in a Wellsian time machine. Except that this is no scenic railway, but a total reorientation of the personality. If we let these buried phantoms master us as they re-appear we'll be swept back helplessly in the floodtide like pieces of flotsam.[98]

As the environment changes in *The Drowned World*, several of the characters experience a pull towards a different world recognized by most of them to be a world of the deep past. It is as if the sun transmits the sound of a beating pulse into Kerans and the others. They become increasingly self-immersed, defying a logic of anthropocentric rational action: "The light drummed against his brain, bathing the submerged levels below his consciousness, carrying him downwards into warm pellucid depths where the nominal realities of time and space ceased to exist. Guided by his dreams, he was moving backwards through the emergent past."[99] It is important not to confuse this self-immersion with a mere psychological state. The new geo- and hydrophysical conditions activate layers of deep time memories, neuronics, which are encoded in the characters' neurological and genetic structures. The invention of a complex and speculative scientific theory, here a theory on Neuronics, is a literary device often associated with the genre of science fiction. In *The Drowned World*, it enables Ballard to represent evolutionary movement in form of slow change and deep time as concentrated in one individual.

The Drowned World is a novel of barrier transgressions and dissolutions. It is fascinated by the concept of One in the Many, or the One that connects the Many. With art as medium, the novel promotes correspondences between inner and outer, as when Kerans "strolled over to look at the painting by Ernst at the far end of the lounge, while Bodkin gazed down at the jungle through the window. More and more the two scenes were coming to resemble each other,

---

[98] Ballard, *Drowned World*, 44–45.
[99] Ballard, *Drowned World*, 83.

FIGURE 33   Max Ernst, *Europe After the Rain II* (1940–42)
© WADSWORTH ATHENEUM, HARTFORD, CONNECTICUT

and in turn the third nightscape each of them carried within his mind."[100] The outside world is mirrored in the painting's world is mirrored in the inner world.

Underlying evolutionary variety and distinction are elements that traverse distinctions. Water plays a crucial role. The outer world is flooded, the air is humid, and the former cities are submerged under seawater. At one point, Kerans wishes that he could "walk straight down into the water, dissolve himself." Deeper than the personal level of the human unconscious exists a species level of a common mnemonic ocean mirroring the external flooded world: "A more important task than mapping the harbours and lagoons of the external landscape was to chart the ghostly deltas and luminous beaches of the submerged neuronic continents," also referred to as "the amniotic paradise." Ballard also invokes the uterine state of the foetus as a phase comparable to humanity's shared sea of deep time. When Kerans dives into the old planetarium he nearly drowns. The building is associated with a uterus, and when Kerans' lungs fill with water, he senses a strong connection with the sea of deep time, "the soothing pressure of the water penetrating his suit so that the barriers between his own private blood-stream and that of the giant amnion seemed no longer to exist."[101] It is as if Ballard insists upon the destruction of highly developed forms, among them humans, in order for the planet to be able to regenerate. It is suggested that human minds are faster at adapting to the speed of devolution and at reconnecting with deep time than human bodies are.

---

100   Ballard, *Drowned World*, 81.
101   Ballard, *Drowned World*, 56, 45, 70, 110.

5.1 Science Fiction and the Anthropocene

If the "serious" novel is to remain relevant in the Anthropocene, according to Ghosh, the challenge is whether or not it can break free of a series of formal-aesthetic restraints that sedimented during the nineteenth century: probability, lifetime, nation-state, the individual. Science fiction is a genre potentially more aligned with the Anthropocene than the "serious" novel. Instead of the regularity of bourgeois life filled with predictable, uneventful everyday events, science fiction revolves around the extraordinary and speculative. In his classic study, Darko Suvin describes the constitutive elements of sci-fi as being "*radically or at least significantly different from the empirical times, places, and characters* of 'mimetic' or 'naturalist' fiction." As a result, the genre estranges the reader cognitively. To Suvin, this "attitude of estrangement [...] has grown into the *formal framework* of the genre," and he elaborates by drawing attention to sci-fi as a fictional discourse that employs factual strategies: "The effect of such factual reporting of fictions is one of confronting a set normative system—a Ptolemaic-type closed world picture—with a point of view or look implying a new set of norms; in literary theory this is known as the attitude of *estrangement*." To him, estrangement is both an underlying attitude (vision) and a dominant formal device (detached, defamiliarizing point of view), both cognitive and creative. It is creative because the cognitive potential of science fiction is not so much linked to its reflection *of* reality as to its reflection *on* reality, and because its approach to reality valorizes dynamic transformation rather than static mirroring. Consequently, science fiction is critical, rooted in reason and doubt: "In the twentieth century SF has moved into the sphere of anthropological and cosmological thought, becoming a diagnosis, a warning, a call to understanding and action, and—most important—a mapping of possible alternatives."[102]

The estrangement often hinges upon a technological invention, a scientific theory, or a remarkable event that at the time of composition transgresses the achievable, the state of the art, or the plausible respectively.[103] In *The Drowned World*, the fictional universe owes its strangeness, a flooded planet, to an implausible unstableness in the sun. That life on the planet seems, implausibly, to be regressing biologically is explained by Bodkin's theory of neuronics. Neither the implausible event nor the implausible theory is completely

---

102 Suvin, *Metamorphoses of Science Fiction*, viii, 7, 6, 12. Suvin's concept of estrangement draws on Skhlovskij's *ostranenie* and Brecht's *Verfremdungseffekt*.
103 These observations are mine. Suvin downplays the roles of science and the future (to him, they are merely two themes out of the many other themes), and instead links cognitive estrangement to *locus* and/or *dramatis personae*.

unthinkable; indeed, it is essential that they can be "perceived as *not impossible* within the cognitive (cosmological and anthropological) norms of the authors epoch."[104] Ballard seems in alignment with Suvin when he claims that good science fiction morphs into bad science fiction when "the stuff isn't won from experience."[105] The insistence of "a strange newness, a *novum*," that produces estrangement sets science fiction apart from naturalist or empiricist fiction as it developed from the eighteenth century to the twentieth century with its "ideal extreme of exact recreation of the author's empirical environment." It is then the "*not impossible*" aspect combined with sci-fi's view on norms as being historical and variable—its cognitive dimension—that contribute to differentiating science fiction from adjoining literary forms such as myth, fairy tale, and fantasy despite their shared opposition to naturalist or empiricist literature.[106] Sci-fi takes off from an empirical environment characterized by cognitive laws (as opposed to myth, folk (fairy) tale, and fantasy), but then it pursues this environment's variable and future-bearing elements, which always comprise the alternative-fostering question "What if?" (as opposed to naturalist-empiricist fiction).

Sci-fi novels are often less restricted to short time spans and narrow spaces than "serious" novels. This is due in part to their commitment to wonder in the form of machines, universes, or events. In Jules Verne's *Vingt mille lieues sous les mers*, the invention of the *Nautilus* allows access to a planetary submarine space in which national borders are meaningless. In H. G. Wells's *Time Machine* (1895), the Time Traveller invents a machine for travelling through the fourth dimension and uses it to venture into the distant future. In *The Drowned World*, there is no invention of a complex machine, but the implausible event of solar storms and the subsequent flooding of the planet create a fluid planetary space in which the landbased national-territorial borders and the maritime boundaries just beyond their coastlines become negotiable or are eliminated. Although set in primarily London, important locations in the Arctic and the Antarctic as well as in southern Europe contribute to the transnationalization of the novel's space. The solar storms and the flooding also cause processes of devolution, and combined with the theory of neuronics, this warrants a temporality beyond human lifetimes. Although the action unfolds over just a couple of months, Ballard introduces additional temporal

---

104 Suvin, *Metamorphoses of Science Fiction*, viii.
105 J. G. Ballard, "Science Fiction Monthly Interview," interview by David Pringle and Jim Goddard, *Science Fiction Monthly*, January 4, 1975, accessed January 31, 2020, https://www.jgballard.ca/media/1975_jan4_science_fiction_monthly.html.
106 Suvin, *Metamorphoses of Science Fiction*, 3–4.

planes, most notably the deep past and a future that has an uncannily resemblance to this deep past.

Science fiction novels resemble "serious" novels in their interest in individual biographies. Liu Cixin's *The Three-Body Problem* (2006/2008), categorized as hard science fiction, is a Chinese novel of immensely vast temporal and spatial scope excelling in the art of complicated plots defying summary. Despite the presence of a large number of characters, the novel's narrative attention is primarily directed towards Ye Wenjie, an astrophysicist, and Wang Miao, a professor in nanotechnology. In Ursula K. Le Guin's *The Left Hand of Darkness* (1969), the author explores human life on several planets, but the plot revolves around one main character, Genly Ai, a resident of planet Terra, who is sent to Gethen, another planet, in order to persuade the nations of Gethen to join the Ekumen, a loose federation of planets. In *The Drowned World*, Ballard zooms in on Robert Kerans, a biologist, with only a few other characters playing significant roles in the plot.

One major difference between the characters of "serious" novels and science fiction novels is their varying degrees of singularity and generality. The history of the novel is characterized by a development towards individualization and concretization. Despite their individual qualities, attributes, and traits, the characters in sci-fi often transcend their own individuality and become representatives of universal principles or humanity as such. This is partly a result of sci-fi being "a basically allegorical mode,"[107] partly a result of the transformation of the fictional universe from an unremarkable naturalist world into a strange world often characterized by urgency. If the everyday life of the outer world is one of regularity, authors naturally direct their attention towards the protagonists and their uniqueness. When the outer world is out of joint, authorial attention is redirected to more transpersonal and nonhuman challenges. This is why Kerans will not only be remembered by readers as the biologist living in a Ritz penthouse suite, who was erotically engaged with the aloof and stylish Beatrice Dahl, and who performed as Neptune in a staged incarnation while having the head of a freshly decapitated alligator pressed down over his human head. These singular traits, surreal in their juxtaposition, are to some extent surpassed by Kerans' role as *representative* of the principle of species transformation, as someone who leads by example when he embraces the annihilation of the human species as we know it. What is more, the nonhuman, in the form of water, winds, light, vegetation, and animals, plays a vital

---

107   Ballard, "Science Fiction Monthly Interview."

role in *The Drowned World* and generally contributes to de-anthropocentricize the Ballardian universe.

The poetics of Ballard's sci-fi novel, some of them inherent in the genre, meet the criteria proposed by Ghosh for novels to be capable of representing the Anthropocene. In Ballard's drowned world, the unthinkable becomes real and the extraordinary becomes everyday. Although Ballard does not ascribe past human activities to the extreme climate changes that have transformed the planet in *The Drowned World*, the novel opens up immense vistas of time and space in which the causes and effects, some astrophysical, some geo- and hydrophysical, others psychological or biological, of the environmental cataclysm can be explored. If Ghosh found the novel's occupation with individual moral adventure insufficient when facing a warming world, Ballard finds ways to supplement its subscription to a traditional biographical format. First, the characters become carriers of urgent ethical principles, for example preservation or transformation, just as they become vehicles for exploring transindividual psychobiological processes. Second, the nonhuman is granted massive power in *The Drowned World*. Astral processes caused temperatures to rise, which subsequently led to planetary flooding. Humans could not but accept the cataclysmic metamorphosis of the environment. Situated in that environment, they still cling to their scientific and geopolitical habits of mapping and surveying, to their preferences for foie gras and Beethoven, and to their ideas of individual autonomy and anthropogenic agency. Each in their own way, Riggs and Strangman are the two characters who most strongly represent the belief that humans can continue to inhabit the planet and even reoccupy the lost European cities. But they are wrong for two reasons: temperatures and sea levels continue to rise and will eventually result in the uninhabitability of even the Arctic and Antarctic Circles, and the human species is in the process of a fundamental psychological, physical, and biological transformation corresponding to the astrophysical, hydrophysical, and geophysical changes in their environment.

It sounds bleak. It even brings to mind nihilism and fatalism. It certainly seems dystopic, but it isn't, at least not to Ballard and Kerans. Reminiscent of Pope's "Whatever is, is right," of Leibniz's "le meilleur des mondes possibles," and also of Rousseau's modification of Voltaire's ironic "Tout est bien" into "Le tout est bien, ou tout est bien pour le tout," Kerans' final words, which are conveyed in letter form to any future reader on the novel's last page, tell us so: "All is well."[108] *The Drowned World* is a utopia disguised as a dystopia. Thirteen

---

108 Ballard, *Drowned World*, 165.

years after the publication of *The Drowned World*, Ballard had the opportunity to look back and reflect upon his work in an interview with David Pringle and Jim Goddard:

> People seem to imply that these are books with unhappy endings, but the reverse is true: they're books with happy endings, stories of psychic fulfilment. The geophysical changes which take place in *The Drought*, *The Drowned World* and *The Crystal World* are all positive and good changes—they are what the books are about. The changes lead us to our real psychological goals, so they are not disaster stories at all. [...] In a sense, all these are cataclysm stories. Really, I'm trying to show a new kind of logic emerging, and this is to be embraced, or at least held in regard.[109]

The "new kind of logic" is what Suvin refers to as "a *novum*" and "a new set of norms," which produces cognitive estrangement. Later in the interview, Ballard expands on his earlier comments:

> In *The Drowned World*, the hero, Kerans, is the only one to do anything meaningful. His decision to stay, to come to terms with the changes taking place within himself, to understand the logic of his relationship with the shifting biological kingdom, and his decision finally to go south and greet the sun, is a totally meaningful course of action. The behaviour of the other people, which superficially appears to be meaningful—getting the hell out, or draining the lagoons—is totally meaningless. The book is about the discovery by the hero of his true compass bearings, both mentally and literally.[110]

Ballard asks quite a lot of us. While Kerans experiences an epiphany on the personal level, this epiphany has implications for the human species level. The biological, physical, and psychological transformations happening to Kerans are positive, says Ballard, and of great intensity, but it would be naïve to think that they—especially the biophysical processes—can keep pace with the devolutionary processes taking place in the geophysical and hydrophysical environments and in the animal kingdom. Sooner or later, the human species will die out in Ballard's drowned reptilized world. To Ballard, and considered

---

109 Ballard, "Science Fiction Monthly Interview."
110 Ballard, "Science Fiction Monthly Interview."

5.2 Surrealism and the Anthropocene

Ballard was fascinated with surrealism. He found inspiration in principles common to both surrealist literature and painting, more specifically in the worldly visions in paintings by Max Ernst (Figure 33) and Paul Delvaux (Figure 34 and 35) and by the style and choice of words in Jean Genet and Alfred Jarry. Surrealism is another aesthetic strategy that furnishes his novels with a poetics different from that found in the "serious" novel. Surrealism is sci-fi's sister. Through the fusion of dream images and expressions emerging from the unconscious with the logic of empirical reality, surrealism is also defined by and employs formal devices that promote an underlying attitude of estrangement. One surreal device is the startling juxtaposition of distant realities: "the somber green-black fronds of the gymnosperms, intruders from the Triassic past, and the half-submerged white-faced buildings of the 20th century still reflected together in the dark mirror of the water, the two interlocking worlds apparently suspended in some junction in time, the illusion momentarily broken when a giant water-spider cleft the oily surface a hundred yards away."[111] Like science fiction, but unlike myth, fairy tale, and fantasy, surrealism is grounded in cognitive laws from the empirical outer world but supplements them with cognitive laws of our inner world. Ballard considered the exploration of human psychology under the circumstances of cognitive estrangement (say, a flooded world) to be his original contribution to the evolution of the sci-fi genre. Surrealism provided an arsenal of aesthetic strategies that were necessary for him to realize his vision. This vision comprises the entanglement of inner and outer, of psychohydrographies, and of the entanglement of past, present, and future, of psychotemporalities, as in the quote above in which the colorful Triassic period and white modernity are superimposed.

Ballard's style merges some of the potent aesthetic devices of surrealism. He uses language evocatively to create estranged psychohydrographies that are intensely visual. He has been compared to Conrad, especially in relation to *The Drowned World*, and although Ballard had not read Conrad before writing the novel, the comparison is valid. They share a belief in the entanglement of environment and psychology, a fascination with psychohydrography, realized as Martin Amis has aptly said of Ballard's poetic style "in a prose style of hypnotically varied vowel sounds":[112] "Golden waves glimmered up into the

---

111   Ballard, *Drowned World*, 10–11.
112   Martin Amis, "Introduction," in *The Drowned World*, 5.

boiling air, and the ring of massive plants around them seemed to dance in the heat gradients like a voodoo jungle."[113] If one slows down the tempo of reading Ballard's words and sentences, detailed images of moving colors and light and even imaginings of smells and tastes are certain to surface.

If the Ballardian psychohydrography in *The Drowned World* has a lot in common with Max Ernst's *Europe After the Rain II* with its intense colors and baroque fractal forms (Figure 33), there is also a fascination with whiteness in the novel. As indicated, the colors are associated with "jungle time," the Triassic past re-emerging in the present. In opposition to this colorful world, Ballard evokes a world dominated by whiteness and represented by Strangman, twice referred to as a "white devil."[114] If Ernst surrealistically captures the visual qualities of the drowned world, it is Delvaux whom Ballard promotes as the painter of his world's whiteness. In her apartment, Beatrice has a painting by Ernst and one by Delvaux on her wall. The Ernst painting strongly resembles *Europe After the Rain II*, whereas the Delvaux tableau comprising half-naked, ashen-faced women, and dancing skeletons wearing tuxedos is probably a merging of several Delvaux paintings such as *Sleeping Venus* (1944) (Figure 34), *Ecce Homo* (1949) (Figure 35), *The Break of Day* (1937), and *The Awakening of the Forest* (1939).

Other elements in the novel fall into the category of whiteness. An albino python is one among several creatures associated with Strangman's uncanny albino radiance. Apart from Strangman's, perhaps the most significant whiteness is expressed by Kerans in response to Strangman's pride as he shows off all his treasures—"a huge ornamental altarpiece," "a dozen pieces of statuary," "stacks of heavy gilt frames," "triptychs," "an intact pulpit," "statues," "cathedral doors," "a large tiered marble fountain" etc.—plundered from the museums, cathedrals, private mansions, and public institutions in the old European cities: " 'They're like bones,' he said flatly." In a world in which human preservation, reoccupation, and agency were not delusions, Strangman's endeavors would be cause for exhilaration, praiseworthy efforts to salvage relics symbolizing the high points of human civilization. But they *are* delusions. Seen from the perspective of the near future (which is also the deep past), the relics are mere "fossils of tomorrow." This is why Strangman is regarded as greedy, not noble. Through Delvaux, Kerans sees him as he really is: "Kerans nodded, watching Strangman in his white suit, the bare-legged Beatrice beside him. Suddenly he remembered the Delvaux painting, with its tuxedoed skeletons. Strangman's

---

113   Ballard, *Drowned World*, 16–17.
114   Ballard, *Drowned World*, 134, 158.

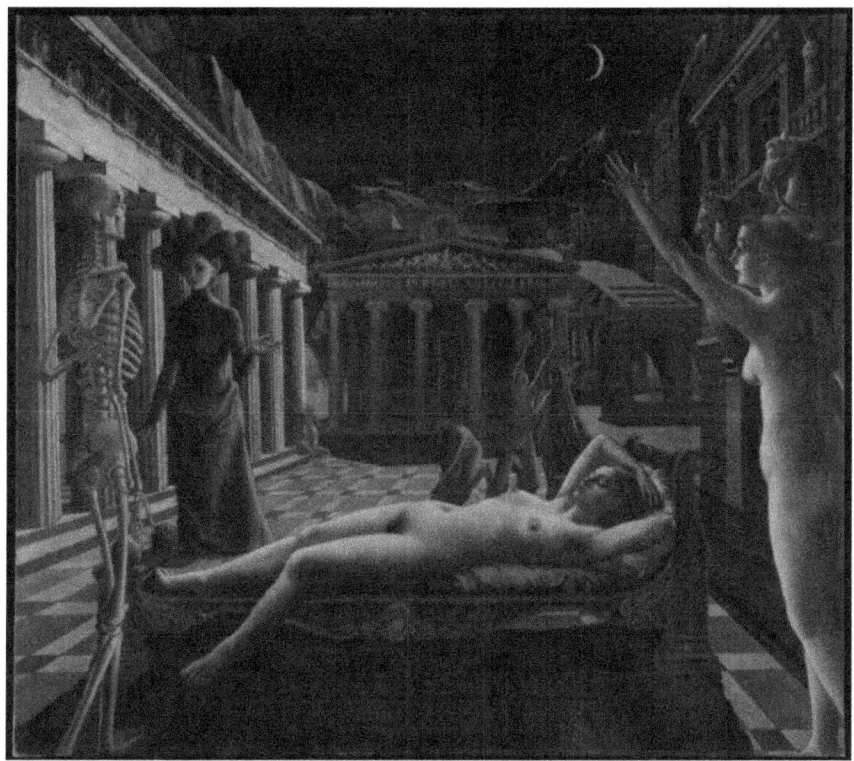

FIGURE 34   Paul Delvaux, *La Vénus endormie* (1944). Presented by Baron Urvater 1957. Tate
© FONDATION PAUL DELVAUX, ST. IDESBALD, BELGIUM/DACS, LONDON 2020

chalk-white face was like a skull, and he had something of the skeleton's jauntiness."[115] In *The Drowned World*, the *memento mori* motif underlines the connection between whiteness, civilization, modernity, and death.

Hydrography and geography are important in the novel, especially the North-South axis. There are entire imaginaries associated with the Poles and the North and with the Equator and the South. As civilization has developed, it has simultaneously migrated northward toward the Arctic region. Here, it has become associated with whiteness, cooling, and mere preservation, with ice, bones, and death. Kerans' southward migration is not accidental. It is a movement away from stagnation and towards the sun—into heat, light, and life, but not life as we currently know it. In *The Drowned World*, the sun represents a vitalist utopia, a Dionysian principle of metamorphosis that dissolves humans

---

115   Ballard, *Drowned World*, 95, 94.

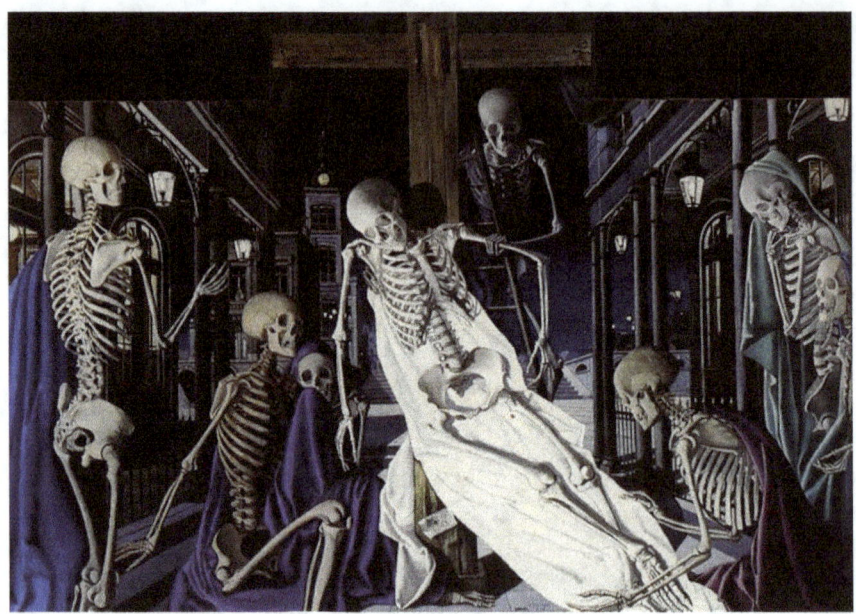

FIGURE 35   Paul Delvaux, *Ecce homo* (1949).
© FONDATION PAUL DELVAUX, ST. IDESBALD, BELGIUM, C/O PICTORIGHT AMSTERDAM 2022

and triggers an evolutionary acceleration during which all forms and barriers liquefy. It is through this evocation of the great dissolve (Alaimo), the *Ursuppe* (Michelet, Serres), that Ballard prepares the conditions he believes to be necessary to restart planetary life.

Ballard achieves his vision through literary devices associated with surrealism such as startling juxtapositions of words or images and the entanglement of inner and outer worlds. His poetics combines elements from science fiction and surrealism in a way that produces cognitive estrangement. This is applied to explore cataclysmic scenarios that did not seem possible when written. Decades later we would label them extraordinary, but not impossible, events of the Anthropocene era.

6   Empire of Thalassa in *Havbrevene*

In Siri Ranva Hjelm Jacobsen's *Havbrevene*, Gaia may constitute the underlying foundation of the planet, but the puppet master, the one pulling the actual strings, is Thalassa, the primeval female spirit and embodiment of the sea. Humans are assigned the role of mere puppets. It is a book that disrupts the poetics of the "serious" novel on several levels. James Joyce's *Ulysses* recounts around 18 hours of Dublin life on 730 dense pages, and Jacobsen's *Havbrevene* encompasses deep time and the entire planet on 64 airy pages, some of which are full-page illustrations by Dorte Naomi. The epistolary novel, designated "Prosa" on the title page, is divided into four chapters: "The Plan," "The Rebellion of the Land," "Icarus," and "We Become a Mother." In what follows, I will discuss the roles played by humans and nonhumans and the book's configurations of time and space as it conveys a history of the planet through the eyes of the oceans.

6.1   Evolution, Devolution

Havbrevene tells the story of Earth's history from its creation four billion years ago to our present and thus operates within a time frame unconstrained by the traditional dictates of narrative. A future of rising sea levels is hinted at. It addresses the relationships between evolutionary theory and myth, science and fable, humans and nonhumans, and spectatorship and agency. It makes references to global warming, ocean pollution, forest fires, U.S. border politics, and what Europeans refer to as the refugee crisis. *Havbrevene* mixes elements from "The Book of Genesis," most notably the image of a planet covered entirely by water until God gathered the waters in one place and lets dry land appear, with elements from natural science, such as the notion of Earth's history being billions of years old and unfolding through a combination of gradual evolution and catastrophic events. In *The Earth After Us* (2008), Jan Zalasiewicz observes that "It is hard, as humans, to get a proper perspective on the human race."[116] That challenge is met innovatively by Jacobsen. With a twist of Aldo Leopold's 1949 dictum, "Thinking Like a Mountain,"[117] *Havbrevene* is a book that thinks like the oceans, adopts a marine perspective on humans, and imagines the earth after them. It does so from a feminist perspective: Thalassa, not Oceanus.

Though not similar in length to Fernand Braudel's seminal *La Méditerranée et le Monde Méditerranéen à l'Epoque de Philippe II* (1949), Jacobsen's book structurally and methodologically compares to Braudel's work and the principles of the Annales School in that it prioritizes the *longue durée* over *histoire événementielle* and the long-term historical structures over individual events or group of events. Braudel's observation in the concluding paragraph to the second edition anticipates the vision in *Havbrevene*:

---

[116]   Jan Zalasiewicz, *The Earth After Us: What Legacy Will Humans Leave in the Rocks?* (New York: Oxford University Press, 2008), 1.
[117]   Aldo Leopold, *A Sand County Almanac: And Sketches Here and There* (New York: Oxford University Press, 1949), 129–33.

> So when I think of the individual, I am always inclined to see him imprisoned within a destiny in which he himself has little hand, fixed in a landscape in which the infinite perspectives of the long term stretch into the distance both behind him and before. In historical analysis as I see it, rightly or wrongly, the long run always wins in the end. Annihilating innumerable events [...] indubitably limits both the freedom of the individual and even the role of chance.[118]

Perhaps somewhat paradoxically given this statement by Braudel and my linking it with *Havbrevene*, Jacobsen's story unfolds as a letter exchange between two sisters, the Atlantic Ocean, aged one hundred and eighty million years, and the Mediterranean Sea, aged five million years. The epistolary genre is traditionally the form of intimacy and the personal. The reader gains access to one, two, or several points of view and voices that are often conveyors of inner thoughts and personal feelings. By anthropomorphizing the two oceans, Jacobsen exploits these generic conventions to give the reader "proper" perspectives on the human race. The choice of the epistolary form seems less paradoxical because the perspectives are both nonhuman and personalized, *longue durée* and *événementielle*.

The two saltwater basins produce contrasting associations. While the Atlantic, even after the voyages of Columbus and Magellan, continued for at least two more centuries to play the role of the great unknown and the radical other in the history of Western imagination, the Mediterranean is traditionally considered to be the cradle of Western civilization. While related as sisters and being elementally and materially alike, their temporal and spatial scales are wide apart. Compared to the anciency and vastness of the Atlantic, the Mediterranean's juvenescence and enclosedness bring it closer to human history and its relative insignificance (if considered from a geological time frame).

To young Michelet, while lecturing at the École Normale in 1830–31 on the history of the Middle Ages, the Mediterranean almost presented itself as mankind's friend, when he experienced it personally on a journey to Gênes and the Apennines in March 1830: "This sea is the Mediterranean, that is to say the most beautiful, the most charming of all the seas. It is no longer the ocean with its menacing mists and waves. It is a pretty sea, always sparkling under the sun, almost always peaceful; in addition, limited on all sides."[119] The

---

118 Braudel, *The Mediterranean and the Mediterranean World in the Age of Philip II*, 1244.
119 The passage, which can be found in Michelet's *Cours d'histoire du moyen âge*, handwritten lecture notes from his 1830–31 course, is quoted by Paul Viallaneix in Jules Michelet, *Journal*, vol. 1, 724–25, note 1 to his journal entry from March 30, 1830.

Romantic Michelet, dreaming of sublimely "menacing mists and waves," was perhaps disappointed in his encounter with the "beautiful sea." Only a year later, Michelet visits Le Havre and for the first time comes into contact with the Atlantic, more specifically the English Channel, a sea that is more alive and changing, a sea dominated by tides, whose calms are exceptional and always full of menaces.[120] His journal entry of August 5, 1831, testifies to an experience that differed from the one in Italy the previous year. He now refers to the ocean as "this sublime space of freedom" and only regrets that it belongs to the English.[121] During the days that followed, the ocean got under Michelet's skin. Its infiniteness and threatening might make him feel infinitely small. The radical divergence between himself and the ocean is supplemented with a convergence. When Michelet realizes the chasmic nature of the ocean, he realizes that he too suffers from an internal abyss of emptiness.

Michelet's impressions of the two seas and their different characteristics are good to bear in mind when we examine *Havbrevene* more closely. From his reflections on his encounter with the Atlantic, we can extrapolate a more general observation on creative impulse that can serve as an epigraph, not merely for Jacobsen's letter exchange but for all writers of the sea from Homer, Horace, and Hugo to Camões, Conrad, and Carson: *A poetic elevation of the ocean is always informed and inspired by the contrast between the might of the sea and the relative weakness of humans.*

In *Havbrevene*, Jacobsen's choice of oceanic focalization provides the reader with nonhuman perspectives on planetary evolution and human history. Events in *Havbrevene* are geological, hydrological, and global in scale, but stories of human destinies and deeds are also told by the two oceans. Jacobsen's version of Genesis goes like this. In the beginning, probably more than four billion years ago, the planet was covered entirely by water. This initial oceanic harmony was disrupted when tectonic movements and underwater eruptions caused landmasses to appear: "The first land erupted red and pimplelike, then browned into a scab and tasted of a fierce mineral."[122] Ever since that unwanted (and ugly) intrusion, the oceans have been collaborating on a comprehensive plan of action whose purpose is a complete flooding of the planet to bring about a reunion. To assist them, the oceans began to foster "creep," tiny organisms, some of which eventually developed into birds, animals, and humans. The idea was that these organisms as "living vessels" would carry water across

---

120   E. de Saint-Denis, "Michelet et la mer de la Manche," *Revue d'Histoire littéraire de la France* 61, no. 1 (1961): 38.
121   Michelet, *Journal*, 82.
122   Siri Ranva Hjelm Jacobsen, *Havbrevene* (København: Lindhardt og Ringhof, 2018), 36.

the landmasses, ultimately contributing to heal the separation and transform the planet back into a crystalline sphere of saltwater. It is possible to imagine that such a crystal ball would constantly reflect the sky, stars, and universe and emphasize cosmic congruence between the astral sphere and planet earth.

In the nineteenth century, when ocean science was an emerging discipline and its pioneering scientists struggled to find ways to conceptualize the ocean, they sought analogies from more established scientific fields, especially astronomy and geology. Maury compared the behavior of the Gulf Stream (new discovery) to the orbit of planets (established knowledge) and likened the study of the sea to that of astronomy, claiming that the mariner experienced similar wonder when sounding the depths of the ocean as that experienced by the astronomer when stargazing in the darkness and stillness of the night. According to Rozwadowski, Maury analogized oceanography and astronomy for several reasons. It signaled that exploration of the ocean depths was as important as the scrutiny of the heavens, and it provided an epistemological model for exploring an immense and unreachable place by insinuating that if humans could reach the upper spheres, they could do the same with the lower spheres.[123]

In *Havbrevene*, Jacobsen's analogy between the astral sphere and the ocean, its surface and depths, serves to emphasize the desirable cosmic harmony and correspondence expressed through the image of the crystal ball. However, something has disturbed the oceans' conspiracy, something that will bring about the desired goal of reunification sooner than anticipated. This disruption alludes to the impact of humankind on global ecology, which leads to rising temperatures, the melting of ice caps, and, ultimately, to rising sea levels at a speed faster than that envisioned in the seas' plan.

Jacobsen endows humans with a powerful agency (acceleration), but by subordinating human actions and their effects to a nonhuman scheme (flooding), she simultaneously spotlights human impotence. This impotence is amplified in relation to how we normally understand it. First, the human-activated processes of the Anthropocene eventually spin out of human control, making humans powerless to stop the processes they initiated (as Bonneuil and Fressoz previously stated). Second, a higher force—not the Gaia of James Lovelock and Lynn Margulis, but Thalassa—treats humans as lowly pawns used as part of an endgame strategy. Humans thought that they were in control, but the processes of the Earth system have run amok and left humans

---

123   M. F. Maury, *The Physical Geography of the Sea* (New York: Harper & Brothers, 1855), 202; see also Rozwadowski, *Fathoming the Ocean*, 29–30.

outside the control room. This uncontrollability was part of the plan designed by the oceans all along. The plot situates humans in a position even more precarious and insignificant than the one attributed to them by many climate-change advocates and environmental pressure groups, which, in addition to criticizing human behavior, also believe that humans are the only ones capable of rectifying their own misdeeds.

This explains how *Havbrevene* differs from otherwise like-minded contemporary Scandinavian examples of blue climate and ecofiction, such as Morten Strøksnes' *Havboka* (*Shark Drunk*, 2015) and Maja Lunde's *Blå* (2017). Whereas the former arguably compares best with Hemingway's *The Old Man and the Sea* (1952) in its intense focus on a rivalry between man and animal, and the latter zeros in on the struggles of three persons, two adults and a child, against the simultaneous threats of drought and rising sea levels, *Havbrevene* stages several nonanthropogenic plots and perspectives. In that sense, *Havbrevene* is bluer than *Blue* and *Havboka*.

6.2 *Icarus, Bruegel, and the Echo Chamber of Reception*

In *Havbrevene*, the negotiations of how to act when faced with imminent ecological destruction (present in *Drowned World*) and who is to blame for it (absent in *Drowned World*) are both absent. In Thalassa's empire, human action is meaningless and, consequently, so is human guilt—in regard to climate change at least. Does this mean that Jacobsen promotes a posthuman vision of the world? Is *Havbrevene* a misanthropic, perhaps even nihilistic work? To answer these questions, we first need to introduce the two letter-writing protagonists. The Atlantic Ocean: "Old and gruffy, but not without tenderness. Loves the universe. Nothing can surprise this ocean anymore." And the Mediterranean Sea: "Younger sister to the Atlantic Ocean. Loves to shimmer, Icarus, and when large herds of animals drift along."[124] There is a clear temperamental and axiological difference between the two sisters, the elder being fully committed to the plan, the younger more hesitant because she has a soft spot for humans and animals. Through the voice of the Mediterranean Sea, Jacobsen introduces a sympathetic perspective on humans that relativizes the possible misanthropy or at least indifference of the geological, cosmic plot. As indicated by the quotation, the Mediterranean Sea loves Icarus, the human son of the human master craftsman Daedalus, who manufactured wings from feathers and wax as a means for them to escape from Crete. Daedalus warned Icarus against complacency and hubris, urging him not to fly too low, since

---

124 Jacobsen, *Havbrevene*, 9.

the sea's dampness would congest his wings, nor too high, since the sun's heat would melt the wax. Icarus disregards the advice and flies too high. Falling victim to hubris (or perhaps shear youthful ebullience), the wings fail. Icarus is plunged into Mediterranean Sea and drowns.

Icarus is a double-edged emblem of human pride and courage, open for both denigration and admiration. Depending on scale, he can also be treated with indifference, met with compassion, or even arouse feelings of guilt. In *Havbrevene*, The Mediterranean Sea cannot help but admire and feel sorry for the handsome youth. The importance of the myth about Icarus to Jacobsen's overall vision is underlined by her incorporation of no fewer than six references to it, all of them discursively distinct: 1) a fragment of a poem by William Carlos Williams; 2) a Naomi illustration that visualizes the Williams fragment (Figure 36); 3) an essay-like document, presumably by an art historian, on the autonomy of art and Daedalus' greatness as an artist; 4) a soldier's story recounting his public conversation with a professor about the possible parallels between his personal experiences of patrolling the Mexico-United States border and some artworks; 5) embedded in the soldier's story is an explicit reference to one of these artworks, the painting of the fall of Icarus attributed to Pieter Bruegel the Elder, and also to Williams' ekphrastic poem about it; 6) finally, *Havbrevene* ends with a short passage printed on the inside of the book cover which, through a third-person narrator using internal focalization through Daedalus, describes the arrival of the craftsman to the Sicilian coast and the fall of his son just off that coast.

Apart from these explicit references to the Icarus myth, there is a series of other intertextual sources not explicitly referred to by Jacobsen (e.g., Ovid, W. H. Auden). A discussion of these sources will assist us in better understanding Icarus' role in *Havbrevene*, as will a closer examination of the genealogy of Bruegel's painting. It is my contention that a genuine echo chamber has enclosed around Bruegel's painting—Williams' poem is only one of "over sixty poetic *ekphrases* in some half-dozen languages"[125]—and the question is if Jacobsen and Naomi end up amplifying or disturbing the resonance of these echoes in the chamber?

Jacobsen first alludes to the myth of Icarus in an epigraph that frames the letter exchange. It consists of the last stanza of Williams' "Landscape with the Fall of Icarus" (1960): "a splash quite unnoticed / this was / Icarus drowning." Above the epigraph is one of Naomi's illustrations. It shows a segment of the ocean, which is represented mostly in black, but with white lines representing

---

125 Ruth Bernard Yeazell, "The Power of a Name: In Bruegel's *Icarus*, for Instance," *Raritan: A Quarterly Review* 33, no. 2 (2013): 113.

FIGURE 36   Dorte Naomi, *Icarus* (2018)
© DORTE NAOMI

wavelike forms and currents giving structure to the ocean. Williams' last stanza is cleverly composed. While the first line stresses the indifference of the surroundings—possibly human onlookers, nature, Daedalus—to Icarus' fate, the two final lines of the poem contradict this indifference by directing the reader's attention to Icarus: "this was Icarus drowning." It is as if the poet has the power through words to zoom in on and highlight what others have considered "unsignificant," in this case a human drowning.

Naomi's illustration (Figure 36) emphasizes Williams' word "unnoticed" and brackets the rest of the quotation. Icarus and the splash are nowhere to be seen, not even a trace of his sinking is discernible. In that sense, we can only read Naomi's title (*Icarus*) as blatantly ironic. The two first versions of the Icarus myth in *Havbrevene*—more precisely of Bruegel's painting—point in opposite directions, one drawing attention to human suffering and neutralizing the indifference toward it, the other providing us with a glimpse of a world in which humans are absent or at least unimportant. It could be significant that Naomi's illustration precedes Williams' stanza and represents the reader's first (visual and thus more immediate) encounter with what are (interpretations of) Bruegel and Icarus.

The third reference to the Icarus myth occurs at the beginning of the third chapter entitled "Icarus." Here, the Mediterranean Sea hesitantly admits to her older sister that she has been thinking a lot about Icarus again. Worried about her sister, the Atlantic Ocean tries to convince her that "Icarus is not the exemplary creep you make of him, and he is certainly not your 'son' as you have previously referred to him."¹²⁶ To get her point through, the Atlantic Ocean encloses a document in her letter, which it took her a long time to locate in her underwater library. The document, written by a human, distinguishes itself typographically from the letters written by the two seas by being italicized (this applies to all the fragments of human texts, stories, and memories in *Havbrevene*).

The document mimes an academic discourse and presents an alternative version of the story of Daedalus and Icarus. The author, whose focus is on Daedalus, argues that the architect left Crete voluntarily to pursue his creative talents. Consequently, the common belief of an escape necessitated by political intricacies is untrue. Daedalus was not interested in politics, he just wanted to build and create, which is why it could benefit our understanding of his genius and artistic rigorousness to compare him with Albert Speer or Giuseppe Terragni, the author tells us. During the completion of the Minoan palace (the author must be referring to Knossos), especially the underground prison facilities and the dormitory of the temple priestesses, Daedalus became increasingly interested in what has later been labeled "the wearable slim-fit architecture." An example of this intersection between space production, clothing, and prosthesis is the wooden cow that he donated to Pasiphaë: "*Although the wooden construction could accommodate a human on all four and allowed for the exposure of the genitals by the opening of a hatch under the tail, it is not likely that Queen Pasiphaë has used it herself.*" Just as the author of the document refutes that the cow was a commissioned work or that it was ever used by Pasiphaë to facilitate mating with the white Minoan bull, the author also denies that the wings built by Daedalus were an invention made in distress and dictated by the need to escape. Instead, they should be considered "*as the culmination of a long-lasting artistic and philosophical work: the result of an absolute re-thinking of the relationship between edifice, body, and nature. As to the maiden voyage, nothing suggests that Daedalus have made stay or later attempted to initiate a search for Icarus. By all accounts he considered the fall as a less significant event.*"¹²⁷ The document repeats the message from Naomi's illustration and to a certain extent also that of Williams' stanza, that Icarus is not all that important. This time the insignificance is not the consequence of a nonhuman, oceanic perspective indifferent to the pettiness of humans and their minuscule time scale, but of art's unconditional detachment from and uncompromising superiority to politics, kinship, and religion as articulated by someone who is probably an art historian.

---

126   Jacobsen, *Havbrevene*, 41.
127   Jacobsen, *Havbrevene*, 43, 43–44.

Does Jacobsen subscribe to the same theory of art? This is doubtful, as both Daedalus' cynicism towards his son's death and the comparison with Speer and Terragni indicate. However, one of the lessons we can learn here is that in *Havbrevene*, everything depends on the scale from which things are perceived and judged. One of the book's forces is its capacity to juggle with a variety of very different scales and its ensuing production of a dynamic space of verities. Seen from the perspective of art, the document's author is right in praising Daedalus for his inventiveness. His creations deserve to be admired. But to the Atlantic Ocean, the document bears witness of an evolutionary experiment gone wrong: Daedalus' indifference towards Icarus' death is a sign of human cold-heartedness, and human inventions are futile on the scale of geological time anyway.

The document even makes the Mediterranean Sea doubt the very evolutionary experiment that she formed herself: "When you liberated the creep from the form they are born in—gave them the will to own and the longing for spooning together—you created the world anew. None of us imagined that it would lead this far. Yes, perhaps it was a little unwarranted, but it *was* also virtuoso," writes the Atlantic Ocean. To which her sister replies curtly: "Perhaps if we had given them a little more longing and a little less will? What do you think? M." To the Mediterranean Sea, however, and despite these doubts, there remains an emotional bond with Icarus, the young man who fell from the sky and whom she caught. He ended up drowning, and she cannot help comparing him with the many humans, some children, who drown when their overcrowded "pods" capsize on their way to Europe: "I listen to the sinking shoals. The clicking sound of the brains that gradually rise and then ebb out. They stand on the bottom and undulate with lungs that shudder with plankton and krill. When the eels arrive, I look away."[128] The perspective may be oceanic and nonhuman, but it is not without affection and empathy towards humans. A parallel to this scene can be found in Jason deCaires Taylor's sculpture *The Raft of Lampedusa* (2016) exhibited at the underwater Museo Atlantico off the island of Lanzarote.

In addition to the contextless, pure emphasis on Icarus' ultimate obliteration in the Naomi illustration (and, partly, in the Williams fragment), the document's praise of Daedalus' ingenuity and agency signals another type of hubris to the one sometimes ascribed to Icarus. If the son can be found guilty of flying too close to the sun and thus symbolically approaching the sphere of the gods, the father can be found guilty of designing the very wings that made such high-flying possible in the first place and thus symbolically taking the power of a god. This line of thinking involving an alternative hubris is not

---

128   Jacobsen, *Havbrevene*, 23, 24, 18.

the art historian's take on the matter, but it can be derived from Jacobsen's overall composition. Again, everything is a question of scale, and by introducing the oceanic perspective's scale of deep time and structurally and compositionally prioritizing this perspective, Jacobsen signals a relativization of all things human.

The fifth reference to the Icarus myth is embedded within the fourth, a four-page italicized narrative by a young American soldier who used to study art history before he joined the army and got stationed in Nogales to help patrol the Mexico-United States border. The soldier has been chosen by the army's public relations department to participate in a public conversation with a Professor Rydon about the possible connection between a series of artworks and the soldier's border experiences. One of these artworks is the painting (presumably) by Pieter Bruegel the Elder, *Landscape with the Fall of Icarus* (c. 1558/1560), of which Williams' entire poem is an ekphrasis. The Bruegel painting (Figure 37) is also Jacobsen's fifth reference to the Icarus myth following the Naomi illustration, the Williams fragment, the art historian's essay, and the soldier's narrative.

In the soldier's story we are presented with several interpretations of the Icarus myth: Bruegel's canonized version, the professor's understanding of Bruegel's painting and inclusion of quotations from Williams' poem, and

FIGURE 37   Pieter Bruegel the Elder, *Landscape with the Fall of Icarus* (c. 1558/1560). Musées royaux des Beaux-Arts de Belgique, Brussels, Belgium
© BRIDGEMAN IMAGES

the soldier's response to the professor's attempt to link the soldier's job and Bruegel's choice of perspective in his painting. "*My talk and the subsequent conversation with Rydon were supposed to be a layer on top of art, an experience that heightened the audience's understanding of the artworks and my work and human nature, that sort of thing*," the soldier tells us. We are also told that Rydon quoted from a poem by Williams, "*which was probably about the sea's indifference towards Icarus' fall.*" After the soldier's brief talk, the professor asks him whether he has ever fired his gun at the border and how that has affected him as a human being. Placed in an asymmetrical and awkward position for leading a conversation (the professor standing and positioned next to Bruegel's painting while the soldier sits in a chair facing the audience and further forward on the scene than the professor), the soldier feels an urge to stand up, but forces himself to remain seated and tries to answer the professor's questions: "*At first, we went for the men, believing that that would make the women turn around. We just had to keep them away from the fence. As soon as they were out of the zone, we could let them run. It was only the children who made them turn around.*" After this attempt to introduce the audience to border policing experiences, "*Rydon lifted the hand and drew a gentle curve from me to the painting.*"[129] The professor explains:

> On Pieter Bruegel's 'Landscape with the Fall of Icarus,' Icarus is only visible as a couple of helpless legs at the motif's lower right corner. That is what makes the painting so heartbreaking and why it can arouse this immediate feeling of guilt in some people. William Carlos Williams writes in his poem about the painting that Icarus' fall goes unnoticed, but that is not entirely true. In the first place, one could argue that Icarus is seen from Daedalus' point of view in the painting. But this point of view is also ours, the spectators'. We are all spectators to the drowning off Sicily, we sit here in the gentle humming from the aircon and watch.[130]

After this professorial explanation linking Bruegel's painting to contemporary American and EU border politics (and perhaps drawing on Blumenberg's ideas in *Shipwreck with Spectator*), while at the same time completely ignorant of his own hegemonic and privileged position towards the soldier in an asymmetrical spatial constellation that mimes that in the painting, Rydon shifts his attention to the soldier, "*glanced at me, a hyena's gaze*," and asks: "*And you? What do you*

---

129 Jacobsen, *Havbrevene*, 48, 49, 49.
130 Jacobsen, *Havbrevene*, 49–50.

feel when you look at such a poor Icarus?" Clearly uncomfortable with the role he has been put in and the answer expected from him, the soldier reflects: *"The correct answer would be that I felt guilt or sorrow, perhaps both, that duty tormented me. I would like to have answered truthfully like the Israeli soldier in the book with testimonies from Hebron who, when asked how he handled the daily encounter with human misery, answered: You start finding interesting things to do.*" Instead, and in yet another example of perspectival juggling, the soldier answers what Rydon and the audience want to hear: *"When I have to go again, I would like to go to the coast. I would like to go to the ocean."*[131]

The soldier's story contributes with new perspectives on some of the questions already discussed. In contrast to the document, which presented a view of art as autonomous and thus detached from any political, religious, and didactic purposes, Professor Rydon sees art as entangled with politics and ethics and uses it to instruct the audience and the soldier in a moralizing and didactic manner. Verbally (but not spatially), the professor assumes a humanist position by refusing to accept the oceanic scale and the sea's indifference to human suffering as a viable standpoint. Instead, he opts for the empathetic route, which to some extent affiliates him with the position of the Mediterranean Sea. But unlike Rydon, the Mediterranean Sea refrains from moralizing, and she does not participate in or encourage any blame game. In a review in the Danish newspaper *Politiken*, Lilian Munk Rösing criticizes the museum conversation and the essayistic document for being "too artificial and instructive."[132] If the standpoints expressed in those discourses could be attributed to Jacobsen, I would agree with Rösing. But they cannot. Each discourse makes up one part of a complex composition of converging and diverging perspectives, scales, and focalizations. Rather than being a too instructive and unambiguous discourse on art's potential for political activism and human moral awakening framed as a museum talk that the reader is supposed to buy into, the purpose of incorporating this discourse in *Havbrevene* is to provoke a mistrust in the reader towards the professor's didactic, moralizing methods. Such a reaction from the reader is not simply a matter of coincidence or personal taste. It has been prepared formally by Jacobsen through the book's multiscalar orchestration, which has trained the reader to adopt a variety of different scales, both human and nonhuman, moral and scientific, and historical and evolutionary.

---

131 Jacobsen, *Havbrevene*, 50, 50, 50.
132 Lilian Munk Rösing, "Lille bog med stor forestillingskraft: Et hav, der taler om busstoppesteder, må jeg bede om mine himmelblå!" *Politiken*, March 2, 2019, accessed November 10, 2019, https://politiken.dk/kultur/boger/art7057748/Et-hav-der-taler-om-busstoppesteder-må-jeg-bede-om-mine-himmelblå.

The final explicit reference to the Icarus myth appears on the inside of the book's back cover: "*The wings sing, he has hit a thermal uplift. Great, soft strokes—away from the sea, and inland. Sicily: a silver green rocky coast, fields, mountains ahead. He looks back and spots the boy. If it was possible, he would prefer the moment without the naked, jerking legs. The feet are white from reflected sun. They fumble in the sea's surface.*"[133] Again, Jacobsen provides us with a fresh interpretation of the myth, although it is also one that picks up the mantles passed on from the essay on Daedalus and Professor Rydon's interpretation of the Bruegel painting. The short passage is narrated by a third-person narrator and focalized through the eyes and mind of a cynical Daedalus. In fact, it is an aesthetic gaze that not only mimes that in the iconic *Landscape* but also adjusts Bruegel's gaze: the landscape without the legs would be preferable. As in the essay, the focus is on Daedalus, but in contrast to the essay, Icarus becomes the paradoxical center of attention in the latter half of the passage. I call the attention paradoxical, because Icarus is not mentioned by name but merely referred to pejoratively as "boy" and through rather unflattering descriptions of his legs. Like Rydon's explication of Bruegel's painting, the perspective is Daedalus', but unlike Rydon, the passage does not attempt to establish a feeling of guilt in the reader. If the passage builds a bridge between Daedalus and the reader as Rydon does, this bridge transfers the uncompromising negativity of the former's perspective, which in its non-neutrality blocks for any feelings of guilt in the reader. If, as Rydon claims, we are spectators in Bruegel's painting as Daedalus is and see what he sees, then we must assume that the same applies to the inside back cover passage where Daedalus' explicitly egocentric point of view is highlighted.

The above shows how Jacobsen draws on canonical sources and how she and Naomi supplement those by creating their own. I will now examine the genealogy of Bruegel painting in relation to both its production and reception. In addition, we shall discuss some of the Icarus sources not mentioned in *Havbrevene*. This will allow us to better understand the originality of Jacobsen's project and how she and Naomi create disturbance and syncopation within the echo chamber that has enclosed around Bruegel's painting.

Perhaps the best-known literary commentary on Bruegel's painting is W. H. Auden's poem "Musée des Beaux Arts" written in 1938. It is not a coincidence, I think, that Jacobsen has chosen not to refer explicitly to Auden's poem, but to William's instead. Her intervention in the Bruegel/Icarus echo chamber is an attempt to forge new interpretative paths and introduce scales different

---

133 Jacobsen, *Havbrevene*, inside back cover.

from those taken by Auden and others. Auden's poem falls in two parts, a first more general part on human suffering and the indifference of the surroundings, and a second part zooming in on Bruegel's *Landscape with the Fall of Icarus*:

> About suffering they were never wrong,
> The old Masters: how well they understood
> Its human position: how it takes place
> While someone else is eating or opening a window or just walking
>   dully along;
> How, when the aged are reverently, passionately waiting
> For the miraculous birth, there always must be
> Children who did not specially want it to happen, skating
> On a pond at the edge of the wood:
> They never forgot
> That even the dreadful martyrdom must run its course
> Anyhow in a corner, some untidy spot
> Where the dogs go on with their doggy life and the torturer's horse
> Scratches its innocent behind on a tree.
>
> In Breughel's *Icarus*, for instance: how everything turns away
> Quite leisurely from the disaster; the ploughman may
> Have heard the splash, the forsaken cry,
> But for him it was not an important failure; the sun shone
> As it had to on the white legs disappearing into the green
> Water, and the expensive delicate ship that must have seen
> Something amazing, a boy falling out of the sky,
> Had somewhere to get to and sailed calmly on.[134]

Auden visited the Musées Royaux des Beaux-Arts de Belgique in Brussels in 1938 and took in several paintings by Pieter Bruegel the Elder (*The Census at Bethlehem* (1566) inspired the writer in lines 5–8). What Auden did not know at the time was not only that *Landscape with the Fall of Icarus* is presumably a copy made by someone else than Bruegel, although this copy is probably based on an original by him, but also that the painting's title cannot be attributed to him or the artist that made a copy of his original. What Auden and many others take "as evidence of artistic intention is instead the work of middlemen—a

---

134   W. H. Auden, *The Collected Poetry of W. H. Auden* (New York: Random House, 1945), 3.

label applied centuries after the fact by persons who were themselves engaged not in making the picture but in interpreting it."[135]

This later discovery may not diminish the potency and unique vision of Auden's poem, but it serves as a cautionary tale of possible misreading or overreading in which Auden's choice of zooming in on Icarus is problematized, and his poem's correspondence with the painting is questioned. According to Ruth B. Yeazell, Arthur C. Danto played with the ideas that if the painting had merely been identified as a landscape, the legs of Icarus would remain relatively unimportant, or if it had been called *Industry on Land and Sea*, the legs could have been those of a pearl diver or oysterman, while *Works and Pleasures* might have identified them as belonging to a swimmer. Danto, also unaware of the fact that the title had been given to the painting much later than its date of composition, draws the conclusion that the title, unequivocally identifying the legs as Icarus', changes the whole work, because the painting itself does not in any obvious way indicate the centrality of the legs, let alone Icarus' presence. As summarized by Yeazell: "Once the viewer knows the painting's title, those partly submerged legs become the focus of interpretation, such that their very lack of salience in the composition as a whole proves the key to its meaning."[136] This was exactly what happened to Auden.

But before we comment on "Musée des Beaux Arts" we need to establish the facts about the painting:

> The canvas is neither dated nor signed. No record of it surfaces until 1912, when it was purchased from a London gallery by its current owner, the Musées royaux des Beaux-Arts in Brussels. It is not clear whether the seller had already identified the drowning boy or whether that was the work of the Brussels curators. But from 1913, when the picture appeared in a museum guide as *La chute d'Icare*, to the present, when a label on the wall repeats the short title while an inscription on the frame gives *Paysage avec la chute d'Icare*, scholars seem to have had little doubt that those white legs belong to the mythical figure who plummeted into the sea when he flew too near to the sun. They have been more certain, in fact, about the name of Icarus than that of the painter, whose identification with the elder Bruegel has been debated ever since the work was first displayed in public a century ago. Yet there is a crucial difference between

---

135   Yeazell, "The Power of a Name," 115.
136   Yeazell, "The Power of a Name," 114.

FIGURE 38   Circle of Pieter Bruegel the Elder, *The Fall of Icarus* (c. 1590–95)
© LE MUSÉE ET JARDINS VAN BUUREN, BRUSSELS

the sort of iconographic research that served to establish the figure as Icarus and the decision to name the picture after him.[137]

Yeazell's point is that even though it can be established with certainty that the Icarus myth is a motif in (the copy of) Bruegel's painting, this does not justify naming the painting after him.

The certainty of Icarus' presence in the painting stems from a variety of sources, some of them inventories of collections, others related images, still others written sources that inspired the composition:

> The strongest verbal evidence for the picture's current title comes from a 1621 inventory of the imperial collection at Prague, which records "Eine Historia vom Daedalo und Icaro vom alten Prügel" (A History of Daedalus and Icarus by the elder Bruegel). A subsequent entry of 1647–1648 refers to "Eine Landschaft. Dédalo und Icaro" but doesn't name the painter. Though some scholars have been tempted to identify these records with

---

137   Yeazell, "The Power of a Name," 115.

FIGURE 39   Simon Novellanus after Pieter Bruegel the Elder, *River Landscape with Daedalus and Icarus* (c. 1595)
© THE TRUSTEES OF THE BRITISH MUSEUM

the painting celebrated by Auden and others, the absence of Daedalus from the present work calls that identification into question—especially since there exists another version of the image, now at the Musée van Buuren in Brussels, that shows both figures (fig. 4 [Figure 38]). That version, which first surfaced in a private collection in 1935, has long been viewed as a copy. An engraving and an etching after Bruegel also show a pair of tiny figures in the sky, one flying and the other plunging; and an inscription on the etching, which dates the design to 1553, includes a passage about Daedalus and Icarus from Ovid's *Tristia* (fig. 5 [Figure 39]). The latter must be treated cautiously—not only because the inscriptions on Bruegel's prints typically originated with the publisher rather than the artist, but because the etching was only published several decades after the date it records, by which time the artist was dead. There is also the possibility that the mythical figures in both prints were added by other hands. Yet even without the support of sixteenth-century emblem books and editions of Ovid, which also feature images of a falling Icarus, details in the painting itself help to confirm the connection to the version of the myth in Ovid's *Metamorphoses*.[138]

Yeazell, like others before her, refers to specific lines in *Metamorphoses* (c. 8 AD) that point the way forward to Bruegel's painting, as they feature the three characters included by the Flemish painter, a *captat* (an angler), a *pastor* (a shepherd), and an *arator* (a plowman): "An angler fishing with his quivering rod, / A lonely shepherd propped upon his crook, / A plowman leaning on his plow, looked up / And gazed in awe, and thought they must be gods / That they could fly."[139] Interestingly, a comparison between the Ovidian source and the painting shows the latter performing a radical modification of the poem. In Ovid, all three characters raise their heads and look in wonder at Daedalus and Icarus, mistaking them for gods. In Bruegel's painting, only the shepherd looks up—perhaps at Daedalus, but we cannot be sure about this—while the plowman and the angler are both absorbed in their daily chores and completely unaware of Daedalus and Icarus.

Do all these sources, documents, and images confirm the legitimacy of the title of the Bruegel painting? No, not at all. Especially the drastic deviation in the painting from the Ovidian rendering in *Metamorphoses* indicates that Bruegel wanted to express a different vision. As Yeazell pointed out earlier, the verification of the presence of the Icarus myth in the painting does not necessarily justify entitling the artwork after the Greek youth. She adds: "Picture titles can have a zooming effect, as Leo Hoek has shrewdly noted, and no title better demonstrates that effect than *Landscape with the Fall of Icarus*. The process is circular; the painting acquired its title from knowledgeable viewers who recognized the drowning Icarus in the small figure to the right, and that title in turn prompts subsequent viewers to zoom in on the figure."[140] Auden's poem quoted above is a good example of that.

Auden's first stanza speaks generally about how the old masters understood that suffering, miracles, and martyrdom always happen peripherally and unnoticed while the world moves along unaffected. In the second stanza, he zooms in on a concrete example, Bruegel's *The Landscape with the Fall of Icarus*. The zooming in does not end here, though. Yeazell again:

---

138   Yeazell, "The Power of a Name," 115–16.
139   Ovid, *Metamorphoses*, trans. A. D. Melville, introduction and notes by E. J. Kenney (1986; Oxford: Oxford University Press, 1998), 177–78, book viii, lines 217–20.
140   Yeazell, "The Power of a Name," 118.

The inverted syntax of the first line, like the reduction of the picture's traditional title to the italicized name of the drowning boy, intensifies the zooming effect by turning what is compositionally a small area into the emotional center of the image: Bruegel's picture is "about" the suffering it appears to minimize—or, more precisely, about how "everything turns away" from "the disaster." The painter may have treated Icarus as a mere detail, but only two of the poet's eight lines contain no direct reference to his fate. Auden's focus on the drowning figure is not surprising. "To me, Art's subject is the human clay," he had written two years earlier, "And landscape but a background to a torso."[141]

Auden's poem is anthropocentric, oriented towards "the human clay" and less interested in landscape. In his poem, this is found in both stanzas and the general semantic progression of the poem and is also enhanced in the condensed formulation "In Bruegel's *Icarus*," a symbolic amputation of the conventional title which begins with *Landscape*.

Something similar happens in William Carlos Williams' poem, but it differs from Auden's in important ways. First, the poem repeats what we now realize is a problematic title of the painting, "Landscape with the Fall of Icarus." As readers, we are thus zoomed in on Icarus from the very beginning. And the zooming effect continues in the poem's first stanza, after which Williams loosens its grip in the next five, only to allow it to return in the last stanza, the one quoted in *Havbrevene*:

> According to Brueghel
> when Icarus fell
> it was spring
>
> a farmer was ploughing
> his field
> the whole pageantry
>
> of the year was
> awake tingling
> near

---

141 Yeazell, "The Power of a Name," 119.

> the edge of the sea
> concerned
> with itself
>
> sweating in the sun
> that melted
> the wings' wax
>
> unsignificantly
> off the coast
> there was
>
> a splash quite unnoticed
> this was
> Icarus drowning[142]

If the first stanza contributes to the echo chamber that constantly repeats the centrality of Icarus in Bruegel's painting, and if the last stanza negates its own initial insistence on the indifference of the surroundings towards Icarus' fall by bringing forth what was otherwise unnoticed, "this was / Icarus drowning," then the five middle stanzas do something else.

Auden's poetics valorized the human clay and relegated landscapes to background, but Williams is famous for his maxim "No ideas but in things," first coined in an early 1927 version of "Paterson."[143] Williams is truer to his principle in stanzas 2–6, the body of the poem, than in stanzas 1 and 7. In the middle stanzas, he pans out on the landscape, becomes panoramic rather than partial. Auden's description of various indifferences to Icarus' fall was grounded in what he considered to be human limitations. The indifference evoked by Williams is *eco*centric, not egocentric, a result of the landscape's inertia when set against the ephemerality of human affairs. True, he mentions the plowman in the first line of stanza 2, but this figure merely functions as a steppingstone into "the whole pageantry," which is positively affected by the spring season and being situated near "the edge of the sea" and only "concerned / with itself" and "sweating in the sun." Williams evokes an ecological spectacle of panoramic dimension with sea, spring, sun, and pageantry. If wings of a human melt, they do so "unsignificantly" instead of "insignificantly," that is, "not just

---

142 William Carlos Williams, *The Collected Poems of William Carlos Williams. Volume II: 1939–1962*, ed. Christopher MacGowan (1988; New York: New Directions, 2001), 385–86.
143 Williams, *Collected Poems 1939–1962*, 263–66.

trivially, but without signifying at all."[144] However, despite the centrality that Williams reserves for *tópos* and *georgikós*, formally underlined with their position in the poem's middle stanzas, we cannot disregard the fact that he entitled the poem "Landscape with the Fall of Icarus" and also structured it to begin and end with Icarus. This seems to be an attempt to follow the movements of the spectator's eyes as they scan the painting in search of Icarus. *Ánthropos* gets the first and last words and, admittedly, also dominates portions of the middle of the poem since the landscape is to some extent urban and cultivated (ploughing, field, pageantry, tingling, concerned, sweating).

Interestingly, among the several paintings in which Bruegel seems to obscure his real focus—*The Census at Bethlehem*, *The Procession to Calvary* (1564), and *Landscape with the Fall of Icarus*—the latter is the only painting not based on scripture but on classical myth. This has led art historians to speculate that the foregrounded plowman is the painting's moral centroid, because his constant attention on tending the soil acts as a counterweight to Icarus' rash and frivolous flight, thus bearing witness to a social order more geocentric than anthropocentric. There are numerous sources, biblical (e.g., "Luke," 9:62) and proverbial, as well as details in the painting itself (e.g., the dignity of the plowman's attire) that support such a reading. Ovid is also invoked from his *Tristia* (8–17 AD): "He who lies low, lives well, believe me; one should / Remain within the limits of one's lot."[145] Such an interpretation shifts the attention from the indifference toward human suffering (indifference of humans in Auden, of nature in Williams) to a georgic world order in which the insignificance of Icarus' destiny is in line with the plowman's devotion to his agricultural duties.

Despite this hermeneutical redirection and change of scale, a stubborn inertia still sticks to the title of the painting. A more recent engagement with the painting challenges the habit of routinely reiterating a title that was never given to the painting by the artist, but only added later by middlemen, a title unsubstantiated, and then continuously reinforced by art historians, artists, and writers. Lyckle de Vries has proposed an alternative title that would make us better understand the painting: "*World landscape at sunset with a plowing farmer, an idle shepherd, a hopeful fisherman, a merchant vessel, a dead body, and the fall of Icarus.*"[146] One consequence of suggesting a more distributive title, which converges better with the painting's multicomponent arrangement,

---

144   Yeazell, "The Power of a Name," 120.
145   Ovid, *Sorrows of an Exile: Tristia*, trans. A. D. Melville, introduction and notes by E. J. Kenney (Oxford: Clarendon, 1992), 49, book 3, section 4a, lines 25–26.
146   Lyckle de Vries, "Bruegel's *Fall of Icarus*: Ovid or Solomon?" *Simiolus: Netherlands Quarterly for the History of Art* 30, no. 1–2 (2003): 18.

is that the spectator recognizes that Icarus is a secondary character rather than a protagonist. In addition, it signals that Bruegel's composition is rooted in the classic Greek interpretation of Icarus as a symbol of excessive pride that led to his fall, rather than as a victim of human suffering unnoticed.

By situating *Landscape with the Fall of Icarus* within the genre of "world landscape" (as theorized by Walter Gibson), de Vries wants to underline the composition's relative subservience of the human characters to the natural environment as well as its staging of "an armchair traveler's look upon the structure of the earth compressed into a narrow space" resulting from "its high horizon and helicopter view."[147] The orchestration of this point of view means that multiple other activities or iconographic components call for our attention: the cultivation of the land, the preparation of an ocean-going ship, the town on the coast, the sea, the mountains, and the setting sun. The ship, for example, has not received much attention. But instead of seeing it in relation to the drowning Icarus, which would make it exemplify another instance of human indifference to human suffering, the generic lens of world landscape enables us to see the ship as a homage to human industry, international trade, and global exploration thus endowing the painting with an outward movement and a dimension of world order.

It has puzzled commentators that Icarus falls into the sea as a result of the sun melting the wax of his wings, because the painting shows a setting sun. De Vries explains the setting sun (and further dismantles the centrality of Icarus) by referring to "Ecclesiastes" as an important source for the painting. Here, images of human labor, both during mornings and evenings, are simultaneously depicted as dignified and vain, and human life in general is portrayed as being subordinated to the forces and eternal rhythms of nature. The Teacher's wisdom is one that converges well with the painting's Ovidian allusions, especially in *Tristia*. The intention of de Vries is to propose a corrective—based on the formal features of the painting itself and on alternative sources used by Bruegel—to the misreadings by Auden, Williams, and several other poets. According to de Vries, these poetically licensed misreadings have subsequently made scholars blind to the painting's composition and thus outmaneuvered scholarly discipline.[148] As Yeazell points out, the poets were indeed following earlier generations of scholars who built on the tradition of those who first titled the painting *Landscape with the Fall of Icarus*.[149] She somewhat surprisingly proceeds by stressing the legitimacy behind that entitling, pointing to the

---

147   de Vries, "Bruegel's *Fall of Icarus*," 9.
148   de Vries, "Bruegel's *Fall of Icarus*," 18.
149   Yeazell, "The Power of a Name," 124.

precision and clarity with which the legs of Icarus are painted: "The title of the painting tells the viewer where to look, and the style of the painting reinforces the title."[150]

Yeazell's defense of the conventional title is surprising, because she has previously stressed a decisive distinction between the iconographic investigation that helped establish the figure as Icarus and the choice of naming the painting after him. However, Yeazell's maneuver may be seen as an attempt to make an impact with a correction even more important, one not concerning the title but the artist:

> it seems increasingly certain that the attribution to the master's hand may be more misleading than the titular emphasis on the drowning boy. [...] According to the latest word from the laboratories of Belgium's Royal Institute for Culture Heritage, the painting that has inspired so much poetry should now be identified as just another copy: an anonymous artist's version of an absent original. What remains of Bruegel himself is at best the composition, though we still don't know which of the two copyists followed it more closely.[151]

Yeazell does not aim to contradict her previous warnings about the epistemological consequences of (inauthentic) titles; instead, she adds yet another potentially misleading zooming effect, that of the artist's name. She seems to rejoice in the postmodern idea of aesthetic artifacts circulating among us and feeding the cultural imagination, each of them full of meanings perhaps ascribed to them automatically through names of titles or artists, but also through dynamic processes of appropriations and reappropriations occurring in a variety of different media and forms, from images, movies, and music to poems, novels, and academic articles.

The complexity of Jacobsen's vision is rooted in a formal logic of representation that W. J. T. Mitchell has labelled "mixed media," the idea that the border between image and text is always blurred: "the interaction of pictures and texts is constitutive of representation as such: all media are mixed media, and all representations are heterogeneous; there are no 'purely' visual or verbal arts, though the impulse to purify media is one of the central utopian gestures of modernism." To Mitchell's, this representational logic of mixed media is not only a matter of form, it is also linked to "issues of power, value, and human

---

150   Yeazell, "The Power of a Name," 126.
151   Yeazell, "The Power of a Name," 126, 127.

interests": "Images, like histories and technologies, are our creations, yet also commonly thought to be 'out of our control'—or at least out of 'someone's' control, the question of agency and power being central to the way images work."[152] *Havbrevene* is an example of how this picture theory of "all media are mixed media" works in practice. This is not the time and place to discuss the assumptions behind and implications of Mitchell's picture theory, but by importing its ideas of blurring borders between media and of thematical complexity resulting from this formal impurity, we are able to better understand the mechanisms of appropriation and reappropriation in what I have termed the echo chamber.

Jacobsen's *Havbrevene* is a reappropriation of Bruegel's *Landscape with the Fall of Icarus*, although the painting is presumably not by Bruegel and the title may be misleading. Her book, a collaborative endeavor between visual artist Dorte Naomi and verbal artist Siri Ranva Hjelm Jacobsen, is also a creative commentary on Williams' poem. Whether Jacobsen was fully aware of the complicated genealogy of the painting when she conceived *Havbrevene* is not so important. Her project—an orchestration of different scales, a giving voice to multiple interpretations of the Icarus myth, and a reappropriation of the painting traditionally ascribed to Bruegel—succeeds through the six references to the Icarus myth and their multimodal interplay. My introduction to the complex discussions of authorship and entitling only supports Jacobsen's project by deepening the foundation of its basic dilemmas: Should Icarus be regarded as a victim of human pride or of human suffering unnoticed? Does it matter whether his suffering is ignored by humans or the ocean? What is the role of humans, and Icarus, in the world and in nature? Should art be regarded as autonomous, didactic, or even moralizing? How does the inclusion of different temporal scales, human time and deep time, influence our answers to such questions?

I will argue that the problematization of the painting's conventional title not only amplifies the resonances of Jacobsen's basic dilemmas, but it also contributes to her disturbance of the echo chamber that grows out of and encloses Bruegel's painting. Consequently, this supports her overall vision. Remember, the echo chamber around the painting was heavily dependent on the title. By naming Icarus, the title emphasized his importance. Through the voices of poets such as Auden and Williams, who confirmed in individual distinct ways the centrality of Icarus in Bruegel's painting, the echo chamber subsequently

---

152 W. J. T. Mitchell, *Picture Theory: Essays on Verbal and Visual Representation* (Chicago and London: The University of Chicago Press, 1995), 5, 5 6.

harmonizes and produces loud reverberations which layer like sediment. However, Jacobsen's Atlantic Ocean and, most radically, Naomi's illustration above the book's epigraph by Williams both represent versions of Bruegel's painting in which the sea, landscape, and nature are essential, not Icarus. Naomi does not include Icarus at all, we see only the surface of a dynamic ocean, whereas the Atlantic Ocean embodies deep time in which humans are insignificant, considered to be no more than evolutionary experiments gone wrong, although, importantly, never so wrong as to threaten the rehydration plan or the planet.

6.3 Life, but not Human

Havbrevene poses fundamental questions about the relationship between humans and nature, the effects of human activities, and the future of life on the planet. With its oceanic purity, Naomi's revisionist illustration echoes the words of Rachel Carson in her preface to the 1961 edition of *The Sea Around Us*: "It is a curious situation that the sea, from which life first arose, should now be threatened by the activities of one form of that life. But the sea, though changed in a sinister way, will continue to exist; the threat is rather to life itself."[153] With humans reduced to an evolutionary experiment invented by the Mediterranean Sea as an attempt to help carry out the master plan of the oceans, and with human history reduced to a microscopic parenthesis in earth's history, the question is whether or not life as such—human life, animal life, plant life—will continue to exist when the oceanic master plan reaches its conclusion, and the planet is transformed to all-blue.

Through the Mediterranean Sea, Jacobsen creates a voice that counters the mercilessness of the Atlantic Ocean. The Mediterranean Sea cares for Icarus and regards him as a son. She sympathizes with the refugees whose drowning she witnesses and absorbs. She was even the one who created the human experiment. In that sense, the Mediterranean is the mother of all humans, and Jacobsen mobilizes her long history of entanglement with human culture and her function as the cradle of Western civilization. In the end, though, the opening for a potential future *with humans* and the glimpse of affective hybridity as expressed by the Mediterranean Sea cannot curb the general devolution— only temporarily and seemingly an evolution—initiated four billion years ago into a world *after us*.

There is much evidence supporting that Naomi's Icarus-free illustration shows the most likely, perhaps even the most desirable, future as envisioned

---

153   Rachel Carson, *The Sea Around Us* (1951; New York: Oxford University Press, 2018), xxv.

by Jacobsen in *Havbrevene*. It is a posthuman world, in which the planet is covered by a unified ocean. But it is not a world after organic life as such. The title of the last part, "We become a mother," signals that life in some form or another will continue or begin again. The Atlantic Ocean's final words to her sister supports this: "Soon great forests will once again grow in us, thick and black of nourishment. Just think about that. We will be the only sound in the world." Jacobsen evokes rebirth and a renewal of life in the great mother ocean, which is portrayed—like in Josh Keyes' beautifully chilling images *Phantom* (2016) and *Glider* (2017)—as a fertile and lush incubation vessel for a future re-enchanted submarine world. It may be that the Mediterranean Sea is uncomfortable with such a scenario: "Forgive me. But precisely that thought can be terribly lonely."[154] But such words and feelings are not enough to prevent a blue planet, one that is bluer than the one we call blue today. The final words of the Mediterranean Sea can serve as a reminder to the reader that now is the time for humans to take the condition of our planet seriously. Why? Not so much for our own sake as for the sake of nature. Through anthropomorphism as enunciatory strategy, Jacobsen indicates that nature herself may have a desire for company, at least so if the next evolutionary experiment with humanoid creatures turns out more successful than the first, and that unlike past generations, future humans will possess more "longing to spoon together" than "will to own."

6.4 *Anthropomorphism*

Zalasiewicz claims that it is difficult, as humans, to get a "proper" perspective on the human race. By "proper," he refers to a perspective by nonhuman species (as opposed to human species) that encompasses geological time (as opposed to human lifetime or human history) as well as planetary space (as opposed to place-bound human space). But with "proper," Zalasiewicz could also have an *embedded* perspective in mind, what Donna Haraway has influentially termed "situated knowledge."[155] The combination of nonhuman, geological, planetary, and situated is precisely what makes such a perspective difficult. It should at one and the same time be distant, detached, and different from a human perspective yet still possess recognizable elements: maximum (although not too much) alterity plus minimum (although not too little) familiarity.

In that sense, Jacobsen's oceanic perspective is "proper." We see ourselves from the outside, but not merely from a different cultural (and, thus,

---

154 Jacobsen, *Havbrevene*, 63.
155 Donna Haraway, "Situated Knowledges: The Science Question in Feminism and the Privilege of Partial Perspective," *Feminist Studies* 14, no. 3 (Autumn 1988): 575–599.

anthropocentric) perspective as in, say, Montesquieu's *Lettres persanes* (1721), or, for that matter, in Swift's *Gulliver's Travels* (1726) where scaling of size was added to Montesquieu's purely cultural inversion. The perspective—or at least one of the most important perspectives, since *Havbrevene* stages several perspectives—is properly nonhuman, geological, and planetary, yet Jacobsen also *situates* this perspective through anthropomorphisms such as endowing the oceans with a human language and the ability to write letters as well as humanoid temperaments that are distinguishable from one another. But is it possible to grasp a nonhuman perspective? Is it even possible for a human writer to create such a perspective? Is there not danger of anthropocentric hubris when attempting to adapt nonhuman perspectives since it ultimately eliminates the radical otherness of the nonhuman? Is there not something inherently inauthentic in a nonhuman perspective on the human that is created by a human?

As we saw earlier, Jane Bennett believes that the principal problems associated with this equation are outweighed by the advantages: "We need to cultivate a bit of anthropomorphism—the idea that human agency has some echoes in nonhuman nature—to counter the narcissism of humans in charge of the world."[156] Bennett's demand was met innovatively in the mid-twentieth century by one of the most respected scientists in the field of blue environmentalism, the pioneering Rachel Carson who throughout her career maintained a writing style that combined scientific accuracy and rigor with poetic language and literary generic models. Carson never did so to embellish or blemish the state of the natural world; instead, she had a keen awareness that any epistemological interface between humans and nature is always determined or prefigured by specific generic models and by the specific bodies that see, hear, smell, taste, and feel.

In *Silent Spring*, Carson entitles the first two-page chapter "A Fable of Tomorrow" and opens it with the fairy-tale formula "There was once a town in the heart of America where all life seemed to live in harmony with its surroundings." Carson evokes a pastoral landscape that "delighted the traveller's eye," and which is "famous for the abundance and variety of its bird life." The rural idyll includes "prosperous farms," "fields of grain and hillsides of orchards," where "oak and maple and birch set up a blaze of colour" in the autumn all the while "foxes barked in the hills and deer silently crossed the fields." The generic model underlying Carson's first lines is the pastoral, which signals harmony, peace, and changelessness. This vision is enhanced by

---

156 Bennett, *Vibrant Matter*, xvi.

Carson's poetic vocabulary. But in the third paragraph, Carson abruptly disturbs the image of tranquility and harmony: "Then a strange blight crept over the area and everything began to change. Some evil spell had settled on the community: mysterious maladies swept the flocks of chickens; the cattle and sheep sickened and died." Soon, the melodious spring is replaced by "a spring without voices:" "On the mornings that had once throbbed with the dawn chorus of robins, catbirds, doves, jays, wrens, and scores of other bird voices there was now no sound; only silence lay over the fields and woods and marsh." In the movement from sound to silence, Carson replaces the pastoral with another generic model, the apocalypse, but continues to employ a vocabulary of the fairy tale and poetic language ("evil spell," "mysterious maladies").[157] Peace, harmony, and repetitive seasonal rhythms make way for mass death, antagonism, and unnatural, fatal changes. Bountiful past, ominous present, barren future—this is the generically scripted and poetically articulated narrative Carson presents.

In *Silent Spring*, one of the founding texts of modern environmentalism, Carson employs literary scripts such as the parable, the pastoral, and the apocalypse, the latter two providing her with preexisting visions of the relationship between humans and nature that can be found in "The Book of Genesis" and "The Book of Revelation," the opening and concluding chapters of the Bible. The parable is a short narrative that visualizes or exemplifies a truth, principle, or morale by didactically underlining a tacit analogy with something familiar. It is thus allegorical in its basic structure in that it narrates a coherent set of circumstances (here, the death of birds in a small town caused by a man-made insecticide) that signify a second order of correlated meanings (here, the end of nature on a global scale caused by human behavior in general). In Carson's writing, two important elements must be emphasized. One is her initial speculation that the silencing might be caused by supernatural forces, an idea she soon rejects: "No witchcraft, no enemy action had silenced the rebirth of new life in this stricken world. The people had done it themselves." Responsibility can be placed, *humans* are at fault, and silence is not a result of geological, planetary, or nonhuman evolution. The other is Carson's admission that the town described does not actually exist, yet it could nevertheless "easily have a thousand counterparts in America or elsewhere in the world." Every disaster she describes in the opening chapter has happened somewhere, so Carson's fictional town is a *condensation* of events taking place around the world. This literary device helps illustrate matters of

---

157   Rachel Carson, *Silent Spring* (1962; London: Penguin, 2000), 21–22.

concern that would otherwise seem fragmented and dispersed and therefore difficult to grasp.[158]

If Carson's style combines scientific data with literary tropes and genres in *Silent Spring*, in her debut book, *Under the Sea-Wind: A Naturalist's Picture of Ocean Life* (1941), she fashions a perspectival heterogeneity and alterity, a strategy similar to that applied by Jacobsen in *Havbrevene*. Originally published as an essay in *The Atlantic Monthly* in 1937 under the title "Undersea," Carson was encouraged by publisher Simon & Schuster to expand her essay into a book, as readers were captivated by her poetic ability to access to maritime life on its own terms. *Under the Sea-Wind* is a scientific book, but by focalizing the narrative through a female sanderling called Silverbar (first part), a mackerel named Scomber (second part), and Anguilla, an eel (third part), Carson produces a novel as much as a book of natural history. In each of the book's three parts, we follow a different organism throughout a whole year as it migrates and interacts with the sea. For most of the time, everything that happens is seen from the personified organism's perspective. In the preface to the first edition, Carson writes that her objective with employing a novelistic-poetic prose and with personalizing ocean life was "to make the sea and its life as vivid a reality for those who may read the book as it has become for me during the past decade."[159] Interestingly, Carson acknowledges the potentially unsurmountable epistemological barrier between those who have personal experience with the sea and its depths and those who merely have mediated access to it through books and movies. This distinction is a recurring motif in literary history in authors such as Fenimore Cooper (remember his discussions of Scott's *The Pirate*), Melville, and Conrad, all of whom were engaged in the challenge of conveying the distinctive oceanic experience to their landlubber readers. Like her male predecessors, Carson finds a solution to the epistemological problem: the use of literary genres, tropes, and devices, here anthropomorphism and animal focalization. In that sense, Siri Jacobsen is an obvious heir to Carson.

Carson's stated goal anticipates Bennett's reflections on anthropomorphism: "an anthropomorphic element in perception can uncover a whole world of resonances and resemblances—sounds and sights that echo and bounce far more than would be possible were the universe to have a hierarchical structure." Like Jacobsen, Carson aims to de-hierarchize the human and

---

158 Carson, *Silent Spring*, 21–22; see also Greg Garrard, *Ecocriticism*, 2nd edition (London and New York: Routledge, 2012), 1–2.
159 Rachel Carson, *Under the Sea-Wind* (1941; London: Penguin, 2007), 3; see also Arlene Quaratiello, *Rachel Carson: A Biography* (Westport, CT: Greenwood Press, 2004), 26–27.

nonhuman phenomena, so that humans once again become beings with an intrinsic relationship to their surroundings. Bennett again:

> If a green materialism requires of us a more refined sensitivity to the outside-that-is-inside-too, then maybe a bit of anthropomorphizing will prove valuable. Maybe it is worth running the risks associated with anthropomorphizing (superstition, the divinization of nature, romanticism) because it, oddly enough, works against anthropocentrism: a chord is struck between person and thing, and I am no longer above or outside a nonhuman "environment."[160]

It is a precarious and fluid balance. If anthropomorphism strengthens anthropocentrism by hubristically confirming humanity's godlike power and our separation from those phenomena to which and whom we give a voice, it also works in the opposite direction in that it undermines anthropocentrism by fashioning confederations and intimacies between humans and nonhuman organisms and matter. *Havbrevene* adds a twist to this dual structure, subscribing to both possibilities and adding a third: the vision of a planetary evolution superficially caused by human actions, but substantially master planned by the world's oceans. So, Jacobsen not only uses anthropomorphism to strengthen anthropocentrism and to create intimacy between humans and nonhuman beings, but she also uses it to completely overturn the hierarchy between mankind and matter, here the ocean.

---

160 Bennett, *Vibrant Matter*, 99, 120.

Conclusion

Literary history reveals a modernity that has a substantial and crucial maritime component, but a maritime component that has often been overlooked. This is one main argument of *A Poetic History of the Oceans*. In fact, the varied sources analyzed in the previous chapters—historical and philosophical ones, logbooks, paintings and (moving) images along with all the literary texts—inform us that history is also deeply maritime and oceanic. What does that even mean? How does literature reveal this insight? The chapters of this book have contributed multiple and different answers to these and other questions.

The objective of the first chapter on history was to delineate (Western) humanity's changing conceptions of the ocean. I did so through a reading of a wide variety of sources spanning from biblical and Greek-Roman texts and an Icelandic saga to texts by writers such as Camões, Jens Munk, Jules Michelet, Jonas Lie, and Jens Bjørneboe. To understand the maritime world picture of each individual text, I employed a similar approach by examining their temporal configuration (their figure of time and their conception of past, present, and future), their articulation of a distinct relationship between gods, humans, nature, and technology, their image of the ocean, and their poetics. This generic method revealed shared features and conceptions across time but also showed how humanity's conception of the ocean has evolved from a theocentric (–1450) to an anthropocentric (1450–1850) maritime world picture, which was first replaced by a technocentric (1850–1950) and then a geocentric (1950–) maritime world picture.

In the theocentric epoch the dominant component are the gods. The motto of the period is *Non Plus Ultra*, and the ocean is regarded mainly as a barrier that is believed to host monstrous creatures. This is the era of oar and sail during which humans are advised to know their limits. Sea journeys are generally associated with high risks not worth taking. The anthropocentric epoch replaces faith in the gods with a belief in human mastery over nature. *Plus Ultra* replaces *Non Plus Ultra*, and the ocean as barrier is supplemented with the ocean as an enchanting means of passage whose glittery surface allures with fantasies of adventure, wonder, and wealth. During the centuries-long Age of Sail and Discovery, superstitions and sea monsters are replaced by exploration and fish. The contingency of ocean voyages is no longer associated exclusively with risk but also with chance. In the technocentric epoch, modern technology begins to dominate, resulting in a perpetuation of *Plus Ultra* and the understanding of the ocean as a place of passage. In this era of steam, the sea is transformed from fish into a disenchanted machine, and the glitter of the previous age morphs into a grid of saltwater trade routes and scientific mapping. Supplementing the dimensions of risk and chance are powerful humanmade means of control and calculation. Belief in progress prevails as does fascination with knowledge gained through scientific explorations. In the geocentric epoch, nature and the blueness of the planet gain heightened significance. The *Non Plus Ultra* attitude returns, cautioning humans against limitless expansion and growth, and the ocean is understood to be a coherent ecosystem vital to all forms of life on the planet and the planet itself. This is the era of diesel and inorganic chemicals during which the saltwater sea is transformed into a plastic ocean or, in some works, is re-enchanted in an attempt to foster human care through words and images. Belief in human control over nature is replaced by a realization of our impotence, and a suspicion toward calculation as miscalculation sets in.

If there is a self-conscious simplicity on my part in this stage-by-stage chronological construction, there are nevertheless two points. One is that efforts to synthesize always entail the danger of erasing nuances and downgrading the odd singularities that might contest the beauty of the construction. But these four maritime world pictures tell nuanced stories with a lot of historical truth. The second and perhaps more important point is that I consider my amphibian approach of analyzing poetic strategies, ocean images, figures of time, conceptions of the past, present, and future, and articulations of the relationship between gods, humans, technology, and nature to be a cohesive method applicable to further readings into maritime literature. I also activated this generic method in greater detail in my reading of Melville's *Moby-Dick*, while drawing on philosophies of time developed by Koselleck and Gumbrecht, which concluded the historical chapter. This reading had a dual function in that it offers a simultaneous summation and deconstruction of the previous stage-by-stage narrative. That is, it confirmed the fundamental chronology and content of the narrative, but the reading also undermined the narrative by showing how maritime texts are often composites of several maritime world pictures, and how they frequently employ a variety of poetic strategies to mime and construct the oceanic. *Moby-Dick* may be a preeminent example of such "composture" poetics, as Mentz calls it, but it is not the only one. In general, maritime literature is associated with a crisis of representation and therefore also with innovations in formal and aesthetic strategies, partly in response to the immensity of an object (the ocean) that is notoriously difficult to match and figure, and partly in response to technological inventions that have made previous forms obsolete.

In the chapter on maritime rhythms, I replace the hermeneutical approach of the historical chapter with a more sense-oriented method. The ambition of this chapter was to come closer to how it feels for a human body to be on board an ocean-going vessel as well as to examine the moments of homeliness and stability that also characterize maritime existence along with its potential risks, conflicts, and breakdowns. The chapter was motivated by the following question: What contributes to the homeliness of the ship and the sea? Close readings of passages from a variety of literary texts show that maritime literature is a privileged place from which to exercise what Henri Lefebvre called rhythmanalysis with its examination of biological-natural, cultural-social, and aesthetic-formal rhythms. Rhythmanalysis mobilizes a different conceptual vocabulary than the one traditionally associated with a hermeneutical approach: not meaning but presence; less interpreting, more grasping. Interpretation is replaced by description, depth by surface, the bodily by the mind, and sense is less about signification and more about the sensuous. In this chapter, I showed how the body of a sailor acts as a metronome maintaining rhythms as he navigates the ship through storms and in calms seas, to avoid reefs, and to profit from the winds and the waves. The role of the sailor as a human and rhythmic instrument also applies to interactions with fellow crew members as they perform their duties on the ship.

The interior of the ship contains spaces in which seafarers perform sequences of highly choreographed activities. Performances of the scripted body-ballets act as counterweights to the threatening chaos of the surrounding ocean. What a rhythm *means* becomes less important than how it *functions*. Adopting the rhythmanalytical method enabled me to appreciate and demonstrate that shipboard life and maritime existence, clothed in cosmic rhythms of nature and dictated by stringent cultural rhythms, is an extremely a bodily and affective culture, what Gumbrecht calls a presence culture. The analysis of maritime rhythms means that we can read literature and cultural artifacts in new and more rhythmic ways that show greater sensibility toward materialities, moods, bodily effects and affects, as well as the immanent rhythm of physical things. If the ship and the ocean oscillate between being space and place—between being movement and pause, freedom and security, threat and claustrophobia—then the maritime rhythms are what determine the direction and tempo of the oceanic pendulum. As we saw, the cosmic-cyclical and the social-linear rhythms jointly endow the ship life with form and homeliness, yet these same rhythms—if disrupted or stopped altogether—bring forth chaos, disruption, and potential destruction to the ship and those on board.

At the end of the chapter on rhythms, I discuss the implications of the rhythmanalytical method for classroom pedagogy and writing styles. Because rhythmanalysis is descriptive, not interpretive, it is a means of reducing the current focus on ideology and semantics and a way of helping students to become more receptive to the aesthetic and rhythmic qualities of art. Meditating on their own writing practices, Lefebvre and Régulier admit that their ambition is to unite the scientific and the poetic, or at least to minimize any separation between the two forms of knowledge and the two genres. Consequently, they propose a discourse that either poetically and lyrically will evoke splendor or, through a descriptive approach and style, will capture the rhythmic and sensuous dimensions of a city, a place, or a text and make them comprehensible and graspable. Inherent in their suggestions is a call for an expansion of our scholarly vocabulary.

The chapter on technology reignited the hermeneutical approach in that I examined the mediating role of premodern and modern technologies in maritime literature, in particular "Relação da muy notavel perda do Galeão Grande S. João," *Typhoon*, and *Vingt mille lieues sous les mers*, through phenomenological thinkers such as Heidegger, Don Ihde, and Peter-Paul Verbeek. The chapter's central argument was that maritime existence is per definition technological, whether in the form of canoes propelled forward by human strength applied to paddles, or of ships using sails to catch winds and follow ocean currents as their means of motion, or steamships whose propellers are rotated by the power generated by burning coal. With the invention of new instruments, new perceptions emerge. Therefore, I analyzed the distinctive experiences of different technological environments at sea.

The account of the shipwreck of the *São João* revealed an impressive awareness of technological crisis, although the overarching discourse was still religious. The maritime worlds of Jules Verne and Joseph Conrad become intensely technological. If Verne is regarded a writer welcoming the possibilities of scientific and societal progress as well as geographical advancements made possible by the invention of new technologies, Conrad is considered a reactionary critic of modern technology because it entails alienation, disenchantment, and moral corruption. My readings showed how these perceptions are correct, but I also nuanced them by showing that Verne exhibits ambivalent and complex attitudes to modern technologies, and that Conrad finds positive human experiences on board a steamship in distress. It was my intent to steer clear of the rigid dichotomy between utopianism and dystopianism

My reading of *Typhoon* unfolds as an examination of the different technological experiences onboard the *Nan-Shan* and a close reading of Captain MacWhirr's character. My reading reveals that MacWhirr unites the complementary viewpoints of calculative and meditative thinking, the technological and contemplative approaches, and the challenging and collected attitudes into a single point of view: the composed attitude. Maintaining composure is Conrad's means of preserving a unique maritime-technological form of experience that is an acceptable and nonreductive world-disclosure with a capacity to safeguard the sailor and increase chances of survival in his encounters with extreme natural phenomena. Conrad's profound explorations of technology's role as mediator between man and his environment makes *Typhoon* one of the great existentialist novels.

In *Vingt mille lieues*, Verne also stages an experiment with technology as mediator between man and his surroundings, but his novel is not existentialist. Verne's interest is not in the transformation of human psychology by technological innovations; instead, he focuses on technology as a motor for scientific and geographical discoveries. This is one reason why I claimed that Conrad is an author of the *passé recent*, whereas Verne is an author of the *futur proche*. My reading of Verne shows that his underwater voyage is genuinely global. Verne organizes a recapitulation and completion of a century's disconnected conquests into a conclusive epistemological system and explication of the (submarine) world. The genuinely new in *Vingt mille lieues sous les mers* is the world of the underwater depths and, by implication, the potential planetarity of its vision. As we saw, Verne's universe is one of the marvelous and the extraordinary, but it is at the same time saturated by poetic techniques of vraisemblance. In *Vingt mille lieues*, science is elevated to primary focus in that it absorbs state-of-the-art knowledge from several domains such as ichthyology, conchyliology, hydrography, and meteorology. Science and classification are supplemented with poetry and lyricism in a poetics comprising both Apollonian and Dionysian elements. The scientifically infused encyclopedic impulse and the stylistic oscillations make Verne's novel into one of the true books of the sea.

In the chapter on materiality, my focus was on maritime entanglements between humans and nonhumans and between organic and inorganic matter. I first discussed the aesthetic strategies of maritime immersion in the experimental documentary *Leviathan* by Lucien Castaing-Taylor and Véréna Paravel and used this discussion to frame the subsequent analysis of Hugo's *Les Travailleurs de la mer*. The objective was to read the novel as a poetic staging of a reimagined relationship between humans and nonhumans. To do so, my reading mobilizes theories by Jane Bennett, Stacey Alaimo, Jeffrey J. Cohen, Bill Brown, and Maurizio Boscagli as I situated Hugo's protomodernist novel in the context of new materialism. This context allowed us to acknowledge and appreciate the crucial role of the novel's extensive introduction that almost reads as a travel guide to the Channel Islands with its blend of natural history and anthropological observations. Supplementing this chapter are several additional chapters in the book that challenge anthropocentrism and introduce a universe of material and nonhuman forces.

Les Travailleurs de la mer, like *Moby-Dick*, thematically centers on the relationship between gods, humans, technology, and nature, and in some passages, it anticipates contemporary discourses and ideas about human-caused climate change. My reading, which included illustrations by Gustave Doré and Hugo, showed that sections of *Les Travailleurs* express a radical posthuman vision of the world, incorporating deep time and depicting the energetic forces of inorganic matter such as stones, rocks, and steamships, forces that constantly oscillate between creation and effacement. The toilers of the sea are both humans and nonhumans, organic and inorganic matter.

In the final chapter on the Anthropocene, the objective was to examine how writers have imagined the ocean and its possible role in a warming world. I started out by introducing the Anthropocene and its characteristics of both slow, accumulating violence and the suddenness of fierce and freak weather events, which seem to become the new normal. I then introduced different theories of the novel by Moretti, Ghosh, Pavel, Underwood, and others to discuss the genre's (in)capacity to embrace and match the Anthropocene challenges of a new world order produced by a powerful humanity, and a condition in which humans have been left impotent in the face of potentially catastrophic Earth system processes run amok. The dominant form of the novel, sometimes referred to as "the serious novel," displays three key features, which make it difficult for this form to match the Anthropocene: concealment of exceptional moments, concretization of individual perspective, and contraction of narrated time and space. Subsequently, I analyzed three literary works, Krarup Nielsen's *En hvalfangerfærd*, Ballard's *The Drowned World*, and Jacobsen's *Havbrevene*. Their generic differences were important since my intention was to show the representational limitations and strengths of different formats when confronting the Anthropocene Ocean.

My reading of Nielsen's travelogue emphasizes how it registers human activities and a mindset that we can read today as origins to fossil fuel-driven climate change and species extinction. *En hvalfangerfærd* was written prior to our acknowledgment of the Anthropocene, but by presenting a fragment of political and environmental history around the year 1920, it offers valuable insights into our current predicament. With Andreas Malm we can say that "invisible missiles aimed at the future" are at work in *En hvalfangerfærd*. The most important "missiles" are the belief in human exceptionalism, the confidence in capitalistic growth, and the reliance on nature as stock. These attitudes are consolidated into missiles more tangible, as in the burning of coal and the killing of whales. Underlying this, and with reference to Conrad's theory of three types of geographical thinking, Nielsen promotes what I call a monetary geography and subscribes to a geometrical scientific impulse. The travelogue form allows Nielsen to incorporate a more collective scope loosened from any individual perspective and traditional plot demands by centering on the whaling industry through an anthropologically oriented discourse.

Ballard's focus in *The Drowned World* is to envision the potential psychobiological effects of the hydro- and geophysical effects of inundation. The analysis of Ballard's sci-fi novel revealed a radical vision of a species-specific biological transformation for humanity, which on a geological time scale is regarded as a positive event. On a flooded planet, species preservation is pointless since humans in our current form only have a limited existence. In *The Drowned World*, the Holocene human is unfit to survive on the post-Holocene (Anthropocene) planet, but we may reinvent ourselves as a species by descending the evolutionary ladder, returning to the sea, and eventually entering a second Triassic period. To Ballard, preservation of the human species presupposes an unwanted antagonism between humans and nature, so he introduces what he labels a "zone of transit," which is a transformative and hybrid model in which humans comprise dimensions of geology, hydrology, biology, and psychology, a model defined by metabolism, entanglement, and exposure. I argue that Ballard collapses the future into familiar vistas of the deep past. The clocks moving forward really signal an evolution moving backward. Evolution is, ultimately, devolution. Ballard's choice of the sci-fi form makes it possible for him to escape the narrow poetics of the "serious" novel. *The Drowned World* is not limited to the portrayal of a protagonist's lifetime but opens up vistas of evolutionary deep time. Kerans may be an individual with singular attributes and experiences, but he also becomes a type, a representative of species transformation, in part because of sci-fi's allegorical mode. The novel takes place in a fluid, planetary space that overrides and overwhelms the old geopolitical borders of nation-states. Finally, probability, the most important characteristic of the serious novel, has morphed into the unthinkable, but not impossible.

The same degree of radicalness characterizes the vision in *Havbrevene*, in which Jacobsen also points toward a posthuman blue planet on which nonhuman life may reemerge and regenerate in the fertile conditions of the submarine world. Where Ballard's novel has a significant psychological component, Jacobsen's work is characterized by its innovative enunciatory strategy: letters written by oceans combined with evocative illustrations, textual sources and narratives by humans, and an elaborated meditation on the Icarus myth. The epistolary form, the anthropomorphizing of the oceans, and the multimodality of *Havbrevene* allow Jacobsen to exploit a formal elasticity that transgresses the poetic limitations of the serious novel. With scales and perspectives ranging from site specific to planetary space, from personal history to geological history, and from human perspectives to oceanic perspectives,

Jacobsen and Naomi stage a virtuoso play with a happy ending (from an oceanic perspective): a de-anthropocentricized world. From the perspective of the Mediterranean Sea, Jacobsen upholds an affective link to humanity, as personified by Icarus. Though her numerous readaptations of the Icarus myth, most notably the Bruegel painting, she explores multiple interpretations of Icarus and feelings toward him that we would describe as human. However, the outcome of the plot ultimately points toward a posthuman world in which all seas are reunited, and the planet Earth is once again entirely covered in blue. As in *The Drowned World*, *Havbrevene* foresees a biological restart made possible by the incubatory forces of the submarine world.

•••

A Poetic History of the Oceans has shown the importance of the ocean in human and planetary history through readings of various sources, most of them literary, from different epochs and areas. Some of these sources have upheld a canonical status for decades or even centuries, while others have led a more anonymous life. Including both was a deliberate choice. The book features some of the big names in the canon of English language maritime literature: Shakespeare, Defoe, Cooper, Turner, Melville, Conrad, and Ballard. Alongside those, I analyzed non-Anglo canonical authors such as Homer, Camões, Michelet, Hugo, and Verne. In addition, I also introduced writers and texts from the Nordic archive, which may be less familiar to a global readership, but which are essential to include in a comprehensive oceanic and maritime cultural history; examples are "The Saga of the Greenlanders," Jens Munk, Jonas Lie, Holger Drachmann, Jens Bjørneboe, and Siri Ranva Hjelm Jacobsen. My intention to make a global Blue Cultural Studies readership more familiar with important maritime sources from the Nordic countries represents not only an archival but also an interventionist purpose. The readings of these sources mean that *A Poetic History of the Oceans* is more than just another introduction to oceanic literature in the West. It is also intended to be an intervention in and an original contribution to the shape of that discourse.

By demonstrating that a transgressive mentality and "nautical original sin" already existed before the great Spanish and Portuguese transoceanic voyages, the analysis of "The Saga of the Greenlanders" softened the traditional view of a historical break around 1500 conceptualized as an oceanic turn by Carl Schmitt and others. My reading of Munk shows that he epitomizes a new anthropocentric spirit and is also an important precursor to Defoe's *Robinson Crusoe*. As we saw, Lie deconstructs Fenimore Cooper—*The Pilot* morphs into *The Pilot and His Wife* and signals more generally the important role of active female characters in Nordic maritime fiction—and his Rejer Jansen Juhl is a Nordic relative of Ahab and Nemo. I put forward that while Drachmann implicitly went along with Hegel's idea of the novel as a modern bourgeois epic, his micro-poetics of literature as articulated in "Ørnen" and other documents move in a different direction to Hegel's. Drachmann used words such as *wet* and *salt* to describe his poetics more than a century before Steve Mentz elevated them to keywords in Blue Humanities. With *Haiene*, my analysis suggested how Jens Bjørneboe emerges as a worthy Scandinavian heir to Conrad. And with *Havbrevene*, we saw how Siri Ranva Hjelm Jacobsen innovatively intervenes in a global discourse on climate change. A new thalassology from the Scandinavian realm is also represented by writers such as Maja Lunde and Morten Strøksnes.

The ambition to reinsert the ocean in the engine room of human and planetary history is fueled by a revisionist resolve as well as the contemporary climate crisis. Our historiographical perspectives have been primarily terrestrial, meaning that the massive role of the ocean as both premise for and motor of development when it comes to phenomena such as societal development, imperialism and colonialism, the transformation of mercantilism into capitalism, advances in aesthetic theory and new thematic and formal paths in literary history, the invention of new technologies, the emergence of an empirical and materialist epistemology, and the circulation of books, cultural artefacts, and ideas has been minimized or absent in the majority of cultural and literary histories.

The revisionist resolve is founded on a dual acknowledgement, that the Ocean is a mighty presence in human life from which we are radically separated and with which we are also extremely intimate. From an evolutionary perspective, we emerged as species from the saltwater basins covering Planet Earth, hence the senses of familiarity and intimacy many of us feel whenever we are near the ocean. However, there is no apparent chance of us turning back on the evolutionary ladder. Our shared destiny remains firmly on *terra firma*, hence the sense of separation we feel at times when the ocean threatens to absorb us. From a cultural perspective, humans live their lives and conduct their business in cities and megacities, in the green countryside and industrialized rural areas, or on semi-barren mountainsides, all separated from the ocean. Only a small minority of us spend our lives at sea. However, the various sources analyzed in this book also demonstrate that human history is only terrestrial in a superficial sense; actually, it is profoundly marked by a maritime component. Shifting from a human to a geological perspective, planetary history is deeply oceanic. Finally, literary history as we are used to reading it is admittedly a history authored by humans about human earthbound existence;

however, on closer examination it is also a history of entanglements between the human and the nonhuman, between the terrestrial and the nautical. Hence the need for an amphibian approach to literature.

The historical importance of the ocean has become dramatically more apparent because of our contemporary climate and existential crises. Earth's history is now striking back against human history with a vengeance. The human species face a present and a future with rising sea levels and potentially violent, but definitely wet weather events such a floods, cyclones, and heavy cloudbursts. Planetary history is unstable with or without human intervention. The Earth has been flooded before, but now there are close to eight billion people inhabiting the Earth, and together with our recent forefathers many of us are implicated in bringing about an accelerated heating of the planet. Naturally, the effects strike back on us in unpredictable and uneven ways far beyond our control. Literature and the arts envision such scenarios of a dark blue future in a variety of ways. Although literature and the arts cannot shield us from tsunamis and the rising seas, they could, through their imaginative power, creative language, and innovative forms, help us prepare for or even cope with changes in our existential conditions. What is literary form if not an attempt to manage chaos and articulate a world picture? *A Poetic History of the Oceans* demonstrates how their exploration of the frontiers of the unknown and their poetic reactions to crisis make the wet fables, old and new, especially instructive for humanity.

Bibliography

Abulafia, David. *The Boundless Sea: A Human History of the Oceans.* London: Allen Lane, 2019.

Abulafia, David. *The Great Sea: A Human History of the Mediterranean.* 2011. London: Penguin, 2012.

Achebe, Chinua. "An Image of Africa: Racism in Conrad's 'Heart of Darkness.'" *Massachusetts Review: A Quarterly of Literature, the Arts and Public Affairs* 18 (1977): 782–794.

Achterhuis, Hans. *American Philosophy of Technology: The Empirical Turn.* 1997. Translated by Robert P. Crease. Bloomington: Indiana University Press, 2001.

Agnew, John. "The territorial trap: the geographical assumptions of international relations theory." *Review of International Political Economy* 1 (1994): 53–80.

Alaimo, Stacy. *Exposed: Environmental Politics and Pleasures in Posthuman Times.* Minneapolis and London: University of Minnesota Press, 2016.

Amis, Martin. "Introduction." In J. G. Ballard. *The Drowned World.* 1962. London: Fourth Estate, 2014.

Anand, Ram P. *Origin and Development of the Law of the Sea.* The Hague: Martinus Nijhoff, 1983.

Anderson, Benedict. *Imagined Communities: Reflections on the Origin and Spread of Nationalism.* New York: Verso, 1983.

Auden, W. H. *The Collected Poetry of W. H. Auden.* New York: Random House, 1945.

Auden, W. H. *The Enchafèd Flood: or, The Romantic Iconography of the Sea.* New York: Vintage, 1950.

Bachelard, Gaston. *Water and Dreams: An Essay on the Imagination of Water.* Translated by Edith R. Farrell. Dallas: Pegasus Foundation, 1983.

Bacon, Francis. *The instauratio magna part II: Novum organum and associated texts.* 1620. Edited by Graham Rees and Maria Wakely. Oxford: Oxford University Press, 2004.

Bache-Wiig, Harald. *Med lik i lasten: Subjekt og modernitet i Jonas Lies romanunivers.* Oslo: Novus Forlag, 2009.

Ballard, J. G. *The Drowned World.* 1962. London: Fourth Estate, 2014.

Ballard, J. G. "Reality is a Stage Set." Interview by Travis Elborough. In *The Drowned World.* 1962. London: Fourth Estate, 2014.

Ballard, J. G. "Science Fiction Monthly Interview." Interview by David Pringle and Jim Goddard. *Science Fiction Monthly.* January 4, 1975. Accessed January 31, 2020. https://www.jgballard.ca/media/1975_jan4_science_fiction_monthly.html.

Ballard, J. G. "Time, Memory and Inner Space." In *The Drowned World.* 1962. London: Fourth Estate, 2014.

Baucom, Ian. *Specters of the Atlantic: Finance Capital, Slavery, and the Philosophy of History*. Durham and London: Duke University Press, 2005.

Bauman, Zygmunt. *Liquid Modernity*. 2000. Cambridge: Polity Press, 2012.

Beebee, Thomas O. "Carl Schmitt's Myth of Benito Cereno." *seminar* 42, no. 2 (2006): 114–34.

Bellow, Saul. "The Search for Symbols, a Writer Warns, Misses All the Fun and Fact of the Story." *New York Times*. February 15, 1959.

Bennett, Jane. *Vibrant Matter: A Political Ecology of Things*. Durham and London: Duke University Press, 2010.

Benvéniste, Emile. *Problems in General Linguistics*. Volume 1. Translated by Mary Elizabeth Meek. Miami: Miami University Press, 1971.

Bercovitch, Sacvan. *The American Jeremiad*. Madison: The University of Wisconsin Press, 1978.

Berthoud, Jacques A. *Joseph Conrad: The Major Phase*. Cambridge: Cambridge University Press, 1978.

Bjørneboe, Jens. *The Sharks: The History of a Crew and a Shipwreck*. 1974. Translated by Esther Greenleaf Mürer. Norwich: Norvik Press, 1992.

Blackmore, Josiah. *Manifest Perdition: Shipwreck Narrative and the Disruption of Empire*. Minnesota: University of Minnesota Press, 2002.

Blum, Hester. *The View from the Masthead: Maritime Imagination and Antebellum American Sea Narratives*. Chapel Hill: The University of North Carolina Press, 2008.

Blumenberg, Hans. *The Legitimacy of the Modern Age*. 1966. Translated by Robert M. Wallace. 1976. Cambridge, MA: The MIT Press, 1999.

Blumenberg, Hans. *Shipwreck with Spectator: Paradigm of a Metaphor for Existence*. 1979. Translated by Steven Rendall. London and Cambridge, MA: The MIT Press, 1997.

Bonneuil, Christophe and Jean-Baptiste Fressoz. *The Shock of the Anthropocene: The Earth, History and Us*. 2013. Translated by David Fernbach. London: Verso, 2017.

Boscagli, Maurizia. *Stuff Theory: Everyday Objects, Radical Materialism*. New York and London: Bloomsbury, 2014.

Bouhour, Père Dominique. *Les Entretiens d'Ariste et d'Eugène*. Paris: Mabre-Cramoisy, 1671.

Boyesen, Hjalmar Hjort. *Essays on Scandinavian Literature*. New York: Charles Scribner's Sons, 1895.

Bradbrook, M. C. *Joseph Conrad: Poland's English Genius*. Cambridge: Cambridge University Press, 1941.

Braudel, Fernand. *The Mediterranean and the Mediterranean World in the Age of Philip II*. 1949. Volume 1. Translated by Siân Reynolds. 1972. Berkeley: University of California Press, 1996.

Brombert, Victor. "*Les Travailleurs de la mer*: Hugo's Poem of Effacement." *New Literary History* 9, no. 3 (Spring, 1978): 581–590.

Brombert, Victor. *Victor Hugo and the Visionary Novel*. Cambridge, MA., and London: Harvard University Press, 1984.

Brown, Bill. *A Sense of Things: The Object Matter of American Literature*. Chicago and London: The University of Chicago Press, 2003.

Brown, Wendy. *Walled States, Waning Sovereignty*. 2010. New York: Zone Books, 2017.

Bruss, Paul S. *Conrad's Early Sea Fiction*. London: Associated University Presses, 1979.

Buchanan, Brenda J. "Editor's Introduction: Setting the Context." In *Gunpowder, Explosives and the State: A Technological History*. Edited by Brenda J. Buchanan. Aldershot: Ashgate, 2006.

Buell, Lawrence. *The Environmental Imagination: Thoreau, Nature Writing, and the Formation of American Culture*. Cambridge, MA, and London: Harvard University Press, 1995.

Butcher, William. "Introduction." "Appendix." "Explanatory Notes." In Jules Verne. *Twenty Thousand Leagues under the Seas*. 1869–70/1871. Translated and with introduction and notes by William Butcher. Oxford: Oxford University Press, 1998.

Camões, Luís Vaz de. *The Lusíads*. Translated, introduction, and notes by Landeg White. 1997. New York: Oxford University Press, 2001.

Carson, Rachel. *The Sea Around Us*. 1951. New York: Oxford University Press, 2018.

Carson, Rachel. *Silent Spring*. 1962. London: Penguin, 2000.

Carson, Rachel. *Under the Sea-Wind*. 1941. London: Penguin, 2007.

Casarino, Cesare. *Modernity at Sea: Melville, Marx, Conrad in Crisis*. Minneapolis: University of Minnesota Press, 2002.

Casey, Edward S. *Getting Back into Place: Toward a Renewed Understanding of the Place-World*. 1993. 2nd edition. Bloomington and Indianapolis: Indiana University Press, 2009.

Catcott, Alexander. *A Treatise on the Deluge*. London: E. Allen, 1768.

Celan, Paul. *Der Meridian: Endfassung, Vorstufen, Materialen*. Frankfurt am Main: Suhrkamp, 1999.

Chamier, Frederick. *The Life of a Sailor*. Volume 3. 1831–32. London: Richard Bentley, 1832.

Chandra, Satish. "Introduction." In *The Indian Ocean: Explorations in History, Commerce, and Politics*. Edited by Satish Chandra. New Delhi: Sage, 1987.

Chesneaux, Jean. *Une lecture politique de Jules Verne*. Paris: Maspéro, 1971.

Clarke, Jim. "Reading Climate Change in J. G. Ballard," *Critical Survey* 25, no. 2 (2013): 7–21.

Clavel, Marcel. *Fenimore Cooper and His Critics*. Aix-en-Provence: Imprimerie Universitaire de Provence, 1938.

Clavel, Marcel. *Fenimore Cooper: Sa vie et son œuvre: La jeunesse (1789–1826)*. Aix-en-Provence: Imprimerie Universitaire de Provence, 1938.

Cohen, Jeffrey Jerome. *Stone: An Ecology of the Inhuman*. Minneapolis and London: University of Minnesota Press, 2015.

Cohen, Margaret. "The Chronotopes of the Sea." In *The Novel, vol. 2: Forms and Themes.* Edited by Franco Moretti. Princeton, NJ: Princeton University Press, 2006.

Cohen, Margaret. "Fluid States: The Maritime in Modernity." *Cabinet* 16 (Winter 2004–2005): 75–82.

Cohen, Margaret. "Literary Studies on the Terraqueous Globe." PMLA 125, no. 3 (2010): 657–662.

Cohen, Margaret. *The Novel and the Sea.* Princeton and Oxford: Princeton University Press, 2010.

Cohen, Margaret. "Traveling Genres." *New Literary History* 34, no. 3 (2003): 481–499.

Coleridge, Samuel Taylor. "The Rime of the Ancyent Marinere." In *Lyrical Ballads.* William Wordsworth and Samuel Taylor Coleridge. 1798. London: Henry Frowde, 1911.

The Congressional Globe: The Debates, Proceedings, and Laws of the First Session of the Thirty-Second Congress. Volume XXIV. Part II. City of Washington: John C. Rives, 1852.

Conrad, Joseph. "Certain Aspects of the Admirable Inquiry into the Loss of the *Titanic.*" In *Notes on Life and Letters.* 1921. In *Collected Edition of the Works of Joseph Conrad.* 1926. London: J. M. Dent & Sons, 1970.

Conrad, Joseph. "The Character of the Foe." In *The Mirror and the Sea: Memories and Impressions—A Personal Record: Some Reminiscences.* 1906/1912. In *Collected Edition of the Works of Joseph Conrad.* 1923. London: J. M. Dent & Sons, 1975.

Conrad, Joseph. *The Collected Letters of Joseph Conrad.* Volume 5. Edited by Frederick Karl and Laurence Davies. Cambridge: Cambridge University Press, 1996.

Conrad, Joseph. *The End of the Tether.* 1902. In *Youth, Heart of Darkness* and *The End of the Tether: Three Stories by Joseph Conrad.* 1902. In *Collected Edition of the Works of Joseph Conrad.* London: J. M. Dent and Sons, 1960.

Conrad, Joseph. "Falk: A Reminiscence." 1901/1903. In *Typhoon and Other Stories.* In *Collected Edition of the Works of Joseph Conrad.* 1923. London: J. M. Dent & Sons Ltd, 1950.

Conrad, Joseph. "Geography and Some Explorers." 1924. *Tales of Hearsay and Last Essays.* In *Collected Edition of the Works of Joseph Conrad.* 1928. London: J. M. Dent and Sons Ltd, 1955.

Conrad, Joseph. *Heart of Darkness.* 1899/1902. In *Youth, Heart of Darkness* and *The End of the Tether.* 1902. In *Collected Edition of the Works of Joseph Conrad.* 1923. London: J. M. Dent & Sons Ltd, 1960.

Conrad, Joseph. *The Mirror and the Sea: Memories and Impressions—A Personal Record: Some Reminiscences.* 1906/1912. In *Collected Edition of the Works of Joseph Conrad.* 1923. London: J. M. Dent & Sons, 1975.

Conrad, Joseph. *The Nigger of the "Narcissus": A Tale of the Sea.* 1897. In *Collected Edition of the Works of Joseph Conrad.* 1923. London: J. M. Dent & Sons Ltd., 1950.

Conrad, Joseph. "Ocean Travel." 1923. In *Tales of Hearsay and Last Essays.* In *Collected Edition of the Works of Joseph Conrad.* 1928. London: J. M. Dent and Sons Ltd, 1955.

Conrad, Joseph. "Tales of the Sea." 1898. In *Notes on Life and Letters*. 1921. In *Collected Edition of the Works of Joseph Conrad*. 1926. London: J. M. Dent & Sons, 1970.
Conrad, Joseph. *Typhoon*. 1902. In *Typhoon and Other Stories*. 1903. In *Collected Edition of the Works of Joseph Conrad*. 1923. London: J. M. Dent & Sons Ltd., 1950.
Cooper, James Fenimore. *The Two Admirals: A Tale*. 1842. In *The Writings of James Fenimore Cooper*. Historical introduction by Donald A. Ringe. Text established by James A. Sappenfield and E. N. Feltskog. Albany, NY: SUNY Press, 1990.
Cooper, James Fenimore. *Gleanings in Europe: England*. 1837. In *The Writings of James Fenimore Cooper*. Historical introduction and explanatory notes by Donald A. Ringe and Kenneth W. Staggs. Text established by James P. Elliott, Kenneth W. Staggs, and Robert D. Madison. Albany: SUNY Press, 1981.
Cooper, James Fenimore. *Notions of the Americans: Picked up by a Travelling Bachelor*. 1828. In *The Writings of James Fenimore Cooper*. Text established with historical introduction and textual notes by Gary Williams. Albany, NY: SUNY Press, 1991.
Cooper, James Fenimore. *The Pilot; A Tale of the Sea*. 1824. In *The Writings of James Fenimore Cooper*. Edited, historical introduction, and explanatory notes by Kay Seymour House. Albany, NY: SUNY Press, 1986.
Cooper, James Fenimore. *The Red Rover: A Tale*. 1827. In *The Writings of James Fenimore Cooper*. Edited by Thomas and Marianne Philbrick. Albany: State University of New York Press, 1991.
Corbin, Alain. *Le ciel et la mer*. Paris: Bayard Culture, 2005.
Corbin, Alain. *The Lure of the Sea: The Discovery of the Seaside 1750–1840*. 1988. Translated by Jocelyn Phelps. 1994. London: Penguin, 1995.
Corbin, Alain, and Hélène Richard. *La mer, terreur et fascination*. Paris: BNF, 2004.
Correspondance inédite de Jules Verne et de Pierre-Jules Hetzel: 1863–1886. Volume 1, 1863–1874. Edited by Olivier Dumas, Piero Gondolo della Riva, and Volker Dehs. Genève: Slatkine, 1999.
Cox, C. B. *Joseph Conrad: The Modern Imagination*. London: Dent, 1974.
Crutzen, Paul J., and Eugene F. Stoermer. "The 'Anthropocene.'" *IGBP Newsletter* 41 (2000): 17–18.
Crutzen, Paul J. "Geology of Mankind." *Nature* 415, no. 6867 (2002): 23.
Daleski, H. M. *Joseph Conrad: The Way of Dispossession*. New York: Holmes & Meier, 1976.
Daley, Christopher. "The Not So Cozy Catastrophe: Reimagining the British Disaster Novel in J. G. Ballard's *The Drowned World* (1962) and Brian Aldiss's *Barefoot in the Head* (1969)." In *Apocalyptic Discourse in Contemporary Culture: Post-Millennial Perspectives on the End of the World*. Edited by Monica Germanà and Aris Mousoutzanis. New York and London: Routledge: 2014.
Damrosch, David. "World Literature in a Postcanonical, Hypercanonical Age." In *Comparative Literature in an Age of Globalization*. Edited by Haun Saussy. Baltimore, MD: Johns Hopkins University Press, 2006.

Davis, Thomas S. "Fossils of Tomorrow: Len Lye, J. G. Ballard, and Planetary Futures." *Modern Fiction Studies* 64, no. 4 (Winter 2018): 659–679.
de Certeau, Michel. "Writing the Sea: Jules Verne." In *Heterologies: Discourse on the Other*. Translated by Brian Massumi. Manchester: Manchester University Press, 1986.
de Saint-Denis, E. "Michelet et la mer de la Manche." *Revue d'Histoire littéraire de la France* 61, no. 1 (1961): 36–47.
de Vries, Lyckle. "Bruegel's *Fall of Icarus*: Ovid or Solomon?" *Simiolus: Netherlands Quarterly for the History of Art* 30, no. 1–2 (2003): 4–18.
Defoe, Daniel. *Robinson Crusoe*. 1719. Edited an introduction by Thomas Keymer. Notes by Thomas Keymer and James Kelly. Oxford: Oxford University Press, 2008.
Dekker, George and John P. McWilliams, eds. *Fenimore Cooper: The Critical Heritage*. London and Boston: Routledge and Kegan Paul, 1973.
Delbanco, Andrew. *Melville: His World and Work*. New York: Alfred A. Knopf, 2005.
Deleuze, Gilles. *Différence et répétition*. Paris: P.U.F., 1968.
Deleuze, Gilles. *Essays Critical and Clinical*. 1993. Translated by Daniel W. Smith and Michael A. Greco. London and New York: Verso, 1998.
Deleuze, Gilles. *Expressionism in Philosophy: Spinoza*. 1968. Translated by Martin Joughin. New York: Zone Books, 1992.
Deleuze, Gilles, and Félix Guattari. *A Thousand Plateaus: Capitalism and Schizophrenia*. 1980. Translated by by Brian Massumi. Minneapolis: University of Minnesota Press, 1987.
Derrida, Jacques. "La Structure, le signe et le jeu dans le discours des sciences humaines." In *L'Écriture et la différance*. Paris: Seuil, 1967.
Doklady: biological sciences sections. Volume 132–135. American Institute of Biological Sciences, 1960.
Döring, Tobias. "The Sea is History: Historicizing the Homeric Sea in Victorian Passages." In *Fictions of the Sea: Critical Perspectives on the Ocean in British Literature and Culture*. Edited by Bernhard Klein. Aldershot and Burlington: Ashgate, 2002.
Drachmann, Holger. "Havets Sang." In *Ungdom i Digt og Sang*. København: Gyldendal, 1879.
Drachmann, Holger. "Nogle erindringsord." *Ude og Hjemme*, 1879.
Drachmann, Holger. "Ørnen." 1874. In *Poetiske skrifter IV: Sømandshistorier*. København: Gyldendalske Boghandel Nordisk Forlag, 1927.
Duffy, Eve M., and Alida C. Metcalf. *The Return of Hans Staden: A Go-between in the Atlantic World*. Baltimore: The Johns Hopkins University Press, 2012.
Durkheim, Émile. *The Rules of Sociological Method: And Selected Texts on Sociology and its Method*. 1982. 2nd edition. Edited and introduction by Steven Lukes. Translated by W. D. Halls. Basingstoke: Palgrave Macmillan, 2013.
Earle, Sylvia. Introduction to Rachel Carson. *The Sea Around Us*. 1951. New York: Oxford University Press, 2018.

Ellis, Erle C. *Anthropocene: A Very Short Introduction*. Oxford: Oxford University Press, 2018.

Eriksen, Thomas Hylland. *Overheating: An Anthropology of Accelerated Change*. London: Pluto Press, 2016.

Ernst Jünger—Carl Schmitt. Briefe 1930–1983. Stuttgart: Klett-Cotta, 1999.

Ette, Ottmar. "European Literature(s) in the Global Context: Literatures for Europe." In *Literature for Europe?* Edited by Theo D'haen and Iannis Goerlandt. Amsterdam and New York: Rodopi, 2009.

Ette, Ottmar. "Literature as Knowledge for Living, Literary Studies as Science for Living." Translated by Vera M. Kutzinski. *PMLA* 125, no. 4 (2010): 986–987.

Ette, Ottmar. *ZwischenWeltenSchreiben: Literaturen ohne festen Wohnsitz*. Berlin: Kadmos, 2005.

Foucault, Michel. *Discipline and Punish: The Birth of the Prison*. 1975/1977. 2nd edition. Translated by Alan Sheridan. New York: Vintage, 1995.

Foucault, Michel. "Des espaces autres." 1967/1984. In *Dits et écrits*. Volume 4. Paris: Gallimard, 1994.

Foucault, Michel. "Of Other Spaces." *Diacritics* 16, no. 1 (Spring 1986): 22–27.

Foulke, Robert. "Life in the Dying World of Sail, 1870–1910." In *Literature and Lore of the Sea*. Edited by Patricia Ann Carlson. Amsterdam: Rodopi, 1986.

Foulke, Robert. *The Sea Voyage Narrative*. New York and London: Routledge, 2002.

Frank, Søren. "7. januar 1824: James Fenimore Cooper og den maritime romans fødsel." *Kritik* 198 (2010): 54–67.

Frank, Søren, and Marlene Marcussen. "Jonas Lie mellem det maritime og det hjemlige: Stedets rolle i *Lodsen og hans Hustru*, *Rutland* og *Gaa Paa!*" *K & K* 118 (2015): 205–225.

Frank, Søren. "Litteraturhistoriske fragmenter: Billeder af havet." In *Digtning og virkelighed: Studier i fiktion*. Edited by Søren Frank, Leif Søndergaard, and John Thobo-Carlsen. Odense: Syddansk Universitet, Institut for Kulturvidenskaber, 2013.

Frank, Søren. "Maritime rytmer: En analyse af livet ombord på skibet." In *Stedsvandringer: Analyser af stedets betydning i kunst, kultur og medier*. Edited by Malene Breunig, Søren Frank, Hjørdis Brandrup Kortbek, and Sten Moslund. Odense: Syddansk Universitetsforlag, 2013.

Frank, Søren. "Melvilles Ambivalenz gegenüber Vater Mapples Rhetorik und Weitsicht." *Neue Rundschau* 1 (2013): 183–94.

Frank, Søren. "Melville's Broad Present: Nostalgia, Presentiment, and Prophecy in *Moby-Dick*." *Aktuel Forskning* (March 2015): 67–85.

Frank, Søren. "Rhythms at Sea: Lefebvre and Maritime Fiction." In *Rhythms Now: Henri Lefebvre's Rhythmanalysis Revisited*. Edited by Steen Ledet Christiansen and Mirjam Gebauer. Aalborg: Aalborg Universitetsforlag, 2019.

Frank, Søren. "The Seven Seas: Maritime Modernity in Nordic Literature." In *Nordic Literature: A Comparative History*. Edited by Tom DuBois and Dan Ringgaard. Amsterdam: John Benjamins Publishing Company, 2017.

Frank, Søren. "The Tensions between Domestic Life and Maritime Life in Sea Novels." In *Navigating Cultural Spaces: Maritime Places*. Edited by Anna-Margaretha Horatschek, Yvonne Rosenberg, and Daniel Schäbler. Amsterdam: Rodopi, 2014.

Frank, Søren. "Thalassas imperium: Siri Ranva Hjelm Jacobsens *Havbrevene*." NLvT 2 (2021): 81–96.

Garborg, Arne. *Jonas Lie: En udviklingshistorie*. Kristiania: H. Aschehoug & Co. Forlag, 1893.

Garrard, Greg. *Ecocriticism*. 2nd edition. London and New York: Routledge, 2012.

Ghosh, Amitav. *The Great Derangement: Climate Change and the Unthinkable*. Chicago and London: The University of Chicago Press, 2016.

Gilroy, Paul. *The Black Atlantic: Modernity and Double Consciousness*. London: Verso, 1993.

Gohin, Yves. "Préface." in Victor Hugo. *Les Travailleurs de la mer*. 1866. Paris: Gallimard, 1980.

Golding, William. *Fire Down Below*. 1989. London: Faber and Faber, 2013.

Gould, Stephen Jay. *Time's Arrow, Time's Cycle: Myth and Metaphor in the Discovery of Geological Time*. 1987. London: Penguin, 1988.

Grieg, Nordahl. *The Ship Sails On*. 1924. Translated by Arthur G. Chater. New York: A. A. Knopf, 1927.

Grotius, Hugo. *The Freedom of the Seas: or, The Right Which Belongs to the Dutch to Take Part in the East India Trade*. 1609. 1633. Edited by James Brown Scott. Translated by Ralph van Deman Magoffin. Union, NJ: The Lawbook Exchange, 2001.

Guerard, Albert J. *Conrad the Novelist*. Cambridge, MA: Harvard University Press, 1958.

Gumbrecht, Hans Ulrich. *After 1945: Latency as Origin of the Present*. Palo Alto: Stanford University Press, 2013.

Gumbrecht, Hans Ulrich. *Our Broad Present: Time and Contemporary Culture*. New York: Columbia University Press, 2014.

Gumbrecht, Hans Ulrich. *Stimmungen lesen: Über eine verdeckte Wirklichkeit der Literatur*. München: Carl Hanser Verlag, 2011.

Hadot, Pierre. *The Veil of Isis: An Essay on the History of the Idea of Nature*. 2004. Translated by Michael Chase. Cambridge, MA, and London: Harvard University Press/Belknap, 2008.

Hansen, Thorkild. *Jens Munk*. 1965. København: Gyldendal, 1989.

Haraway, Donna. "Situated Knowledges: The Science Question in Feminism and the Privilege of Partial Perspective." *Feminist Studies* 14, no. 3 (Autumn 1988): 575–599.

Harrison, Robert Pogue. *The Dominion of the Dead*. Chicago: University of Chicago Press, 2003.

Hegel, G. W. F. *Aesthetics: Lectures on Fine Art*. 1835–38. Volume 2. Translated by T. M. Knox. Oxford: Clarendon, 1998.

Hegel, G. W. F. *Elements of the Philosophy of Right*. 1821. Edited by Allen W. Wood. Translated by H. B. Nisbet. Cambridge: Cambridge University Press, 2003.

Heidegger, Martin. *Being and Time*. 1926. Translated by John Macquarrie and Edward Robinson. 1962. Oxford and Cambridge, MA: Blackwell, 2001.

Heidegger, Martin. "Memorial address." 1959. In *Discourse on Thinking*. Translated by John M. Anderson and E. Hans Freund. New York: Harper Perennial, 1966.

Heidegger, Martin. "The Question Concerning Technology." 1953. In *The Question Concerning Technology and Other Essays*. Translated by William Lovitt. New York and London: Garland Publishing, 1977.

Heise, Ursula K. *Sense of Place and Sense of Planet: The Environmental Imagination of the Global*. Oxford: Oxford University Press, 2008.

Hesiod, The Homeric Hymns and Homerica. Edited and translated by Hugh G. Evelyn-White. London: William Heinemann Ltd./New York: The Macmillan Co., 1914.

Hewitt, Douglas. *Conrad: A Reassessment*. Cambridge: Bowes and Bowes, 1952.

Heydenreich, Titus. *Tadel und Lob der Seefahrt: Das Nachleben eines antiken Themas in den romanischen Literaturen*. Heidelberg: Carl Winter, 1970.

Heyerdahl, Thor. *Early Man and the Ocean: The Beginning of Navigation and Seaborn Civilizations*. London: George Allen and Unwin Ltd., 1978.

Hirth, Friedrich. *The Ancient History of China: The End of the Chóu Dynasty*. New York: Columbia University Press, 1908.

Holmer, Joan Ozark. *The Merchant of Venice: Choice, Hazard and Consequence*. New York: Macmillan Education, 1995.

The Holy Bible. KJV King James Bible 1611. London: Robert Barker, 1611.

Homer. *The Odyssey*. Translated by A. T. Murray. 1919. Cambridge, MA: Harvard University Press/London, William Heinemann Ltd., 1945.

Horace. *The Odes and Carmen Saeculare of Horace*. 23 BC. Translated by John Conington. London: George Bell and Sons, 1882.

Horden, Peregrine and Nicholas Purcell. *The Corrupting Sea: A Study of Mediterranean History*. Oxford: Blackwell, 2000.

House, Kay Seymour. "Historical Introduction." In James Fenimore Cooper. *The Pilot; A Tale of the Sea*. 1824. Edited, historical introduction, and explanatory notes by Kay Seymour House. Albany, NY: SUNY Press, 1986.

House, Kay Seymour. "The Unstable Element." In *James Fenimore Cooper: A Collection of Critical Essays*. Edited by Wayne Fields. Englewood Cliffs, N.J.: Prentice-Hall, 1979.

Huet, Marie-Hélène. *L'Histoire des* Voyages extraordinaires: *Essai sur l'œuvre de Jules Verne*. Paris: Minard, 1973.

Hugo, Victor. *Correspondance*. Volume II, 1849–1866. Edited by Cécile Daubray. Paris: Albin Michel, 1950.

Hugo, Victor. *The Toilers of the Sea*. 1866. Translated by James Hogarth. New York: The Modern Library, 2002.

Hugo, Victor. *Les Travailleurs de la mer*. 1866. Paris: Gallimard, 1980.

Hutchins, Zachary. "*Moby-Dick* as Third Testament: A Novel 'Not Come to Destroy but to Fulfill' the Bible." *Leviathan* 13, no. 2 (2011): 18–37.

Ibsen, Henrik. *Brev fra perioden 1880–89. Henrik Ibsens skrifter*. Universitetet i Oslo. Accessed April 19, 2022. http://www.edd.uio.no/cocoon/ibsenarkiv01_01/BREV_1880-1889ht%7CB18820622JLi.xhtml.

Ihde, Don. *Technology and the Lifeworld: From Garden to Earth*. Bloomington and Indianapolis, Indiana University Press, 1990.

Jacobsen, Siri Ranva Hjelm. *Havbrevene: Prosa*. København: Lindhardt og Ringhof, 2018.

James, Henry. "Preface to The Tragic Muse." In *The Tragic Muse*. New York: Charles Scribner's Sons, 1922.

Jensen, Carsten. *We, The Drowned*. 2006. Translated by Charlotte Barslund with Emma Ryder. London: Vintage, 2011.

Jensen, Johannes V. "Forord." In *De islandske sagaer*. Volume 1. Edited by Johannes Larsen. 1930. København: Gyldendals Bogklub, 2001.

Joyce, James. "Daniel Defoe." Translated (from Italian manuscript) and edited by Joseph Prescott. *Buffalo Studies* 1 (1964): 24–25.

Joyce, James. *Ulysses*. 1922. London: Penguin, 1995.

Kant, Immanuel. *Critique of the Power of Judgement*. In *The Cambridge Edition of the Works of Immanuel Kant*. Edited by Paul Guyer. Translated by Paul Guyer and Eric Matthews. Cambridge: Cambridge University Press, 2000.

Kellogg, Robert. "Introduction." In *The Sagas of Icelanders: A Selection*. Edited by Önólfur Thorsson. New York: Penguin, 2001.

Kinzel, Ulrich. "Orientation as Paradigm of Maritime Modernity." In *Fictions of the Sea: Critical Perspectives on the Ocean in British Literature and Culture*. Edited by Bernhard Klein. Aldershot and Burlington: Ashgate, 2002.

Klein, Bernhard. "Camões and the Sea: Maritime Modernity in *The Lusiads*." *Modern Philology* 111, no. 2 (November 2013): 158–180.

Koselleck, Reinhart. " 'Space of Experience' and 'Horizon of Expectation': Two Historical Categories." In *Futures Past: On the Semantics of Historical Time*. Translated by Keith Tribe. New York: Columbia University Press, 2004.

Kundera, Milan. *The Curtain: An Essay in Seven Parts*. Translated by Linda Archer. London: Faber and Faber, 2007.

Lagerkvist, Pär. *Pilgrim at Sea*. 1962. Translated by Naomi Walford. New York: Random House, 1964.

Lassen, Anette. *Islændingesagaernes verden*. København: Gyldendal, 2017.

Latour, Bruno. *Aramis, or the Love of Technology*. Cambridge, MA: Harvard University Press, 1996.
Latour, Bruno. *We Have Never Been Modern*. 1991. Translated by Catherine Porter. Cambridge, MA: Harvard University Press, 1993.
Lawrence, D. H. *Studies in Classic American Literature*. 1923. London: Penguin, 1971.
Leavis, F. R. *The Great Tradition*. London: Chatto and Windus, 1948.
Lefebvre, Henri. *Éléments de rythmanalyse: Introduction à la connaissance des rythmes*. Paris: Éditions Syllepse, 1992.
Lefebvre, Henri, and Catherine Régulier. "Le projet rythmanalytique." *Communications* 41 (1985): 191–199.
Lefebvre, Henri. *Rhythmanalysis: Space, Time and Everyday Life*. Translated by Stuart Elden and Gerald Moore. London and New York: Continuum, 2004.
Lehmann, Mette Harbo. "Havet som selvportræt: Maleren Holger Drachmann." In *Jeg er hav: Holger Drachmann med pen og pensel*. Edited by Mette Harbo Lehmann. Skagen: Skagens Kunstmuseer, 2019.
Leopold, Aldo. *A Sand County Almanac: And Sketches Here and There*. New York: Oxford University Press, 1949.
Lesky, Albin. *Thalatta: Der Weg der Griechen zum Meer*. New York: Arno Press, 1973.
Lévi-Strauss, Claude. *Les Structures élémentaires de la parenté*. Paris: Presses universitaires de France, 1949.
Lie, Jonas. *Gaa Paa! Sjøfortælling*. Kjøbenhavn: Gyldendalske Boghandels Forlag, 1882.
Lie, Jonas. *The Pilot and His Wife: A Norse Love Story*. 1874. Translated by Mrs. Ole Bull. Chicago: S. C. Griggs and Company, 1876.
Lie, Jonas. *Tremasteren "Fremtiden" eller Liv nordpaa: En fortælling*. Kjøbenhavn: Forlagt af den Gyldendalske Boghandel, 1872.
Lim, Dennis. "The Merger of Academia and Art House: Harvard Filmmakers' Messy World." *The New York Times*. August 31, 2012. Accessed September 9, 2021. https://www.nytimes.com/2012/09/02/movies/harvard-filmmakers-messy-world.html?pagewanted=all&_r=0.
Linebaugh, Peter, and Marcus Rediker. *The Many-Headed Hydra: Sailors, Slaves, Commoners, and the Hidden History of the Revolutionary Atlantic*. Boston: Beacon Press, 2000.
London, Jack. *The Sea-Wolf*. 1904. New York: Random House, 2000.
Lothe, Jakob. *Conrad's Narrative Method*. Oxford: Clarendon Press, 1989.
Loti, Pierre. "Avant-propos." In Jules Michelet. *La Mer*. Paris: Calmann-Lévy, 1900.
Lowry, Malcolm. *Ultramarine*. Revised edition. 1933. London: Jonathan Cape, 1969.
Malm, Andreas. *Fossil Capital: The Rise of Steam Power and the Roots of Global Warming*. London: Verso, 2016.
Mariani, Giorgio. "'Chiefly Known by His Rod': The Book of Jonah, Mapple's Sermon, and Scapegoating." In *Ungraspable Phantom: Essays on Moby-Dick*. Edited by John

Bryant, Mary K. Bercaw Edwards, and Timothy Marr. Kent: Kent State University Press, 2006.

Marsh, George Perkins. *The Earth as Modified by Human Action: A Last Revision of "Man and Nature."* 1864. 1874. New York: Charles Scribner's Sons, 1885.

Martocq, Bernard. "Note bibliographique sur l'História Trágico-Marítima," *Cahiers d'études romanes*, no. 1 (1998): 19–29. Published online January 15, 2013. Accessed March 31, 2017, http://etudesromanes.revues.org/3428.

Marx, Karl. *Das Kapital: Kritik der politischen Ökonomie*. Volume 1. 1867. Berlin: Dietz Verlag, 1962.

Maury, M. F. *The Physical Geography of the Sea*. New York: Harper & Brothers, 1855.

McNeill, J. R., and Peter Engelke. *The Great Acceleration: An Environmental History of the Anthropocene since 1945*. Cambridge, MA: Harvard University Press, 2014.

Melville, Herman. *Billy Budd, Sailor (An Inside Narrative)*. In *Billy Budd, Sailor and Other Uncompleted Writings*. In *The Writings of Herman Melville*. Volume 13. Edited by Harrison Hayford, Alma A. MacDougall, Robert A. Sandberg, and G. Thomas Tanselle. Historical note by Hershel Parker. Evanston and Chicago: Northwestern University Press and the Newberry Library, 2017.

Melville, Herman. *Correspondence*. In *The Writings of Herman Melville*. Volume 14. Edited by Lynn Horth. Evanston and Chicago: Northwestern University Press and the Newberry Library, 1993.

Melville, Herman. *Journals*. In *The Writings of Herman Melville*. Volume 15. Edited by Howard C. Horsford and Lynn Horth. Evanston and Chicago: Northwestern University Press and the Newberry Library, 1989.

Melville, Herman. *Moby-Dick; or, The Whale*. 1851. In *The Writings of Herman Melville*. Volume 6. Edited by Harrison Hayford, Hershel Parker, and G. Thomas Tanselle. Evanston and Chicago: Northwestern University Press and the Newberry Library, 1988.

Melville, Herman. *White-Jacket: or, The World in a Man-of-War*. 1850. In *The Writings of Herman Melville*. Volume 5. Edited by. Harrison Hayford, Hershel Parker, and G. Thomas Tanselle. 1970. Evanston and Chicago: Northwestern University Press and The Newberry Library, 1988.

Mentz, Steve. *At the Bottom of Shakespeare's Ocean*. London and New York: Continuum, 2009.

Mentz, Steve. "Blue Humanities." In *Posthuman Glossary*. Edited by Rosi Braidotti and Maria Hlavajova. London: Bloomsbury, 2018.

Mentz, Steve. *Ocean*. New York: Bloomsbury, 2020.

Mentz, Steve. *Shipwreck Modernity: Ecologies of Globalization, 1550–1719*. Minnesota: University of Minnesota Press, 2015.

Michelet, Jules. *Journal*. Edited by Paul Viallaneix. Volume 1. Paris: Gallimard, 1959.

Michelet, Jules. *La Mer*. Paris: Librairie L. Hachette et Cie, 1861.

Mitchell, W. J. T. *Picture Theory: Essays on Verbal and Visual Representation*. Chicago and London: The University of Chicago Press, 1995.
Moretti, Franco. *Atlas of the European Novel 1800–1900*. 1997. London: Verso, 1998.
Moretti, Franco. "Conjectures on World Literature." *New Left Review* 1 (2000): 54–68.
Moretti, Franco. "Serious Century: From Vermeer to Austen." In *The Novel*. Volume 1. Edited by Franco Moretti. Princeton, NJ: Princeton University Press, 2006.
Moretti, Franco. *The Way of the World: The Bildungsroman in European Culture*. 1987. London: Verso, 2000.
Morton, Timothy. *Dark Ecology: For a Logic of Future Coexistence*. New York: Columbia University Press, 2016.
Morton, Timothy. *The Ecological Thought*. Cambridge, MA: Harvard University Press, 2010.
Mumford, Lewis. *Technics and Civilization*. 1934. Chicago and London: University of Chicago Press, 2010.
Munk, Jens. *Navigatio, Septentrionalis. Det er: Relation eller Bescriffuelse, om Seiglads oc Reyse, paa denne Nordvestiske Passagie, som nu kaldis Nova Dania, igiennem Fretum Christian at opsøge*. København: Heinrich Waldkirch, 1624.
Munk, Jens. *Navigatio Septentrionalis: That is, A Relation or Description of a Voyage in Search of the North-West Passage, now called Nova Dania, through Fretum Christian*. In *Danish Arctic Expeditions, 1605 to 1620, In Two Books, Book II: The Expedition of Captain Jens Munk to Hudson's Bay in Search of a North-West Passage in 1619–20*. 1624. Edited, notes, and introduction by C. C. A. Gosch. London: The Hakluyt Society, 1897.
"Naufrage du grand Galion *São João* sur la Côte du Natal en l'année 1552." In *Histoires tragico-maritimes 1552–1563: Chefs-d'œuvre des naufrages portugais*. Edited by Anne Lima and Michel Chandeigne. Translated by Georges Le Gentil. Preface José Saramago. Paris: Chandeigne, 2016.
Nayder, Lilian. "Sailing Ships and Steamers, Angels and Whores: History and Gender in Conrad's Maritime Fiction." In *Iron Men, Wooden Women: Gender and Seafaring in the Atlantic World, 1700–1920*. Edited by Margaret S. Creighton and Lisa Norling. Baltimore, MD: The Johns Hopkins University Press, 1996.
Needham, Joseph. *Science and Civilization in China: Volume 4, Physics and Physical Technology, Part 1, Physics*. Taipei: Caves Books Ltd., 1986.
Needham, Joseph. *The Shorter Science & Civilisation in China: 3*. Cambridge: Cambridge University Press, 1986.
Nerlich, Michael. *Ideology of Adventure*. Volume 1. Translated by Ruth Crowley. Minneapolis: University of Minnesota Press, 1987.
Nexø, Martin Andersen. *Days in the Sun*. 1903. Translated by Jacob Wittmer Hartmann. New York: Coward-McCann, 1929.
Nexø, Martin Andersen. *Vejs Ende*. 1939. In *Erindringer II*. København: DSL/Borgen, 1999.

Nielsen, Aage Krarup. *En hvalfangerfærd: Gennem troperne til Sydishavet.* 1921. 2nd edition. København: Gyldendal, 1935.

Nietzsche, Friedrich. *On the Uses and Disadvantages of History for Life.* 1874. In *Untimely Meditations.* Translated by R. J. Hollingdale. Cambridge: Cambridge University Press, 1983.

Nixon, Rob. *Slow Violence and the Environmentalism of the Poor.* Cambridge, MA: Harvard University Press, 2011.

Noiray, Jacques. "Préface." In Jules Verne. *Vingt mille lieues sous les mers.* 1871. Paris: Gallimard, 2005.

Olson, Charles. *Call Me Ishmael.* San Francisco: City Lights Books, 1947.

Orr, Linda. *Jules Michelet: Nature, History, and Language.* Ithaca and London: Cornell University Press, 1976.

Osborn, Fairfield. *Our Plundered Planet.* Boston: Little, Brown and Company, 1948.

Ovid. *Metamorphoses.* Translated by A. D. Melville. Introduction and notes by E. J. Kenney. 1986. Oxford: Oxford University Press, 1998.

Ovid. *Sorrows of an Exile: Tristia.* Translated by. A. D. Melville. Introduction and notes by E. J. Kenney. Oxford: Clarendon, 1992.

Palmer, Sarah. "Coal and the Sea." In *The Sea in History: The Modern World / La Mer dans l'Histoire: La Période Contemporaine.* Edited by N. A. M. Rodger. Woodbridge: The Boydell Press, 2017.

Parker, Hershel, and Harrison Hayford. "Preface." In Herman Melville. *Moby-Dick; or, the Whale.* New York and London: W. W. Norton, 2002.

Parry, J. H. *The Discovery of the Sea.* 1974. London: Weidenfeld and Nicolson, 1975.

Pages and Pictures: From the Writings of James Fenimore Cooper. Edited and with notes by Susan Fenimore Cooper. New York: W. A. Townsend and Company, 1861.

Pavel, Thomas. "The Novel in Search of Itself: A Historical Morphology." In *The Novel.* Volume 1. Edited by Franco Moretti. Princeton, NJ: Princeton University Press, 2006.

Pavel, Thomas. *La Pensée du roman.* Paris: Gallimard, 2006.

Payen, Jacques. "De l'anticipation à l'innovation: Jules Verne et le problème de la locomotion mécanique," *Culture Technique*, no. 19 (1989): 309–317.

Peck, John. *Maritime Fiction: Sailors and the Sea in British and American Novels, 1719–1917.* Gordonsville, VA: Palgrave Macmillan, 2001.

Pérez-Mallaína, Pablo E. *Spain's Men of the Sea: Daily Life on the Indies Fleets in the Sixteenth Century.* 1992. Baltimore and London: The Johns Hopkins University Press, 1998.

"Permian-Triassic extinction event." Accessed January 28, 2020. https://en.wikipedia.org/wiki/Permian–Triassic_extinction_event.

Pesce, G.-L. *La Navigation sous-marine.* Paris: Vuibert & Nony, 1906.

Philbrick, Thomas. "Cooper and the Literary Discovery of the Sea." *Canadian Review of American Studies* 20, no. 3 (1989): 35–46.

Philbrick, Thomas. *James Fenimore Cooper and the Development of American Sea Fiction.* Cambridge, MA: Harvard University Press, 1961.

Quaratiello, Arlene. *Rachel Carson: A Biography.* Westport, CT: Greenwood Press, 2004.

Radkau, Joachim. *The Age of Ecology: A Global History.* 2011. Translated by Patrick Camiller. Cambridge: Polity Press, 2014.

Rediker, Marcus. *Between the Devil and the Deep Blue Sea: Merchant Seaman, Pirates, and the Anglo-American Maritime World, 1700–1750.* Cambridge: Cambridge University Press, 1987.

Rediker, Marcus. *Villains of All Nations: Atlantic Pirates in the Golden Age.* London: Verso, 2004.

Robb, Graham. "Introduction." In Victor Hugo. *The Toilers of the Sea.* 1866. Translated by James Hogarth. New York: The Modern Library, 2002.

Robb, Graham. *Victor Hugo.* 1997. London: Picador, 1998.

Rodner, William. "*Snow Storm—Steam-Boat off a Harbour's Mouth 1842.* Painting by J. M. W. Turner." In *Encyclopedia of the Romantic Era, 1760–1850.* Volume 2. Edited by Christopher John Murray. New York and London: Fitzroy Dearborn, 2004.

Roesdahl, Else. *The Vikings.* 1987. 3rd edition. Translated by Susan M. Margeson and Kirsten Williams. London: Penguin, 2016.

Ropp, Theodore. *War in the Modern World.* 1959. Baltimore and London: The Johns Hopkins University Press, 2000.

Ritchie, Hannah, Max Roser, and Pablo Rosado. "CO2 and Greenhouse Gas Emissions." Our World in Data. May 2017. Last modified August 2020. Accessed April 20, 2022. https://ourworldindata.org/co2-and-other-greenhouse-gas-emissions.

Roser, Max, Hannah Ritchie, and Esteban Ortiz-Ospina. "World Population Growth." Our World In Data. 2013. Most recent substantial revision in May 2019. Accessed April 20, 2022. https://ourworldindata.org/world-population-growth.

Rösing, Lilian Munk. "Lille bog med stor forestillingskraft: Et hav, der taler om busstoppesteder, må jeg bede om mine himmelblå!" *Politiken*, March 2, 2019. Accessed November 10, 2019. https://politiken.dk/kultur/boger/art7057748/Et-hav-der-taler-om-busstoppesteder-må-jeg-bede-om-mine-himmelblå.

Rozwadowski, Helen. *Fathoming the Ocean: The Discovery and Exploration of the Deep Sea.* 2005. Cambridge, MA: Harvard University Press, 2008.

Ruddick, Nicholas. *Ultimate Island: On the Nature of British Science Fiction.* Westport, CT: Greenwood Press, 1993.

Rushdie, Salman. *Midnight's Children.* 1981. London: Vintage, 1995.

Ruskin, John. *Modern Painters.* Volume 1. 1843. In *The Complete Works of John Ruskin.* Volume 3. Edited by E. T. Cook and Alexander Wedderburn. London: George Allen, 1903.

The Sagas of Icelanders: A Selection. Edited by Önólfur Thorsson. New York: Penguin, 2001.

"The Saga of the Greenlanders." Translated by Keneva Kunz. In *The Sagas of Icelanders: A Selection*. Edited by Önólfur Thorsson. New York: Penguin, 2001.

Sager, Eric W. *Seafaring Labour: The Merchant Marine of Atlantic Canada, 1820–1914*. Montreal: McGill-Queen's University Press, 1989.

Said, Edward. *Culture and Imperialism*. New York: Alfred A. Knopf, 1993.

Sand, George. *Correspondance*. Edited by Georges Lubin. Paris: Classiques Garnier, 1985.

Sandemose, Aksel. *Mutiny on the Barque Zuidersee*. 1963. Translated by Maurice Michael. London: Neville Spearman, 1970.

Saramago, José. "La mort familière." In *Histoires tragico-maritimes 1552–1563: Chefs-d'œuvre des naufrages portugais*. Edited by Anne Lima and Michel Chandeigne. Translated by Georges Le Gentil. Preface José Saramago. Paris: Chandeigne, 2016.

Schmitt, Carl. *Land and Sea*. 1942/1954. Translated by Simona Draghici. Washington DC: Plutarch Press, 1997.

"The Seafarer." Anglo-Saxons Net. Accessed September 7, 2021. http://www.anglo-saxons.net/hwaet/?do=get&type=text&id=Sfr.

Seamon, David. "Body-Subject, Time-Space Routines, and Place-Ballets." In *The Human Experience of Space and Place*. Edited by Anne Buttimer and David Seamon. London: Croom Helm, 1980.

Sedgwick, Eve Kosofsky. *Epistemology of the Closet*. Los Angeles: University of California Press, 1990.

Sekula, Alan. *Fish Story*. 1995. 2nd edition. Düsseldorf: Richter Verlag, 2002.

Serres, Michel. "Michelet, la soupe." *Revue d'Histoire littéraire de la France* 74, no. 5 (1974): 787–802.

Shakespeare, William. *Hamlet*. 1599–1602. Edited by Ann Thompson and Neil Taylor. Arden Shakespeare. London: Methuen Drama, 2006.

Shakespeare, William. *The Merchant of Venice*. 1596–98. Fully annotated and introduction by Burton Raffel. New Haven and London: Yale University Press, 2006.

Sivasundaram, Sujit, Alisan Bashford, and David Armitage. "Introduction: Writing World Oceanic Histories." In *Oceanic Histories*. Edited by David Armitage, Alisan Bashford, and Sujit Sivasundaram. Cambridge: Cambridge University Press, 2018.

Sloterdijk, Peter. *Spheres II: Globes*. 1999. Translated by Wieland Hoban. South Pasadena: Semiotext(e), 2014.

Smollett, Tobias. *The Adventures of Roderick Random*. 1748. Oxford: Oxford University Press, 1999.

Sobecki, Sebastian I. *The Sea and Medieval English Literature*. Cambridge: D. S. Brewer, 2008.

Sophocles. *Antigone*. In *The Tragedies of Sophocles*. Translated by Richard C. Jebb. 1904. Cambridge: Cambridge University Press, 1912.

Spanos, William. *The Errant Art of* Moby-Dick: *The Canon, the Cold War, and the Struggle for American Studies*. Durham: Duke University Press, 1995.

Spivak, Gayatri Chakravorty. *Death of a Discipline*. New York: Columbia University Press, 2003.

Sprondel, Walter M. "Entzauberung." In *Historisches Wörterbuch der Philosophie*. Volume 2. Edited by Joachim Ritter and Karlfried Gründer. Darmstadt: Wissenschaftliche Buchgesellschaft, 1972.

Stape, J. H. " 'The End of the Tether' and Victor Hugo's 'Les Travailleurs de la mer.' " *The Conradian* 30, no. 1 (Spring 2005): 71–80.

Steffen, Will, Jacques Grinevald, Paul Crutzen, and John McNeill. "The Anthropocene: Conceptual and Historical Perspectives." *Philosophical Transactions of the Royal Society A* 369, no. 1938 (2011): 842–867.

Steffen, Will, Paul Crutzen, and J. R. McNeill. "The Anthropocene: are humans now overwhelming the great forces of Nature?" *Ambio* 36 (2007): 614–21.

Steinberg, Philip E. *The Social Construction of the Ocean*. Cambridge: Cambridge University Press, 2001.

Stoppani, Antonio. *Corso di geologia*. Volume 2. Milano: G. Bernardoni and E. G. Brigola, 1873.

Strabo. *The Geography of Strabo*. Translated by H. L. Jones. 1917. Cambridge, MA: Harvard University Press, 1949.

Suvin, Darko. *Metamorphoses of Science Fiction: On the Poetics and History of a Literary Genre*. Yale University Press, 1977.

Taussig, Michael. "The Beach (A Fantasy)." *Critical Inquiry* 26, no. 2 (2000): 248–278.

Thompson, Christina. *Sea People: In Search of the Ancient Navigators of the Pacific*. London: William Collins, 2019.

Underwood, Ted. *Distant Horizons: Digital Evidence and Literary Change*. Chicago and London: The University of Chicago Press, 2019.

Updike, John. "Satan's Work and Silted Cisterns." In *Odd Jobs: Essays and Criticism*. New York: Knopf, 1991.

Urry, John. *Mobilities*. Cambridge: Polity Press, 2007.

van Doren, Carl. *The American Novel: 1789–1939*. New York: MacMillan, 1940.

Varberg, Jeanette. *Viking: Ran, ild og sværd*. København: Gyldendal, 2019.

Verbeek, Peter-Paul. *What Things Do: Philosophical Reflections on Technology, Agency, and Design*. 2000. Translated by Robert P. Crease. Pennsylvania: The Pennsylvania State University Press, 2005.

Vernadsky, Vladimir. *La Géochimie*. Paris: Librairie Félix Alcan, 1924.

Verne, Jules. *The Adventures of Captain Hatteras*. 1864–65. Translated, introduction, and notes by William Butcher. Oxford: Oxford University Press, 2005.

Verne, Jules. *Twenty Thousand Leagues under the Seas*. 1869–70/1871. Translated and with introduction and notes by William Butcher. Oxford: Oxford University Press, 1998.

Verne, Jules. *Vingt mille lieues sous les mers*. 1869–70/1871. Paris: Gallimard, 2005.

Walker, Warren S. *James Fenimore Cooper: An Introduction and Interpretation.* New York: Barnes and Noble, 1962.

Watson, Frank. *The Sailor in English Fiction and Drama, 1550–1800.* New York: Columbia University Press, 1931.

Watt, Ian. *Essays on Conrad.* Cambridge: Cambridge University Press, 2000.

Watt, Ian. "Impressionism and Symbolism in Heart of Darkness." In *Joseph Conrad: A Commemoration.* Edited by Norman Sherry. London: Palgrave Macmillan, 1976.

Watt, Ian. *The Rise of the Novel.* London: Chatto and Windus, 1957.

Weber, Max. "Wissenschaft als Beruf." In *Wissenschaft als Beruf. Politik als Beruf.* In *Max Weber-Gesamtausgabe.* Volume I/17. Edited by Wolfgang J. Mommsen and Wolfgang Schluchter. Tübingen: Mohr Siebeck, 1922.

Werberger, Anette. "Überlegungen zu einer Literaturgeschichte als Verflechtungsgeschichte." In *Kulturen in Bewegung: Beiträge zur Theorie und Praxis der Transkulturalität.* Edited by Dorothee Kimmich and Schamma Schahadat. Bielefeld: transcript, 2012.

"The Whale. By Herman Melville, Author of 'Typee,' &c. &c." *London Athenæum* 1252 (October 25, 1851): 1112–13.

"What is Ocean Acidification?" NOOA Ocean Acidification Program. Accessed November 5, 2019. https://oceanacidification.noaa.gov/OurChangingOcean.aspx.

White, Landeg. "Introduction." In Luís Vaz de Camões. *The Lusíads.* Translated, introduction, and notes by Landeg White. 1997. New York: Oxford University Press, 2001.

Wilk, Richard. *Home Cooking in the Global Village: Caribbean Food from Buccaneers to Ecotourists.* Oxford and New York: Berg, 2006.

Williams, William Carlos. *The Collected Poems of William Carlos Williams. Volume II: 1939–1962.* Edited by Christopher MacGowan. 1988. New York: New Directions, 2001.

Wills, John H. "Conrad's *Typhoon*: A Triumph of Organic Art," *The North Dakota Quarterly* 30 (1962): 62–70.

Wilson, Thomas. *A Discourse upon Usury.* 1572. Edited and historical introduction by R. H. Tawney. London: Frank Cass & Co., 1962.

Winner, Langdon. *The Whale and the Reactor: A Search for Limits in an Age of High Technology.* 1986. Chicago and London: Chicago University Press, 1989.

Wood, Sarah Florence. " 'Narrow Passages': Captive Sailors and National Narrative in James Fenimore Cooper's *The Pilot,*" *Atlantic Studies* 3, no. 2 (2006): 245–255.

Woodworth, Samuel. *The Champions of Freedom; or, The Mysterious Chief.* New York: Charles N. Baldwin, 1816.

Wright, Nathalie. *Melville's Use of the Bible.* Durham, NC: Duke University Press, 1949.

Yeazell, Ruth Bernard. "The Power of a Name: In Bruegel's *Icarus,* for Instance." *Raritan: A Quarterly Review* 33, no. 2 (2013): 110–127.

Yi-Fu Tuan, *Space and Place: The Perspective of Experience.* 1977. Minneapolis and London: University of Minnesota Press, 2001.

Zacharek, Stephanie. "'Leviathan': Of Fish And Men, Without Chats." *National Public Radio*. February 28, 2013. Accessed May 21, 2018. https://www.npr.org/2013/02/28/172981501/leviathan-of-fish-and-men-without-chats?ft=1&f=1045.

Zalasiewicz, Jan. *The Earth After Us: What Legacy Will Humans Leave in the Rocks?* New York: Oxford University Press, 2008.

Zhu Yu. *Pingzhou ketan*. 1111–17. Shangwu yinshuguan, 1936.

Østerberg, Dag. *Det moderne: Et essay om Vestens kultur 1740–2000*. Oslo: Gyldendal, 1999.

Index

Age of Reason 17
Age of Sail 14, 29, 34, 112, 142, 144, 147, 206, 241, 242, 203, 413
Amphibian Comparative Literature 10–11, 16, 35, 40–41
Andalusia 2–3
Antarctica 46, 71, 271, 272, 325, 327, 354, 357, 359–360, 363, 364, 359, 375, 377
Anthropocene 10, 37–40, 42, 44, 46–50, 143, 145, 269, 303, 323–340, 342, 345–346, 348, 351–352, 358, 361–363, 367–368, 374, 377, 379, 382, 386, 418–419
anthropocentrism 4, 12, 40–41, 44, 49, 51–52, 54, 66, 70, 77, 82, 86, 89, 91, 112, 142–143, 146–147, 150, 154–155, 159, 160–163, 165–167, 169–170, 204, 214, 280, 292, 298, 300, 303, 307, 309, 311–314, 320, 322, 335, 344–348, 355, 360–361, 372, 401, 403, 409, 412–413, 417, 420
Antilles, the 122–123
Arctic 78, 86, 352, 363–364, 368, 375, 377, 381
Armitage, David 10, 25
Atlantic Ocean 3–4, 14, 19, 28, 42, 47, 60, 63, 67, 96, 108–109, 111, 112, 114, 132, 149, 159–160, 166–167, 206, 213, 216, 301, 320, 325–326, 334, 351, 384–385, 387, 389–391, 407–408, 411
Atwood, Margaret 342
 The Handmaid's Tale 342
Auden, W. H. 52, 116, 388, 395–397, 399–404, 406
 "Musée des Beaux-Arts" 395, 397
Austen, Jane 27, 111, 127, 129, 337–338, 348
 Mansfield Park 111, 348
 Persuasion 111
Australia 234

Bacon, Francis 18–19, 152, 208, 212–216
 Novum Organon 18, 214–215
 The New Atlantis 215
Ballard, J.G. 8–9, 29, 38, 42, 44, 47, 334, 351, 362–373, 375–382, 418–420
 The Drowned World 9, 29, 38, 42, 44, 47, 143, 334–335, 351, 362–365, 367–368, 372–381, 418–420

The Drought 365, 378
The Crystal World 365, 378
Balzac, Honoré de 163–164, 200, 342
 Les Chouans 342
barometer 121–122, 229, 243, 246, 250–253, 258–259
Baucom, Ian 25, 213
Beckett, Samuel 7, 153
Beckford, William 147
Benjamin, Walter 22, 25, 49
Bennett, Jane 46, 296, 300, 303, 305, 308, 310–311, 409, 411–412, 417
Benvéniste, Émile 184–185, 194
Bering, Vitus 60
Bible 37, 42–43, 44, 50–52, 54, 58, 61, 114, 154–159, 172, 195, 299, 319, 324, 403, 410, 413
Biblical flood 51, 52, 160
Bildungsroman 2, 133–134, 137, 138
Bjørneboe, Jens 2, 8, 42–45, 112, 127, 143–145, 173, 177–178, 188, 191, 193, 361, 413, 420–421
 The Sharks 40, 45, 143, 173, 177, 188, 191, 193, 421
Bjørnson, Bjørnstjerne 127
Blackmore, Josiah 25, 202
Blue Cultural Studies 16, 35, 40, 420
Blue Ecology 35–42
Blue Humanities 8–9, 11, 12, 16, 26–27, 34–35, 39, 421
Blum, Hester 13, 25, 146, 165, 177, 195
Blumenberg, Hans 21, 52, 59–60, 213, 393
Bougainville, Louis Antoine de 60, 270
Bonneui, Christophe and Jean-Baptiste Fressoz 39, 328, 330–331, 333, 336, 386
bourgeois 10, 17, 23, 25, 128, 129, 130, 131, 133, 138, 266, 280, 320, 337, 342, 374, 421
Brandes, Georg 2
Bruegel the Elder, Pieter 387–388, 392–407, 420
 Landscape with the Fall of Icarus 388, 392–393, 396, 400–401, 403–404, 406
Burke, Edmund 256
Burney, William 127, 129
Butler, Judith 227

INDEX

Cádiz 3–6, 16, 157
Callenbach, Ernest 40
Camões, Luís Vaz de 8, 59, 66–73, 77, 385, 413, 420
  The Lusíads 44, 59, 66–72
Camus, Albert 7, 116, 153
cannibalism 28, 131, 235
capitalism 17, 20, 22, 98, 166, 304
Carlyle, Thomas 147
Carson, Rachel 44, 114, 331, 385, 407, 409, 410–411
  Silent Spring 409, 410, 411
  The Sea Around Us 44, 331, 407
  Under the Sea-Wind 411
Casarino, Cesare 31, 129
China 2, 18–19, 71, 160, 212, 234
Chivalric romance 162
Christianity 28–29, 37, 50–51, 61–63, 68, 70, 72–73, 78–79, 86, 91, 93, 130, 145, 152–156, 173
claustrophobia 6, 198, 415
Cohen, Jerome 46, 300, 302–303, 318, 321, 417
Cohen, Margaret 16, 19, 22, 25–30, 32–34, 97–102, 111–112, 162, 202, 216, 257, 270, 292, 299, 315–317
Coleridge, Samuel Taylor 45, 178, 194
  "The Rime of the Ancyent Marinere" 45, 194
colonialism 20, 28, 59, 98, 169, 270, 348–349, 352, 421
Columbus, Christopher 9, 19, 60, 79, 83, 384
compass 18–19, 210, 212, 214–216, 222, 229–230, 280, 378
Conrad, Joseph 2, 6, 8–9, 13, 26–32, 42, 44–46, 100–101, 105, 111, 112–113, 125, 127, 129–132, 138–145, 175, 178, 186–188, 193, 196–197, 206–208, 212, 214–215, 222, 231–254, 257–259, 261, 263–267, 273, 275, 239, 299, 351–355, 361–362, 379, 385, 411, 416–418, 420–421
  Heart of Darkness 27, 131, 175, 233, 273
  Lord Jim 26, 32
  "Ocean Travel" 140–142, 206, 236, 239, 242
  "The Character of the Foe" 231, 236, 239–241
  The End of the Tether 131, 206, 230, 233–235, 243, 293, 306

  The Mirror and the Sea 13, 100, 231, 236
  The Nigger of the "Narcissus" 32, 131, 196–197, 232
  The Secret Sharer 32, 129
  Typhoon 9, 44–46, 100, 129–131, 186, 188, 193, 207, 214, 231–232, 243–255, 257–259, 261, 264–271, 416–417
Cook, James 34, 77, 90, 262, 270–271, 274, 283, 353
Cooper, James Fenimore 8, 24, 28–31, 33, 43, 92–100, 102–112, 127, 129, 172–123, 184, 214, 352, 362, 411, 420
  Homeward Bound 111
  Notions of the Americans: Picked up by a Travelling Bachelor 96
  The Deerslayer 97
  The Last of the Mohicans 96–97
  The Pathfinder 97
  The Pilot 24, 26, 33, 43, 93–112, 127–129, 420
  The Pioneers 97
  The Red Rover 111, 172–173, 184, 187
  The Sea Lions 111
Copernicus, Nicolaus 37
Corbin, Alain 25, 50, 213

Dana, Richard Henry 28, 30, 283
Dante 14–15, 73
Darwin, Charles 37, 283, 367–368, 371
de Freitas, Seraphim 20–21
Defoe, Daniel 9, 24, 26, 30, 44, 85–86, 90–92, 96, 106, 148, 162, 283, 338, 420
  Captain Singleton 30, 96, 106
  Robinson Crusoe 9, 24, 26, 30, 32–33, 44, 85–86, 90–91, 92, 96, 106, 162, 299, 349, 420
Deleuze, Gilles 149–150, 296, 304
Deleuze, Gilles and Guattari, Félix 113, 176–177, 186
Denmark 19, 23, 78, 79
Derrida, Jacques 181, 227
Dickens, Charles 111, 350
Döblin, Alfred 8, 166
Drachmann, Holger 2, 6, 13, 23, 34, 127, 420, 421
Durkheim, Émile 43, 184, 215
dystopian 143, 208, 215, 224, 231, 377, 416

Egypt 19
Eiriksson, Leif 63, 64–65

Eliot, George 111, 200
Ellul, Jacques 227
Engels, Friedrich 22, 49, 100
England 19–20, 27–28, 61, 64, 75–76, 94–108, 110
Enlightenment 17, 29–30, 32, 41, 92, 215, 303, 337, 341
epistemology 13, 34, 149, 183, 195, 215, 220, 272, 273, 421
Eurocentrism 14, 29

Faulkner, William 342–343
   Absalom, Absalom! 343
Faust 57, 155, 168, 282
Flaubert, Gustave 337, 344
Forester, C. S. 8, 112
Foucault, Michel 17, 22, 49, 175, 176–177, 227
Foulke, Robert 30, 216, 267–268
France 20, 28, 61, 121, 181, 216, 385
Frankfurt School 34
Fulton, Robert 30, 216, 267

Gama, Vasco da 9, 19, 66–72, 74, 83, 202, 354
Genesis, Book of 50, 51, 54, 172, 383, 410
geocentrism 44, 143, 150, 154, 169, 310, 313
German Romanticism 37
Ghosh, Amitav 8, 46, 112, 145, 335–342, 345–350, 358, 361, 362, 374, 377, 418
   The Great Derangement 336–342, 346, 349–350
Gibraltar 3, 4, 19
globalization 20, 50, 58, 59, 97
Goethe, Johan Wolfgang von 147, 213–214
Golding, William 8, 92, 112, 361
Great Britain 38, 46, 129, 343
Greene, Robert 90
Greenland 61, 63– 65, 363, 368
Grieg, Nordahl 100, 112, 187
   The Ship Sails On 100, 187
Grotius, Hugo 20–22
   Mare liberum 20–22
Gulf Stream 26–27, 386
Gumbrecht, Hans Ulrich 7, 150–151, 153–154, 170, 179–184, 238, 414–415

Hadot, Pierre 35–38
Hakluyt, Richard 60, 77–78, 84, 90
Hawthorne, Nathaniel 147–148

Hegel, Georg Wilhelm Friedrich 10, 19, 23, 128–129, 134, 137, 172, 181, 342, 421
   Aesthetics: Lectures on Fine Art 23, 128
   Elements of the Philosophy of Right 19, 172
Heidegger, Martin 17, 45, 50, 208, 214, 217–220, 222–226, 228, 231, 238, 242, 252, 263
   Being and Time 217–224, 226–227
   "Memorial Address" in *Discourse on Thinking* 238, 260
   The Question Concerning Technology 219, 222–225, 264
hermeneutics 180, 184, 199, 217, 229–230, 232, 236, 250, 252–253, 258–259, 403, 414, 416
Hesiod 53, 55, 60
   Works and Days 55, 60
heteroglossia 137
Jacobsen, Siri Ranva Hjelm 2, 8–9, 29, 42, 44, 47, 145, 334–344, 351, 362, 382–385, 387–389, 392–398, 408–412, 414, 416, 418–421
   Havbrevene 9, 29, 40, 44, 47, 143, 334–335, 351, 366, 382–385, 387–389, 391–393, 395–398, 404, 409–412, 414, 416, 418–421
Homer 8–9, 14–16, 40, 42, 44, 53–55, 67–68, 99, 114, 128, 385, 420
   The Odyssey 9, 40, 54–55, 67, 99
homosexuality 131, 168, 193
Horace 8, 44, 55–56, 58, 172–173, 385
   The Odes 55–56, 172–173
Hudson River 30, 216
Hugo, Victor 8–9, 20, 28, 31, 32, 42, 43–44, 46, 112, 125, 145, 291–324, 347, 385, 417–418, 420
   Les Misèrables 292
   Notre-Dame de Paris 292
   The Toilers of the Sea 9, 32, 43–44, 46, 121, 291–293, 298, 300, 301–304, 306–308, 311–316, 318, 320–324, 347, 417–418

Ibsen, Henrik 127–128, 138
Ihde, Don 45, 207–208, 214–215, 225–231, 232, 236, 241–242, 250, 260, 416
imperialism 28, 421
India 19–20, 46, 66–68, 70–71, 73–74, 76, 83, 114, 202–203
Indian Ocean 66–67, 71, 159, 204

INDEX   445

individualism   60, 269, 357, 358
Industrial Revolution   17, 29, 30, 151, 329
industrialism   5, 98, 113, 155, 163
Ingemann, B. S.   26
   Valdemar Seier   26
Italy   1–2, 5, 28, 78, 328, 385, 388

Jaspers, Karl   227
Java   122–123
Jensen, Carsten   8, 112, 127, 145, 173–174, 361
   We, the Drowned   173
Joyce, James   24, 166, 172, 383
   Ulysses   172, 383

Kant, Immanuel   152, 164, 244, 255–257, 259, 263, 303
   Critique of the Power of Judgement   255–256
Kielland, Alexander   23, 112, 127
Kirk, Hans   112, 298
   Fiskerne   298
Klein, Bernhard   59, 69
Koselleck, Reinhart   6–7, 150–153, 163–164, 171, 414

Latour, Bruno   178, 181, 205, 208–209, 213, 338, 346–347
Lefebvre, Henri   178–187, 189, 191, 193, 195, 199–202, 264, 415–416
Leggett, William   30
Leibniz, Gottfried Wilhelm   117–118, 124, 152, 341, 377
Lessing, Gotthold Ephraim   152
Leviathan   46, 149, 154, 160, 287– 291, 347, 417
Lie, Jonas   2, 8, 23– 27, 43–44, 112–113, 127, 133, 413, 420
   Gaa Paa!   113, 127–128, 133–140
   Rutland   127, 133–134, 138–139
   The Family at Gilje   138–139
   The Pilot and His Wife   25, 43, 127–128, 133–134, 138–139, 198, 420
London, Jack   45, 112, 195–196
   The Sea-Wolf   45, 195–196
Lowry, Malcolm   45, 100, 112, 188–189
   Ultramarine   45, 100, 188
Lukács, György   10, 342, 344–345, 347–349
Lunde, Maja   2, 8, 143, 145, 362, 387, 421
   Blå   40, 143, 387, 394
Lynch, David   290

Magellan, Ferdinand   9, 11, 19, 60, 354, 384
Málaga   3
Malta   4
Manzoni, Alessandro   26
Marquez, Gabriel Garcia   348
Marryat, Captain Frederick   28, 30, 60, 106, 111
Marx, Karl   22, 24, 31, 49, 100, 304
Marxism   24, 39, 269
materialism,   see new materialism and vital materialism
McFee, William   112
Mediterranean Sea   1–4, 14, 19, 42, 44, 53, 54, 56, 60, 129, 201, 334, 351, 384, 387–389, 391, 394, 407–408, 420
Melbye, Vilhelm   3–4, 16
Melville, Herman   2, 6, 8, 9, 14–17, 24, 26, 28, 31, 33, 36, 39, 41–44, 48, 100, 111, 112, 125, 127, 129, 131, 132–133, 138, 145–150, 153–170, 176, 212, 280, 298–299, 308–310, 347, 350, 359, 361, 400, 403, 411, 414, 420
   Billy Budd   6, 100, 132, 133
   Mardi: and A Voyage Thither   31, 147
   Moby-Dick   9, 14, 17, 24, 26, 31–32, 36, 38–39, 43–45, 48, 50, 121, 146–150, 153–170, 282, 298, 308–309, 347, 348, 350, 414, 418
   Omoo: A Narrative of Adventures in the South Seas   132, 147
   White-Jacket   131–132, 176
   Typee: A Peep at Polynesian Life   132, 147, 170
Mentz, Steve   12–16, 25–27, 35–36, 39–41, 43, 146–147, 202–203, 209, 414, 421
mercantilism   20, 22, 73, 421
Mexico   75–76, 329, 388, 392
Michelet, Jules   9, 11, 38, 42–44, 48, 107, 113–126, 140, 216, 260, 267, 272, 280, 281, 283–286, 321, 430, 431, 353–354, 382, 384, 385–413, 420
   L'Insecte   114
   L'Oiseau   114
   La Mer   9, 11, 38, 42, 44, 48, 107, 113–118, 120–121, 124–126, 140, 216, 260, 286, 327, 330–331, 353–354
Middle Ages   21, 99, 384
Milton, John   147
Mobilities Studies   22

modernism   32, 167, 405
modernity   4–5, 16–19, 26–30, 32–39, 42, 49, 69, 89, 97, 100, 113, 142, 145, 151, 161, 183, 211, 216, 219, 231, 235, 303, 338, 346, 347, 350, 379, 381, 413
Moretti, Franco   26, 43, 46, 69, 138, 257, 337, 340, 345, 350, 418
Munif, Abdel Rahman   348–350
Munk, Jens   2, 8–9, 33, 42–44, 78–81, 82–84, 86–90, 119, 222, 394, 413, 420
   Navigatio Septentrionalis   9, 40, 78–80, 82–84

nationalism   17, 28, 31, 107–108, 110, 119, 127, 133, 269
navigators   13, 15, 270
Neptune,   see Poseidon
Netherlands, the   20
new materialism   46, 304, 417
New York City   30, 216
Nexø, Martin Andersen   1–7, 16
   Days in the Sun   1–4, 7, 16
   End of Road   1
Nielsen, Aage Krarup   46–47, 325–334, 351–361, 418–419
   En hvalfangerfærd   46, 325–327, 335, 351–361, 418
Nietzsche, Friedrich   2, 14, 199, 304
   On the Uses and Disadvantages of History for Life, Untimely Meditations   14
North Africa   3
North America   63–65, 363
North-West Passage   33, 78, 88
Norway   19, 24–25, 27, 63–64, 78, 127, 137, 327, 354
nostalgia   6, 8, 100, 128, 142–143, 148, 242, 351, 361

O'Brian, Patrick   8, 14, 112
Oceanic Studies   8, 34
Oceanic turn   9, 25, 58, 60, 62, 420
Odysseus   16, 54, 55, 67–68, 128, 172, 383
Olson, Charles   14, 15, 16
Ovid   56, 388, 399–400, 403
   Metamorphoses   400
   Tristia   399, 403–404

Pacific Ocean   8, 14–15, 26, 40, 71, 77, 167, 169, 207, 215, 353

Pavel, Thomas   46, 344–345, 347, 349, 418
Poe, Edgar Allan   28, 31, 112, 136
   The Narrative of Arthur Gordon Pym   31, 136
Polynesian   14, 60, 149
Portugal   20, 42, 44, 46, 59, 66–72, 86, 202–205, 216, 353, 420
Poseidon   53, 54, 55, 67, 70, 72, 281, 376

racism   28, 149, 169
realism   4, 9, 98, 105, 119, 163, 166, 167, 280, 340, 348
Renaissance   17, 73, 180, 182
rhythm   45, 172, 180, 181, 183–184, 186, 194
rhythmanalysis   180, 181, 182, 186–187, 198–201, 415
Richardson, Samuel   34, 127, 129, 162, 166, 167, 338
Riche, Barnaby   90
Robinson, Kim Stanley   8, 40
Romanticism   5, 92–93, 108, 121, 124, 303
Rousseau, Jean-Jacques   32, 34, 152, 162, 341, 377

"Saga of Eirek the Red"   62–63
"Saga of the Greenlanders, The"   40, 60, 62–66, 420
sagas   2, 8, 62, 63, 65, 413
sailing ship   4–6, 19, 46, 144, 148, 192, 208, 237, 238, 242, 265, 299, 304, 352
Sandemose, Aksel   2, 6, 8, 23, 32, 34, 112, 127, 144, 145, 361
   Horns for Our Adornment   32
   Mutiny on the Barque "Zuidersee"   144
São João, shipwreck of the   9, 46, 86, 202–205, 222, 236, 416
Sartre, Jean-Paul   7, 153
Saussure, Ferdinand de   179
Scandinavia   8, 25, 34, 89, 127, 211, 335, 387, 421
Schiller, Friedrich   37
Schmitt, Carl   8, 18, 24, 58, 113, 132, 134, 137, 169, 213, 216, 420
Scott, Walter   26, 96, 102–103, 106, 344
   Waverley   26, 103, 344
   The Pirate   96, 102–104, 106, 112
secularization   17, 33
Selden, John   20, 21, 209
Seneca   56

INDEX

Shakespeare, William 12–15, 35, 40–41, 73–78, 147–148, 172, 204, 420
  Hamlet 89, 172
  The Merchant of Venice 73–77, 204
Shelley, Mary 129
shipwreck 9, 16, 60, 65, 86, 90, 98, 202, 295, 416
Sicily 1, 329, 395
Sidney, Philip 90
Simmel, Georg 22, 49
Skram, Amalie 2, 23, 34, 112, 127
slavery 169, 202, 205, 213
Sloterdijk, Peter 11, 20–21, 25, 41
Smollett, Tobias 92–93, 96, 104–106, 148, 172–173
  Peregrine Pickle 105
  Roderick Random 93, 96, 105–106, 172
socialism 208, 269
Sophocles 53–54, 159
  Antigone 53–54, 159
Sørensen, C. F. 13
South America 28
Spain 1–4, 20, 28, 83, 206, 216
Stefánsson, Jón Kalman 2
Strabo 11
Strøksnes, Morten 2, 8, 145, 387, 421
Sturm und Drang 213
submarine 140, 207, 230, 266, 267–268
Sue, Eugène 28, 60
Sweden 1

Taussig, Michael 14–16
technocentrism 44, 49, 113, 140, 142–143, 145, 154, 163, 165–167, 214
The Strait of Gibraltar 3, 4, 19
theocentrism 44, 50, 53–54, 56, 70, 142–143, 150, 154, 159, 204, 214
Thoreau, Henry David 348
Tolstoy, Leo 200, 344, 350
transnational 17, 28, 29, 42, 98, 342, 350

unionization 5
United States, the 13–14, 20, 24, 26–28, 30–31, 32, 43, 64, 77, 93–98, 105–112, 119, 148, 156–157, 159–160, 173, 175, 213, 216, 226, 267, 270, 287, 304, 328, 348, 392–393
utopianism 2, 132, 207–208, 214–215, 266, 269, 284–285, 405, 416

Verne, Jules 8–9, 26, 28, 44, 46, 112–113, 120, 140, 142, 207, 214–215, 224, 231, 265–276, 280, 282–285, 375, 416, 417
  Five Weeks in a Balloon 266–267
  From Earth to the Moon 267
  Journey to the Centre of the Earth 266–267, 275
  The Survivors of the Chancellor 270
  Twenty Thousand Leagues Under the Sea 9, 26, 37, 44, 107, 120, 207, 214, 228, 231, 265–266, 268–272, 274, 276, 280, 282–283, 285–286, 375, 416–417
Vikings 9, 60–65, 353
violence 28, 38, 93, 158, 172, 184, 193, 239, 243, 255, 321, 335, 339, 418
Virgil 16, 40, 67–68, 71, 147
  Georgics 40
  The Aeneid 16, 40, 67–68, 71
vital materialism 304–305, 308, 313

Watt, Ian 24, 244, 273, 338
Whitman, Walt 35, 40
Wilde, Oscar 213
Williams, Raymond 34
Williams, William Carlos 388, 389, 390, 391
  "Landscape with the Fall of Icarus" 388, 389, 390, 391
women 25, 60, 65, 129, 136, 138, 380, 398

Zhu Yu 18
Zola, Émile 215, 298, 350
  Germinal 350

www.ingramcontent.com/pod-product-compliance
Lightning Source LLC
Chambersburg PA
CBHW071355300426
44114CB00016B/2067